SOUTH AFRICAN

WINE

SOUTH AFRICAN

WINE

DAVE HUGHES ❦ PHYLLIS HANDS ❦ JOHN KENCH

CONTRIBUTORS

MICHAEL FRIDJHON PROFESSOR CHRIS ORFFER
DAWID SAAYMAN PETER DEVEREUX
AND SIMON RAPPOPORT

PRINCIPAL PHOTOGRAPHER

DARYL BALFOUR

STRUIK

Struik Publishers. A member of
The Struik Publishing Group (Pty) Ltd
80 McKenzie Street
Cape Town 8001

Reg. No.: 63/00203/07

First published as
The Complete Book of South African Wine 1983
Second edition 1988
Second impression 1991
First published as *South African Wine* 1992

Project co-ordinator and editor: Christine Riley
Editors, previous editions: Peter Borchert, Ellis Pender and
Bev Bernstone
Art director: Joanne Simpson
Design concept: Neville Poulter
DTP design, typesetting and layout: Kevin Shenton
Proof-reader: Tessa Kennedy
Indexer: Leonie Twentyman Jones
Cartographers: Angus Carr and Donald McIntyre

Reproduction by Unifoto (Pty) Ltd, Cape Town
Printing and binding by Tien Wah Press (Pte) Ltd, Singapore

ISBN 1 86825 270 1

Principal photographer: Daryl Balfour

The publisher and the principal photographer are indebted to
the following individuals and organizations who provided
additional photographic and other illustrative material:

The Africana Museum, Johannesburg 17, 18, 25 • The Berg-
kelder 30 right • Cloete Breytenbach 37 above, 39 left, 40, 42
right, 44, 45 left, 52, 53, 68 • The Cape Archives 11, 12, 13, 16 •
De Kock & Kerkhoff 97 • Gilbey Distillers and Vintners 32 right
• Klein Constantia Estate 10 • Mandy Moss 34, 62, 73, 109 •
Neethlingshof Estate 161 right • Nicci Page 38, 41, 50 •
Alain Proust cover, back flap, 32 left, 37 below, 39 right, 42 left,
43, 45 below, 58, 64, 89, 90, 92, 93, 94, 95, 96, 108•
Stellenbosch Farmers' Winery 19, 20, 21, 72, 74-86 •
Janek Szymanowski 88 • Erhardt Thiel 30 left, 31 left, 47 below,
48, 143 right, 144, 146 left, 147 right, 148, 174, 215, 217 right,
218 below, 225 • Mark van Aardt 60, 236, 239

With the exception of graphs and illustrations, the copyright
for the above material remains with the photographers or
organizations listed.

TITLE PAGE: *Vineyards below the Simonsberg.*
RIGHT: *Table Mountain seen from the Helderberg above
Alto Estate in Stellenbosch.*
PAGE 6: *An aerial view of Boschendal, in the Groot
Drakenstein valley.*
PAGE 8: *The tasting rooms at Oude Nektar.*

CONTENTS

Contributors   7

Acknowledgements   9

A HISTORICAL PERSPECTIVE   10

THE WINE INDUSTRY TODAY   26

IN THE VINEYARD   36

WINE-MAKING   58

WINE-GRAPE VARIETIES   72

THE ENJOYMENT OF WINE   88

THE WINE ROUTES   98

THE WINELANDS OF SOUTH AFRICA   106

CONSTANTIA   110

DURBANVILLE   118

STELLENBOSCH   124

PAARL   188

FRANSCHHOEK   208

SWARTLAND   222

TULBAGH   228

OLIFANTSRIVIER   236

WORCESTER   240

OVERBERG   248

ROBERTSON   252

KLEIN KAROO   264

Glossary   272

Bibliography   279

Index   280

Dave Hughes – Principal Author
Dave Hughes has been a guest lecturer at the International Wine Educators' Conference in the United States, and delivered papers at the Masters of Wine International Symposium at Oxford in 1982, at the eighteenth Congress International de la Vigne held in Cape Town in 1983, and at the second cold climate Wine Making Conference held in New Zealand in January 1988. He has worked in the wine industry all his adult life, both in southern Africa and Europe. He established the Cape Wine Academy for Stellenbosch Farmers' Winery in 1979. A wine taster and judge of great repute, he has done much to promote local wine societies and his expertise is sought after internationally. Dave was made an honorary member of the Institute of Cape Wine Masters in 1990. He has written several other books on wine and the Cape winelands and his popular *South African Wine Buyer's Guide* is published annually by Struik.

Phyllis Hands – Principal Author
At the age of 23, Phyllis Hands went to live in the Stellenbosch district, hub of the Cape winelands. Four years later she found herself mistress of a small vineyard and, against the advice of veteran wine farmers, was determined to 'learn it all'. That she did, riding her show horses across adjoining fields observing, discussing, learning, and pruning her own 3 000 trellised vines. In time she became a wine consultant, buyer, judge and taster of repute. Since 1979 she has been principal of the Cape Wine Academy. She has written many articles for local and international magazines and her voice has become familiar to thousands through lectures and worldwide broadcasts. She has travelled extensively to overseas winelands and led numerous wine study tours to Europe and South America. Phyllis was made an honorary member of the Institute of Cape Wine Masters in 1990 and has been *Bailli* of the Cape Chapter of the *Confrérie De La Chaîne des Rôtisseurs* since 1985.

John Kench – Principal Author
John Kench has a long association with the Cape – he arrived in South Africa at the age of 17 – and has developed an abiding interest in its people and their history. He wrote the text for the widely acclaimed *Cape Dutch Homesteads* (Struik, 1981) and it is not surprising that his attentions were soon turned to another unique aspect of the Cape's history – its wines. His writing talent provided the catalyst for the first edition of this book; for more than two years his keen mind and eloquent pen were devoted to co-ordinating

the research, knowledge and experience of his colleagues and weaving the story of wine in South Africa. He has written or co-authored *The Coast of Southern Africa* (Struik, 1984), *South Africa - An Aerial Close Up* (CNA/Colour Library, 1986), *Cottage Furniture in South Africa* (Struik, 1987), and *Know Table Mountain* (Chameleon Press, 1988).

Daryl Balfour – Principal Photographer
Daryl Balfour is one of South Africa's leading photographers. His keen interest in wildlife and conservation has resulted in the publications *Okavango: An African Paradise* (Struik, 1990), *Rhino* (Struik, 1991) and *Etosha* (Struik, 1992). His first photographic excursion into the world of wine was to illustrate *Stellenbosch: A Place of Gables, Oaks and Vines* (Struik, 1992). For *South African Wine*, Daryl and his wife and assistant, Sharna, ventured further into the winelands, capturing images of the historic estates, modern co-operatives, and colourful personalities which make up the wine industry in South Africa today.

Michael Fridjhon – Writer: The Wine Industry Today
After completing his B.A. (Hons.) in 1975, Michael Fridjhon spent a year in Montpellier in France as well as in the wine-making regions of Burgundy and Bordeaux. On his return to South Africa, he took up the position of director responsible for the imported wine and spirits division of what was then the world's largest liquor supermarket. With this experience behind him, he established South Africa's first liquor consultancy. Michael is now a director of several companies, including the United Kingdom-based New World Auctions Limited. In 1986, he obtained his Master's degree in the Theory of Literature. He holds the position of wine correspondent for the *Financial Mail* and *Business Day* and in addition writes for several other publications. He is co-author of *Conspiracy of Giants – An analysis of the South African Liqour Industry* (Divaris Stein, 1986) and is presently engaged in completing *The Penguin Book of South African Wine*.

Chris Orffer – Consultant and Editor: In the Vineyard
In 1947 Chris Orffer graduated from the University of Stellenbosch with a B.Sc. (Agric.) majoring in chemistry, viticulture and oenology, subsequently obtaining his M.Sc. (Agric.) in 1954 for experiments on the grafting over of mature vines. Seven years after receiving his Doctorate from the University of California, Davis, he was made a professor in the Department of Viticulture and Oenology at the University of Stellenbosch. Chris has acted as consultant to Ernita, SFW's nursery

farm, and to Klein Constantia Estate and his knowledge of ampelography has resulted in several written papers. Chris retired from the University of Stellenbosch in 1986 but continues his research.

Dawid Saayman – Consultant and Editor: In the Vineyard
Dawid Saayman majored in soil science and chemistry at the University of Stellenbosch, obtaining his M.Sc. (Agric.) in 1973. In August of the same year he was appointed head of the Soil Science Section of the Agricultural Research Council. In 1983 he became head of the Raisin Grape Section. Dawid is now a senior lecturer in the Department of Soil and Agricultural Water Science at the University of Stellenbosch and a member of the demarcation committee of the Wine and Spirit Board. Dawid has authored and co-authored several general and scientific articles, including a substantial contribution to the book *Wingerdbou in Suid Afrika* (Maskew Miller, 1981).

Peter Devereux – Contributor and Editor: The Enjoyment of Wine
An advertising career, liberally laced with travel and entertaining, inspired Peter Devereux's interest in wine and haute cuisine. He is a founder member and was third chairman of The South African Society of Wine Tasters, the Transvaal's first wine club. Peter has launched several wine and restaurant competitions and functions, including the Diners' Club Winemaker of the Year Award and the annual Swaziland Wine Tasting Weekends. Peter is a member of wine and food societies locally and overseas – he is the chairman of the Johannesburg branch of the International Wine & Food Society – and holds the Honorary Grande Diplome of the Cordon Bleu, and *Chevalier* of the *Confrérie de Tastevin du Bourgogne*. Currently the wine editor of Style magazine, he also writes the annual Reader's Digest Wine Feature.

Simon Rappoport – Writer: The Wine Routes
Simon Rappoport has been a wine writer since 1978. He has contributed to a number of publications both locally and overseas including a series of articles in the wine magazine Wynboer, tracing the history of every co-operative winery in South Africa. He is also known for his writing on the wine-producing countries of the New World, researched during his extensive travels. Simon has served as a wine judge on several panels, including that of the South African Championship Wine Show. He is also a wine consultant, specializing in the compilation of wine lists for hotels and restaurants.

ACKNOWLEDGEMENTS

It would be impossible for us to acknowledge by name everyone who has contributed so much to this new edition of *The Complete Book of South African Wine* as so many have parted with so much information over the years. However, we would like to thank Ronnie Melck and Lothar Barth, whose constant inspiration and support encouraged our fascination with the world of wine.

Special thanks to all the 'outside' contributors; Michael Fridjhon, Chris Orffer, Dawid Saayman, Peter Devereux and Simon Rappoport. Thanks, too, to all the other winemakers, viticulturists and wine-associated people — especially the ever helpful people at Stellenbosch Farmers' Winery, such as Paul Wallace. Mention must be made of John and Erica Platter, two fine friends, who could not contribute to this book as they were occupied with the annual revision of *John Platter's South African Wine Guide*.

Last but certainly not least, thanks to Daryl and Sharna Balfour, who took the majority of the photographs for the book, as well as to all those involved in the cartography, design and layout of the book. Thanks are also due to the ever painstaking and patient Peter Borchert and, of course, the editor, Christine Riley, without whom the book would never have been published.

PHYLLIS HANDS & DAVE HUGHES
Stellenbosch, 1992

I offer my sincere thanks to David Rawdon and Bob Toms, without whose encouragement I would have remained a grape grower and private wine drinker. And most of all I acknowledge great debt to my family, and especially to my husband, Harry, who has been so tolerant of my abiding passion for wines, and of the days and nights I have spent working on this book.
P.H.

Thanks must go to those wine-tasting groups, in particular 'The Wine Swines', who have always helped me to obtain a broadly based opinion on wines. Thanks are also due to the many ladies that have been willing guinea pigs to try new wines: Kathy Hughes, Sue Wardrop, Laura van Niekerk, Sally Simson and Sally Leslie.
D.H.

A photographic undertaking of the magnitude of this book is possible only with the support, assistance and co-operation of many people, too numerous to list here. To all those who assisted in whatever way, including several who probably made a lasting impression on my capacity for imbibing the fruit of the vine, I say a heartfelt thank you. However, I feel I must single out a few people who played an important part in making my sojourn in the western Cape more comfortable and companionable. The inimitable humour of co-author Dave Hughes kept me going through the inevitable depressions and blues. Rijk Melck and Kim Swemmer at Muratie Wine Farm became valued friends and companions. Marj van der Merwe of the Stellenbosch Wine Route made many initial introductions. Gert Lubbe at D'Ouwe Werf in Stellenbosch and Basie and Sandy Maartens of Mountain Shadows in Paarl, offered welcome hospitality in their marvellous establishments, while Norma and Stan Ratcliffe of Warwick Farm provided more than a roof over our heads.

I must also thank my sponsors and patrons, in particular Erich Michel of SA Canvas & Tent in Johannesburg, Delta Motor Corporation in Port Elizabeth, John Matterson, and Sean, Nina and Maia Beneke.

To my family, all of whom have been greatly supportive and encouraging, and my wife Sharna, without whose love, assistance and sheer hard work none of this would have been possible, I offer my deepest gratitude.

DARYL BALFOUR
Cape Town, 1992

— PUBLISHER'S NOTE —

When *The Complete Book of South African Wine* was first published in September 1983 it was received with great enthusiasm, and not surprisingly, for it was the first truly comprehensive volume on the wines of this part of the world. The book was not without its flaws, and this was to be expected given its broad compass and the fact that it was in many respects a pioneering work, but it won critical acclaim both locally and abroad where, in 1984, at the 64th Assembly of the *Office International de la Vigne et du Vin* it won the award for 'Monographs and Specialized Studies'.

Since 1983 some 50 000 copies of the book embracing several printings and a revised edition have been sold. No one likes to break with a winning formula, but when the book came up for review some fifteen months ago we, the publishers and the senior authors, decided that a few cosmetic changes would not be sufficient to reflect the dynamic changes that had taken place and indeed were ongoing in the South African Wine Industry of the 1990s. And so it was decided to revise the text comprehensively – this involved not only updating, but also necessitated substantial rewriting and the inclusion of many new entries – and to commission a new design and many new photographs.

We did not simply change for the sake of change and there seemed no point whatsoever in altering or rewriting sections that were accurate and had stood the test of time. For this reason much of John Kench's fine original prose has been retained and great editorial effort has been expended in ensuring that the new or revised sections do not jar with the original style. The major departure from the original, however, was to broaden the creative input to include the writing, consulting and editorial comment of a number of wine authorities such as Michael Fridjhon, Simon Rappoport, Peter Devereux, Dawid Saayman and Professor Chris Orffer. There is no doubt that their contributions have broadened the perspective and authoritativeness of the book considerably and we thank them for being prepared to take part.

Another major departure from the original printings was the inclusion of maps of individual estates and wineries showing the position, type and extent of their plantings. We would have liked to have included maps for all estates and wineries, but this was not possible as some owners, although willing, were not able to provide the information while others, despite repeated badgering, were not prepared to part with it. The many maps that we included are meaningful and interesting and our team of cartographers led by Angus Carr did a fine job of drawing information of varying shapes and extent into a standard presentation.

It is perhaps unusual for the publisher to thank members of the editorial and design team for their input, but in this instance it is appropriate as the book would simply not have been possible without the unstinting commitment of Christine Riley and Kevin Shenton, and it would be wrong not to acknowledge this.

Despite the new design, the updated and expanded text, and the many other innovations, the pedigree of the book lies clearly in the previous editions and impressions. For this reason the title of the book was debated long, hard and often heatedly, but in the end *The Complete Book of South African Wine* gave way to the simpler and less pretentious *South African Wine*. It is published at a time when the wine industry is more dynamic and challenging than ever before.

South African Wine attempts to reflect the excitement and diversity of the wine industry today and to live up to the reputation of its forebears as the standard work on the subject.

PETER BORCHERT
Cape Town, 1992

A HISTORICAL PERSPECTIVE

The first winemaker in South Africa was Jan van Riebeeck. It was he who imported the first grapevine cuttings, who was responsible for laying out the first vineyards and made the first wine – albeit in small quantity and of dubious quality. But his example was soon followed by the local farmers who were impressed by the resilient qualities of the Commander's vines and by the weight of their crops.

Thereafter, the wine and the society of the 'free burghers' (employees of the Dutch East India Company who had been released from service and given small parcels of land to farm) grew up together, gradually gaining independence and an identity of their own. This identity became established in the second half of the eighteenth century, when a new and surprising affluence came to the world of the wine farmers of the Cape. It was then that they built their splendid homesteads, the stately *opstalle* which have become a feature of the winelands, part of the lingering nostalgia for that time.

For it was a period which came and went. It was followed by political conflicts and, for the wine farmers, increasing economic distress with the gradual loss of their overseas market and withdrawal of the protective tariffs by the Palmerston Government in Britain. All these culminated in the legendary disaster of the winelands in the late nineteenth century: the epidemic of a near microscopic plant aphid, *Phylloxera vastatrix*, which included the South African vines in its destruction of most of the world's vineyards.

Recovery in the Cape was relatively rapid; by an ironic twist, too rapid. Hardly had the winelands recovered from the grape pest than there loomed the problems of an uncontrolled over-production.

It was a testing time. Millions of litres of excess wine had to be poured away. Many farmers went bankrupt, many moved to the towns. Organization was needed, not least among the farmers themselves.

LEFT: *The historic Groot Constantia homestead, originally built by Simon van der Stel.*

Jan van Riebeeck, the Dutch East India Company's first Commander at the Cape.

But survival was at stake, the survival of the winelands and of everything which they had stood for in the vision and tradition both of the Cape and of the country at large. A new outlook was needed, a new unity of purpose. And, in the first decades of the present century, the form of this unity was found in the co-operative movement of the winelands.

All this grew from the modest vineyard planted by the first Commander of the Cape, Jan van Riebeeck. It is a remarkable triumph of a tenacious spirit in an often hard and intractable land. And this spirit and purpose was already visible in the career of the first winemaker himself.

Not that he was not human. There was, for example, the small matter of a somewhat mysterious lapse in conduct in the Far East, that had never quite been cleared up. But, still, he was a personable young man – he was in his early thirties at this time – and his report on the possibilities for settlement at the strange and rather mysterious outpost of Africa known as the Cape of Good Hope was certainly intelligent: intelligent enough to suggest him as a possibility for the position of first Commander of the post. Moreover, it would give him a chance to reinstate himself.

Such thoughts as these must have occupied the mind of Secretary van Dam on that day in 1650 when he and his fellow council members in their chamber in Amsterdam summoned Company servant Johan Anthonisz van Riebeeck, to interrogate him upon certain matters pertaining to the Company's wealth and welfare.

The Company, of course, was the Dutch East India Company, in the words of Louis Leipoldt, 'that most profitable combination of unblushing piracy and commercialized Protestantism'. And Mr van Dam and the Council were gathered to debate a relatively minor but nevertheless important venture. This was the establishment of a halfway house on the route to the East Indies, the apparently inexhaustible source of their wealth in spice – several hundred per cent profit on a single voyage raised no eyebrows. Dotted among the resonant Dutch accents were the magic names: Java and Batavia, Malacca and Tandjong Priok. These were the important places where the Company's senior servants were sent. But there was still a job to be done at the Cape, and this young man might be the one for it.

They took a risk and decided on Van Riebeeck. At the age of 33, he found himself no longer an assistant ship's surgeon or an assistant factor, but a fully fledged Commander. As he mused his way through the thronged and bustling streets of Amsterdam on the way home to tell his wife, he must have been a thoughtful and somewhat nervous man. Of course, he knew the Cape. That was partly the reason he had been given the job. The year before he had spent 18 days wandering around the lower slopes of the precipitous mountain with its

East India House, the headquarters of the Dutch East India Company in Amsterdam.

tablecloth of cloud, while they were rescuing the crew of the *Haarlem* which had run aground on that windy and treacherous coast. But it was a command: moreover, something might be made out of it. If nothing else, it would be a challenge and an adventure .

They gave him three ships which together would have fitted comfortably into today's Church Square in Cape Town. His flagship was a 200-tonner, however, done up with all the trimmings, including a nicely gilded camel – the *Dromedaris* – and the Commander's quarters were stately, and by the hard standards of the seventeenth century, comfortable.

They had need to be, over a three-month voyage through the tropics, tacking out through a great arc of the Atlantic. And there were some nervous souls even among the old hands, while some of the few women on board were naturally apprehensive of what they were to expect.

Their anxieties, however, must soon have been forgotten in the impact of arrival. For they beheld a beautiful wilderness – and a magnificent natural monument: the vast mountain with its great buttresses on either side rose high over a deep, sandy valley which ran up from the blue edge of the ocean. After the months of speculation, this was the reality, this was the raw material of their future, of the lives they and their descendants were to make in this land of which they were to become a part.

The first boats were dropped, and the Commander and his party were rowed ashore where they scrambled out of the water onto the beach on the sixth of April 1652. Soon they had their belongings gathered around them. At this time of the year strong winds could be blowing, and the clouds gathered around the mountain tops might presage the coming autumn. There was urgent work to be done.

The nucleus of a small community soon sprang up at the water's edge. A rough wood-and-mud fort was a priority, and was soon built. Sailors' stories dwelt upon the terrors of the great black-maned Cape lion; and a smaller but not necessarily less malevolent threat came from those diminutive human figures that flitted among the scrub on the slopes and darted among the boulders at the end of the beach.

There were not many of these bands of Hottentots (or Khoikhoi), the only indigenous population here – about 60

all told, broken up into family-size bands. They had no settled community or agriculture, living meagrely off shellfish and fruit, including the berries of a wild vine, *Rhoicissus capensis*, later to become popularly known as 'bobbejaanstou' or monkey creeper.

Perhaps that was what gave Van Riebeeck the idea, or perhaps he already had it. At all events, it is certain that it had crystallized within a month or so after the landing, even as the fort was being laid out and the first simple thatched houses were being built: he would introduce the cultivation of the European vine to Africa.

It was a novel idea. It might work. Van Riebeeck had spent his life in Holland and in the tropics, but he was educated enough to know something about the conditions of the Mediterranean wine-growing countries. And the Cape seemed to offer the same type of climate. The winters – their first was on its way – were wet, but without severe frosts; and the summers were long and hot, with a steady temperature. True, the earth did not appear very fertile, but he had the assurance from Hendrik Boom, his head gardener, busy laying out the Company's garden further up the valley, that the vegetables they had brought with them were taking well in this dry soil, with the help of irrigation from the Fresh River trickling down the valley.

And if the vines took, if they were successful? The possibilities were, if not infinite, at least exciting. His brief from those cautious gentlemen back in their candlelit council chamber in Amsterdam had been to establish a station,

revictualling and watering-place, as well as a repair depot for the Company's fleets on their way around the Cape of Good Hope to the Orient. It had long been needed, and the increase of the fleet and its traffic had made it imperative. The Fresh River would supply the water, increasing flocks of sheep and cattle would supply the meat and vegetables were being cultivated. But the vines would supply something extra, something more than the familiar basic staples.

Sitting in his newly built but somewhat dusty Commander's quarters down by the busy water's edge, one thought must have been foremost in Van Riebeeck's mind. *De wijn!* Wine! What they had up till now had been tossed halfway around the world, frozen half to death in Holland, beaten up and all but evaporated in the tropics, a pale, thin, bitter travesty of the vision of healthy vines which must have been in the new Commander's mind.

If all went well they would be able to grow enough vines to make sufficient wine for the community, for his hundred men and their handful of sturdy wives, supplies for the passing ships, and even perhaps for a little private trading with those wine-starved Dutch East India Company servants in the East. But further thought was needed in an exercise of intelligence allied with cunning. It was necessary to acquire vine-cuttings, and the Company must be persuaded to send them out. In order to achieve this, solid reasons had to be advanced to sway the minds of those sceptical old men who perpetually suspected their overseas employees of attempting to feather exotic nests at their expense.

Ships sailing to and from the East regularly anchored in Table Bay.

Scratching assiduously with his quill pen, the Commander wrote eloquently to Secretary van Dam. The community was coming along, building was going forward apace, the Company's gardens were already healthily productive. Vegetables had been planted, and wheat had been sown on a fine, flat site further along the beach. But now there was a further matter which he would like to discuss. The Council did not immediately show much interest in the Commander's idea. True, many of his arguments were persuasive. The climate was promising, near enough to that of France or Spain. But one other argument was particularly effective, more so in view of Van Riebeeck's surgical training. This was the question of scurvy. Although the Dutch of the seventeenth century had no clear idea of what caused this disease, they were all too aware of its effects. Deficiency of the vitamins represented by fresh fruit and vegetables could cause up to a 40 per cent death rate on a long voyage (an extreme case was that of the voyage of Magellan; by the end of the journey all but 20 of his 200 sailors had died of the disease). But though the cause of scurvy was not fully understood, it had come to be general knowledge, particularly among the fleets of the wine-making countries of France, Spain and Portugal, that wine, especially young, red wine which contains some vitamins, could help to counteract the effects of the deficiency. A further advantage of wine was that though it could be chemically unstable, it generally travelled and tasted better than water kept in a leaky keg in the hold of a small wooden ship.

Compared to the fleets of the Mediterranean countries, the Dutch ships had hitherto fared badly. But by Van Riebeeck's time the advantages of carrying wine had come to be recognized by the officials of the Dutch East India Company who had written a daily ration of wine for each of their sailors into their regulations.

The response to Van Riebeeck's request was not immediate. It was, after all, an unusual one, and one which would have put the Secretary to some inconvenience. Eloquence and good sense, however, finally activated the old gentleman, who obtained some grapevine planting material, and sent it out to Van Riebeeck 18 months after his first request.

The small vine cuttings were packed into wet earth and sewn up in sailcloth which the sailors were instructed to keep damp. Perhaps they were over-zealous, for by the time the samples arrived at the Cape and were opened, their contents had rotted. But at least his project had been approved, and within a few months the first new healthy vine plants arrived on the shores of Africa, packed in earth. It must have been a moment of intense excitement and anticipation for the Commander, as he watched the cloth wrappings fall away to reveal the small, twisted plants.

Much research has been devoted to identifying these first vine plants, and to tracing their origins. Both these and their successors appear to have come from the French vineyards, which is natural enough since these were the nearest vineyards to Holland. Van Riebeeck refers to some of them as his *Spaanse druyfen*, which reveals little. He was in fact to re-

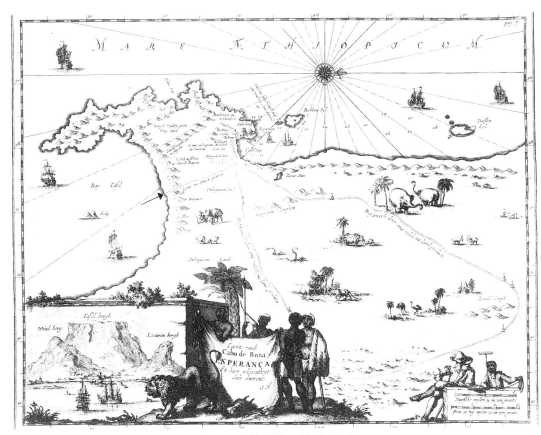

A map of the south western Cape, with the travel routes established by 1660 clearly shown.

ceive a good number of consignments of planting materials over the next few years, most of which he notes as coming from France, not Spain as his choice of name for them would imply. In 1656 two ships, the *Dordrecht* and the *Parel*, both brought French vines and the following year Van Riebeeck again noted that he had received a supply of cuttings from France. It is possible that his 'Spanish grapes' were Hanepoot, otherwise known in France as Muscat d'Alexandrie (this is an early example of the kind of multiple nomenclature which still confuses South African wine lovers). Steen, the French Chenin Blanc, was also probably introduced at this time.

The exact identity of his first vine samples probably mattered less, if at all, than the simple fact that they were alive and well after their long voyage and ready to be planted. And planted they soon were, by the head gardener, the appropriately named Hendrik Boom and his assistant Jacob Cloete van Kempen, the ancestor of the later aristocrats of Constantia. The new vines were introduced alongside the vegetables in the Company gardens, Mediterranean strangers among these Dutch crops.

If the Commander had any worries about their success they were soon dispelled, for the vines grew and flourished. The wind blew strongly under the great sandstone slab of mountain, but the young vines weathered its attacks. They even survived Hendrik Boom and Jacob Cloete van Kempen, for neither Boom nor his assistant had the least idea about

how to run a vineyard (neither, of course, had Van Riebeeck). The Dutch were not a wine-making people, and in this wind-blown extremity of the earth they were even more sorely lacking in viticultural and oenological information, though they were to receive some help and advice on the matter of pruning from a passing German sailor with a memory of the Rhineland.

Once planted, the vines were largely left to fend for themselves, which they did, for the vine is generally an adaptable and resilient plant. The hot summers came and went, and the wet, grey Cape winters nurtured the vines, which put down ever deeper roots. In their neat rows in the Company gardens they bore each year a stronger crop of grapes, ripened to a high degree of sweetness by the summer sun.

Van Riebeeck was enthralled by all this. Of course, it would have been less than human not to have felt pride in his own achievement. But, though it is difficult to confirm across a three-century span of history, there seems little doubt that the vines went to his head – even before any of the wine was pressed.

He constantly pestered his superiors in Amsterdam for further supplies of cuttings (and this at a time when they were wondering whether the little Colony would ever pay for itself). And once the nursery was well established in the Company gardens, he began casting around for larger and better sites for his vines. The first of these was in the area where attempts had been made to grow wheat – what is now Green

Point – where there was a wide space of flat land with a shallow lake which should have provided irrigation for the crops. Unfortunately, the wind seared the leaves off the plants and stripped the corn from its husks. And in winter the lake, which was brackish anyway, overflowed and flooded these promising-looking fields.

A new site was sought, and soon found, in the area of the source of the present-day Liesbeek River, then called the Amstel by the colonists after the river which runs through Amsterdam. Here the ground was sheltered, and here the Company's first large-scale farm was laid out. At first named 'Wijnbergen', but later renamed 'Bosheuvel', this 101-morgen site was also to be that of the first substantial vineyard in the Cape, though the experimental nursery in the Company's gardens was retained, supplying rooted cuttings for the new vineyard. In August 1658, for example, Van Riebeeck recorded that he 'with the aid of certain free burghers and some slaves, took the opportunity as the moon waned of planting a large part of Bosheuvel with young rooted vines and cuttings'. Within four days 1 200 rooted vines and cuttings were thus transported and planted.

The Commander was getting into his stride. The progress of these plantings was witnessed by a number of travellers at this time. Among them was Commissioner Rijkloff van Goens. Impressed with Van Riebeeck's efforts, he reported of the young vineyard that 'it is only one year old, but stands green and flourishes'. His enthusiasm for the venture on his return to Holland helped to overcome much of the residual resistance of the Lords Seventeen, expediting the delivery of yet more planting stock.

The vineyards were expanding, but another kind of expansion was also taking place: the community itself. And with this went changes of structure, among them the appearance of the first free burghers.

It had early become apparent to Jan van Riebeeck that the farming resources of the Dutch East India Company alone would not be enough to cover the needs of the fleet. It was therefore proposed that a number of the Company's servants be released from service to farm their own land in the neighbourhood. It was understood that this privilege would be granted only in return for good and steady service – the men were normally contracted on a five-year basis.

The first nine of the free burgher farmers were given their formal discharge from the Company's service in February 1657, and were immediately installed on grants of land along the Amstel River, near to the Company's farm, from which they received supplies of planting materials and tools to help get them started. In a short while they were followed by a further 40 aspirant farmers, and soon the banks of the river grew into a settled network of smallholdings, few of them larger than 50 hectares in extent. It was a sensible and, on the surface, quite casual move in response to a given situation. The last thing that probably entered Van Riebeeck's mind at that moment was that he was setting up a new society.

If the vines were one innovation, grants to the free burghers were another. These were men with little cultural background. In general they came from the lower ranks of the Company's service, mercenary soldiers, sailors and runaway sons, the rabble of the Dutch overseas empire: the dispossessed, the ones without land or status.

Now, if not status, they were given land. Not a great deal of land, but enough to thrust in tenacious roots. Of course, some of them gave up, for the work was hard, the returns uncertain, and there were other hazards. The Hottentot population appears belatedly to have realized that they had been elbowed away from their ancestral lands. So they took to raiding and plundering, which became part of the pioneers' way of life. Small wonder, then, that many of the free burghers lost heart and returned to the Company's safe bondage or drifted back to sea. But the majority set their teeth and persisted, slowly breaking the land and becoming familiar with the character and demands of farming in a hot, dry climate with a limited topsoil. They planted wheat, bred small herds of sheep and cattle, and built themselves starkly simple mudbrick dwellings thatched with the tough local reed.

At first they showed no interest in planting vines, preferring their more familiar crops. But gradually the Commander's determination began to affect them and they started introducing a few vines on their farms. They were encouraged by the evident success of the vineyards at Bosheuvel, and by the hardiness of the vines – the wind was a constant threat to their exposed fields of wheat (the oak trees and stone pines which are part of the present image of this area did not exist in what was still a virgin Cape landscape).

Their vines did well, and this in spite of the fact that, as with the Company's gardeners, they knew little about their culture. Their methods were simple. The vines were set out in rows about a metre apart, with about a metre between each vine, a compact formation which must have drawn heavily on the soil's resources. The vines were not trellised; instead, the growing canes of the young plants were tied to stakes thrust into the earth. This method, commonly used in Germany, may have been shown to them by the German mercenaries who were part of the Dutch East India Company during that period.

The community by the Amstel took root, as did its vines. But the expansion of farming activity brought with it another problem. More land was being tilled, but the population had not increased. Labour was urgently needed to work these new developments and it was supplied by the Company in the form of slaves.

In the ancient world, slavery was a norm rather than an exception. In one form or another the institution of the bonded labour force had persisted through the Middle Ages – the medieval villein was little more than a serf in terms of absolute status. And if slavery had died out in Europe by the time of the Renaissance, the opening-up of new lands and colonies had revived it. From the sixteenth century onwards Africa had become a vast reservoir of slaves, exploited largely by the Arabs, and sold through European agents to the men who were building up the colonies of the New World and the Orient. In common with the other colonizing nations, the Dutch also took advantage of this supply of cheap labour in their own overseas possessions. Batavia had its slaves, and very soon so did the Cape.

There had been a few in the Cape from the beginning, a dozen or so individuals dropped off by passing ships from Batavia and Madagascar. Then, in 1658, the labour situation changed abruptly and the structure of the population altered radically, when two Dutch ships arrived bringing 200 slaves. They were drawn from a variety of sources. They included both men and women, and came from Africa, from Madagascar and from the Far East.

These people were to become crucial in the expansion and consolidation of the Colony and in the development of agriculture and viticulture. At first the majority was retained by the Company. Special regulations were made concerning them, together with concerted efforts to adapt them to a European outlook. To this end Van Riebeeck's first regulation about them laid down that they were to be taught the doctrines of the Christian church (which presumably omitted any proscription on slavery).

In April 1658, a school for their instruction was started in the charge of the Commander's brother-in-law, Pieter van der Stael. The slaves were given Dutch-style names and were sent to 'school' for a few hours each day. When it first opened, Jan van Riebeeck himself made a formal visit of inspection to check that it was being properly run. As a reward for Christian diligence the slaves were given a glass of brandy and a supply of tobacco, inducements which must have warmed them to the pleasures of conversion.

In spite of all these blandishments, a fair number of these slaves opted for the outback, escaping to take their chances with the mountains, the Hottentots and the Bushmen. A dangerous freedom was perhaps a fair exchange for the hardships of their present existence, the comfort of tobacco and brandy notwithstanding.

It may be as well to emphasize at the outset that the winelands were not based on an egalitarian social structure. The fact that this system worked, altered nothing of its unfairness at a human level. The principles the first slaves learned at 'school' did not for one moment square with the brute reality they encountered from one day to the next.

They were given to and later bought by the free burgher farmers, whose property they became. The farmers asked no questions. There was work to be done, land to be broken, more vines to be planted, cattle to be slaughtered, slave quarters to be built. If the sun scorched the crops in summer, or the mountain brought down floods in winter, what time or leisure, what objectivity of mind was there to debate the niceties of their moral situation? The free burghers were a people on the move, alone in a hostile environment, in a dangerous paradise. They had to conquer or die. Those were the only alternatives they were aware of, from one day to the next. All else was swallowed up in this central question, and by the accepted convention of the period.

They held in their hands the seed of a future society, and in the vine an element that would trigger the tremendous growth which was to sweep it to power and affluence – both economic and symbolic. It was not the vine alone, but the beautiful juice which was made from it, which underwent mysterious metamorphoses, mysteries they felt known only to God, but which they could now perform.

Even with the knowledge of hindsight, and the intellectual equipment of modern science and viticulture at our command, it is still possible to feel the sense of wonder, of mystery, which the natural process of fermentation must have aroused in the early winemakers, in all parts of the world. And something of this sense of wonder lingers like a bouquet over the making of the first wine in the Cape, even over the meagre amount that Van Riebeeck made on the second day of February in 1659, at the Company's original nursery in the gardens near the fort.

The Commander's vineyards had given promise. Now, in the seventh season after the pioneers had set foot in the Bay, this promise was fulfilled. The first small crop of French grapes was harvested, and the first wine made. Given the limited circumstances, the method must have been very simple and straightforward.

Van Riebeeck is curiously silent about the quality of his first wine-creation. The plain fact is that it may have been almost undrinkable. But of course, this mattered neither to Van Riebeeck nor to posterity. He had made wine, and that was all that mattered. He had overcome the caution of 17 Dutchmen (in itself no easy matter), he had imported the vines, he had watched over them, he had made the first wine. His entry in his official journal for that day, scratched out at his desk by the window of his now rather elegantly appointed chamber in the fort, soberly records this small but historic moment: '*Heeden is Gode loff van de Caepse druyven d'eerste mael wijn geparst…*' 'Today, praise be to God, wine was pressed for the first time from Cape grapes, and from the virgin must, fresh from the vat, a sample taken – pressed from the three young vines that have been growing here for two years, yielding 12 mengels must from French and Muscadel grapes, the Hanepoot Spanish not yet ripe.'

The scratching stops. The grave figure with its long, curled seventeenth-century wig, its frilled cuffs, gazes out of the window with shadowed eyes. On the waters of the Bay the Company's ships bob, tugging at their anchor chains. On the dusty road that runs up from the newly built jetty to the gardens, a wagon creaks, the horse urged on by a languid slave in no hurry. On the dark, polished wood of the desk before him the sunlight catches the rim of a slightly cloudy glass of the first wine to have been made in the Cape.

For Van Riebeeck, though he perhaps did not realize it, the adventure was over, at least for him. From now on it was to belong to others: above all, to the thickset man in a slouch hat sitting on the farm cart on the road past the fort, return-

ing to his farm by the Amstel after delivering supplies to the fleet. His shirt lacked cuffs – neither it nor he had any frills. He smoked a clay pipe, and spat when he felt like it. His eyes were narrowed against the sun. His children, already at work on his farm, were bigger and sturdier than he had been at their age under the cloudy skies of Holland.

Growth was in the air. Within a few years a thrusting, driving expansion had taken these people from the Peninsula across the dust-blown wastes of the Cape Flats, the *Kaapse Duinen*, to the watered and fertile valleys beneath the distant, brooding mountains.

Van Riebeeck himself helped to inspire, if not the expansion, the explorations which preceded it and which began within a few years of settlement. In 1657, for example, a small party of burghers crossed the Cape Flats to the foot of the mountains in the north-east. It is thought that it was they who first named this area of the barrier of mountains the Hottentots-Holland (it was about this time that it was first mentioned).

Early in the following year, the Commander himself commissioned a party under Sergeant Herwaarden to conduct a further and more systematic exploration. This group included the surveyor, Pieter Potter, whose job was to record and chart the journey, of which he left a vivid description, through what is now the Paarl Valley, then teeming with game, with great herds of zebra, with hippo wallowing in the mud of the Berg River. Searching for an entrance to the hinterland they eventually reached the Roodezand Pass, which looks down into what is now the valley of Tulbagh, before turning back. The journey was marred by three deaths, two from dysentery and one when a lion gnawed off the arm of a soldier almost within sight of the fort.

The following year saw the last expedition sent by Van Riebeeck, a curiously forlorn affair which throws an odd sidelight on the hopes of a colonial administrator in a strange land far from home. Led by Christiaan Janssen, the party of explorers was detailed to search for the fabled land of gold, Monomotapa. Reluctant, but propelled by the Commander's passionate eloquence extended over several hours, the group trekked off to the north. With half of Africa still to traverse, they collapsed on the banks of the Great Berg River, on the outskirts of what is now known as Piketberg district, all their lust for gold expended.

There *was* gold further on, of course, but it was to be many decades before it was to see the light of day, and by that time Van Riebeeck's bones had long turned to dust on the island of Malacca in the East Indies, for that was where the life and career of this remarkable man ended. After his departure from the Cape in 1662, his career, if successful, was perhaps a little short on adventure. It was also saddened by the death of his first wife, Maria de la Quellerie, who had borne him seven children, four of them at the Cape. The life of a pioneer was not easy.

He himself died as Governor at Batavia on the eighteenth of January, 1677, at the age of 58. It is to be hoped that the

17 grave but shrewd gentlemen in their candlelit council chamber in Amsterdam offered a prayer for his soul when they heard of his death. He had, after all, turned out well; in spite of that youthful indiscretion, whatever it was, he had justified their confidence and hopes.

But the vines, they heard, lived on; the vineyards at the Cape were doing well, very well. This, in spite of the fact that some of the free burghers were not the most expert of farmers or winemakers at that. But the sunburnt farmer with his pipe, trundling back through the dust to his holding by the Amstel, was learning his craft. His methods were simple in the extreme. His vineyards were cultivated by hand – the close spacing of the rows precluded the use of horse and plough, which did not make their appearance in the local vineyards for a further century. No irrigation was used; in the Peninsula area the rain was generous enough. In this early period, the vines were blessedly free of the diseases which were later to cause havoc, and the main natural pest was the birds which descended in ravening flocks particularly at harvest time. The Hottentots also made periodic raids on the vineyards, and they were discouraged with musket shot, and the birds driven off by slaves with whips patrolling the vineyards.

Because of the birds the harvesting was often done too early, which affected the quality of the wine. The early crops were mostly table, rather than wine grapes, the bulk of the Colony's wine still being imported. Harvesting was done with crude baskets, and grapes, pips and stalks were crushed together with energetic abandon in the wooden vats. Later in the eighteenth century sizeable wooden wine presses came into use, but at first the grapes would be crushed by foot or hand (this method was used at Constantia until well into the nineteenth century). The rough juice was drained from the vat and fermented in *velkuipe*, or ox-hides suspended from four vertical wooden poles. The resulting wine contained many impurities, though it was sometimes filtered through baskets to remove most of the fragments of skin, leaves and pips which it contained.

In general the first free burgher winemakers were innocent of any knowledge of the importance of hygiene or cleanliness. Wines were transferred from one container to another with blithe disregard for their previous contents, whether wine, spirits or arrack.

In terms of bulk, the amount of this local wine was still small. And whatever its quality, the quantity gradually increased. The first modest exports of the burghers' wines were made, and the first reports on them returned to their makers.

If these reports, mostly from the Company's servants in Batavia, tended to be negative to outright hostile, this was not necessarily the fault of the wine itself. As the burghers themselves knew, wine, whether imported or exported, fared badly through the long tropical voyages, its fragile physical and chemical structure easily disturbed by micro-organisms and by changes in temperature and humidity, as well as by the vibrations of the small wooden ships. The foreknowledge that this problem of wine transport from South Africa was to persist well into the nineteenth century would have been little consolation to the burghers receiving biting epistles from the Orient from Company servants complaining that they were being poisoned with sulphur.

They were in sore need of help and informed advice, which they indeed were soon to receive, though not always with unmixed enthusiasm. The source of this much-needed guidance was their new Governor, Simon van der Stel. He arrived at a propitious moment, for the 17 years since Van Riebeeck's departure had seen an increasing disorganization in the administration and a lack of direction from the Company. Van Riebeeck had been succeeded by the ailing and disgruntled Zacharias Wagenaar, and he in turn had been followed by a series of temporary commanders. One of the few positive actions in this interregnum had been the start made to the building of a new and larger stone castle to replace the old fort.

It was in this fine new castle that the fine new Governor van der Stel now settled. There was much to be done, and he had every intention of seeing to it. Everywhere there were signs of disorganization, the Colony was losing money, the unkempt colonists perpetrated the most primitive of farming methods. However with energy and determination perhaps something could be made from this shambles.

Van der Stel set about putting his mark upon the Colony, a mark still visible. For the inhabitants of the winelands of the Cape, the monuments to Van der Stel are still there for them to see.

Van der Stel himself made certain that they would be. He was an interesting personality and, like his son and successor Willem Adriaan, a curious mixture of altruism and self-interest. There is no doubt, however, that he did much for the growing community and its expanding but unsophisticated wine industry.

Within a few weeks of his arrival in 1679, he made one of the most important contributions to the early structure of Cape society. On the way back from a tour of inspection of the Hottentots-Holland area he turned aside from his original route to explore a long, verdant valley which he decided would make excellent farming land, and a fine spot for settlement. The area had hitherto been named the 'Wildebosch'. Resting on the banks of the river which ran through the valley, Van der Stel dreamed up what he felt would be an appropriate name for his new settlement, with its projected church and school.

It was thus that Stellenbosch was 'born' in the head of Simon van der Stel in November, 1679 – the first time that the name appeared in his journal at the Castle.

With this action, the new Commander created a centre for the growth of a new community, separate from the seaboard town under the mountain of the Cape. It was to be specifically a colonists' town, a free burgher town, and one in which from the beginning wine was to form a major element.

He was to have a personal effect upon the quality of this wine. On his arrival at the Cape he found the local product to

Among Simon van der Stel's other achievements was the settling of a new community, Stellenbosch, which soon became the centre of rural life.

be 'exceptionally harsh'. In reply to this criticism the free burghers bluntly maintained that the wines could not be improved – a fine and determinist excuse, perhaps, for their own ignorance. Van der Stel set out to prove them wrong by producing wine of a quality not before found at the Cape, and one which for the first time received favourable comment when exported to Holland.

At the same time he began to impose the rudiments of an administrative apparatus on the local wine industry, such as it was at the time. He also sought to find a balance between one kind of farming and another. Thus he not only encouraged the growing of grapes, but, to ensure that the main object of settling at the Cape was not forgotten, he decreed that for every morgen of grapes planted, six morgen of other crops, particularly of wheat, should be planted as well. The varieties he introduced (or re-introduced) probably included Muscat de Frontignan and Pontac. And of course, he was responsible for the introduction of thousands of oak trees throughout the area, lending a graceful intimacy to the grandeur of the landscape.

At the practical level he demonstrated the importance of pressing grapes only when they were fully ripe – the practice of harvesting early to avoid the attack of birds on ripe fruit gave a raw edge to the wine. He set up a committee whose duty it was to visit the vineyards and who had to be satisfied that the grapes had reached the required level of maturity: failing which a fine of 60 *rijksdaalders* was imposed. The general importance of orderliness and cleanliness, particularly with regard to the casks, was also emphasized. Fining – a method of cleaning the wine – was done with ox blood, white of egg and with imported isinglass (a gelatinous extract from a sturgeon's air bladder).

If the establishment of Stellenbosch was Van der Stel's most public memorial, it is for a more private creation that he is also remembered. This was his estate of Constantia, still one of the Cape's most gracious monuments to a past age, in the valley which bears that name. Here, in this cool valley beneath the Constantiaberg, a few hours' ride from the Castle, the Governor set up a model farm. As dubious as the way in which he acquired this superb piece of real estate might have been, there can be no doubt that his farming methods set a good example, especially in the making of good wine.

In the year of his purchase of the Constantia land, there occurred in Europe an event which was to have a delayed effect both on the character of the Colony's population, and on the quality of its wines. For it was in this year that the king of France, Louis XIV, revoked the Edict of Nantes which had guaranteed religious tolerance of the French Protestants since its promulgation by Henri IV in 1598.

In the wake of this change in their circumstances, some 200 Huguenots (their name was a corruption of the word *Eedgenoot*, or 'oath-associate'), assisted by the Dutch East India Company, emigrated between the years 1688 and 1690 from France through Holland to the Cape. They were a great asset to the newly established Colony of the Cape as they were hard-working and skilled in many trades (the Huguenot weavers were particularly valued) and their loss was a blow to the French economy.

France's loss was the Cape's gain. The free population of the Colony at this time did not exceed 600, so the Huguenot infusion undoubtedly made a significant change in the make-up of the burgher society. Moreover, they derived from a different stratum of society from the rough-and-ready Dutch free burghers and introduced a certain cultural flair.

The title deed to the farm L'Ormarins in the Drakenstein valley in Franschhoek was granted to the French Huguenot Jean Roi, in 1694.

The Huguenot farmers were readily given grants of land on the same terms as those made to the free burghers. The farms which they were allocated were mostly in the areas of what are now Franschhoek, Paarl and Drakenstein, the newly established farming areas beneath the mountains. One valley became their domain. Previously called De Olifantshoek, it now acquired a number of new names, from the Fransche Quartier, to Le Coin Français, or the settlers' own name for the area, La Petite Rochelle, before coming to its present one, Franschhoek.

Many of the new settlers came from the south of France, where, if not directly involved in wine-making, they were at least familiar with its methods and procedures. In May 1689, for example, the Chamber of Delft wrote to Simon van der Stel, informing him that the brothers Pierre, Abraham and Jacob de Villiers had a good knowledge of viticulture, and that he should assist them on their arrival; the brothers François and Guillaume du Toit were also noted as wine farmers.

The expertise of the Huguenot winemakers was thus added to the free burghers' limited store of knowledge and experience. The newcomers quickly settled down in the area, becoming absorbed in the larger community and exchanging their own language for Dutch within a generation or so – though they remembered the land of their origin in the names of their farms, from L'Ormarins to Champagne to La Provence. And if the atmosphere at first was one of suspicion from the local farmers, any resistance was soon submerged in the common antagonism felt by both groups towards the

new Governor of the Colony, Simon van der Stel's eldest son and successor, Willem Adriaan, or, as it was then spelt, Wilhem Adriaen.

The elder Van der Stel retired as Governor – he had been given this new title as a reward for his services – in 1699. He spent his remaining days in seclusion at Constantia. The earlier distrust between the first Governor of the Colony and the burghers, a symptom of an increasing discord between the Company servants and the free landed farmers, became an open rift during the career of the able but ruthless and self-serving younger Van der Stel.

The trajectory of Willem Adriaan's career is well known. The tendency to stretch rules, already evident in the father, became excessive in the son. At the same time, the intelligence and resourcefulness of the family remained. It shows in Willem Adriaan's passionate interest in the horticultural and agricultural possibilities inherent in this new land. The questing, probing mind of the scientist, of the man of reason hovering on the verge of the eighteenth century, found expression in extensive farming experiments.

These experiments were carried out at the Governor's palatial but illegally acquired country estate of Vergelegen in the Hottentots-Holland district (600 of the Company's slaves were siphoned off to build his famous mansion) and they included meticulous investigations into viticulture. In his comprehensive *Gardener's Almanack*, Van der Stel reported on the progress and care of these vines for the benefit of the community at large.

This early 'vineyard calendar' provides a fascinating glimpse into the methods of the eighteenth-century viticulturalist. In July, to which he refers as the 'second winter month', Van der Stel advised that, 'When a vineyard is intended to be planted, it is best to dig the ground to a depth of three feet and clear it of stones and weeds, and, immediately after the canes are cut, tie them into bundles of a hundred each, and so bury them until the end of September or the beginning of October, when they are to be taken up and planted in moist weather; although they will have shot while under the ground, these leaves fall off, and new ones bud out.' In the same month he advised the farmer to 'Prune old Vines early this month; young Vine stalks may be planted in the place of those that have been removed. The Vine stalks or Sets intended to be planted must be fourteen or fifteen inches in length, and have at least two or three buds above soil level; those that have been slipped or torn from the stalk are the best; they should be planted regularly in a S.E. or N.W. direction. It has happened that a Young Vine has borne Fruit the same year of its being planted, and that 800 old Vines have yielded three Leaguers of good red Wine. It has also happened that a small bough of an Apple Tree, being put into the ground has borne Fruit the following year.

'When a Vine has died, it should not be replaced by a new set; for the old Vines, having possession of the ground, would draw all the nourishment from the new one, and prevent its growing; but a hole, of about a foot deep, should be dug close to the nearest Vine, a Cane of the same laid down, and this covered, that only a couple of inches of it appears. When it is found to grow, then, the year following, it should be cut half through, closer to the Mother Vine; the second year it should be cut off quite'.

He further advises that if 'anyone wishes to have Vines to run up by the side of Trees, they should be planted at the same time, and close together'.

In October he recommends that 'the vineyard be kept clean; and if it grows too rank, let the shoots be topped, and the ground be hoed'. In November, 'The Vineyard must now be attended to, and the long shoots tied up.'

And then, in March, 'Now is the season for gathering the Grapes and making Wine.'

The harvest that Van der Stel himself reaped was the bitter one of exile. Though, like his father, he had begun well, encouraging further immigration and opening up for settlement the 'Land van Waveren' – now known as the Tulbagh Valley – he soon allowed the temptations of self-interest to overcome him. This in itself might have been tolerated by the colonists had it not been set off by an intolerant and autocratic temperament.

It was a confrontation with the wealthier and more established of the burghers, men such as Henning Huysing and his fiery nephew Adam Tas, which led to his downfall. Van der Stel misread the tenacity of his opponents; he also misunderstood their power of organization as well as their power of protest. In the few decades since Van Riebeeck, a political

Willem Adriaan van der Stel's palatial estate of Vergelegen in the Hottentots-Holland district.

nucleus, however crude, had been created among the farmers, now strengthened by the addition of the relatively articulate and sophisticated Huguenots.

Mounting tension led to open rebellion. In a furious over-reaction to this defiance, the Governor rounded up the ring-leaders, first imprisoning them and then dispatching five of them to Holland for trial before the Council in Amsterdam.

It was a crucial mistake. Not only had Van der Stel mis-read the power of those beneath him but he also failed to gauge the mood of those above. The Governor had been liv-ing like a lord at their expense. When the men sent for trial before them pleaded an eloquent case against Van der Stel's corruption and tyranny, a dramatic reversal took place. The Governor found his powers effectively pruned; then relieved of his post, he paid the price of his lack of human acumen and was sent into exile to Holland. Much of the benefit which his intelligence and vision could have given to local farming methods, including wine-making techniques, went into exile with him. An enigmatic personality (it is one of the curios-ities of his life that no record of what he looked like, either visual or verbal, has survived), the effect of venality on the spirit of enquiry destroyed its potential for good.

With the passing of the Van der Stels – Willem Adriaan went into exile in April, 1708 and his father died in June, 1712 – went the larger defeat of the ambitions of the local servants of the Dutch East India Company. To an increasing degree the Cape of Good Hope came to be the land of the free burghers, under their control and bearing the imprint of their personality.

They were assisted in this by a number of factors, the most important of which was the fortunes of the Dutch East India

Company itself during the following century. The mid-seventeenth century, the moment at which the Cape had been established, had been the high point of Dutch power. Released from the repressions of the Spanish occupation, armed with a profound knowledge of the sea and with a powerful expansionist appetite, they had thrust the Spanish and Portuguese aside and, uneasily sharing the newly charted oceans with the equally ambitious British, had begun acquiring an overseas mercantile empire.

But the eighteenth century saw the beginnings of its slow disintegration, largely from within. A series of European wars weakened Dutch resources and the administrative grip on the overseas possessions. But the European wars in which Hol-land became embroiled were also, if only indirectly, respon-sible for the first great affluence of the free burgher society of the time, their first great harvest and one which was going to be long remembered.

By the end of the eighteenth century, the descendants of those first pioneer farmers had become rich and prosperous beyond the wildest dreams of their forebears. The series of military entanglements between France, the Low Countries and England during this period, culminating in the French Revolutionary Wars and the succeeding Napoleonic Wars, ef-fectively cut off the French wine trade from the opposing countries. For the first time the Cape wine farmers found a market and a large-scale demand for their products outside those of their own society and the passing fleets.

They also, for the first time, if indirectly, made the ac-quaintance of the English, whose drinking habits were to give them much joy: for in this period they consumed with enthusiasm all forms of alcohol. The Elizabethans had

drowned themselves in raw ale and sack. Beer and gin had contested for the soul of the seventeenth- and eighteenth-century Londoner (as Hogarth had mordantly illustrated), and the middle- and upper-class drinker had discovered wine, specifically French wine. Of course, a flank attack was being mounted in the same period by an obscure oriental beverage absurdly derived from boiled leaves brought from India, but no sensible wine drinker would have taken this competition seriously or have imagined that on a steaming brown tide of tea a global empire would soon be floated.

In the late eighteenth century the British drank wine, with a prejudice in favour of very sweet wines, ports and sherries, whose high calorie content was excellent for keepingout the chill of the northern winters.

When the French Wars cut them off from French wines, the British turned to the Cape for their supplies. A trade was established, and with it the first apparatus of wine marketing and promotion, represented by the wine dealers of London who imported the burghers' wines. For the first time, wines from the Cape were being tasted in Europe.

Like the Dutch the British knew nothing of the making of wine, but the machinery of import and marketing was of long-standing, going back to the early Middle Ages (the poet Chaucer's father, for example, was a wine merchant in the port of London in the fourteenth century).

The English demand for Cape wines was such that the pre-cise assessment of the quality could be disregarded, at least for the time being. The British gentry sipped their newly en-countered Cape wines with perhaps the occasional delicate grimace, but were glad enough to get it.

If the English asked few questions, the Cape farmers asked none at all. British money bought their wines, and the bur-ghers spent their guilders.

The spending spree lasted for 50 years. With British gold they made their grand homesteads, pulling down or modi-fying the simple, traditional Dutch-style dwellings that had sufficed their forefathers, and built great mansions, with high, gleaming white gables fashioned to ornate shapes by Malay slaves whose temperamental subtlety inspired a rich and florid design. On either side of the gables stretched smooth, tightly bound thatch. Below were green-painted teak window-frames and doors, and within was elegant yellow-wood and stinkwood furniture with burnished brass handles, the finest that money could buy. Out in the fields the slaves harvested the grapes from vineyards stretching away over the rolling foothills of the great mountains.

The land had borne fruit, and for the farmers it was a time without precedent, and one which had no sequel. It was a justification and a celebration of the adventure of their forefathers, and of the generations whose lives had gone into its creation. A Cape farmer, born in 1750 and living through his appointed three score years and ten, could look back in his sunset hour on a life for which there were few parallels in terms of freedom and comfort in the old world of Europe, torn by wars and, as the century wore on, by moral and intellectual conflicts, beset by a mounting crescendo of political, social and philosophical questions.

It was at this moment that the Cape tradition was born, never to be forgotten; one in which the questions of Europe, including those of the Rights of Man, had no part. It included none of the northern currents of thought which were to lead to the creation of a liberal vision in the nineteenth century. It had no prophets and no analysts. Its memory survived not so much in history books, but as group consciousness, even through the upheavals of the coming decades.

Among the many famous farms and homesteads preserved from this time, one in particular stands out. It was in this period that the wine-making *genius loci* of the Constantia Valley came into its own, represented by Simon van der Stel's historic estate of Groot Constantia. Here Van der Stel the elder made wine that was widely acclaimed, especially his sweet 'Constantia' which gained great favour among English and European society.

Little had been heard of Constantia wine after 1699, however, when Simon van der Stel had retired there. After his death in 1712 his estates were sold by auction. Of the various subsequent owners none achieved the success of the estate's creator and it was only one Johannes Colijn who appears to have had any constructive effect. This was reflected in the first notable export of red and white Constantia wine: in 1761 and 1762 both were sold in Amsterdam, the white fetching £120 to £196 and the red £270 to £333 a leaguer.

In 1778 Groot Constantia experienced its most important change in ownership, when the Cloete family, descendants of Van Riebeeck's under-gardener, purchased it for 60 000 guilders. Under their ownership, which lasted till 1885 when it was purchased by the Colonial Government as a viticultural training centre, it was to achieve its highest renown.

The legend of Constantia wine was created against an increasingly shaky political background. Wealthy, independent, and with sophisticated tastes reflecting their increased affluence, the burghers' world was illusory in its sense of security. Among its memories, along with white gables and the smell of dark cellars and the cool shadows of oak trees, went the breath of freedom, of political autonomy.

By this time the rambling, far-flung mercantile empire of the Dutch East India Company was in full disarray, and the farmers were wealthy, but without real political or military influence. They mistook a power vacuum for freedom. That vacuum was soon to be filled. In 1780 war was declared between Britain and France, and the news reached the Cape in 1781. The Netherlands were in alliance at this time with the French and there was much fear that the British would attempt to take the almost defenceless Cape. Temporary relief arrived in the form of the French fleet in June 1781 under Admiral de Suffren. Among the members of the Swiss Meuron Regiment in the pay of the Dutch was the French architect Louis Michel Thibault, who abandoned military life in 1785, to make a distinctive mark on winelands architecture.

Lady Anne Barnard, wife of the Secretary to the Governor.

The French departed, having spent liberally on local wine. A decade later, in 1795, Europe once more returned to Africa. The first British occupation, which lasted seven years, was preceded by the invasion of General Clarke and Admiral Elphinstone. As few changes as possible were made: a Governor with supreme power replaced the Council of Policy housed in the Dutch East India Company's offices near the Parade; however, local government and the Dutch legal system remained largely unchanged.

Thus, the British were somewhat casual conquerors. After all, their acquisition of the Cape had been chiefly motivated by expediency and by the need to head off French expansion at sea. They observed the local scene with interested curiosity, and for the first time had an opportunity to observe the places from which many of their imported wines came. One of the most vivid reports of the period was written by Lady Anne Barnard, wife of the Secretary to the Governor. An intelligent and observant personality, an enthusiastic letter writer and amateur artist, she appears to have struck up a friendship with Hendrik Cloete of Groot Constantia, and in her letters to Lord Macartney makes several references to him.

'Mynheer Cloete took us to the wine press hall,' she wrote, 'where the whole of our party made wry faces at the idea of drinking wine that had been pressed by three pairs of black feet; but the certainty that the fermentation would carry off every polluted article settled that objection with me. What struck me most was the beautiful antique forms, perpetually changing and perpetually graceful, of the three bronze figures, half-naked, who were dancing in the wine press beating the drum (as it were) with their feet to some other instru-

ment in perfect time. Of these presses, there were four with three slaves in each.

'Into the first the grapes were tossed in large quantities and the slaves danced on them softly, the wine running out from a hole in the bottom of the barrel, pure and clean. This was done to soft music. A quicker and stronger measure began when the same grapes were danced on again. The third process gone through was that of passing the pulp and skins through a sieve; and this produced the richest wine of the three, but the different sorts were ultimately mixed together by Mynheer Cloete, who told us that it had been the practice of the forefathers to keep them separate and sell them at different prices, but he found the wine improved by mixing them together.'

Not only did Cloete blend his wines, but he evolved other techniques, including the twisting of the branches of the vines to reduce the supply of nutrients and in this way to concentrate the flavour and sugar content of the grapes, the result being a wine of a rich, almost syrupy quality.

The first British occupation finally came to a close in 1802, when the Treaty of Amiens secured a break in the hostilities. But the brief Batavian Republican Government of General Janssens lasted no more than four years, a last flicker of independence before the British returned once more, this time permanently. Their century-long dominance began in January, 1806 with the Battle of Blaauwberg. Heavily outnumbered by General Baird's forces, the Dutch troops retreated in disorder (cannonballs said to be the relics of the battle are fixed on the pillars near the corner of Groot Constantia homestead); and the power vacuum in the lives of the Cape farmers was ended.

Their immediate situation suffered little change. While the European wars lasted so would a major source of their wealth, but within a few years the situation with regard to their market in Britain was to change drastically. Trafalgar broke the French sea power, Russia broke the army, and Waterloo broke Napoleon. Half a century of wars were over, redirecting the wine market upon which much of the free burgher affluence had been founded. There followed a long, slow process of isolation and increasing economic hardship in the winelands, for with the end of the Napoleonic Wars the wine trade between France and Britain was gradually restored; and as it did so the supply of British revenue to the Cape dried up. The winelands became an industry without an overseas market.

At first the reality of the situation was not fully apparent. Assuming responsibility for their acquisition, the new rulers attempted to protect the local farmers. At the same time they tried to establish controls over the quality of the local vine product which had hitherto largely been left to the individual farmer who, with a booming seller's market and a high demand, had not always been too scrupulous in such matters.

On the nineteenth of December 1811, a proclamation issued by Sir John Cradock promised the Government's 'constant support and patronage to the cultivators and

—WINE-MAKING IN SOUTH AFRICA—

A HISTORICAL CHRONOLOGY OF MAJOR EVENTS AND INFLUENCES

1652 The Dutch East India Company, in the person of Jan van Riebeeck and his party of Company servants, establishes the first European settlement at the Cape of Good Hope

1657 First free burgher farmers released from Company service to work their own land

1658 First shipment of slaves arrives in the Colony

1659 February 2: Van Riebeeck records the making of the first wine at the Cape

1662 Departure of Van Riebeeck for the East Indies

1679 Appointment of Simon van der Stel as Governor of the settlement; later in the same year, his foundation of the town of Stellenbosch

1688 Arrival of the first Huguenot immigrants

1699 Simon van der Stel retires to his estate of Constantia; his place as Governor is taken by his son, Willem Adriaan van der Stel. The first modest exports of wine from the Cape take place in the same year

1708 Willem Adriaan departs to exile in Holland

1761 The first notable exports of red and white Constantia wine take place

1778 Groot Constantia is acquired by the Cloete family. The following decades see the sweet Constantia wine winning acclaim throughout Europe

1795 The first British occupation of the Cape

1802 End of the first British occupation

1806 The Battle of Blaauwberg and the start of the second British occupation

1811 Quality control instituted by British authorities in the Cape on wines exported from the Colony

1825 The British Government imposes heavy tariffs on importation of French wines and sales of Cape wines in Britain increase rapidly

1834 Emancipation of the slaves and the start of the Great Trek

1860 First appearance of the phylloxera epidemic in the French vineyards

1861 Palmerston Government reduces tariffs on French wine imports to Britain which had hitherto protected the Cape wine market

1863 Louis Pasteur's investigations into diseases of wine in France

1885 Appearance of phylloxera in the Cape vineyards

1886 Discovery of gold on the Witwatersrand

1899 Start of the second Anglo-Boer War

1906 Formation of the first South African wine co-operatives, the first being the Drostdy in Tulbagh

1909 Over-production causes a slump in wine prices to an all-time low

1910 The Union of South Africa is established

1918 Serious over-production leads to great quantities of unsaleable wine being allowed to run to waste. KWV is formed

1924 KWV empowered to fix the minimum price for distilling wine

1925 Professor Perold crosses various vines which eventually give rise to the first specimens of the Pinotage variety

1935 Formation of Stellenbosch Farmers' Winery

1940 KWV empowered to fix the minimum price for good wine

1945 Formation of Distillers Corporation. The years following the Second World War see the further development of cold fermentation, which gives impetus to the production of quality white wines

1950 Gilbeys (SA) formed

1955 Oenological and Viticultural Research Institute established at Nietvoorbij outside Stellenbosch

1959 First Lieberstein marketed

1961 First bottled Pinotage appears

1965 Amalgamation of Stellenbosch Farmers' Winery, Monis of Paarl, and Nederburg

1971 Stellenbosch Wine Route opened

1973 South African Wine of Origin legislation implemented

1975 First auction of rare Cape wines at Nederburg

1979 Formation of Cape Wine and Distillers

1980 The newly formed Cape Wine Academy begins courses for the trade and the general public

1983 The Mouton Commission recommends a less monopolistic structure for the wine industry, but this is not accepted by the Government

1985 Liquor Amendment Act is gazetted allowing greater uniformity of selling hours in liquor retailing and extended hours for restaurants with liquor licences

1991 Douglas Green and Union Wine combine to form Douglas Green Bellingham

1992 Cape Wine Academy and KWV wine courses merge KWV suspends quota system.

PRIME MOVERS IN THE SOUTH AFRICAN WINE INDUSTRY

The legendary William Charles Winshaw, founder of Stellenbosch Farmers' Winery.

Professor C.J. Theron headed the department of viti- and viniculture at the University of Stellenbosch in the 1940s and 1950s.

Charles Kohler, founding chairman of KWV.

Professor Abraham Izak Perold, pioneer of viticulture in South Africa.

Dr J.G. Niehaus, who made a fundamental contribution to the creation of South African sherry.

merchants, to give serious and lively attention to their interests as their wines are losing their reputation', and further went on 'that no means of assistance should be left unattempted to improve the cultivation and every encouragement given to honest industry and adventure to establish the success of the Cape Commerce in her great and native superiority'.

In the same month Cradock appointed an official taster, one W. Caldwell; and much advice on how to improve their product was issued to the farmers. It seemed that the wine trade was going to have the opportunity to flourish.

The moves to protect the wine trade at the Cape culminated in 1825 with the introduction by the British Government of heavy tariffs on French wines, which resulted in a rapid increase in the sale of Cape wines in Britain. These revitalized links were set up notwithstanding much opposition from many of the London wine merchants and importers whose traditional and understandable prejudice was in favour of the better quality and more accessible French wines. They instigated something of a campaign of slander against the Cape wines in an attempt to strengthen their ties with Europe. It has even been maintained that they went so far as to adulterate the Cape wine upon its arrival in England, although this may not always have been necessary – the prob-

lem of the long sea voyage and its effect on the wines was still unsolved.

But if, with these tariffs, the Government at the Cape gained favour with the farmers, one further piece of legislation was to have long-term and deep-seated effects – the emancipation of slaves in 1834.

It split the traditional burgher society down the middle. Slavery was the base of their social structure and of their agriculture, including viticulture. As an institution it was as old as their society. The new legislation, although changing very little in practical terms, had a profound symbolic meaning for the burghers, bringing to the surface a rebellion of spirit which had been lying dormant since the first British invasion. This was their country, and not only had it been taken away from them but the foundation of their labour force was threatened as a result.

The reaction was mass migration. The Great Trek was to open up the interior, to see the establishment of the Boer Republics of the Transvaal and to usher in a new era in South African history. It also marked a change in the structure of Cape society.

A new kind of pioneer had been born, created as a clone from the burgher stock. In the following decades he was to become embodied in the heroic figure of the Boer, to confront for the first time the black peoples of southern Africa, and to leave behind for ever the enclosed valleys and the vine-clad hills of his ancestors.

Those who joined the Trekkers confronted hard and unambiguous choices. Those left behind found themselves confronted with an increasingly complex economic world and a mounting sense of loss of traditional identity. Among these new uncertainties was a phenomenon not hitherto found in the early vineyards of the Cape: vine diseases.

Whatever planting stock Van Riebeeck had received had evidently been fine and healthy, and for the better part of two centuries little disease was recorded. It is recorded that, in 1819, a farmer Van Breda reported a type of 'rust' which was detrimentally affecting his Muscat d'Alexandrie and, to a lesser degree, his Chenin Blanc vines, but it seems to have disappeared of its own accord.

Then in 1854, powdery mildew, a form of fungus indigenous to North America, found its way to France and devastatingly reduced the French wine crop by a quarter, in a matter of four years. It was not long before the disease was found in the Cape vineyards, but by this time it had been discovered that dusting with flowers of sulphur successfully combated the fungus. This treatment was promptly followed wherever the fungus's characteristic small spots and white, powdery, cobweb-like growth appeared, with the result that by the early 1860s it had been brought conclusively under control.

The immediate picture by the mid-century, notwithstanding these natural hazards, was hopeful. The result of the increase of the export trade during this period of protective tariffs had been the rapid expansion of the vineyards – there were some 55,3 million vines in the Cape winelands by this

time. But then in 1861 an event occurred which was to prove to the wine farmers that their security was as fragile as had been their earlier prosperity, when the abolition of the preferential tariffs which had kept the trade afloat brought about the collapse of the export market.

In 1861 the Palmerston Government entered into a treaty of commerce with France which reduced the existing import duties on wine from that country to three shillings a gallon. The following year, in April, 1862, the duty was reduced still further, to one shilling a gallon on wine with less than 26 degrees proof, and to 2s 6d on wines of more than 26 but less than 42 degrees proof spirit.

This change in duties hit the Cape wine industry hard. The Cape winemakers had, of course, not been consulted by Gladstone, the Chancellor of the Exchequer, and were badly shaken by this turn of events. Protest meetings were held at which the wine industry, commerce and the professions were represented, and the Cape Parliament agreed to appoint a Select Committee to enquire into the effects of the amended tariff on the local wine industry.

Their findings were brought to the attention of the Imperial Government, which, however, did not alter its tariffs; and many of the Cape farmers were forced to sell up and leave their farms.

The Cape exports dropped from 126 951 gallons (approximately 577 120 litres) in 1861 to 30 679 gallons (approximately 139 466 litres) in 1864, while French imports to Britain after 1860 totalled more than two million gallons (approximately 909 200 litres) annually. Notwithstanding this healthy trade, the French wine industry was soon to face problems of its own, from which it – and the winelands of the world at large – was to be rescued by the genius of a French chemist; for it was in these mid-century years that some of the most important developments in wine-making history took place, leading to the beginnings of the modern science of viniculture. And of this science Louis Pasteur was the pioneer.

For centuries man's knowledge of the vine had been pragmatic. The processes whereby the wine was made were discovered by accident. But what actually happened during the process of fermentation was unknown. Then, in 1863, the unknown became the known.

In that year the French Emperor Napoleon III asked Louis Pasteur, who had already made studies of the souring of milk, to look into the problems besetting the French wine trade which were causing a rapid loss of the newly established links with England. The making of the famous French natural wines was accompanied by serious financial loss, owing to several ills, the most common of which was souring.

Pasteur retired to his laboratory with samples of the offending vines, and proceeded to do something which had never been done before. He looked at wine through a microscope. In doing so he made the fundamental discovery of its organic 'living' nature. 'The wine', Pasteur enthusiastically observed, 'is a sea of organisms.'

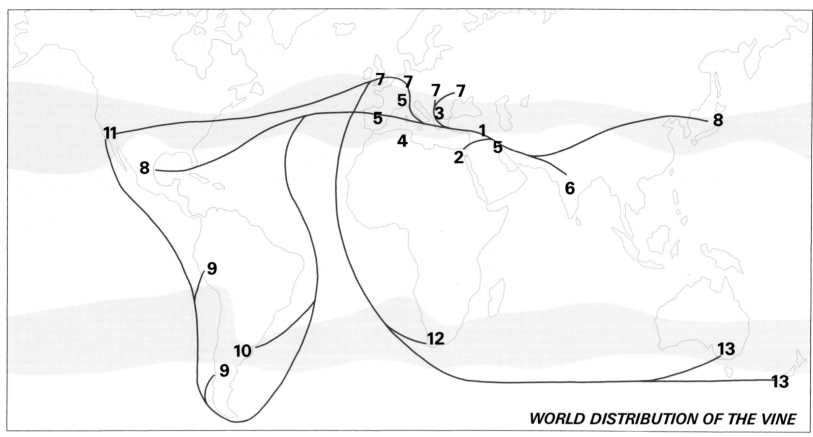

WORLD DISTRIBUTION OF THE VINE

*It is generally accepted that the vine was first cultivated in the Middle East during the period 6000-4000 BC and from the area south of the Caspian Sea **1** spread throughout the temperate regions of the world. In chronological order the distribution was: Egypt and Phoenicia – ± 3000 BC **2**; Greece and Crete – ± 2000 BC **3**; Sicily, Italy and Western North Africa – ± 1000 BC **4**; Spain, Portugal, Southern France, South-western Arabia – ± 500 BC **5**; Northern India and China 100BC **6**; the south of England, Northern Germany, the Rhineland, Northern France and the Balkans – 100-400AD **7**; Japan and Mexico – 1528-1545 **8**; Peru and Chile – 1548 **9**; Argentina 1557 **10**; California 1600-1610 **11**; South Africa –1655 **12**; South-western Australia and New Zealand 1813 **13**.*

For the first time the hidden world of wine was revealed to man. For the first time, with this knowledge, the possibility of control of the wine-making process, from the vineyard to the modern bottling plant – and including Pasteur's innovative method of 'pasteurizing' the wine by heating it to 55 degrees centigrade to destroy unwanted souring bacteria – suddenly became feasible. Vast improvements were promised, at the level of both quality and quantity.

But the full realization of the degree of control open to the winemaker was as yet far in the future, and in the next few years was to seem even more remote. During the three decades following Pasteur's remarkable discovery occurred a salutary reminder of the power of nature and the vulnerability of human aspirations. In the years after the repeal of the protective tariffs, the winemakers of the Cape and their European counterparts were to find both their competition and their legislation brutally overshadowed: benign nature, often taken for granted, turned against them with the start of the largest disaster in the history of wine, the great *Phylloxera vastatrix* epidemic which swept the winelands of the world in the second half of the nineteenth century.

Like the powdery mildew, *Phylloxera vastatrix* originated in North America. However, it was not a fungus but an

aphid and one whose lifecycle was closely and destructively bound up with that of the vine whose roots and branches it preyed upon at various stages of its life. Though not in itself bacterial, its ravages left the plant vulnerable to rot which effectively killed it.

In north-east America this near microscopic aphid was found living in a naturally parasitic relationship with about 60 species of a locally found form of wild grapevine, including *Vitis riparia, V. aestivalis* and *V. rupestris*. The roots of resistant *Vitis* species generate corky layers in wounds caused by phylloxera, allowing the plant to heal itself and prevent secondary rot.

In the early 1860s specimens of these wild grapevines were taken from America to France. Breeding experiments to incorporate resistance to powdery mildew in European grapevines using the tough wild stock had been mooted. Unknown to the experimenters, however, the vines carried specimens of the aphid in the earth about their roots.

The more sensitive European cultivated vine lacks the inherent resistance to phylloxera of the North American species. Within a few years of its first appearance the disease had caused widespread devastation, from the point of entry in the south-west of France in 1861 to the north and the Bur-

gundy area, resisting all attempts at control, and eventually wiping out some 75 per cent of the European vineyards – and this in spite of the fact that its only mode of locomotion was pedestrian, from one plant to the next.

The vine growers of the Cape watched the progress of the disease from what at first appeared a safe distance – with varied reactions. The diamond magnate Cecil John Rhodes, for example, saw an opportunity to profit from the disaster in Europe and promptly became a major shareholder in a syndicate to export Cape wine. This optimistic piece of opportunism, however, was defeated by the poor quality of the local product, which had deteriorated further on its bumpy voyage through the tropics. In the meantime, the Cape Government banned the importation of grapevine material from Europe, a move which was supported by the Austrian viticulturalist, Baron Carl von Babo, who had been invited to the Cape by the Colonial government to take over as its wine expert at the farm of Groot Constantia, then being purchased by the Government from the Cloete family as an experimental wine farm.

Von Babo's report endorsed the official ban on the importation of vines, which had kept out the phylloxera. He also suggested as a cure for the problem one which was already being implemented in Europe – the grafting of *Vitis vinifera* onto rootstock derived from resistant American stock, the initial bearer of destruction, but which was now to be the main agent of its control.

His advice proved crucial to the survival of the Cape winelands, for notwithstanding the Government's measures, phylloxera found its way into the local vineyards. It was first noticed in the Mowbray area in 1885, and was then found on the vines at Constantia and in the Helderberg area, two of the oldest wine-farming regions. Within a few years it had spread unchecked from its initial point of entry to lay waste most of the Cape winelands. It was a disaster of the first magnitude, and it shook the already tottering local wine industry to its foundations. The results were devastating. Many farmers went bankrupt, long family relationships with farming areas were broken, and the idealistic vision of security, natural as well as human, sank into the ruined fields.

The first and most powerful instinct of the farmers in the face of this calamity had been to save their vines. When the disease first appeared steps were taken to combat it directly, even though no successful and economically feasible chemical remedy had been found in Europe.

It soon became clear that a complete new start would have to be made, and that the vineyards would have to be cleared and reconstructed on a basis of grafted vines, as had been done in Europe.

To this extent the Cape vine growers had the benefit of the European experience. With the backing of the Vineyards Protection Act there began the gradual replacement of all the vineyards with vines grafted onto resistant American rootstock. The Government appointed a Phylloxera Commission with powers to destroy the infested stock, for which some small compensation was paid. The dissatisfaction which this caused among the growers led to the appointment of a select committee in 1889 to investigate the complaints. It was reported that although the regulations were causing tensions, there was no way in which they could be relaxed.

The Committee not only insisted upon continued strong action, but also made other recommendations which were subsequently adopted. These included restrictions on the import of any grapevine material from abroad and more stringent quarantine regulations; it also disallowed the use of any part of the vine for packaging. More importantly for the farmers' morale, it granted larger compensation for grapevines marauded by phylloxera.

The cleared vineyards were slowly rebuilt. The enforced grafting was soon appreciated by the farmers as the only way to overcome the disease and ensure against its return, and they and the nurserymen soon mastered the art of wholesale grafting – one which is still a feature of modern vineyards.

A major crisis of winelands history was thus overcome. As Hugh Johnson aptly writes in his *Wine Atlas of the World*, the phylloxera was 'undefeated but outmanoeuvred'. Other ailments, however, were not so easily cured. In 1886 gold was discovered in the Witwatersrand. Like Van Riebeeck's gold of

Monomotapa it beckoned adventurers, among whom was Cecil Rhodes. The clouds of war gathered with mounting tensions between Boer and Briton. The twentieth of December, 1895 saw the Jameson Raid as the curtain-raiser, political tensions culminating in 1899 when the Boer Republics of the Transvaal and the Orange Free State declared war on Britain.

The Anglo-Boer War and its rearguard action lasted until the Peace of Vereeniging in 1902, when the Boer Republics lost their independence and became part of the British Empire. In the years after the war the Boer Republics as such ceased to exist, and so did the traditional world of the Cape, both of which were incorporated by the Act of Union in 1910 into a new country, the Union of South Africa.

These were not easy years in the winelands. The hardships of the war were followed by uncertainty and economic stress exacerbated by the increasing problem of over-production. By 1904 the number of vines, now all grafted onto imported rootstock, had increased to some 78 million. Exports in 1905 were negligible, and a large surplus was carried over from the 1904 vintage. This was reflected in the Cape winemakers' old adage: 'Good crop bad cash; bad crop good cash.' Again it was the growers who were faced with ruin, this time of a different kind from that presented by phylloxera.

It was in response to this situation of over-production and resultant low prices for the wine that one of the most important features of the modern winelands was created – the co-operative movement.

This began in 1905 with the appointment of a government commission to examine the depression in the wine and brandy industry. It recommended the creation of the first co-operative wineries. The objective of the co-operative system was to secure the benefit of collective bargaining and marketing, as opposed to the traditional system of individual wine farmers competing with each other to market their own wine at the best prices they could obtain.

A further advantage of the co-operative winery was that plant and machinery could be used more effectively with less outlay of capital investment. Unit costs of production could be considerably reduced through the large volume of grapes being processed, and technical knowledge centralized at the co-operative. It would obviate the need for each grower to have a wine-production cellar on his farm. From now on the grower would be able to choose his degree of involvement with the wine-making process, making his own wine or distributing it in barrels, or simply delivering his grapes at harvest time and leaving the production of the wine to the co-operative and its chosen winemaker.

The Government made £50 000 (an enormous amount of money for those days) available for the establishment of these wineries. The first – the Drostdy in Tulbagh – came into operation in 1906. Over the next four years a further eight such pioneers were established at Helderberg, Helderfontein, Groot Drakenstein, Paarl, Wellington, Bovlei, Over Hex, and Montagu – of which, however, only four survive as originally constituted.

Most co-operatives were – and still are – run by committees elected from the member farmers contributing grapes to them. There would always be an elected chairman who was often the farmer who sold a part of his property as a site for the co-operative.

This system had intrinsic advantages but remained for a time somewhat limited. Power supply in these early days was apt to be a problem, often being supplied at harvest time by steam-engines or tractors. Moreover, the position with regard to over production in the winelands continued to deteriorate owing to the limited authority of the co-operatives themselves. Not all of them survived the strain: four were soon forced to close, even though the Government wrote off the balance of their loans.

Continued over-production led to a slump in prices; 1909 saw the lowest ever received for wine – £1 17s 6d a leaguer (577 litres). Prices during the years of the First World War, particularly from 1915 to 1917, also saw extremely low levels of between £2 10s and £3 a leaguer.

The burdens of this period were only slightly alleviated by, curiously enough, the phenomenon of the ostrich boom. From 1906 to 1913 ostrich feathers were high fashion in Europe, and excessive prices were paid. During this period about 10 million vines were uprooted in the Oudtshoorn area to make way for fields of lucerne to feed these valuable birds. At the height of the boom the ostrich population had spread down from the Karoo to the Breede River Valley, where the lucerne (alfalfa) grown on the lime-rich soil provided a highly beneficial diet. But the boom came to an end in 1913. Whereas horse-drawn transport made little feminine flutter, the advent of the motorcar made billowing plumage disconcerting and the feather market collapsed. The ostrich population retreated to Oudtshoorn and most of the farmers went back to planting vines.

They planted far too many. By 1918 there were almost 87 billion vines in the winelands, producing an annual 56 million litres of wine. Unsaleable and unsold, millions of litres were allowed to run to waste.

By hard experience the co-operative principle was being brought home to the growers. At the same time it gradually became clear that for the co-operative movement to be fully effective all farmers would have to belong to it. This was the thesis put forward by Charles W.H. Kohler, and it was a concept which was to bear fruit in 1918 with the foundation of 'Ko-operatieve Wijnbouwers Vereniging van Zuid-Afrika Beperkt' – the sonorous full title of what is commonly referred to as KWV.

For several years as Chairman of the Cape Wine Farmers' and Wine Merchants' Association, Kohler had been involved in the mounting problems of the wine industry. This first organization collapsed in due course but he continued to refine his concept of the co-operative principle, which crystallized in 1917 when he handed a draft constitution for a new organization to a committee of growers which had been formed to draw up a memorandum.

His concept was accepted, and a new co-operative formed. Registered on the eighth of January, 1918, it was an organization which was to alter the structure of the winelands, providing them with a new unity, an all-important bargaining power in relation to the wine merchants, and a legal and administrative machinery which provided the basis for the present system.

The main objective which KWV set itself in 1918 was 'So to direct, control and regulate the sale and disposal by its members of their produce, being that of the grape, as shall secure or tend to secure for them a continuously adequate return for such produce'. And central to the achievement of this aim was the necessity of persuading the growers to join the new co-operative.

In due course more than 95 per cent of the wine-grape growers joined KWV. Through this joint action they were in a position to conclude agreements with local merchants in terms of which the market price of wine was increased and stabilized. The merchants agreed to make their purchases only from members of KWV, with the result that prices gradually rose, standing in 1919 at £10 a leaguer. A high price, however, did not necessarily mean a stable one: and when the years between 1921 and 1923 saw particularly heavy crops, the farmers once again received only £3 a leaguer. During this period 91 000 leaguers of wine were run off into the Eerste River. In these dire circumstances the farmers took matters into their own hands. Dealers succeeded in buying wine direct from them at lower prices than those of KWV. As low prices continued some of its members lost faith in the organization and withdrew from it.

Then in 1924, KWV received Government ratification of its powers when the Smuts Government passed Act 5 of 1924. This was the Wine and Spirit Control Act which empowered KWV to fix the minimum price to be paid to farmers for their distilling wine each year. It was the start of a progressive process of legal protection and control of the wine industry which was to be refined over the coming decades to meet a wide range of contingencies. Among its immediate effects, apart from securing for the growers a 'continuously adequate return' for their produce, was a sharp reduction in the number of wine merchants who, deprived of a manipulable market, disappeared.

The developments in scientific viniculture which had followed Pasteur's discoveries were now gaining acceptance in South Africa. In 1925 at the Stellenbosch University farm of Welgevallen there occurred an event whose significance was not to be realized for many years, when the well-known viticulturist Professor Abraham Izak Perold produced the first seedlings of the Pinotage vine. This, the first successful locally bred variety, was developed from a cross of the varieties Pinot Noir and Cinsaut, then commonly known as Hermitage. The work was later continued by Professor C.J. Theron who saved and propagated Perold's original seedlings and began the long and arduous task of evaluating the variety which, two decades later under the name of Pinotage, was to

make its debut, achieving fame as the first successfully developed South African variety, one which was superbly adapted to the local conditions, yet which possessed a strongly individual character of its own.

There were a number of such developments in the 1920s, but many of them remained dormant with the advent of the World Depression from the early Thirties onwards. The year 1935, however, saw the emergence into public status of an important new company, that of the Stellenbosch Farmers' Winery, the inspiration of an immigrant American, William Charles Winshaw.

Trained originally in medicine, Winshaw arrived at the Cape in 1899 with a consignment of mules ordered by the Cape Government. A one-time acquaintance of Buffalo Bill, and a vivid personality in his own right, he stayed on in South Africa after the 'English War', and turned from medicine to wine. In 1924 he joined forces with one Gabriel Krige Jnr, whose father had purchased in 1870 a section of Adam Tas' historic farm, Libertas, on the northern bank of the Eerste River. They named their jointly owned farm 'Oude Libertas' and began making and selling wine on the farm.

Even though the local taste at this time was largely for brandy and sweet fortified wines, as a medical man Winshaw considered a natural wine more beneficial to the public health, and so from the outset he made it his business to concentrate upon this type of wine, exemplified in his Chateau Libertas and La Gratitude wines.

In spite of the development of natural wines and improvements in quality, overseas markets remained largely closed to South African wine. Only South African sherry and port continued to enjoy a healthy market in Britain (Perold made an extensive study of their production in this period, while Professor Theron concentrated on port and Dr Niehaus on sherry). The advent of the Second World War put heavy restrictions on the import of equipment, and the co-operatives in particular marked time during this period.

But 1940 saw major new legislation extending the powers of KWV and laying down the framework for the system of total control which now includes primary producers, wholesalers, retailers and importers.

The powers vested originally in KWV had been limited to wine for distilling purposes only. The minimum price measures did not cover 'good' wines – wine not for distilling – as it had been assumed that once the price of distilling wine had been fixed the price of good wine would automatically become stabilized. In the event this proved false, and good wine prices have fluctuated dangerously. After investigation, the problem was resolved by also vesting in KWV control over the production and marketing of good wine in terms of Act 23 of 1940. A minimum price was fixed for good wine; all transactions between merchants and producers had to carry the approval of KWV; and all payments for wine had to be made through the organization.

The Act further stipulated that no person might produce wine except under a permit issued by KWV. Such permits

would only be granted if KWV was satisfied that the producer was in possession of the necessary cellar equipment, tanks and vats for the making of good wine. The problem of overproduction was met by empowering KWV in terms of its constitution to fix annually the percentage of each member's vintage which was not saleable on the local market. This portion of the crop, which became known as the surplus, had to be delivered to KWV without payment or, if the farmer could sell this fraction, he had to make an equivalent reimbursement to KWV. The 'surplus' was processed by KWV into wines, brandies and spirits.

The conclusion of the Second World War marked an increasing change of pace in the wine industry.

These developments were both accompanied and made possible by technical advances. Perhaps the most important of these, and one which is still central to the white wine aspect of the industry, was that of the process known as 'cold fermentation'. KWV had made a study of the process in the pre-war years, but had advised the farmers against it. The post-war period, however, saw renewed experiments, the most important of which came from the Graue family, an immigrant German father-and-son team who established the process on a large scale at their farm Nederburg in the Paarl Valley. At much the same time N.C. Krone was also experimenting in the Tulbagh Valley. His attempts, however, were less practical than the method of the Graues, which was to be exploited on a large scale, and permitted fine control in the making of natural white wine in the hot South African conditions. Developments both in equipment and methods accompanied this expansion.

In the period following the Second World War, the influence of producing wholesalers increased parallel with the enlarged role of KWV and the co-operatives. Among them, of course, was that of Stellenbosch Farmers' Winery, still the largest of the producing wholesalers.

In spite of the 1940 controls the old problem of overproduction (enhanced by streamlined modern methods) again threatened in the 1950s. This led to the introduction of the 'quota system', which provided a legal limit to the amount of vines which the farmer might grow . The first modern South African quotas were fixed in terms of vines growing on the farmer's property as at the twenty first of June, 1957, an allowance being made for vines uplifted immediately prior to that date in order to renew the vineyards. Increases in quota took place in subsequent years.

The 1956 Act recognized the principle of declaring the surplus each year and price fixing by KWV, and made these provisions applicable to all producers of wine, whether members of KWV or not. The Act further stipulated that all purchases of wine had to be made through or from KWV and that no one might obtain or distil wine without the permission of the organization. It also provided the basic administration machinery of the winelands as it exists today. In 1992 KWV suspended the quota system.

—CONSTANTIA—
THE VALLEY OF THE VINES

In 1695 Van der Stel contrived to have himself granted 891 morgen (approximately 770 hectares) of land. It was later supplemented with grazing rights amounting to a staggering 10 000 morgen (approximately 8 500 hectares), virtually the whole of the Peninsula. In the midst of all this cunningly acquired chunk of paradise, he built Groot Constantia, now a symbol of the country's wine-making heritage.

In laying out the estate Van der Stel employed the expert help of the Dutch East India Company's gardeners and personally supervised the bringing-in of the harvest. The meticulous and patient handling of the vineyards was matched by care and attention in the wine cellar. The result was a wine of an aristocratic quality which presaged its future fame. Having mastered the art of making natural wines, Van der Stel extended his ambitions and set about the making of a sweet fortified wine similar to those which were coming into fashion in Holland and England at this time. He succeeded in making a wine which compared more than favourably with the contemporary European product. It was this wine to which the Governor gave the name of 'Constantia'.

In 1699 Van der Stel retired from public life and withdrew to his estate. In the years after his death in 1712 , little further is heard of Constantia wine. The estate was initially divided into three sections , Groot Constantia, Bergvliet and Klein Constantia, and the grazing rights to the surrounding land expired. Groot Constantia was later further subdivided, the subdivision confusingly being called Klein Constantia. The property originally called Klein Constantia later came to be called Hoop op Constantia, the name it retains to this day. Bergvliet was also later subdivided, a portion becoming Buitenverwachting.

But it was the next owner who was to recreate the legend of Constantia in all its splendour. In 1778, Jan Serrurier, the then owner of the farm, sold it to Hendrik Cloete. A direct descendant of Jacob Cloete van Kempen, Van Riebeeck's undergardener at Table Bay, Cloete took over a farm which still appeared in poor condition. Hendrik was to take a firm grip on its fortunes within a few years. Under Hendrik Cloete, Constantia's European reputation expanded rapidly. By 1783 he had begun exporting his wines to Europe, including to a number of its monarchs. The King of Prussia was a favourite customer.

Few travellers visiting the Cape during this period failed to include Groot Constantia on their itineraries, a steady flow of visitors which continues unabated to the present day. The flamboyant French explorer, Le Vaillant, for example, called on Cloete in 1783, referring to him as '*le prince vigneron*' – the prince of vine-dressers. The first invasion by the British occurred in 1795 and the following year Percival visited the 'village' of Constantia, where he enjoyed the 'sweet, luscious and excellent wines'. Cloete's son, also Hendrik, continued

Groot Constantia in the early days of the Cloetes.

the making of his father's fine, rich, sweet wines. John Burchell, the famous explorer, visited the farm in 1811, during the ownership of the younger Cloete. Like others before him, he commented on the 'dwarf vines' and on the fact that the grapes were left on them so long that they shrivelled and their juice turned to syrup. The Cloetes employed a technique of twisting the grape bunches on the vine, so arresting the flow of sap and turning the grapes into semi-raisins.

But the halcyon days of Groot Constantia were almost over. Many changes were taking place in the society of the free burghers which cast their shadows over Constantia. Amongst them, of course, was the permanent presence of the British. From the wine farmers' point of view, however, other changes had a deeper meaning and effect. The repeal of the protective tariffs by the Palmerston Government in 1861 was followed two decades later by the start of the phylloxera epidemic – the disease was first noticed a few kilometres away, near Mowbray, in 1885. In the same year, after 100 years of ownership, the Cloete family sold its estate to the Colonial Government. After the epidemic the farm became a Government experimental wine farm and the homestead was converted into a hostel for the viticultural students.

During the present century Constantia, slowly encroached upon by the expanding suburbs of Cape Town, has continued in this educational and experimental role, only one incident marring the even passage of its days. In December of 1925 a spark from the kitchen chimney set alight the old building with its thatched roof. The house as it stands today is an architectural phoenix, a meticulous restoration. After completion of the work the homestead was refurnished through the gift of a Cape Town shipping magnate, Alfred Aaron de Pass, and opened as a museum to the public in 1927.

Klein Constantia passed through the hands of two other owners before returning to the Cloete family in 1870 when it was bought by Dirk Gysbert Cloete as a simple wine farm. He sold the farm in 1873 for £1 699 to William Brading. The next owners, the Van der Byls, worked hard on the farm, but it was not all work and no play in nineteenth-century Constantia as there were continual picnics, luncheons, and all-day shooting parties. The whole emphasis at Klein Constantia changed from farming to lavish entertainment when Abraham Lochner de Villiers took possession in 1913 with his American steel millionairess wife, Clara Hussey.

In 1963 Diana and Ian Austin took over this property and it reverted to a genuine farm. Ian, as chairman of the Constantia Heritage Group, supported its request that adequate facilities be made available to private farmers for the making and distribution of Constantia wine. However, partly because of urban development encroaching upon Klein Constantia over some decades, the farm was in a derelict condition when it was bought and saved by Duggie Jooste, whose family had controlled the producing wine and spirit company, Sedgwick Tayler Limited, for three generations. Duggie had been chairman when the company merged with SFW in 1970.

The third of the subdivisions of the original Constantia Estate was named Bergvliet, 200 morgen of which was bought in 1793 by Cornelis Brink. He sold most of the farm a year later to his brother Arend, who called the property 'Buitenverwachting' – 'Beyond expectation'. He sold the property in 1797 to Ryk Arnoldus Cloete, brother of the famous Hendrik Cloete of Constantia and the farm reached its heyday in 1825. The next owner was Ryk's nephew, Pieter Lourens Cloete, who bought it in 1827. Five years later, however, Pieter had sold the farm to his brother Johan Gerhard who, like their uncle, also went insolvent.

In 1852 Buitenverwachting was bought by Abraham de Smidt but sold a year later to Jacob Willem Brunt whose brother owned the adjoining farm of Klein Constantia. In 1866 it was sold yet again, this time to Johannes Wynand Louw. Through the female line of this family, the Lategans arrived in the valley, taking over no less than five farms. Buitenverwachting was eventually inherited by Stephanus Petrus Lategan and later by his son Daniel, whose daughter Olivia then lived there with her husband George Louw. His nephew Willem Lategan owned the neighbouring farm Constantia Uitsig until his death a few years ago. The farm is now owned and run by Willem's son Stephen.

This brief history of the Constantia valley would be incomplete without a reference to Alphen. The Alphen Estate is no more, and the wines are no longer made in Constantia (Alphen is now merely a brand name for some of the wines distributed by Gilbeys) but it is one of the oldest names in the Cape wine story. Originally granted to a free burgher in the late seventeenth century, the property of Alphen was transferred to Simon van der Stel who, however, never incorporated it into his own estate of Constantia.

After Van der Stel's death, the Dutch East India Company refused his heirs their claim of Alphen as a part of Constantia and it was regranted instead to Theunis Dirkz van Schalkwyk in 1714. There followed several changes of ownership, till Abraham Lever came into possession of the five morgen property in 1748, and it was he who began building the magnificent homestead which today forms a part of the Alphen Hotel (now owned by Peter Bairnsfather Cloete, a descendant of the first Cloete of Groot Constantia). The dignity of the old Cape Georgian homestead and its gracious outbuildings still recall the atmosphere of the past in this wine-making valley.

THE WINE
INDUSTRY TODAY

Wine was produced at the Cape within seven years of Van Riebeeck's settlement in 1652. By then, the employees of the Dutch East India Company had already brewed their own beer with grain harvested from their first crops. A distiller (together with two stills) arrived at the Colony at about the same time, though the first record of successful distillation of Cape wine is 1672.

Within 50 years of its establishment, the Cape wine and spirits industry had acquired many of the features which are still, to some extent, with us today: firstly, wine production exceeded domestic consumption; secondly, the annual yield of wines and brandies was sold through a monopoly (the Company) whose primary function was not the commercialization of the crop; finally, the overall standard of the Cape's produce was poor, despite a few quality examples to vindicate the industry's potential.

The history of the South African liquor industry has pretty much followed this pattern since the seventeenth century, irrespective of who ruled the subcontinent and determined the country's commercial practices. At the heart of the matter is a concentration of power at the manufacture/wholesale point of the product cycle, together with a dissipation of power at the agricultural and retail ends of the spectrum.

Wine producers have enjoyed periods of plenty, just as they have suffered immense hardship. Sudden and substantial swings from the one to the other extreme characterize their lives. In the mid nineteenth century, the era of Imperial Preference brought a seemingly boundless demand from the English market. The end of this boom coincided with a series of crop failures, as first oïdium and then later phylloxera devastated the vineyards. For many farmers these catastrophes spelled bankruptcy. A mere handful of years earlier Imperial Preference had brought sales in line with the vast supply.

These patterns, and the experiences they have imprinted, go some of the way to explaining the present structure of the

LEFT: *Wineries along the railway line, below the Papegaaiberg in Stellenbosch.*

Pietman Hugo, the chairman of KWV.

industry. Like King Priam of Troy, the steps taken to prevent the fulfilment of a prophecy cause it to come to pass. The manoeuvres aimed at avoiding a repetition of past disasters have flung the country's wine farmers headlong towards the fate they have been at such pains to avoid.

In order to understand the workings of the Cape wine industry in the last decade of the twentieth century, it is necessary to be familiar with the significant role played by Kooperatiewe Wijnbouwers Vereniging (KWV). The powerful organization was formed in 1918 as a kind of national wine co-operative, a trade union of the country's grape growers seeking to present a united front to the wholesale or processing sector of the trade.

The circumstances leading to the creation of KWV were the perennial problems of over-supply in the midst of an economic downturn. Wine farmers desperate to obtain some income on the stocks in their cellars were being negotiated by the wholesale trade into accepting prices which were well below an acceptable rate of return.

The discovery that their interests were better served by creating a producer price cartel inspired the country's wine farmers to extend the principle of united action. Initially KWV protected the price of the distilling wine crop, its authority to do so being embodied in the Wine and Spirit Control Act No. 5 of 1924. Subsequently this was extended to cover so-called good wine (Act 23 of 1940). Later amendments empowered KWV to grant production quotas to aspirant wine farmers, fixing the potential size of the country's wine crop, the regions in which wine grapes might be grown, and therefore the minimum income a farmer might be guaranteed. Only in 1992 was the quota system suspended. In doing so, KWV acknowledged that the high cost of entry into wine farming ensured that no new players could afford to come into the business solely on the strength of the guaranteed minimum good wine price.

In 1979 the South African liquor industry underwent a substantial re-alignment. A protracted price war between market leaders South African Breweries (SAB) and the Rembrandt Group's Intercontinental Breweries was settled through mediation provided by the Sanlam Group's late chairman Fred du Plessis. In terms of the arrangements concluded at the time, the Rembrandt Group disposed of their brewing interests to SAB, effectively granting them a monopoly. In return for this arrangement, SAB agreed to sell its shares in Stellenbosch Farmers' Winery (SFW), the country's major wine and spirits wholesaler, to a newly formed holding company which would also own the Rembrandt Group's wine and spirits interests, Distillers/Oude Meester. This new behemoth came to be called Cape Wine and Distillers (CWD). It controlled more than 80 per cent of the country's wine and spirits turnover, as well as South Africa's major retail chains. Since the Rembrandt Group also owned 49 per cent of Gilbey Distillers and Vintners, as well as its retail chain, the concentration of power came closer to 90 per cent.

The shareholding in CWD was divided equally between the former owners of Distillers/Oude Meester and SFW

La Concorde, the headquarters of Kooperatiwe Wijnbouwers Vereniging (KWV) in Paarl.

(30 per cent each) with a further 30 per cent allocated to KWV and the remaining 10 per cent offered to members of the public. Ostensibly the shareholders of the former major competitors in the wine and spirits industry would enjoy equal power in the new company and would represent the interests of the old production/processing/wholesaling sector. KWV's 30 per cent slice of CWD was intended to represent the interests of the wine farmers who could, in addition, subscribe for the 10 per cent of the shares issued to members of the public.

No sooner was the Cape Wine and Distillers deal formalized when some of the key players set about re-aligning the power structure within the company. The Rembrandt Group pooled its 30 per cent parcel of shares with those of KWV in a jointly owned holding company which effectively controlled 60 per cent of the shares of CWD. In other words, SAB had been finessed out of any real say in the management of the wine and spirits industry. It is reasonable to assume that the brewing giant had anticipated this strategy. The beer monopoly which had been carrot to these arrangements, together with the advantages of ending the price war between SAB and the Rembrandt-controlled Intercontinental Breweries, must have justified the risk of entering the CWD venture as a possible minority.

From 1979 until 1988 the Cape wine and spirits industry was managed by Rembrandt and KWV, through CWD Holdings. During this time several state-appointed commissions of enquiry criticized the oligarchical nature of the wholesale trade. In addition considerable debate centred on the question of vertical integration in the liquor industry. The country's largest wholesalers also owned the country's largest

retail chains. At the time of the 1979 industry re-alignment it had been agreed that CWD would sell off its retail operations. At the same time the Government fixed at 12 the maximum number of stores in any new retail operation. This decision effectively ensured that the retail sector would never develop a countervailing power likely to equal the domination at wholesale of CWD.

By the mid 1980s it was clear that the 1979 dispensation was politically inept. The State could hardly claim to support free trade principles while it condoned a virtual and unnecessary wine and spirits monopoly and prejudiced the prospects of a strong independent retail trade by allowing the continued existence of the powerful, vertically integrated outlets of CWD. Various scenarios were planned and subsequently abandoned. Finally two solutions were arrived at – one for the wholesale sector and one for the retail trade.

The wholesale trade was to be rendered cosmetically more competitive by the separate stock exchange listing of the two key players who had been united in the formation of CWD. The marriage of the two Stellenbosch-based wholesalers was to be annulled, with each company recording its activities separately, and each company's shares separately quoted on the Johannesburg Stock Exchange. On the surface, competition had returned to the wholesale sector. In reality, however, the same shareholders retained control. KWV and the Rembrandt Group jointly held 60 per cent of Distillers and 60 per cent of SFW.

In the time that has elapsed since the implementation of these arrangements, evidence of the Rembrandt Group's direct control of the affairs of both companies has been widely acknowledged. Changes in the executive management of

SFW have been imposed by the shareholders, with key personnel joining the wholesaler from other operations within the Rembrandt fold. Hence it is true to say that about 85 per cent of South Africa's wine and spirits industry is partly controlled by the organization charged with managing its regulations and protecting the interests of the individual farmer.

Since KWV became directly involved in the commercial management of the wine and spirits industry, opinion has been divided as to whether or not the organization is fulfilling the terms of its charter. Formed originally in the midst of great over-production, KWV was directed to bring into harmony the relationship between supply and demand in the wine industry.

In the 60 years between the formation of KWV and the organization's entering the wholesale sector of the local wine industry in the 1979 re-alignment, its role was indisputably that of a union battling for the rights of its members. It fought to keep taxes and excise duties as low as possible, wielding considerable influence to achieve these results. The country's producer/wholesalers learned at their cost that a rampant KWV was a difficult, if not intransigent, opponent. The rigorous imposition of a minimum wine price system, setting floor prices for distilling wine and subsequently for table or 'good' wine, made it impossible for the brand owners to force farmers to accept uneconomically low prices. KWV steadfastly re-wrote the laws of supply and demand, ensuring that no bulk trader enjoyed a position of privilege commensurate with his size. At the same time it ensured that few, if any, farmers went to the wall, no matter how inefficient.

The basic operation of the KWV-imposed system was very simple: you could only farm wine grapes in districts approved by KWV. The total quantity you were authorized to produce was firmly circumscribed by the allocation of a quota, fixing your maximum tonnage. KWV guaranteed to take up any portion of your distilling wine crop that you were unable to sell, agreeing in advance to pay at least the advance price for distilling wine.

The recent suspension of the quota system has changed very little. Farmers can now plant vineyards wherever they consider the land and climate suitable. They can deliver any quantity of distilling wine to KWV, which is still obliged to take up this production, and to pay for it on the same basis as it takes in distilling wine. However, the cost of establishing new vineyards is so prohibitively high that no new player would enter the market solely on the strength of the guaranteed minimum income. Only serious producers of quality wines could conceive of a return on investment at the current entry cost. In other words, the long-established operations which cynically abuse the minimum wine price system will continue to flourish, despite the scrapping of production quotas. At the same time the industry provides no financial encouragement to entrepreneurs seeking to open up new wine-producing regions.

Until recently (when a more segmented pricing system was introduced) all wine and wine grapes were divided into two categories: good (table) wine and distilling wine. Just prior to the annual harvest KWV estimates the likely national production, as well as the probable demand for good wine, distilling wine and for grapes used for non-alcoholic purposes. Anything surplus to this amount accrues to the surplus account, calculated as a percentage of the distilling wine crop. Hence, if the estimated national yield is nine million hectolitres, with a demand for good wine of three million hectolitres and a demand for distilling wine of three million hectolitres, the surplus of three million hectolitres is taken to represent a 50 per cent 'nominal' over-production.

KWV would then pay out initially only 50 per cent of the distilling wine price to any farmer not selling his wine as table wine. Thereafter, the organization takes up the production for distilling wine purposes and grape juice on a contract purchasing basis, processing and disposing of it in the best possible way to ensure that the Cape is not swamped with a wine lake. The income from this stock disposal is then handed over to the farmers in proportion to the quantity received from them, less the KWV's management costs. Such income might take a year or two to materialize. It is known as the 'bonus' or *agterskot* portion of the farmers' income. While it is unlikely to exceed the upfront payment on distilling wine, it frequently comes close enough to this amount for farmers to earn the listed distilling wine price on the entire portion of their crop not sold as table wine.

This system has innumerable advantages for the country's bulk wine farmers: they are guaranteed an income, and the certain disposal of their production; to the extent that they are able to sell a portion of their harvest as table wine, their average income is always greater than the product of their yield and the distilling wine price; this frees them to cultivate tonnage without assuming responsibility for the marketing of their harvest. Farmers, in other words, are there to grow grapes; someone else – the co-ops or KWV – takes on the business of selling what has been brought into the cellars.

Unfortunately, this same arrangement has innumerable disadvantages for the country's wine drinkers: there is only a limited incentive to farmers to aim for quality: unless the producer is already actively involved in marketing his own crop, he is better served if he sacrifices quality for quantity to maximize the income provided by the KWV's guarantee.

The effect of these arrangements over the years has been the polarization of the wine market itself. Premium wine producers who are either marketing their own wines to the trade or directly to the public are not dependent on the KWV's fallback position. They are committed to quality, and in general produce less than the potential yield of their vineyards in order to maintain it. They operate from the high-quality table wine areas, use minimal if any irrigation, and plant market-oriented varieties. They succeed because they earn high revenues per tonne, albeit on low yields.

On the other side of the spectrum are the most efficient producers of pure wine litreage. They farm in areas where

Bottles left for further maturation in The Bergkelder Vinotèque.

there is plenty of sun and unlimited supplies of water for irrigation. They maximize their yield per hectare through high tonnage at low income per tonne. They depend entirely on KWV as a buyer of last resort, processing their grapes or wine to make grape juice concentrate or distilling wine. It is a tribute to the KWV's skill in operating within the system it has created that the industry disposes of its own surpluses without subsidy, save for the inflationary effect of a minimum pricing structure.

Perhaps where KWV is not fulfilling its wider responsibilities to the wine industry as a whole is in middle ground between the two extremes of the spectrum. Here the attrition of low income with insufficient resources for growth continues to take its toll. Farmers who are trying to upgrade their production through improved planting material and lower yields need more capital than is normally available to them to finance the shift from the volume to the quality end of the spectrum. Those who have embarked on costly upgrading projects often run out of funds on the way; those who simply try and sit it out have found their position deteriorating over the years.

Vineyards have always seemed like sound assets to the banks. Many farmers in the western Cape have been kept going through increased loans secured by the supposedly enhanced value of their farms. Now, in much the same way as Third World debt has rendered the western banking system impotent to act, South African financial institutions find themselves literally over a barrel when it comes to foreclosing on any important wine farming debt.

In summary, the role played by KWV has not promoted wine quality to the same extent that it has encouraged the

production of surpluses. The premium wine farmers derive little benefit from the organization, and often find themselves at odds with it, at least to the extent that it appears to support the interests of the major wholesalers in which it is now a joint controlling shareholder. The country's bulk grape growers have, however, become increasingly dependent on KWV: the efficient disposal of production surpluses requires a capital intensive infrastructure which only KWV can maintain. The intertwining of cause and effect, of administration and self-interest, has produced a Gordian knot which will, in the long run, require an Alexandrian solution.

Distillers Corporation is the listed controlling company of The Bergkelder and the Oude Meester Group. Prior to the 1979 liquor industry re-alignment these companies were part of the Rupert family/Rembrandt tobacco group empire. They were subsequently incorporated in Cape Wine and Distillers Ltd, together with Stellenbosch Farmers' Winery. Overall control of Cape Wine and Distillers was vested jointly in the hands of KWV and the Rembrandt Group. In 1988 the former Cape Wine companies were separately listed on the Johannesburg Stock Exchange. The effect of this was largely cosmetic inasmuch as it appeared to reduce the concentration of power in the wholesale wine and spirits industry. In reality, however, the same shareholders controlled the two companies.

Distillers Corporation was altogether the more attractive investment prospect at the time: by the late 1980s it dominated the most profitable sectors of the wine and spirits trade. All but one of the country's leading brands of brandy came from its cellars. Moreover, through The Bergkelder it handled the wines of most of South Africa's best-known

The Bergkelder Vinotèque cellar, in which conditions of temperature and humidity are meticulously controlled.

Dr Anton Rupert, chairman of Rembrandt Holdings Investment Limited.

estates, operating some on a joint venture basis, but with outright ownership of several of them.

This kind of business was far more profitable than the declining trade in low price table wine and cane spirits, the two staples of Stellenbosch Farmers' Winery. Brandy was already in the midst of an upswing, having benefited enormously from the role played by the Brandy Foundation in countering the growth of whisky. Distillers' brands were all strong, and effectively segmented the local brown spirits market. Premium brandies like Oude Meester, a range of proprietary names like Viceroy, Klipdrif and Richelieu and a couple of discount lines all contributed to ringing out the opposition.

Distillers also distributed several of the country's leading brands of whisky. In some cases the company also enjoyed exclusive importation rights, thereby ensuring the maintenance of healthy margins. Products like Johnnie Walker and White Horse were the exclusive preserve of the Group until the establishment of a joint venture in 1991 between the former Cape Wine companies and the UK-based United Distillers Group.

The Bergkelder had been a growing force in the premium wine trade in South Africa from the early 1970s. Initially conceived by Anton Rupert, the operation was elegant in its simplicity and commercially successful. The introduction of wine of origin legislation in 1973 focused attention in South Africa for the first time on the potential of estate, rather than branded wines. While many farming enterprises qualified for registration as estates in terms of this legislation, they all faced similar problems when it came to marketing their crops. All lacked a sales, distribution and marketing infra-

structure able to get the wines from the estates in the Cape to the market in the Transvaal – over 1500 kilometres away. The wine farmers were also generally not familiar with the politics and practices of the retail liquor trade. Sales networks, deals, promotions and incentives are terms which seemed strangely foreign to families which had owned and managed wine farms in the Western Cape for several generations. Distillers' wine estate infrastructure, called The Bergkelder (meaning mountain cellar), provided exactly the marketing and distribution support so vital to the estate wine producers.

On the surface, the partnership between the estates and the Rupert organization through The Bergkelder has countless advantages and no downside risk. The Bergkelder undertakes to market the entire crop of each of the participating estates. A portion of this wine is bottled and distributed under the name of the estate. The technical side of the business is owned by The Bergkelder, who provide storage tanks, bottling equipment, depots and the requisite sales force. The Bergkelder also takes up all the bulk wine produced at the estates for use in its own brands such as Fleur du Cap, Drostdyhof and Stellenryck.

Some of the producers have come to recognize that there is a hidden downside to this arrangement: both partners share equally in the marketing costs of the estate wines; both draw equally from the profits. While wines are in the 'pipeline' however they are usually stored in The Bergkelder's cellars, with ownership technically in the hands of The Bergkelder itself. This makes it very difficult for any producer to terminate the partnership: several vintages of his wines have

passed out of his control. If he wants to make it on his own, he faces a potential absence from the market place of a couple of years. This same liability affects the saleability of the estate. It is not an attractive prospect for a buyer to know that, in the event of his not wishing to continue the arrangement with The Bergkelder, it will be some time before he has wines to offer to the market. This has meant that when estate owners want to sell their farms, the buyer is inevitably The Bergkelder, or someone associated with the group.

Notwithstanding this problem, The Bergkelder operation has proved to be singularly successful. The estates distributing through its infrastructure have enjoyed the widest possible access to the market. The wines are better known than many of those of the more independent wineries. The proprietors have been free to get on with their grape growing, secure in the knowledge that the entire crop will be disposed of, either in bottle or in bulk.

On the technical side, the estates enjoy access to some of the country's finest viticulturists. State-of-the-art planting material, superb quality French barrels, ideal ageing conditions and the sheer muscle of the group are all benefits of great value, even if they are difficult to quantify.

In addition, The Bergkelder (through its 'Vinotèque') runs its own special release schemes in which the estates are free to participate. These include the annual pre-release, a futures sale where the buyer is able to reserve wines prior to their release, paying current prices to anticipate inflation. The Bergkelder also holds an annual tender sale, where buyers (through trade licensees) submit sealed tenders for more mature wines. This particular selling strategy has an advantage over conventional auctions for the wine buyer. The Bergkelder agrees to charge all those who have tendered successfully the lowest price applicable on the complete sale of the parcel. In other words, if there are 100 cases on offer and the various tender bids range from 100 rand per case to 60 rand per case, the highest tenderers whose combined bids total the 100 cases obtain the stock, and they pay the lowest

Dr Julius Laszlo, manager of wine production at The Bergkelder.

Stellenbosch Farmers' Winery, South Africa's largest producing wholesaler.

price of any of their successful bids. As a result, all customers pay the same amount, thus ensuring price and image stability in the trade.

The Bergkelder's own range of quality wines includes Stellenryck and Fleur du Cap. Both of these are proprietary brands, the grapes which go into their production deriving either from contracted estates, or from individual farmers whose viticultural practices comply with the company's specifications. Several of these wines enjoy the same treatment or *élevage* as the estate wines; special selections, such as the Cellarmaster's Choice, are arguably amongst the finest red wines produced in South Africa. Given the range of quality grapes purchased by The Bergkelder and the facilities available for wine-making and maturation, it is hardly surprising that limited quantities of such select wines rival even the best produced on the individual estates.

The other major wine-producing and wholesaling group, Stellenbosch Farmers' Winery, was the brainchild and creation of William Charles Winshaw, a larger-than-life American who settled in South Africa at the turn of the century and developed an enterprise which in time became the most successful wine wholesaler in the country. Prior to the 1979 liquor industry re-alignment, SFW was the wholly owned subsidiary of South African Breweries. Perhaps due to the synergy of popular priced brands in the two companies, and the directors' grasp of the industry, in the 1960s and 1970s SFW dominated the wine and white spirits industry.

Until it was eclipsed in the 1980s by Smirnoff vodka, Mainstay cane spirit was South Africa's largest selling white spirit brand. Its sales represented over 90 per cent of the cane spirit category and at one stage its volumes exceeded 70 per cent of all white spirits, including gin and vodka. At the same time SFW marketed the leading brand of gin. While the company enjoyed only limited success with local brandies, it drew reasonable revenues from the sale and distribution of Scotch whisky and substantial income from the sale of white spirits.

During the 1970s its wine sales were the envy of the industry. It owned the dominant brands at the popular end of the market, with volumes in Lieberstein, Virginia and Oom Tas running to over 30 million litres per year: at one stage Lieberstein was the world's largest selling wine. In addition, the company's prestige brands of Zonnebloem and Nederburg controlled their respective market segments. Nederburg in particular enjoyed a unique position: it was known to be a deluxe quality affordable product insofar as its regular release wines were concerned; at the same time its annual Paarl auction imbued its special selections with a status and credibility unrivalled by any other producer.

The Nederburg Auction was launched in 1975, one of the first such selling arrangements. It has become the best known and most respected of the special release forums, with annual turnovers around the two million rand mark. The auction is a trade event. Only liquor licensees are permitted to bid for the nearly 10 000 cases of wine on offer each year. The sale takes place after the harvest and before the late autumn rains set in. In the past decade this has meant a date not later than mid-April and the auction has almost always enjoyed the kind of perfect weather which enhances its reputation as *the* gala event on the Cape wine calendar.

The Nederburg Auction is usually opened by a leading international figure associated with the European or New World wine industry. More and more the speakers provide a policy guideline for South Africa's wine producers. This famous auction is one of the few events in the year when most of the country's leading winemakers are assembled together at a single venue.

For those members of the public lucky enough to secure an entrance ticket to the day's proceedings, the auction is an opportunity to wine, dine and socialize in the gardens of the Nederburg homestead. For the dedicated traders, it is a hard day's work with the usual haggling, counter-bidding, buyer's rings and purchasing monopolies to colour the activities.

The Auction today maintains a link with the style of the old Stellenbosch Farmers' Winery of the 1970s. Little else remains of what was the country's most powerful wine house. The industry re-alignment of 1979 and the subsequent collapse of the cane spirit market and the low price wine market wreaked havoc with the company's margins. New managers and new directors – a consequence of the Rembrandt/KWV controlling interest – are slowly restoring its trading fortunes. Two entirely separate sales forces operating under the almost forgotten names of Sedgwick Tayler and Monis of Paarl represent the various brands owned and managed by Stellenbosch Farmers' Winery. A new wood maturation cellar for the Zonnebloem range, new vineyards in the cool climate of Elgin contributing grapes to Nederburg, and the considerable investment in upgrading old favourites like Chateau Libertas all appear to be paying dividends in terms of quality and image. The next few years will see further changes as turnover is concentrated on the more profitable premium wines and the spirits business is refocused.

What remains a matter of considerable curiosity is who will be in a position to exploit the indisputable volumes that exist, at present, in the low-price wine market, and further what will happen to the goodwill that is inherent in the company brands at the moment.

—THE NEDERBURG AUCTION—

Wine auctions have long been a feature in Europe, at places such as the Hospice de Beaune in France and Kloster Eberbach in Germany. London, too, sees regular auctions of rare wines, conducted by Sothebys, Christies and Bonhams.

On the eighth of March 1975, the first Nederburg Auction of South African wines was held, and though there had been auctions before, it was the first to draw extensive interest locally and abroad. Since then, it has been held every year. Presided over by the well-known British wine-auctioneer, Patrick Grubb, the event has all the excitement that goes with competitive bidding and high prices.

Every producer of wine in the country is invited to participate at the auction and must submit their selection to a panel of judges who, in a blind tasting, select some 35 to 40 of South Africa's best wines to be auctioned alongside those of Nederburg. SFW's chief wine buyer, Jeff Wedgwood, has been involved in obtaining the wines from all outside participants since the inception of the auction. Mrs Arlene Johnston has been the administrative officer for all but the first three auctions.

Nowadays all the major wholesalers participate, except for The Bergkelder, which runs its own wine tender scheme. Such names as Bellingham, Bertrams, Boschendal, Douglas Green and Laborie (KWV) are to be found in the Nederburg Auction catalogue. Some 50 estates, co-operatives and private cellars have participated to date. At the end of the day's proceedings a number of items are auctioned for charity. At the sixth auction in 1980, a half-bottle of 1791 Constantia wine changed hands in a good cause for R2 500, and in 1982 a Grande Fine Champagne Imperial Cognac of 1811 was purchased by Mr Bennie Goldberg for R16 000. In 1987 the Goldbergs bid the extremely generous sum of R20 000 for a half-bottle of Constantia, vintage *circa* 1790, donated by the retiring manager of the auction, Sue Wardrop. In 1992, Graham Beck purchased a 1,5-litre magnum of Robert Mondavi

Reserve Cabernet 1979, for an unprecedented R230 000. The proceeds of this auction went to the South African Hospice Association.

If these good prices spell good publicity both for Nederburg and for the buyers, there are other more important general credits for the Auction. It provides a showcase for the best of the local products as well as offering an incentive to local winemakers to aim for yet higher standards of quality. At the same time, overseas buyers are attracted to the auction and thus to South Africa, and though they may buy relatively little at the Nederburg event (an average of about 10 per cent of the total), the amount is increasing and their visits help to forge links between the winemakers of the Cape and possible future markets for their wines in Europe and America. They also purchase other wines for export to their home countries while in South Africa and so all in all the Nederburg Auction has a wider beneficial effect on the South African wine industry than merely the amount of money realized on the day.

Over the years the auction has been attended by many international personalities of the wine world, including Robert Drouhin of Burgundy, Marchese Piero Antinori of Italy, Miramar Torres of Spain and North America and Robert Mondavi of California.

After the success of the annual Nederburg Auction and having been made aware of the need for wine collectors to be able to trade their wine legally, the Minister of Justice (under whose department the Liquor Act was administered) announced when opening the fifth Nederburg Auction in 1979 that the law would be altered to allow auctions at which the consumer could participate. It took some years, however, until the law was changed.

Nowadays, regular auctions are held by Stephen Welz and Company in association with Sotheby Park Bernet of London. South African vintage wine auctions (Julius Buchinsky) and a whole host of charity auctions are regularly held throughout the country.

The prestigious Nederburg Auction, which has become a highlight of wineland's life.

Peter Fleck, group managing director of Gilbeys.

Aside from the two wine and spirit giants of SFW and Distillers Corporation, there are few companies of any real significance in the South African industry. Those of note include Gilbey Distillers and Vintners. The history of Gilbeys in South Africa is one of the great success stories of the liquor trade. From its humble beginnings less than forty years ago, the company has grown in stature and profitability through determined brand building and dedicated perseverance.

Gilbeys is controlled by the UK-based International Distillers and Vintners, though the Rupert/Rembrandt Group owns 49 per cent of the shares. This means that while the company is nominally independent of the management structure of Distillers Corporation and Stellenbosch Farmers' Winery, it tends to align with them in matters of industry policy. Line management is certainly committed to competition, but always within the constraints acceptable to the shareholders. This has left Gilbeys free to take over from SFW the dominance of the white spirits market in the last decade. This usurpation of Mainstay by Smirnoff (Gilbeys' brand) has taken place in the era in which both companies had common shareholders. In other words, both wholesalers fight for the same share of the consumer rand. No one is in any doubt, however, that if the spirit of competition between them led to massively eroded margins because of a long-term price war, the shareholders would intervene.

The bulk of business is conducted in the lucrative spirits trade. In addition to Gilbeys' Gin, the company handles Smirnoff vodka (South Africa's largest spirit brand), J&B whisky (the number two standard brand in the country), Cinzano, all Seagrams products, Moët, Bollinger and a whole range of very profitable locally produced cream-based liqueurs.

There is only a limited involvement in the wine side of the trade. For many years Gilbeys has bottled and distributed the wines of the Twee Jongegezellen estate in Tulbagh. In the mid 1980s it assisted the Krone family – who have owned the estate for centuries – in re-packaging and modifying the brand. The success of this strategy substantiated Gilbeys'

Bertrams' winery in the Devon Valley in Stellenbosch.

claim to be the most innovative brand builders on the South African wine scene and inspired a substantial re-appraisal of the company's own brands.

Gilbeys had managed the Bertrams Devon Valley operation for many years. Despite a series of wine show successes in the 1970s, the brand was showing marked signs of decline by the mid 1980s. Gilbeys has since undertaken a considerable programme of investment. The Bertrams cellars have been upgraded, new wood vinification introduced, vineyards have been replanted and the Bertrams brand re-packaged. A similar re-think of the company's Alphen brand leaves no doubt that Gilbeys is firmly committed to the fine wine market.

Arguably the most significant recent event in the wine industry has been the merger of Douglas Green of Paarl and Union Wine. This has created a producer/wholesaler with a share of about 10 per cent of the South African market and the potential to offer a semblance of competitive muscle to the Rupert/KWV monolith. The firm of Douglas Green dates back to a Paarl trading operation formed shortly before the Second World War. A small wine and spirits merchant, Douglas Green acquired most of its bulk wines from KWV. These were marketed under a variety of brand names, including St Augustine and St Raphael.

In 1976 the Rennies Group (which subsequently assumed the trading style of Kersaf Liquor Holdings) purchased Douglas Green, as well as the independent liquor merchants J.D. Bosman and Avrons, and an option to buy Superior Im-

ports Ltd. This gave the company a national distribution grid and an important range of lucrative imported spirits and liqueurs. Recognising that the political and economic situation required a secure profit source in local goods, Kersaf invested substantially in building its wine business in the 1980s. However, the money spent in acquiring market share was always at risk as long as the company did not control its own winery. With the increasing involvement of KWV on the trading side of the local wine industry, and the national co-operative's close working arrangement with Rupert/- Rembrandt, Douglas Green could not discount the possibility that its bulk wine source might one day dry up on it.

Union Wine, on the other hand, was a company with a reasonably sophisticated winery and only a limited number of brands. Its key product was Bellingham, a proprietary wine enjoying a dominant, but declining position in the table wine market. There was an overwhelming logic behind a merger of the two operations and discussions between both parties were an on-off item on the wine trade agenda for years. Only after the Picard family disposed of its shares to Graham Beck's Kangra Holdings was the way opened for the consummation of a deal.

Douglas Green Bellingham trades in a wide range of local and imported products. In addition to the Douglas Green and Bellingham ranges – both of which enjoy a strong supermarket and restaurant presence – it offers Portuguese wines imported by its Pagan International subsidiary, as well as Allied-Hiram Walker and Remy Cointreau imported products

and the full range of wines from several of South Africa's leading estates and private producers. The economies of scale and the increased efficiencies which the merger should provide will take a few years to work through to the level of operations. There is however no doubt that the new company is a force to be reckoned with in the Cape wine industry.

With the wholesale/production side of the industry divided between so limited a number of players, it is hardly surprising that competition in the traditional sense is more or less absent from the sector. Trading terms, discount structures and even price increases reveal an air of quiet orchestration about the arrangements. The few surviving producing cellars, and the regional wholesalers/distributors tend to operate in the shadow of the key players. The so-called rats-and-mice are tolerated primarily because they do not rock the boat, and because a natural process of attrition is thinning their numbers every year.

Everything appears to conspire against their continued existence: the decline of the low-priced wine market has undermined the prospects of any new producing wholesalers in the western Cape. Only new export initiatives would provide an opportunity for some of the stronger estates and private producers to consolidate their efforts and to extend their operations to include an independent wholesale relationship with the local industry. Even so, without a national sales and distribution grid, there would be only a limited likelihood of success. The estates are more likely to increase their own direct marketing efforts, building up mailing lists of private customers and supplying the major retailers straight from the farm. In time this process will undermine the margins of the few independent distributors left in the trade. More and more these operators will have to concentrate on low cost, no-name-brand spirits and niche products. Further consolidations will then take place, and it is likely that in the next five years most of these traders will be operating under one roof to survive.

The growth of the auction wine business in South Africa is also having its impact on the margins of the wholesale and retail trade. In the early 1980s the liquor laws were changed to enable bona fide wine collectors to dispose of their cellars. Sotheby's, and its successor, Stephan Welz & Company, conduct several such auctions annually. The growth of this secondary market has obviously been a boon to serious wine buyers: they now have the right to upgrade their collections, selling off surplus quantities of wines which may be reaching their peak, or buying in mature stocks when their own supplies have been exhausted. Inevitably however these sales take place outside the traditional channels. More and more private wine buyers are coming to use the auction room as a point of purchase, in place of conventional retailers who buy from wholesale distributors.

The Sotheby's/Stephan Welz and Company salesroom is also the venue for the annual auction of the wines of the Cape Independent Winemakers' Guild. This special selection of the finest young wines from the cellars of the Cape's Inde-

THE SOUTH AFRICAN WINE INDUSTRY

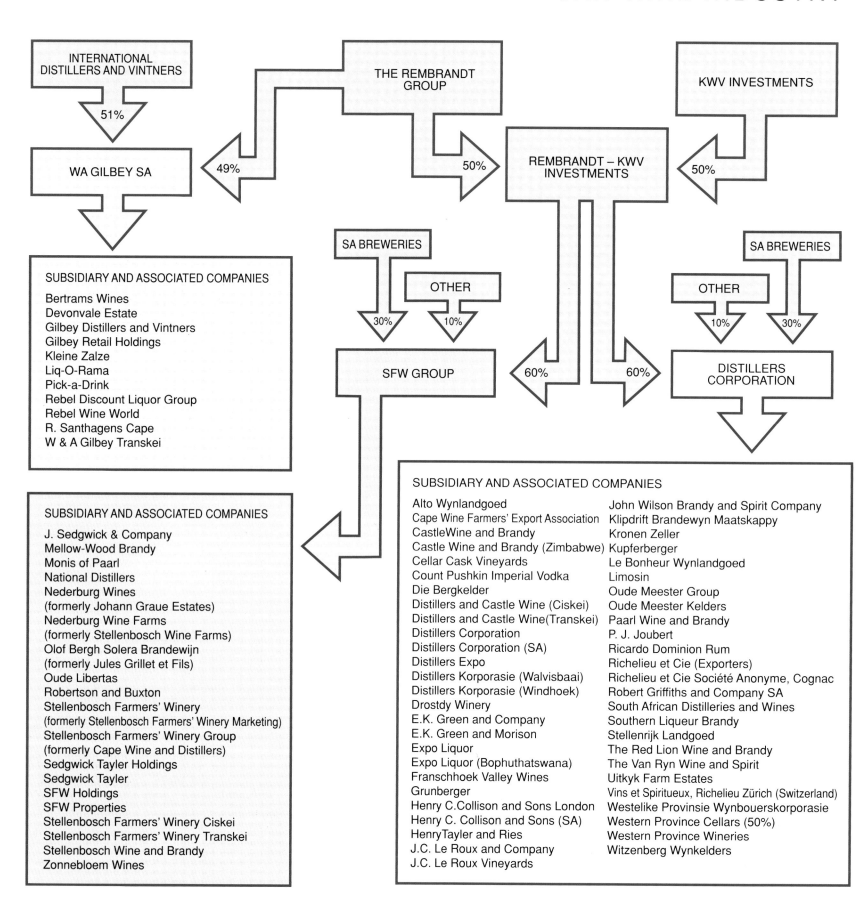

INTERNATIONAL DISTILLERS AND VINTNERS

THE REMBRANDT GROUP

KWV INVESTMENTS

51%

WA GILBEY SA

49%

50% **REMBRANDT – KWV INVESTMENTS**

50%

SA BREWERIES

OTHER

30% 10%

SFW GROUP

60% 60%

SA BREWERIES

OTHER

10% 30%

DISTILLERS CORPORATION

SUBSIDIARY AND ASSOCIATED COMPANIES

Bertrams Wines
Devonvale Estate
Gilbey Distillers and Vintners
Gilbey Retail Holdings
Kleine Zalze
Liq-O-Rama
Pick-a-Drink
Rebel Discount Liquor Group
Rebel Wine World
R. Santhagens Cape
W & A Gilbey Transkei

SUBSIDIARY AND ASSOCIATED COMPANIES

J. Sedgwick & Company
Mellow-Wood Brandy
Monis of Paarl
National Distillers
Nederburg Wines
(formerly Johann Graue Estates)
Nederburg Wine Farms
(formerly Stellenbosch Wine Farms)
Olof Bergh Solera Brandewijn
(formerly Jules Grillet et Fils)
Oude Libertas
Robertson and Buxton
Stellenbosch Farmers' Winery
(formerly Stellenbosch Farmers' Winery Marketing)
Stellenbosch Farmers' Winery Group
(formerly Cape Wine and Distillers)
Sedgwick Tayler Holdings
Sedgwick Tayler
SFW Holdings
SFW Properties
Stellenbosch Farmers' Winery Ciskei
Stellenbosch Farmers' Winery Transkei
Stellenbosch Wine and Brandy
Zonnebloem Wines

SUBSIDIARY AND ASSOCIATED COMPANIES

Alto Wynlandgoed
Cape Wine Farmers' Export Association
CastleWine and Brandy
Castle Wine and Brandy (Zimbabwe)
Cellar Cask Vineyards
Count Pushkin Imperial Vodka
Die Bergkelder
Distillers and Castle Wine (Ciskei)
Distillers and Castle Wine(Transkei)
Distillers Corporation
Distillers Corporation (SA)
Distillers Expo
Distillers Korporasie (Walvisbaai)
Distillers Korporasie (Windhoek)
Drostdy Winery
E.K. Green and Company
E.K. Green and Morison
Expo Liquor
Expo Liquor (Bophuthatswana)
Franschhoek Valley Wines
Grunberger
Henry C.Collison and Sons London
Henry C. Collison and Sons (SA)
HenryTayler and Ries
J.C. Le Roux and Company
J.C. Le Roux Vineyards

John Wilson Brandy and Spirit Company
Klipdrift Brandewyn Maatskappy
Kronen Zeller
Kupferberger
Le Bonheur Wynlandgoed
Limosin
Oude Meester Group
Oude Meester Kelders
Paarl Wine and Brandy
P. J. Joubert
Ricardo Dominion Rum
Richelieu et Cie (Exporters)
Richelieu et Cie Société Anonyme, Cognac
Robert Griffiths and Company SA
South African Distilleries and Wines
Southern Liqueur Brandy
Stellenrijk Landgoed
The Red Lion Wine and Brandy
The Van Ryn Wine and Spirit
Uitkyk Farm Estates
Vins et Spiritueux, Richelieu Zürich (Switzerland)
Westelike Provinsie Wynbouerskorporasie
Western Province Cellars (50%)
Western Province Wineries
Witzenberg Wynkelders

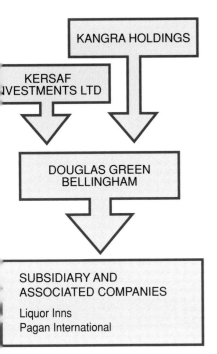

KANGRA HOLDINGS

KERSAF INVESTMENTS LTD

DOUGLAS GREEN BELLINGHAM

SUBSIDIARY AND ASSOCIATED COMPANIES

Liquor Inns
Pagan International

Although the two major groups of companies in the South African wine industry (Stellenbosch Farmers' Winery and Distillers Corporation) are listed separately on the Johannesburg Stock Exchange, the following chart shows that wine-making and wine and spirit marketing is effectively controlled by KWV and the Rembrandt group through their jointly held Rembrandt-KWV Investments Ltd. The only other companies of note are Gilbey Distillers and Vintners, in which the Rembrandt group has a substantial direct investment, and the independent, new Douglas Green Bellingham group which is the result of the recent marriage of Douglas Green of Paarl and Union Wines Limited.

— CAPE INDEPENDENT WINEMAKERS' GUILD —

The Cape Independent Winemakers' Guild was founded in 1983, at the instigation of Billy Hofmeyr of Welgemeend, with the aim of promoting the production, bottling and marketing of excellent wine by its members. An aim of the Guild is 'to contribute to the advancement of the quality of Cape wines by mutually developing the knowledge, capabilities and horizons of the members'. Members must be active winemakers themselves, and be prepared to share their knowledge and experience with each other and to learn from each other. They must be independent, that is, free of connection with wholesalers or co-operative groups. Their methods of promoting their wines include an annual auction, group export arrangements and general publicity.

The Guild held seven annual auctions at Sotheby's in Johannesburg and has now moved the event to the Cape where it combines with their annual barrel tasting on the Victoria & Alfred Waterfront development. All the bottles at each year's auction are individually numbered and display the Cape Independent Winemakers' Guild label. Tastings of the wines to be auctioned are held beforehand in all the main cities of the country. One does not need to be physically at the auction to be able to take part in the bidding – postal bids may be submitted. Features of the auction are the good prices fetched, and the relative youth of most of the wines. The Guild is scrupulous in satisfying itself, through rigorous self-scrutiny, that the wines on offer measure up to the best of wine-making standards. None of the wines offered is ever older than five years and all have been selected with a view to long life and good

A pre-auction tasting of the wines being offered for sale at the auction.

bottle maturation potential. The auctions generally take place in the month of September.

Winemakers currently belonging to the Guild include Jannie Engelbrecht and Kevin Arnold of Rust-en-Vrede, Jan 'Boland' Coetzee of Vriesenhof, Janey Muller of Lemberg, Braam van Velden of Overgaauw, Johan Malan of Simonsig, Etienne le Riche of Rustenberg and Schoongezicht, Jeff Grier of Villiera, Beyers Truter of Kanonkop, Kurt Ammann of Rozendal and Norma Ratcliffe of Warwick Farm, Hilko Hegewisch of Boschendal, Neil Ellis of Neil Ellis Wines, Danie Truter of Hartenberg, Abraham Beukes of Lievland, Gyles Webb of Thelema, Carel Nel of Boplaas, Walter Finlayson of Glen Carlou, Eric Saayman of Zevenwacht, Philip Constandius of Delheim, Pieter du Toit of Groot Constantia, Jean Daneel of Buitenverwachting, Jacques Kruger of Blaauwklippen, and Achim von Arnim of Clos Cabrière.

pendent producers has become something of a highlight on the annual wine calendar. Unlike the Nederburg Auction, which is a major social event at which only trade licensees are permitted to bid, the Guild sale is also open to members of the public. Over the years it has attracted an increasing number of private buyers. This has led to the alienation of some retailers who see in the presence of private collectors at the auction an inevitable conflict of interests. They argue that there is no incentive to invest in stocks which are available at the same forum to people who are normally their own customers.

In reality the trade buyers are not disadvantaged: members of the public tend to buy the smaller lots at the Guild auction, and these sell for a premium because of the competition to acquire them. The trade buys the larger parcels, which sell at a discount because there are only a few licensees able to invest in this sort of stockholding. The success of the sale suggests that an uneasy compromise will be reached: the public will not be chased away from the auction room, and the more sophisticated wine merchants cannot afford to

boycott the event. What is certain, however, is that such specialist occasions, where the auction room replaces the role of the traditional distributor, contribute in the long term to the decline of the independent wholesale trade. It is a curious feature of the South African wine industry that the produce of over 5000 farmers is sold through over 8000 licensees to millions of consumers via fewer than 10 wholesalers, several of whom are already members of an endangered species. This means that in the long term the distribution sector may disappear entirely, in which case there is little likelihood that the industry will achieve any real growth. Alternatively, producers will come to realize that their access to the market must be through wholesalers with a vested interest in building brands. The opportunity for testing this theory will only arise if the concentration of power in the wholesale/production sector is broken up. Since monopoly is the inevitable result of success in business, future governments will have to weigh up the cost of interfering with this process rather than letting the industry run its natural course to whatever destination awaits it.

IN THE VINEYARD

ESTABLISHING A VINEYARD

The cultivated grapevine of the winelands of the world is a member of the botanical family Vitacae. It is a family with a long traceable lineage, as is witnessed by the discovery of fossilized vine leaves.

The 12 genera of the Vitacae embrace numerous species of wild vine as well as the type found at the Cape by Van Riebeeck, *Rhoicissus capensis*. The species from which the modern cultivated varieties are descended is believed to have originated in the region between, and south of, the Black and Caspian seas, in the 'fertile crescent' where the first agricultural peoples settled. Its scientific name is *Vitis vinifera* – *vinum* being Latin for 'wine', and *ferens* for 'bearing'.

From its first settlement at the eastern end of the Mediterranean, in about 6 000 BC, the vine slowly spread, first down the Levant as far as Egypt, and then, by about 2 000 BC, westwards to Greece. From there, during the next millennium, it spread to encompass the whole Mediterranean seaboard. It was the expansion of the Roman conquests, however, which led the vine to perhaps its most important modern homelands, namely Italy, Spain and France. The bulk of the early vineyards in Western Europe was settled by the Romans in the wake of Julius Caesar's conquest of Gaul, completed by 51 BC. Starting from the already well-established vineyards of Provence, they spread up the Rhine Valley and thence to the Bordeaux area, generally following natural watercourses. By the second century AD vineyards were established in Burgundy and on the Moselle and the Rhine; the following two centuries found them settled on the Loire and in Champagne, thus defining roughly the northern borders of Europe's present wine-making community. By the tenth century of the Christian era the heartland of the modern wine world had been fully laid down.

Further expansions were to follow with the opening up of new lands during the Renaissance. By the mid-sixteenth cen-

LEFT: *Neat rows of trellised vines on Simonsig Estate.*

tury there were already plantings of *Vitis vinifera* in Central and South America. Driven by their need for Communion wine, Jesuits introduced the vine to Mexico in 1545. In 1548 a priest by the name of Father Francisco brought the first vines to Chile from Peru, and in 1557 they were established in Argentina. By the early 1600s the grapevine had been taken to California and the first wine was made there in 1620. In the same century explorers began to discover in other countries of the southern hemisphere climatic conditions suited to the vine and similar in many respects to those conditions of the Mediterranean basin. These new wine-making countries included South Africa, and in due course Australia and New Zealand.

In all these areas *Vitis vinifera* grows to advantage. Although the wild grapevine is a hardy plant and flourishes under astonishingly different conditions (there are varieties which can survive extreme cold), the classic cultivated vine is more specialized in its needs.

Under such conditions it grows easily – and also in variety. Indeed, over the centuries of its cultivation a wide range of different varieties of the basic red and white types of grapevine have been evolved.

Upwards of 12 000 of these varieties are at present known. Until the twentieth century they were generated by a process of evolution, of natural selection aided by man. Those varieties known best in the South African vineyards were originally developed mainly in the French vineyards, and the dominant influence of the French is reflected in their traditional names. These are Cabernet Sauvignon, Cinsaut, Merlot, Pinot Noir, Pontac, Petit Verdot, among the red wine varieties, and Chenin Blanc, Muscat d'Alexandrie, Clairette Blanche, Sémillon and Raisin Blanc among the white wine varieties.

Other varieties, often for the making of fortified wines such as sherry and port, were developed in Spain and in Portugal. These include Tinta Barocca, Souzão, Tinta Francisca and Tinta Roriz; and in Germany, white wine varieties were created well suited to the cooler conditions of the Rhineland. Among these being the famous white wine variety, Weisser Riesling, and the recently developed Bukettraube.

Together with these varieties specific, at least originally, to one region, have been others which have come to be generally grown because of their versatility. They have tended to arise with different names in different countries, or with different versions of the same name. An extreme example of this confusing phenomenon is the Shiraz variety which, in one area or another, has been called Syrah, Schiras, Sirac, Syra, Sirah, Petite Sirah, Serenne, Serine, Biaune, Hignin Noir and Marsanne Noire – no less than 11 seductive titles for the same basic vine.

Some degree of such traditional confusion exists in all grape-growing countries. The early winemakers at the Cape,

Workers collecting rootstock material from a mother plantation.

Pruning the rootstock to the required length prior to grafting.

THE VINE AND ITS ENVIRONMENT

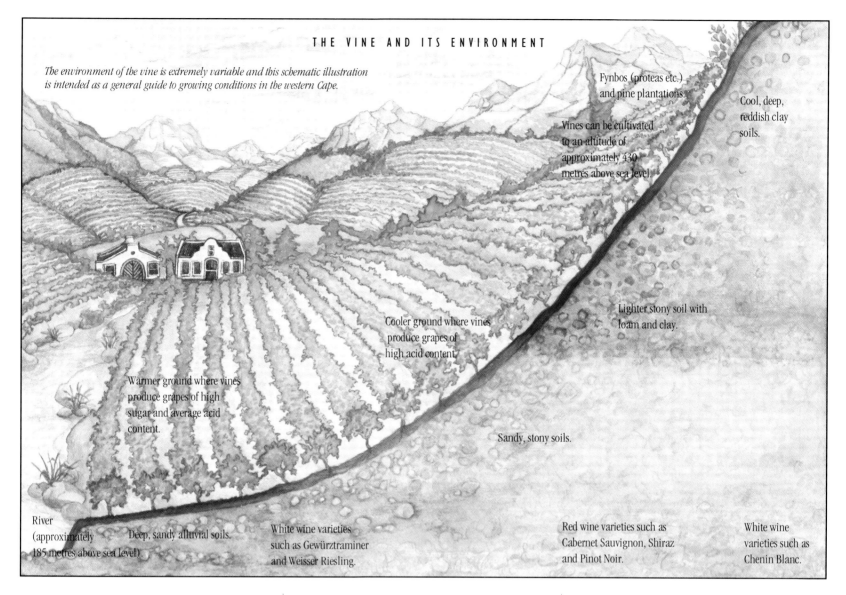

The environment of the vine is extremely variable and this schematic illustration is intended as a general guide to growing conditions in the western Cape.

Fynbos (proteas etc.) and pine plantations.

Cool, deep, reddish clay soils.

Vines can be cultivated to an altitude of approximately 430 metres above sea level.

Lighter stony soil with loam and clay.

Cooler ground where vines produce grapes of high acid content.

Warmer ground where vines produce grapes of high sugar and average acid content.

Sandy, stony soils.

River (approximately 185 metres above sea level).

Deep, sandy alluvial soils.

White wine varieties such as Gewürztraminer and Weisser Riesling.

Red wine varieties such as Cabernet Sauvignon, Shiraz and Pinot Noir.

White wine varieties such as Chenin Blanc.

not always certain of the European identity of their varieties, often gave them alternate names. In time, the idea arose that these were specifically local varieties, different from those in Europe, and gradually this belief acquired the force of tradition. In recent decades, however, investigations by such prominent South African viticulturists as Professors Perold, Theron and Orffer have confirmed that certain local varieties are the same as their European counterparts; for example, Steen has been identified as Chenin Blanc, Hanepoot as Muscat d'Alexandrie, White French as Palomino, and Green Grape as Sémillon, while the red wine grape Hermitage was found to be the same grape as Cinsaut. The variety which came to be known as South African Riesling was found to be unrelated to the Weisser Riesling; instead it has been identified as the French variety, Cruchen Blanc.

In nature, the evolution of a new variety of vine takes many generations of adaptation to specific conditions of soil and climate, but in the past century scientific methods of breeding new varieties have been developed, of which Pinot-

age and Chenel are well-known local examples. These new varieties are generally bred from selected stock to present certain features or advantages which fit them for use in a particular area or mesoclimate, or for the making of a certain style of wine.

Each variety produces its own characteristic type of wine, with its own bouquet and flavour, its own private poetry. To a greater or lesser extent this inherent character can be modified or heightened by other factors, the first and most obvious of which is the way the wine is made, but others play a part at a more basic level. A common adage in the winelands holds that good wine is made in the vineyards, which is true. Good wine begins with healthy, well-tended vines and with sound vineyard practice.

The life of a vine begins before it reaches the vineyard proper – in the nursery with the propagation of the young plant. There are two main ways in which grapevines can be reproduced. One is that designed by nature, sexual reproduction by means of seeds, in this case the pips of the grapes.

When the flowers of the vine are mature, pollen is released onto the stigmas, and fertilization takes place in the ovary, after which the berry develops. If a new variety is to be bred it is necessary to cross-pollinate artificially by depositing the pollen from one strain on the stigmas of another. The seedling resulting from this cross pollination may bear the characteristics of the parent plants.

This method is only used in the breeding of new varieties. By far the most common method of reproduction, and one that guarantees replication of individual characteristics, is asexual. Here the large-scale reproduction of existing varieties is effected by taking cuttings and grafting them, on the domesticated *Vinifera* vine and selected rootstock varieties which reproduce themselves easily from cuttings. If a portion of cane is cut from a vine and placed in good, moist soil in protected conditions, it will quickly produce roots and shoots, eventually growing into a young vine which will almost certainly be genetically identical to the plant from which the original cutting was taken.

After the workers have collected the rootstock material from the mother plantation, the canes are bundled and then transported to the nursery where they are debudded and trimmed for grafting to the desired 300-millimetre length. Subsequently, the trimmed canes are dipped and disinfected to prevent the transmission of fungal diseases.

─ GRAFTING ─

This simple and indirect method of propagation was the one used from time immemorial in the winelands of the world. However, since the phylloxera epidemic of the 1860s the process of reproduction has included the grafting of cuttings onto rootstocks taken from vines which are resistant to the phylloxera aphid and to other pests such as nematodes.

The cutting, or scion, of the variety required for fruition is grafted onto cuttings taken from the rootstock vine. With good contact between the cambium and living bark layers of the two vines, tissue-bridging takes place to produce what, in effect, will henceforth be a single plant. Soon this new vine puts forth roots and shoots, and when it is growing healthily and strongly it can be safely transferred from the nursery to the vineyard.

Most vines in Europe and South Africa are grafted onto rootstock derived mainly from crosses of a number of indigenous species found in North America. These include Richter 99 (a cross of *Vitis berlandieri* and *V. rupestris*), Mgt 101-14 (a cross of *V. rupestris* and *V. riparia*), and Jacquez (crosses of *V. aestivalis, V. cinerea*, and *V. vinifera*).

In recent years viticultural researchers have focused on these and other neglected wild vines, calling on their genetic make-up to develop a wide range of varieties suited to exigencies of different soils and climates. Reflecting the predominant local conditions, the two most commonly used in South Africa are the Richter 99 and Mgt 101-14. Richter 99 should be used only on well-drained soils, usually red and yellow-brown soils, because of its susceptibility to a water-borne fungus. Mgt 101-14 is able to cope with shallower and wetter soils. Others used for specific conditions include Richter 110 for more fertile soils in order to control

vigour; Ramsey for poor, sandy areas under irrigation; Richter 110 for clayey soils.

The rootstock must not only accord with its physical environment, but must remain compatible with the chosen scion. In general this is not a problem, but occasional cases of a bad marriage of scion and rootstock occur. Certain clones of Cape Riesling and Colombard, for example, are not compatible with certain clones of Mgt 101-14 (it has been proved that some compatibility problems are associated with certain virus combinations).

Vigour and resistance to pests and diseases are important in the rootstock but other and more complex qualities are supplied by the scion, or top-variety. Selection of good-quality material for the scion part of the graft is an essential skill of the vine-grower or nurseryman. Scions are obtained from producing vineyards by selection over a number of years of close observation on the progress of the established vines. The material is collected during pruning in the winter months and cut into 250- to 300-millimetre lengths which are bound together and stored in a cool, moist place or in cold storage until required.

In choosing material for the rootstock, one-year-old canes from the mother vine are selected, cut, bound and stored in the same way as for the fruiting material.

Grafting of young cuttings usually takes place in winter between July and August. In the post-phylloxera era it was largely done by hand, but recent decades have seen the development of machines capable of making grafts at speed and with a fine degree of accuracy. But whether performed by hand or by machine, the basic principles remain simple.

The two components of the vine – the scion and the rootstock cuttings – are prepared in such a way that they fit together. The cut is designed to present the largest

growing face between one part and the other. To this end, two traditional types of cut were evolved which could be done relatively quickly by hand: the long-whip and short-whip methods.

The long-whip graft (see page 41) is the oldest method in South Africa, and is still very widely used. Here, both components are cut diagonally through the wood, a 'tongue' is made on the cut surface of both, and they are then fitted together. The scion in this case usually has two buds.

This is a simple method whereby a skilled grafter can complete up to 2 000 unions a day. Moreover, when employing this method, heated rooms are not necessary for the subsequent callusing which bonds the scion to the rootstock. However, it has the unfortunate disadvantage that the callus sometimes fails to form completely.

The short-whip graft (see page 41) is similar to the long-whip except that here the incision is about half as long and usually only one-bud scions are used. The advantage of this method is that it is not necessary to tie the graft – waxing alone is sufficient – and also that there is less danger of the graft drying out.

As well as these hand-cut methods a number of different machines and configurations of cut are available, of which the most well known are the Omega and Hengl grafting machines (see page 41). The Omega makes matching omega-shaped cuts in the rootstock and scion which are punched in endways, from both ends of the machine. The join is automatically made. The Hengl makes a crenel joint on the scion and the rootstock which are pushed in endways in two different saws of the machine. The two components are then fitted together by hand and will callus.

Machine grafting has many obvious advantages over hand grafting. It is easy to operate, requiring less skill or

Rootstock for grafting is stored in a cold room.

A graft produced by the Omega grafting machine.

labour, and gives good callus formation because it ensures better contact of the generative layers.

As well as the Omega cut, a number of other configurations are possible with machine grafting. Although rarely used nowadays, these include the Jupiter or Zig-Zag graft, and the Heitz or Wedge graft.

No matter which grafting method is used, once the two components of the graft have been fitted together, the union and scion are dipped in warm wax to prevent loss of moisture from the incisions (when grafting was first introduced, rootstock and scion were normally tied with raffia). The grafted cuttings are then placed in callusing boxes and stored under ideal conditions of temperature (24 to 28 °C) and humidity (70 per cent) to ensure good knitting of the unions. This is done by packing the vines in porous material such as sand or sawdust to keep them moist. A callusing box can contain about 1 000 grafted vines.

During this period, the callusing box into which the grafted cuttings have been placed, is put on a moist floor in order to keep the lower section of the box cool. This is important as it helps to prevent excess rooting, because if too many roots are formed they are likely to be damaged during handling of the small vines.

After root formation has taken place, the cuttings are moved from the hothouse and acclimatized to the open air, usually in a *lat huis* or 'shade-house', which lets sun and air

in but protects the young vine from excessive sunlight and from the danger of strong winds.

This entire initial process usually takes about eight weeks, after which the vines are transferred to the nursery, where they remain for a year before being planted in the main vineyard for the rest of their growing and fruit-bearing lives.

Besides the propagation of young vines in the hothouse and the nursery, there are other ways in which new vineyards can be established or old ones refurbished. These are also based on the principles of grafting, but are here applied directly in the field (as distinct from 'bench-grafting' or indoor methods used for vines propagated in the nursery).

There are three basic methods of such grafting: chip budding, amphi grafting and soil grafting.

Chip budding (see page 41) takes place in summer, in November and December. A small bud is grafted onto a rootstock which has been planted out during the previous winter; an incision is made about 30 millimetres above the soil level on the rootstock, and the bud is inserted and then tied with rubber or plastic tape.

Wedge, or amphi grafting (see page 41), the so-called 'winter bud on green shoot' method, was developed by Professor Orffer of the University of Stellenbosch in the early 1950s. It is done in early November when the green shoot is about 450 millimetres long. The bud of the scion must be completely dormant. The rootstock in the vineyard is pruned early

and severely and, when its green shoots have grown about 450 millimetres long, the strongest and straightest is chosen and trained along a stake. All the leaves on the shoot are left intact until after healing of the graft unions, since transpiration helps to reduce excessive bleeding which hinders callusing. An incision of about 40 millimetres is then made between the nodes on the green shoot, the scion wedge is inserted, and the graft is tied with plastic tape. About two weeks after the bud has burst, the shoot is cut away at the node above the graft union. All the rootstock shoots that subsequently develop are continuously removed so that growth can be concentrated in the scion.

Chip bud and amphi grafting have four principal advantages: the rootstock is not lost if the scion does not take, the percentage take is generally high, the vine can begin production almost immediately since the root system is already established, and mature vines can be re-grafted to another variety without losing more than one harvest.

Chip bud and amphi grafting also render possible the grafting of very thin scions. These grafts are therefore approximately 99 per cent successful. The few disadvantages of these methods are that they are slow (a good grafter can do only 300 vines a day), and that suckers are troublesome with rootstocks such as Richter 99.

Soil grafting (see page 41) takes place from September to mid-October at about soil level. A scion with two buds is grafted onto the rootstock using the cleft or whip-graft method – the rootstock here can be either in the nursery or in the vineyard. In making the graft, particular care must be paid to ensure good contact between the cambium of scion and rootstock. It is also important to make sure that the incision in the rootstock is made at right angles to the prevailing wind to prevent being dislodged by it. If necessary, the graft is covered with soil or tied so that the grafting twine or string does not overlap, to allow bleeding sap to escape. Plastic strips are then used to trap the excessive moisture and no callus initiation will proceed.

Aftercare is important with soil grafting, and these 'molehills' must be replaced after rain. The young shoots are also susceptible to wind damage and should be staked or topped regularly to reduce that risk.

Soil grafting gives better results than bench grafting in areas with warm light soils. It is easier to perform and fits well into the farm work programme, since it is done shortly after bench grafting has been completed. Disadvantages are that weather conditions must be favourable, and that only light, well-pulverized, warm and well-serrated soils are really suitable. Moreover, if the scion does not bud the rootstock is lost for it will not bud again.

By these various methods the vine is prepared for and introduced to the vineyard, However, this is not the only form of preparation, for just as that vine must be prepared for the land, the land must also be made ready to support and nurture it, and to provide it with ideal conditions for optimum growth and production.

GRAFTING TECHNIQUES

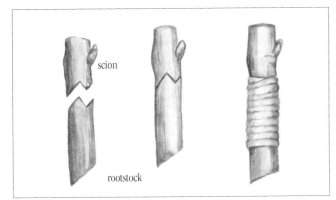

JUPITER GRAFT

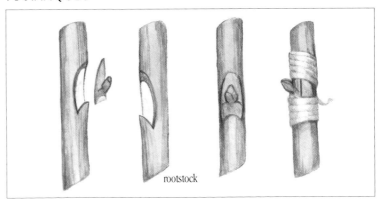

CHIP BUDDING

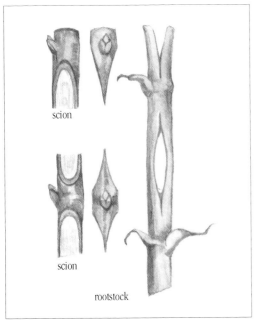

AMPHI GRAFT

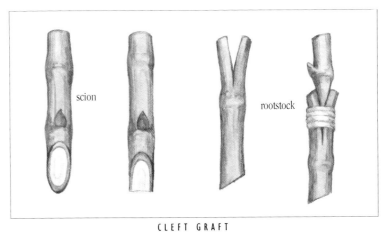

CLEFT GRAFT

LONG-WHIP GRAFT

SHORT-WHIP GRAFT

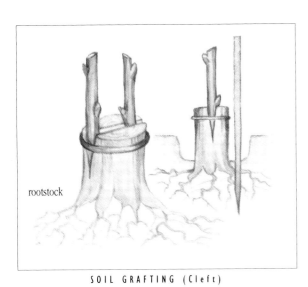

SOIL GRAFTING (Cleft)

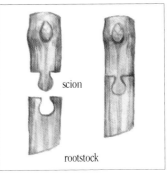

HENGL OR SAW GRAFT

OMEGA GRAFT

The nursery bed being prepared for the planting of the callused vines.

A newly planted nursery vineyard.

— S O I L —

A balance must be found between the plant and its environment, the complex conditions in which it will live for about 30 years. They involve not only the soil and its specific properties of structural and chemical composition but also the particular climatic conditions.

Both the wine farmer and his vines are largely at the mercy of the elements: heavy frost in spring, hail or a wet summer can write off the year's wine production, and in a relatively erratic climate such as that of Europe (in France the local vignerons claim God makes the wine) this can be a fairly regular occurrence, drawing heavily on human reserves of patience and resignation. Notwithstanding the occasional act of God, the winemakers of South Africa generally have little about which to complain. Compared with the average temperatures of many other wine-making countries, those here are relatively high; the weather is commendably steady; and the summers ideal for fine, ripe grapes and good crops. And if the land is not always very fertile, this in itself is not necessarily a disadvantage. 'The worse the soil, the better the wine', is an old adage among wine farmers, for a poor soil encourages restricted growth which in turn concentrates the richness of the grape.

A combination of rich soil, high temperatures and judicious irrigation makes for large crops of grapes high in sugar content, but does not ensure complexity of character or quality. The mountain valleys of the Cape, the 'inland' areas of the Olifantsrivier, and the Breede River districts of Worcester and Robertson, with their rich alluvial soils and high summer temperatures unrelieved by a prevailing wind from the sea (with a few notable exceptions), tend to produce such grapes. Here are many of the country's co-operatives, and from these areas large quantities of grapes for distilling wine and for making raisins have grown from the nineteenth century onwards. Although various new methods have helped to improve much of the wine made in these grape-growing areas, the emphasis, with certain happy exceptions, remains largely upon quantity rather than quality.

Tulbagh provides a contrast. By any agricultural standard, this seems an unattractive prospect – a deep, wide and in mid-summer furiously hot valley, where the river banks are relatively fertile but the old, higher river terraces and slopes of the mountains little more than rock, with virtually no topsoil. Yet it is these stony slopes which yield some of South Africa's finest white wines.

The needs of the vine are therefore not always immediately predictable: indeed for the first wine pioneers, seeking to establish a crop with which they had not long been acquainted, the only guide was a kind of inspired trial and error. And if they had successes, they also had many failures, planting specific types of vines in conditions of soil and irrigation, or the lack of it, to which they were barely adapted.

It was a hit-or-miss system. While there are still many uncontrollable variables in the life of the modern vine grower, however, he can operate many more conscious controls, both of the vine and the conditions under which it lives. Above all, he has a far clearer knowledge of the way these work together, of the precise nature and influence of soil and climate than had his predecessors.

Modern viticulture, for example, informs the grower that the vine is a plant with comparatively low nutritional needs. With its long growing season of about seven months and its large root system, sometimes going down to a depth of more than 7 metres in soils without physical, chemical or water table restrictions (a deciduous creeper, the vine has no taproot), it can usually meet its own particular growth requirements, even in poor soil.

Thus almost any soil which allows the necessary conditions of mild and stable growth will provide the ideal medium in which the well-chosen and appropriate variety will be able to develop to its full potential.

The characteristics which affect its quality can be both chemical and physical. The chemical composition of the soil is currently regarded as less important than its physical and water regulating properties. In particular, the degree of acidity or lack of it will influence the growth of the vine and the resultant wine. A soil with free lime present (common in the Breede River area, for example) is alkaline – in scientific terms this is referred to as a soil with a high pH. Lime-rich soils, however, do not automatically give high-quality wine.

Soils containing an excess of potassium make for high pH grapes which tend to produce unbalanced wines, and in the reds, of poor colour. On the other hand, too little potassium results in poor carbohydrate production and thus poor colour and sugar formation.

Nitrogen is essential for the stimulation of growth. Too much, however, causes too rapid growth, leading to vigorous growth but low quality. Too much nitrogen can also result in an increased sensitivity to disease.

Piercing the black plastic mulch in which the young vines are to be planted.

Planting the new nursery.

The chemical composition of the soil is important, but more so are its physical aspects. In fact it is these physical properties that determine the eventual excellence of the wine. They include such characteristics as the depth of the soil, its rockiness, the degree of structural layering, the clay content, its ability to drain well during wet periods, and to supply adequate water during dry spells.

As far as the general physical needs of the vine are concerned, soils of good depth and drainage are better for both quality and growth. They create a more effective buffer against drought (an important consideration locally) and also against unseasonable rain. Deep soils ensure more stable growth in both dry and wet areas.

The soil's capacity to retain moisture can have a considerable effect on the vine. It is determined by its depth, texture, and the amount of organic matter it contains; it is also affected by the presence of rocks or stones. Soils with a high clay content will retain far more water than sandy soils, but this is not necessarily an advantage. Too much water can lead to rank growth or excessive moisture in the berries at ripening time, which can result in detrimental unbalanced sugar-acid ratios and mould infections. That is why in those regions which are cool and moist, soils that retain too much water, especially during the ripening phase of the grapes, are to be avoided for quality wine grapes.

Most countries have their own system of soil classification. In South Africa, soils are classified into 'soil forms' according to the presence and sequence of defined soil horizons or layers. These forms are further subdivided into 'families', presently distinguished by four-digit codes, based on struc-

ture, degree of wetness and leaching, clay accumulation, colour and presence of lime.

Each of these different soil types has its advantages and drawbacks in relationship to the growing vines. Many of the specific disadvantages, however, can be removed or at least modified by the appropriate treatment of the soil, ranging from straightforward ploughing to various forms of deep ploughing (delving), or ripping ('ripping' involves the breaking-up of underlying rocky layers in the soil without disturbing the topsoil structure). With deep ploughing, lime and chemical or organic fertilizers can be added to the soil.

Before this preparation can take place, an assessment of the soil must be made. South African soils are extremely heterogeneous – sometimes varying markedly from one part of the farm to another – and this necessitates meticulous soil screening and evaluation. A soil survey, often carried out by the technical staff of Government laboratories, private consultants or those associated with the producing wholesalers, charts the various soil types present on the farm. 'Profile holes' as deep as 1,2 metres are made at points in the planned vineyard area, from which a complete 'underground map' of the land can be plotted.

From a producer's point of view, soils can be loosely grouped into five categories, namely 'Structureless' (further divided into Hutton and Clovelly soils and Fernwood soils), 'Duplex', 'Shallow' and 'Alluvial'.

Structureless may at first appear an odd name for a soil. In fact, it simply indicates that this type contains no restrictive layers in the subsoil which would impede growth, such as compacted, heavy textured layers, hardpans, cemented

layers, or layers of a generally stratified nature. Several types of these structureless soils have been recognized at the Cape, the most important being the Hutton and Clovelly and the Fernwood forms. Hutton and Clovelly are well-drained soils of red and yellow colour respectively, while Fernwood is represented by dry, sandy soils.

In general, the local Hutton and Clovelly forms require little preparation. It has, however, been shown experimentally that most of them in the coastal region which have a fairly high clay content (20 to 30 per cent), show compaction in the subsoil. Here it is advantageous to delve the soil to a depth of 700 to 1 000 millimetres. In areas in the interior where fine sandy types of these soils are found, sub-surface compaction takes place as a result of fine-sand fraction and prolonged cultivation. Therefore, a relatively shallow delve cultivation is an advantage here also.

It is often found that the subsoil of the Hutton and Clovelly types in the coastal areas is very acid, allowing little deep root growth, and thus resembles a shallow soil. In such cases careful consideration must be given to deep delving accompanied by the addition of lime to provide a chemical balance. However, the determination of the necessary requirements must be made before delve ploughing in order not to exceed the optimum ploughing level.

The dry and sandy Fernwood form is generally inhospitable to the vine. Deep cultivation of such soils is usually ineffectual, and the addition of straw serves little purpose. Well-rotted organic material or dung may help, for that temporarily increases the water-retaining capacity and nutritional value of the soil. But this practice is not generally

Testing the strength of the graft union.

A close view of the graft union.

The vines are tied into bundles of 50 plants which are then dipped in a fungicide.

economically viable, and the farmer working with this kind of soil usually prefers to give his vines frequent light irrigation and to keep the surface covered by an organic mulch.

The second major category of soil is the Duplex category. As the name implies, these are soils which feature a noticeable difference of texture between that of the topsoil and that of the subsoil.

There are a number of local variations of the Duplex category of soil, including the Kroonstad, Sterkspruit and Estcourt forms which make up a very large proportion of the soils in the western Cape coastal region. They have a relatively sandy topsoil, with an underlying clay pan. Of these three forms, Kroonstad has a sandy top layer with an iron-bearing

pan of peculiar hard, nuggety forms known as *ouklip*, just above the clay. Sterkspruit, on the other hand, has a topsoil which is relatively light-textured, changing sharply to a strongly structured, heavy-textured subsoil.

Structured soils are represented by the Swartland and Valsrivier forms. They are derived from shale and have a dense, clayey subsoil with underlying fragmented shale, which usually has a high salt content. Preparation of Duplex and Structured soils is problematical. After incorrect delve ploughing, they are often in a poorer condition than before, because the clay subsoil is ploughed to the surface. The 'raw' soil is thus uppermost, inhibiting the establishment of the vines. The clay subsoil is often very acid or brackish, which compounds the problem. Moreover, most of these soils are inherently wet, and disturbance of the underground drainage can affect the natural balance. Because of the variability of these soils, proper preparation is never easy and expert advice is usually called for. Use of the modern, specially designed 'shifting' delve ploughs, which break up the subsoil restric-

tion and cause a fair amount of topsoil to sieve into the subsoil, without lifting the subsoil to the surface, gives excellent results in most cases. Drainage must also be installed in the case of wet duplex soils. The ripping operation must be carried out against the contour to promote healthy drainage. When dealing with the Kroonstad form, the iron-cemented *ouklip* just above the clay pan must also be broken to ensure effective root penetration. Large stones displaced by this method may be removed, but the gravel of the *ouklip* must be left undisturbed.

Shallow soils, the fourth category, feature a layer of topsoil directly over rock. These soils are known as 'Mispah' or 'Glenrosa', depending on the state of disintegration of the underlying rock, Glenrosa being at a more advanced stage of disintegration. They are nevertheless very suitable for grapegrowing provided that the underlying rock can be broken or ripped, particularly where the underlying rock is sloping or vertical shale. For greater effectiveness the ripping action must be carried out against the vertical layering of the shale.

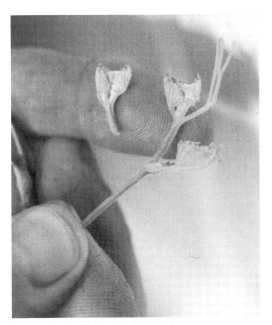

The growing tips of virus-tested material.

Tossie Louw, nursery manager of Ernita, in the heat therapy room.

With this method, however, steps must be taken to guard against salination of lower-lying soils. The shallow shale ground is often rich in salt, which may cause serious bracking through the rapid seepage of water through such soils and the subsequent damming against the lower, usually more heavily textured soils.

The fifth main soil category is Alluvial. Deposited by the rivers over the ages, it is made up of alternating layers of soils of different textures. These layered alluvial soils are known as the 'Dundee' form. Alluvial soils are mostly encountered near river courses – the Eerste, Olifants, Berg and Breede rivers are the main sites in the Cape winelands for this alluvial type of soil.

With alluvial soils of the Dundee form, any intense layering, that is, sharp transitions from coarse texture layers (such as sand) to fine texture layers (such as silt or clay), must first be corrected by deep ploughing to produce a more uniform texture, since root distribution and water penetration are invariably impeded by the layers. Intensive ripping cultivation is also less effective with this type of soil in creating channels for root and water passage.

When the type of soil in the projected vineyard has been analyzed and assessed, the physical operations involved in soil preparation can begin. This procedure may involve a number of implements and machines, of which the deep plough and the ripper are the most important.

Both the delve plough and the ripper can usually cultivate to a depth of approximately 1,2 metres. It is the nature of the particular soil that will determine the choice of the appropriate implement. The delve plough generally mixes the various soil layers together, whereas the ripper breaks up the lower layers, but does not mix them with the top strata.

If there is doubt as to which will be the more effective, expert advice is usually called in. Both the delve plough and

After grafting, the vines are placed in callus boxes.

Mist beds in the hothouse, a controlled growing environment.

A bud sprouting on a Chenin Blanc vine.

Although invisible, a miniscule 'bunch' of grapes is formed.

At a further stage of development, a 100-mm shoot from the base bud can be seen.

ripper usually require powerful caterpillar tractors. In extreme cases it may even be necessary to first break the soil with a ripper before it can be delved properly. These days powerful wheel tractors are also available, which give excellent results to a depth of 700 to 800 millimetres if the soil is not too hard or has been ripped beforehand.

If soil preparation takes place before winter, green cover crops are planted, generally oats, rye or barley. After soil preparation, it is important to restrict traffic only to the future interrow zones in order not to recompact the soil. For this purpose, the future vine rows should be carefully and clearly marked after deep preparation, before any further operation such as treating the soil against nematodes or other detrimental organisms, or sowing a cover crop, takes place. The cover crop plays an important role as it guards against soil erosion and stabilizes the newly created soil structure.

Before planting the vines, the cover crop, which until now has protected and stabilized the soil, should preferably be killed with an environment-friendly chemical weed killer and flattened on the soil surface to create a beneficial organic mulch. This mulch is crucial for three principal reasons; it serves as a biological pre-emergence weed killer, conserves moisture and protects the soil against excessive heat. Vines can be planted in this mulch or a narrow zone can be cleared for this purpose.

The young vines from the nursery are introduced into this well-prepared earth. With a consistent and well-drained soil and a good supply of nutrients, they are given a firm foundation for their future working life.

Of relatively greater importance than the influence of the soil is that of the significant influence of the climate – the sun, wind and rainfall which from now on will to a high degree condition the quantity and quality of its crops.

— CLIMATE —

The optimum development of the vine and its grapes is dependent upon a balance of climatic conditions at different times during its yearly cycle of growth and dormancy.

Winter is the dormant period. For three months the vine must be allowed to rest. During this time the soil should stay wet. At the same time, temperatures must not rise too high during this dormant period – warm spells in winter induce unseasonal growth which can deplete the reserves of the vine, thus upsetting the natural growing cycle. Severe spring frosts injure the young shoots, while strong winds can prevent good pollination at flowering time. Now, too, temperatures should not markedly fluctuate. Cold snaps during blossoming time can lead to poor setting of the young grapes, or give rise to small seedless berries – an effect referred to as millerandage.

During the long summer growing season the vine needs a steady supply of warmth. This is expressed both in terms of temperature and the amount of sunshine received. Ideally, the temperature should average 18 °C; the amount of direct sunshine should be about 2 000 hours a year. Again, the 'not too much, not too little' principle operates. Heat and sunlight are needed to bring the grapes to fruition, for it is photosynthesis that produces the major element, namely sugar, in the grape. Without this supply of sunshine the sugar content would be low, thereby resulting in a light wine which would be high in acid and low in alcohol (it is the fermentation of the sugar which makes the alcohol).

At the opposite extreme, problems can arise in a climate with too much sunshine. In general, in a very hot climate the aromatic qualities of the grape (with the exception of Muscat flavours) are not as delicate or rich as those which can develop in more temperate conditions. The high rate of photosynthesis which takes place results in a high sugar content and the high rate of respiration results in a low fruit acid production, having the undesirable tendency to yield an unbalanced wine which is difficult to preserve.

Lack of direct sunlight is rarely a problem in South Africa; rather the reverse. Problems are often encountered with the 'burning' of flavour compounds from grapes, especially with the heavy concentration of sunlight in the late afternoons in summer on north- and west-facing slopes. In areas where this happens ingenuity must be exercised in the siting of the vineyards, either in the shadow of a mountain, or where there is a strategically placed row of trees to block the late afternoon sun, and thereby protect the vines.

The effect of wind is important, too. The areas in the Cape winelands within reach of the cooling breezes from the sea are provided with a natural compensation for the effects of the heat. When accompanied by the protection of a mountain or a valley site, as in Constantia or the valleys of the Simonsberg, natural conditions prevail for the making of fine wine with a high fruit acid content, well balanced with sugar.

Together with sunlight and warmth, a continuous supply of moisture is needed throughout the summer. In the coastal region the ideal water supply to a vine during the growing season would be between 300 and 350 millimetres. Too

—PLANT IMPROVEMENT—

The breeding of new wine-grape varieties is pursued in South Africa. Here and abroad, new clones with improved characteristics are continuously being selected. These new clones need screening for the possible presence of viruses and, if present, the necessary eradication thereof. Imported varieties and clones are screened for exotic pests and diseases under quarantine by the Plant Protection organization of the Department of Agriculture at Stellenbosch. After release, these varieties and clones go to private or co-operative organizations such as Ernita or KWV for further treatment if harmful viruses are still found to be present.

Although there are many excellent vine nurseries in South Africa, presently only two have their own selection and heat therapy programme. These are Ernita of SFW (under the management of Tossie Louw and consultancy of Ernst le Roux M.Sc. (Agric.) and Johannes van Rensburg) and KWV in Paarl. These programmes require special technology and involve the selection of the best performing clones, followed by heat therapy to rid the vine of dangerous viruses. With the rapid growth of the vines under these artificial conditions, together with the adverse effect of heat on the propagation of the virus, the vines are able to outgrow the viruses.

The vines are placed in a chamber for about 100 days at 38 °C in a carbon dioxide-enriched atmosphere, an artificial climate which encourages rapid growth. The first 0,5 millimetres growth is then cut off at the tip of the vine and rooted in a test tube. Thereafter the vines are stored in a growth cabinet (phytotron) at a much lower temperature. From there they are transplanted into pots. When five or six new leaves are visible, the process named 'milking' begins. One internode together with one leaf is cut off and transplanted. The process is repeated a number of times, and when the resulting plants are large enough they are propagated and indexed for viruses. Indexing can

Young virus-free rooted and grafted vines.

take a number of forms, but usually means grafting the plants onto indicator varieties (such as LN33, Baco 22A, Mission Seedling No. 1, and others) to show up the virus – the three main virus groups under observation being fan leaf, leaf roll, and corky bark. However, this may take several years. Fortunately, fan leaf can now also be detected using the rapid ELISA technique. Based on serology, this method consists of injecting the virus into rabbits to produce an anti-serum, which is then used for detecting fan leaf virus in the new plants. Recently an anti-serum has also been developed for the detection of type 3 leaf roll virus and promising progress is being made with the development of another one for corky bark.

Whereas Ernita mainly looks after the needs of SFW producers, KWV serves the rest of the wine-grape industry, having supplied more than 90 per cent of the 27,89 million rootstocks and 88 per cent of the 22,7 million scions given out to nurseries and producers in 1991. Presently KWV has more than 390 hectares of rootstocks and more than 500 hectares of scion-variety mother plantations all over the wine regions, that need regular screening and upgrading. Control over wine-grape improvement is exercised by the privatized Wine Grape Improvement Board.

much water can be harmful, resulting in plants and fruit with soft cell structures which become susceptible to mould. The presence of excessive moisture can also lead to the growth of denser foliage, causing variations of the same problem. Heavy falls of rain when the grapes have almost reached their optimum ripeness can invariably cause the berries to split and rot; the sugar content of the grape will also decline considerably owing to dilution.

Local preference tends to favour drought rather than flood, for a deficiency in natural rainfall can be made up by judicious irrigation. In very low rainfall areas, this is essential to obtain any kind of crop at all; in the coastal belt it is sometimes used as a supplement to rainfall.

As a general principle, under South African conditions, the vine grower looks for altitude, for a cooling breeze, for a

site with relatively less sunshine hours and sheltered in the late afternoons in summer, and for a good accessible supply of water – a farm with numerous dams is not exceptional in the hotter areas. He also looks for varieties appropriate to his particular conditions. For example, certain varieties, such as Pinot Noir, are very sensitive to warm temperatures, and only achieve excellence under very specific temperatures and conditions of cultivation. Assessment of these climatic influences will determine not only the type of vine to be planted but its location, the orientation of the vineyard, and the type and degree of irrigation to be used.

Once the vineyard is established, however, the farmer's focus shortens from the imponderables of sun and rain to the more mundane but equally important matter of the day-to-day running of the vineyard and the care of his vines.

This college, which includes an important wine-making course in its curriculum, is situated 11 kilometres from Stellenbosch, on the farm of Elsenburg, once one of the grand total of 10 farms owned by Martin Melck in the late eighteenth century. Its origins go back to 1887, when a minuscule College of Agriculture was established in the Victoria College (the precursor of Stellenbosch University). Its human resources were one principal and five students, while its agricultural resources were half a hectare of rented land.

In 1898 the Elsenburg farm was purchased by the Colonial Government, and the College. When in 1918 the Victoria College became the University of Stellenbosch it was endowed with a Faculty of Agriculture; in 1926 this was amalgamated with the Elsenburg College to form the Stellenbosch-Elsenburg School of Agriculture of the University of Stellenbosch, which in the 1960s was brought under the auspices of the Department of Agriculture and Fisheries.

Today the college is the immediate responsibility of the Director of the Winter Rainfall Region, Dr Johan Burger, the former head of the VORI. He has two deputy directors, Johan Bloemaris in charge of extension services and Mike Walters in charge of research and responsible for the Elsenburg Agricultural College. One of five assistant directors, Mr L.S. Erasmus, is the head of the college.

The buildings of Elsenburg Agricultural College.

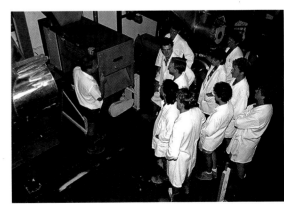

Cellar technology students in the cellar at Elsenburg.

The viticulture and wine-making course now consists of two years of viticulture with a third optional year of Cellar Technology. Theoretical studies in chemistry and physics, in plant physiology and microbiology, accompany study of vineyard practices such as pruning, grafting and trellising, cellar methods, including cellar hygiene, wine analysis and fining, and practical exercises in wine-making. Microvinification of all the major types of wine is followed by experimental wine-making on a commercial scale. The students of the college have excelled in recent years, winning many medals and occasional trophies for their wines on the young wine shows in the country.

—THE DEPARTMENTS OF— VITICULTURE AND OENOLOGY
FACULTY OF AGRICULTURAL SCIENCES, UNIVERSITY OF STELLENBOSCH

The departments of Viticulture and Oenology at Stellenbosch University have played a pioneer role in the development of scientific vine growing and wine-making in South Africa since 1917. In that year the Department of Viticulture and Oenology was formed under its first professor, Abraham Izak Perold. It was he who began the scientific examination of the local vines, research into their origins (he was responsible for the identification of many of the local varieties with their European counterparts), and the study of their behaviour under many different conditions of soil and climate. Together with these studies went the crossing of standard vine varieties to breed new types, the most famous of these being the creation of Pinotage from Pinot Noir and Cinsaut, or Hermitage as it was then generally known. Besides these practical contributions, Perold made many theoretical advances, summed up in his *Treatise on Viticulture*, published in the 1920s and the first major local work of its kind.

His work was further developed by his successor, Christiaan Jacobus Theron, who succeeded to the post in 1930. Theron was responsible for much of the patient spade-work of testing which ensured the survival of the Pinotage vine and its commercial emergence after the Second World War.

Professor Theron held the post at the University for 32 years, until his retirement in 1962. His successor as Head of the department was one of his former students, Chris Orffer.

Appointed professor in 1965, Chris Orffer made extensive contributions to local viticulture, including many published articles on this subject, and was editor of the book *Wine Grape Cultivars in South Africa*. In the practical sphere he has been responsible, among other innovations, for the introduction of two new scion varieties designed for the local environment, those of Chenel and Weldra, as well as 10 new rootstock varieties. Professor Orffer retired at the end of 1986 and his post has been filled by Pieter Goussard, his assistant for many years. Professor Goussard's place has in turn been

taken by Eben Archer from the Agricultural Research Council, otherwise known as the ARC.

Until the 1960s the department had been known simply as that of 'Wynbou', a handy word which covers all aspects of wine agriculture. After the foundation of the Research Institute of the ARC at Nietvoorbij in 1967, however, the department was split at Orffer's suggestion, to create a separate Chair of Oenology, or the science of wine-making. Joël van Wyk was appointed professor of this new department; among his specialist interests are the identification and determination of the aromatic substances in grapes and wine and their evaluation as they emerge in the wine's bouquet, and the study of malolactic fermentation in local red table wine. In addition attention is also focused on phenols of wine and their relationship to wine quality and stability. Joël van Wyk is now also Chairman of the Wine and Spirit Education Trust.

Though technically separate, the two departments are closely linked in their work, sharing premises in the University of Stellenbosch's agriculture building, where both teaching and research take place.

Much of the Viticulture Department's work, however, takes place out in the open, at Welgevallen, one of the University's two experimental farms on the outskirts of the town of Stellenbosch. It is here that students can both observe the department's test programmes in action in the vineyards and conduct experiments of their own.

If the ultimate end of vine growing and wine-making is largely practical, the viticultural and oenological courses provided here are well rooted in theory. All students begin their courses with a first year of the standard B.Sc. course before beginning viticultural and oenological studies in their second year.

The full B.Sc. (Agric.) course, majoring in both viticulture and oenology, takes four years — many of the prominent local winemakers possess this qualification. A B.Sc. Honours course of one year in viticulture or oenology is also offered. And upon submission of a thesis on research conducted under the guidance of the teaching staff of either department, an M.Sc. (Agric.) degree can be obtained. Advanced

Students at Kromme Rhee Agricultural College.

students may go on to take a Ph.D. in certain specialist aspects of their subject.

The complexities of contemporary wine-making theory are well evidenced in Joël van Wyk's Department of Oenology. Here the students all work on an individual basis, studying all aspects of cellar technology 'in miniature' in the laboratory, performing small-scale vinifications to make their own individual wines which are then rigorously analyzed and assessed — only in their final year do the students become directly involved in the outside world of the winelands, usually spending a term at the beginning of the year at work in a co-operative winery.

At the higher student level of M.Sc. and Ph.D., as well as among the staff, active research is an important part of the calendar. Under Professor Chris Orffer, the Department of Viticulture built up a broad base of studies. These include ampelography, or the study of grape varieties, the breeding of new scion and rootstock varieties, and studies on the compatibility of scions and rootstocks. Carried out at Welgevallen, these are protracted experiments, calling for careful control and patience of a high order: it is rare for a new cross to be released in less than 20 years.

Further studies examine the resistance of the plants to pests and diseases, and assessment of different ways of treating these — a few vines are grown ungrafted to allow the students to witness the effect of the phylloxera aphid. Heat treatment of vine propagating material to reduce viruses and virus-like infections was one of Orffer's special interests, as was the development of new training and trellising systems.

The study of the rapid reproduction of new vine cuttings and their development *in vitro* in an agar medium, carried out by Pieter Goussard, has been of great benefit to the industry. He works in a small forest of test tubes, each containing a tiny plant, in a temperature-controlled culture room.

In the Department of Oenology, research includes microvinifications of grapes from the crosses developed by the Department of Viticulture. Particular attention is paid to the separation and analysis of the wine's components, which are recorded in graph form by a mass spectrophotometer and then computer-stored; these spectra are then compared with many thousands of the records which have been compiled from the literature to make a rapidly expanding library of the myriad possible tastes and aromas of the wines. An even more recent development has been the introduction of oak wood chips into white wine during fermentation, in comparison with the traditional ageing of such wines in small barrels. The flavour substances of oak wood and their significance to the quality of the wine are at present also being thoroughly investigated.

A two year course on general agriculture is run by the Kromme Rhee Agricultural College for workers on grape-growing farms. At the college, short courses on specialized subjects such as 'vineyard pruning' and 'trellising systems' may also be taken, as well as courses on tractor driving and the use of mechanical implements.

VINE CULTIVATION

Vines have been known to reach an impressive old age: a hundred years is not uncommon, though few come within reach of the country's oldest vine citizen, a 125-year-old still going strong in Graaff-Reinet.

The average life of a commercially grown vine is about 25 to 30 years, but its productive life only begins after the first three to four years. At the end of its productive period it is uprooted, and the land planted with a cereal crop before a new vineyard is laid out.

During its working career the vine must be given constant physical and chemical attention – physical support in the form of stakes and trellises to which it is trained; its degree and pattern of growth must be regulated and assisted by pruning if required; its soil must be enriched with fertilizers; irrigation applied where necessary; and a variety of vine diseases and ever-hungry pests must be kept at bay.

All this requires considerable planning. Supplies of material and tools must be ensured and fertilizers and pesticides ordered well in advance. The disposition of labour must be planned, and farm machinery, from the irrigation equipment through to the tractors and cultivators, must be kept serviced and in good repair.

All this organization reaches a climax at the time of harvest, the high point of the wine farmer's year. In a period of about two months the annual crop must be brought in. On a large farm or estate this can amount to several hundred or even thousand tonnes of grapes, which must be delivered as quickly as possible to the grower's production cellar, or to the crusher at the local co-operative or producing wholesaler. The complexities of harvesting and delivery are increased when a range of different varieties is concerned.

Different varieties mature at different times, some earlier than others. Pinotage, for example, matures early in the season, whereas Cabernet matures later. Others such as Shiraz and Tinta Barocca are ready for harvesting in mid-season. To avoid uneconomic gaps in the harvest and his labour force being idle, the wine farmer plans his production to suit this. In particular, red-wine producers often 'pad' their harvest programme with a white wine variety such as Chenin Blanc to ensure a sustained level of activity throughout the vintage period. (South Africa is one of the few wine-making countries where the vineyard workers live year-round on the farm.)

At the end of the harvest, if the farmer is producing his own wine in his own cellar, much of his time and attention will be taken up with the complex mysteries, the aromatic secrets of his wine cellar. Outside in the sun, now shadowed a little with a hint of approaching autumn, the vineyards' long rows stand lightened of their burdens. In a few months the winter will come. By then the wine will have been made and been bottled or set aside in oak casks to mature. With the winter rains comes the ebb of the year, the dormant period for both the vines and the people on the farm, for the farmer and his family, the farm manager and the workers – all bound to the cycle of nature, the slow turn of the seasons.

It is a time of regeneration in the communal life of the farm. This is not a world which is often seen or penetrated by the *stadjapies*, the city folk who flock to the winelands in the golden height of summer; it is a secret winter world.

It is also one with a beauty of its own. The full, ripe splendour of the summer winelands has often been celebrated, but the subtle magic of the winter in the valleys, however windand rain-swept, has been the subject of less frequent praise.

After the hectic days of summer, this is the wine farmer's chance to take stock and to start planning ahead. It is also a time for renewing valuable contacts with the many members of the extended family of the farm. For a South African wine farm is a small community which can range from a dozen to a couple of hundred people. The bonds that operate between them, however casual on the surface, are deep, silent and powerful, of ancestral tenure in this part of the land. A South African farmer, talking to his foreman, both of whom, like their ancestors, will usually live and die on this piece of earth, have the language of the mountains between them, a common heritage and bond.

Theirs is largely a silent communion. And by comparison the matter in hand will appear very ordinary indeed. A casual visitor from the town might make little of this muttered debate, intent and frowning, this plucking at half-fallen leaves, this muttering of 'mildew', of 'tandpyn' and 'anthracnose', of 'dead arm' and 'snout beetle', of pruning and trellising.

— TRELLISING AND PRUNING —

Most vines are trellised, by one method or another, to keep them off the ground, to make the bunches of grapes more accessible and, with certain types, to provide a larger leaf-cover for the crop.

The trellis is designed for the particular type of vine that is to be introduced to the vineyard and is usually erected after the vines have been growing for a year. In the course of its growth towards maturity the vine is both pruned and trained to adapt to the advantages of the specific form of trellis that is being used.

Not all vines are trellised, however, although all are trained in some fashion. A proportion is grown as bush or goblet vines, generally in the more arid areas where there is nevertheless enough rainfall for the vines to grow. In this method, the simplest way of establishing a vineyard and the one largely used in the early vineyards, the vines are trained and pruned into a neat 'goblet' shape. The main methods of trellising used locally are the three-wire system and the fence system (a four-wire vertical trellis).

Table grapes are trained onto larger trellises than those used for the support of wine grapes. This is because table grapes are generally more vigorous growers and higher levels of fertilizer and irrigation are applied to support a much heavier crop, for which the delicate balance between flavour compounds, sugar and acid contents is not as important as for wine grapes.

The most common method of training the vines on this variety of structures is the cordon system. By this method the trunk of the vine is trained to about 200 millimetres below the lowest wire of the trellis, the so-called 'cordon-wire', and then divided horizontally into two branches which extend in opposite directions, along the cordon. This system has the effect of disposing the growth of the vine along the full extent of the length of the wires.

But if the trellis provides the basic support for the vine, it is through the craft of pruning that its growth, development and yield of grapes is controlled.

Pruning comprises the removal of canes, shoots, leaves and other vegetative parts of the vine (the removal of flower clusters is known as thinning). By this process of selective removal, the growth of the young vine is controlled in proportion to its vigour and the depth of its root-system. A good balance between vigour and capacity to produce quality fruit must be found. This means that weaker vines must be allowed fewer fruiting buds than vigorous vines. Pruning is therefore individual to each vine. At the same time, dead and unproductive arms, spurs and canes are removed.

The vine is also pruned according to its situation, that is, whether it is grown as a bush vine or on one or other kind of trellis. It is also pruned according to its age, particularly in its youth – if it were not thus restrained it would develop very rapidly in the first few years of life, exhausting its growth and shortening its lifespan. It would bear less fruit and the quality of its grapes would be poor.

There are a number of different styles of pruning. Spur pruning, for example, is used for grape varieties which have fruitful buds at the base of their canes; of these, one to three are retained. With cane or semi-long pruning, the principle of the system is that each arm should have a long cane in combination with one spur with one to two buds. A cane will have between eight and 12 buds. In this instance the canes are for grape production, and the spurs for producing shoots to serve as canes and spurs the following year.

It is important when pruning to know which buds are fruitful. As a rule the fertile buds of the vine occur on the one-year-old canes that arise from two-year-old wood. The buds of vigorous water-shoots (canes arising from three-year-old wood, or older) are frequently unfruitful.

It is also necessary to know if the fruitful buds are situated at the fifth to the tenth node, but in most of the wine varieties the basal buds are sufficiently fruitful to allow spur pruning. With varieties whose basal buds are unfruitful, cane pruning should be practised.

Before planting, the vine is pruned as shown in fig. 1. The strongest and/or the most upright cane is retained and pruned back to two to three buds. Frequently during the first summer no training or trellising is done. During July or August of the following year the first winter pruning takes place

PRUNING AND TRELLISING

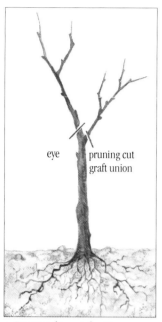

1. Pruning the rooted cutting

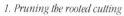

2. Pruning after the first growing season

3. Pruning after the second growing season

all growth below the
first wire is
completely removed

4. Pruning after the third growing season

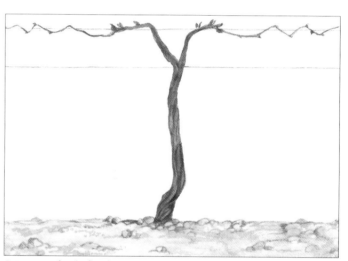

5. Pruning after the fourth growing season

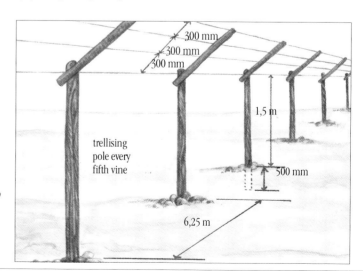

6. Trellising is a precise technology which, together with proper pruning methods, is aimed at obtaining optimum results from the vine. Among the trellising systems used in South Africa is the four-wire system shown here

300 mm
300 mm
300 mm

1,5 m

trellising
pole every
fifth vine

500 mm

6,25 m

— SPRING —

Mild weather with dry spells is needed at this time when the new period of growth commences. Continuous rain makes control of fungoid diseases difficult. Mild frost can help to control insects, but very cold weather and heavy frost can be very detrimental during the flowering period, resulting in poor berry set and millerandage.

— SUMMER —

In the summer season long, warm to hot days are needed; in particular, once the grapes have started ripening dry weather is needed. Humidity in summer causes fungus diseases and encourages insect pests. Rain at the time of full ripening causes the grapes to split and rot.

— AUTUMN —

Rain or irrigation after the crop has been harvested is beneficial to the vine. At this time spraying to prevent fungal diseases is still important, and fertilizers should be applied to ensure the build-up of reserves.

— WINTER —

In winter the vine lies dormant and during this period temperatures should remain low, without being too low, preferably not below 0 °C. There must be sufficient rain to fill catchment dams, for irrigation and to ensure a filled soil water reservoir at bud burst. If the weather remains too warm unseasonable growth may take place which replenishes reserves and may be killed by frost.

(fig. 2). Again, the strongest cane is chosen and pruned to two or three buds, all other shoots being removed.

During early spring the two strongest of the new green shoots are selected and the remaining shoots are removed. The strongest is then tied loosely to the stake. The other shoot is kept as a reserve. Lateral shoots arising from the main shoot are removed, but the leaves are retained.

After the second season, the strongest shoot is tied to the second lowest wire and is cut off at this point. All the other shoots are removed, to leave one stem (fig. 3).

During the third growing season, all the bottom shoots developing from the upright stem are removed, leaving only the top four shoots below the wire – this is done at the end of September. At this time excessive bunches should also be removed, leaving only one bunch to each shoot. After the third growing season the two strongest shoots are selected, one on each side of the stem. These are pruned back to six buds, and the shoots are tied to the wire (fig. 4).

In the next dormant season, the short bearing units (spurs) are cut back to two buds, providing 16 fruit-buds on each vine. Spurs growing upright are selected (fig. 5).

In the following dormant season the cordon is lengthened and finished to leave a vine with between 10 and 12 two-bud short bearers, or spurs. The advantage of this method is that it permits the cordons to be short and sturdy.

The mature plant receives its most thorough pruning during the dormant season of the winter. The first pruning usually commences in May or June, after all the leaves have dropped, and consists of removing all the canes which will not be required as spurs or canes. This is known locally as 'skoonsnoei', and is preliminary to the final pruning, which takes place at any time between mid-July and late August, depending on the variety. In areas where spring frosts are prevalent or where varieties are concerned which set their berries badly, pruning is done as late as possible – in late August or early September.

— PESTS AND DISEASES —

Through careful pruning and trellising, a disciplined use of the vine's resources is obtained. Against these well-ordered battalions of the vineyards, however, are ranged the armies, some visible, some invisible, of viruses, of bacteria, of rot and fungus, and their high command led by a variety of miscreants. It is for these long-standing enemies that the farmer and his assistant will be most prepared and alert.

There are four major pests which, when not effectively combated, are likely to cause serious damage in the local vineyards. These are phylloxera, nematodes, snails, snout beetles, and mealy bugs. Besides these, there are a number of fungus diseases, of which five are paramount. These are, in order of importance, powdery mildew (oïdium), downy mildew, rot, dead arm, and anthracnose. All precautions possible must be taken to prevent these pests from causing damage of any kind to the vines.

Dactylosphaera vitifoliae, is the current scientific name for **phylloxera**, the most widely known of the aphid family. This destructive aphid has caused considerable historic grief in the winelands of the world. In South Africa, *Dactylosphaera vitifoliae*, or phylloxera, attacks the roots and the characteristic effects of its predations are that the affected vines stop summer growth sooner than healthy vines, that leaf colour changes to dull green and later to yellow, and that the symptoms tend to spread relatively quickly so that a patch of weak or dead vines can be observed in the vineyard.

Phylloxera in this country is spread mainly by man. The insect spreads naturally by crawling slowly in the soil from vine to vine, but flood waters and man (through rooted plants, implements and boots) can distribute the pest rapidly over great distances.

The control of phylloxera is mainly a matter of prevention, since no effective chemical control has yet been found. The basic method remains the now almost universal one of grafting onto resistant rootstocks; but the planting of vines in sandy soil (generally avoided by the aphid) can have a limiting effect on the pest.

Nematodes, or **eelworms**, are microscopic worm-shaped pests which attack the roots of the vine and cause damage similar to that of phylloxera. Unlike phylloxera, however, they favour, sandy soils. Their control involves the use of resistant rootstock such as Richter 99, Dog Ridge, or Ramsey, and the fumigation of the vineyard soil before new plantings are made.

Snout beetles are insects which eat young shoots, leaf petioles, and young flower clusters, and in serious cases can lead to the destruction of all the green parts of the vine. They eat mainly at night, and hide during the day in the soil or under the bark of the vines, and are usually active from October to December.

Mealy bugs are lice which form a sticky, sweet and shiny deposit on the shoots, leaves and on the bunches of grapes. This inevitably causes the grapes to be unfit for normal wine-making purposes. This deposit also attracts ants which in turn protect the mealy bug from its natural enemies, namely the ladybirds. By spraying with suitable pesticides to kill the ants (traditionally this was with Dieldrin, now made illegal and replaced by several others), and leave the field clear for the ladybirds, natural control of the mealy bugs can be ultimately obtained.

Powdery mildew (oïdium) first made its appearance in the Cape vineyards in 1859. It is caused by a fungus which exhibits certain characteristic and easily recognized symptoms. On the lower surface of the leaves, small spots occur, and on the upper surface a white, powdery cobweb-like growth appears around the spot where the fungus begins to grow. The young shoots can be adversely affected, but most of the damage is reserved for the grapes. Mature berries, if infected, will crack and dry up. The initial cracking of the berries provides a site for other micro-organism infections, such as that of *Botrytis cinerea*. A characteristic of powdery mildew is that if the normal white powderiness on the shoots and the berries is rubbed off, a brown or black discoloration is revealed underneath.

Powdery mildew and other forms of mildew, such as downy mildew, are easily spread in the vineyard. The fungus prefers warm, humid weather, but the spores will not germinate in wet conditions.

Oïdium is best controlled with vineyard sulphur, or with other systemic chemicals.

Downy mildew (*Plasmopara viticola*) registers its appearance on the lower surface of the leaf when a white downy mass of spores is formed. On the upper surface of the leaf an oily-looking spot, at first light yellow but later turning to a reddish colour, can be seen.

Young bunches of grapes are also infected, a white powdery covering being observed. This may cause the berries to shrivel and drop; in comparison, the shoots are little affected by the fungus.

Susceptible to disease, roses provide the farmer with an early warning system if planted at the head of vineyards.

Noble rot, which is desirable for the making of sweet wines.

Grapes showing symptoms of sour rot.

Powdery mildew, or oïdium, in its early stages.

Oïdium in a more advanced stage.

Downy mildew is best controlled by the use of copper-containing compounds such as copper oxychloride and with organic or systemic fungicides.

Besides these different types of fungi, there are two main kinds of bunch-rot found in South African vineyards. These are **botrytis**, or **grey mould**, rot (*Botrytis cinerea*), which may develop into **noble rot** under favourable conditions; and **sour rot** (Rhizopus). Noble rot is advantageous to the winemaker but sour rot is a grievous nuisance in the vineyard. Usually botrytis rot occurs first, after rains during harvest time. Sour rot is usually a secondary infection.

Chenel, Weldra, Colombard, and to a certain extent Cabernet Sauvignon, are most resistant to botrytis rot because their bunches are loose compared with those of other varieties such as Chenin Blanc, which are compact. Fungicides may aid control with susceptible varieties, which can also be helped by the removal of leaves from the inside of the vine to expose the grapes to the sun and improve ventilation.

Dead arm (*Phomopsis viticola*) is characterized by small cankers which form on the basal parts of the shoots and by small spots which appear on the leaves. These spots usually have a black centre and a yellow border.

Anthracnose (*Gloeosporium ampelophagum*) shows as small, circular, greyish-black spots on the leaves; sometimes these spots are bordered by a yellow discoloration. The spots enlarge, and often the middle portion falls out. On the shoots sunken cankers form and the bark is eventually destroyed, the shoot becoming hard and black. Organic fungicides again provide good control for anthracnose.

From planting to the first harvest some years later, is a long and complex journey for the vine. Many people are involved in its upbringing, from the workers in the field to the farmer, the foreman, the farm manager, to the supplier of chemicals, of fertilizers and pesticides to control the prevalent pests and diseases, to the viticultural expert giving the farmer advice on his plantings and the type of variety he should use, to the expert grafter and nurseryman.

— NIETVOORBIJ INSTITUTE —
FOR VITICULTURE AND OENOLOGY

The headquarters of the Nietvoorbij Institute for Viticulture and Oenology is situated on 200 hectares of the farm Nietvoorbij, on the northern outskirts of the Stellenbosch municipal area. Here are performed a number of important functions which have a bearing on general viticultural and oenological research.

The institute was founded in 1955, in response to a long-felt need for exact research into the local conditions of viticulture and its allied disciplines. Launched with a R1 million state grant, it began as a scattered collection of offices and laboratories in Stellenbosch, Elsenburg, Paarl and Cape Town. Since this state of decentralization seriously hampered its activities, the present complex was built. Completed in 1968, it

The phylloxera aphid usually attacks the root system of the vine but the insect can also feed on the foliage, the mucus deposited during feeding causing the formation of galls or lumps on the underside of the leaves.

Damage caused by the erinose mite is similar to that caused by the phylloxera aphid, but in this instance the galls form on the upper surface of the leaves.

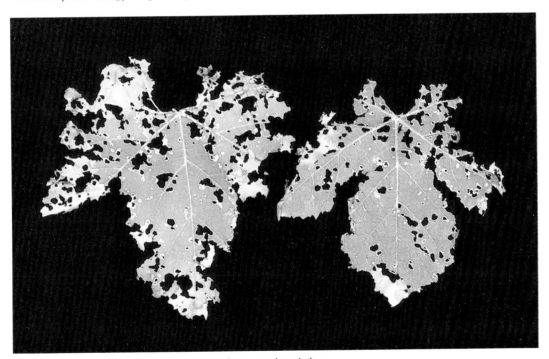

Snout beetles are one of the most destructive vineyard pests, attacking the leaves and young shoots early in the growing season.

The sticky, shiny substance deposited by the mealy bug renders the grapes unsuitable for wine-making.

Later in the season, the damage caused by snout beetles extends to young bunches.

was officially inaugurated by the then Minister of Agriculture, Mr D.C.H. Uys. As from the first of April 1992, the Viticultural and Oenological Research Institute for the Department of Agricultural Development, together with all its personnel and assets, were transferred to the Agricultural Research Council (ARC or LNR in Afrikaans). Officially the institute is now known as the Nietvoorbij Institute for Viticulture and Oenology. 'Nietvoorbij' is now used as a 'trade' name in a similar fashion as Rothemstead and Longashton in Britain and Geisenheim in Germany. No changes are contemplated in the operations of the institute with development being an integral part of its task.

The present resources of the ARC include its main building, consisting of offices, laboratories, and an experimental

—VINEYARD COMPETITION—

Originally sponsored by Stellenbosch Farmers' Winery and judged by a panel of experts drawn from the Oenological and Viticultural Research Institute, Elsenburg College, KWV and Stellenbosch Farmers' Winery, this annual competition seeks to encourage rigorous vineyard practices based on the common winelands maxim that 'good wine is made in the vineyard'. The entrants are judged on a regional basis, the overall winner receiving a carved wooden floating trophy and an overseas study trip to a wine area of his own choice; regional winners also receive a floating trophy and a cash prize.

Competing vineyards must be at least five years old, and a minimum of 1 hectare in size. Judgement is made on the basis of a number of criteria. Yield, of course, is important, and is judged in relation to the potential of the soil in the area of the vineyard. Plant material must be of a high quality; the disposal of the vines should be uniform, without gaps in the rows; there should be good affinity between rootstocks and varieties; pruning methods, crop or yield control and the use of fertilizers and irrigation (where applicable) are also examined. General management and vineyard records are also assessed. After the final judging, the vineyard practices of the winners are analyzed and discussed.

Winners of the competition to date are: **1981** – B. van Velden of Overgaauw in the Stellenbosch district; **1982** – S. Fouché, supplier to the Klawer Co-operative in the Olifantsrivier district; **1983** – P. Bruwer of Uitsig in the Worcester district; **1984** – H. Joubert of Hooggenoeg in the Stellenbosch district; **1985** – P. Hugo of Onderplaas in the Worcester district; **1986** – T. Louw of Diemersdal in the Durbanville district; **1987** – S. Louw of Opstal Estate in the Worcester district; **1988** – J. van Lill of Doringboom in the Olifantsrivier district, R. du Toit of Uitgezocht in the Paarl district, W. Steytler and son of Riverhouse in the Robertson district, D. Jooste of Klein Constantia in the Constantia district, L. Naudé in the Worcester district; **1989** – W. van der Merwe of Het Sluis in the Olifantsrivier district, W. Dreyer of Rustenburg in the Paarl district, D. Erasmus of Wansbek in the Robertson district, D. Jooste of Klein Constantia in the Constantia district, P. Hugo of Hugoskraal in the Worcester district; **1990** – N. Laubscher of Doornboom in the Olifantsrivier district, J. du Toit of Uitsig in the Paarl district, D. Erasmus of Wansbek in the Robertson district, J. Marais of Leef-op-Hoop in the Stellenbosch district, A. Stofberg of Swartwalle in the Worcester district; **1991** – G. Webb of Thelema in the Stellenbosch district, H. Jonker of Signal Hill in the Paarl district, A. Stofberg of Swartwalle in the Worcester district, Steytler Boerdery of Riverhouse in the Robertson district, J. Kotze of Lutzville Proefplaas in the Olifantsrivier district, S. du Toit of Goedertrou in Malmesbury, J. van Zyl of Aden in the Oranjerivier district and D. Stassen of Uitkyk in the Klein Karoo district

distillery and winery, one of the most modern of its kind in the world. There are also extensive nursery facilities, and a *glashuis* and *lathuis* where young vines are propagated and established before being transferred to the vineyards of the experimental farm. The soil and climate at Nietvoorbij are fairly typical of those found in the Boland region in general; research, however, requires close study of vine performance under specific local conditions across the winelands as a whole. The institute therefore runs a number of further experimental farms at Robertson (to serve the Breede River area) and at Lutzville (for the Olifantsrivier region), as well as the farms Bellevue in Paarl and Hexvallei in De Doorns, both of which produce table grapes.

Trial plots are also maintained on the experimental farms of other Departmental institutions at Upington (for the Lower Orange River Irrigation Scheme) and at Roodeplaat (north of Pretoria) and Messina.

There is little in the culture of the vine that is not included in the Agricultural Research Council's investigations. One area of particular concern is that of the improvement of the country's grape varieties (the rising cost of energy and the competing demand for the water supply by the expanding towns make the development of better quality and more economical varieties a priority). The institute's grape improvement programme is based on the evaluation of imported varieties and the selection of the most promising vines in existing vineyards. The imported varieties begin with a period of quarantine at the Research Institute for Plant Protection. Upon release from quarantine, the immigrant vine stocks are planted on a small scale at the Nietvoorbij Institute, and their growth and bearing characteristics meticulously evaluated in the first phase of screening.

In the second phase of screening the most promising clones are planted on a larger scale in statistically planned experiments on all the farms of the ARC.

Together with the development of the necessary scion varieties goes the development of suitable rootstock varieties. Successful growth and bearing of the resultant plant depends principally upon the grafting of the top variety onto a rootstock variety with which affinity problems do not occur; the resulting plant must also adapt well to soil and climate conditions. To determine the adaptability of the various rootstock varieties in the many viticultural regions, series of experiments are carried out both on the institute's farms, and on certain private farms on a co-operative basis.

Research is also done into soil and its preparation, into general vineyard practices, trellising and spacing (the relationship between the number of vines and the quality changes with the density of the vines), pruning and crop control, the effect of fertilizers, methods of cultivation and of irrigation, and into the control of diseases and pests (tested in special 'disease gardens').

And together with viticultural research goes oenological research. This includes investigations into wine chemistry and microbiology, as well as into the full gamut of cellar technology – the grapes from the experimental vineyards are fermented in rows of 20-litre steel tanks.

Besides all its other departments, the ARC also administers a National Oenothèque, which is more often referred to as the National Vinotèque, which is its official English name. It consists of a wine library where samples of wines made and marketed in South Africa are kept. Wine producers partake in this venture on a voluntary basis, and after every vintage 24 bottles of wine selected by the producer are delivered to the Oenothèque. All relevant information regarding these wines is stored in a computer. The Oenothèque has accommodation for 84 000 bottles of wine, and at present there are 36 000 bottles of 1 800 different wines in storage, including their most precious possessions, a number of bottles of Constantia wine dating from 1793 and 1823, which have been donated to the institute.

The dissemination of information about new developments is regarded by the ARC as one of its most important functions. To this end well-attended courses on all aspects of vine growing and wine-making are held throughout the year and scientific as well as popular publications are issued on a regular basis. The present director of the ARC is Dr Jakob Deist and its public relations officer is Eugene Booysen, while long-time stalwart of Nietvoorbij and very popular Christo 'Kokkie' Kok has been transferred to Paris, France as the South African Agricultural attaché, which should help to promote South African wine.

— THE VINEYARD — CALENDAR

The climax of the wine farmer's year comes with the vintage which takes place at the height of summer, generally from February through to March and later still for certain of the vines. In a sense, everything which takes place during the remainder of the year is a preparation for this event. The arrangement of this 'vineyard calendar' therefore abandons the traditional western January to December arrangement in favour of Nature's calendar of March to February, beginning immediately after the conclusion of the harvest.

— MARCH —

By the end of March, most wine farmers will have brought in their crop. It is still hot in the land, but the edge of the coming autumn is now approaching. Immediately after the harvest has been brought in the vineyards are irrigated if

Overhead irrigation sprinklers in a vineyard in Stellenbosch. Irrigation is a necessary supplement to rainfall in many parts of the South African winelands.

possible, preventing early defoliation and allowing the wood to mature properly.

At this time seed and fertilizers for the winter cover crop are ordered to ensure an early sowing. By now, too, quick grass (fast-growing, hardy grass) on new soils and in the vineyards must be removed and destroyed.

— APRIL —

New vineyards are now prepared. The farmer prepares the soils to be planted in the coming winter before the heavy winter rains begin. Advance planning of new plantings is also undertaken. Organic matter and/or fertilizer and lime are applied during soil preparation, this being the only opportunity the farmer has to introduce it into the subsoil. Sources of organic matter include natural vegetation, which should never be removed completely when veld or bush is cleared. Sown cover crops will also supply a considerable quantity of organic matter. Before the heavy rains begin contours and stormwater ditches are constructed. Existing contours and ditches are also inspected, and repaired and

cleaned where necessary. Drainage pipes are put in new soils where these tend to become waterlogged.

— MAY —

By this time the winter cover crops have generally been sown. By now, too, soils for new plantings are fully prepared. At the same time, preparations for pruning the vineyards are under way. All pruning equipment, particularly shears, is checked for condition – the shears should make a clean cut to prevent harm caused by bad pruning wounds. When pruning certain basic guidelines are followed. Clearing is started as soon as the leaves have fallen – the final pruning of the bearers is done late in the winter. The best time to start pruning is after a good rain. This will prevent the pruning wounds from drying out – dry wounds may give access to disease organisms. Fortunately, a sealer for large wounds is now available. Varieties which bear and grow well and are not inclined to millerandage are generally pruned early. Early pruning will also, to a certain extent, encourage the earlier ripening of the grapes.

— JUNE —

By now important decisions are made regarding the type of trellises to be used in the new vineyards. Trellising and the size of the trellis depend upon the vigour of growth, which in turn is determined by the variety planted, the soil fertility and depth, the water supply and the spacing between the vines, that is, the relationship of supply by the soil and demand by the vine. Trellising poles must then be planted. It is especially important to plant the end posts now to allow time for them to settle firmly in the soil before the wires are put up. During this month it must also be remembered to control ants, otherwise trouble with mealy bug may occur in the coming season.

— JULY —

If weather permits a start can now be made on ploughing and cleaning around the vines. This may save trouble when the soil becomes hard later in the season.

The 'skoonsnoei', or clean pruning, has been completed and 'stompsnoei', or final pruning, is started.

Workers in Stellenbosch vineyards during the growing season.

Blocks are planned and laid out for new vineyards and sometimes planting is started towards the end of the month. The drying-out of vines has to be carefully avoided, planting being done if possible directly from the nursery. It must be remembered to fill the gaps in young vineyards while planting is taking place. This replanting of missing vines is done the year after the original planting.

—AUGUST—

The farmer usually tries to complete the planting of new vineyards during this month. Orders for grafted vines for new plantings in the following year are usually placed now.

The final pruning of the vineyards is done. Where there is a danger from frost, however, pruning should be done later.

The green manure crop (sown or natural weed growth) must be ploughed into the soil before the end of August. Some farmers prefer to kill the weed growth with herbicides, rather than plough it in. If weather conditions are right, the vines start growing now and competition for nutrients and water by weeds and other crops must be eliminated. This is especially important for unirrigated vineyards where growing weeds or crops will deprive the vine of valuable moisture. If the ploughing in of the green manure is delayed for too long the soil may become too hard and make cultivation difficult. The farmer should avoid working the soil too finely. A few stalks protruding here and there will do no harm.

The spring fertilization is applied this month, or in September, depending on weather conditions. Where anthracnose, erinose and dead arm occur the vineyards are sprayed with lime sulphur prior to bud burst.

—SEPTEMBER—

If new vineyards are being planted and it is already hot and dry, the farmer generally waters the planted vines. Cleaning around the vines is done, before the soil becomes too hard.

Where one or other of the diseases bacterial blight, anthracnose, dead arm or downy mildew occur, the farmer sprays the vines with copper oxychloride, this being done when the shoots are between 2,5 and 5 centimetres long. Oïdium (powdery mildew) and erinose are controlled by vine sulphur. The first dusting is applied when the shoots are 15 to 25 centimetres long. Dusting is done on windless days, early in the morning. The control of oïdium is of the utmost importance and the sulphur-dusting programme is neglected by the wine farmer at his peril.

—OCTOBER—

Where cultivation is practised, the second ploughing is done in this month. The soil is ploughed back towards the vines without ridging the stems.

Young vines are generally supported with stakes to enable them to form a straight line from the start. Dead vines can now be replaced if some grafted vines are left. Young vineyards should be regularly inspected for insect damage and it is essential that the insects, especially caterpillars and vine beetles are controlled where necessary.

'Tipping' is the removal of the first 2 to 5 centimetres of the growing shoot early in the season, and is done this month and in early November. The procedure is recommended where growth is strong as it has the effect of temporarily curbing excessive shoot growth. When tipping is done

at the commencement of flowering, it usually follows that the fruit sets better, particularly in the case of the variety Muscat d'Alexandrie.

In trellised vineyards all the shoots are removed from the stem. Shoots growing from the rootstock are cut off below the soil surface to prevent regrowth. The removal of these unnecessary rootstock shoots is important since they are mere passengers on the vine.

—NOVEMBER—

In unirrigated vineyards, if cultivation is practised, the second disc-cultivation is done in October while the soil is still moist. In irrigated vineyards this cultivation can be left until after the irrigation in November. Weed control is the only justification for any further summer cultivation. Here the tine-cultivator is used in preference to the disc-cultivator which makes the soil too fine and creates subsoil compaction. These cultivations are done only when weed growth demands, and not at predetermined times.

Irrigation, if used, must not be postponed until the soil is quite dry. Later in summer, when the soil has dried out to a considerable depth, wetting of the topsoil will be of little value, as the roots there will already be damaged. The vines need moisture especially now in the early summer for sufficient growth and leaf surface. Depending on the soil, a light irrigation of 25 to 50 millimetres is therefore can be given now, even if the soil is still moist.

Only slight topping is done now so that the biggest possible leaf surface is maintained. 'Topping' is the removal of the first 15 to 25 centimetres of a young growing shoot, either by machine or by hitting it off with a strong switch or thin stick. There are several reasons for topping, which is usually done in November, the most important being that it allows more sunlight through, and controls fungus diseases and rot by allowing a good circulation of air. Topping also gives protection against wind damage. The farmer should tie up shoots of trellised vines regularly.

During this month flowering and berry set are completed. At this stage the tiny bunches are very susceptible to damage by downy mildew, which is controlled by preventative sprays. Snout beetles, too, usually appear from October onwards. Although damage by oïdium is usually observed only in December, prevention is already started with sulphur dusting or a systemic fungicide.

—DECEMBER—

Summer cultivation is limited to an absolute minimum, weed control being the only justification.

Ground which will be used for new plantings during the following season and is contaminated with quick grass, is sprayed, ploughed and disc harrowed during the summer months – to date this is the only effective method of eradicating quick grass. It is, however, important to destroy this weed before the vines are planted, since it is extremely difficult to control in an established vineyard.

December is an important month for irrigation, if there has been no rain. The vine still grows at this stage and the berries begin to enlarge. Adequate moisture is needed for this.

The main shoots of young trellised vines are tied up and superfluous shoots are removed. This ensures a good, strong stem. The main anchor poles of vineyards which are to be trellised next season are put in now. Topping of vineyards should only be done slightly and must be concluded before growth stops.

Mealy bugs, snout beetles, erinose, oïdium and botrytis must be well controlled now. The spray programme against downy mildew is kept up as long as weather conditions are favourable for the disease. Grapes are most susceptible to botrytis from the time when the berries begin to ripen until picking time. The nearer to picking time, the greater becomes the danger. Healthy grapes can be infected if they are wet for a period of time, while damaged grapes can be infected at any time. To prevent this disease the bunches must be adequately aerated so that they dry easily after rain or dew – damaging of the grapes must be avoided. The infection can be controlled to a certain extent by dusting with copper oxychloride from within six weeks before the harvest.

— JANUARY —

By now the heat of the year is intensifying in the vineyards. At this point the grapes have already been growing a few months, and some of the earlier varieties are beginning to ripen. Bearing vineyards are no longer irrigated, except in cases where soils are very shallow and where the vines are inclined to wilt or scorch. Excessive irrigation or rain especially shortly before the harvest, not only adversely affects grape quality, but also creates favourable conditions for botrytis. Where water is available, young vineyards are irrigated, as they are still growing strongly. The root systems of young vines have not yet developed strongly and deeply, and therefore suffer more readily from drought. At this stage, too, grapes that have not yet developed are vulnerable to damage .

In this month weeds must be eradicated, particularly those growing close to the vines. Strong weed growth near the vines impedes aeration of the bunches, creating favourable conditions for the growth of botrytis infection.

Within six weeks prior to the harvest no toxic insecticides may be applied in the vineyards. It is important, too, at this time to watch for late attacks of oïdium. Judicious sulphur dusting can be done where necessary, but sulphur must never be used when it is very hot, since scorching of leaves and grapes may result. Sulphur-containing fungicides must not be applied later than six weeks prior to harvesting. Grapes become more susceptible to botrytis as harvesting approaches. Excessive nitrogen application, as with excessive irrigation, encourages this disease.

In preparation for the pressing season, the farmer who makes his own wine will clean the cellar in readiness and make certain that all his machinery is in good order. The steel bins in which grapes are transported are thoroughly cleaned, loose rust being removed with a steel brush; they are then painted with acid-resistant paint. Sulphur dioxide, bentonite and other wine-making requirements should now be in stock in the cellar. Yeast must be ordered in time. The containers for propagation of the yeast must be made clean and sterilized before they are used.

All possible care is taken in this hot season to improve the aeration of the grape bunches; in particular, windbreaks must allow sufficient circulation of air through the vineyards and there should not be tall weeds growing between them.

— FEBRUARY —

This is generally the hottest month of the year in South Africa. The vineyards (except for the younger plantings) are left unirrigated. Now, before the harvesting of the grapes, the farmer will generally take stock of the condition of his vineyards, noting aspects which may need improvement in the following season.

Vineyards or patches growing too vigorously and where rot occurs should receive less irrigation and nitrogen in future. Aeration can be improved to a certain extent by the pruning method adopted. Vineyards bearing too heavily should be pruned more heavily to restore the balance between growth and yield.

Note should be made of where diseases such as oïdium, anthracnose, or bacterial blight, and insects such as snout beetle and mealy bug, have harmed the vines. This will ensure that more efficient precautions will then be taken against these pests in the following season.

At this time, too, the farmer consults his fertilizer company about autumn fertilization of the vineyards, green manure crops, and new lands which are to be prepared. The fertilizer company should be allowed enough time for the analysis of the farm's soils, and to work out a fertilization programme. This enables the farmer to order the fertilizer early and to have it delivered well in time.

If the farmer does his own grafting or supplies a nursery, vines must be selected for cutting scions during the winter. This must be done before harvesting. The quantity of scions needed must be estimated, and a sufficient amount of these vines to supply this need must be marked.

Harvesting is only commenced when the grapes are fully ripe. Apart from a low sugar content, unripe grapes will not yet have developed a full flavour.

The grapes are harvested according to a fixed plan. Most farmers arrange their vineyards so as to dispose the ripening pattern of the different varieties, early-, middle-, or late-season ripening varieties, across the whole vintage period.

Grapes should not be left to become over-ripe. The fruit acids which are essential for good quality then decrease rapidly. Furthermore, the must of over-ripe grapes has a high polyphenol content.

Grapes of good and bad quality should be kept apart in the cellar. If the farmer delivers to a local co-operative or wholesaler's cellar, a harvesting programme is decided well

— RIPENING —	
WHITE VARIETIES	RED VARIETIES
EARLY	**EARLY**
Gewürztraminer	Pinot Noir
Muscat Ottonel	
Morio Muscat	
Pinot Gris	
Pinot Blanc	
Chardonnay	
Fernão Pires	
Kerner	
Sylvaner	
EARLY-MID	**EARLY-MID**
Sémillon	Pinotage
Sauvignon Blanc	Merlot
Weisser Riesling	
Bukettraube	
Chenin Blanc	
Palomino	
MID	**MID**
Hárslevelü	Cabernet Sauvignon
Cape Riesling	Gamay
Chenel	Pontac
	Malbec
LATE-MID	**LATE-MID**
Colombard	Carignan
Furmint	Cinsaut
Muscat d'Alexandrie	Grenache
Weldra	Souzão
	Tinta Barocca
	Shiraz
	Cabernet Franc
	Cabernet Sauvignon
LATE	**LATE**
Clairette Blanche	Zinfandel
Raisin Blanc	
Trebbiano	

in advance through consultation between the supplying farmer and the cellarmaster. This programme, however, has to be reasonably flexible to allow for the vagaries of weather and other unforeseen factors.

Good quality grapes, following the old European practice, are harvested early in the morning, the more zealous beginning before sunrise, avoiding deterioration in the quality of the grapes brought about by the heat of the day. However, picking continues throughout the day at those larger cellars that have cooling facilities.

W I N E - M A K I N G

The technology of a modern wine cellar, with its rows of gleaming steel tanks and its rich aroma of the wine, unseen but very present, is a far cry from the simple, rough wooden vats, casks and *velkuipe* of the pioneer wine farmers. It is far even from the nineteenth-century basket-presses, now objects of industrial archaeology, mellowed to become treasured museum pieces and mementos of the past, their once busily clanking parts slowly welding together with time. For it is in the winemaker's cellar more than in any other area of the winelands, that the images of yesterday have more visibly given place to those of today.

But under the surface of these changes some things, of course, persist. The raw material of the vine, the grape, remains, even if it is a healthier entity than its forebears. The basic process of fermentation, the root chemical reaction of wine-making, exploited for thousands of years before it came to be understood, has always been and will remain the same. The wooden casks in which the red wine (and ever increasing amounts of white wine) is matured have a familiar and traditional look too, for no modern technology could replace their subtle function in the life of the wine.

Many of the other steps in the process of wine-making have been modified and streamlined to an altogether new level of efficiency. This applies particularly to some of the ancillary machinery which the modern era has introduced into the wine-making process. A tank is a tank, whether made of stone a thousand years ago, of concrete 50 years ago, or of stainless steel or glass fibre today. However decorated with dials and festooned with pipes, its basic function remains the same, namely to contain the wine before it is bottled. But a large-scale modern bottling machine – such as the splendid cacophonous specimens at many of the modern Cape cellars – is a far cry from the simple but effective appliance of the nineteenth century which thrust a cork into a bottle, one bottle at a time (and still works perfectly well, if somewhat slowly, for a small farm with a modest output).

At the chemical level, understanding of the complexities of fermentation has led to many refinements of the process in terms of the growing of pure yeasts, of methods of effective filtering, cleaning and polishing of the wine, and of the stabilization of its chemical composition; and knowledge of the need for hygiene has swept away the haphazard methods of the past. A modern winery is a meticulously clean and well-maintained place, so that wine which comes from it is healthy and rich in its natural composition of acids, esters and many other compounds.

Indeed, one of the arts of the winemaker, of the skilled oenologist, is to strike a balance between chemical control of the wine and a respect for its natural complexity. While cleanliness and hygiene are background factors in the making of the wine, in the foreground stand the qualities which have always made wine one of the companions of mankind, its complexity and variety of sensation (wine contains over 200 different compounds), its subtleness of aroma and bouquet and flavour. The winemaker, however often he refers to his pipettes, his hydrometers, pycnometers and refractometers, his microscopes and temperature and humidity gauges, must never lose sight of the inherent life and character of the wine. It is this delicate balance between the consciously objective and the elusively poetic and mysterious, between instinct and intelligence, which informs the modern wine-making process; a process which begins simply enough, with the image of the harvest.

It evokes, even in today's urban dweller, a sense of the past when his forebears once took part in this ancient ritual. In Europe this moment usually began on the name-day of the vignerons' patron saint, Saint Vincent. It is reflected in the work of artists and poets from antiquity to today, from that Greek farmer-poet of old, Hesiod, celebrating the abundance of summer in his *Works and Days*, through to the *Four Seasons* of Pieter Brueghel, with their musical counterpart in the *Four Seasons* of Vivaldi, to the harvest paintings of Van Gogh, a brief but violent harvest of creation before the artist's private winter descended.

Their works reflect a sense of the self-enhancing power of the earth, of the land as 'the mother who never dies'; an

image barely touched by the hand of time or technical progress in the vineyards. Though various machines have been devised to replace them, most of the world's vineyards are still harvested by the workers in the field, moving with steady rhythm along the rows of vines, cutting free the heavy bunches, transferring them to baskets or lug-boxes, to be emptied into the trucks or tractor-drawn carts which trundle away along the early morning roads – grapes are often harvested at dawn or even earlier to gather them in the best condition before the heat of the day. Picking at night has become a feature in some South African vineyards, such as Twee Jongegezellen and L'Omarins, where the workers, like miners, wear head-mounted lamps. Other vineyards use tractor-mounted floodlights to provide illumination.

At the entrance to the winery the truck is weighed together with its cargo of grapes. Then a sample of the grapes is taken and measured with a Balling hydrometer or a refractometer for its sugar content. At this point the natural fruit acid of the grapes is also determined, as is the overall quality. The truck tips the grapes into the crusher at the entrance to the winery and is then weighed empty to give the mass of the grapes. The farmer, if he is delivering to a co-operative or merchant wholesaler, is paid for his crop on the basis of its weight, and sugar content and quality.

Today the producing wholesalers pay a considerable bonus for grapes of high quality brought in at the sugar and acid levels of the high calibre required for modern wine-making. In some instances this bonus paid by the producing wholesalers can be substantially more than the minimum price set down by KWV per tonne of grapes.

The brief independent life of the grape comes to an end at this point, with the process of crushing and possible destemming which marks the beginning of the making of the wine. During this process the stems of the grapes may be mechanically removed, where necessary, from the berries. The grapes are then gently crushed between rollers which release the juice but do not crush the pips – so as to avoid releasing the oil and tannin they contain and which would impart an acrid, biting taste to the wine. The stems, containing many phenolic compounds, undesirable because they

A load of grapes is weighed on the weighbridge.

After being weighed, a sample of grapes is taken for analysis.

The grapes are then tipped into a receiving bin.

render the wine susceptible to oxidative browning, may also give rise to a bitter taste in the wine if they are not removed.

During the crushing, sulphur dioxide (SO_2) can be added to the grapes in carefully regulated small doses. This functions as an anti-oxidant and inhibits micro-organisms such as the yeasts and bacteria, which normally breed on the grapes, from reacting.

There is a gradual decrease in the amount of sulphur dioxide used in modern wine-making. Only rarely nowadays are the natural yeasts, occurring in the waxy 'bloom' of the grapes, allowed to develop spontaneously, a healthy selected yeast culture being preferred.

From the crusher the juice or the must of the grapes is run off. In the case of both red and white grapes, it is almost colourless. The colour of the red grapes is usually contained in the skin – the Pontac variety, which has a natural red juice, being one of the few exceptions.

It is at this point that the two processes of white and red wine-making, as well as those of rosé, sparkling and fortified wines, begin to diverge.

— WHITE WINE —

The juice of the white grapes (and in some instances of red grapes, since the juice of most red grapes is also almost colourless) is run off from the pulp through patent drainers which are, in effect, giant sieves. To inhibit the growth of micro-organisms it is cooled to 12-13 °C, and allowed to settle for periods of up to 24 hours. Modern mash coolers are now fairly commonplace in Cape wineries where extended skin contact enhances the flavours.

During the settling of the must, the suspended particles of skin, seeds and dust not removed or left behind in the crushers are allowed to sink to form a sediment at the bottom of the tank. The removal of these particles eliminates the off-odours they would otherwise produce in the wine. In the modern winery this process of settling may be aided by the use of pectolytic enzymes.

Many wineries use centrifuges to expedite the separation of the juice from its unwanted passengers. This reduces the time needed for clarification from a day to a few hours. The degree of clarification achieved, however, does not match that of proper settling. Some wineries use first the centrifuge and then settling to achieve a high degree of clarification.

When the process of juice clarification is completed, the must is run off into a fermentation tank, the modern equivalent of the *velkuipe* of old. In this fermentation tank, which varies considerably in design from one winery to the next, the process of fermentation is initiated in most instances by the addition of an active selected yeast culture.

To understand this process it is necessary to take a close-up look at the anatomy of the grape. As the seed-bearer of the vine, it is highly complex. Its three main components are the husk, or skin, the flesh, and the pip. The latter, which because of its astringency and tannin content is removed before fermentation, carries the basic woody structure of the vine.

The skin of the grape contains colour pigments, tannin, flavouring substances, fruit acid and aromatic compounds, plus innumerable other substances in minute quantities.

It is these components, mostly stored in the skin of the grape, which are released during the fermentation process and give the wine its character. The major difference, in fact, between white and red grapes lies in the skin. Most red and some white grapes are richly endowed with qualities which the winemaker aims to capture.

The flesh or pulp of the grape contains water (70-80 per cent), carbohydrates, pectins, traces of proteins, and a range of vitamins. It is the grape sugar in the flesh of the grape, produced by photosynthesis during the long summer, which is the component involved in fermentation. The element that causes the reaction is yeast.

Yeasts are forms of microscopic unicellular plant organisms which are widely spread in nature. They are used commercially in the production of a number of commodities, including bread and pharmaceuticals, as well as wine. They occur naturally on the grape in the 'bloom', a watertight, protective layer on the skin of the berry. The bloom has a slightly waxy feel and is responsible for the characteristic dull sheen on the surface of the ripe fruit.

When the skin of the grape is broken, the yeast on the outside of the skin and the sugar in the juice (which is an almost perfect balance of nutrients for the growth of the yeast cells) meet in a reaction which converts the sugar into ethyl alcohol, or ethanol, and carbon dioxide and energy. Most of the carbon dioxide is released as a gas during the reaction, but some is retained, giving liveliness to the wine.

If the naturally occurring yeasts sufficed the world's winemakers for centuries, their modern descendants have increasingly tended to replace them with more reliable cultured strains. In the modern winery the wild yeast in the bloom is subdued by the sulphur dioxide added at the start of the winemaking process, and fermentation is started with the inoculation of a three to five per cent actively fermenting pure yeast culture to the clear juice.

From its many components the fermenting must yields a resultant wine which is broken down into 80-90 per cent water and alcohol, sugar, fruit acids (tartaric, malic and citric acids among them), colouring matter, and pigments. Varying amounts of tannin can also occur.

The amount of sugar remaining after the reaction can also vary. Left to itself, fermentation runs its natural course, that is, it proceeds until all the sugar is used up and converted to alcohol. With the assistance of the winemaker, the process can be halted to give varying ratios of unfermented sugar and alcohol. The quantity of sugar in the liquid determines its sweetness or 'dryness' – a dry wine being simply one with a low sugar content (in practice, less than four grams of sugar in a litre of wine).

Energy, in the form of heat, is released during fermentation. In the white wine process the heat is removed by cooling, and fermentation temperatures are usually maintained between 14 °C and 16 °C. The innovation of this 'cold fermentation' technique during the 1950s was a major development in enabling the making of quality white wine in warm climates. At the high temperatures prevalent in the South African summer, fermentation tends to be very fast and tumultuous if left to its own devices, and can all be over in a few hours, with carbon dioxide evolving rapidly, often sparging many of the aromatic flavour compounds from the wine: at temperatures of above 20 °C the aromatic compounds become more readily volatile.

Moreover, if the heat is not removed, the fermentation temperature may rise to a level where the yeast is destroyed,

Steel cold fermentation tanks with glycol cooling jackets.

thus halting further fermentation. In this condition the partly fermented must is very susceptible to bacterial spoilage.

Thus, there is both an upper and a lower temperature limit to active fermentation: above 32,2 °C (90 °F) the yeast cells are killed by the heat, while below 4,4 °C (40 °F) they are rendered dormant by cold.

With the conclusion of fermentation, which in the case of white wines normally takes up to 14 days but can take longer at a reduced temperature, a procedure known as 'racking' takes place. This procedure is identical for both white and red wines and involves the running off the wine from its lees. If this is not done, off-odours can arise in the wine as a result of yeast cell autolysis.

The first racking takes place two to four days after the completion of fermentation. At this stage the wine is usually dry, that is, there are no fermentable sugars left in it. With this first racking, sulphur dioxide is usually added to the newly made wine. Every effort is made in modern wine-making to keep the additions of sulphur dioxide to an absolute minimum. Thereafter the so-called 'free SO₂' is carefully monitored and maintained at a hygienic level of 30 milligrams a litre as a control against further oxidation. For this reason it is also important to protect the white wine from contact with air.

A distinction must be made between 'free' and 'fixed' sulphur dioxide: the 'free' sulphur dioxide which was originally added to the crushed grapes reacts during fermentation with such products of the fermentation as acetaldehyde, -ketoglutaric acid, and pyruvic acid, and becomes 'bound', or 'fixed' sulphur dioxide. The acetaldehyde-bound sulphur dioxide has no anti-oxidant or preservative properties and is therefore of no practical use to the winemaker; it is the 'free' sul-

phur dioxide which is the active assistant. Some of the remaining, loosely bound forms of sulphur dioxide can replenish 'free' sulphur dioxide 'on demand' during oxidation. However, malic acid fermentation cannot occur if the fixed sulphur dioxide rises above 120 parts per million.

Some 14 to 21 days after the first racking, there is a second and sometimes even a third racking to remove further impurities which have settled down. Some winemakers use a centrifuge for this, which is quicker than racking but, as with the earlier stage of separating impurities from the must, it is not a universally accepted method.

After the final racking the young wine is filtered so that it is ready for blending and for the final stabilization procedures before it is bottled. It is then protein stabilized, usually before final filtration, with bentonite. There is a growing belief in leaving wine as natural as possible and not subjecting the wine to fining and filtration.

Oddly enough the tendency towards making wine with the emphasis on keeping it as natural as possible is only the case with some of the best quality and most expensive wines. For most regular wines, what is described here is fairly common practice. (Some winemakers, a relative few, blend their wines at the outset of the process, mixing grapes of different varieties at the crusher.)

The blending of wines is an almost universal practice, even when the winemaker is ostensibly dealing with a single variety, where a small percentage of other wines will be used to round off the character of the basic wine-type. It has developed over the years into a fine art and one central to the winemaster's rôle. The wines he selects must blend harmoniously and achieve a level of excellence within the limitations imposed upon him. These include not only the specific char-

acter of the variety or varieties themselves, but the particular character of area and vintage as well.

After blending, the wine is stabilized, in order to restore its equilibrium after the disturbances of the blending, and to prevent it from undergoing any unwanted changes after bottling. There are four main kinds of stability which must be ensured: oxidative, protein, tartrate and microbiological.

In white wines, unwanted oxidation leads to browning and sometimes to the formation of sediments which result in a characteristic and unpleasant odour and taste. To prevent this, contact with air is avoided as far as possible throughout the wine-making process, and judicious quantities of sulphur dioxide are used as an anti-oxidant.

As soon as a white wine is blended it is protein stabilized. The protein content of wines can vary substantially from a few to several hundred milligrams in a litre, but it remains one of the most important causes of white wine cloudiness. Virtually all young white wines will become cloudy if the proteins are not removed from the wine.

This is done by fining the wine with bentonite, a purified, complex, hydrated aluminium silicate, the predominant constituent of which is montmorillonite clay. A pre-determined amount is mixed with the wine whose proteins are absorbed by the clay which settles at the bottom of the tank. When the settling process is completed, the protein-stable wine is filtered off the fining lees, and is tartrate stabilized.

Tartaric acid is the most common fruit acid found naturally in wine. In young wines the concentration of bitartrate and potassium ions as well as tartrate and calcium ions, often exceeds their solubility in the wine and they separate out. In the case of potassium bitartrate (KHT), commonly known as 'cream of tartar', and calcium tartrate (CaT), a crystalline precipitation of potassium bitartrate often occurs in the wine after fermentation. If that took place after bottling, a formation of unsightly (though harmless) crystals would greet the consumer.

To make wine tartrate stable it is cooled to 1 °C above the freezing point of wine, and held at this temperature for four to eight days. After the wine has been cooled for this time, it is filtered at this temperature to remove the crystals which have formed – at low temperatures KHT and CaT become progressively more insoluble, enhancing the process of crys-

A semi-automatic red-wine bottling line.

THE WINE-MAKING PROCESS

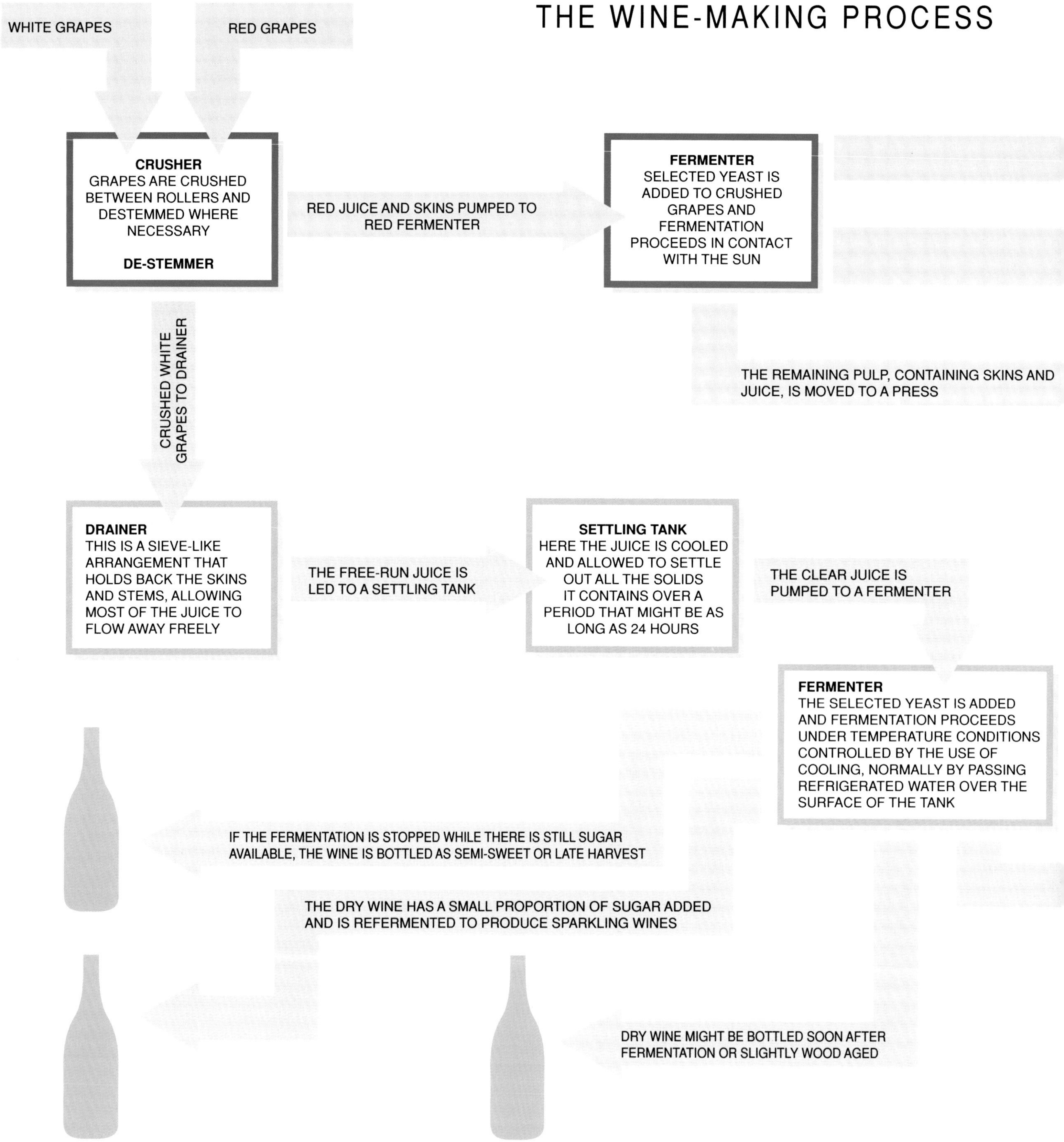

WHITE GRAPES

RED GRAPES

CRUSHER
GRAPES ARE CRUSHED
BETWEEN ROLLERS AND
DESTEMMED WHERE
NECESSARY

DE-STEMMER

RED JUICE AND SKINS PUMPED TO
RED FERMENTER

FERMENTER
SELECTED YEAST IS
ADDED TO CRUSHED
GRAPES AND
FERMENTATION
PROCEEDS IN CONTACT
WITH THE SUN

CRUSHED WHITE
GRAPES TO DRAINER

THE REMAINING PULP, CONTAINING SKINS AND
JUICE, IS MOVED TO A PRESS

DRAINER
THIS IS A SIEVE-LIKE
ARRANGEMENT THAT
HOLDS BACK THE SKINS
AND STEMS, ALLOWING
MOST OF THE JUICE TO
FLOW AWAY FREELY

THE FREE-RUN JUICE IS
LED TO A SETTLING TANK

SETTLING TANK
HERE THE JUICE IS COOLED
AND ALLOWED TO SETTLE
OUT ALL THE SOLIDS
IT CONTAINS OVER A
PERIOD THAT MIGHT BE AS
LONG AS 24 HOURS

THE CLEAR JUICE IS
PUMPED TO A FERMENTER

FERMENTER
THE SELECTED YEAST IS ADDED
AND FERMENTATION PROCEEDS
UNDER TEMPERATURE CONDITIONS
CONTROLLED BY THE USE OF
COOLING, NORMALLY BY PASSING
REFRIGERATED WATER OVER THE
SURFACE OF THE TANK

IF THE FERMENTATION IS STOPPED WHILE THERE IS STILL SUGAR
AVAILABLE, THE WINE IS BOTTLED AS SEMI-SWEET OR LATE HARVEST

THE DRY WINE HAS A SMALL PROPORTION OF SUGAR ADDED
AND IS REFERMENTED TO PRODUCE SPARKLING WINES

DRY WINE MIGHT BE BOTTLED SOON AFTER
FERMENTATION OR SLIGHTLY WOOD AGED

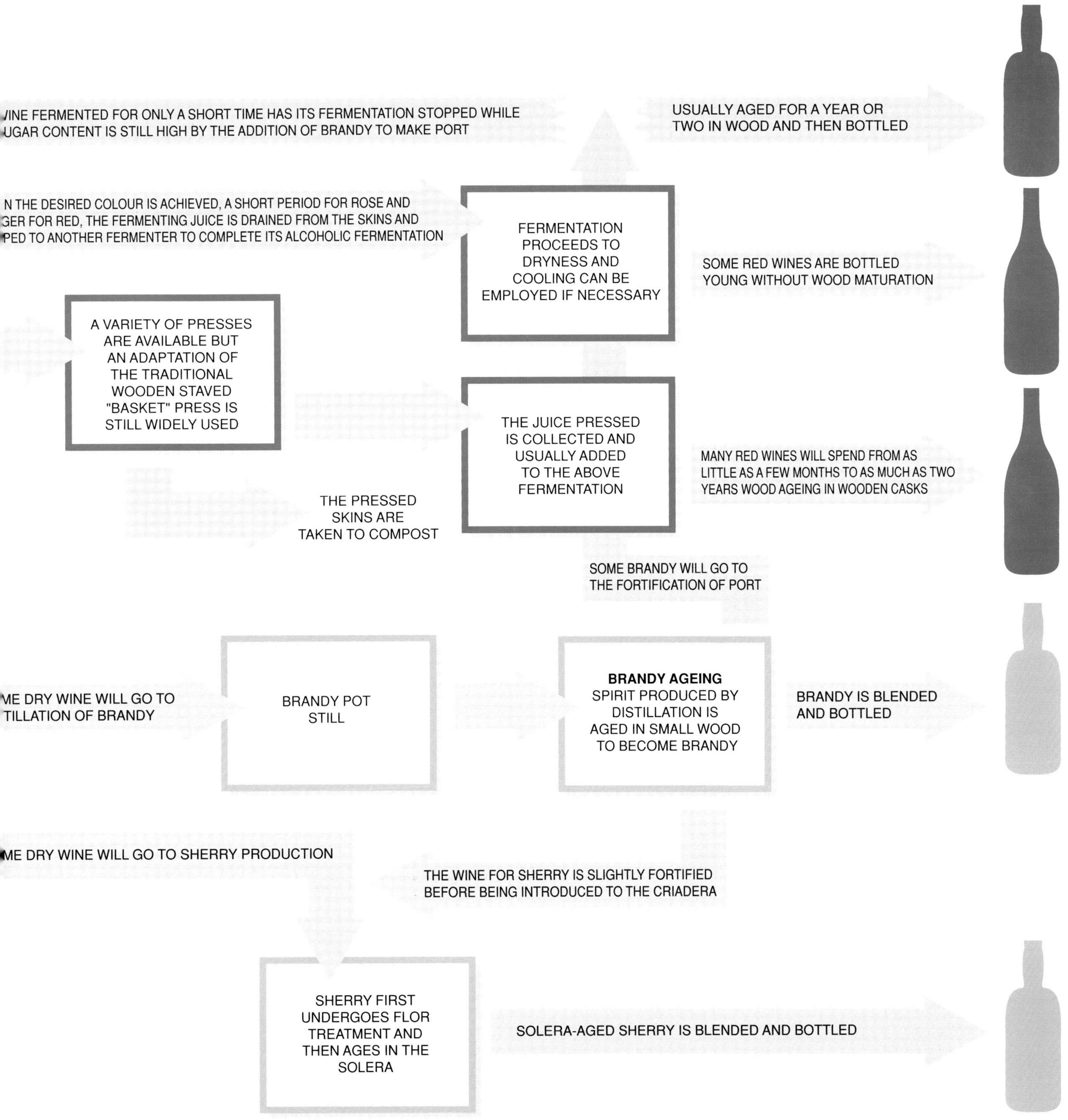

VINE FERMENTED FOR ONLY A SHORT TIME HAS ITS FERMENTATION STOPPED WHILE
UGAR CONTENT IS STILL HIGH BY THE ADDITION OF BRANDY TO MAKE PORT

USUALLY AGED FOR A YEAR OR
TWO IN WOOD AND THEN BOTTLED

N THE DESIRED COLOUR IS ACHIEVED, A SHORT PERIOD FOR ROSE AND
GER FOR RED, THE FERMENTING JUICE IS DRAINED FROM THE SKINS AND
PED TO ANOTHER FERMENTER TO COMPLETE ITS ALCOHOLIC FERMENTATION

FERMENTATION
PROCEEDS TO
DRYNESS AND
COOLING CAN BE
EMPLOYED IF NECESSARY

SOME RED WINES ARE BOTTLED
YOUNG WITHOUT WOOD MATURATION

A VARIETY OF PRESSES
ARE AVAILABLE BUT
AN ADAPTATION OF
THE TRADITIONAL
WOODEN STAVED
"BASKET" PRESS IS
STILL WIDELY USED

THE JUICE PRESSED
IS COLLECTED AND
USUALLY ADDED
TO THE ABOVE
FERMENTATION

MANY RED WINES WILL SPEND FROM AS
LITTLE AS A FEW MONTHS TO AS MUCH AS TWO
YEARS WOOD AGEING IN WOODEN CASKS

THE PRESSED
SKINS ARE
TAKEN TO COMPOST

SOME BRANDY WILL GO TO
THE FORTIFICATION OF PORT

ME DRY WINE WILL GO TO
TILLATION OF BRANDY

BRANDY POT
STILL

BRANDY AGEING
SPIRIT PRODUCED BY
DISTILLATION IS
AGED IN SMALL WOOD
TO BECOME BRANDY

BRANDY IS BLENDED
AND BOTTLED

ME DRY WINE WILL GO TO SHERRY PRODUCTION

THE WINE FOR SHERRY IS SLIGHTLY FORTIFIED
BEFORE BEING INTRODUCED TO THE CRIADERA

SHERRY FIRST
UNDERGOES FLOR
TREATMENT AND
THEN AGES IN THE
SOLERA

SOLERA-AGED SHERRY IS BLENDED AND BOTTLED

Harvesting commences in February, when the grapes are picked at the optimum ripeness.

tallization. The continuous process of tartrate stabilization is used on large volume lower-priced wines.

If the wine were to be aged for a year or more this crystallization would to some degree take place automatically; the reduced-temperature method makes it happen quickly and more reliably.

Quite a large volume of wine sold in South Africa is semi-sweet. To prevent micro-organisms from using this sugar in the bottle, giving rise to turbidity and off-odours, the wine must be microbiologically stabilized before and during bottling. This is usually done by one of two methods, and follows tartrate stabilization.

The most common method with lower-priced wines is to pasteurize the wine during bottling by raising it to a temperature of between 55 and 60 °C – this was the method Pasteur initiated in the 1860s during his investigations into the souring of French wines.

With quality wines the favoured method of microbiologically stabilizing the wines is that of cold-sterile bottling. Here all micro-organisms are physically removed from the wine by extremely fine filtration, and all apparatus which comes into contact with the wine after filtration, including bottles, is sterilized.

South Africa produces far more white wine than red. Depending on the period of fermentation, different styles of white wine are made; these are characterized as dry, medium-dry or off-dry (resulting from a complete or near-complete fermentation), semi-sweet or sweet.

In the case of many commercial semi-sweet and off-dry white wines the must is allowed to ferment dry and a sweeter grape juice is added to the wine in order to achieve the desired sweetness. (A table of sugar levels appears in the glossary, under 'Sugar level laws'.)

— ROSÉ, BLANC DE NOIR — AND BLUSH WINES

Rosé wines can be made by blending red and white grape must, but most winemakers make their rosé by leaving the red grape skins on the must during fermentation in the same way as for a red wine, but only until the desired amount of colour has been extracted to produce its clear, delicate, characteristic hue – usually no more than 24 hours, as opposed to the four days or more which give the red wines their full colour. The juice is then run off the skins and treated for the remainder of the process in the same way as white. The grape variety used in making rosé wines is optional; the result can be either dry, medium, off-dry or semi-sweet. A variation on the theme is Blanc de Noir, literally white from black, which is in fact an almost white wine made from red grapes. The method of its making differs from that of rosé wines, for the skins are not kept in contact with the juice for long. Instead the juice is drained away immediately, but in the process small quantities of pigment are released, which are sufficient to give the faintest blush of colour to the wine. The wine is then made as if it were white.

Blanc de Noir as a colour-term almost certainly derives from the Champagne area of France where wines made in this style have been blended with Chardonnay wine to pro-

duce the really great Champagnes. These wines lose their Blanc de Noir colour during ageing but some (where the proportion of the white wine made from red grapes is greater) retain their youthful colour described as '*Oeil de Perdrix*', 'Eye of the Partridge'.

Blanc de Noir wines made for marketing as such rather than for blending in Champagne were given real impetus in California a little more than 25 years ago. In this wine-making region of the United States there were excessive plantings of Pinot Noir and the cellarmasters were having very little success in their attempts to produce wines of good colour from these grapes. Rosé wine from Pinot Noir was a possible answer but was considered too risky because of the poor market image such wines had in California at the time. And so Blanc de Noir wines were made and enjoyed considerable success.

Although these wines took a long time to reach South Africa (they were first introduced by Boschendal Estate in Franschhoek), many are now available from local cellars. Some are very good and many are certified with the variety from which they have been made.

Because of the manner of its making, all Blanc de Noir wine in South Africa has to be certified by the Wine and Spirit Board. However the Board at one time would not certify any wine marketed in a container larger than 2 litres, and so Blanc de Noir was only available in bottles and 2-litre 'Bag-in-Box' packs or 2-litre jugs. To overcome this restriction the term 'blush' was and still is being applied to some wines made in the Blanc de Noir manner. These can then be packed in a container of any size allowed by Weights and Measures without reference to the Wine and Spirit Board. However, such wines cannot be guaranteed as having been made by the usual Blanc de Noir process, although most of them are. There is nothing to stop a marketer calling his rosé wine, for example, by the term 'blush'. In any event it is the wine that counts and not the terminology.

— SPARKLING WINES —

Sparkling wines as we know them today are a relatively new phenomenon, emerging in France in the late seventeenth century. Before that, certain wines were sold with a slight bubble in them. This effect was called *spritzig* in Germany, and *pétillance* and later *perlé* in France. They were due to the vagaries of the European climate: if the winter began early and the newly made wine had not completely fermented then it became dormant and still, since the low temperature inhibited further yeast activity. It was then bottled with its slight yeast content and sealed with a waxed hemp. When the weather warmed in the spring, the yeast became active once more. Since there was little sugar left in the wine, the activity was not vigorous but just enough to create bubbles, to the extent that when the stopper was removed and the wine was poured it was sparkling, *spritzig*, or *pétillant*.

Wines of this kind still exist today (the best-known examples are probably the slightly bubbly Vinho Verdes of Portugal, although these owe their bubbles to malic fermentation and not to alcoholic fermentation). The *perlé* wine of today is a natural development of this type. What would otherwise be a straightforward table wine is given a slight lift by adding bubbles to it. In South Africa, as in most other wine-making countries, if the pressure of the bubbles is less than two atmospheres it is not considered sparkling but *perlé* – if the pressure exceeds that amount the wine would be liable for champagne duty, which is normally at the luxury tax level.

Champagne is, of course, the most famous of all sparkling wines. Its development is generally accredited to the Benedictine monk, Dom Perignon, who was appointed chief cellarer at the Monastery of Hautvillers in 1668. Before his time all the wine of Champagne had been still, but he experimented for some 20 years to produce a sparkling wine. His early efforts were further developed by his successors until today's refined product was perfected.

The production of *le vin chantant* – the singing wine – of Champagne is the most intricate of all wine-making procedures and is known as *méthode champenoise*. The grapes are picked, weighed and then pressed in broad, shallow presses. The must is settled, and the clear juice is drawn off for fermentation with selected yeasts under optimum temperature-controlled conditions at 12 to 16 °C. The wine is fermented to complete dryness in modern tanks – very few French champagne-makers still employ the traditional small casks for fermentation.

At least three rackings take place to remove the sediment from the wine, after which the selection of the wines takes place: those to be kept for future years are put away in vats. The current wines are blended with older ones and it is this blend which is called the *cuvée*.

After fining and clarification, the clear wine has a measured amount of cane syrup added to it, together with a special yeast which will ferment under pressure. It is then bottled and closed with a temporary cap. Thereafter, the bottles are stacked to undergo their second fermentation – it is this fermentation which will introduce the bubbles into the wine.

The bottles are stored until they are ready to be released onto the market. For non-vintage champagne, the wine must be at least one year old before this takes place; for vintage champagne the minimum is three years, although most respectable houses exceed both these legal minima.

When the wine is required for sale, the bottles are removed from their stacks and placed in racks, neck down, for the process that is known as *remuage*, or riddling. The bottle is given a sharp, oscillating spin before being dropped back into the rack. Initially the bottle will be in a near horizontal position in the rack, and each time it is jolted and rotated the position of the rack alters, so that eventually the bottle rests in a vertical position, neck down.

This procedure causes the sediment to collect in the neck of the bottle against the crown cork which is used as a

Bottles in pupitres *in the* méthode champenoise *cellar at Twee Jongegezellen.*

temporary closure during champagne making. When *remuage* is complete, the bottles are placed neck down in a refrigerated bath so that a quantity of champagne in the neck of the bottle, enough to lock in the sediment, is frozen solid. The bottle is then turned upright and the closure removed, taking with it the frozen sediment and leaving behind sparkling clear wine.

The champagne then has a predetermined amount of sugar syrup added to it to bring it to the required degree of sweetness, and is closed with the familiar cork, dressed and packaged for sale.

Early South African sparkling wines were made in this method but it gave way to tank production during the 1930s. In the tank fermentation process the wine is fermented in sealed tanks to capture the carbon dioxide resulting from the reaction; it is then filtered and bottled under pressure directly from these tanks. This modernized procedure has great advantages in cost saving, and produces excellent wines, particularly if they are allowed to bottle age.

Some of the local sparkling wines are produced by tank carbonation. Here syrup is added to the wine as is the case with all methods of making sparkling wines, but in this process it is added for sweetness and not for the process of fermentation. The wine is then refrigerated and carbon dioxide is passed through it by means of a carbonator. These modern machines are extremely effective and give the wine an incredibly fine bubble. Then it is stored in pressurized tanks to allow the carbon dioxide to be thoroughly absorbed before being filtered and bottled under pressure. This results in an inexpensive product of good quality.

The local estate of Simonsig in the Stellenbosch district was the first to reintroduce the *méthode champenoise* in preference to the tank method, to make Simonsig Estate's 'Kaapse Vonkel' in 1971.

Many other winemakers have followed (there are now over 20 producers), including the estates of Boschendal, Villiera, Clos Cabrière, Backsberg, Twee Jongegezellen and major merchants such as SFW and The Bergkelder. The latter has been very successful in international competition with their J C Le Roux Pinot Noir Méthode Champenoise and J C Le Roux Chardonnay Méthode Champenoise.

— RED WINE —

The making of red wine begins, as does the process for making white wine, with the crushing of grapes. Thereafter, however, the two methods diverge. The juice of red grapes, like that of white, is almost colourless and in the making of red wine it is the pigment and other components in the skins which are leached out during fermentation to impart and influence colour, taste and flavour. Skin contact during fermentation is of paramount importance in the eventual composition of the wine.

Thus, after the grapes have been destemmed and crushed, the juice is not separated from the skins. Some winemakers might leave the juice and allow spontaneous fermentation to begin. However, the more common practice is to use a selected yeast culture. A 3 to 5 per cent actively fermenting pure yeast culture is added to the crushed grapes, and a controlled fermentation on the skins takes place for a specific period, usually about four days, depending on the cellarmaster's desired result; the longer the skin contact, the greater the extraction of colour and flavour held in the skin. During this time the skins and must are regularly mixed as the escaping carbon dioxide (CO_2) tends to lift the skins to the surface where they form a 'head' or 'cap' on the developing wine. In earlier times this was done by hand, the head being punched down and submerged with long wooden poles, a method that can still be seen at some wineries. This took place every three hours, or even more frequently, and was a precarious occupation, since the worker had to balance on the edge of the concrete tank; from time to time a worker fell and, like the Duke of Clarence, met a vinous end.

Later and less hazardous methods included pumping the juice from the bottom of the tank over the cap, but all these 'traditional' methods, though still practised in some cellars, were labour intensive and exposed the wine to the risk of excessive oxidation. With the advent of closed fermentation tanks, the problem of the skins rising remained, but at least the enclosed environment reduced the risk of oxidation.

Nowadays many successful systems have been developed to ensure skin contact and mixing without danger of oxidation. Some of the more commonly used and better devices are pressure tanks, roto tanks and stirring tanks. In the first, CO_2 released during fermentation is prevented from escaping and pressure builds up in the tank. When the gas is released the skins and liquid are thoroughly mixed in the resultant agitation. This system prevents oxidation and as no mechanical stirring or mixing takes place, relatively little sediment is produced. The roto tank principle employs a horizontal cylindrical tank mounted on a device that rotates the tank at regular intervals.

As with the previous method, thorough mixing takes place in the absence of oxygen; carbon dioxide is released through valves to prevent any dangerous, and therefore unwanted build-up of gas during fermentation. Mixing is achieved by long metal blades welded perpendicular to the inside surface, as in a concrete-mixer. In stirring tanks various mechanical methods are used, sometimes in conjunction with pumping over, but the system produces very high sediments.

During the course of the mixing the colour and flavour compounds are extracted from the skins, the process being facilitated by the high fermentation temperature of between 20 and 25 °C. Heat actually breaks down the colour cells, resulting in the effective release of their colour. However, the presence of excess heat would destroy the yeast. Cooling is therefore also essential to maintain the temperature during fermentation within the required parameters.

The period of fermentation on the skins is critically important; if too long, too many tannins (polymers of phenolic compounds which are responsible for the astringent taste in wine) are released along with colour and flavour compounds; too short, and the colour of the wine will be too light. In both cases the character of the final wine will be un-

WINE SHOWS

Each year the wines of the vintage are judged at a number of 'young wine' shows, organized by KWV on both a regional and a national basis. The regional shows are held in Stellenbosch, Paarl, Robertson, Worcester, Olifantsrivier and Klein-Karoo districts; from these the best of the wines go forward to compete in the South African Champion Wine Show, which, until 1991, was held at the Goodwood Show Ground. In 1991, the National Young Wine Show was combined with the newly instituted National Bottled Wine Show. With much fanfare from the media, the year's champion young wines are selected, and the champion winemaker awards made.

These shows judge the abilities of individual winemakers on the basis of their young wines of the season, which often bear little direct resemblance to the wines eventually marketed. The red wines will need a period of maturation, and the whites will usually be blended before bottling. In addition to the 'young wine' shows, Stellenbosch and Robertson hold bottled wine shows at which wines are judged as they will greet the consumer in the bottle-store, restaurant or hotel – a more meaningful event as far as buyers and the wine lover are concerned.

The National Bottled Wine Show, introduced in 1991, has been called the 'biggest wine show in Africa'. The judging takes place a few weeks before the show, which is held at the Johan Graue Hall at Nederburg. A total of 104 judges representing every aspect of the wine industry select the best wines from over 2 600 entries. Overseas judges are also represented, in 1991 by Paul Pontallier, the oenologist of Château Margaux. The first person to chair the show was Lourens Jonker. The top award at the show is termed the 'double gold' and given when at least five of the seven judges on the panel give the wine a score of 17 or more points out of a possible 20.

Besides the local shows, many South African wines are submitted to shows and exhibitions overseas. Important among these are the Monde Sélection, administered from Brussels but held in a different country each year, Vinexpo in Bordeaux and the 'International Wine and Spirit Competition' (I.W.S.C.), judged in Britain by panels drawn from all over the world. The wines at the I.W.S.C. are first screened on a chemical basis and only after passing this do they go forward for organoleptic analysis. The wines are then judged on a regional basis; for example, South African wines are judged as a group as are those from Germany, France, Spain and so on. Winners of gold medals in these regions then compete internationally for top honours in specific categories.

The top award at the I.W.S.C. is the Robert Mondavi trophy, awarded to the most successful winemaker of the year. This was won in 1986 by Günter Brözel, then of Nederburg. In 1991, Beyers Truter became the first South African-born winemaker to be given the award.

Award-winning wines from Simonsig at the National Bottled Wine Show.

balanced although today it is not altogether uncommon to ferment on the skins to total dryness and even then to leave the wine in contact with the skin for a number of days.

In addition to the methods of colour extraction already outlined, further methods make use of heat without fermentation. This procedure involves heating the must in hot-water/wine-exchange units and holding the temperature at a required level for a short time. However, rising temperature not only increases colour extraction but also promotes the activities of polyphenol oxidative enzymes which can cause the wine to brown. To prevent this the liquid is quickly heated to 55 °C, a temperature at which the enzymes become inactive. The temperature is then raised to between 60 and 75 °C for best results. Above 85 °C the wine develops a 'boiled' flavour as a result of partial caramelization of sugars, especially if held at that temperature for any length of time. This method is only used for less serious wines.

Irrespective of the method used, when the right degree of extraction has taken place the winemaker separates the juice from the skins, which are usually given a final light press; and the press-juice is added back to the must, which is allowed to continue fermenting until dry.

When fermentation is complete, the wine is racked a number of times in the same way as for white wine.

After racking and filtration, the young red wine is ready for ageing in wood. Not that all red wines are matured in wood; the light, fruity young red wines are often stored in stainless steel tanks until needed for blending and/or bottling purposes. Wines which have not been aged in wood are sometimes blended with wood-matured wines, in the combination desired by the winemaker.

The word 'wood' is the winemaker's vernacular for a wooden barrel or cask. Such barrels were originally used simply for transport or storage until it was realized that the period in the wood added something to the flavour and the character of the wine, which was also thus given a chance to 'mature', that is, to evolve its latent characteristics.

The barrel can be made from various types of wood, but oak is probably the most frequently used for better quality wines – most of the oak used for casks in South Africa being imported from France, though some now comes from Germany and, with increasing importance, from North America.

The most important physical aspect in maturation is the size of the container, for the surface-to-volume ratio affects the rate at which certain exchanges take place and the degree to which these influence the character of the wine. Containers can range in size from as little as five to as much as a hundred thousand litres, but the most commonly used size is a barrel of between 225 and 250 litres. This size appears to provide optimum conditions for maturation, and has been used empirically in many different areas in the past. In general, smaller barrels were developed for holding wines for topping up and for transport, while larger fixed vessels were made for storage and for use over many years.

The most obvious physical action involved in maturation is the absorption by the wood of some of the wine, and the leaching out of flavour from the wood by the wine. Besides this, five general factors influence the process of maturation: the relative humidity, temperature, air movements around the cask, the physical characteristics of the wood, and the frequency of the topping up.

The first three factors are self-evident, while flavour pick-up will be greatly affected by the type, porosity, and thickness of the wood from which the cask is made. Topping up of the wine at regular intervals is important, for as the level of the liquid drops in the cask so the wood becomes drier and slightly more porous owing to shrinkage of the wood tissue. This may not only lead to increased loss of wine (through evaporation) but also allow more air in.

As a result of the introduction of air in the cask, excessive oxidation, and therefore browning of the wine, may occur. The presence of oxygen also stimulates the growth of bacteria which produce acetic acid. This could increase the volatile acidity to levels which would spoil the wine. Frequent topping, done from an enclosed wine reservoir, is therefore necessary in order to avoid the presence of oxygen.

At the same time oxygen trapped in the cask on filling leads to certain chemical reactions. These include the extraction and development of tannic and related compounds from the wood. On the interior surface of the cask a layer develops with a high concentration of tannic compounds extracted from the wood by the wine. The minute amounts of oxygen present react with the phenols. These various compounds slowly diffuse and are replaced by fresh wine; as an inevitable result, the process is thus continuous.

On the inner surface, besides the tannins, there is present a certain amount of colour, of resinous substances, and of some bitter compounds which occur in wood and which will affect the eventual taste of the wine. These vary with the type of wood, and with the manner in which it has been treated. In particular, aromatic substances exist in the wood and contribute to the wines' bouquet.

In the presence of minute amounts of oxygen certain slow reactions also occur and are not necessarily influenced by the flavour of the wood; and aldehydes, carboxyl acids and acetyls are also formed. Most of these complex reactions will occur in a cask of any size, but more quickly in smaller ones as the surface-to-volume ratio decreases. But if the cask is too small the reaction becomes relatively quick, with a too heavy absorption of the flavour of the wood at the expense of that of the wine. At the opposite extreme, in very large containers the change is so slow that it is rarely feasible to leave the wine for the length of time required for these reactions to take place. Biochemical or biological reactions take place as well, of which the most important during maturation is that of malolactic fermentation.

There are no precise rules as to the length of time red wine should be allowed to mature in wood. This will depend upon various considerations, including the style of wine for which the winemaker is aiming. He must take into account the specific properties of the wine, its particular vintage characteristics, the variety from which it is derived, the biological and chemical make-up, and its eventual destiny. He must also take into account the nature of the wood, including its porosity, as well as the size of the container.

Equitable conditions of temperature and humidity are of great importance during maturation in the wood. A cool, slightly humid cellar with little temperature variation will allow for a long, slow maturation which can vary from two months to two years. However, wine is seldom aged in wood for a longer period than this.

Once the red wines have been matured to the winemaster's satisfaction they are blended (some blends comprise matured and unmatured wines) and tartrate stabilized before bottling. It is interesting to note that red wines seldom have problems with protein instability. Phenols and polyphenols have a negative electrical charge in wine, while proteins have a positive charge. With the excess of phenolic compounds in red wines, the proteins are consequently 'neutralized' and removed from the wine naturally.

Young red wines are filtered and stored in stainless steel tanks, where they are allowed to 'rest' for a period of three to eight months. The rest period is necessary to ensure that they will be sufficiently stable before bottling and to allow the desired complexity of flavour to develop.

After this rest period, the wine is sterile-filtered and cold sterile-bottled. Some of the lower-priced red wines, especially the few which are semi-sweet, might be pasteurized during bottling. As with the making of white wine, oxidation is to be avoided, because it results in a loss of colour as well as a change from red to brown, accompanied by a deterioration of aroma and taste.

Red wines are described as being either full- (or heavy-) bodied, medium-bodied or light-bodied. The degree of body depends largely upon the selection of the variety from which the wine is made, and the wine-making process used.

Besides the basic type of white and red natural wines, other forms of wine have been developed, including the rosé wines, sparkling wines (some made by the *méthode champenoise*), and fortified wines such as sherry and port.

CORKS AND OTHER CLOSURES

A seemingly innocuous issue, the much debated problem of the best way to seal a bottle of wine is one which causes perennial discussion in the wine industry. The traditional, and still most widely used closure for high-quality wines, of course, is that of cork. This is derived from the bark of the cork oak, *Quercus suber*, which is found in Portugal, Spain and North Africa.

In recent years, however, a number of other closures such as those made from metal, plastic, and various ingenious combinations of these, have been developed, because of the need for convenience of opening and in an attempt to improve on the time-hallowed traditional cork closure.

Cork has certain advantages which have stood it in good stead down the three centuries in which it has been in common use. Because of its air-filled cells containing fatty acid, each a watertight, flexible compartment, cork is an effective insulating medium against heat, cold and vibration, as well as being impervious to liquids.

In addition to these practical advantages, cork is a vegetable product, free of toxic ingredients, and does not impart odour, taste or cause deterioration of the wine unless it has been contaminated by bacteria or fungi of some kind.

But the substance of cork does have a number of disadvantages. A bottle which has been closed with a cork, once opened, is not easy to reseal effectively. Cork is also somewhat prone to shrinkage under certain conditions. Corked bottles must be 'laid down'; that is, stored lying flat so that the wine remains in constant contact with the cork. The purpose of this is to keep it wet thereby preventing it from drying out, tending to crumble and allowing air into the bottle and wine out of it. 'Laying down' is no problem in the private cellar, but is a disadvantage, for example, in supermarkets or in aeroplanes, or during transport, where there is a preference for bottles which can be stored upright.

A popular belief persists that a wine 'breathes' through its cork. In fact, if what is described as 'breathing' were to take place it would soon lead to the oxidation of the wine, and its degeneration and discoloration.

Notwithstanding the romantic prejudice in favour of the traditional cork (like wine itself, it is a 'natural' product), most of the newly developed metal and plastic screw tops, none of which are either 'natural' or particularly alluring aesthetically, are definitely considerably more efficient both in hermetically protecting the wine, and also because they can be used to reseal the bottle.

Man-made closures are also non-perishable, lend no flavour to the wine, and furthermore are not susceptible to either the drawbacks of distortion or shrinkage. They are also notably cheaper to produce. Thus, with the increased expense of cork, traditional though it may be, there appears little doubt that its use will dwindle, if not entirely die away, in the coming decades. Already over the past 30 to 40 years the use of cork has been steadily reduced, to the extent that, today, it is used as a closure in less than 12 per cent of all wine bottled in South Africa.

—BOXES AND OTHER PACKS—

The idea of the 'wine box' originated in the 1960s in Australia as a handy way of marketing large quantities of ordinary wine of no particular distinction. It was picked up and introduced in South Africa by the Simonsig Estate, but later withdrawn because of lack of support owing to serious quality problems in the manufacture of the boxes. These difficulties were resolved and in the early 1980s the box, as a container of ordinary wine, made a serious comeback.

'Chateau Cardboard' swept the country in the early eighties, with sales of almost nine million boxes annually (about half of these being marketed in the Transvaal), about 30 per cent of all wine made in South Africa. Today sales have settled down to some 10 per cent of the total wine sales.

The success of the wine box is not fortuitous. The quality of the wine has often not been of award-winning level but it is usually good, dependable 'drinking' rather than 'tasting' wine. It is easily stored and carried and, since the box is almost unbreakable, is particularly suited to outdoor occasions where a jug or bottle would be at risk. Moreover, the design of the box itself ingeniously preserves the wine against oxidation, allowing it to be kept safely for upwards of a month or more after being broached. Its principle is simple. A cardboard outer casing holds a laminated metallized polyester bag which is filled with wine. As the wine is dispensed through the non-drip tap at the bottom of the box, the hermetically sealed bag collapses without allowing air in, thus preventing the deterioration of its contents.

After Simonsig's attempt the first box to be marketed locally was 'Cellar Cask', introduced in the Transvaal in 1979. The present range of brand names includes Autumn Harvest, Drostdy-Hof, Valley Wines, Witzenberg, Kellerprinz, and Huguenot; the old national favourite, Tassenberg, has also appeared in a box. Nowadays many 'House-Brands' and 'No-Name' brands are available from many outlets at unbelievably low 'budget' prices. The popular brands no longer dominate the national market but the 'House' and 'No-Name' sector has become the most popular sector of the box market due to competitive prices.

A number of variations of the theme included the Kiesenbosch Keg, which contained a 5-litre wine bag connected to a permanent dispenser in the keg, the bag being replaced when

At Monis of Paarl flor sherry is made according to the traditional Spanish method of criadera and solera. A glass-fronted cask in the winery provides a fascinating glimpse of sherry in the making – the film of yeast is clearly visible on the surface of the developing wine.

necessary. Recently similar soft packs without outer cardboard have been used in an effort to minimize packaging costs. Today many hotels, public houses, clubs and fairgrounds are supplied with bags with a capacity of as much as 20 litres for dispensing through patent machines equipped with chilling apparatus.

Withal, the 'bag-in-a-box' is ideal for any generally jolly gathering, and has become and will remain a feature of the urban landscape.

In recent years a number of patent packs have appeared on the market with varying degrees of success. Cans (aluminium and tin), 'Tetra Pak', 'Combibloc', 'Hypa-pack', PVC and PET bottles are all available. Maybe the future will bring further innovations such as 'See thru' cans and cans that will chill themselves when opened.

—FORTIFIED WINES—

A further important category of wine is that of fortified wines – thse are wines that are strengthened by the addition of spirits to bring their alcohol content to a level higher than that produced naturally by fermentation. Until the 1950s, most wines were fortified. This had the advantage of increasing their longevity – the alcohol effectively acting as both a preservative and as a stabilizer. The development of natural wines in the last century, itself dependent upon increased technical controls, has reduced the proportion of fortified wines produced, the increased popularity of one being at the expense of the other.

Of the range of fortified wines, two retain their importance: sherry and port, both prominent in the South African winemaker's canon in that they represent an important element in the country's wine exports (although the word 'sherry' is Spanish property and can no longer be used by South Africa outside the Republic).

—SHERRY—

The different styles in which sherry can be made include dry (or *fino*), medium, and full sweet (or *oloroso*). Grapes with a high sugar content and a good total acidity are normally chosen. They are crushed in the usual way, and the juice is separated. Those musts which are to be matured into dry sherries, or *finos*, are inoculated with selected strains of yeast which will, under the right conditions, develop the special *flor* yeasts which are essential to the making of sherry. The wine is fermented dry, and after one or more rackings, is subjected to chemical analysis and testing. It should be sound, fairly delicate, and have a low tannin content (since tannin inhibits *flor* growth in *finos*).

On the basis of this initial examination it is passed for the further stages of production, and pumped into stainless steel or concrete tanks.

In these stainless steel or concrete tanks, it is fortified by the addition of pure wine spirit to a 14,5 per cent alcohol level, at which vinegar-forming bacteria are killed, but at which the *flor* yeast can still grow. The young wine is then pumped into large 500-litre vats in the *criadera* ('nursery'), which are filled leaving approximately 10 per cent ullage. The vats are subsequently loosely bunged. This ensures that air can reach the wine, since oxygen is essential for the existence of the *flor* yeast.

Under these conditions, a film of *flor* starts to develop within two to three weeks on the surface of the wine. It can be left at this stage for as long as two years; after which the best of the *criadera* wine is transferred to the *solera*. The *criadera* is not cleaned after the wine has been removed, but merely filled with the new vintage. The barrels may be washed after about four years, but they are never sterilized.

The *solera* is traditionally a three-tier or more stack of casks. When it is established the lowest one is filled from the year's production of sherry. When the annual sherry blend is required, a proportion, seldom more than a third, is carefully drawn from the bottom cask which is then topped from the top cask. The top cask is refilled from the *criadera*. On this basis it takes about seven years for a wine to pass from the *criadera* through the *solera*.

The wines leaving the bottom of the *solera* are blended according to the taste and characteristics desired. They are adjusted for sweetness by the addition of a small percentage of jerepigo matured in wood, and for colour with the addition of *shermos*, which is grape juice that has been concentrated and caramelized by boiling in open pans. Blended with *oloroso* wine, they are then fortified to 17 to 18 per cent by volume and matured in wood.

This final blending is carried out in blending vats. Should the alcohol level need adjusting, wine spirit is added to increase it, or well-aged sherry is then fined with gelatine and bentonite, racked, analyzed chemically, and cold stabilized for tartrates at -7 °C for 10 to 14 days. Before bottling a light filtration is carried out.

The making of the sweet *oloroso* sherries is similar to that of the *finos*, but with certain important differences. The must of the initial fermentation is inoculated with a strain of yeast different from the *flor*-producing yeast used for the *finos*. In this case the yeast used is one which does not develop *flor*. The selected *oloroso* wines are fortified with an addition of pure wine spirit to between 17,5 and 18 per cent by volume – this alcohol content further inhibits any growth of *flor*.

The young wines are then clarified by fining with gelatine and bentonite, racked and filtered. They are then adjusted for sulphur dioxide level, and transferred into 500-litre barrels which, unlike those used for the *fino* wines, are completely filled, leaving no room for ullage.

The sherries, once put into the 500-litre barrels, are allowed to mature for up to 10 years, during which time they are checked at least once a year. Also unlike the *finos* at a similar stage, they are not topped or racked during this time. In South Africa, *finos* are produced mainly in the Boberg region, and *olorosos* are made both there and in the Little Karoo. The main varieties used locally are Chenin Blanc, Palomino, Sémillon and Pedro.

—PORT WINE—

The second major form of fortified wine is port, which is usually made from selected red grapes, by means of an art demanding considerable time and expense and experience. Besides the apéritif-type white port, there are three main types of red port: Tawny, Ruby and Vintage Port. Tawny, as its name would suggest, is an amber-coloured wine, the colour arising from long wood ageing – a Tawny Port spends about 10 years in wooden barrels. Ruby is much brighter in colour, and fruitier on the palate. It is aged for about five years in wood before being bottled. Both types are ready for consumption when bottled.

The basic difference between sherry production and port is that sherry is fortified at the end of its fermentation and then sweetened with sweetish wine. Port obtains its sweetness from the actual grape sugar with the fermentation being stopped at the required level by the addition of pure grape alcohol in sufficient quantities to inhibit further yeast action.

Vintage port is the classic port of the type made in the Douro region of Portugal, selected from years of exceptional quality. Before the wine undergoes bottle maturation, it should be deep in colour and full-bodied. These properties are obtained, partly, by storing the young wine in wooden barrels called 'pipes' for two years. The young wine is then bottled, after which it should be aged further for up to

20 years or more. As most of the ageing takes place in the bottle, there may be a natural sedimentation, and it is therefore often necessary to decant a vintage port before drinking in order to clear the sediment.

The principal problem in the making of port is the extraction of sufficient colour from the skin during the restricted period of fermentation: the particular method depends upon the grape varieties used as well as upon the optimum temperature of fermentation.

Included in the Cape varieties used are Pontac, Shiraz, Mataro, Tinta Barocca, Souzão, Cinsaut and Grenache; it is also possible to use Chenin Blanc for the production of white port. Port should be a combination of several different varieties, some providing richness of colour, others aroma, fruit acid and sugar, resulting in complex blends.

Grapes for port wines should be harvested at full maturity to over-ripe. As with red wines, the skins tend to rise during fermentation and the 'cap' so formed must be constantly mixed by various methods with the liquid to obtain maximum contact for colour and flavour extraction. The winemaker allows the must to ferment to the point where, with the fortification – usually with good quality brandy – the fermentation will cease. Hereafter, the basic port undergoes further maturation and is blended.

—BRANDY—

While not strictly belonging to the family of wine, brandy is nevertheless a close relative. Moreover, particularly in South Africa, its production has considerable bearing upon the workings of the industry as a whole.

Brandy is a distillate of natural wine – its name is a corruption of the Dutch *brande-wijn*, or 'burned-wine'. In the process of distillation the wine is heated until the alcohol, which boils at a lower temperature than that of the other liquid components of the wine, is driven off in the form of a vapour, which is then led away to be cooled and condensed again as a liquid. This retains much of the flavour and aroma of the original wine, though it is now very much higher in alcohol content.

Traditionally, this process took place in simple but highly effective copper brandy-stills, or pot-stills. These copper pot-stills, modelled on those of the Cognac region of France, are used in South Africa by all the South African distilleries as a requirement of the law. All brandy must contain a minimum of 25 per cent of pot-still brandy, usually referred to as 'rebate' brandy, aged a minimum of three years in approved 'small wood'. A contemporary distillery includes equipment not only for the making of rebate brandy, but for the production of pure wine spirit. Separated off by fractional distillation in modern column stills, this is a purified form of wine alcohol which does not include the flavour components which are of prime importance in the making of brandy. This spirit is usually aged for a short time in wood and is

—BRANDY—

The new regulations in the Wine and Spirit Control Act now make provision for grape spirit, husk brandy, pot-still brandy, and vintage brandy.

Grape spirit is produced from wine in continuous stills at strengths of not less than 75 per cent and not higher than 92 per cent alcohol by volume. In its final form it must not be reduced with water to lower than 43 per cent alcohol by volume.

Husk brandy is made from fermented grape husks through steam distillation or after water has been added to release the alcohol at strengths not exceeding that of 86 per cent alcohol and then reduced to not lower than 43 per cent alcohol.

Pot-still brandy must contain at least 90 per cent alcohol by volume. This is calculated on the basis of absolute alcohol of a distillate made from wine in a pot-still at not higher than 75 per cent alcohol. It must then be matured for a minimum of three years in wooden casks of a capacity not exceeding 340 litres. At bottling it must have a strength of at least 38 per cent alcohol by volume.

Brandy must be at least 30 per cent alcohol calculated on the basis of absolute alcohol of matured pot-still brandy as described above. The other 70 per cent can be grape spirit as described above or other brandies of ages of more than the minimum three years of age. The final strength must not be less than a minimum of 43 per cent alcohol by volume.

Vintage brandy must be 90 per cent alcohol by volume calculated on the basis of absolute alcohol as brandy. The aged portion must be matured for at least an extra five years after its initial minimum of three years. This extra ageing can be in larger oak casks but must not exceed a capacity of 1 000 litres. The other portion must also have been matured for a minimum of eight years in oak. The ultimate product can be bottled at a strength of at least 38 per cent alcohol by volume.

then blended with the pot-still product to the formula of the particular brand.

Palomino, Chenin Blanc, Sémillon and Cinsaut are the grape varieties most commonly used for the making of wine for distilling in South Africa, though others include Ugni Blanc (Trebbiano) and Colombard, which are important varieties prescribed in the Charente region of France for the production of high-quality Cognac.

The chief aim in the making of distilling wine is to produce a clean wine, with a high acid content relative to the alcohol, and without any off-flavour. In South Africa therefore, after a light crushing of the grapes, the juice is immediately separated from the skins and fermented without the otherwise usual addition of sulphur dioxide.

The distillation begins as soon as the wines have been fermented dry (that is, they no longer contain fermentable sugar), the wine being stored for as short a time as possible. In South Africa's hot climate this is a necessity, since wines unprotected by the antiseptic action of sulphur dioxide would soon deteriorate.

The wine at this stage comprises some 10 to 12 per cent of alcohol, the balance being water. With the first distillation (or the first series of distillations) this concentration is increased to a strength of about 50° proof spirit, equal to 28 per cent alcohol by volume. Besides the alcohol and a reduced amount of water, this liquid contains volatile substances such as aldehydes and esters, carried over from the wine. The residue contains most of the water and the non-volatile constituents such as mineral salts, sugar, colouring matter and fruit acids. Not yet technically a brandy, this first distillate is called a 'low-wine'. It is then further distilled and the resultant distillate is put into wood for ageing. In the pot distillation the 'heads' or 'foreshot', are 'cut away', and only the succeeding product of the distillation, the 'heart' or 'cream' of the wine, is collected in a separate vessel. When the heart has been condensed, the last vapour, the 'tails', is also 'cut off'. It is the heart which is used for ageing.

The young brandy as collected in the brandy receiver is as clear as water, an aromatic liquid but still far from ready for consumption. Its strength is reduced to 60 per cent alcohol by the addition of distilled water, and it is transferred into imported Limousin oak casks of about 300 litres capacity where it is matured for not less than three full years. During this period the brandy extracts colour from the wood, becoming tea-coloured. The somewhat raw character of the liquid is slowly mellowed, its 'rough edges' rounded off, and a pleasant, slightly woody smell is derived from the cask.

At the end of three years, the brandy is blended, the blender sampling from each cask to decide how they may be combined, before being bottled.

Brandy, which was first distilled about 20 years after Van Riebeeck's arrival, has a strong separate tradition of its own in South Africa. *Dop*, *Witblits* ('White Lightning'), *Boerblits*, and 'Cape Smoke' (a corruption of *Kaapse Smaak*, literally 'Cape Taste') were some of the names by which local brandy was known. The precursor of the modern South African brandies required an iron constitution for its consumption.

Cape Smoke was made from the wet mash of husks, pips and stalks which remained after the fermented must of the grapes had been run off in the traditional process of winemaking. Probably similar to the French *Marc* or the Italian *Grappa*, it was not considered necessary to distil it more than once. In spite of its roughness it continued to have its devotees long after the more modern product had emerged.

Much of the improvement in the local brandy followed the arrival of the French brandy-maker, René Santhagens, who shipped his own copper stills from Cognac in the 1890s. After his death in 1937, Santhagens' name was perpetuated in those of his famous brandies; but perhaps his most enduring monument resides in the design of the South African pot-stills, all of which by law must operate on the principles of his original Cognac model.

Brandy has been a long-time favourite with South Africans, and accounts for about 50 per cent of all spirit sales. The quantity of wine flowing through South African distilleries amounts at present to some 250 million litres annually.

Recent legislation now allows for the production on farms of pot-still brandy and we can look forward to individual estate brandies in the future; both the estates of Clos Cabrière and Backsberg are now distilling small quantities of brandy. The law now also allows for fine-aged brandy to be sold at 38 per cent alcohol by volume rather than the regular strong strength of 43 per cent. This allows for a more natural and finer flavoured product. Reference to age and even vintage will be a feature of fine Cape brandy in the future.

—COOPERAGE—

Coopering, or the making of wooden casks, is an ancient craft. Records of early wine casks survive on the walls of Egyptian tombs from the third millennium BC. By the time of the classic period of Greece and Rome, however, wine tended to be carried in clay *amphorae*, rather than in the more perishable wooden containers. But by 100 AD casks had generally replaced clay in the Roman wine world.

By the time of the Roman withdrawal from Britain, the use of coopered vessels was general throughout Europe. But the cooper's trade as we know it today emerged clearly about the time of the Norman Conquest, when new words entered the winemaker's vocabulary, including the word barrel, from the French *baril*, and butt from the old French *bot*.

Eventually, three main types of cooperage were recognized: wet, dry and white. The wet cooper was the most skilled, and could carry out any type of cooperage; he made casks with a bulge to hold liquids. The dry cooper made a similar kind of container, but for holding dry materials. The 'white' cooper made straightsided, splayed vessels, such as milk pails. Within these broad categories were others; barrels for wine, spirit and beer required greater precision than those for oils and tar for example.

Since the First World War, traditional wood containers have been increasingly replaced by cheaper and more effective materials, from metal to plasticized hessian. Wooden beer casks, too, have yielded to ones of aluminium and stainless steel. The wine and spirit coopers, however, survive, the last representatives of their ancient *métier*.

The desired characteristics derive from a particular kind of oak. Wood for the earliest casks came from palms. Since

The cooperage of Tonnellerie Radoux.   *Barrels being shaped on an open fire.*   *A cooper fitting the staves in the barrel.*

—TONNELLERIE RADOUX—

Great confidence has been shown in the Cape wine industry by the family firm of Radoux whose president, Monsieur Christian Radoux, extended the family-owned cooperage, Tonnellerie Radoux, from France to Stellenbosch in 1991. The Radoux family have been master coopers in France for many generations. Today they are the second largest cooperage in France. In their Stellenbosch concern, the family has invested extensively in coopering equipment, as well as in intensive training programmes for local coopers.

The Radoux operation starts with a site selection of oaks in the forests of Nevers, Limousin, Fontainebleau, Vosges, Allier, Tronçais and central France. Much of the wood from these oak forests is used for furniture but 5 to 6 per cent of the annual forest quota is carefully selected for the production of barrels for wine and brandy. The trees are selected while still growing in the forest and then bid

for at annual auctions. The staves cut from the trees spend two to three years seasoning out of doors in tall stacks that are open to the effect of all the elements, allowing only natural changes to take place.

Ready-cut staves are imported by Radoux from their cooperage in France to the Cape to be made into barrels at their Stellenbosch cooperage. The toasting of the barrels and all other finishing treatment is done at the Stellenbosch cooperage under the eye of a fourth generation cooper, Norman Sowter.

Radoux hold the majority share in Tonnellerie Radoux which is situated alongside the Van Ryn Brandy Distillery at Vlottenburg near Stellenbosch. Minority shares are equally held by Stellenbosch Farmers' Winery and Distillers Corporation. The cooperage was opened with a production capacity of approximately 6 000 barrels a year, but this can easily be extended.

---

then many other types have been used, but wine coopering is basically concerned with oak casks. Of the 500 odd species of *Quercus*, the oaks, only a few find their way into the wine industry and the most famous of those used for wine are those from the French province once known as Limousin. Today the oak comes mainly from the Department of Haute-Vienne, near the city of Limoges.

Though oaks are a familiar feature of the Cape landscape, the local species does not produce timber with the qualities required for wine-maturation. Most of the oak used locally to make barrels is imported from Limousin and Nevers.

—BOTTLES—

As with the cask, the wine bottle was originally used simply for transport. By the end of the eighteenth century, however, the enhancing effect of storing wines in the bottle was ap-

preciated, encouraged by the discovery of the cork and its ally, the corkscrew. The traditional squat, flat-bottomed bottle came to be superseded by a design which could be easily stored for the period of time needed for the softening, maturing and 'rounding' of the wine's qualities to take place.

Modern wine bottles come in a number of shapes, sizes and colours. The following are some of the main styles encountered (though idiosyncratic variations, such as the Bellingham flask, enliven these basic categories).

Burgundy. A sloping-shouldered bottle of 750-millilitre capacity with a punt (the 'punt' is the indentation in the bottom of the bottle); this is the ubiquitous red and white wine bottle used around the world. It is usually green or amber in colour; the colour acts as a filter for ultra-violet rays in sunshine which can spoil the wine.

Hock. The name 'Hock', from Hochheim, was given by Queen Victoria to the white wines of the Rhine Valley in general. These 750 and 375 millilitre bottles hold both white

and rosé wines; the colour ranges from amber for sweet white wines to dark green for the dry white and flint, or natural glass, for the rosés.

Claret. This is the usual shouldered bottle with a punt, used for red wines of the kind normally laid down for bottle maturation; it is available in a capacity of 750 and 375 millilitres.

Sparkling wine. This is a sloping-shouldered bottle with a punt. 750 millilitres in capacity, it is thicker and more heavily built than the still wine bottles, to withstand an internal pressure of about 18 atmospheres. The pressure of Champagne and similar sparkling wines inside the bottle at room temperature is about six atmospheres.

Sherry and Port. These dark green bottles with a marked shoulder have a 30 millimetre extra deep drawn seal to replace the traditional cork; this closure allows the bottle to be stored upright, as against the traditional port bottle with a long cork which had to be stored on its side.

Jug. Usually containing 'house wines', the jug can be of 1,5- or 2-litre capacity.

Jar. This is a 4,5-litre container used for inexpensive natural and fortified wines of lesser quality.

375-millilitre bottle. or half-bottle is still sometimes used for natural wines and champagne.

250-millilitre bottle. This has a twist-off metal cap, and it is both easy to open and can be stored upright. It is particularly useful for the practice of tasting, since each bottle yields approximately eight 'tastes'. It is also known as a 'Wynette' or 'Dinky', but these are trade names registered by produciwng holesalers in the Cape Wine and Distillers Limited group of companies.

Besides these common containers various large sizes of bottle, for display or ostentation, are made, often for champagne. Compared to a standard 750-millilitre bottle they are:

Magnum	2 bottles.
Jereboam	4 bottles.
Rheboam	6 bottles.
Methuselah	8 bottles.
Salmanazar	12 bottles.
Balthazar	16 bottles.
Nebuchadnezzar	20 bottles.

The range of closures, casks and bottles, all forming an integral part of the wine-making process, is as wide as the variety of methods by which the different kinds of wine, white wine and red wine, dry and sweet, rosé, sparkling and perlé, sherry, port and brandy, are produced in the modern wineries and distilleries. These are the main classes of vine product, but the complete family of wines has a vastly wider spectrum and complexity, comprising within each of the main types many further subdivisions of type and character. And these finer distinctions are based on the qualities brought to the wine, both singly and in blended form, by the many different grape varieties, by the character, strengths and limitations of the individual varieties.

WINE - GRAPE VARIETIES

The wine-grape varieties are the building blocks of the wine-master's craft, the colours of his art. And like a true artist, he must know the strengths and limitations of his medium, what it can or cannot be made to do. Respect for the essential character of each variety must be rigorously observed through the procedures of wine-making.

For the wine lover, a knowledge of the varieties is central to the assessment and comparison of wines.

The most obvious and major division of the varieties is between those which go to make white wines and those for red wine-making. There are others which specifically favour the making of fortified wines such as sherry and port.

Within the main classes are further divisions between those varieties which are generally termed 'noble' or 'classic', that is, varieties which are 'shy' bearers and produce a relatively small yield of high-quality grapes, and those which are more suited for high-quantity production, giving large crops of high sugar content.

Other varieties, such as Chenin Blanc, are more versatile than 'shy' bearers. This is because they are adaptable to bulk or quality production under certain conditions of climate and soil, or of style of growing or of wine production.

The extent to which a particular variety is grown depends upon a number of factors. These include the traditions of the area – even when these traditions have not always matched the appropriate variety to the local conditions. They also include the pressures of public demand, as well as the changes in popular taste (not easily predictable). These developments are particularly evident in the increased plantings in recent decades of varieties suitable to quality natural wines, and the post-Second World War reduction of fortified wine varieties such as Souzão and Tinta Barocca.

LEFT: *Chenel, a relative newcomer to the range of white wine varieties, was developed between the 1950s and the early 1970s by Professor Chris Orffer of Stellenbosch University. A cross between Chenin Blanc (Steen) and Trebbiano, the variety has prospered under widely varying conditions in South Africa, producing grapes which are resistant to berry split, botrytis and sour rot.*

VARIETY TRENDS

More than 300 million vines are grown in South Africa, covering some 100 000 hectares. Of these approximately 92 per cent comprise wine grape varieties, with table grapes accounting for a further 5 per cent. The balance comprises rootstock and currant varieties.

In all about 80 wine-grape varieties are cultivated, but of these relatively few are grown to any meaningful extent. The accompanying graph shows a marked increase in plantings of classic varieties during the last five years.

Also interesting is that one white variety, Chenin Blanc, alone accounts for 31,9 per cent of the total surface area given to vines. More than any other variety it has grown in popularity over the past decades; and not surprisingly, for this prolific bearer will yield, depending on the skill of the cellar-master, virtually any wine of quality asked of it, from dry to sweet, from sparkling to fortified, to wines of superb botrytis character and even brandy.

Among the red wine varieties, Cinsaut remains the most widely grown and at some 7 per cent of the total number of vines is ahead of rival varieties such as Cabernet Sauvignon. However, Cinsaut has decreased considerably in popularity in the last decade.

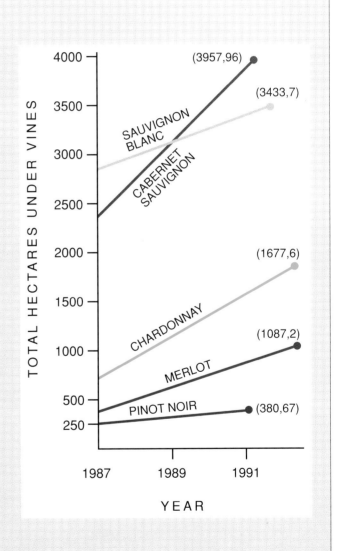

The dominant factors remain those of the land, the climate and the specific qualities of the individual varieties in terms of weight of crop, resistance to disease and extremes of heat and cold and, above all, of their qualities of fragrance, taste and character. Thus each variety has its own definite character, which the winemaker must recognize.

The following is a 'portrait gallery' of a selection of the most important varieties in the local vineyards.

WHITE GRAPE VARIETIES

—CHENIN BLANC— (STEEN)

This, the most planted grape variety in South Africa, probably originates from the Loire Valley of France – more specific-ally, the Anjou-Touraine area. Very popular there for more than five centuries, it has proved itself to be a reliable import in many other countries. Other than South Africa, California has the largest plantings of Chenin Blanc. It is also grown in Australia where it was called Albillo and Sherry (depending on the region where it was planted) until the mid-1970s when it was correctly identified by a French ampelographer. Chenin Blanc is also grown in Chile, the Argentine and New Zealand where it is the third most important variety grown.

In the Loire Valley area, some delightful wines are pro-duced from Chenin Blanc. The Saumer area is particularly known for its *méthode champenoise* sparkling wines. Some of the French Chenin Blancs with their racy acidity can age for a decade or more, a good example being Bourguiel. The late harvested grapes are used to produce sweeter wines, the best known being Moulin Touche and Quart de Chaune. Chenin Blanc wines away from the Loire vary in character from country to country, while certain other varieties, such as Cabernet Sauvignon, steadfastly retain their varietal iden-tity regardless of where the vines are planted.

Chenin Blanc (Steen).

Although Jan van Riebeeck did not record the names of the varieties that he imported to the Cape from France, sub-sequent records show that Chenin Blanc has been planted here for over three hundred years. Thus it may be assumed that Chenin Blanc could have been one of the varieties planted here in 1655. Local growers called it Steen and it was only in 1965, that thorough scientific tests proved that Steen was in fact Chenin Blanc. To add to the confusion of con-sumers, both names are allowed to be used. Most growers still speak of Steen, but it is a name that is gradually disap-pearing from wine labels.

Chenin Blanc is extremely versatile and has adapted well to the conditions in the wine-producing regions of South Af-rica. Generally speaking, the best wines come from dryland and goblet (bush) vines in the Swartland and Paarl districts.

Chenin Blanc is pruned and trellised according to the style of wine to be made. In some instances, lower yields are encouraged. There are still vineyards of bush vines to be found which produce grapes of special quality.

In South Africa Chenin Blanc grapes produce all styles of wine – sparkling wine, natural wines that are very dry, off-dry, semi-sweet and luscious late harvest styles. Special men-tion must be made of Chenin Blanc Noble Late Harvest wines which are made from grapes affected by noble rot (*Botrytis cinerea*) as these are among the finest to be found anywhere in the world and of course have great ageing potential.

In certain heavily irrigated and bulk-producing areas, large crops of up to 40 tonnes per hectare produce grapes with good acid for brandy production and for South African sherry-style fortified wines.

An extremely small proportion of late ripening Chenin Blanc grapes is also used in the production of white port. The advent of Lieberstein, a semi-sweet natural table wine, and its spectacular burst of popularity during the 1960s, resulted in the planting of Chenin Blanc vines in even greater numbers.

CHENIN BLANC

Bunch: Medium in size, conical, compact; winged bunches prominent; short tough peduncle.
Berries: Small, oval; thin skin with little bloom; yellowish-green; soft texture, very juicy.
Ripening: Early mid-season.
Cultivation: Moderate vigour, good yield and fertility; well adapted to various soil and climatic conditions and very resistant to wind; susceptible to oïdium, medium resistant to downy mildew and very resistant to anthracnose, also susceptible to botrytis and sour rot on rich soils.
Rootstocks: Good affinity to most rootstock varieties.
Total Plantings: 31,9%.
Wine: Approximately 40 dry Chenin Blanc wines are bottled and about 100 off-dry to semi-sweet. There is a great variance in quality and it is as well to be selective. Many of these labels bear the word Stein, which is the name for a semi-sweet style of German wine. In South Africa, Stein is usually a blended wine of predominantly Chenin Blanc.

Palomino (White French).

—PALOMINO— (WHITE FRENCH)

This variety is one of the oldest known to have been grown at the Cape. In the local vineyards it was traditionally known as White French or *Fransdruif*, but was identified by Professor Perold in 1926 with one of the famous sherry varieties of Spain, Palomino Fino. Palomino is also grown in Portugal, California and Australia with a small quantity grown in the area of the Midi in France.

On rich, irrigated lands very high yields are obtained and the resultant wines are mainly used for distillation. It was particularly successful in the Vredendal irrigation area where it was grown on its own roots prior to the phylloxera invasion (the Vredendal area remained free of phylloxera for some 60

PALOMINO

Bunch: Large, well-shouldered, long conical, loose; long, brittle peduncle that can snap easily.
Berries: Medium in size, perfectly round; thick, tough skin with medium bloom; yellow-white, and fairly brown when fully mature; firm texture; yield little free run-off must.
Ripening: Early mid-season.
Cultivation: Vigorous grower; well adapted to various soils and climates, performs especially well on higher pH soils under irrigation in warmer climates; trellising is best to ensure optimum yield; susceptible to anthracnose and downy mildew in areas of high rainfall, and very susceptible to bud mite disease and erinose, but reasonably resistant to oïdium.
Rootstocks: Good affinity to most rootstocks.
Total Plantings: 9,7%.
Wine: Wines from this variety are no longer bottled and are used for the production of sherry and brandy.

years after it had devastated most of the rest of the vineyards of the Cape). Those who can remember back to the 1950s considered the wines made from Vredendal Palomino grapes to have been a far better quality before the vines had to be grafted onto American rootstock.

A vineyard of Palomino grapes is easily identified by its particularly dark green leaves, which are deeply lobed showing a fairly white felted type covering, or tomentum below. Palomino is fully ripe at about 18 to 20 °Balling, rarely reaching a higher sugar content than this. The modest sugar content of the must and low fixed acid do not give the winemaker much scope. It needs good leaf development to allow for a slower ripening and a higher sugar content, as well as for protection from sunburn in the hotter areas. Care must be taken to ensure that the must does not oxidize.

— CLAIRETTE BLANCHE —

In the late 1940s and up to the mid-1950s Clairette Blanche gained popularity as a wine eminently suited to the production of sparkling wines and it still plays the rôle.

Used on its own as a natural wine it gives a delicate, fruity aroma which is very pronounced and distinctive when young. Unfortunately, this tends to disappear when the wine is about 12 to 18 months old.

The winemaker has to use all his skill with Clairette Blanche since the must and the young wine have a tendency to oxidize fairly rapidly. The use of stainless steel tanks and cold fermentation have helped to limit this traditional problem and enhance the making of fine, flowery, low-acid wines.

In France Clairette Blanche is considered to be somewhat susceptible to botrytis rot, but this has not been the case in South Africa where it has been grown in summer-rainfall areas with considerable success. Clairette Blanche matures

Clairette Blanche.

late in the season which helps the farmer to 'stretch the harvest time'; this is particularly important because of the great number of different grape varieties grown here.

In Australia it is also known as Blanquette and wines made from it are considered of reasonable quality. It is mainly planted in the Hunter Valley region. It is also grown in Sardinia, Algeria and Israel.

CLAIRETTE BLANCHE

Bunch: Medium in size, cylindro-conical; well-filled to loose; medium thick, long, brittle peduncle that breaks easily.
Berries: Medium to small, long oval; thin, tough skin with little bloom; light yellowish-green when mature; pulp firm and juicy with a neutral flavour.
Ripening: Late season.
Cultivation: Moderate vigour; performs well as a trellised vine; best in cool areas on deep, well-drained, fertile soils; loses leaves easily; tends to overproduce and has brittle shoots which are easily damaged in windy regions; very susceptible to downy mildew and bacterial blight, reasonably resistant to oïdium and anthracnose, good resistance to botrytis rot.
Rootstocks: Good affinity to most.
Total Plantings: 3,8%.
Wine: Presently only five wines are bottled under the varietal name.

— MUSCAT D'ALEXANDRIE — (HANEPOOT)

Thought to have been cultivated by the ancient Egyptians as well as by the Greeks and Romans, Muscat d'Alexandrie, known locally as Hanepoot, is believed to be one of the earliest cultivated plants. Since it was propagated asexually, that is, from cuttings rather than seeds, it is probably one of the oldest living plants on earth with an unchanged genetic make-up. The origin of its name is French and suggests that it may have originated in the region of the ancient North African port of Alexandria. It is also known in France as Muscat Romain, as Moscatel Gordo Blanco in Spain, and as Muscat Gordo Blanco or Muscat Gordo in Australia and in the fresh fruit industry as Moscatel.

Muscat d'Alexandrie requires considerable heat to bring it to full maturity and so tends to be found in the warmer wine regions of the world. An early immigrant to the Cape winelands, it is thought to be the variety to which Van Riebeeck referred as his *Spaanse Druyfen* – his 'Spanish grapes'. The vine found a natural habitat in the warmer inland regions, though in earlier years it also thrived in Constantia and was grown with success in many of the cooler coastal areas where it produced a slightly higher acid content than inland, yielding a natural wine of a slightly different style.

The name Hanepoot was attached to the vine at some time in the course of its local history. Professor Perold held that it was an intentional corruption of the Dutch word Hanekloot or cock's testicles which, according to those competent to make the comparison, bear a strong resemblance to the

Muscat d'Alexandrie (Hanepoot).

berries of the Muscat d'Alexandrie vine. The identification of the local plant with the ancient French Muscat d'Alexandrie was established in the 1920s. Professor Perold imported Muscat d'Alexandrie from Montpellier in the south of France and determined conclusively that the existing local variety and the imported strain were the same plant.

Muscat d'Alexandrie is not an easy vine to grow. Nevertheless it remains one of South Africa's most planted vines. It gives mellow, sweet wines of low acidity, but possesses an unmistakable 'muscat' flavour. By percentage, more Muscat d'Alexandrie is grown here than anywhere else in the world.

A considerable quantity of the production is sold as table grapes on the local market as they do not travel or last very well even if refrigerated – the berries being inclined to drop off the bunch. Its versatility is reflected in its use in raisin production, grape juice, grape concentrate, natural table wine and some liqueur wines.

In the Cape a number of mutations of the Muscat d'Alexandrie variety are known, of which three are grown on a modest commercial scale. Le Roux Hanepoot was named after the first farmer to grow it on its own. It has

---

MUSCAT D'ALEXANDRIE

Bunch: Medium to large, conical; well-branched and loose; peduncles long and thick.
Berries: Large, obovoid; skin thin but tough with conspicuous bloom; pulp firm, juicy and sweet with a pronounced muscat flavour.
Ripening: Late mid-season.
Cultivation: Prefers a deep soil with optimum water conservation capacity and a moderate climate, with warm conditions at the flowering stage; low trellising is best; susceptible to most diseases and pests and also to sunburn.
Rootstocks: Affinity weak with a variety of rootstocks, one of the best being Richter 99, but combines quite well with certain clones of Mgt. 101-14.
Total Plantings: 5,7%.
Wine: Only about six wines are presently bottled but Muscat d'Alexandrie is also used to form part of some blended wines.

---

smaller bunches than the original variety and looser berries which do not require thinning; it is generally grown more as a table grape than for wine. Red Muscat d'Alexandrie grows well in the cooler regions and was derived from the white as a bud variation which is now constant and which retains its distinctive characteristics. Of this red mutation some 230 000 vines are known to exist. There is also a longer-berried Muscat d'Alexandrie strain which dries rapidly and is therefore suitable for making raisins.

Its distinctive flavour and rich sweetness have led many a newcomer to the country to mistake the name of the grape for 'honeypot'. It also makes a delicious jam.

— WEISSER RIESLING — (RHINE RIESLING)

The Weisser Riesling vine is the most noble of the German varieties, producing a good deal of the classic Spätlesen, Auslese and Trockenbeerenauslese styles of wine for which Germany is famous. It also produces very good dry white wines.

Most authorities agree that this variety is indigenous to the Rhine Valley and was used by the Romans for wine-making when they occupied that area. It is thought to be a descendant of a wild vine found there, which was of the *Vitis vinifera* family. In Germany the existence of Weisser Riesling is recorded as far back as 1435. Because of its late-ripening characteristics, a problem in the cooler, northerly German vineyards, Weisser Riesling has been superseded over the last 50 years by Müller-Thurgau as the most widely cultivated vine in Germany. Although Müller-Thurgau is a cross of Riesling and Sylvaner it does not have the noble character of Riesling, being a producer of quantity rather than quality. Weisser Riesling remains the dominant variety in certain areas, though, such as the mid-Moselle, the Saar-Ruwer, Rheingau and Mittelrhein, and is still grown throughout the country.

Weisser (Rhine) Riesling.

Weisser Riesling is considered by many to be one of the world's great varieties. In spite of this, however, it is the only noble variety that is not planted in France, except in Alsace, which for historical reasons is more German than French in character. In France, for some reason known only to the French, Weisser Riesling is not allowed to be grown more than 50 kilometres from the German border. Outside Europe, it has travelled as far as Australia, California, Chile and South Africa, adapting well to the new and varied environments in which it is now grown.

While still retaining its identity, Weisser Riesling reflects the differences of climate and soil in which it is grown. In hot climates it is inclined to become a fatter wine and loses some of its elegance, but remains distinctive with a honeyed, spicy nose and hints of a certain flowery sweetness. It is described by French winemakers as *'le petit aromatique'* or 'the small, fragrant' grape.

In South Africa Weisser Riesling has only really become known in the last decade. Now that the vines are more mature, and the Cape winemakers have come to terms with the idiosyncrasies of the variety, some fine wines have been produced. Weisser Riesling produces a full-flavoured wine noted for its good acids; generally, it ages well and develops a distinctive nose. On the palate it gains complexity with age. Well adapted to various soils, Weisser Riesling prefers the cooler areas of the Cape winelands, although these are still considerably warmer than those of its German homeland. It is found mainly in the districts of Paarl and Stellenbosch.

WEISSER RIESLING

Bunch: Small, cylindrical tending to conical, shouldered compact; peduncle quite red, very short and tough, held tightly against cane.
Berries: Medium to small, round; skin medium thick, greenish-yellow; soft and very juicy with an aromatic fragrance.
Ripening: Early mid-season.
Cultivation: Extremely well adapted to various soils but prefers medium potential soils in cool climates; medium yield potential; not very susceptible to oïdium and downy mildew but prone to botrytis due to the compact bunches.
Rootstocks: Good affinity to most well-known rootstocks, particularly Richter 99.
Total Plantings: 0,14%.
Wine: Most attractive, aromatic, full flavoured with almost perfectly balanced fruit acids, Weisser Riesling ages well and then develops an oily terpene character very acceptable to those who know this variety. About 80 wines are commercially available and most are made off-dry.

— CAPE RIESLING — (SOUTH AFRICAN RIESLING)

Like so many varieties, Cape Riesling originated in the far south-west of France, where it is known as Cruchen Blanc. In South Africa it is also known as Paarl Riesling. For many years it was mistakenly thought to be the same variety as Weisser or Rhine Riesling because it looks so similar. Ex-

Cape (South African) Riesling.

tremely good wines with their own different and distinctive character are made from it.

A delicate variety, it is choosy about soil and climate: it only tolerates cool climates and soils having a medium yield potential. If planted in very rich and fertile soil, it is susceptible to botrytis and sour rot. Botrytis, while necessary in grapes intended for certain sweet dessert wines, is most undesirable in grapes intended for a dry table wine. The grapes and juice of Cape Riesling have to be carefully handled, as this variety is particularly prone to oxidation which causes a slight browning of the wine.

However, under ideal conditions, Cape Riesling can produce a wine of quality with a distinctive forthcoming bouquet which, when the wine is young, is quite fruity but never overpowering. It is at its best when steely dry. Not only are Cape Riesling wines delightful to drink when young, but with selected plant material, fruit of optimum ripeness, and expert wine-making, wines of special quality, which have good ageing potential, can be produced. Nederburg is one of the few producers to have aged some Rieslings in wood. The wood, subtly used, adds an interesting flavour dimension.

CAPE RIESLING

Bunch: Medium small, medium length, very compact; short thick peduncle.
Berries: Small, round or slightly oval; thin soft skin, green in colour, covered with a white bloom; firm texture, very juicy with a distinctive grassy taste.
Ripening: Mid-season.
Cultivation: Vigorous grower, medium yield potential; susceptible to sunburn, oïdium and downy mildew; tolerant of wind if vines are not allowed to grow too vigorously.
Rootstocks: Good affinity to most rootstocks including Mgt. 101-14 clones.
Total Plantings: 3,8%.
Wine: This wine has absolutely no resemblance to Weisser Riesling. Cape Riesling will always have a faithful following in South Africa where about 80 different wines are made from this variety.

Sémillon (Green Grape).

— SÉMILLON —
(GREEN GRAPE)

Most plantings of Sémillon are found in France and mainly in Bordeaux, and the Sauternes area of this region is thought to be Sémillon's original home. For the great white wines of Bordeaux, Sémillon is usually blended with Sauvignon Blanc with the latter variety predominating in the best wines. Its rôle is reversed with the wines of Sauterne where Sémillon predominates in the blend.

In the early days of wine-making at the Cape, Sémillon was the most popular variety for the production of wine – records reveal that in 1822, 93 per cent of the vineyards were planted to the *Wyndruif* or 'Wine Grape' as it was then known. Plantings dropped dramatically this century.

At the Cape, Sémillon traditionally produced a good wine of a distinctive character. Its earlier popularity was enhanced by the fact that it yielded a reasonable crop and was resistant to anthracnose. It has a reputation for yielding to a ripe old age and Sémillon vines of up to 80 years of age can still be found making a contribution to the crop. It is argued that this variety gives a better wine with a longer life when grown as a goblet vine than when trained on a trellis.

Until fairly recently the local name for this variety was Green Grape (*Groendruif*), derived from the colour of its foliage and not from that of its berries. In the early growing season, the leaves of the Sémillon vines are much lighter than most other vines. As the leaves mature they become more vivid, making the vineyards easily identifiable. Most green growth in South Africa is duller than that of European vineyards.

After France, Chile has the greatest plantings of Sémillon. It has also found a home in the Argentine and New Zealand,

and is fairly extensively planted in Australia. In California, on the other hand, its distribution is sparse. It is considered to be one of the varieties that is most sensitive to the environment it is moved to, and the resultant wines vary accordingly.

SÉMILLON

Bunch: Medium in size, conical, compact; short tough peduncle.
Berries: Medium in size, tending to short oval; thin soft skin with light bloom, greenish-yellow; flabby texture.
Ripening: Early mid-season.
Cultivation: Suited to medium to high potential, deep alluvial soils; medium to high yield potential; susceptible to wind during early growth; resistant to anthracnose and fairly resistant to oïdium and downy mildew.
Rootstocks: Good affinity with most rootstocks.
Total Plantings: 1,5%.
Wine: A few commercially available wines are bottled, the remainder disappearing into blends. There is no doubt that this variety is gaining popularity and being re-established in the Cape vineyards.

— COLOMBARD —

Originating in the Cognac area of France, Colombard adapted well to South African conditions where it has been cultivated for a considerable time. Colombard might have lost favour in France but the reverse has happened here. In South Africa it was primarily planted for brandy production until an error resulted in its sudden emergence as an extremely palatable table wine.

In 1954 Wouter de Wet, a farmer in the Robertson district, was mistakenly supplied with Colombard vines instead of the St Emilion he had ordered. Since he considered that they were equally suited to the making of rebate wine for brandy he proceeded to cultivate the variety, which he supplied to the Robertson Co-operative Winery.

The vines did very well in the local Breede River Valley conditions and other farmers began to follow suit. It was the manager and winemaker of the Robertson Co-operative, the late Pon van Zyl, who was the first to realize the potential of this new variety for the making of a natural wine.

Colombard's ability to produce a quality wine under the hot conditions of the inland areas was quickly appreciated. At first the authorities were wary of this new development, since recent data had showed Colombard wine to be very prone to oxidation. However, modern wine-making has dispelled this fear, and its public acceptance was signalled by a series of first prizes in the late 1970s for this hitherto unknown wine at the Cape Championship Young Wine Show.

Thus, while Colombard has not lost favour in South Africa as a brandy-producing grape, it has gained it as a natural wine producer.

When grown in the hotter regions it produces a high natural fruit acid content and a highly characteristic and fragrant aroma – variously and lyrically described by Pon van Zyl as 'rose-garden', or as resembling the scent of the koeke-

Colombard.

makranka flower – of a quality which few other varieties can achieve under these conditions. Grown in the cooler coastal regions it produces an unmistakably aromatic wine, but one which is somewhat softer than its inland sibling. The distinctive qualities of the wine are very prominent when young, but it remains an interesting wine when aged, and lends itself well to blending, adding a refreshing fruitiness to many wines.

COLOMBARD

Bunch: Medium conical, well-branched, medium loose; peduncle medium long.
Berries: Medium in size, short oval (elliptical); skin thin and tough, yellowish-green with a purple tinge when fully mature; pulp medium firm but juicy; neutral acid flavour.
Ripening: Late mid-season.
Cultivation: Vigorous grower, performs well on a variety of soils, especially on high potential soils in warmer climates; high yield; susceptible to wind damage early in the season; reasonably resistant to diseases, especially to botrytis rot.
Rootstocks: Performs best with Richter 99.
Total Plantings: 6,2%.
Wine: Approximately 21 dry and close to 50 off-dry to semi-sweet Colombards are bottled.

— GEWÜRZTRAMINER —

Gewürztraminer is grown in most wine-making countries to a greater or lesser extent. It is an important variety in the winelands of Alsace, where it makes up some 22 per cent of plantings. Elsewhere its distribution is limited, though its reputation stands relatively high. With its full, flowery, highly spiced taste, it is considered essentially a sipping wine, and

Gewürztraminer.

for general purposes tends to take second place to the rounder flavour of the Weisser Riesling.

The German word *Gewürz* means spicy. The Gewürztraminer vine is ampelographically identical to the Traminer variety. There are, however, selected clones which perform better than others, and these sought-after spicy clones are those normally referred to as Gewürztraminer.

Deriving from and adapted to a cold climate, the Gewürztraminer does not always do well when transported to a warmer one, and its success in the newer wine areas of the world has usually been in very localized cool conditions. In South Africa the percentage grown to date has barely made the statistics; the bulk is cultivated in the Stellenbosch region, with token quantities elsewhere, particularly in the Paarl area.

The problems of obtaining above-average growth are compounded by those of making the wine itself. Some winemakers maintain that the precise moment of picking is important, the grape only developing its fullest and most

GEWÜRZTRAMINER

Bunch: Medium to small, fairly short and compact; winged bunches often present.
Berries: Small round to short oval; tough skin; firm pulp; delicate, characteristically perfumy flavour.
Ripening: Early mid-season.
Cultivation: Moderate vigour; prefers deep, medium to high potential soils with abundant moisture and cool climate; susceptible to oïdium and, due to the compact bunches, to botrytis rot; bird damage is a problem.
Rootstocks: Good affinity for commercial rootstock varieties.
Total Plantings: Minimal.
Wine: About 30 wines are bottled, few of which are sweet.

characteristic spiciness in the last stages of maturity. The disadvantage of awaiting this crucial moment is that the acid tends to be lost, and wines of a very low acid content may result. Nevertheless, some outstanding Gewürztraminer wines have been made in the Cape.

— BUKETTRAUBE —

Developed from unknown parents in the winelands of Germany, this is a fairly recent addition to local vineyards, being first imported in 1967. Since the first wines from these grapes were made at Nietvoorbij, it has been adopted by a number of prominent winemakers and just over a million vines have been planted. This variety has adapted well and gives its best wines in the cooler coastal area.

BUKETTRAUBE

Bunch: Medium large, conical, well-shouldered, quite compact.
Berries: Medium large, round and firm; thin, tough skin, yellowish-green at maturity; juicy with a slightly Muscat flavour.
Ripening: Early mid-season.
Cultivation: A vigorous grower under irrigation; well adapted to various climatic conditions; does well on medium to high potential soils; susceptible to wind damage, oïdium, downy mildew and botrytis.
Rootstocks: Richter 99.
Total Plantings: Minimal.
Wine: About 25 producers make a wine from this variety and they are all off-dry, semi-sweet or sweet. It is also used as part of a blend.

Bukettraube.

Bukettraube (*bukett* is German for bouquet) makes a highly characteristic wine and one, as its name suggests, with a prominent bouquet. Besides making a very commendable and individual wine on its own, Bukettraube also works well in partnership, adding a most complementary bouquet to any wine that is not dry.

— SAUVIGNON BLANC —

Sauvignon Blanc has been grown in France for centuries and is found in the Loire and Bordeaux regions. In the Loire the Sauvignon Blanc wines are unblended, the best known being Pouilly-Fumé and Sancerre. In the Bordeaux region Sauvignon Blanc is usually blended with Sémillon and sometimes a little Muscadel. From the end of the 1960s to 1979, about half of the Sauvignon Blanc and Sémillon vines in the Gironde were uprooted because of the good prices being realized for red wines. In Sauternes, Sauvignon Blanc is a less important part of the blend of the lush wines of this region but is nevertheless necessary, as it increases the acid and adds interest to the aroma of the wine. Sauvignon Blanc is also planted in Italy and Eastern Europe and fairly extensively in California, Argentina, Australia and New Zealand where it is producing some particularly good wines.

Mistakenly, Sauvignon Blanc is considered to be a new variety in the Cape winelands, but it was extensively planted here in the eighteenth century. It lost favour earlier this century because it produced poor crops, the reason for this being

Sauvignon Blanc.

the propagation of inferior plant material. It is also very sensitive to dying arm or eutypa disease. In the last decade Sauvignon Blanc vines have been grown in ever-increasing quantities, mainly in the districts of Paarl and Stellenbosch. Some excellent wines are being produced.

SAUVIGNON BLANC

Bunch: Medium to small, conical, slightly shouldered to almost cylindrical, compact; short, tough peduncle.
Berries: Medium to small, oval; greenish-yellow with a thin, tender skin; very juicy with a markedly delicate, grassy flavour.
Ripening: Early mid-season.
Cultivation: Performs well on medium potential soils in cool climates; low yield potential; on very fertile soils the bunches are very compact and extremely susceptible to botrytis rot; moderately susceptible to oïdium and downy mildew.
Rootstocks: Good affinity to most commercial rootstocks.
Total Plantings: 3,6%.
Wine: About 100 unwooded and 40 wooded Sauvignon Blanc wines are bottled.

— CHARDONNAY —

Originating in north-east France, Chardonnay is one of the oldest and most popular of the classic varieties. Like Cabernet Sauvignon it has travelled happily to most wine-producing regions of the world, proving to be relatively easy to grow. Chardonnay has certainly been the most popular white variety for producing quality wines in the 1980s and demand continues to grow in the 1990s.

In France the legendary wines of Burgundy such as the best Meursalts, Chablis Grand Crûs and the great Montrachets, have been the benchmark for many winemakers throughout the world.

Chardonnay also holds the distinction of being the only white variety planted in the Champagne region permitted for the making of champagne. It is blended with the black grapes Pinot Noir and Pinot Meunier to produce the famous sparkling magic. In the best years some Champagne houses blend a particular Cuvée called 'Blanc de Blanc' which is made entirely from Chardonnay grapes.

Chardonnay is planted in other regions of France, such as in the Loire Valley and in Alsace, where it lends its acidity and noble character to certain blends. Outside France the first country to cultivate this variety was the United States. The majority of American plantings are in California, and it is often difficult to distinguish the best Chardonnay wines of California from the good wines of Burgundy. Today extremely good Chardonnays are also produced in Australia, with the variety being grown in countries as far afield as the Argentine, Chile, New Zealand and Italy.

In South Africa one of the first modern winemakers to plant Chardonnay was Sydney Back of Backsberg. With the addition of new producers each year, there is no doubt that this variety will go from strength to strength, as determined

Chardonnay.

winemakers persevere to produce a very special wine from this most noble of noble varieties.

If the plant material is free of harmful viruses, Chardonnay is an easy variety to grow. In South African conditions it is found to prefer medium to high potential soils and cooler areas. Chardonnay ripens in early mid-season and has a low yield potential. Most plantings are in the Stellenbosch and Paarl districts with some plantings in Constantia, Tulbagh, Worcester, Barrydale and the Overberg.

The meteoric rise of Chardonnay plantings in South Africa, is due to international trends in wine drinking and, more importantly, the availability of good propagation material.

CHARDONNAY

Bunch: Small cylindro-conical, compact when not subject to millerandage; short and thin peduncle.
Berries: Small, round; normally only one seed or seedless; light green to yellow with a thin, tough hyaline skin; pulp tender and juicy with a neutral flavour.
Ripening: Early mid-season.
Cultivation: Moderate vigour, low yield potential; prefers medium to high potential soils and cool climates; fairly susceptible to oïdium, downy mildew and bunch rot.
Rootstocks: Richter 99.
Total Plantings: 1,5%.
Wine: About 90 Chardonnays of varying styles and quality are being bottled. The majority would benefit from a few more years of bottle ageing after their release. The few unwooded Chardonnays are proving to be popular.

Chenel.

— CHENEL —

This is a South African-bred variety, specifically developed to respond to the local conditions of soil and climate. The creation of Professor Chris Orffer, it was developed from crosses first made in 1950.

This new variety, derived from a cross of Chenin Blanc and Trebbiano, was released in the early 1970s, after some two decades of patient testing and research. A representative panel decided on the name of the new variety. The final choice was derived from the name of Chenin Blanc and the first syllable of the teaching and research establishment of Elsenburg, where much of the development work was carried out.

CHENEL

Bunch: Medium in size, cylindrical, well-filled; winged bunches frequently present; peduncle medium long.
Berries: Short oval; thin tough skin, conspicuous bloom.
Ripening: Mid-season.
Cultivation: Vigorous grower; medium dense vine which is well adapted to various climatic conditions; high production potential; reasonably resistant to oïdium and downy mildew and practically immune to botrytis and sour rot.
Rootstocks: Weak affinity when grafted onto some clones of Mgt 101-114 rootstocks.
Total Plantings: Minimal.
Wine: Only two wines are sold commercially – Chenel is otherwise used successfully in blends.

Since its introduction, Chenel has proved very successful on a wide range of soils under intensive irrigation and trained on a high trellis. With such treatment it has prospered both in the Karoo region and in the coastal belt. Its vigorous growth and high production under intensive cultivation have been an unexpected bonus for this variety.

—KERNER—

This white grape is unusual in that it has as one of its parents the red grape Trollinger, the other being Weisser Riesling. The cross was produced at Weinsberg in Germany in the early 1960s and registered there in 1969 as a variety. It is planted in quantity in seven of the 11 German wine-producing regions, with the largest plantings being in the Rheinfalz. Unlike the Weisser Riesling, it has good frost resistance and bears about 10 per cent more than the noble Riesling.

Some authorities say that it was named after the poet and physician Justinus Kerner (1786 – 1862), who 'cured his patients by the use of wine', others that its name derives from

---

KERNER

Bunch: Very compact, medium large, prominent winged bunches; peduncle medium short and tough.
Berries: Medium large, round, green; medium thick skin; medium soft pulp; juicy without a pronounced flavour.
Ripening: Very early in the season.
Cultivation: Performs best on medium potential soils in the coastal area; good resistance to wind damage; susceptible to botrytis rot, moderately susceptible to oïdium, not very susceptible to downy mildew; medium yield of good-quality grapes, trellising preferred.
Rootstocks: Good affinity to most rootstocks and performs particularly well on Richter 00.
Total Plantings: 0,08%.
Wine: Kerner has a fairly distinctive fruity nose when young and ages well from two to five years, developing an interesting nutty character. Fewer than 10 wines are bottled under the varietal name.

Kerner.

the German *kernig*, meaning not only that the variety is strong and resistant, but also that the grape has a taste of the kernel, or pip. As a result of this latter quality, wine made from Kerner sometimes tastes as though it has spent some time in wood, thereby acquiring a distinctive savour of tannin. It ages well.

RED GRAPE
VARIETIES

—CABERNET SAUVIGNON—

By general consensus, Cabernet Sauvignon is the finest of the red wine varieties. It has a long and illustrious tradition in Europe – it has been speculatively identified with the Biturica mentioned by the Roman writer Pliny. In the Gironde region it is the oldest continuously grown variety.

It supplies much of the essence of the aroma and the flavour of the fine Médocs of Bordeaux, where it is one of the five varieties allowed for the production of red wine, the others being Cabernet Franc, Merlot, Petit Verdot and Malbec.

Cabernet Sauvignon produces a small crop in Bordeaux, compared to other areas. Larger crops are obtained from this variety beyond the borders of France, particularly in Australia, California, Chile and South Africa. The French do not consider this small crop a disadvantage, however, as their Appellation Contrôlée law limits the production per hectare of quality wines. The planting of Cabernet Sauvignon in France nearly doubled between 1968 and 1979 and now exceeds 22 000 hectares. Three-quarters of the vines are in Bordeaux and the balance mainly in the Loire (Anjou-Touraine) area, with some in the Midi and the Languedoc-Rousillon vineyards. Merlot, however, remains the most planted vine in the Bordeaux region.

The best French Cabernet Sauvignon wines come from the Bordeaux districts of the Médoc and Graves, where they are usually blended with Cabernet Franc and Merlot. Cabernet Sauvignon berries are almost black and can produce extremely rich dark wines, which when not blended, are inclined to be rather austere. They need long ageing. The addition of Merlot and Cabernet Franc not only softens the austerity and gives complexity but also makes the wines accessible sooner.

It is not known precisely when the variety was first introduced to the Cape, but it has been grown locally for a considerable time: by the 1920s it was regarded as one of the local varieties of quality. In the early days it was not uncommon to find Cabernet being blended with Cinsaut at the crusher, a method still practised at Rustenberg. When pressed on its own, however, a beautifully coloured red wine is obtained, with a very dominant, characteristic flavour of green walnuts.

Cabernet Sauvignon.

Because of its astringent nature and high fruit acid content, Cabernet Sauvignon needs a fairly long period of wood maturation and bottle ageing before the wine can produce its rich rewards.

CABERNET SAUVIGNON

Bunch: Small, conical to cylindrical, occasionally somewhat shouldered, generally loose; poor setting can occur.
Berries: Round and small; seeds are relatively large in relation to the berry size; skin thick and tough, black, thick bloom; pulp firm with characteristic grassy flavours.
Ripening: Mid- to late-season. Clones not infected by viruses might ripen earlier.
Cultivation: Vigorous grower but fertility can be below average; requires medium to high potential soils and limited nitrogen; fairly susceptible to oïdium and downy mildew, resistant to botrytis rot and wind.
Rootstocks: Good affinity with most commercial rootstocks.
Total Plantings: 2,6%.
Wine: As well as the 120-odd Cabernet Sauvignon wines made, there are now more than 50 traditional 'Bordeaux-style' blends of extremely good quality being produced with Merlot and Cabernet Franc used to blend. The only producer to use all five recognized Bordeaux varieties is Welgemeend Estate. Some traditional Cabernet Sauvignon wines have Shiraz, and less frequently Cinsaut, as part of the blend.

—CABERNET FRANC—

Originally known as Bouchet, records dating back to the late eighteenth century show that Cabernet Franc was considered eminently suitable for the Libournais area of France. It is thought that Cabernet Franc was originally planted in Pomerol, Fronsac and St Emilion and then moved to the Médoc. In the 1960s there was considerably more Cabernet Franc planted in France than Cabernet Sauvignon. It was only at the end of the 1970s that Cabernet Sauvignon plantings became more extensive than those of Cabernet Franc.

Though somewhat austere in character, wines made from Cabernet Franc are nevertheless softer than those made from its cousin Cabernet Sauvignon, which is generally considered the nobler variety. Wines containing a high proportion of both varieties are hard and rigorous when young and need ample time in which to develop their mature complexities of rich bouquet and flavour.

Both Cabernets blended together produce a harmonious wine, particularly if, as is usually the case in Bordeaux, Merlot is also used. Unlike Cabernet Sauvignon, Cabernet Franc

---

CABERNET FRANC

Bunch: Larger than Cabernet Sauvignon.
Berries: Round; thick, tough skins; black with a prominent bloom when fully mature.
Ripening: Late.
Cultivation: Like Cabernet Sauvignon it is vigorous, with somewhat better yield under similar conditions; requires medium to high potential soils, cool areas and fertile growth conditions.
Rootstocks: Good affinity for commercial rootstocks.
Total Plantings: 0,15%.
Wine: Only two wines are marketed, the balance being used in blends.

Cabernet Franc.

seems to be well suited to both hot and cooler regions, producing its most typical wines in the latter. It is also found in the Midi and the Anjou-Saumur region of the Loire Valley where much the same area is planted as in Bordeaux.

Cabernet Franc is a more prolific bearer than Cabernet Sauvignon, one of the reasons for its popularity in Italy and Chile. It is also extensively planted in Bulgaria, Hungary, Romania and Yugoslavia.

—PINOT NOIR—

Botanists recorded accurate descriptions of Pinot Noir as far back as the first century AD. Even the invading Romans wrote of the luxuriant wines that were produced from the grape and in the fifteenth century the reigning Duke of Burgundy ensured its supremacy by banning the Gamay variety from the northern Burgundy district, even though it was hardier and more prolific than Pinot Noir.

The finest wines made from Pinot Noir have been produced in France, in the Department of Burgundy known as the Côte d'Or (the slope of gold), a thin, 60-kilometre north-to-south strip of superb vineyards beginning just south of the city of Dijon and sloping down to the charming village of Chagny. This ideal southern slope provides everything that Pinot Noir needs, namely the required sunlight exposure, optimum climatic conditions and extremely well-drained soils for this temperamental variety.

Two-thirds of all champagne is made from Pinot Noir, which has a 'black' skin but a white pulp – the must is drained off immediately after pressing to ensure that it is not coloured. Its reputation for quality has led to its being planted in many other countries – northern Italy, Switzerland, Austria, Germany, Hungary, North and South America and South Africa, but in all these countries it has yet to demonstrate the greatness it has achieved in France. A sensitive and rather temperamental vine, which tends to prefer the cooler regions, Pinot Noir remains a considerable challenge to winemakers outside France.

PINOT NOIR

Bunch: Fairly small, fairly compact, mostly cylindrical; short thick peduncle.
Berries: Small and round; skin fairly thick and tough, dark violet blue to black when fully mature; pulp sweet and juicy.
Ripening: Early mid-season.
Cultivation: Moderate vigour, medium production; well adapted to medium high potential soils and cool areas; medium production; reasonably resistant to diseases, excluding downy mildew.
Rootstocks: Good affinity with commercial rootstocks.
Total Plantings: 0,37%.
Wine: Just over 30 wines are available and there are some pleasant wines among them. Except for a few notable exceptions, it remains elusive and most winemakers still need to come to terms with this variety.

Pinot Noir.

The exact date of the original introduction of Pinot Noir to South Africa is unknown, although by the late 1920s it was grown by an immigrant German painter-turned-winemaker, Georg Canitz at Ou Muratie, his estate in the Stellenbosch district. A noble variety, Pinot Noir is a medium- to low-volume producer.

After a rather shaky start the improvement in the local Pinor Noir wines has been encouraging considering that the oldest vines, using new improved plant material, are only now reaching full maturity of about 12 years. New vineyards are still being established.

—CINSAUT—

The Cinsaut variety (previously known in South Africa as Hermitage) originated in France, in the vineyards around the small town of Tain-l'Hermitage on the banks of the Rhône. The town takes its name from the sharply rising hill which towers over it and on which once stood a hermitage of great renown. For it was to this spot in the thirteenth century that a French knight named Gaspard de Sterinburg retired from a life of war and crusades to become a hermit, dividing his time between religious meditation and the cultivation of his vineyards on the slopes of the hill. His wine soon became famous and acquired the name of the hill on which it was grown.

Its renown lasted through to the nineteenth century. Along with most of the European vineyards, however, those of the Hermitage hill were destroyed by phylloxera. After the devastating epidemic they were replanted on resistant rootstock, but according to contemporary wine lovers something of the original quality of the wine had been lost, never to be completely recaptured.

Cinsaut.

First introduced here in the 1850s, it was generally known within the industry as Hermitage, though the name was more commonly rendered in the Cape as 'Hermitake'. The name Cinsaut, however, was virtually unknown outside wine-making circles, although Professor Perold had identified Cinsaut and Hermitage as being one and the same. In terms of the so-called 'Crayfish Agreement', made with France in 1935, the local winemakers agreed to refrain from using French place-names such as Hermitage on their labels, although Hermitage was used up to the introduction of the Wine of Origin legislation in 1973, when the name Cinsaut began to appear on many of the local labels.

Under South African conditions, Cinsaut is a heavy bearer and is also the most profitable of the local wines, both of which considerations – together with its high sugar content – made it popular with early growers. Unfortunately, when grown for bulk, Cinsaut makes a wine which is thin and light in colour, as well as somewhat lacking in character. Only when grown correctly does it give the palate-pleasing smooth wines of varying fullness of body.

On trellises in the irrigation areas Cinsaut produces insufficient colour and can be used for light wine which must be drunk early or distilled for brandy-making. In the cooler coastal regions, grown as a goblet vine with an average yield, it makes an interesting red wine. It is also used for the making of rosé wine.

Owing to its relatively poor colour, a percentage of the juice is often drained away at the time of crushing so that the skins are concentrated in a lesser amount of juice, resulting, with fermentation, in a deeper colour. When fermented for a longer time on the skins a very pleasant, fragrant and soft early drinking light red wine is produced. If the vine is pruned to give a much smaller crop and the fruit allowed to generate a higher sugar content, medium-full to very dark and full-bodied wines can be made; these stand well on their own, but can also be used for blending with other high-

quality red wines. Some ports have also been made entirely from Cinsaut.

Thus in general, though it can be grown for bulk production, the best Cinsaut wines are made from grapes grown on goblet vines on unirrigated hillsides and pruned to prevent excessive yields. Many a palate prefers the almost sweet character (although the wines are dry) of these well-made Cinsauts to the stronger-flavoured Cabernet; it also functions well as a supporter in Cabernet blends or in partnership with Shiraz.

CINSAUT

Bunch: Large, conical, shouldered, medium compact.
Berries: Large, oval; skin thick and tough, dark blue under fertile conditions, black under less fertile conditions, conspicuous bloom; pulp medium firm and juicy.
Ripening: Early mid-season.
Cultivation: Low to moderate vigour, high yield potential; over-production, over-fertilization and over-irrigation cause low quality; high humidity frequently causes berry cracking and rot; a mutation, Cinsaut Blanc (Albatross), bearing white grapes, originated locally and is cultivated on a small scale – corresponds viticulturally to the red variety.
Rootstocks: No affinity problems.
Total Plantings: 7,0%.
Wine: Almost 30 wines are bottled under the Cinsaut label. It is used in varying proportions in some of South Africa's very good blended wines.

— PINOTAGE —

This famous variety, the first grape developed in South Africa to prove a commercial success, originated from a cross made in 1925 by Professor Abraham Perold. In that year he bred crosses of two varieties, Pinot Noir and Cinsaut, or Hermitage (as it was then called), to produce a new variety which he named Pinotage, taking an element from the names of each of the newcomer's parents.

The choice of two such parents was based on consideration of their qualities, which Perold hoped to bring together in the new cross. The Cinsaut, a relatively well-established and trustworthy variety in the local vineyards, would bring its high productivity to the match, while the Pinot Noir, one of the great traditional noble vines of Burgundy, would contribute its complexity, richness of flavour and bouquet and colour – and this notwithstanding its none-too-steady performance in the local vineyards at the time. A newcomer in the country, it was prone to non-setting, or millerandage, and old clones of the variety were susceptible to leaf-roll virus.

Perold himself could hardly have anticipated the future success of his creation. The new vine proved to be an earlier-ripening variety than most other varieties, and so had much in its favour from the outset. Its ability to mature early in the vintage meant that it could be harvested before the other varieties, thus stretching the period of the vintage. It gave good colour, high sugar, and a reasonable if not outstanding acid content. Depending upon its pruning and trellising, it could

Pinotage.

also be a good yielder, a fact generally approved by early growers when volume seemed more important than quality. Today, however, it has been established that if stringently pruned, Pinotage will give a smaller crop, but one which, if allowed to mature fully on the vine, will yield a truly remarkable wine, with a unique and immediately recognizable personality of its own.

Being generally a light- to medium-bodied wine, a quality Pinotage is ready for drinking sooner than a quality Cabernet Sauvignon, for example. On the other hand, it can develop into a very interesting wine if aged in bottle. When young it sometimes possesses a very different nose which, while intriguing to some, is strange to others; it disappears with time, leaving a delightfully fruity and full-flavoured wine.

Although Pinotage was developed in South Africa, it has not remained confined entirely to the local vineyards. Cuttings have found their way to many experimental plots as widely spread as Zimbabwe, Germany, California and New Zealand – in recent years New Zealand Pinotage wines have found a small market in the United States.

PINOTAGE

Bunch: Medium sized, cylindrical, compact.
Berries: Small, oval; tough, thick skin, dark in colour; soft, juicy pulp.
Ripening: Early.
Cultivation: Moderate vigour, medium yield potential; best on low trellising; not particularly susceptible to any vine disease.
Rootstocks: No affinity problems.
Total Plantings: 2%.
Wine: Almost 100 wines are bottled under the varietal name and Pinotage is also used in many blends.

— SHIRAZ —

The origins of the Shiraz variety are obscure, though it is believed that they were in the ancient Persian town of that name. It was mentioned frequently by classical writers, who often conferred legendary qualities upon it, and it was encountered by Marco Polo on his travels to the Far East. He described how the vine was grown over the Persian houses, the buildings being used, in effect, as a kind of trellis. Following the prohibition by Mohammed on the making and drinking of alcohol, the cultivation of Shiraz for this purpose fell away. Thereafter, grapes were grown only on a small scale for consumption as fresh fruit; today viniculture in Iran concentrates on a large table-grape production.

From ancient Persia the vine set out on its travels, gathering on its way a rich harvest of synonyms, including Syrah, Schiras, Sirac, Syra, Sirah, Petite Sirah, Serenne, Serine, Biaune, Hignin Noir, and Marsanne Noir. Its establishment in France came early, when the Roman Emperor Probus made the planting of Syrah compulsory in the province of Gaul, though later legends gave the credit for its introduction to France to the returning Crusaders, or even laid it at the dusty door of the hermit of Hermitage himself.

Shiraz was brought to the Cape at an early stage, but it was never widely cultivated, although excellent dessert and red table wines could be made from it. It proved very susceptible to 'Shiraz disease', a disorder similar to corky bark which killed thousands of the vines. It was also prone to

Shiraz.

wind damage and therefore needed costly trellising and cane pruning.

It has never been a dominant variety but the development of selected, virus-tested clones of Shiraz has to a degree improved its status, an advance reflected in its use in blends with Cabernet and sometimes with Cinsaut. With the move towards varietal wines Shiraz has become a sought-after wine in its own right.

SHIRAZ

Bunch: Medium in size, cylindrical, usually loose with a long brittle peduncle that breaks easily.
Berries: Medium small, conspicuously oval, bloom heavy, thin skin, juicy pulp with light flavour.
Ripening: Mid-season.
Cultivation: Vigorous grower, performs well on medium high potential soils, adapts well to various climatic conditions; susceptible to wind damage and reasonably resistant to disease.
Rootstocks: Weak affinity for some Mgt. 100-14 and Metallica clones.
Total Plantings: 0,9%.
Wine: About 50 Shiraz wines are currently bottled with some excellent wines among them. Some of the wines have extremely good ageing potential. Shiraz is also popular in blends, often adding an interesting dimension to a Cabernet Sauvignon wine.

— PONTAC —

Many early references in the literature of Cape wine speak of Pontac as a vine peculiar to South Africa, but this claim has since proved to be false. According to Professor Perold, Pontac originated in Bohemia. Nevertheless the variety retains the distinction of being one of the first to have been found on local shores, if not during Van Riebeeck's time, then certainly by the time of the Van der Stels.

As early as 1772 the ship *De Hoop*, after depositing a corps of militia at the Cape, returned to the Netherlands with a cargo which included an oddly named Red Steen and a leaguer of Pontac (which fetched a substantial 166 guilders as compared with a low
88 guilders for the same amount of Cape brandy).

Since the making of this Pontac coincided with the advent of the Huguenot immigration during Simon van der Stel's governorship, it has been speculated that they may have brought cuttings of the vine with them, perhaps naming it after the famous Pontac family, who were important vineyard owners in the Médoc.

In the local vineyards this variety came to be valued as a producer of high-quality grapes and in the days of Constantia's hegemony it formed an important component of the estate's famous wines. The Cloete family sold a rich red dessert wine under the name of Pontac, which by the mid-nineteenth century was regularly considered the best of the Cape wines — according to one local newspaper of the day, the *South African Commercial Advertiser*, it was '... almost, if not altogether, equal to European wine'.

Pontac.

Its prestige lasted into the present century. Many old-timers nostalgically remember the Pontacs of 50 years ago; and it was also considered indispensable in giving body and superb colour to Karoo port. Remembered too are the magnificent matured dessert wines in which the variety of Pontac was the principal element and which left the legacy of a long, lingering and memorable aftertaste.

Pontac has now all but disappeared from the Cape's vineyards. A shy and light bearer, its vines have tended in recent decades to develop problems, particularly in the more humid areas such as Constantia and Stellenbosch. A virulent form of the vinegar fly found its way into the pedicel end of the tightly packed bunches, souring the grapes and making them unsuitable for red wines of high quality. Because of the wine's high volatile acidity it was also unsuitable for rebate brandy distillation, and thus tended to end up as distilling wine, a poor fate for a noble grape.

In an attempt to save one of the Cape's oldest and now most neglected varieties, Professor J. Theron stressed the need

---

PONTAC

Bunch: Cylindrical though somewhat conical and small; fairly compact; short, thick peduncle.
Berries: Round, medium in size; skin thick, tough and black.
Ripening: Towards late season.
Cultivation: Moderate to low vigour, performs best on relatively fertile soils in warmer areas; low yield because of small bunches; susceptible to oïdium and botrytis rot but reasonably resistant to other diseases.
Rootstocks: Weak affinity to Mgt.101-14.
Total Plantings: Minimal.
Wine: No wines are bottled using the varietal name but Pontac is used in port.

for strict selection. During the past two decades this has resulted in clones superior to those featured in the old commercial vineyards. Professor C.J. Orffer also produced an interesting new cross of Pontac and Cabernet which has scored well with the experimental wines made from it. Thus even if the Pontac variety itself does not survive into the future, perhaps some of its character may be preserved through its descendants.

—MERLOT NOIR—

Merlot Noir is generally known as Merlot. In fact, a distinctly different variety known as Merlot Blanc exists.

Merlot Noir is one of the very old varieties in Europe. It was recorded that Merlot was planted in the Pomerol and St Emilion areas in the eighteenth century. However, it only seems to have reached the Médoc last century. Today Merlot Noir is of significant importance in the Bordeaux and Languedoc regions of France.

The popularity of the variety is due to the fact that it adapts well to a great variety of microclimates and soils, and if not over-cropped produces excellent wines of a distinct character which mature quickly. Its thick, blue-black skin results in a wine of a good, deep colour. The greatest wine produced from Merlot is a Château Petrus from Pomerol in Bordeaux, and it is no coincidence that it is the most sought-after red wine produced in the world. Merlot Noir is also one of the few Bordeaux grapes that is pleasant to eat - as is evidenced by the local grape pickers in the heat of the vintage time.

Merlot is more productive than Cabernet Sauvignon and, as the resultant wine is rich in fruit and without the astringent tannins of a Cabernet Sauvignon, it is accessible much sooner. This is a very good reason for it being one of the five grape varieties allowed to be used in a classic Bordeaux blend. In Pomerol and St Emilion it usually dominates the blend with Cabernet Franc being less than 40 per cent. The

Merlot Noir.

opposite applies in the Médoc and Graves where Cabernet Sauvignon usually makes up most of the blend.

Planting Merlot in Europe, where rain and cooler weather can start inconveniently early, has its advantages and disadvantages, an advantage being that it ripens before Cabernet Sauvignon and a disadvantage being that because of its early budding and flowering, there is a danger of damage from spring frosts. The dropping of flowers and berries during the initial period of development (the first seven to ten days), known as 'coulure' or shelling, can also be a problem.

Merlot was introduced to the Cape by Professor A.I. Perold in about 1910. It is only since the early 1980s, however, that it has been re-introduced and become of importance.

Merlot is also planted in Hungary, Bulgaria, Romania, and Italy, where it is extremely popular. It is also found in the U.S.A. with most plantings being in Washington State rather than in California. Small plantings are also found in Australia and New Zealand.

MERLOT NOIR

Bunch: Cylindrical; medium in size to fairly large; well-filled to loose; peduncle medium long and thick.

Berries: Medium in size; round; skin very thin; black in colour at full maturity.

Ripening: Mid-season.

Cultivation: Performs well in cooler climates on medium potential soils; in hot areas the acidity will often be too low and on very fertile soil matured grapes are susceptible to bunch rot; medium production; susceptible to downy mildew; inclined to poor berry set.

Rootstocks: Good affinity with most commercial rootstock varieties.

Total Plantings: 0,93%.

Wine: At its best, the wine is luscious and rich in fruit with wood maturation giving it added complexity. Just over 20 Merlot varietal wines are bottled, a few of which are excellent.

Malbec.

—MALBEC—

Malbec, one of the old traditional varieties, is one of the lesser grapes of Bordeaux, but one which contributes good colour and bouquet. It is normally included in a blend only in small quantities. It has settled in many of the world's winelands, particularly in Argentina, where it has become the most extensively grown variety and is the backbone of their considerable wine production.

The variety ripens in the late mid-season and prefers medium to high potential soils in the coastal area. Malbec has a good resistance to most vine diseases, except for downy mildew. The eventual wine should be enjoyed young.

It is not yet available in the Cape in any appreciable quantity, but as more vines come into production it is being blended with Cabernet Sauvignon to complement that variety with its colour, bouquet and taste. It also makes a pleasant wine in its own right.

In the local vineyards the largest concentration of the few thousand existing Malbec vines are found around Stellenbosch and particularly in the Paarl district.

—GAMAY NOIR—

A number of Europe's classic varieties which are grown in South Africa have not excelled as they have in their homelands or in other wine-making countries. Among these reluctant travellers is Gamay Noir.

It is a native of Burgundy where, traditionally, Pinot Noir is grown on the hillsides for quality and Gamay Noir on the lower slopes for quantity; but where it is grown on the hill slopes, as in the Beaujolais region, it responds with a better

---

MALBEC

Bunch: Mostly conical, medium large and fairly loose to well-filled; peduncle fairly long, thick and rose coloured; poor setting does occur.

Berries: Medium large and round; thin skin; black with a heavy bloom.

Ripening: Late mid-season.

Cultivation: Preferably on medium to high potential soils in coastal area; except for downy mildew, good resistance to vine diseases.

Rootstocks: No affinity problems.

Total Plantings: Minimal.

Wine: Only one wine is bottled under the varietal label. Wines made from this variety have a good colour and are usually meant to be enjoyed young.

Gamay Noir.

quality wine. Gamay Noir ripens in the early mid-season and prefers medium fertility soils in cool areas. The wines resulting from this variety are usually fruity and made for drinking young.

In the Cape, Gamay Noir experienced mixed fortunes, having been planted by numerous growers from the 1920s onwards, only to be removed to make way for the heavier bearing and more consistent Cinsaut. Only some plantings of Gamay Noir have survived.

However, when Günter Brözel, then of Nederburg, launched a nouveau-style Gamay Noir at the 1985 Nederburg Auction lunch, only 55 days after it was harvested, he revived the interest in this variety. The following year there was a scramble for fruit from existing vines and a sprinkling of Gamay Noir labels appeared on the market. Gamay Noir continues to be planted in districts such as Constantia, Durbanville, Stellenbosch and Paarl, in order to meet the increasing demand for nouveau-style wines in general, and wines from this variety in particular.

GAMAY NOIR

Bunch: Medium in size, compact; cylindrical; occasionally somewhat branched.
Berries: Medium in size, slightly oval; thin, tough skin, black, bloom-covered; juicy.
Ripening: Early mid-season.
Cultivation: Strong growth, average production; preferably medium fertility soils and cool areas; susceptible to oïdium, leaf roll and stem grooving.
Rootstocks: No problems with compatibility if virus-tested clones of the commercially grown rootstock varieties are used.
Total Plantings: 0,04%.
Wine: Only two wines are currently bottled under the varietal name, both wines being fruity and traditionally made for drinking young.

LESS FAMILIAR VARIETIES

Old varieties, which have been long established in Europe and various other vine-growing areas, are being tried out in the Cape vineyards. At the same time new and experimental varieties, both from home and abroad, are systematically tested. However, only a few of these are likely to become commercially viable.

The entire procedure regarding the importation of new vines from various other parts of the world to revitalize South African vineyards underwent meticulous scrutiny by the Commission of Inquiry.

This inquiry was headed by Mr Chris Kloppers, retired president of the Northern Transvaal Regional Court, assisted by Professor Chris Orffer, retired from Stellenbosch University. The past lengthy procedure of quarantine and eventual propagation and distribution of the approved material through the various official bodies has been streamlined and the system has become more efficient, bringing dramatic developments in the Cape vineyards.

The Klopper Commission of Inquiry was originally set up to investigate the alleged illegal importation of the varieties Chardonnay, Olasz Riesling, Pinot Gris and Auxerrois, and the varietal purity of the illegal material.

Many hectares of established Auxerrois vines, originally thought to be Chardonnay vines, unfortunately had to be uprooted or regrafted. Auxerrois is now a registered variety for the production of table wine.

Locally developed varieties produced by Professor Orffer such as Weldra, Therona, Grachen and Roobernet, are being planted in various areas to test their acceptability. Some of the more recently introduced varieties from Europe have proved their worth and have become acceptable to, and enjoyed by, the South African wine drinker, but some are still not all that readily available.

These recently introduced varieties include Nemes Furmint, a new clone of Furmint, a well-known Hungarian variety used to make Tokay wines; and also from Hungary, Hárslevelü, which has proved a reliable all-rounder locally and is now commercially planted in both the coastal and inland regions. From Portugal, Fernão Pires has made its mark as a variety of interest.

Minority red varieties include those such as Alicante Bouschet, Carignan, a much-grown vine in the south of France, where it contributes a high percentage of the so-called *vin ordinaire* of the region, and Zinfandel, a leading Californian variety which gives a good, medium-coloured red wine when handled carefully.

A recent cross from the wine-making areas of Germany, a variety called Heroldrebe is still experimental and to date it has yielded a wine of only average quality. Small numbers of other varieties such as Emerald Riesling are to be found scattered across the vineyards of the Cape.

Pinot Blanc.

— PINOT BLANC —

A white wine variety described by more than 20 synonyms, Pinot Blanc has an unsure ancestry. It has however been established that Pinot Blanc is a Pinot, and that it is a mutant of Pinot Gris. For a long time the variety was thought to be closely related to Chardonnay. This is incorrect. Pinot Blanc is more prolific and its wines less distinctive and complex than Chardonnay.

France and Italy have substantial plantings of Pinot Blanc. In Alsace where it is planted mainly in the flat, lower-lying vineyards, and called Gros Pinot Blanc, plantings have increased. It is used in blends with a more acidic wine such as Sylvaner. A few varietal wines are produced.

In Germany Pinot Blanc is called Weisser Burgunder. In Italy, where it has been cultivated for almost two hundred years, it is known as Pinot Grigio. In California, plantings are also increasing, and it is becoming a popular variety for making sparkling wine.

— PINOT GRIS —

This well-travelled mutation of Pinot Noir is found in many European countries with the greatest plantings in Germany where it is normally called Ruländer. A white wine variety, it is also planted fairly extensively in Italy as well as in Hungary, Switzerland and Alsace in France. Pinot Gris seems to adapt well to the conditions in the country where it is planted. To a much lesser extent it is also grown in Yugoslavia, Germany and New Zealand. The grapes and wines vary as much in character as the inhabitants of the different countries. The colour of the grapes can be anything from white to a pinky brown or black. Some of the most complex and inter-

Pinot Gris.

esting wines made from this variety come from Alsace and Germany, and in the best years are not unlike a white Burgundy. If it should be a particularly hot year, the wines could lack acid and be a bit flabby.

Pinot Gris is a relatively new variety to the Cape; plantings are mainly to be found in Constantia, Stellenbosch, Paarl and Robertson. To date 11 wines are bottled under the varietal name with plantings accounting for 0,14 per cent of the total.

— GRENACHE —

Spanish in origin, this red wine variety migrated around the world in the wake of the Spanish conquistadors – one of their gentler gifts to mankind. Today the variety has spread not only to Argentina and Chile, but also to Australia, California, North Africa and South Africa, where it is still used in sweet, fortified wines.

In France its clear pink colour has made it one of her most sought-after rosés, and when chilled it makes a light, refreshing and thirst-quenching wine. In the Cape, as on the Alto Douro of Portugal, Grenache was used traditionally for port, even before Professor Perold imported Grenache vines from Spain and France in 1910 to establish the provenance of the local variety.

The variety was never particularly popular among local winemakers. It ripens in mid-season and gives a substantial quantity of wine, but it lacks the vigour demonstrated by its relatives in Europe and the New World. Its wines, moreover, lack colour, as well as acidity and tannin, and their flavour generally lacks distinction.

These drawbacks are compounded in the vineyard where Grenache is selective about its site, and by a susceptibility to

Grenache.

downy mildew and mealy bug, though on the credit side it is reasonably resistant to oïdium and anthracnose, as well as to wind and drought.

Thus, Grenache is grown to a very limited extent in the Cape, almost half of the vines planted in the Paarl district, and a quarter in the Olifantsrivier district, with even less in the Malmesbury and Worcester areas.

— RUBY CABERNET —

We have the University of California at Davis to thank for this red wine variety. Fairly new to South Africa, it is an innovative cross between Carignan and Cabernet Sauvignon (Olmo 1948). Dr Olmo's aim was to cross a peasant or prolific variety, namely Carignan, with royalty, namely Cabernet Sauvig-

Ruby Cabernet.

non. This cross follows the same principle as that of the well-known Pinotage.

The resultant wines are not particularly complex. If the wines undergo subtle wood ageing, some interest can be added. They are, however, meant to be enjoyed young. If it were a good example of this variety, the young wine would have the deep colour of Carignan, and the aroma of Cabernet Sauvignon, but generally would lack complexity on the palate. Some of the most successful wines from Ruby Cabernet have been made in the hotter areas.

A prolific producer, it is important to ensure that Ruby Cabernet is not allowed to overcrop as quantity would be at the price of quality. Ruby Cabernet is fairly resistant to disease but prone to developing leaf roll, and is also susceptible to sunburn so a good canopy with ample foliage is necessary. Only two wines are bottled under the varietal name.

— ZINFANDEL —

For many years Zinfandel, a red wine variety, in hectareage and total production, was the leading wine-grape variety in California. Very much the workhorse of Californian winemakers, Zinfandel can produce very fine red, white or rosé wines, or even be used for a port-type wine.

Zinfandel is very similar to the Italian variety Primitivo di Gioia which is grown in southern Italy. Plantings of this variety are almost a rarity anywhere else with only very small plantings in Australia and at the Cape.

Goblet training is preferred for the Zinfandel variety, with medium spacing, as it is very susceptible to bunch and sour rot. Zinfandel is most successful in the drier areas providing that the soil is not too fertile. Four wines are bottled under the varietal label.

Zinfandel.

—PORT VARIETIES—

In South Africa, port-style wines have been made from early times. In the nineteenth century their production was encouraged by that enthusiastic port-drinking nation, the British, and the demand continued through to the years before the Second World War. It was at this time that a number of new varieties were imported from the Douro region of Portugal in an attempt to enhance the quality of the local South African ports. They included such grape varieties as Alvarelhão, the prolific Bastardo, Donzellinho do Castello, and Touriga. This last is a reasonable producer giving good colour and aroma, and is one of the best all-rounders among the Douro varieties.

Since 1945, further attempts have been made to improve the local ports, in particular by Professors Perold and Theron, who imported further varieties together with better selections of existing varieties. Extensive experiments were made with these vines, which included such exotically titled types as Mourisco Tinto, Tinta Barocca, Cornifesto, Tinta Francisca, Tinto Roriz, Souzão and Malvasia Rey.

Most of the varieties introduced continue to be grown, but on a much reduced scale – they now amount to less than 0,01 per cent of the total vines in the Cape winelands. Moreover, many of them are no longer used in the production of port, but instead are blended with dry red wines to add a touch of the unusual to them. Among these varieties are a number which make the statistics and manage to have their voices heard above the crowd.

Recently, however, the production of good port along the lines of Portuguese vintage port is enjoying something of a revival in the Cape, albeit on a small scale. With the more relaxed attitude of the authorities regarding the importation of

Souzão.

new varieties, fresh vine stocks are being introduced to the Cape vineyards. This new development should encourage the increase in port production.

—SOUZÃO—

Only about 80 000 Souzão vines are still grown locally. A traditional port variety deriving from the Douro and Minho regions of Portugal, it makes a natural wine of an intense dark colour, a deep red bordering on black, and with a high fruit acid content which gives it good potential for maturation. Though Souzão still has a limited use for port, its main use is in blends with other red wines.

—TINTA BAROCCA—

When the Stellenbosch-Elsenburg College of Agriculture and KWV conducted a series of experiments over a decade or more to find the most promising port varieties, Tinta Barocca proved to be one of the best under local conditions. This resulted in a great deal more Tinta Barocca being planted than almost all the other rival varieties put together.

With the decline of the port market, the variety was diverted for the making of a dry red wine, though, when overripe and shrivelled, it continues to make an excellent port, and one which matures with great benefit. Its natural varietal wines are well coloured, medium to full and characteristic in style, with an average maturation potential.

Tinta Barocca is grown mainly in the Stellenbosch, Paarl and Malmesbury areas with vines making up 0,5 per cent of the total plantings.

Tinta Barocca.

—THE MUSCAT GROUP—

The Muscat vines are subgenera of the *Vitis* group. Their best-known and most versatile member is Muscat d'Alexandrie, better known locally as Hanepoot. Others include White Muscadel and Red Muscadel, an important component of the old Constantia wines, originating as a mutation of Cape Muscadel. It is grown in much larger quantities than its progenitor going to make a characteristic, often sweet wine. There are also small amounts of Muscat Ottonel and Morio Muscat planted.

White Muscadel.

—DISTILLING WINE VARIETIES—

While many of the white wine varieties are cultivated both for their varietal potential and for the more traditional use of distilling wine, there exists a number of others which are retained in the Cape winelands specifically for distilling wine purposes. The following are some of the most important of these.

Raisin Blanc, which totals more than 6,5 million vines, is an old South African grape which has been identified with the Servan Blanc of the French vineyards. The light and generally straightforward wine resulting from Raisin Blanc grapes is largely used for brandy distilling. Kanaan, which yields very large bunches of grapes, is used for the same purpose.

Trebbiano, called Ugni Blanc in the south of France, is also a copious producer, mostly used for distilling but also occasionally for blending. Some 1,7 million Trebbiano vines are now grown, mostly in the Breede River area. Sultana, or Thompson's Seedless, is a famous raisin grape, widely grown from the early nineteenth century onwards; much of the wine made from this variety goes for distilling.

The practical art of the winemaker ends with the bottling of his wines. Their distribution to the public can then be through restaurants, hotels or bottle stores, and in some cases direct. From this moment on, the wine becomes the creative province of the individual wine lover.

The relationship between wine and drinker may be simple or sophisticated. It may be a casual matter of the odd glass of wine over lunch, the occasional bottle with a good dinner, a passing but pleasurable acquaintance. Or it may be a deeper and fuller commitment. All aspects of wine and its culture, from its history to its growing and making, from its storage to its presentation, and above all, its tasting and appreciation, may become areas of exploration and delight in their own right. The pleasures of wine may thus be developed with knowledge and experience into something more complex, rewarding and enduring, a lifetime's pursuit.

As with art, music and literature, wine appreciation is a matter of aesthetics, for a wine too has properties of balance, harmony and complexity. And like art, there are no simple equations which exist for its evaluation; the way to understand it is through conscious effort.

Region, producer, vintage and price all have a bearing on the quality of wine but it is the sensory attributes of the wine in the glass that are important and not the words on the label, the price, or the excellence of the advertising. The intelligent wine connoisseur develops sufficient sensory skill and aesthetic appreciation to be able to ignore with confidence both advertising agencies and 'wine snobs' who contend that expensive and imported products are automatically better and that wines from certain vineyards, producers, estates or vintages are superior.

The gradual ageing and mellowing of all better wines over time is what endlessly fascinates their admirers. This explains the attraction of wine clubs, wine books and wine courses which guide the initiate along wine's infinite byways, leading to the ultimate pleasure of home cellars.

LEFT: *A home cellar, whether simple or sophisticated, is the sure, affordable way to enjoy properly aged wines at full, sublime maturity.*

WINE TASTING

Wine appreciation is a learned response comprising sensory pleasures, social custom and personal experience. Individual preferences and prejudices certainly increase the complexity of understanding wine but there is a rational basis for its appreciation which provides general aesthetic principles. Wine puts tasters to the test with its honesty for, when tasted blind (decanted or made anonymous by any other means), it has nothing behind which to hide. The following guiding principles will help you to gain confidence in wine tasting, thereby adding immeasurably to your enjoyment of wine.

—THE GLASS—

A clear wineglass should be used – preferably one with a tulip-shaped bowl to capture and hold the bouquet. A coloured glass will make the assessment of a wine's clarity or colour impossible. The glass should be rinsed with a little of the wine to be tasted. Warm glasses are unsuitable since temperature plays a vital role in the evaluation of wine.

Pour the wine into the glass to a depth of 20 to 25 millimetres. This will be sufficient for you to swirl the wine so that it coats the maximum surface area inside the glass, thereby giving off sufficient bouquet.

Three different types of tasting glasses; the second is the international wine-tasting glass while the third is more commonly used.

Learning to distinguish the full spectrum of white-wine colours takes time and experience. Initially, it is important to be able to differentiate between those of dry white, dry wooded white, special late harvest, noble late harvest, blanc de noir and rosé.

Hold the glass by the stem or base and not by the bowl so that the wine is not obscured by fingers or finger marks, This also prevents the bowl being warmed. Furthermore, the glass can be swirled with ease.

—THE WINE—

Wine must have a lively, living appearance and not the flat, dull or lifeless look of a liquid that has been standing for too long. Ideally, the wine should be bright and clear, although in many of the best red wines a sediment can be an indication of great quality.

Swirl the wine in the glass and note the 'tears' or 'legs' which form on the sides and run back into the wine. These are thought by some to show wines of high quality. Legs are a sure indication of high alcohol, however, as they form as a result of rapid evaporation of alcohol from the thin film of wine adhering to the sides of the glass. High sugar and/or glycerol levels could further enhance this effect.

Small bubbles may be seen inside a bottle of 'still' wine and these adhere to the wineglass at the edge of the wine after pouring. They are often a desirable characteristic; in fact people in Europe prefer wines with a slight 'sparkle'. Such bubbles can result from carbonic acid which dissolves in wine during the fermentation process and is eventually released as a natural liveliness, when the wine is opened and served. The bubbles can also result from the modern pressure filling machine designed to ensure that wine reaches the consumer in peak condition.

THE COLOUR

As you look at your wine, preferably against a white surface, note the gradations of colour. There will be more in a red wine (particularly in a full-bodied red wine that has had some bottle maturation) than in a white wine. In a poorer wine only a few will be noticeable, but in a wine of quality whether young or old there will be many more. Bear this in mind during a 'blind tasting' when you might be asked to assess the quality of, or identify, a particular wine. Generally, white wines tend to darken with age while red wines lighten, but become somewhat browner in hue.

White wines range in colour from pale lemon to amber. Young wines are often paler. Wines made from grapes grown in cool areas are sometimes lighter in colour, while grapes grown in warmer regions produce wines that can be more gold than yellow in colour.

When white wines are stored over a long period, they eventually turn amber or brown mainly as a result of oxidation. you can distinguish an oxidized wine from one that is well bottle-aged by appearance: oxidized whites have a brownish, misty look, while bottle-aged whites show yellowness rather than brownness and do not lose their clarity. The process of browning and oxidizing is loosely called maderization, as the wine thus affected tastes slightly like Madeira wine and is related to the presence of ethylic aldehyde in the wine. Such wines give off a caramel-type odour but they do not always deteriorate as a result.

Blanc de noir wines have only the faintest blush of colour, a pale salmon pink variously described as 'onion skin' or '*Oeil de Perdrix*', 'The Eye of the Partridge'.

The subtleties of colour in red wine depend on various factors. Shown here are a light red, a medium-bodied blended red and a full-bodied red.

Rosé wines made in South Africa should preferably be pink without traces of brown or orange. Usually brown and tawny hues in rosé wines indicate that the wine has aged too long or has become oxidized.

Red wines have a wide range of acceptable colours depending on style and vintage conditions, the age of the wine, the type of grape used and the style of wine-making. Some very young reds may be purple-red, while others are more ruby and develop a tawny tint with age.

The colour of red wine is pH dependent: the lower the pH (or the higher the acid content), the more purple the colour of a young red wine; and the higher the pH (or the lower the acid content), the greater the tendency to have traces of yellow and orange intermingled with the purple.

As red wines mature their colour changes in hue from ruby to a brick red. This change results from polymerization or the linking together of pigment molecules. Sediment developing in very old wines results when such chains become too heavy to remain suspended and as a result collect at the lowest point of the bottle.

THE NOSE

A good sense of smell is essential for the proper appreciation of wine, not only because the nose perceives and recognizes various subtleties of bouquet and aroma but also because the sense of smell constitutes some 75 per cent of taste perception.

The biggest problem facing all wine lovers, experts and connoisseurs alike, is that they find it very difficult to express their perceptions of various smell and taste sensations verbally, and each publication on wine seems to have evolved its own lengthy list of sometimes meaningless terms, thus confusing the issue to an even greater extent.

How to smell or nose a wine. Swirl the wine in the bowl of the glass and then sniff it hard to assess the bouquet. The best method is to sniff the wine quickly, then remove the glass and sniff again after about 30 seconds. The first sniff, however, is all important and is often the basis of judgement.

Try to memorize the smell by associating it with something personally experienced.

Wine odours (or smells) may be divided into two groups: bouquet and aroma; and the so-called off-odours. Although bouquet is used generally when discussing the fragrance or smell of the wine, some experts maintain that the term is only correctly applicable to odours derived from the fermentation, processing, or maturation. The range of pleasant and desirable wine odours derived from the grape itself is called the aroma. The serious taster should develop a clear impression of these basic, easily identifiable varietal aromas so that when faced with an unknown wine sample, the grape variety from which the wine was made can be identified.

Desirable odours include fruity, flowery, clean, positive, spicy, penetrating, heady, sweet, fine, fresh and piquant.

Undesirable odours include mousy, acetic, oxidized, maderized, musty, corky, acidic, baked, dumb, green, stemmy, yeasty, and those of sulphur and bacteria. All these terms are explained in the glossary.

TASTE

In appreciating wine, taste usually serves to confirm information given by the nose. However, if the wine is poorly balanced in that it has the characteristics of being too sweet, too tannic, too acidic or too astringent, it will be rejected on taste though not necessarily on smell.

The four primary tastes perceived by the tongue are sweetness (the tip), sourness or acidity (the upper edges and sides), bitterness and astringency (the back), and saltiness (the middle). Usually only sweetness, bitterness and sourness are important in tasting wines, but saltiness may be noticed in some very dry sherries.

Although the taste buds are predominantly concentrated on the tongue, they are also spread throughout the mouth, albeit in lesser numbers. In fact the cheeks, palate and throat are most important in the assessment of wine as in addition to taste they are receptive to temperature, which greatly affects taste and smell, and to touch.

How to taste wine. First take a sip, rinse your mouth with the wine, effectively cleaning out other tastes, then spit it out into the nearest spittoon. Take another sip and hold the wine in your mouth, rolling it around the tongue so that it reaches the sides and root of the tongue where the most delicate taste buds are situated. Try opening your lips as you roll the wine and draw in air through the mouth as this will help to release volatile ingredients and to draw them into the upper reaches of the olfactory system where they can be sensed. Then breathe out gently through the nose, swallow or spit out the wine and then assess it.

A good memory will help you to relate past tasting experiences to those you are presently acquiring. Notes, however, are a great aid to memory and should be made as you nose and taste the wine; notes made an hour or more later will never be as effective. Every time you taste a wine also consciously try to commit outstanding characteristics to memory. After making your notes, clear your palate by chewing a dry biscuit. While cheese has been traditionally associated with wine tastings it is discouraged when making an accurate assessment since it contains fat which dulls the taste buds and may leave a flavour in the mouth.

Sweetness is usually one of the easiest taste elements to detect but the intensity ranges widely from the slightest hint of sweetness in off-dry wines to sweet and very sweet. This quality is usually derived from natural glucose and fructose, traces of which sometimes remain in the wine after the fermentation process has been completed. Sweetness usually serves to improve the palatability (roundness and smoothness) of the wine and in this respect enhances the organoleptic harmony. When unbalanced in relation to acidity, sweetness can produce an undesirable flat sweetish taste. Tannins, compounds responsible for astringency of taste, reduce the detectable sweetness of a wine. In young red wines this effect is predominant but it also occurs to a lesser extent in whites. As red wines age, the effect of tannins becomes less detectable and the wine softens.

Dryness occurs when all the sugar naturally present in grape juice has been converted to alcohol (and carbon dioxide) during fermentation, producing a dry wine. Because virtually no sugar remains in such a wine it often seems sour or acidic to the novice taster.

Acidity is an essential element in the composition of wines; without it wine would be a flat, lifeless liquid. Wines with a relatively high acid content usually have the best finish and are eminently suitable for maturation (as long as the other required components are present) but too much acid results in a hard, thin wine which is just as unpalatable as a wine with too little acid.

Fruit acids occurring naturally in grapes are, of course, also present in wine and include malic and tartaric acids which account for approximately 98 per cent of all the acid found in wine. Other acids such as succinic, lactic and minute quantities of acetic acid, are the natural by-products of fermentation.

Acids, which give the wine sharpness and freshness, essentially have no taste but rather produce a sensation which many people confuse with the effect of tannin. Tannin tends to be abrasive and is 'felt' on the top of the tongue, roof of the mouth and as a 'furriness' on the teeth. Acids on the other hand have the effect of hitting the tip of the tongue, then the sides and then dissipating.

Bitterness is often confused with astringency (a mouth-puckering sensation) but with sufficient experience the two can be distinguished. Both result from the presence of polyphenolic compounds (tannins) which are most abundantly found in the stalks, skins and pips.

During red-wine processing the skins and pips are left to ferment with the juice so that the colouring matter may be extracted. As a result, tannins are also extracted and therefore red wines usually have a marked degree of astringency. Unless excessive it usually indicates a wine with good maturation potential. With bottle ageing the tannin content actually decreases, resulting in a wine that is less astringent and therefore more palatable.

In making most white wine it is usual to remove the stalks, skins and pips before fermentation and therefore bitterness and astringency are not usually found in white wines.

Body is best described as the feel of 'weight' of a wine in the mouth. It is a result of the combined effect of both glycerol and ethyl alcohol. Wines of high ethyl alcohol and glycerol content are full in body (glycerol is a normal by-product of alcoholic fermentation).

Balance is that elusive quality of harmony in a wine. Tasted individually the various wine constituents may often be unpleasant but when found in perfect combination they produce wines with exquisite flavour and balance.

Aftertaste – or 'follow through', if pronounced, is usually the hallmark of a great wine and refers to the length of time the taste lingers on the palate.

As with nosing the wine the most difficult part of tasting is finding the words to express the sensations experienced. The following terms all have reasonably standard applications in the appreciation of wine and are explained in the glossary.

Desirable qualities include big, delicate, elegant, fat, fresh, luscious, fruity, rich, mellow, noble, nutty, ripe, rich, robust, silky, smooth, soft and supple.

Undesirable qualities include acetic, astringent, bitter, coarse, common, cloying, dull, flat, green, hard, harsh, metallic, overripe, rough, sharp, oxidized, sour, tart and thin.

ASSESSING WINE

The ability to judge wines on their appearance, smell and taste varies from person to person. Some people are more naturally sensitive to colour differences than others. A person with good colour sense will, for example, be able to discern the full spectrum of red wine colours – purple, ruby, red, red-brown, mahogany, tawny and amber-brown – while someone with a poor sense may only be able to differentiate between purple, red and amber-brown. To ensure that tasters use their natural colour sense to best advantage it is important that the correct lighting is used at a tasting. Natural daylight is, of course, ideal.

As with colour, sensitivity to smell varies from one individual to another. There is little evidence that a smoker's tasting ability is inferior to that of a non-smoker, as many fairly heavy smokers are excellent tasters. However, some non-smokers are disturbed by the smell of tobacco smoke while judging wines and at a serious tasting the 'no smoking' rule should be strictly enforced. By the same token women should avoid wearing strong perfume or powder, while men should steer clear of powerfully scented deodorants and aftershave lotions. By attending to these finer points your natural sense of smell will not be distracted from the bouquet of the wine.

— THE TASTING TECHNIQUE —

First, tilt the glass and assess the colour of the wine.

Then swirl the wine in the glass and sniff the bouquet.

Lastly, take a sip, in order to taste the flavour.

People may not realize it, but they are at their freshest both mentally and physically in the morning, and for this reason, many professional tastings are held at this time. Sensitivity to taste is also highest before a meal. A light lunch may be served after the tasting.

To help your palate, you should taste wines in the most appropriate order: dry before sweet, young before old and modest before fine. Whether red wines are tasted before whites depends on their relative 'weights'; light dry whites are better before fuller bodied reds, but light, young red wine is better tasted before full-bodied, sweet white wines.

— CONDUCTING A WINE TASTING —

Tasting, whether a simple affair with a few friends at your home or a grander more sophisticated event, can take many forms, from the comparison of different vintages, grape varieties, quality grades and wine-producing regions, to a comparison of wines at various stages of maturity. The relatively inexperienced taster, however, should restrict the scope of tasting, gradually attempting more 'sophisticated' or complicated tastings as experience is gained.

Whatever the level of sophistication of the tasting it becomes rather vague and unsatisfactory without a system of scoring the wines. There are a number of systems available, but the internationally accepted 20-point system is best understood and most widely used in South Africa.

In this scoring system a high score for an individual wine is 18 points out of a total of 20. A wine in this category would score full points on colour, and perhaps miss one point on the nose and one on the taste. The comment column may be used to exercise your descriptive powers. In this system, reasonable wines usually gain 11 to 13 points, rather good wines 14 or 15, excellent wines 16 to 18, while scores of 19 or 20 are reserved for masterpieces.

Remember the order in which wines should be tasted and guard against tasting too many wines; for the novice taster two to four wines are sufficient, with eight or nine being the maximum for someone reasonably experienced.

The number of people present at a tasting may vary from two upwards, but for a meaningful, yet manageable, home tasting, 10 to 20 guests would be optimum.

Once you have decided how many people will attend the tasting you can calculate how much wine you will need. With a small number of people at a tutored tasting, one bottle will comfortably serve 20 tasters. Use plastic waste bins or jugs for the taster to empty his glass before proceeding to taste the next wine. It is not considered impolite to spit out a wine you do not like, or feel might impair your judgement as the alcohol takes effect. A few jugs of water for guests to rinse their glasses should be provided.

Early evening is probably the most convenient time for a wine tasting. At a dinner party, a pre-dinner 'blind tasting' can be great fun. This type of wine tasting can be organized quite simply by slipping a paper sleeve over the bottle so that the label is covered. Try to guess the grape variety, vintage and wine-growing region.

Holding a wine tasting, even a modest event, takes careful planning, but the following checklist should aid its smooth running:
- Set a theme for the tasting.
- Set a date and send out invitations.
- Make certain that you have all the wines to be tasted.
- Check the availability of chairs, tables, glasses, corkscrews, paper napkins and spittoons.
- Use white tablecloths, as coloured cloths affect colour judgement of the wine.

- Lighting will also affect colour judgement. Ordinary tungsten or warm white fluorescent lighting is best.
- Supply score cards, a list of the wines to be tasted, notepads and pencils.
- Supply jugs of water for rinsing glasses.
- Have dry biscuits at hand for cleaning the palate.
- Allow the wines to settle well in advance.
- Serve wines at the correct temperature: red wines at approximately 18 to 20 °C; rosé and white wines at approximately 16 °C. Chill white and rosé wines for not longer than two or three hours before tasting, as over-chilling can cause loss of flavour and aroma.

WINE SOCIETIES

Wine societies are of long standing in Europe, particularly in France, where each of the more important wine-making districts has its own society or *confrérie*. Elaborate ceremonies attended by growers and shippers of wine, decked out in mediaeval costumes, are invariably followed by a vast, wine-laden banquet. Without the mediaeval panoply, the local South African wine societies have nevertheless proliferated in recent decades, making up in enthusiasm what they lack in history. They provide a vital link between the public at large and the producers, stimulating a heightened interest in the one and providing an indication of shifts in public taste to the other. A few lay the emphasis equally upon food and wine but the majority concentrate on the wine itself.

LES TASTEVINS DU CAP

Les Tastevins du Cap was the inspiration of an immigrant Frenchman, Dr I.C. van Oudenhove de St Géry, who first visited the Cape as a young man in the late 1940s, then returned in 1958 to settle. The first official assembly of *Les Tastevins* took place at their Spring Dinner of 1963. The 38 enthusiasts present elected themselves as the founder members of the group and the French Consul, Count Max de Montalembert, became the first Honorary President. *Les Tastevins* continues to flourish. Many of the original members came from France or from other European wine-making countries and over and above the generally convivial aims of the society persists a desire to promote goodwill between these countries and 'L'Afrique du Sud' with wine as the diplomatic language of these contacts.

THE SOUTH AFRICAN SOCIETY OF WINE TASTERS

In the early 1970s a Cape Town advertising executive, Roger Sinclair, was transferred to Johannesburg. A long-standing member of the Cape Wine Tasters Guild, Roger soon discovered that no wine society then existed in the Transvaal and promptly set about filling the gap. Thus, in 1972, was born the South African Society of Wine Tasters, now one of

There are many different corkscrews from which to choose, including, from left to right, the gas-operated corkscrew which is not recommended; traditional winding corkscrews; the practical and commonly-used 'waiter's friend'; the winged corkscrew; devices to assist in opening champagne bottles and at bottom right, the highly recommended 'screwpull' with a capsule remover.

the most energetic in the country and one particularly dear to expatriate *Kaapenaars*. The third chairman and one of South Africa's most respected wine writers, Peter Devereux, was instrumental in putting the society on the map.

DURBAN WINE SOCIETY

With not a living grape in sight, surrounded by sugar cane, mangoes and bananas, in the midst of a community with a deep traditional allegiance to the joys of beer, whisky, cane spirits and gin, the Durban Wine Society might appear at first blink to be little more than a cheerful anachronism. It flourishes, however, for since its inception in 1974 under its first chairman, Cas Dreyer, it has grown rapidly. The society has its own cellar and holds well-attended wine tastings, with a monthly newsletter relaying members their scores in these

tastings. With the waiting-list for membership of the Durban Wine Society, some of the members have helped to start similar societies elsewhere in Durban and in Pietermaritzburg.

THE INTERNATIONAL WINE AND FOOD SOCIETY

This international organization was founded by the late André Simon and the Cape Town branch enjoyed at least two visits from this 'grand old man' of the wine trade. The local chapter was inaugurated at 'Steenberg', then the home of Nico Louw, on the ninth of February 1947 and was one of the earliest branches to be formed outside the United Kingdom. In South Africa today, there are also active branches in Durban and Johannesburg, the latter being chaired by the wine expert, Peter Devereux.

THE WINE TASTERS' GUILD OF SOUTH AFRICA

This society is probably the oldest in the country, having been established in 1938. It has a strong core of members in the southern suburbs of Cape Town.

Other well-known wine societies are the Grahamstown Wine Circle, the Bacchanalian Society, Johannesburgse Wynproewersgilde, Free State Wine Tasters' Guild, The Stellenbosch Wine Circle, The Wine Swines, and around 300 others.

Encouragement is given to these societies, not only by KWV and Stellenbosch Farmers' Winery-controlled Cape Wine Academy, but also by *'Die Wynboer'* – the official mouthpiece of KWV and South Africa's only wine magazine – whose enthusiastic editor, Henry Hopkins, is generous in providing publicity to the various societies.

YOUR OWN WINE COLLECTION

Like most forms of art, wine can be toweringly serious, simply above average, or just plain commonplace. And with approximately 3 000 different Cape wines available (vintage duplications excluded), it's clear that most are utility wines for everyday enjoyment.

In strong contrast are the wines bought by wine lovers to lay down for some years of bottle-ageing. Due largely to the tannin content, some red wines can taste coarse and astringent during their early years. While it lends longevity to wine, tannin can take three to ten years or more to soften and become part of the balanced whole. Other elements which comprise sediment are proteins, pigment, polyphenols and anthocyanins; and their dropping out of the wine also adds to its mellow smoothness when mature, as well as to the emergence of its richly fruited ripeness on both nose and palate. It follows that most higher-priced, more serious wines are at their best only when optimally mature. The simple answer is to collect some favourite, above-average bottles (or cases) and leave them until they are ready. To do this, you will need a storage space, preferably in a home cellar.

— THE IDEAL HOME CELLAR —

It is not necessary to have a huge underground room to begin keeping wine in your home. Most folk begin with a simple rack or cupboard filled with shelves. Another possibility could be to use the end wall of a garage and brick up about a metre in depth, providing a door for access – insulating the walls and roof and installing a small air-conditioning unit. Your cellar should be kept dark and have an even temperature of between 12 and 16C. If you are handy at carpentry, build a unit containing a series of classical wine 'bins' – diamond-shaped pigeon holes big enough for 12 bottles placed horizontally. If your cellar grows to more than 200 bottles, you cannot rely on memory, so it is advisable to keep a cellar book.

— WINE STORAGE —

Wines are generally quite sensitive to their surroundings. They should be stored in total darkness as prolonged exposure to light adversely affects the quality. Try to prevent excessive movement of the bottles as this can disturb the sediment and damage the flavour.

The ideal temperature at which wine should be stored lies between 12 and 16 °C, the general temperature range of cellars in Europe. The higher the temperature, the less time chemical reactions need to complete their cycles. The maturation potential of the wine could be impaired if stored at temperatures much above 18 °C. At the other extreme, at 10 °C or below, the maturation process is slowed to a near standstill. It is essential to maintain a constant temperature in the storage space as great fluctuation in temperature within 24 hours is even more dangerous to wine than warmth.

The very dry South African climate often causes the cork to dry out, and consequently, the wine to leak from the bottle. Several collectors have installed humidifiers in their cellars, while others cover the floor with damp sand or keep several buckets of water in the cellar so that the air isn't completely dry. The bottles should be placed on their sides to keep the cork moist and swollen.

— STARTING YOUR WINE COLLECTION —

Should your cellar be about the size of a single-car garage and you line its walls with shelves 40 centimetres deep (with a vertical space of 40 centimetres), it will be possible to store over 200 cases on their sides, each containing 12 x 750 millilitre bottles. This will leave you space for a table as well as room for more wine cartons stacked in pyramid form.

— CHOOSING YOUR WINE —

Your favourite everyday wine may be bought by the case, which will bring both a price advantage as well as the possible discovery that it markedly improves with age.
Sparkling wine is the finest welcome to any guest.
Whites, such as Cape Riesling, Chenin Blanc, Weisser Riesling, Colombard and Gewürztraminer, represent the single biggest category of the South African wine industry and unlike the reds, do not need long bottle maturation.
French-style whites such as Chardonnay, Sauvignon Blanc and Pinot Gris are becoming more fashionable.
Pink wines are declining in popularity, although some labels still have very strong followings.
Good everyday red wines continue to be well liked. South African red wines are traditionally full-bodied, needing a long period of maturation. However, today there are a number of light-bodied wines available. These are either ready for immediate drinking or need less maturation. You'll find good value among boxed wines as well as among the house brands of bottle stores and supermarkets. While they're made to be enjoyed soon after purchase, you can safely let most of them age a while: the cheaper ones for perhaps a year or two and the more expensive for three to five years.
Serious red wines are the chief target among connoisseurs and collectors and are consequently more expensive and often out of stock. There are six major categories:
• Cabernet Sauvignon wines can be quite tannic when young but sublime after six to ten years' maturation, depending on the wine concerned.

Fortified wines, such as (from left to right) pale dry sherry, medium cream sherry and port, also vary in colour.

• Bordeaux-style blends are often pricey due to the varieties used for the style of wine. Usually drinkable earlier than Cabernet Sauvignon, they are at their best after four to nine years' maturation.
• Cape-style blends are usually a combination of Shiraz and another variety. They are often wood-matured in large vats instead of in small casks. These classics are not as complex as French-style blends yet can astound even experts with their richness and depth of flavour when eight to twelve years old.
• Pinot Noir is a newcomer to the Cape, and therefore predictions about its longevity would be presumptuous. Current experience, however, shows marked improvement up to six years with the wine showing signs of at least three years more to go to full maturity.
• Pinotage is the Cinderella of the industry for only recently was it discovered that several Pinotages develop distinct Burgundy-like smells and flavours following long bottle maturation of over 10 years.
• Other serious reds certainly exist. Merlot is a fashionable grape now hinting of greatness, and there are collectibles to be discovered in Shiraz and several red blends.
Unfortified sweet wines (late harvest, special late harvest and noble late harvest) should be served cool for tasting and assessment but preferably quite chilled for drinking alone or with fresh fruits or dessert.
Fortified wines are the grand bass notes of wine and there are three main categories:
• Sherry from South Africa can be good enough to be confused with sherry from Spain.
• Port can be the 'grand finale' to any great dinner. In South Africa it is usually in *colheita* style and from grape varieties different to those used in Portugal.
• Muscadel can be white or red and is usually made in Jerepigo style.

— CAPE VINTAGE GUIDE —

South Africa is fortunate enough to have wonderful summers, and yet one is never the same as the next. The Cape's Mediterranean climate sometimes brings rain during

To open a bottle of sparkling wine, begin by removing the foil from the neck of the bottle.

Untwist the wire loop, loosen the wire cage underneath and lift it from the bottle.

Grip the cork very firmly with one hand, turning the base of the bottle. with the other hand.

When pouring, angle the bottle sharply to ensure that a large surface area is created.

And finally, enjoy!

the vintage (January to April) and early onset of winter brings clouds which delay ripening of Cabernet Sauvignon, the last grape variety to be harvested.

In reading the vintage ratings below, which are each rated out of 10 points, bear in mind that they are necessarily generalized and that exceptions in either direction will always exist. The ratings are intended to indicate comparative quality and performance.

YEAR	WHITES	REDS	YEAR	WHITES	REDS
1991	8	9	**1985**	6	6
1990	6	8	**1984**	5	8
1989	6	7	**1983**	5	5
1988	7	7	**1982**	8	7
1987	5	8	**1981**	6	6
1986	6	9	**1980**	5	8

SERVING WINE

There is nothing to stop you drinking wine straight from the bottle. Much would be lost in this process, however, and with quality wine possessing values beyond mere price it is sensible to safeguard and enhance every quality that it has to offer. The protocol involved in serving wine raises many questions but ultimately depends on the degree of formality or informality of the particular occasion.

— OPENING AND CLOSING — BOTTLES

If ever you have sunk a cork into the bottle, wrestled with a sparkling wine, or screwed an old cork into crumbly bits you will appreciate that there is a technique to master. The first

step is to remove the capsule down to well below the glass collar on the bottleneck. This is an important step as it has recently been discovered that lead capsules on wine bottles can put lead into the wine you drink.

Today there are many and varied instruments for removing corks but the most effective and readily available are the openers that employ the use of the screw process. Some corkscrews operate on a lever principle and are very effective for easing stubborn corks. Corkscrews which save on muscle power include the 'winged' corkscrew. The only drawback is when the cork crumbles in the centre the screw cannot be repositioned as it is designed to operate on the centre of the cork. With the good old fashioned corkscrew such as the 'waiter's friend', you can reposition it on some other part of the cork if the centre crumbles. The only corkscrew worth using is one with a hollow helix such as the 'Screwpull', favoured by most serious wine lovers around the world.

Wine served in a table-wine carafe.

Brandy served in a traditional cut-glass decanter.

stop pouring. The residue in the wine bottle can be thrown away. The result should be limpid, polished wine in your decanter without the slightest trace of sediment or cloudiness.

It is generally believed that red wines improve by exposure to the air for some hours in a decanter before being served. Some controversy surrounds this concept with several experts maintaining that decanting should be done just before serving and that any aeration necessary can simply be achieved by swirling the wine around in the glass. Others claim that hours of aeration, or 'breathing', do not reduce the tannins in the wine. In fact, the effect of air on wine is said to diminish the bouquet and the taste.

The general consensus is, with the exception of very old reds, that most wines can be safely left to 'breathe' for some hours in a decanter. They will either remain the same or show some enhancement in aroma, flavour, and character. A recently released young red may be left for 24 hours, while six hours would suffice for a six year old and around three hours for anything from seven to ten years old.

Finally bear in mind that a decanter for table wines is quite different to the cut-glass traditionals used for spirits or sherry. Table-wine decanters should be at least 12 to 15 centimetres in diameter to allow a large surface area of wine to be exposed to the air.

To open any bottle of sparkling wine, remove the foil, untwist the wire loop, loosen the whole wire cage and then remove it. Grip the cork very tightly in one hand and turn the base of the bottle with the other. You should keep as much vivacity within the wine as possible which precludes popping the cork 'Hollywood' fashion. Angle the bottle quite sharply immediately it's open to prevent foam from surging out of the neck. Doing so will create a large surface area of wine within the neck allowing any foam to dissipate quickly within the bottle. The wine may then be easily poured into the glass, and then enjoyed.

—DECANTING—

Decanters can be used to serve boxed wines or any bottled wines closed with screwcaps. However, the principal aim of all fine wine decanting since the 1700s has been the separation of wine from its sediment. Allow the bottle to stand vertically for three days to allow all the loose sediment to settle to its base. Then take the decanter by its neck in one hand and the wine bottle carefully in the other and let the wine flow slowly and gently until you discern the first streaks of sediment moving into the neck of the bottle. At this point

—CHOOSING THE RIGHT— GLASSES

For everyday home use, the following wineglasses are sufficient to cope with any situation:

• The tall, narrow champagne flute is preferred for sparkling wines as it allows the effect of the rise of the bubbles to be appreciated. This type of glass must be rinsed thor-

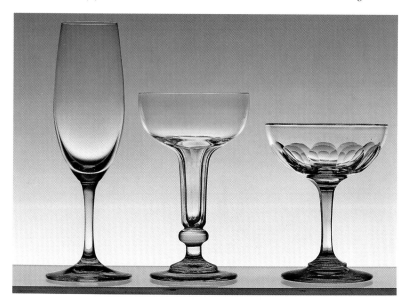

Three different types of sparkling-wine glasses – the narrow champagne flute (left) is recommended as it enables the rise of the bubbles to be appreciated.

A wine decanter and a range of glasses to be used for (from left to right) red wine, white wine, special late harvest, noble late harvest and port.

oughly to remove all traces of detergent as any residue will affect the aroma and the rise of the bubbles.

• An all-purpose table-wine glass can be used for white, red, pink and even inexpensive sparkling wines.

• A sherry glass can also be used for port or even liqueurs.

• A brandy balloon is essential for presenting specialities such as Armagnac, Calvados, single malt whisky, or old Cape brandy.

— THE ART OF POURING — AND DRINKING

Considering the 'correct' procedure for the service of wine will help you to decide what would be most appropriate in your home. At a restaurant the wine steward should present the bottle, prior to opening, on the right hand side of the host to ensure that it is in fact the wine he ordered and to allow the host to check the temperature.

Once the host has given his approval the steward will cut the capsule, remove the upper portion and wipe the bottle clean with a napkin. He will then gently pull the cork, once again wiping the lip of the bottle with a clean napkin to remove any particles of cork which might have adhered to it. All this should be done within the host's sight.

Serving from the host's right the steward will pour about a third of a glass into the host's glass for approval, holding the bottle in his right hand. The steward gives the bottle a slight twist as he takes the bottle away from the glass to prevent wine dripping.

Once the wine has been approved the steward may proceed. Ladies will be served first, then the men and finally the host. Once all the glasses have been charged the steward should place the bottle on the table to the right of the host. A white or a sparkling wine which needs to be kept cool will be placed by the steward in an ice bucket within reach of the host. Red wines should be served at the temperature at which they are stored in the cellar.

In a private home where there is no steward the host should serve the wine, inviting the most appropriate guest to taste if he so wishes.

WINE AND FOOD

In planning wines with food it's important to try and keep the sequences right: white before red; young before old; dry before sweet. The meal should also follow the principle of the crescendo: lighter dishes and wines first, followed by stronger, more characterful ones towards the end, finishing with a sweet flourish when the palate is tired. Remember that most wines are ruined by chocolate and strong coffee flavours. You should also keep anything citric far away from good table wines as these will otherwise taste bitter.

Good wine and good food – the perfect combination.

— FOOD AND WINE CHECKLIST —

Some wines, such as a good dry sparkling wine, partner almost any food successfully, and most people find it quite acceptable to drink the same wine throughout a meal. However, for those who prefer to match wine to food, the list below suggests types of wines which best complement certain dishes. As with personal taste , there can be no rules , only suggestions and recommendations.

SOUP

Clear consommé: medium sherry.
Strong seafood: wooded Chardonnay.
Pea soup with ham: wooded Blanc Fumé.
Oxtail: Shiraz or medium sherry.
Mixed vegetable or meat: medium sherry.

FISH

Oysters: wooded Chardonnay.
Prawns: any unwooded dry white.
Crayfish: (char-grilled) grassy Sauvignon Blanc; (richly sauced) Chardonnay.
Calamari: Sauvignon Blanc.
Crab: Cape Riesling.
Pink Salmon: (smoked) grassy Sauvignon Blanc or off-dry Weisser Riesling; (grilled) dry Weisser Riesling.
Perlemoen: dry Chenin Blanc.
Tuna: (char-grilled) wooded dry white; (with onion & tomato) off-dry Chenin Blanc.
Trout: (panfried) grassy Sauvignon Blanc; (smoked) unwooded Chardonnay or off-dry Weisser Riesling.

POULTRY

Chicken: (roast) Pinot Noir.
Duck: (roast) French-style red blend.
Goose: (roast) Merlot or Zinfandel.
Turkey: (smoked) Pinot Noir.

MEAT

Veal: (grilled) off-dry Cape Riesling.
Pork: (roast) unwooded Chardonnay.
Ham: (with a pineapple or mustard glaze) wooded Blanc Fumé; (with melon) Gewürztraminer.
Lamb: (roast) Shiraz or Tinta Barocca; (barbecued chops) Cabernet Sauvignon or French-style blend.
Beef: (roast) Cabernet Sauvignon; (steak and kidney pie) Pinot Noir; (grilled steak or T-bone) Cabernet Sauvignon.
Venison: (roast) Shiraz; (braised) Pinotage.
Curries: (Cape Malay) light fruity red; (Indian) beer.

DESSERT

General: Special late harvest, noble late harvest or sparkling.

CHEESE

Cheddar: French-style red blend.
Sweetmilk: Pinot Noir or light fruity red.
Ripe Camembert or Brie: Pinot Noir or light fruity red.
Goatsmilk: grassy Sauvignon Blanc.
Feta: off-dry Weisser Riesling.
Parmesan: off-dry sparkling white.
Smoked: Gewürztraminer.
Hard blue: Cabernet or dry sherry.
Peppered: Shiraz or Tinta Barocca.

De Akker
country pub & restaurant

LICENCED
Restaurant

PHONE 5512

RIGHT OF ADMISSION RESERVED

Stellenbosch
wine tasting
Centre
←

wine
tasting
daily

DE
AKKER
o
COCKTAIL BAR
& RESTAURANT
o
OPEN FOR
LUNCH &
DINNER

OOP
VIR
MIDDAG
ETE
11-3 n.m.

Tassenberg

THE WINE ROUTES

The Stellenbosch Wine Route was born out of an amalgam of chance and vision. Chance had it that Frans Malan of Simonsig and Niel Joubert of Spier were touring Burgundy with their wives in 1969 when they happened on the *route des vins* of Morey-St-Denis. The vision was the potential such a route held if replicated locally. Back home, Spatz Sperling of Delheim was their first sounding board for the idea. He was an instant convert. The duo, now become a trio, approached others with varying degrees of success. Initially opposition from vested interests was strong.

Joubert, as a director of KWV and member of the Liquor Board – a statutory controlling body – had considerable clout in guiding the concept through the right channels. Getting the nuts and bolts such as signposting through traditional bureaucratic blockades was Kafkaesque. When the Stellenbosch Wine Route did eventually get off the ground in 1971, nobody could have foreseen its cataclysmic effect on the industry in particular, and on tourism as a whole.

Stellenbosch has since spawned a host of other routes, each with its own satellite activities such as arts and crafts shops, antique dealers, vendors of bric-a-brac, farm stalls, restaurants, art galleries and a variety of cultural activities. Accommodation is never a problem on the wine routes as all areas are well served by a choice of hotels, guest houses, and often holiday resorts, camping sites and caravan parks. The economic spin-off from tourism for the communities involved has been immense.

The success enjoyed by the Stellenbosch pioneers coaxed other producers out of their backrooms and encouraged them to display their wares to an eager public. This exposure had a marked influence on upgrading quality. The next decade saw a proliferation of wine routes. Smaller routes grew out of larger ones and groups of producers hived off to form more compact routes, or ones with more specific local focus. At the time of writing, there are 13 examples of the genre and no doubt more will germinate in time. The consequent jostling for attention has resulted in the visitor being offered a diversity of wine styles and tourist-related attractions.

LEFT: *De Akker pub and restaurant in Stellenbosch.*

Closest to Cape Town are the Constantia Valley Wine Route and the more recently established Durbanville Wine Route. Both are situated within easy access of major freeways and can be reached within minutes of the city centre. For those without their own transport or who prefer to be driven around, there are a number of tour operators who will guide you through the Cape winelands. Facilities are available for private tours or for large groups.

—CONSTANTIA—
WINE ROUTE

The longest established of the Cape's viticultural areas is that of Constantia. All current producers on this compact wine route have connections with the original estate laid out by Governor Simon van der Stel in 1685. In recent years the area has undergone a dramatic viticultural revival. The winelands are an harmonious synthesis of old and new, where historic Cape Dutch buildings are juxtaposed with the most modern cellars boasting up-to-the-minute technology.

A popular stop along the route is the Old Cape Farm Stall which is always stocked with a beautifully displayed selection of top-quality fresh fruit, vegetables and herbs, complemented by a wide variety of gourmet foods, breads and confectionery baked on the spot. A restaurant, coffee-shop, wine-tasting facility and conference centre are located in the same complex.

For those wishing to capture the charm of a bygone age, there is the offer of tours along country roads through the Constantia winelands by horse and carriage with the option of stopping for wine-tastings, lunches, teas or dinners at any of the restaurants and estates in the area, or enjoying an upmarket picnic lunch complete with elegant table linen, cutlery and glassware.

The manor house of state-owned Groot Constantia, the seat of Cape Governor Simon van der Stel's empire to which he retired at the end of the seventeenth century, serves as a cultural history museum furnished with priceless period pieces and *objets d'art*. Behind the manor house is a court-

yard leading to the old wine cellar commissioned by Hendrik Cloete and designed by famous Cape architect Louis Thibault. A pediment sculpted in bas relief by Anton Anreith has the date 1791 on its gable. Part of this building serves as a venue for various exhibitions and is hired out for private or business functions. The rear portion of the cellar houses a fascinating wine museum with some valuble pieces going back to Greek antiquity.

The Jonkershuis, a restaurant located in a building dating back to the early nineteenth century, is situated to the right as one approaches the front of the manor house. The estate's old bottling plant is now home to another restaurant. Close to these National Monuments is the vast, modern production cellar. Guided tours through the winery are offered culminating in a wine-tasting. Hiking trails crisscross the estate and permitted riders on horseback are not an uncommon sight in this setting of vineyards and forests.

Richard and Christine Müller bought the run-down Buitenverwachting in 1981. They meticulously restored the sadly neglected manor house to its former graciousness, laid out vineyards and built a cellar equipped with the most modern wine-making technology. Once part of Governor Simon van der Stel's Constantia, Buitenverwachting offers spectacular views across the valley and False Bay 12 kilometres away and is home to one of South Africa's most highly rated restaurants which offers a sophisticated menu.

A bright display of vegetables at the Old Cape Farm Stall in Constantia.

Klein Constantia, also once part of Simon van der Stel's vast estate, was purchased by Duggie Jooste in 1980 and developed into a showpiece wine estate. On the property stands the kramat of Sheikh Abdurachman Matebe Shah, one of the last great sultans of Malacca, banished to the Cape in 1667. Use of the holy shrine was granted to the Muslim community through an arrangement between Duggie Jooste and the Cape Mazaar Society, who restored the building in 1986.

Illustrated brochures detailing the route's attractions can be obtained from wineries on the route or from the offices of Captour in Cape Town.

**WINERIES ON THE
CONSTANTIA WINE ROUTE**

Buitenverwachting, Groot Constantia and Klein Constantia.

—DURBANVILLE—
WINE ROUTE

Durbanville is a thriving little town situated approximately 20 kilometres from Cape Town. The district is set in the Tygerberg hills and was one of the earliest areas to be grazed by the Dutch colonists' cattle herds from the mid seventeenth century. The Durbanville Wine Trust was established in 1990 with the express purpose of creating a greater awareness of the importance of the district as a wine-producing area. While the estates on this route are open to the public for tastings and sales, and then for limited periods or by appointment only, there are 11 other members of the trust who deliver top-quality grapes to The Bergkelder, Nederburg, Stellenbosch Farmers' Winery and the Bottelary and Koelenhof co-operatives.

The estates of Altydgedacht, Bloemendal and Diemersdal are open for tastings and sales on Wednesday afternoons and Saturday mornings. Meerendal, the fourth of the group, markets its wines through The Bergkelder. The Durbanville Food and Wine Feast is held in April and has become a popular annual event and an effective way of introducing the wines of the district to a wider public.

Durbanville has a number of well-maintained buildings linking the town and its immediate environs to the past, among them Oude Molen, one of the few extant tower mills. The municipality of neighbouring Bellville has restored the seventeenth-century Welgemoed homestead which will accommodate the Oude Welgemoed restaurant with a tasting and sales facility for Durbanville wines in the property's old cellar. The Municipal Rose Garden where new rose varieties

**WINERIES ON THE
DURBANVILLE WINE ROUTE**

Altydgedacht, Bloemendal, Diemersdal and Meerendal.

The Lord Neethling restaurant on Neethlingshof Estate specializes in eastern dishes.

are planted and monitored is also worth a visit, as is the small nature reserve. Here, visitors can still enjoy a patch of the local vegetation – a unique *mélange* of strandveld and renosterveld fynbos which typified the area before urban development and the farmer's plough claimed it all.

Information on the route can be obtained from Captour in Cape Town or from the Durbanville Wine Trust.

—STELLENBOSCH—
WINE ROUTE

Established in 1971, the Stellenbosch Wine Route is the granddaddy of them all. The eponymous town itself is the second oldest in South Africa having been established by Governor Simon van der Stel in 1679. It has been aptly described by Spatz Sperling (of Delheim Estate), one of its founders, as 'a world in one wine route'.

There are 20 estates or privately owned wineries and five co-operative cellars on the route which includes the areas of Muldersvlei to the north of Stellenbosch, and Firgrove, near Somerset West and False Bay, to the south. Within its boundaries the visitor has the opportunity to see how wine and brandy are made and how the barrels in which they are matured are coopered.

The scenery, with its spectacular seascapes and mountainscapes, is heart-stoppingly beautiful. In the town itself there are enough wine, brandy and cultural history museums to hold one's fascination for weeks. Stellenbosch is home to the Rembrandt van Rijn Art Gallery with its permanent collections of South African and international art. There are also

privately owned galleries including those on Overgaauw and Spier wine estates and one under the aegis of Stellenbosch University. The University has several lecture halls, theatres and other venues where academic and cultural events are staged, and the Oude Libertas Amphitheatre is the venue for outdoor productions such as music concerts, during the summer months. A popular venue for the students of the university (as well as for anyone else) is De Akker pub, which also has facilities for wine-tasting.

The Stellenbosch Festival, with its focus on the arts and on music in particular, is held in September each year. October is the month when Stellenbosch celebrates its founding and is the time for the annual Simon van der Stel Festival, an event of much pageantry. The immensely popular Stellen-

Colourful balls of handspun wool photographed at Dombeya farm in Stellenbosch.

bosch Food and Wine Festival takes place during the last week of October.

Stellenbosch is a national showpiece of Cape architecture. Among its buildings is Schreuder House, the oldest example of a private dwelling to be found in South Africa. Many of the buildings have been declared National Monuments. In a brochure issued by the Stellenbosch Publicity Association, 62 such points of interest have been identified to date and walking tours of the town are offered.

Although essentially a university town, Stellenbosch has a well-developed infrastructure of shops and supermarkets and arguably more good restaurants than any other South African town of comparable size. Most of the wineries on the route offer light lunches during summer, while Neethlingshof and Spier estates operate full-blown restaurants.

A number of cottage industries operate in the district and there are interesting examples of the potter's, spinner's and knitter's arts to be seen, such as handspun wool at Dombeya farm. Oom Samie se Winkel, an unusual store describing itself as 'yesterday's general dealer', is situated in historic Dorp Street and offers a quaint product mix of wine, food and goods of a bygone age. Colourful scarecrows, whose costumes are changed each season, can be seen in the strawberry patches around Mooiberg Farm Stall.

Within minutes of the Town Hall is the Viticultural and Oenological Research Institute, plus institutes for research into fresh fruit technology, plant protection and other branches of agricultural endeavour. There is a trout hatchery in the Jonkershoek Mountains, Stellenbosch backdrop.

The many opportunities for the mountaineer and hikes are too numerous to mention. For the golfer there are two 18-hole courses. There are opportunities for the freshwater and marine angler within easy distance and facilities for enthusiasts of bowls, squash, tennis, horse riding and rowing are also available. There is even a flying and parachuting club. For the health-conscious, or for those who feel they have indulged too long or too well in the winelands, there is the famous Hydro health resort on High Rustenburg. Alternative accommodation is easy to find, a noteworthy hotel being D'Ouwe Werf, and there are many very commendable homes offering bed and breakfast in the country or in the town.

More detailed information can be obtained from the Stellenbosch Wine Route's permanent office or from the Stellenbosch Publicity Association.

**WINERIES ON THE
STELLENBOSCH WINE ROUTE**

Avontuur, Blaauwklippen, Bottelary Co-operative Winery, Clos Malverne, De Helderberg Co-operative Winery, Delaire Vineyards, Delheim, Eersterivier Valleise Co-operative Winery, Eikendal Vineyards, Hartenberg, Koopmanskloof, Lievland, Morgenhof, Muratie, Neethlingshof, Oude Nektar, Overgaauw, Rust-en-Vrede, Saxenburg Wine Farm, Simonsig, Spier, Uiterwyk, Vlottenburg Co-operative Winery, Vredenheim and Welmoed Co-operative Wine Cellars.

—THE WINE MUSEUMS—

Adjacent to the Oude Meester headquarters in Stellenbosch and within a few metres of each other are the buildings of the Stellenryck Wine Museum and the Oude Meester Brandy Museum, which are models of their kind, compact but comprehensive, well designed and very entertainingly informative.

Stellenryck Wine Museum. This museum draws its exhibits both from local and overseas sources, ranging from clay amphorae, both elongated and spherical, from the classic period of Greece and Rome, to early modern winemaking equipment. There are glasses and goblets from Holland to England to China; there is an early model of the type of machine used for putting the wire on champagne bottles; there is a nineteenth-century wine cooler and a miniature French wine press once used to make samples of wines. In the rear of the museum, which is designed in imitation of a wine cellar, are different types of oak cask for maturing wines, a flor sherry display and a magnificent nineteenth-century Italian oak wine cart. Outside in the sunshine is an enormous antique German wine press which was built in the late eighteenth century and last used in 1936.

The Oude Meester Brandy Museum. Featuring some 1 000 exhibits, this collection is housed in a cluster of labourers' cottages designed in 1904 by Sir Herbert Baker for the farm then owned by his friend, Cecil Rhodes, on the Eerste River. Baker's only known contribution to Stellenbosch architecture, they were rescued from the bulldozers and restored by the Oude Meester Group, to be opened as a museum of the *Eau de Vie du Vin* – the 'Water of Life from Wine' – in 1977.

The museum contains sections on the history of brandy (exhibits include a Dutch miniature of an early

Inside the Oude Meester brandy museum, Stellenbosch.

brandy distillery, and a cognac brandy-still dating from 1818 on loan from Richelieu et Cie of Cognac), modern methods of production, displays on the early nineteenth-century local brandy houses such as Collisons, Greens and Van Ryns, a beautifully reconstructed Victorian period room, a maturation cellar, and fine photographic displays of cask making and *witblits* making in the mountains.

Both museums are open at the following times: From Monday to Friday, from 09h00 to 12h45, and from 14h00 to 17h00; on Saturdays and public holidays, from 10h00 to 13h00, and from 14h00 to 17h00; and on Sundays from 14h30 to 17h30. The museums are not open to the public on Good Friday, Ascension Day, the Day of the Covenant and Christmas Day.

—PAARL—
WINE ROUTE

The Paarl Wine Route is the second oldest of the genre in South Africa and the town itself the third oldest after Cape Town and Stellenbosch. It was the cradle of the Afrikaans language and is the seat of KWV, the industry's controlling body and largest wine co-operative. It is the only town of its size where vineyards can still be seen lining its main street. Situated 56 kilometres from Cape Town off the N1 highway, it lies in the Berg River Valley between Paarl Mountain and the Drakenstein range to the north. A thriving town with a bustling commercial heart and an outlying industrial area, Paarl is steeped in history.

The wine route offers the visitor a rich diversity of attractions. Here, with the aid of a closed circuit television programme, you can take a self-conducted tour of Backsberg Estate, or opt for the comprehensive guided tours of the

massive KWV cellars offered twice daily from Mondays to Fridays. Of particular interest is Zandwijk, on the southern slopes of Paarl Mountain, as it is the only producer of kosher wines in South Africa, and the Paarl Rock Brandy Cellar, as it is the only one of its kind in the country open to visitors

Boats for hire at Wiesenhof Wildlife Park.

The Toringkerk, a National Monument, is one of the many historic buildings in Paarl.

where the complete flow line of brandy production can be seen. At Fairview, the milking of the Saanen herd for the estate's goat's milk cheeses is a source of fascination for both children and adults. The goat tower with its external, spiral walkway on which the animals clamber has become a landmark. Nederburg is the setting for the world-renowned annual Nederburg Auction and the chamber concerts which are staged in the manor house during the winter months.

Paarl and its environs are peppered with historic buildings and museums, among them the Strooidak Dutch Reformed Church, the country's oldest church still in use. The impressive Toringkerk is also a national monument. Walking tours of the main historic sites are provided. One of these is the Afrikaans language monument sited on Paarl Mountain, home also to a nature reserve. The Afrikaans Language Museum is to be found in the town and forms part of the Afrikaans Language Route. This museum was the home of Gideon Malherbe in 1875, one of the founder members of the *Genootskap van Regte Afrikaners* ('Association of True Afrikaners'). It was also the birthplace of the first Afrikaans newspaper *Die Afrikaanse Patriot*. The original printing press is still housed in the museum.

Paarl Mountain is also the venue for the annual Paarl Nouveau Festival held in April each year. This is an occasion of fun and merriment when producers arrive in often highly original costumes and equally ingenious forms of transport, to present their first fruits of the vintage to a celebrity guest of honour. Here wines of the area can be sampled and picnic lunches purchased. This event is the only one of its kind in the country and has become so popular that it is booked out well in advance.

Another type of institution that exists in Paarl and nowhere else, is the Dal Josophat Art Foundation. It is a non-profit organization housed on the adjoining farms of Non Pareille and Goederust – both National Monuments. It is a settlement where artists live and work, hold workshops and further art education. The work of resident and invited artists, as well as works in the organization's permanent collection, are exhibited in the foundation's gallery.

Drakenstein Draai is another route within a route. It has many points of interest which include the Belcher Wine Farm, where spinning and weaving on traditional apparatus can be seen, the Huber Farm art gallery, a pottery, an antique shop, Nic Taylor's nut farm, and Avignon Lace, the only private exhibition of antique bobbin- and needle-lace in the country that is open to the public.

For those with a nostalgia for 'Darkest Africa' there is Wiesenhof Wildpark situated on the R44 where game animals can be viewed. Then there is Safariland holiday resort and game park on the Wemmershoek road and Le Bonheur crocodile farm near Simondium where a well-stocked shop sells products of crocodile and other game animal leathers.

Some of the producers on the route offer light lunches while Rhebokskloof Estate and KWV-owned Laborie operate their own restaurants. There are many sporting facilities, including an 18-hole golf course. Visitors with a head for heights can get a bird's-eye view of Paarl's multi-faceted charms on a balloon flight over the winelands. A number of hotels, including the magnificent Grande Roche, as well as guest houses, serve the area.

Paarl Vintner, Paarl Wine Route's own newsletter, is available free from member wineries along the route or from the organization's office in Paarl. Further information can be obtained from the permanent office of the Paarl Wine Route, the Paarl Publicity Association or from the Information Bureau in Paarl.

WINERIES ON THE PAARL WINE ROUTE

Backsberg, Belcher Wine Farm, Bolandse Co-operative Wine Cellar, Fairview, KWV, Laborie, Landskroon, Nederburg, Paarl Rock (brandy cellar), Perdeberg Wine Farmers' Co-operative, Rhebokskloof, Simondium Winery Co-operative, Simonsvlei Co-operative, Villiera, Windmeul Co-operative and Zandwijk.

—WELLINGTON— WINE ROUTE

Wellington was long the centre of the wainwright's craft and was called Wagenmakers Vallei – later Wamakersvallei – to identify it as such. It was renamed Wellington in 1840. In the early 1780s, when Voortrekker leader Piet Retief was a toddler, his father acquired the farm Welvanpas on which the eponymous Welvanpas Cellars are situated. The property now belongs to Dan Retief, one of Piet's descendants.

The route's members have strong links with the past. The Onverwacht homestead carries the date 1799 on its gable which marks the date when the present dwelling was erected after an earlier one was ravaged by fire. The present-day Wellington Wynboere Co-operative is successor to the original Wellington Co-operative Winery, a contemporary of Bovlei Co-operative Winery formed in 1907 and one of the oldest of its kind in the country. There are also small, family-run wineries in Wellington, such as Claridge Fine Wines, situated on the farm Rustenburg.

A drive across the narrow Bain's Kloof Pass, 50 years ago the only major road link between Cape Town and the northern hinterland, will reward the motorist with vistas of towering mountainscapes where the baboon and his arch enemy, the leopard, still hunt. Today, the Huguenot Tunnel provides the Cape Peninsula and outlying Boland towns with easy access to the north on the fast N1 highway.

Trails in beautiful mountain surroundings are available to hikers and mountaineers. Wellington was one of the first South African towns to be served by rail traffic when the country's second oldest railway line was opened in 1862, first between Cape Town and Eerste Rivier and later it was extended to Stellenbosch. It reached Wellington the following year, successfully establishing a commercial route between Cape Town and Wellington.

The town boasts two museums and a number of historic buildings, including the Dutch Reformed Mother Church made famous by Dr Andrew Murray, the Scottish missionary who ministered there from 1871 to 1906.

Other interesting places to be visited in the area include SAD, the giant dried fruit co-operative, and Oaklands, the only horse stud farm which is listed on the Johannesburg Stock Exchange.

Further details can be obtained from the Information Bureau in the Wellington Town Hall.

**WINERIES ON THE
WELLINGTON WINE ROUTE**

Bovlei Co-operative Winery, Onverwacht, Rustenburg, Wamakersvallei Co-operative Winery, Wellington Wynboere Co-operative and Welvanpas.

—VIGNERONS DE FRANSCHHOEK—

First known as Olifantshoek because of the annual elephant migration to the valley, it was renamed Franschhoek after many of the French Huguenots had established themselves there. It is the home of the Huguenot Monument and the Huguenot Memorial Museum, the main complex of which is housed in a replica of Saasveld, a homestead designed by Louis Michel Thibault in 1791 and originally sited in Kloof Street, Cape Town.

Vignerons de Franschhoek is an association of producers established in this beautiful valley. While some of the members, notably Boschendal, Clos Cabrière, Dieu Donné, La Motte, L'Ormarins and Franschhoek Vineyards Co-operative have their own wine-making facilities, the others, with the exception of Bellingham, have an arrangement whereby their grapes are vinified by the Franschhoek Vineyards Co-operative in a style specified by the grower. Some Bellingham wines are produced in the Wellington cellars of the parent company, Douglas Green Bellingham, while others are made on the farm. Clos Cabrière is the only producer in South Africa specializing in *méthode champenoise* sparkling wine to the exclusion of all else bar an estate brandy. In the town of Franschhoek there is a wine-tasting centre where members' wines can be tasted.

The valley boasts some of the best restaurants in the Cape. The cuisine is varied with the accent mainly on French-style dishes. Franschhoek also supports a flourishing trout farming industry and this delicacy is a regular feature on the local menus.

Le Quartier Français, judged first among the Cape's 'popular' restaurants in 1991.

Some of South Africa's most historic homesteads are to be found in this picturesque valley. The one on Boschendal houses a beautiful collection of Cape antique furniture and a collection of rare kraak porcelain. Many artists, potters and weavers have made their homes in the valley and their work can be seen at exhibitions which are held locally from time to time or by appointment.

Further information can be obtained from the Huguenot Memorial Museum in Franschhoek.

**WINERIES ON THE
FRANSCHHOEK WINE ROUTE**

Bellingham, Boschendal, Clos Cabrière, Dieu Donné et De Lucque Vineyards, Franschhoek Vineyards Co-operative, Haute Provence, La Bourgogne, La Bri, La Couronne, La Motte, La Provence, L'Ormarins, Môreson Blois and Mouton Excelsior.

—TULBAGH—
WINE ROUTE

On the night of the twenty ninth of September 1969, time stood still in the Boland. At four minutes past ten, the clock on the church tower in Ceres shuddered and stopped. An earthquake with Tulbagh as its epicentre had struck and the ripples of this subterranean upheaval were felt as far afield as Durban. Miraculously few lives were lost but damage to property was extensive. Within less than 24 hours, a meeting was convened to discuss ways of restoring historic buildings or saving them from demolition. The ultimate result was the complete restoration of Church Street in Tulbagh. With its restored eighteenth- and nineteenth-century charm, Tulbagh and environs were a magnet to potters, painters and sculptors who came to settle and work there. Their work can be seen in the local galleries, shops and workshops.

Tulbagh, a paradise for mountaineers and hikers, lies in a basin formed by the Witzenberg, Winterhoek and Ubiqua mountains. Viticulture was practised in the valley almost from the time the first Dutch settlers arrived there in the closing days of the seventeenth century. The five estate wineries, one co-operative cellar and one sherry producer are close to the town and to one another.

The area has many 'firsts' to its credit. The Krones, owners of the historic Twee Jongegezellen Estate were pioneers in the process of cold fermentation and night harvesting and are the only producers of *méthode champenoise* sparkling wine in the area. The Tulbagh Co-operative Winery, formed in 1906 as the Drostdy Co-operative, and situated in

---

**WINERIES ON THE
TULBAGH WINE ROUTE**

Kloofzicht, Lemberg, Montpellier, Paddagang Wine House and Vineyards, Theuniskraal, Tulbagh Co-operative Wine Cellar and Twee Jongegezellen.

---

the hamlet of Drostdy, is the oldest in the country, and South Africa's oldest sherry cellar is housed in the Oude Drostdy, once the seat of the Tulbagh magistracy.

Paddagang in Church Street was the first of a series of wine houses established by KWV to promote the enjoyment of wine with food. It is home to Paddagang Vignerons who also produce and sell a range of wines with fun frog labels.

Further information can be obtained from the Tulbagh Publicity Association or the museum.

—WORCESTER—
WINE ROUTE

There are 19 co-operative and five privately owned wineries on this extensive route which stretches from Villiersdorp in the south to Wolseley at its north-western extremity and De Doorns in the north-east. Rawsonville, to the south of Worcester, is the centre of the most heavily vine-populated area in the country. It is served by nine co-operative cellars and two privately owned wineries, all situated within a 15-kilometre radius of the village. Wines can be tasted and purchased from most producers on the Worcester Wine Route and cellar tours can be arranged.

The town of Worcester lays claim to being the capital of the Breede River Valley. Laid out in 1820 on the instructions of Governor Lord Charles Somerset, it was to serve as the centre of a new magisterial district in the Cape Colony. The Drostdy, seat of the magistracy, built in the Cape Georgian style in 1825, is today the oldest building in Worcester.

Worcester offers the visitor a number of unusual attractions. One of them, the Kleinplasie Farm Museum, daily features live demonstrations of the crafts of yesteryear. Presenters, dressed in appropriate period garb, perform numerous procedures from sheep shearing, spinning and dyeing to the distilling of a type of eau de vie, popularly known as *witblits*, or white lightning. In addition, the museum has permanent outdoor and indoor exhibitions of farm implements and machinery. For those interested in outdoor activities, there are water sport facilities on the Worcester and Brandvlei dams and there are many trails for the hiker and mountaineer. The town has its own golf course.

The Kleinplasie complex is the venue for the local agricultural and industrial shows, the regional wine show and the annual Winelands Festival. It also boasts a restaurant where traditional Cape fare is offered and a shop where wines of the district can be bought. A limited number of self-contained cottages on the complex are available for hire.

Worcester boasts several cultural history museums and art galleries, some featuring in permanent collections the work of famous local artists such as Hugo Naudé, Jean Welz, Paul du Toit and Bill Davis. The town also serves as a centre for the education and care of the deaf and visually handicapped. Handicrafts made in the work centres of these institutions are offered for sale.

The Karoo National Botanic Garden is situated 4 kilometres from the centre of the town. Its 144 hectares incorporate 10 hectares of landscaped gardens containing a variety of plants, in particular succulents, from other desert or semi-desert regions of South Africa.

Further information can be obtained from the permanent offices of the Worcester Winelands Association at Kleinplasie or the Worcester Publicity Association.

WINERIES ON THE
WORCESTER WINE ROUTE

Aan-de-Doorns Co-operative Winery, Aufwaerts Co-operative Wine Cellar, Badsberg Co-operative Wine Cellar, Bergsig, Botha Co-operative Wine Cellar, Brandvlei Co-operative Winery, De Doorns Co-operative Wine Cellar, De Wet Co-operative Wine Cellar, Du Toitskloof Co-operative Wine Cellar, Goudini Co-operative Wine Cellar, Groot Eiland Co-operative Wine Cellar, Lebensraum, Louwshoek Voorsorg Co-operative Wine Cellar, Merwida Co-operative Wine Cellar, Nuy Wine Cellar Co-operative, Opstal, Overhex Co-operative Wine Cellar, Romansrivier Co-operative, Slanghoek Co-operative Wine Cellar, Villiersdorp Moskonfyt and Fruit Co-operative and Waboomsrivier Co-operative Wine Cellar.

— ROBERTSON —
WINE ROUTE

The Robertson Wine Trust was formed in 1983 to promote the wines of Robertson, Bonnievale, Ashton and McGregor. Not all member farms of the Robertson Wine Trust are open to the public. However, most have tasting and sales facilities and offer cellar tours. An attractively illustrated booklet issued by the Trust giving details is obtainable from any of the producers on the route or from the Trust's permanent office in Robertson.

The soils of the district are rich in lime, an important element in producing well-balanced wines. Lime-rich soil is equally important for building strong bones in the horses for which the area is famous. It is home to the Bar (Bonnievale-Ashton-Robertson) Valley Horsebreeding Association whose members have bred some of the country's finest racehorses.

The Breede River, which flows into the Indian Ocean between Witsand and Infanta on the Cape's south coast, is the valley's main artery. Viticulture and, indeed, most other branches of agriculture in this thirsty region could not survive without its life-giving water. The area is traversed by a myriad of hiking and mountain trails that weave through a landscape which is transformed into a floral wonderland in the springtime. The Robertson district is also renowned for its roses, and the rose garden at Van Loveren in particular is worth a visit.

Historic sites abound and the village of McGregor appears to have been plucked out of the nineteenth century and placed, Rip van Winkle-like, with modern, tarred access roads, into the present. All sections of the wine route are within easy reach of the towns of Swellendam, with its Drostdy Museum and tapestry of historic buildings, and Montagu,

famous for its hot mineral springs and the charm of its preserved buildings. Another popular attraction is Silwerstrand, a holiday resort 3 kilometres distant from the Robertson Town Hall and set on the banks of the Breede River at a point where many of the hiking trails converge.

Ashton is the centre of a thriving fruit and vegetable canning industry, while Bonnievale is the home of the Bonnita cheese factory to which visitors are welcome. Several antique shops specializing in Cape furniture are located in Ashton, Montagu and Swellendam.

Further information can be obtained from the Robertson Publicity Association.

WINERIES ON THE
ROBERTSON WINE ROUTE

Agterkliphoogte Co-operative Wine Cellar, Ashton Co-operative Wine Cellar, Bon Courage, Bonnievale Co-operative, Clairvaux Co-operative Winery, De Wetshof, Langverwacht Co-operative Winery, McGregor Co-operative Winery, Merwespont Co-operative Winery, Mon Don, Nordale Co-operative Winery, Robertson Co-operative Winery, Roodezandt Co-operative Winery, Rooiberg Co-operative, Van Loveren, Weltevrede and Zandvliet.

— SWARTLAND —
WINE ROUTE

It is believed that the name Swartland is derived from the renosterbos, a plant common to the area, which acquires a black appearance at certain times of the year. Malmesbury, with a population of fewer than 20 000, is the largest centre on this route which is set in the heart of the Cape's grainlands. There are four co-operatives and one privately owned winery on this route, that includes the districts of Mamre, Malmesbury, Riebeek Kasteel and Riebeek West to the south and Porterville and Piketberg, to the north.

Malmesbury is a large milling centre and hosts an annual bread festival. There are several interesting buildings in the town including the synagogue on the banks of the Diep River. The building was granted to the town by the Jewish community and now serves as a museum.

The charming little towns of Riebeek Kasteel and Riebeek West, only 3 kilometres apart, are set against the northern slopes of Kasteelberg. Riebeek West is the birthplace of

A sign indicating the Swartland Wine Route.

General Jan Smuts, a former South African prime minister and international statesman. His house has been declared a National Monument and now serves as a museum. Another centre for deciduous fruit, wine and grain farming enterprises, Piketberg is set at the foot of a mountain range from which it derives its name. All the towns on the Swartland Wine Route are within comfortable distance of the hauntingly stark west coast and the Langebaan Lagoon.

WINERIES ON THE
SWARTLAND WINE ROUTE

Allesverloren, Mamreweg Wine Cellar Co-operative, Porterville Wine Cellars, Riebeek Wine Cellar Co-operative and Swartland Co-operative Wine Cellar.

— OLIFANTSRIVIER —
WINE ROUTE

This route traverses some 200 kilometres of countryside that take the visitor from almost sea level to a point 900 metres above it in the rugged Cederberg range. It stretches between Citrusdal in the south and Lutzville, near the mouth of the Olifants River on the West Coast, to the north.

Only the Khoi and the nomadic San hunters, toughened by countless centuries in nature's school of survival, could withstand the rigours of life in parts of this territory. It was only once the waters of the Olifants River were harnessed that any form of cultivation became possible. To the uninitiated eye much of this land looks like barren wasteland.

Of the seven producers on this route, which follows the course of the river, six are co-operative wineries including Vredendal Co-operative, the largest winery under one roof in South Africa. Cederberg Cellars high up in the Cederberg mountains, is privately owned.

The Cederberg range with its crystal mountain pools, caves and wealth of rock paintings has long been a favourite venue for hikers, mountaineers, nature lovers, anthropologists, ethnographers, artists and archaeologists. Indeed, much of the territory covered by the wine route is a treasure-house of rock art and artefacts from prehistory.

During spring the area teems with visitors who come from all over the world to see the explosive display of floral colour which, after a winter of above-average rainfall, seems to burst from the arid ground as if by magic. Given favourable conditions, this dazzling tapestry of wild flowers stretches in a broad band from the West Coast, just north of Cape Town through the heart of Namaqualand to Springbok, almost 500 kilometres distant and beyond. The area between Citrusdal and Clanwilliam also supports a thriving citrus industry.

Water sports enthusiasts are well catered for with facilities on the Clanwilliam Dam. The town is the centre of the rooibos tea area and boasts a nature reserve and holiday resort which stretches down to the shores of the dam. A museum, a commercial art gallery, quaint country shops and a shoe factory selling footwear largely made by hand are also to be found. Sitting outside the Vanmeerhof Country Stall at the Piekenierskloof Resort Complex, you can enjoy a spectacular view over the Citrusdal Valley.

Sixty kilometres to the west lies Lamberts Bay where the cold Atlantic waters deliver a bounty of crayfish in the summer and snoek in the winter to the local fisheries and the hardy fishing community. Fish and crayfish are not the only harvests taken from the sea. Doringbaai, north of Lamberts Bay, is the base from where diamonds are plucked from the ocean floor by divers and dredgers. The guano islands in these parts have become the roosting and breeding grounds of a diversity of marine birds such as cormorant, gannet, tern and jackass penguin.

An extremely popular attraction is Muisbosskerm, situated 3 kilometres south of the town. This 'restaurant' is set on the beach where the only shelter from the blowing sand and Atlantic spray is a matting of dried bushes piled up to create a windbreak. The appointments are equally primitive and disposable paper plates in wicker holders are provided while mussel shells serve as cutlery.

The food, strongly biased to marine and local traditional dishes, is served al fresco, buffet style. It ranges from bokkoms – whole, unscaled, dried, salted fish; usually harders, or grey mullet – to barbecued snoek, crayfish, stews based on edible plants indigenous to the area and bread baked in a clay oven while you wait.

In parts the route follows the trails of the early Dutch explorers and the countryside is sprinkled with museums and memorabilia that recall these expeditions. One place of particular interest is the Heerenlogement, or Gentleman's Lodge, a cave in the Vredendal district, used as a shelter by the colonist travellers as far back as 1662. Vredendal is a good base from which to tour the producers at the northern end of the route.

Information on the wine route can be obtained from the Olifantsrivier Wine Trust or the West Coast Tourism Bureau.

WINERIES ON THE OLIFANTSRIVIER WINE ROUTE

Cederberg Cellars, Citrusdal Co-operative Wine Cellar, Klawer Co-operative Wine Cellar, Lutzville Vineyards Co-operative, Spruitdrift Co-operative Wine Cellar, Trawal Co-operative Wine Cellar and Vredendal Co-operative Wine Cellar.

— KLEIN KAROO — WINE ROUTE

One hundred years ago such wealth as existed in the parched Little Karoo came from *Struthio camelus*, that ungainly flightless bird. The ostrich barons built ostrich palaces, as their ostentatious dwellings became known. In 1913, when they exported the equivalent of around six million rands worth of feathers, they were barons; in 1914, when the

market collapsed, they were ruined. Many of them then turned their attentions to the vine and in so doing helped create a new problem – overproduction.

Today some of the ostrich palaces still exist as monuments to those halcyon days and ostrich farming is doing very well, albeit on a more modest scale. Viticulture has also become firmly rooted in this semi-desert region and ostriches and vines can still be seen side by side in these parts.

De Rust is at the eastern extremity of this, the furthest wine route from Cape Town. Domein Doornkraal has a shop and tasting room on the road from Oudtshoorn to Beaufort West through Meiringspoort where one can purchase wines with evocative, fun names such as Kuierwyn, Serenade and Tickled Pink.

There is plenty of interest to see in Oudtshoorn with the world-famous Cango Caves 19 kilometres distant, and its ostrich palaces and historic buildings with their distinctive, regional architecture, situated in the town. The town is home to the giant Kango Co-operative of which the winery is only part. Douglas Green Bellingham has a depot there. The C.P. Nel Museum chronicles the history of the town and its environs. Oudtshoorn also boasts the only ostrich abattoir in the country and possibly the world. Visitors can buy a bewildering array of ostrich products from ostrich eggs and jewellery made from their shells, to shoes, clothing, handbags and briefcases made from their leather. Ostrich meat is a delicacy gaining in popularity. In the district there is also a crocodile farm, an angora rabbit farm and several ostrich farms that cater to visitors.

Approximately 50 kilometres to the west lies Calitzdorp where there is a wine route within a wine route. Prior to the formation of the Klein Karoo Wine Route, Calitzdorp Co-operative, Die Krans and Boplaas established the Calitzdorp Wine Route which still operates independently. Boplaas, where wine was first made approximately 150 years ago, is also well known for its fruit rolls, a confection made from minced, dried fruit.

Still moving westwards, now through the Huis River Pass, you arrive at Ladismith, with the Towerkop in the Klein Swartberg range looming in the background like a protecting sentinel. This is the home of the Towerkop cheese factory which invites the visitor to taste its products. The Barrydale Co-operative, some 70 kilometres west of Ladismith, is the only co-operative winery producing brandy. Montagu, the most westerly point of this wine route, where one emerges from the Little Karoo through the scenic Cogmanskloof.

Montagu is the centre of a flourishing fruit farming district renowned for its stone fruits and apples. Its hot mineral springs have made it a popular holiday and health resort. Immaculately maintained examples of nineteenth-century Cape architecture can be seen around the town. A walk down Long Street with its gleaming white dwellings, most of them National Monuments, is like a stroll through a bygone world. The town and environs boast three hotels, some excellent guest houses and restaurants, interesting shops, a museum,

a library with a collection of old documents and photographs relating to Montagu's early history and a number of walking, hiking and mountaineering trails.

The Little Karoo is separated from the coastal belt and Garden Route by an unbroken line of mountain ranges. A series of picturesque mountain passes links the two making it easy for the traveller to enjoy the many attractions of both these wonderful worlds. SIMON RAPPOPORT

WINERIES ON THE KLEIN KAROO WINE ROUTE

Barrydale Co-operative Winery and Distillery, Boplaas, Calitzdorp Fruit and Wine Cellar Co-operative, Die Krans, Domein Doornkraal, Kango Co-operative, Ladismith Co-operative Winery and Distillery, Mons Ruber, Montagu Muskadel Farmers' Co-operative, Rietrivier Wine Cellar Co-operative, Ruiterbosch Mountain Vineyards and Soetwyn Boere Co-operative.

— RESTAURANTS —

RECOMMENDED IN THE WINELANDS

Constantia: *The Old Cape Farm Stall Coffee Shop*, at the entrance to Groot Constantia; *Buitenverwachting Restaurant* on the estate.

Durbanville: *De Oude Welgemoed* off Jip de Jager Street; *Hansel and Gretel* in the Durbanville Centre; *La Verona* in Visserhok Road.

Stellenbosch: *Cameleon* in Dorp Street; *De Cameron* in Plein Street; *Doornbosch* on the Strand-Somerset West Road; *Mamma Roma* in the Stelmark Centre; *Lord Neethling* on Neethlingshof Estate; *Ralph's* in Andringa Street.

Somerset West: *Chez Michel* in Victoria Street; *Die Ou Pastorie* in Lourens Street; *L'Auberge du Paysan* off Firgrove Road between Stellenbosch and Somerset West.

Paarl: *Grande Roche* in Main Street; *Laborie Restaurant and Wine House* in Main Street; The *Victorian Restaurant* and *Victorian Terrace* on Rhebokskloof Estate; *Wagonwheels* in Lady Grey Street.

Franschhoek: *Boschendal Restaurant* and *Le Pique Nique* on Boschendal Estate; *Chez Michel* in Huguenot Road; *La Petite Ferme* on Franschhoek Pass; *Le Quartier Français* in Huguenot Road.

Tulbagh: *Paddagang* in Church Street.

Hermanus: *The Burgundy Restaurant* in Market Square.

Worcester: *Piccola Roma* in High Street.

Robertson: *Brandewynsdraai* in Riebeek West.

Swartland: *The Cook and Gardener Restaurant* in Riebeeck West.

Olifantsrivier: *Die Muisbosskerm* in Lambert's Bay.

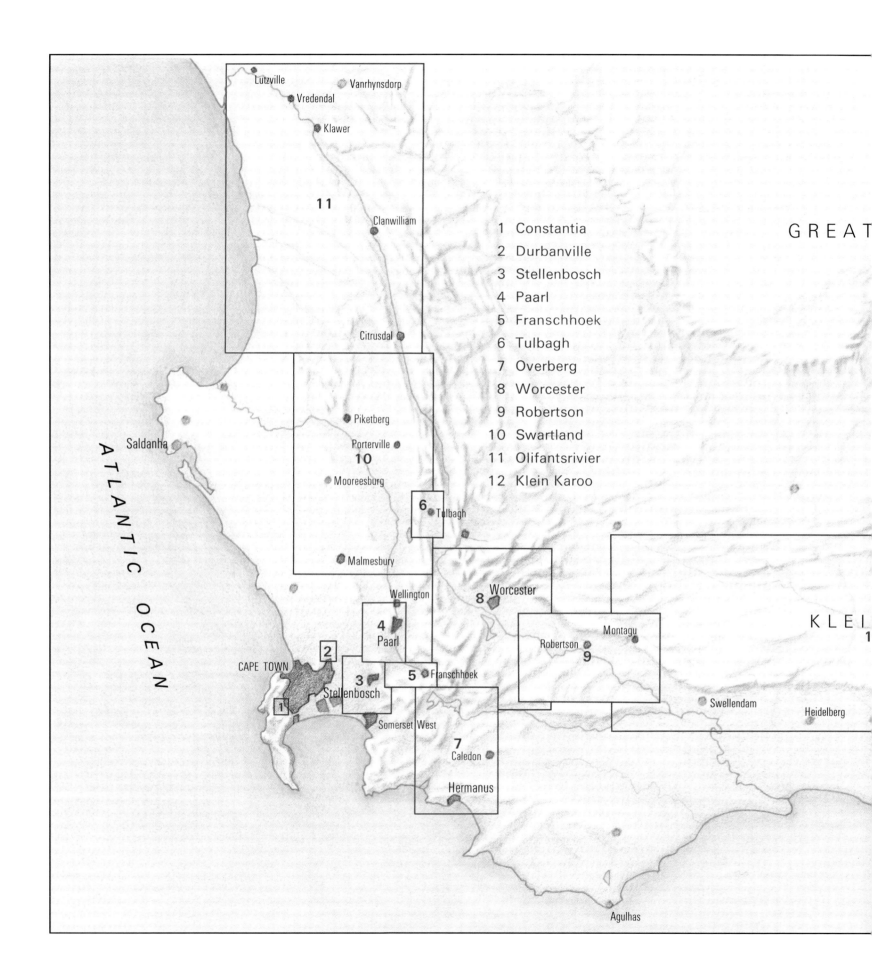

1 Constantia
2 Durbanville
3 Stellenbosch
4 Paarl
5 Franschhoek
6 Tulbagh
7 Overberg
8 Worcester
9 Robertson
10 Swartland
11 Olifantsrivier
12 Klein Karoo

Lutzville
Vanrhynsdorp
Vredendal
Klawer

11

Clanwilliam

GREAT

Citrusdal

ATLANTIC OCEAN

Saldanha

Piketberg
Porterville
10
Mooreesburg

6 Tulbagh

Malmesbury

Wellington

CAPE TOWN

4
Paarl

2

3
Stellenbosch

5 Franschhoek

Worcester
8

Robertson
9
Montagu

KLEI

1

Swellendam

Heidelberg

1

Somerset West

7
Caledon

Hermanus

Agulhas

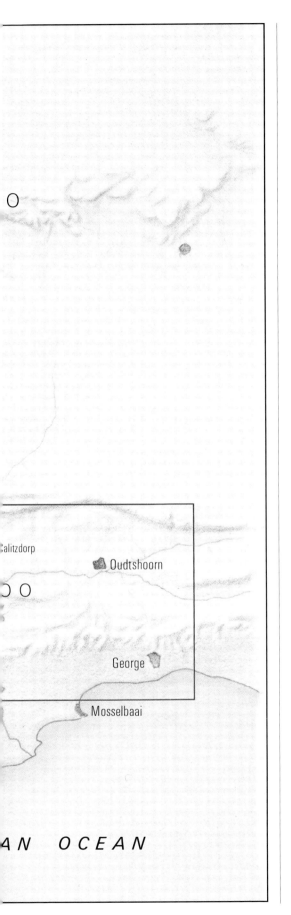

On the map: Calitzdorp, Oudtshoorn, George, Mosselbaai, AN OCEAN

THE WINELANDS
OF SOUTH AFRICA

Wine is a product of the land and its people. It brings together in its complex make-up all the qualities of soil and climate, the personalities of the individual varieties, the specific effects of each year's contribution of sun and rain, and the creativity of the individual wine master. In South Africa winelands life has been formalized and organized both in theory and in practice in the Wine of Origin legislation.

The Wine of Origin legislation came about during the early 1970s, and was developed in the local context from systems of long standing in the winelands of Europe where the relationship of wine to the land and its human society has been a profound part of the culture of countries such as France and Germany. In regions such as Bordeaux and Burgundy such systems have become highly developed, the contrasts of individual vineyards and *crus* being ramified by the vagaries of the French climate.

South Africa's Wine of Origin legislation divided the winelands into a number of official 'areas', now called 'districts'. To a great extent these reflected traditional divisions. From the early days of settlement different areas of the western Cape came to acquire their own character, both social and topographical, and to a remarkable degree these divisions survive today, not only in Divisional Council boundaries, but in the formal divisions of the winelands as well.

There are at present 10 districts. A number of the districts have subdivisions called wards: Simonsberg-Stellenbosch in the Stellenbosch district, Franschhoek in Paarl, and the Walker bay ward of the Overberg district are examples of these.

All these individual areas make up the modern map of the South African winelands, and the concept of Origin relates both to each area and to their sum. A number of groupings of the districts, however, are important both to the winemaker and the wine lover. These 'regions' are based on climate and geography.

The first of these groupings, usually called the Coastal region, includes the districts of Constantia, Durbanville, Stellenbosch, Paarl, Tulbagh and Swartland, which together make up the long crescent of land between the Atlantic Ocean and False Bay and the Cape folded mountains. Over much of this area the prevailing wind from the sea helps to cool the vines in this generally hot climate, leading to a better quality of grape and, of course, a better wine. The rainfall here, too, is relatively high, so that many of the vineyards may be grown with either a minimum of irrigation or with none at all, thereby promoting a rich, slow-growing crop. Thus, in general, much of the local high-quality natural wines are made from grapes grown in the Coastal region.

The Breërievervallei (or Breede River valley) region embraces the great run of the Breede River valley, from Worcester through to Robertson. Here, and throughout other wine-farming areas of the hinterland, hot conditions prevail in which grapes will generally not grow at all without some irrigation to supplement the generally meagre rainfall. With such irrigation, however, vines grow extremely well in the lime-rich soil; sometimes too well, for the speed of growth makes for a grape of high sugar content but with a sacrifice of the flavour constituents needed for the best kinds of wine. Thus, much of the country's distilling wine and fortified wine comes from the Breërievervallei region, though, increasingly, the inland winemakers are finding ways of making good quality natural wines in what were traditionally regarded as adverse conditions.

The Boberg region covers the catchment areas of the Berg River and the Klein Berg River, and comprises the districts of Paarl and Tulbagh, but only with regard to fortified wines. As far as natural wines are concerned, the Paarl and Tulbagh districts fall in the Coastal region.

The Klein Karoo region has no districts and only one ward, that of Montagu. It includes the towns of Oudtshoorn and Calitzdorp.

The Olifantsrivier region also has no districts but does have wards. These are the wards of Spuitdrift, Koekenaap, Lutzville-vallei and Vredendal.

The districts of Swellendam, Piketberg, Overberg and Douglas are not included in any regions, and while the Overberg has a ward, Walker Bay, there are wards which stand on their own, without relation to either district or region. These are the wards of Cederberg, Benede-Oranje and Andalusia.

THE ESTATE PRINCIPLE AND THE WINE OF ORIGIN SEAL

The concept of origin as it was legally applied in the local winelands found form in the principle of the estate. At its simplest, this means that the farmer both grows his own grapes, and makes his own wine from them. These two activities must take place within the boundaries of the estate; in other words, the relationship between the wine and land must be direct. Together with this provision went a number of others regarding cellar equipment and procedures, which had to be up to a rigorous standard before a farm could be granted estate status. The regulations did not cover bottling or distribution, which many estate farmers prefer to leave in the hands of a large wholesaler; nor did they in any way limit the number or type of variety grown or the kind of wine made.

The Wine of Origin seal is the aspect of the Wine of Origin legislation most familiar to the 'wine buyer in the street', and most likely to baffle him. The responsibility of the Wine and Spirit Board, it is affixed to some wines that are marketed. Its purpose is to provide a guarantee of those aspects of the wine related to the origin concept. These are the variety, and whether or not the farm concerned has estate status.

Where applicable all this information is included by the winemaker, with all appropriate flourish, on the main label on the bottle. The official seal simply confirms the veracity of the information by means of coloured bands.

It is interesting that wines with the Wine of Origin seal, important as they are, account for only some 10 per cent of good wine made in South Africa. Many of the most popular blended wines, therefore, do not carry the seal.

— THE LABEL —

For Wine of Origin certification the producer of the wine has to provide certain information on the label.
A Vintage year.
B Name of producer, i.e. estate or co-operative.
C Variety.
D Region, district or ward of origin.

— THE WINE OF ORIGIN SEAL —

Origin

Vintage

Cultivar/Variety

Estate

Superior

This guarantees that claims made on the label relating to origin, vintage and/or variety are certifiably true.

Origin *(Blue Band)* — certifies that 100% of the wine derives from the indicated region, district or ward.

Vintage *(Red Band)* — certifies that at least 75% of the wine is made from the grapes harvested in the indicated year.

Cultivar/Variety *(Green Band)* — certifies that the wine contains the required legal minimum percentage of the variety claimed, and is characteristic of the variety in appearance, smell and taste.

Estate — certifies that the wine is made on the estate claimed, and from grapes grown on the estate. Bottling may take place elsewhere.

Superior — as from March 1982 wines certified as Wine of Origin Superior (WOS) by the Wine and Spirit Board were given a distinctive gold-backed seal. Prior to this date Superior certified wines carried the plain Wine of Origin seal,

and since July 1990, the seal has been discontinued. Superior certification was only given for wines of origin and was the only quality grading that could be claimed for a South African wine. Originally in the case of WOS, 100% variety was required if a varietal claim was made. In December 1977, however, this was reduced to 75%.

The vertical number in the centre of the label is an official identification number and has little relevance for the consumer.

THE WINELANDS OF SOUTH AFRICA

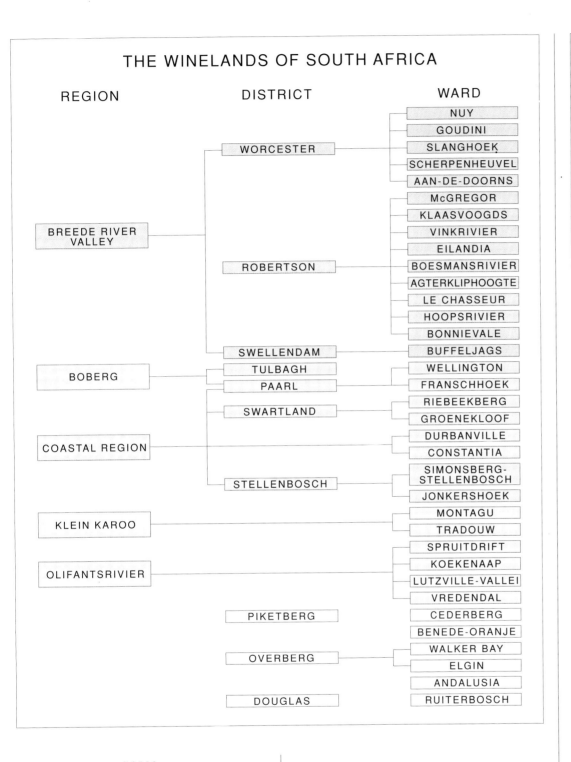

REGION	DISTRICT	WARD
		NUY
		GOUDINI
	WORCESTER	SLANGHOEK
		SCHERPENHEUVEL
		AAN-DE-DOORNS
		McGREGOR
		KLAASVOOGDS
		VINKRIVIER
BREEDE RIVER VALLEY		EILANDIA
	ROBERTSON	BOESMANSRIVIER
		AGTERKLIPHOOGTE
		LE CHASSEUR
		HOOPSRIVIER
		BONNIEVALE
	SWELLENDAM	BUFFELJAGS
BOBERG	TULBAGH	WELLINGTON
	PAARL	FRANSCHHOEK
	SWARTLAND	RIEBEEKBERG
		GROENEKLOOF
COASTAL REGION		DURBANVILLE
		CONSTANTIA
	STELLENBOSCH	SIMONSBERG-STELLENBOSCH
		JONKERSHOEK
KLEIN KAROO		MONTAGU
		TRADOUW
		SPRUITDRIFT
		KOEKENAAP
OLIFANTSRIVIER		LUTZVILLE-VALLEI
		VREDENDAL
	PIKETBERG	CEDERBERG
		BENEDE-ORANJE
	OVERBERG	WALKER BAY
		ELGIN
		ANDALUSIA
	DOUGLAS	RUITERBOSCH

—NOTES—

- The ward of Bonnievale lies mostly in the Robertson district, but part of the ward lies in the Swellendam district.
- Simonsberg-Stellenbosch is so named to identify it as being the Stellenbosch side of the Simonsberg.
- Boberg region is only recognized for fortified wines.
- The Wolseley part of the Tulbagh district is included in the Breëriviervallei region and the rest of the Tulbagh district in the coastal region. (In the case of fortified wines, though, the Tulbagh district falls in the Boberg region.)

—KEY TO VINEYARD MAPS—

RED GRAPE VARIETIES

ALB	Alicante Bouschet
CAF	Cabernet Franc
CAS	Cabernet Sauvignon
CAR	Carignan
CIN	Cinsaut
FDL	Ferdinand de Lesseps
GAM	Gamay
GRE	Grenache
MAL	Malbec
MER	Merlot
MUS	Muscadel (red)
PEV	Petit Verdot
PIN	Pinotage
PNR	Pinot Noir
PON	Pontac
SHI	Shiraz
SOU	Souzão
TIB	Tinta Barocca
ZIN	Zinfandel

WHITE GRAPE VARIETIES

AUX	Auxerrois
BUK	Bukettraube
CHA	Chardonnay
CHE	Chenel
CHB	Chenin Blanc (Steen)
CAN	Canaan
CAR	Cape (South African) Riesling
CIB	Cinsaut Blanc (Albatross)
CLB	Clairette Blanche
COL	Colombard
EAR	Erlihane
EMR	Emerald Riesling
FAP	False Pedro
FEP	Fernão Pires
FUR	Furmint
GEW	Gewürztraminer
HAR	Hárslevelü
KER	Kerner
MUS	Muscadel (white)
MUD	Muscat d'Alexandrie
MUF	Muscat de Frontignan
MUO	Muscat d'Ottonel
MOM	Morio Muscat
PAL	Palomino
PIB	Pinot Blanc
PIG	Pinot Gris
RAB	Raisin Blanc
SAB	Sauvignon Blanc
SEM	Sémillon
SYL	Sylvaner
THE	Therona
TRE	Trebbiano (Ugni Blanc)
WER	Weisser (Rhine) Riesling

CONSTANTIA

The Constantia district is ideally situated as it has a mild climate which is regarded by winemakers as one of the most suitable of its kind in the Cape winelands.

The history of wine-making in the Constantia valley dates back to the late seventeenth century, when Simon van der Stel was the first governor of the fledgling Dutch colony. Van der Stel created the estate of Constantia as the place to which he intended to retire at the end of his working days. Shrewd and acquisitive, he built up the farm piecemeal during his years in office, developing it into the largest single private vineyard in the area. Bought in 1695, at 770 hectares it was vastly out of proportion to the average grant of 12 hectares accorded to the local free burgher farmers. Later, he contrived to have himself granted a further 8 500 hectares of grazing rights, an area which amounted to virtually the whole of the Peninsula. The creation of the farm was crowned by the building of a palatial mansion. He set out to create a model farm, and in particular model vineyards, which were managed strictly in accordance with the rules laid down in the *Gardeners' Manual*.

Van der Stel's painstaking attention to detail and personal involvement in the harvesting and wine-making processes paid dividends and soon his estate was making natural wines of note. Not content with this achievement the Governor set about making a wine in the style of the sweet fortified wines that were becoming fashionable in England and Europe. Again he was successful and his wine, given the name 'Constantia', became widely acclaimed locally and abroad.

After Van der Stel's retirement from public life in 1699 and his subsequent death, Constantia passed through a series of owners. During this time, too, the original estate was divided into three sections: Groot Constantia, Bergvliet and Klein Constantia. In 1778, however, the fortunes of the valley changed for the better when Groot Constantia was bought by Hendrik Cloete, for it was this man – a direct descendant of Jacob Cloete van Kempen, Van Riebeeck's under-gardener – and his son, also Hendrik, who led the estate and the valley into a golden age and made it the focus of society at the Cape.

The story of these early years and the subsequent history of the valley, which in so many ways is the story of wine in South Africa, is told in greater detail in the first chapter of this book, 'A Historical Perspective'. Today the vineyards of Constantia are much reduced from former times, little more than pastoral islands in the midst of Cape Town's ever-extending peri-urban sprawl.

LEFT: *The magnificent Buitenverwachting homestead in the Constantia valley.*

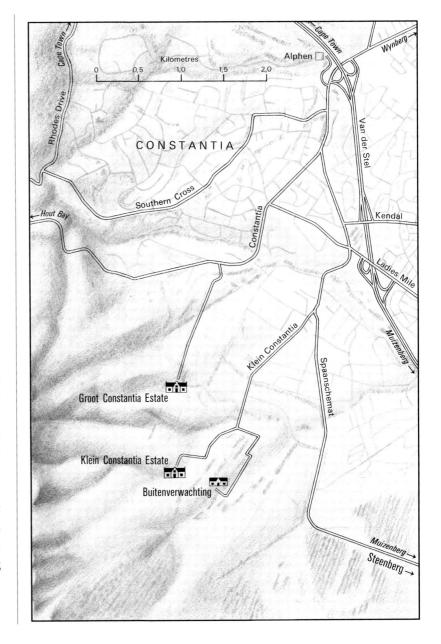

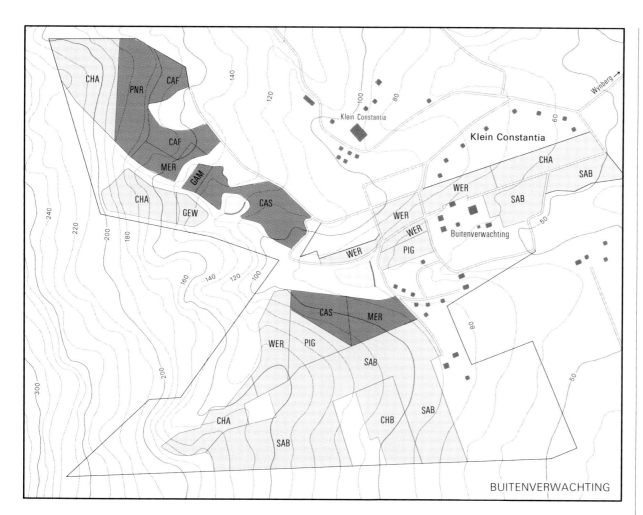

BUITENVERWACHTING

Jean Daneel, the cellarmaster.

The thatched cellar buildings at Buitenverwachting.

—BUITENVERWACHTING—

Buitenverwachting, meaning 'beyond expectations', is situated on the east-facing slopes of Constantiaberg some 12 kilometres from the False Bay coast. The farm, comprising 200 morgen of what was then known as Bergvliet, was sold to Cornelis Brink in 1793 as a subdivision of Simon van der Stel's huge farm Constantia. Since then this excellent wine-producing property has had no less than 16 owners and while several were plagued with insolvency, others such as Ryk Arnoldus Cloete, owner during the 1820s and brother of the famous Hendrik Cloete of Groot Constantia, were crowned with success, with approximately 90 000 vines having been planted by 1825.

From 1866 until the recent past the fortunes of Buitenverwachting were inextricably linked to those of the Louw and Lategan families, but in 1981 a new era for the farm began when the estate was bought by international businessman Richard Müller and his wife, Christina. With the Müllers came infusions of fresh capital and new energy, which, together with careful planning, have brought this historic farm back to life. Extensive replanting of the vineyards began immediately and today 75 hectares have been painstakingly prepared by three-directional ploughing. In so doing, the clay and top soils have been mixed to a depth of 1 metre, ensuring that a regular supply of moisture is maintained in the soil and providing the necessary depth for good root development. The vineyards of Buitenverwachting have been thoroughly planned with regard to soil types and microclimates, and are not irrigated at all, relying instead on the composition of the soils and the natural rainfall. From the first vintage the wines have proved the French saying that 'a good wine must be able to see the sea', as one can do so from the higher slopes.

The maiden harvest of 100 tonnes in 1985 was the first Buitenverwachting had seen for 30 years. Although relatively small in overall terms owing to the strict control exercised to prevent the new vines overbearing in their first year of production, it exceeded all expectations. The 1985 Rhine Riesling obtained a Superior rating. The cellarmaster at Buitenverwachting, Jean Daneel, attributes the excellent balance of the wine largely to the position of the vineyards, for the Constantia valley has long been regarded as one of the finest wine-growing areas in the country, and particularly suited to this variety.

The white wines were the first to be produced in the enormous new cellar. Designed with the traditional high semi-gables, white walls and lofty thatched roof so typical of the Cape, it is nevertheless ultra-modern, with the most up-to-date wine-making equipment. Completed in 1984, the cellar features a refrigerated bottle maturation area which

BUITENVERWACHTING

Varieties planted (ha)

Extended Perold trellis
Sauvignon Blanc 14
Chardonnay 13,2
Weisser Riesling 11,8
Cabernet Sauvignon 7,5
Chenin Blanc 6,4
Pinot Noir 5,86
Merlot 3,67
Pinot Gris 2,6

Total area under vines in 1991/2:
75 ha (5 ha still to be planted).
Irrigation: None.
Average temperatures:
Maximum 25 ˚C; minimum 10 ˚C.
Average annual rainfall: 1 000 mm.
Stock: Rooted vines are bought from a nursery.
**First wines bottled under the
Buitenverwachting label:** Buiten Blanc,
Pinot Gris, Blanc Fumé, Rhine Riesling,
Blanc de Noir (Gamay) and L'Arrivée.
**Wines currently bottled under the
Buitenverwachting label:** Buiten Blanc, Pinot
Gris, Blanc Fumé, Rhine Riesling, Chardonnay,
L'Arrivée and Brut Sparkling Wine. Future bottlings
will include Pinot Noir and a Bordeaux blend.
Wood ageing: Wine is aged in wood on the farm.
Cellar capacity: 7 000 hl.

Buitenverwachting is on the Constantia Wine Route.
Wine tastings take place from 09h00 to 17h00 on
weekdays and from 09h00 to 13h00 on Saturdays.
Cellar tours are conducted at 11h00 and 15h00 on
weekdays and 11h00 on Saturdays.

has a capacity of 3 000 small French barrels, hewn from Limosin and Nevers oak.

The old cellar, which has been restored along with all the other farm buildings and the homestead, is used for special wine-tastings. The kraal, which was converted into one of the most successful gourmet restaurants in the country, burned down in February 1987, but since its restoration in 1988 it has been voted one of the top 10 restaurants in South Africa.

The first red, a Burgundy-style Pinot Noir 1986, was released in 1989 and was followed by two classic Bordeaux-style blends, which were most successful and acclaimed at the 1988 Stellenbosch Young Wine Show. In 1986 one of the Cape's first nouveau-style Gamays in the Beaujolais tradition was made using the carbonic maceration process, and was released under the label L'Arrivée. Since then it has been launched each year at a L'Arrivée festival, along with other new wines.

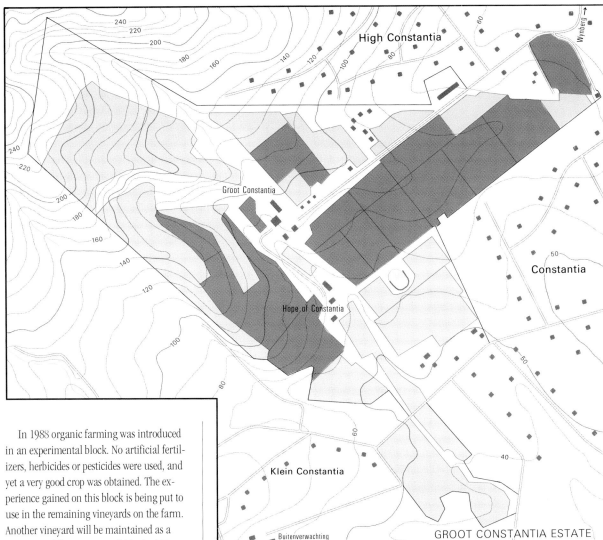

GROOT CONSTANTIA ESTATE

In 1988 organic farming was introduced in an experimental block. No artificial fertilizers, herbicides or pesticides were used, and yet a very good crop was obtained. The experience gained on this block is being put to use in the remaining vineyards on the farm. Another vineyard will be maintained as a memento of the past: a small block of Muscat d'Alexandrie table grapes which is about 100 years old but still bears magnificently.

The future of Buitenverwachting as a flourishing wine farm seems assured. Its wines have won many national and international awards, such as the 1990 SAA Trophy for the best white wine among those selected; a number of medals at the Wine and Spirit Competition in London; and a gold medal at Vinexpo 1989. The farm's achievements so far have indeed been beyond expectation.

GROOT CONSTANTIA
ESTATE

Of all the great wine estates in South Africa, few can compare with Groot Constantia in respect of its historic aura and the popular memory of its near-legendary wines of the late eighteenth and early nineteenth cen-

turies: the rich, sweet wines which, on cold winter nights, kept warm the poets and writers who celebrated them. And now, in the late twentieth century, this estate still makes wines, and very fine ones indeed.

This section of the venerable estate originally granted to Governor Simon van der Stel is a magnificent symbol of a past preserved. It is this historical atmosphere which draws, from all parts of the world, many thousands of visitors who wander along the tree-lined avenues and explore the beautifully restored homestead with its mysterious cellars and underground slave-quarters. The works of man have been lovingly preserved here, notably Hendrik Cloete's majestic two-storey wine cellar, with its allegorical plaster figures designed by Louis Thibault and executed by Anton Anreith, which stand as a tribute to those immigrant artists and

craftsmen who lent lightness and grace of design to the soberly symmetrical Cape Dutch architecture.

This estate has one of the most congenial climates of all the Cape wine districts. The dry summers of the Mediterranean type climate of the Cape are softened by the influence of two oceans, the Indian and the Atlantic which is just behind the Constantiaberg. Groot Constantia also has good soil, derived from Table Mountain sandstone. Some of its lower-lying fields are sandy as distinct from the Hutton and Clovelly forms on the rest of the farm. The bulk of the soils in their natural state are deep and cool with a good water-holding capacity, so irrigation is not used.

It is these general conditions which, for over three centuries, have given birth to Constantia's fine wines, from the sweet wines for which the estate first became famous to the Cabernet Sauvignon, Shiraz and Pinotage wines made today by the estate's winemaker, Pieter Daniël du Toit, a graduate of Stellenbosch University who spent a number of years at Nederburg and the Robertson Cooperative before coming to Constantia.

In spite of the weight of its history and the overtones of the past which linger around the house itself, Groot Constantia still operates very much as a living farm. Though owned by the state, its general activities are now supervised by a Board of Control. It is run on a free enterprise basis and shows a profit.

A registered estate, its wines are entirely grown, pressed, matured, bottled and sold to the public on the estate itself. Of the varieties grown in the earlier days, only Chenin Blanc and Muscat d'Alexandrie remain, albeit new and more effective clones. The 100 hectares of the area now under vines are producing 650 tonnes of grapes annually, but this will be progressively increased to an eventual 950 tonnes.

Problems have been experienced with troops of baboons from the neighbouring mountain, who have made periodic raids on the vineyards. The Weisser Riesling which is planted on the higher ground, appeared to be particularly favoured, and on one occasion so much damage was done to the crop that it had to be harvested early, with a comparatively low sugar content of 19 °Balling, but this notwithstanding, the resultant wine turned out to be as good as ever.

Recent events in Groot Constantia's history include the opening of a wine museum in part of the old cellar. Completed in 1971,

The entrance to the historic estate of Groot Constantia admits thousands of tourists every year.

it was enlarged in 1980. A modern and much larger cellar was also subsequently built in which the 1983 harvest was the first to be processed. Besides the restored homestead and the wine cellar, attractions include two restaurants and the wine museum at the rear of the cellar. The museum provides an ideal introduction both to Constantia and the culture of wine in general.

Some years ago an historic encounter of another kind took place. A number of precious bottles of old Constantia wine were discovered in the cellar of the Duke of Northumberland at Alnwick Castle in the north of England, and some of these were brought

back to South Africa, where they were opened and tasted with all due ceremony. Made from Cloete's famous 1791 vintage, the wine proved to be a magnificent deep amber in colour, with a tinge of yellowy-gold round the edge. When poured into tasting glasses it greeted the twentieth century with a sweet and fruity bouquet, typical of Muscadel-type dessert wines. There were no off-odours, a remarkable achievement in itself after almost two centuries in the bottle. Its flavour proved to be fine and delicate, surprisingly balanced although slightly lacking in acid. Some maderization was present. A little tannin was detected, but the general consensus was that

this was a wine of great richness and character which fully lived up to its legend. Traces of the bouquet of the wine lingered in the glass for many hours after the tasting, surviving as it has through the decades both as a symbol and as a living reality, like Groot Constantia itself.

After this romantic taste of the past a more objective and sober assessment of the wine was made when, on an accepted judging scale, it scored a decisive 18,7 out of 20. It was also subjected to analysis at Nietvoorbij, where it was discovered that it had an alcohol content of 15,03 per cent, a total acidity of 7,1 (remarkable in a wine of this age) and a spectacular sugar content of 128,3 grams per litre.

GROOT CONSTANTIA ESTATE

Varieties planted (ha)

Vertical 3-wire trellis
Cabernet Sauvignon 30
Chardonnay 17
Shiraz 11
Sauvignon Blanc 10
Pinotage 6
Merlot 5
Cabernet Franc 5
Gewürtzraminer 3,5
Weisser Riesling 3,5
Chenin Blanc 2
Muscat d'Alexandrie 2
Sémillon 2
Pinot Noir 2
Tinta Barocca 1

Total area under vines in 1991/2:
95 ha (6 ha still to be planted).
Irrigation: None.
Average temperatures:
Average maximum 20,8 °C; average minimum 12,7 °C.
Average annual rainfall: Approximately 1 253 mm.
Stock: Rooted vines are bought from a nursery.
First wines bottled under the Groot Constantia label: Cabernet Sauvignon 1983 and Shiraz 1983 (Groot Constantia has been famous for its wines since the eighteenth century).
Wines currently bottled under the Groot Constantia label: Pinotage, Shiraz, Cabernet Sauvignon, Stein, Bouquet Blanc, Blanc de Blanc, Weisser Riesling, Heerenrood, Constantia Rood, Sauvignon Blanc, Chardonnay, Vintage Port, Gouverneurs Reserve and Noble Late Harvest.
Wood ageing: Wines are aged in wood on the estate.
Cellar capacity: 9 600 hl.

Groot Constantia Estate is on the Constantia Wine Route and is open to visitors for cellar tours and the sale of wine seven days a week between 10h00 and 17h00.

Ross Gower, the winemaker at Klein Constantia.

—KLEIN CONSTANTIA—
ESTATE

Part of the famous Groot Constantia estate until 1819, Klein Constantia was farmed by a succession of owners until 1913, when it was bought by Abraham Lochner de Villiers of Paarl and his wealthy wife Clara Hussey. This colourful couple entertained on a grand scale, and farming was only of secondary interest to them.

When Cape Town-born businessman Duggie Jooste bought the estate in 1980, only 30 hectares of the total of 146 hectares were planted to vines and these vines were in extremely poor condition. Furthermore the farm was overgrown with alien Port Jackson willows and the buildings were dilapidated and in urgent need of repair.

Fortunately Duggie, heir to a liquor business started by his grandfather, was aware of the potential of the property and realized that everything needed for success was there in the form of excellent soils, mesoclimate and topography. From the start Duggie approached experts for advice about what needed to be done, and now-retired viticulturist Professor Chris Orffer of Stellenbosch and viticulturist and oenologist Ernst le Roux, then chief viticulturist at Nederburg, were consulted on the vineyards.

As far as natural resources and location are concerned, the estate is richly endowed. Distinctive mesoclimatological variations exist, attributable to the variance in elevation above sea level, from 72 metres on the north-facing slopes to 440 metres on the south-facing slopes. This enables the successful cultivation of later-ripening varieties such as Cabernet Sauvignon on the lower slopes and Weisser Riesling and Chardonnay on the higher slopes, where the latter reach full potential under cool growing conditions.

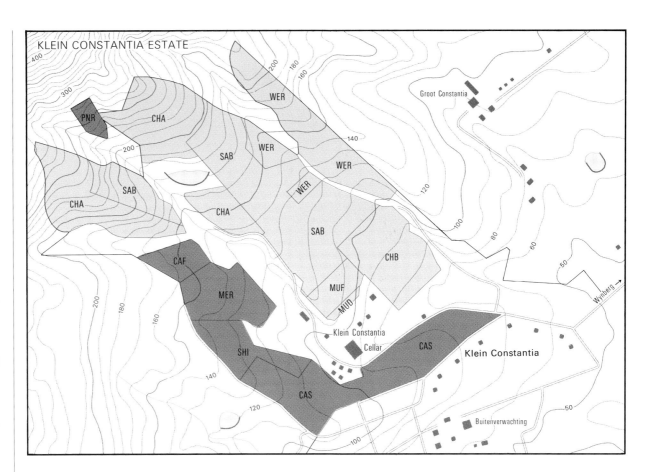

The beautifully restored homestead at Klein Constantia is the home of Lowell Jooste, son of Duggie Jooste, owner of the estate.

Vines on the estate of Klein Constantia, from where the waters of False Bay can be seen.

The kramat of one of the last sultans of Malacca, banished to the Cape in 1667, stands on the estate of Klein Constantia.

Ernst le Roux came to Klein Constantia as general manager and viticulturist and was asked to draw up a development plan for the farm. An even more intensive soil survey was done which showed that the soils were mainly of granitic origin and were deep, red, fertile and well drained, mainly Hutton types with sufficient water-holding capacity to facilitate dryland cultivation. Even the virgin soils were found to have a high pH and to be rich in calcium. The soil was prepared and finally became ready for planting by mid-1982. The very best clonal propagation material from Ernita Nursery was used at Klein Constantia, and the planting of new vineyards – now completed – proceeded at a rate of approximately 15 hectares per year.

The thatched roof of the homestead at Klein Constantia was renewed and the old wine cellar has also been thatched, but is not used for pressing. No wine had been made on this estate for nearly 50 years when, in 1986, the first grapes since 1937 were crushed in the new cellar, which was completed in the same year. Consulting the wine-maker, Ross Gower, about the practical aspects of such a cellar, the well-known Cape Town architect Gawie Fagan designed it partially below ground level to reduce the impact on the beautiful natural surroundings of a large building. The underground cellar provides ideal maturation conditions and the impressive barrel-vaulted ceilings lend a unique atmosphere. A new underground maturation cellar was completed in 1990. The innovative design of the cellar incorporates features such as pre-cast columns, walls and roof, and is connected to the existing winery by a short tunnel, all covered with two metres of soil. Thus, an even, cool temperature

KLEIN CONSTANTIA ESTATE

Varieties planted (ha)

5-wire hedge
Sauvignon Blanc 17,0
Chardonnay 15,8
Cabernet Sauvignon 10,6
Weisser Riesling 9,2
Chenin Blanc 6,4
Merlot 4,3
Shiraz 4,2
Muscat de Frontignan 2,4
Cabernet Franc 2,1
Pinot Noir 0,5
Pontac 0,5

Total area under vines in 1991/2: 73 ha.
Irrigation: Only the Chenin Blanc is irrigated.
Average temperatures: No records are available.
Average annual rainfall: 1 200 mm.
Stock: Rooted vines are bought from a nursery.
**First wines bottled under the Klein Constantia
label:** Sauvignon Blanc and Rhine Riesling
(both 1987 vintage).
**Wines currently bottled under the Klein
Constantia label:** Sauvignon Blanc, Rhine
Riesling, Chardonnay, Cabernet Sauvignon, Shiraz
and Vin de Constance (wines marketed by SFW).
Wood ageing: The wine is aged in wood on
the estate.
Cellar capacity: 800 tonnes of grapes per year.

Klein Constantia Estate is on the Constantia Wine
Route and is open to the public for wine tastings
and sales on weekdays from 09h00 to 17h00 and
on Saturdays from 09h00 to 13h00.
Tours are conducted by appointment.

The cellar at Steenberg, which is to be restored as part of a plan to redevelop the property.

is maintained without the need for expensive air-conditioning.

In the first vintage of the renovated estate, when Sauvignon Blanc, Weisser Riesling, Cabernet Sauvignon and Shiraz were made, winemaker Ross Gower's talent was proved immediately: Klein Constantia won the Johann Graue Memorial Trophy for the

CONSTANTIA WINE OF ORIGIN

**KLEIN
CONSTANTIA**

ESTATE WINE

1987
CABERNET SAUVIGNON

A296 GROWN MADE AND BOTTLED ON THE ESTATE
PRODUCE OF SOUTH AFRICA 750 ml

champion South African dry white wine, with his 1986 Sauvignon Blanc. Ross is no newcomer to wine-making: Prior to starting at Klein Constantia he had 13 years' experience in Germany, New Zealand, France, and at Nederburg, where he worked under Günter Brözel. Two whites, a Sauvignon Blanc and a Rhine Riesling, were released in mid-March 1987 and the first Chardonnay grapes came into the cellar in the same year.

It has taken over 300 years, but immaculate vineyards now stretch well up the mountainside where vines have never before been planted. The build-up of humus in this virgin soil, together with its inherently good water-retaining capacity, enable the vines to be grown without irrigation. Such is the gradient that the higher vineyards have had to be contoured to prevent soil erosion, but one problem Klein Constantia never has is the presence of grape-eating birds, thanks to the preying Steppe Buzzards which migrate from the vast plains of Russia and frequent the Constantia valley between the months of October and March. As soon as they migrate north in April, hundreds of starlings descend on the vineyards, but by then there are only a few grapes left.

Another delight of the Constantia wine-growing area is the cooler climate which allows grapes to ripen slowly without losing volatile flavour compounds. This is why Klein Constantia's crop is picked two to three weeks later than most other areas in South Africa and at a higher sugar level than most. The wines are left on the lees for at least two months, in the French style, and are filtered as little as possible. As a result of the long skin contact (18 and 24 hours for the whites), the wines are slightly deeper in colour and more fully flavoured than most. Only the best wines are bottled under the estate's label and the rest is generally sold in bulk to merchants.

Cultivation practices followed are aimed at producing premium quality grapes for noble wines of distinction. The Klein Constantia Cabernet Sauvignon and Shiraz released in 1990 have built on the early promise shown by previous whites. But there is much more to look forward to from Klein Constantia, as farm manager Kobus Jordaan, Ross, Duggie and his son Lowell, who helps in the day-to-day running of the farm (Ernst le Roux having returned to Nederburg), make a formidable team.

— STEENBERG —

In 1688, the land then known as 'Swaansweide' was granted to Catharina Ras by Simon van der Stel 'to cultivate, to plough and to sow and also to possess'. Six years later it was acquired by Frederik Roussouw who was married to Christina Diemer, to whom it passed on Roussouw's death. Today the land, now known as Steenberg, is owned by Johannesburg Consolidated Investments (JCI) who purchased it in 1990.

It is envisaged that the property will be redeveloped into a flourishing wine farm. The historic homestead, which was built in 1695 by Frederik Roussouw, will be restored to its former beauty, as will the winery and the outbuildings.

The intention is to replant the vineyards with those varieties which will benefit the most from the cool temperatures and cool moist air of the region. Consequently, by 1996, a total area of 48,72 hectares should be under vines, approximately 80 per cent planted with Sauvignon Blanc, Chardonnay, Sémillon, Weisser Riesling and the remainder with Cabernet Sauvignon, Cabernet Franc and Merlot.

DURBANVILLE

Within a few years after the first whites settled at the Cape a tiny hamlet had sprung up at Pampoenkraal ('Pumpkin Kraal'). In those days the hills in the area were mostly devoted to wheat and cattle farming, but later they were shared with the vine. In 1836 the then governor of the Colony, Sir Benjamin D'Urban, was petitioned by the Pampoenkraalers to be allowed to call their village D'Urban. Subsequent confusion with the growing Natal city of Durban led to a further change to the present name of Durbanville.

Like that of Constantia, the arable area of Durbanville is rapidly dwindling, and for the same reason – urban expansion. In the case of Durbanville it is being swallowed by the City of Bellville, which has enclosed the Tygerberg, leaving only an enclave of wheat farmland and a handful of wine farms. These include the estates of Meerendal, Diemersdal, Altydgedacht and Bloemendal.

The location of the Durbanville vineyards suits them particularly to the making of high-quality wines, with an emphasis on fine reds. Lying mainly on the slopes, they receive the benefit of any cool wind off the Atlantic 15 kilometres to the west, and of south-easterly breezes off False Bay. These strong winds prevent the moist conditions on which many vine diseases flourish. The rainfall is modest, being some 357 millimetres per year. During the growing season, which is between the months of September and March, the average temperature is approximately 19 °C.

The soils in the area are predominantly of the Hutton and Clovelly types – deep, cool and well drained, but with a good water-holding capacity. Notwithstanding the low rainfall, the vineyards here, as in Constantia, are cultivated without irrigation, which is rendered unnecessary by the heavy dew and the water-retaining properties of the soil.

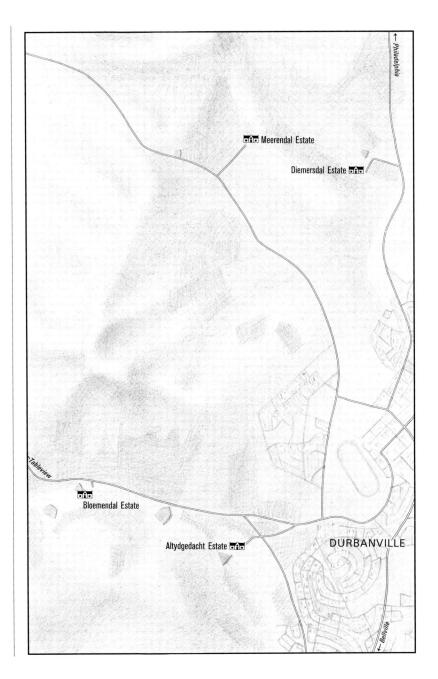

LEFT: *The sharp contrast of the wheatlands and vineyards in the Durbanville area make an arresting sight.*

—ALTYDGEDACHT—
ESTATE

Although boasting an unbroken tradition of wine-making stretching over more than 280 years, this picturesque farm was registered as an estate only in 1985, and produced the first wine bottled under its own label in the same year. Altydgedacht is one of the oldest wine farms in the Cape, with a cellar built in 1705, and inventories showing that wine was sold on the farm as early as 1730. In more recent years (until the mid-1960s) the entire grape crop was made into wine in the cellar and sold in bulk to merchants, notably Monis of Paarl. Lately, however, grapes have been sold directly to Nederburg, while some 10 per cent of the crop is made into wine on the Altydgedacht estate.

Beginning with Elsje van Suurwaarde (after whom is named the Elsieskraal River, commonly known by the abbreviated name of Elsies River), women have continued to play an important role in shaping the destiny of Altydgedacht.

Elsje's husband was an official of the Dutch East India Company, and therefore not permitted to own land; to circumvent this restriction, the farm was officially granted to Elsje in 1698 under the name 'De Tygerbergen'. The title deeds, signed by Simon van der Stel himself, can be seen on the estate, which was renamed 'Altydgedacht' (spelt 'Altijd Gedacht' in some documents) in 1826. Elsje outlived two husbands, both of them high officials of the Dutch East

John and Oliver Parker.

India Company: Andries de Man, and Henricus Munkerus.

The second woman to have a strong influence was Daisy Parker, mother-in-law of the present owner, Jean Parker. During the Depression of the 1930s, Daisy started a tearoom on the farm which proved to be extremely popular and provided an income which she put towards her sons' education.

During World War II Daisy (then widowed) courageously ran the farm while her three sons fought at the front.

For some three decades the farm was owned and run by Jean Parker. When she was widowed in 1954 and left with two sons, John and Oliver (the eldest not yet four years old), her family and her attorneys tried to persuade her to sell the farm, but she would not hear of it. Altydgedacht had belonged to the Parker family for over 100 years and she was determined to keep it. Running a farm is a formidable task, even more so for a woman as young as Jean was when her husband, Dennis, died. But this graduate of Rhodes University (with a degree in fine art and languages) attended courses at Elsenburg Agricultural College and with help from her farm staff and neighbours managed on her own for a few years until she was joined by

Hennie Heydenrych as farm manager. The untimely death of this great character in 1988, after 30 years as manager, mentor and friend at Altydgedacht, was a great loss. As a tribute, a specially selected wine each year bears a special seal with his signature. John is now a qualified viticulturist and chairman of the Durbanville Wine Trust.

Altydgedacht has had an interesting history over the last 300 years, and Jean tells of the time when the farm was used as a 'prison' for Napoleon's secretary, the Comte de Las Cases, who was held there for four months by the British. He had arrived at the Cape from St Helena before returning to

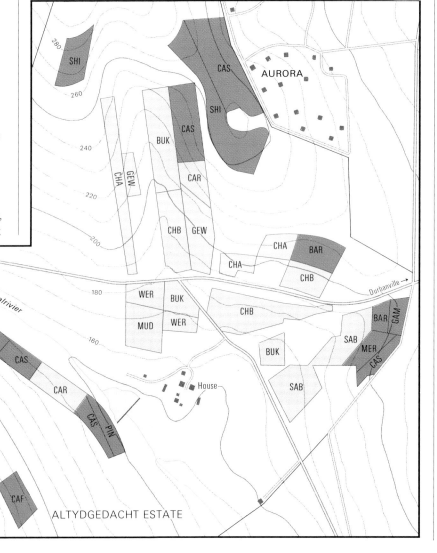

ALTYDGEDACHT ESTATE

ALTYDGEDACHT ESTATE

Varieties planted (ha)

Bush vines
Chenin Blanc 35,7
Perold trellis and bush vines
Cabernet Sauvignon 13,6
5-wire trellis
Bukettraube 8,3
Shiraz 7,2
Cape Riesling 6,7
Chardonnay 6,1
Sauvignon Blanc 5,9
Gewürztraminer 3,6
Gamay 2,6
Merlot 1,6
Pinotage 1,1
Barbera 1
Cabernet Franc 1

Total area under vines in 1991/2: 104,4 ha.
Irrigation: None.
Average temperatures: No records are kept, but Durbanville is regarded as one of the coolest wine-growing regions in South Africa.
Average annual rainfall: 550 mm.
Stock: Some parent stock is used for grafting and rooted vines are bought from the SFW nursery and KWV motherbeds.
First wines bottled under the Altydgedacht label: Bukettraube 1985 and Chenin Blanc 1985.
Wines currently bottled under the Altydgedacht label: Bukettraube, Cabernet Sauvignon, Tintoretto, Tygerberg Wood-aged White, Gewürztraminer, Pinotage, Shiraz and Chardonnay (bottled by the Stellenbosse Botteleringskoöperasie Beperk).
Wood ageing: Wines are aged in wood on the estate.
Cellar capacity: Only 10 per cent of the crop is made into wine on the estate, but the old cellar is being renovated.

Altydgedacht Estate is on the Durbanville Wine Route. Wine tastings and sales take place on Wednesdays between 14h00 and 18h00 and on Saturdays between 09h00 and 12h00.

Europe with his invalid son and it was considered advisable to keep a wary eye on this close associate of the exiled emperor. The count wrote in his diary: 'We left Newlands about the middle of the day on the sixth of April and at night reached Tygerberg. At De Tygerbergen we found ourselves situated at the very extremity of the civilized world'.

As Jean had hoped, John and Oliver studied viticulture and oenology at Stellenbosch University, and followed this by gaining some years' experience in the Napa Valley in California. Oliver also spent a year in Australia and New Zealand, where the wine-making conditions are similar to those in South Africa. Now the two men manage this old Cape farm which also produces fruit, grain and silage for the beef herd.

The vine plantings cover 110 of the 450 hectares at Altydgedacht and comprise Cabernet Sauvignon, Shiraz, Pinotage, Chenin Blanc, Cape Riesling and the only plantings of Barbera in the country. This is Italy's most popular variety, and is also grown in America, particularly in California, where it makes up 10 per cent of the local red wine production. Cooler climates bring out the best in Barbera, producing a high acid level and good fruit. Wine made from the grape should be aged for a few years to enhance the smoothness and flavour. Altydgedacht's Barbera Tintoretto is a blend of Barbera and Shiraz, and was originally called Barberaz; the Wine and Spirit Board forbade the use of this name, however, as being too close to the names of the varieties. At one stage production of the wine dropped dramatically because of the age of the vines, which Jean maintains was 80 years. Originally planted on the recommendation of Italian friends of the Parkers, these old vines have been uprooted and replaced with new plantings of the same variety.

Other grape varieties planted are Weisser Riesling, Gewürztraminer, Bukettraube and Muscat d'Alexandrie, with young vineyards of Sauvignon Blanc, Chardonnay and Merlot now in their sixth and seventh years. The growing of noble varieties is facilitated by the cool winds from the Atlantic Ocean, the deep soils and the varied aspects of the slopes.

Until recently, Altydgedacht was the only estate in the Durbanville district to bottle white wine. The Parkers have also upheld the reputation this area has for excellent red

wine grapes, established by the nearby Meerendal Estate, which originally specialized in port varieties. Indeed, Jean Parker still owns a bottle of 1938 port made by the late 'Oom Willie' Starke of Meerendal, who died in 1988 aged 93 years. The Parker family can justly be proud of their début in the field of estate wines; as they bottle only a small proportion of their crop, demand may soon exceed supply.

—BLOEMENDAL—
ESTATE

The first wines made on this estate, now farmed by Jackie Coetzee , were released in 1987. As rebate wine for brandy was being made at Bloemendal at the beginning of the century, however, it is clear that vineyards have been planted there for many decades.

False Pedro and Cinsaut vines were replaced by Cabernet Sauvignon about 20 years ago under the direction of Koos Coetzee, while Chardonnay, Merlot and Weisser

Riesling have been added in recent years. Jackie's first vintage, a Sauvignon Blanc, was awarded a gold medal at the South African

Championship Wine Show in 1987 and his Cabernet Sauvignon, which was aged in 16 new Bordeaux *barriques*, was judged the

<table>
<tr><td colspan="2">BLOEMENDAL ESTATE</td></tr>
<tr><td colspan="2">Varieties planted (number of vines)</td></tr>
<tr><td colspan="2">Bush vines</td></tr>
<tr><td>Chenin Blanc</td><td>124 000</td></tr>
<tr><td>Chardonnay</td><td>33 000</td></tr>
<tr><td>Shiraz</td><td>19 000</td></tr>
<tr><td colspan="2">Perold trellis</td></tr>
<tr><td>Cabernet Sauvignon</td><td>89 000</td></tr>
<tr><td>Sauvignon Blanc</td><td>78 000</td></tr>
<tr><td>Weisser Riesling</td><td>47 000</td></tr>
<tr><td>Merlot</td><td>25 000</td></tr>
<tr><td>Cape Riesling</td><td>25 000</td></tr>
</table>

Total area under vines in 1991/2: 145 ha.
Irrigation: None.
Average temperatures: Records not available.
Average annual rainfall: 500 mm.
Stock: Rooted vines are bought from a nursery.
Wood ageing: The Cabernet Sauvignon and the Chardonnay are aged in wood on the estate.
First wines bottled under the Bloemendal label: Sauvignon Blanc 1987 and Cabernet Sauvignon 1987.
Wines currently bottled under the Bloemendal label: Sauvignon Blanc, Bloemen Blanc, Chardonnay and Cabernet Sauvignon.
Cellar Capacity: 500 hl.

Bloemendal Estate is on the Durbanville Wine Route and is open to the public on Wednesdays from 13h00 to 18h00 and on Saturdays from 09h00 to 12h00.

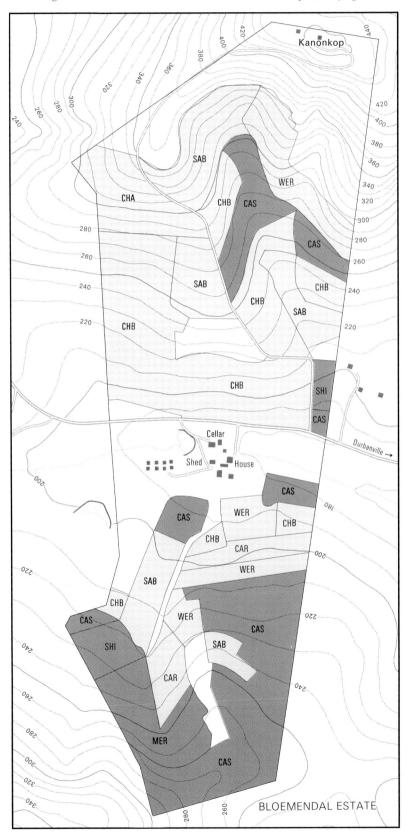

BLOEMENDAL ESTATE

*Jackie Coetzee, the winemaker at
Bloemendal Estate.*

best in the 20-hectolitre class of wooded
Cabernet Sauvignon wines. After further
bottle maturation, it was made available to
the public in 1990. An off-dry white wine,
Bloemen Blanc, is also produced on the estate. The Bloemendal wine labels depict
water lilies of various colours, a large pond
of these beautiful flowers being a striking feature near the homestead and cellar. For the
moment wine-making at Bloemendal is a
hobby rather than a business, as production
will be limited to 2 000 cases annually.

— DIEMERSDAL —
ESTATE

Diemersdal was originally granted in 1698 to
Hendrik Sneewind, whose widow subsequently married a Captain Diemer, after

whom the property was then named. Diemer
was at one time 'fire chief' of the settlement
at the Cape and Master of the Artillery, and
was a son of Jan van Riebeeck's table waiter.

In the 1920s the great-grandfather of the
present owners – Tienie and Beyers Louw –
converted the property from a wheat farm to
a largely wine-making concern. Today, there
is a large and most impressive complex of
farm buildings, including an old Cape Dutch
homestead in which live Tienie and his wife,
Joanita. Beyers lives on the nearby farm
Maastricht, which was bought in 1982 and
where mixed farming is practised. No wine
is made, on Maastricht and the grapes are
delivered to KWV.

Diemersdal is one of two farms (the other
being Vergenoegd in the Stellenbosch district) which have marketing agreements
with KWV going back to 1920. Until recently
Diemersdal sold all its wines to KWV in bulk,
but in 1986 and 1987 retained a total of
about 100 hectolitres (roughly 100 cases) of
red wine which was aged in wood on the estate and released for sale in 1989. This wine
was a blend of Cabernet Sauvignon, Cabernet Franc and Merlot. Otherwise, the red
wine of Diemersdal is sold under the estate's
own label on overseas markets by KWV, and
a small quantity is released to KWV members. A Pinot Noir from Diemersdal won the

Alfa Laval Trophy for the champion new-
variety wine at the 1979 Cape Championship
Wine Show, and a Cabernet Franc from the
estate won the award in 1981.

Although the climate and soil of this area
are eminently suited to red wine varieties,
white grapes are also grown at Diemersdal,
and wine is made from them; this is then
sold in bulk to KWV. All the Kerner and
Weisser Riesling bottled under the KWV label
come from this estate. In fact 60 per cent of
the area under vines is given over to white
varieties, all suitable for making wine of excellent quality. Tienie includes the ubiquitous Chenin Blanc among these as he
maintains, rightly, that outstanding wines
can be made from this variety. The first crop
for wine-making from the 40 000 Chardonnay and 20 000 Pinot Gris vines on the estate

was harvested in 1988. A new 8-hectare
cabernet vineyard has been planted.

Diemersdal produces a large wheat crop
annually and Tienie also keeps German
Merino sheep and beef cattle. Also a wine en-
thusiast, Joanita has started a small Red Poll
stud, and the presence of these beautiful,
richly hued cattle on the rolling pastures
adds to the pleasantness of the place.

— MEERENDAL —
ESTATE

The first estate in the Durbanville area to
produce wine under its own label, Meerendal
is an old farm which for many years produced wheat, as did many of the Durbanville
farms, .before the development of wine-making in the district. As early as 1716, however,
there were vines on the farm – 60 000 of
them, according to the records of the *veld-
kornet* who acted as tax-collector that year.
They were planted and tended by the widow
of Jan Meerland, to whom the farm was
granted by Willem Adriaan van der Stel in
1702. In spite of the governor's munificence,
Meerland was involved, along with Henning
Huysing of Meerlust and others, in the movement to unseat Van der Stel. He sailed to Holland as part of the deputation which put the
complaints of the free burghers to the Chamber of Seventeen (the directors of the Dutch
East India Company) but died on the outward voyage, leaving his widow to run the
farm. His original grant was about 50 morgen and his widow acquired a further 50
morgen, so that her farm extended over 85
hectares in today's measurements. Nonetheless, the tax-collector's count of 60 000 vines
seems inordinately high.

Tienie Louw in his cellar on the Diemersdal Estate, originally a wheat farm.

DIEMERSDAL ESTATE

Varieties planted (ha)

Perold trellis
Chenin Blanc 38
Cabernet Sauvignon 19,8
Sauvignon Blanc 19
Gewürztraminer 15,7
Weisser Riesling 13,5
Pinot Noir 11,2
Chardonnay 7,5
Cabernet Franc 7
Pinot Gris 4
Merlot 3
Ferdinand de Lesseps 2
1-wire trellis
Kerner 14
Pinotage 10,5
Perold and 1-wire trellis
Shiraz 14

Total area under vines in 1991/2: 180 ha.
Irrigation: None.
Average temperatures: Records are not kept.
Average annual rainfall: Records are not kept.
Stock: Rooted vines are bought from a nursery.
First wine bottled under the Diemersdal label:
Dry Red 1987.
**Wines currently bottled under the Diemersdal
label:** Cabernet Sauvignon, Cabernet Franc,
Shiraz and Merlot.
Wood ageing: Wines are aged in wood on the
estate and at KWV.
Cellar capacity: 6 000 hl.

Diemersdal Estate is on the Durbanville
Wine Route and is open to the public on
Wednesdays and Saturdays from 08h00 to 16h00.
Lunches are served.

*William Starke, Kosie Starke's son, is now the
winemaker at Meerendal Estate.*

The gabled façade of the Meerendal Estate homestead in Durbanville.

Meerendal changed hands many times over the years until it was bought by William Starke, whose son Kosie owned and ran the farm until his death in 1991. Kosie Starke's son, also named William, is now winemaker at Meerendal. William Starke the elder's wife was a Faure of Vergenoegd. Through his connections with the Faure family, William was introduced to winebuyers at KWV. He provided Meerendal Shiraz to KWV for use in red wine blends intended for export. On his appointment as wine expert at KWV, Dr Charles Niehaus made Meerendal Shiraz the base of a new blend, revising the standard blend of KWV's red wine Roodeberg. The two most important products of Meerendal at the time were the Shiraz and port supplied to KWV.

There are several Starkes in the Durbanville district, descended from those Starkes who emigrated from the Wash in England in the middle of the nineteenth century; the family had its origins in Germany, but had later settled in England. The well-known Cape garden nurseries, Starke Ayres, were started by one of the sons of the first Starke to arrive in South Africa.

There are three types of soil on Meerendal; stoney, clayey and sandy, and the vineyards are planted accordingly. The summer winds sometimes damage the vines, but provide the cool air essential for optimum ripening. The summer temperatures during the day can be very high, but are balanced by the relatively cool summer nights and heavy dews. In these conditions grapes can reach high levels of sugar without too serious a decrease in acidity. The resultant grapes are thus ideal for the production of full-bodied wines.

When Oom Willie bought Meerendal it was purely a wheat farm, but in the years before World War II he was aware that the climate was ideal for growing vines and he was inspired by the advice of Professor Abraham Izak Perold to set about planting and developing a range of red wine varieties with an emphasis on port varieties. These included such quality varieties as Shiraz, Tinta Barocca, Cornifesto, Souzão and Cinsaut. Post-war changes in taste and the decline of the port market, together with the dramatic advent of Pinotage in the 1950s, persuaded Kosie Starke to make a change in policy when he took over the farm in 1952.

Extending the existing Shiraz vineyards, he also introduced Pinotage vines from which he set about making fine dry red wines, concentrating on them but retaining a minority of some 15 per cent of his vineyards for Chenin Blanc grapes. Grown largely to fill out the harvesting programme, these are not pressed on the estate.

The first Pinotage and Shiraz vintages appearing in 1969 were bottled by KWV as 100 per cent varietal wines under the estate's own label. They were, however, not available to the general public, being reserved for sale to members of KWV.

Kosie soon decided that he wanted to age and bottle his own wines and sell them through retail outlets, but he found that it was not a viable proposition, given the amount of wine he would be able to produce. He thus became one of the earliest of the estates to form an association with The Bergkelder, which now matures, bottles and markets Meerendal wines. The first wine to come from this partnership was the 1974 Meerendal Pinotage; and the first Shiraz was from the 1974 vintage.

In the early 1970s, a period when there was a sudden shortage of red wine, there was a brief diversification when, as did many others, Kosie Starke planted Cabernet Sauvig-

non. But apart from this excursion, the emphasis at Meerendal has remained firmly on Shiraz and Pinotage, the pride of the estate and still the only wines sold under its label.

MEERENDAL ESTATE

Varieties planted (number of vines)

Perold trellis
Cabernet Sauvignon 65 000
Chardonnay 60 000
Shiraz 38 000
Gewürztraminer 30 000
Sauvignon Blanc 27 000
Chenin Blanc 24 000
Merlot 18 000
Bush vines
Pinotage 45 000

Total area under vines in 1991/2: 120 ha.
Irrigation: None.
Average temperatures: Records are not kept.
Average annual rainfall: Approximately 600 mm.
Stock: Rooted vines are bought from a nursery.
Envisaged new variety: Merlot.
First wines bottled under the Meerendal label: Pinotage 1969 and Shiraz 1969.
Wines currently bottled under the Meerendal label: Pinotage and Shiraz. Bottled by The Bergkelder.
Wood ageing: At The Bergkelder.
Cellar capacity: 5 875 hl.

Meerendal Estate is on the Durbanville Wine Route and may be visited by appointment only.

STELLENBOSCH

Stellenbosch is the oldest wine-making centre in South Africa after the Constantia valley. Its roots go back to the day in November 1679 when Simon van der Stel, still in the first flush of excitement and enthusiasm with his new appointment and the new country in which he found himself, turned aside from a visit of inspection to the Hottentots-Holland area to explore the broad and fertile valley of the Eerste River. He liked what he saw, and conceived it as an ideal spot for a pioneer settlement, to be named most appropriately after himself.

The small town thus founded grew rapidly, fed by incoming settlers eager for land and independence. From the start, though wheat and stock-raising were staples of the local economy, wine and its making were an integral part of the burgeoning community's life and culture — as they still are. For while Stellenbosch has contemporary rivals among the other wine-producing districts of the Cape, it still retains its position of *primus inter pares*.

On the official viticultural map, the district of Stellenbosch includes the Regional Services Council area of Stellenbosch itself, as well as those of Somerset West and Sir Lowry's Pass. It also encloses the ward of Simonsberg-Stellenbosch. Topographically, the district is dominated by the complex of high ranges, comprising the Hottentots-Holland mountains, the Helderberg, the Stellenbosch mountains and the Simonsberg. A lower and gentler bastion for the town and its adjacent farms is provided on the west by low hills, including those following the course of the Eerste River, the Papegaaiberg hard by the town (an eighteenth-century shooting range on the crest of this hill featured clay parrots as targets, hence the name), and those of the Stellenbosch Kloof area. Further to the west the area gradually flattens and merges with the infertile dunes of the Cape Flats, which together with the waters of False Bay to the south form natural boundaries to the arable land.

At the heart of this broad stretch of land the modern town of Stellenbosch flourishes as a university and agricultural centre where the quickening rhythms of contemporary life (the university, in particular, provides a lively forum for political and cultural debate) are disguised beneath a carefully preserved historic atmosphere. This is expressed in the formal beauty and dignity of the local eighteenth-century architecture, especially in the region of the central common, *die Braak*, and in the rows of 'senior citizens', the old oak trees, many planted in Van der Stel's day and now declared National Monuments.

As befits its farming and academic role, Stellenbosch is noted for its viticultural institutions. These include the Department of Viticulture and Oenology at the University of Stellenbosch, the only one of its kind in the country, and the Nietvoorbij Institute for Viticulture and Oenology, whose headquarters are at the farm Nietvoorbij on the outskirts of the town. Ten kilometres to the north is a further important grape and wine education centre, the experimental farm and campus of the Elsenburg School of Agriculture, once one of many farms belonging to the redoubtable Martin Melck.

But while these institutions have made a major contribution to local viticulture — not least through creative researchers and wine scientists such as Professors Abraham Perold, Chris Theron, Chris Orffer and Joël van Wyk, to name but a few — the roots of wine culture are in the land. This area provides a fertile earth and a variety of microclimates for growing most of the outstanding quality varieties. The soils tend to be of the Hutton and Clovelly types, with Kroonstad types on the lower lands, and alluvial farms along the banks of the Eerste River — one of the main water sources for vine irrigation. The granitic soils, mostly against the mountain slopes to the east, are well suited to the growing of quality red wines, whereas the vineyards towards the west are located on sandy soils of Table Mountain Sandstone origin, which favour the production of white wines. Along the Eerste River a number of vineyards are found on alluvial soils, most of which are acidic and require deep ploughing and applications of agricultural lime in the subsoil to achieve a balanced medium for good growth.

The Stellenbosch district in general has a moderate and fairly cool climate, with rain largely confined to the winter months, and with fairly hot, dry summers. The average rainfall ranges from 600 to 800 millimetres annually, while the average temperature during the summer growing season is between 18 and 19 °C, depending on the location. The average temperature in the Stellenbosch district varies considerably from one estate to the next. This fluctuation of temperature largely depends on the influence of the south-easterly and southerly winds on the respective properties. Those vineyards which are set against the slopes on Hutton and Clovelly soils, and which are within easy reach of the cooling winds from the sea, do not normally require irrigation. Other sites with different soil types require supplementary irrigation, particularly during the hot months of December and January.

LEFT:*Looking down over the historic town of Stellenbosch from Mulderbosch Estate.*

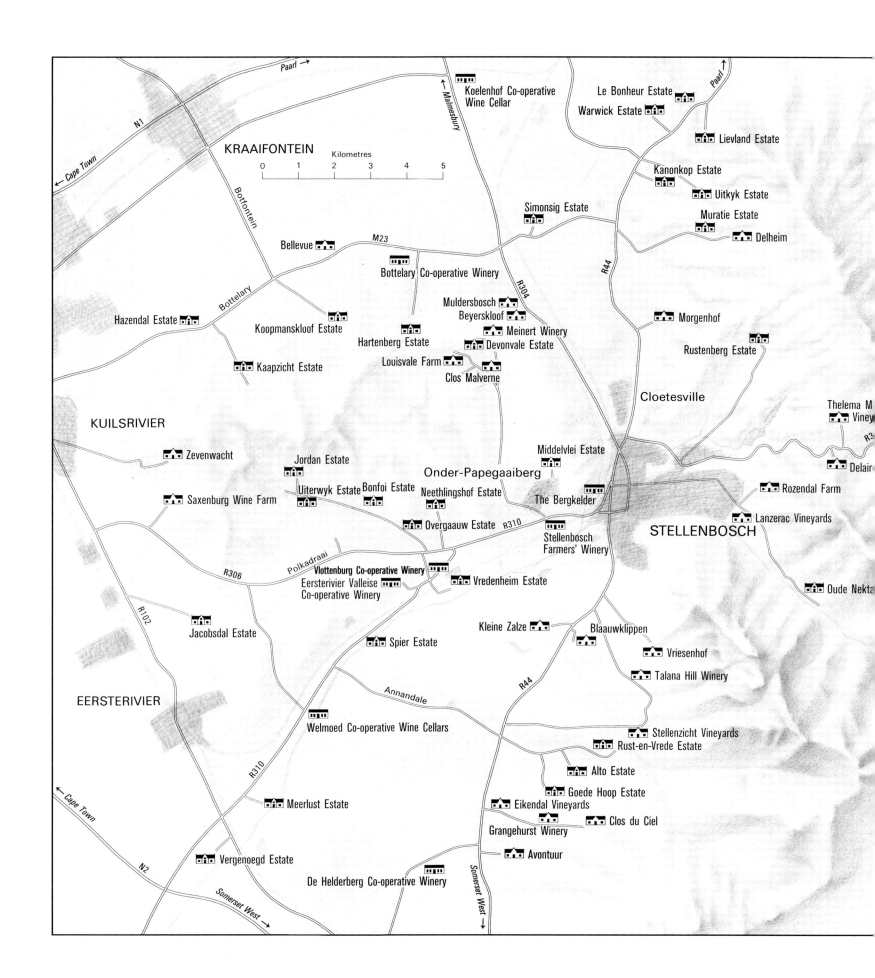

Paarl →

← Cape Town

N1

Boffontein

KRAAIFONTEIN

Kilometres
0   1   2   3   4   5

← Malmesbury

Koelenhof Co-operative
Wine Cellar

Le Bonheur Estate

Warwick Estate

Paarl ↑

Lievland Estate

Kanonkop Estate

Uitkyk Estate

Muratie Estate

Delheim

Simonsig Estate

M23

Bellevue

Bottelary Co-operative Winery

R304

Bottelary

Hazendal Estate

Koopmanskloof Estate

Hartenberg Estate

Kaapzicht Estate

Muldersbosch
Beyerskloof

Meinert Winery

Devonvale Estate

Louisvale Farm

Clos Malverne

R44

Morgenhof

Rustenberg Estate

Cloetesville

Thelema M
Viney

R3

KUILSRIVIER

Zevenwacht

Jordan Estate

Onder-Papegaaiberg

Middelvlei Estate

Delair

R

Saxenburg Wine Farm

Uiterwyk Estate   Bonfoi Estate

Neethlingshof Estate

The Bergkelder

Rozendal Farm

Overgaauw Estate

R310

Stellenbosch
Farmers' Winery

STELLENBOSCH

Lanzerac Vineyards

R306

Polkadraai

Vlottenburg Co-operative Winery

Eersterivier Valleise
Co-operative Winery

Vredenheim Estate

Oude Nekta

R102

Jacobsdal Estate

Spier Estate

Kleine Zalze

Blaauwklippen

Vriesenhof

Talana Hill Winery

R44

EERSTERIVIER

Annandale

Welmoed Co-operative Wine Cellars

R310

Stellenzicht Vineyards

Rust-en-Vrede Estate

Alto Estate

Goede Hoop Estate

Meerlust Estate

Eikendal Vineyards

Clos du Ciel

Grangehurst Winery

Avontuur

← Cape Town

N2

Vergenoegd Estate

De Helderberg Co-operative Winery

Somerset West →

Somerset West

Somerset West →

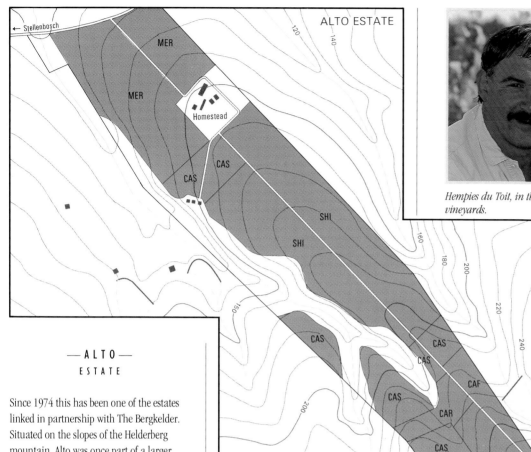

ALTO ESTATE

Hempies du Toit, in the Alto Estate vineyards.

ALTO ESTATE

Varieties planted (number of vines)

Vertical 4-wire trellis
Cabernet Sauvignon 147 000
Merlot 75 000
Pinot Noir 27 000
Cabernet Franc 26 000
Shiraz 21 000

Total area under vines in 1991/2: 93 ha.
Irrigation: None.
Average temperatures: Records are not kept.
Average annual rainfall: 750 mm.
Stock: Root stock and parent stock are supplied to a nursery from which grafted vines are purchased.
First wine bottled under the Alto label:
Alto Rouge 1933.
Wines currently bottled under the Alto label:
Alto Rouge and Cabernet Sauvignon (both wines are bottled by The Bergkelder).
Wood ageing: Wine is aged on the estate.
Cellar capacity: 3 000 hl.

Alto Estate is not open to the public.

— ALTO —
ESTATE

Since 1974 this has been one of the estates linked in partnership with The Bergkelder. Situated on the slopes of the Helderberg mountain, Alto was once part of a larger farm named Groenrivier, the land for which was first granted in 1693. In 1919 the then owner of Groenrivier, Hennie Malan, divided the farm vertically in order to sell half of the land to his brother-in-law.

The development of Malan's share was a co-operative venture between himself and his son, Manie. In the next few years they set about converting this partial wilderness into a wine farm, to which they gave the Latin name, Alto, a reference both to the altitude of the vineyards and the loftiness of their own aspirations. They built a homestead and a cellar, and planted the lower slopes with vines. On the higher slopes they had grazing and grew oats as fodder, as well as onion seed (one of the outbuildings is still known as *Die Saad Saal*).

Malan's choice of varieties was based on a shrewd assessment of the nature of his land, its strengths and limitations. The vineyards were limited in extent — at present they comprise no more than 100 cultivated hectares — but the granite soils found here were well suited to noble vines, situated where both the sea breeze from False Bay and the warmth of the late afternoon sun could reach them.

The main variety planted was Cabernet Sauvignon. But the Malans were not wealthy, and the maturation of Cabernet is a long and expensive business. So Manie planted Shiraz and Cinsaut, which make an earlier maturing wine, to blend with the Cabernet. Without the benefit of sophisticated modern soil or suitability tests, he balanced the quantities of these varieties planted to suit the wine he wished to produce. In the resultant blend, the Cinsaut and Shiraz added smoothness to a dry red wine that could be drunk after only a couple of years' maturation.

The Malans called their new creation Alto Rouge. Almost immediately it began to make its mark, and in an unexpected quarter. In 1923 the elder Malan sent samples of the wine to the reputable firm of wine merchants, Burgoyne's, in London, and received an immediate and enthusiastic order for a

supply for five years. A link was thus set up which continued unbroken for over 30 years, Alto being one of the two red wines which reached the British public in this period (the other was Zonnebloem); both were exported in small casks. With a healthy demand for the wine from overseas, it was some years before Alto Rouge was released on the local market in 1933.

The Alto Estate vineyards on the slopes of the Helderberg.

Winemaker Jean-Luc Sweerts and managing director Manie Kloppers.

Manie Malan continued to supply Burgoyne's until 1956, when he left Alto. Thereafter, the farm went through a number of owners, including Advocate Broeksma and Piet du Toit who was part-owner and winemaker from 1959 to 1983 when he retired, and was succeeded by his son Hempies, a well-known rugby Springbok.

When he first arrived at Alto Estate, neither Piet nor the experts he called in for analysis and advice could fault the planting or the wine created by the Malans.

Thus Hempies has continued the fine red wine-making tradition of his predecessors, while developing and streamlining the farm's vineyard methods. Hempie's signature is on the newly released Alto Rouge label for the first time, the labels having previously carried his father's signature. A 100 per cent Cabernet Sauvignon has been added to the estate's output, but the focus remains the famous Alto Rouge. The wine continues in demand and is now being sold again in London, this time through Henry C. Collison & Sons of St James. Alto Rouge is now a blend of Cabernet Sauvignon, Shiraz, Cabernet Franc and Merlot.

—AVONTUUR—
WINERY

Situated on the south-west slopes of the Helderberg and commanding stunning views across False Bay and the Cape Flats to Table Mountain and the Cape Peninsula, Avontuur is also known as a fine stud farm, having been home to the winner of the 1987 July Handicap, Right Prerogative, amongst others.

A relative newcomer to the ranks of classic wine producers, but fortunately sharing soil types and situation with some of the Cape's great names in red wines, Avontuur's noble varietal vineyard programme was commenced in 1976. Since managing director Manie Klopper's arrival, the farm has been divided into 45 blocks according to soil analysis, degree of exposure, angle of sunlight and microclimatic characteristics, and more than 30 hectares of vineyard have been replanted with classic varieties. Today the impressive sight of neat rows of vines abutting white-fenced paddocks greets the visitor.

The Avontuur production team of Manie and his winemaker Jean-Luc Sweerts make an interesting combination as neither is a

native of the Cape. Manie was previously a successful tobacco farmer in Zimbabwe, while Jean-Luc left his home in the Katanga Province of Zaire in the 1970s to study at the Elsenburg Agricultural College in Stellenbosch. After graduating in 1975 he went to Burgundy to learn about French cellar practices and on his return joined Dr Harvey Illing at Uitkyk, where he made his first wine in 1978, fermenting Cape Riesling and Chenin Blanc in small 225-litre barrels – a novel innovation in those days. In 1990 Jean-Luc came to Avontuur. Attention to detail in both vineyard planning and cellar practices is already paying dividends.

In 1991, Jean-Luc was short of barrels in which to ferment his 1991 Chardonnay. Instead of buying new barrels, he drained 25 barrels which were being emptied of Cabernet Sauvignon, allowed them to dry for a couple of days, and then partially filled them with unfermented Chardonnay juice and yeast. The effect of the colour of the wood inside the barrels was to produce a pink Char-

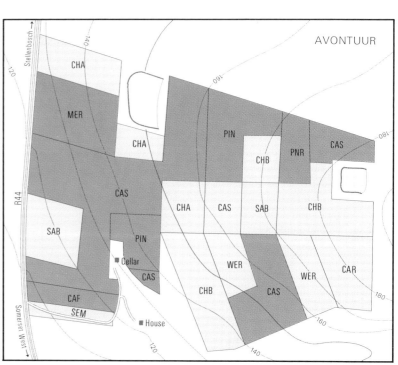

AVONTUUR WINERY

Varieties planted (ha)

4-wire trellis
Cabernet Sauvignon 14
Chardonnay 6
Chenin Blanc 6
Merlot 4,5
Pinotage 4
Sauvignon Blanc 4
Weisser Riesling 2,5
Pinot Noir 2
Cape Riesling 2
Cabernet Franc 1,3
Sémillon 0,5

Total area under vines in 1991/2: 46,8 ha.
Irrigation: None, but water is available if needed.
Average temperatures:
Summer maximum approximately 35 °C;
summer minimum approximately 18 °C.
Average annual rainfall: Approximately 700 mm.
Stock: Rooted vines are bought from a nursery.
First wines bottled under the Avontuur label:
Cabernet Sauvignon 1987, Grand Vin Blanc 1987
and Blanc de Noir 1987.
**Wines currently bottled under the Avontuur
label:** Avon Rouge, Blanc de Noir, Chardonnay,
Cabernet Sauvignon, Merlot, Sauvignon Blanc,
Baccarat, Chenin Blanc and Le Blush.
Wood ageing: Wines are aged in wood in
225-*l* French oak barrels.
Cellar capacity: 15 000 cases.

Avontuur Winery is on the Stellenbosch Wine Route
and is open to the public for wine tastings and sales
on weekdays from 08h30 to 17h00, and on
Saturdays from 08h30 to 13h00.

donnay. Even though the juice was identical to that of previous Chardonnays, the Wine and Spirit Board refused to certify the wine as such, also rejecting the suggestion of calling it a 'Blush Chardonnay' (a Californian term used to describe a Chardonnay/Zinfandel blend). Finally, the name 'Le Blush' was accepted, and the outcome is 500 cases of the first pink Chardonnay in South Africa.

— BELLEVUE —

This farm, once known as 'Houd de Mond', has been owned since the 1860s by four generations of the Morkel family, and is now run by Dirk Cloete Morkel. In a long history of wine-making the farm's finest hour was its dramatic appearance at the 1959 Cape Wine Show with the then almost unknown new variety, Pinotage.

In 1951 the then owner of Bellevue, Pieter Krige Morkel, having failed to obtain Gamay from a nursery, approached the Stellenbosch Agricultural College at Elsenburg for advice as to what other varieties he could plant. Dr Piet Venter suggested that he should try Pinotage, the variety developed almost two decades earlier by Professor Perold. To that date this new variety had been grown at Elsenburg, under the supervision of Professor Theron, on a trial basis only. Morkel accepted the advice and, together with Cabinet Minister Paul Sauer, owner of Kanonkop, became one of the first farmers to develop a commercial Pinotage vineyard – a move which bore fruit in the prize for the best wine on show at the Cape Wine Show almost a decade later. So Pinotage was with us to stay.

The soil in this area, which overlooks the Bellville district, varies from pure, clean Kraaifontein sand to a variety of gravel-based soils, to pure clay, a range which makes farming both interesting and difficult. The average rainfall over the past 40 years has been a little over 600 millimetres annually. In general, dryland farming is practised, with only 15 per cent of the vines receiving irrigation from the two farm dams – those concerned being Cabernet Sauvignon and young plants. Bellevue had its own planting stock, and also sold plant material to other local farmers, but this has ceased. All the good wine produced at Bellevue is delivered to Stellenbosch Farmers' Winery, the distilling wine going to KWV.
(No statistical information available.) Bellevue is not open to the public.

— BEYERSKLOOF —

Beyerskloof is a prime example of the adage that 'small is beautiful', and also that it can be viable and profitable to produce a single, premier wine on a tiny parcel of land. It is the realization of a dream of four ardent wine lovers from Johannesburg, in conjunction with Beyers Truter of Kanonkop, one of the country's most respected winemakers. In 1991, at the 22nd International Wine and Spirit Competition, held in England each year, he won the Robert Mondavi Trophy for the International Wine Maker of the Year in 1991. The partnership counts amongst its ranks Hugh Peatling, managing director of

The gateway to Beyerskloof, one of the smallest wineries in the Stellenbosch area.

Diners' Club SA, who has done a great deal for the wine industry in South Africa, such as sponsoring the Winemaker of the Year Award and encouraging exciting, innovative wine lists in restaurants. The first stage in this collaboration was the search for a suitable property, which was found in the Koelenhof area just outside Stellenbosch.

While thinking about an appropriate name for the farm, it was discovered that it had originally been part of Nooitgedacht, which had been in the Beyers family for five generations until it was sold in 1895. One of the owners had been Jan Marthinus Beyers, from whom Beyers Truter is directly descended on his mother's side. It was unanimously agreed that there could be only one name for the farm – Beyerskloof.

The farm's gravelly soil is similar to that of Bordeaux in France, but is relatively shallow, varying between 300 centimetres and a metre deep. Almost 5 000 vines per hectare were planted, as the relatively dense planting enhances the flavour of the grapes. The vines are furthermore planted north to south, which exposes them to maximum sunlight – considered crucial for the high sugar levels required for quality grapes.

Beyers Truter's wine-making philosophy is that the vintage determines the wine, and he uses the measured, simple vinification techniques which have made the French First Growths the world's most sought-after wines. His contention is that this is made possible by the small size of the operation,

BEYERSKLOOF

Varieties planted (ha)

4-wire verical trellis
Cabernet Sauvignon 7

Total area under vines in 1991/2: 7 ha.
Irrigation: The vineyards are irrigated.
Average temperatures: Records are not kept.
Average annual rainfall: 400 mm.
Stock: Rooted vines are bought from a nursery.
First wine bottled under the Beyerskloof label:
Beyerskloof 1989.
**Wine currently bottled under the Beyerskloof
label:** Cabernet Sauvignon.
Wood ageing: The wines are aged for 18 months
in small French oak barrels.
Cellar capacity: Not available.

Beyerskloof is open to the public during the week
by appointment only.

which allows him to give the wine his undivided attention. His Cabernet Sauvignon is probably the first Cape wine to be 100 per cent matured in new, small oak barrels. All wines are bottled, corked and labelled on the estate by hand.

The enthusiasm and expertise of the Beyerskloof team promises good things for the future. The professionalism which pervades the operation extends to the packaging and marketing of the wines: the distinctive Beyerskloof label and first-release pack of one 3-litre, one 1,5-litre and two 750-millilitre bottles won a Loerie Award, the country's highest advertising accolade.

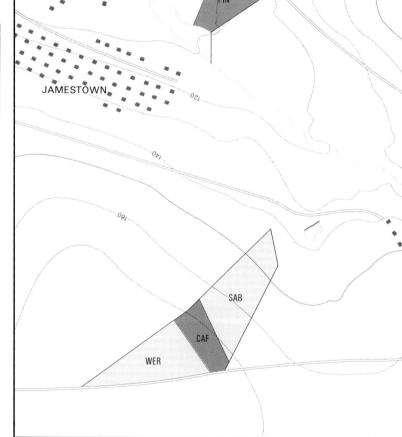

—BLAAUWKLIPPEN—

Originally known as Blaauwklip, as it is situated on the Blaauwklip River, a tributary of the Eerste River, this farm at the foot of the Stellenbosch mountain was first granted by Simon van der Stel to a skilled craftsman named Gerrit Visser in 1692. The present homestead was built in the days of the late eighteenth century, by which time vine growing was well established here.

It remained a wine farm well into the nineteenth century, and indeed wine was sold from Blaauwklippen to Groot Constantia in 1840, but by the middle of the present century the farm's fortunes had declined. Converted into a fruit farm at the time of Cecil Rhodes's attempts to find viable alternatives to wine farming , it had seen no effective wine-making in many decades.

Then, in 1971, it was bought by Graham Boonzaier, an industrialist who had been associated with mining in the Orange Free State for the greater part of his career but who returned to the Cape to pursue a long-standing ambition to farm.

The land was in a sad condition. There was only about half a hectare of open ground out of a total of some 70 hectares. The rest of the remaining land was bush, apart from a neglected orchard of 10 000 apple trees. The soil had been devitalized by heavy afforestation, and all in all the place was badly run down.

The bush was cleared, the existing dams enlarged, and well points set up on the river. The irrigation was replanned, an organic manuring programme was introduced to revitalize the soil, and more land was bought from the municipality to make the present total area of 220 hectares, of which some 107 hectares are now under vines.

In 1975 Graham was joined by Walter Finlayson, previously a very successful winemaker at Montagne, later called Hartenberg. Walter brought with him a pedigree herd of Ayrshire cows (he had originally trained as a dairy farmer), to add to Blaauwklippen's Jersey herd. Soon the existing wine cellar was enlarged and modernized, with complete wine-making facilities as well as new casks for maturing red wines.

BLAAUWKLIPPEN

Varieties planted (ha)

Untrellised
Zinfandel 10,72
Chenin Blanc 2,9
Pontac 1,34

3-wire vertical trellis
Cabernet Sauvignon 20,78
Sauvignon Blanc 14,17
Chardonnay 11,85
Weisser Riesling 11,8
Pinot Noir 7,28
Muscat Ottonel 4,74
Merlot 3,69
Pinotage 3,18
Colombard 3,1
Cabernet Franc 2,99
Sémillon 1,64
Pinot Blanc 0,53

Perold trellis
Shiraz 6,96

Total area under vines in 1991/2: 107,67 ha.
Irrigation: About a third of the vineyards is irrigated.
Average temperatures: Records are not kept.
Average annual rainfall: Records are not kept.
Stock: Parent stock is used for grafting; rooted vines are also bought from a nursery.
First wines bottled under the Blaauwklippen label: White Landau, Red Landau and Late Vintage (all 1976 vintage).
Wines currently bottled under the Blaauwklippen label: Cabernet Sauvignon, Shiraz, Zinfandel, Pinot Noir, Red Landau, Chardonnay, Sauvignon Blanc, Rhine Riesling, Muscat Ottonel, White Landau, Special Late Vintage, Vintage Port and Barouche. The following wines are bottled especially for the Cape Independent Winemakers' Guild Auction: Cabernet Sauvignon Reserve, Cabriolet and Chardonnay Reserve.
Wood ageing: Wines are kept in wood on the farm.
Cellar capacity: 5 387 hl.

On the Stellenbosch Wine Route, Blaauwklippen is open on weekdays from 09h00 to 17h00 for wine sales, and from 09h00 to 12h45 and 14h00 to 16h45 for wine tastings, as well as on Saturdays from 09h00 to 12h30.

In July 1989 Jacques Kruger was appointed as winemaker when Walter left to work at Glen Carlou. Jacques obtained an Elsenburg Agriculture Diploma in 1978 with Viticulture and Viniculture as major subjects. In January 1981 he joined Blaauwklippen as assistant winemaker to Walter Finlayson, but in 1984 went on to make wine on the farm Morgenhof before returning to Elsenburg for further studies in 1985. After obtaining his diploma in Cellar Technology in 1986, he rejoined Blaauwklippen to take responsibility for the production cellar.

Well-kept vineyards in the district of Stellenbosch, the primary wine-making area in South Africa.

The soils on Blaauwklippen are generally alluvial, with Hutton and Clovelly soils on the higher ground. The latter are ideal for vineyards, having good water-retention properties. The vineyards on these soils are not irrigated, though micro-spraying or sprinkler irrigation is used on the rest of the farm. Cultivation is purely by herbicide, since much of the alluvial soil is stony and hard on implements. The soil is aerated in alternate years by putting a ripper through it.

A broad range of grape varieties is now planted. These include varieties such as Cabernet Sauvignon, Cabernet Franc, Merlot, Shiraz, Zinfandel, Pinot Noir, Pinotage, Pontac, Chardonnay, Sauvignon Blanc, Weisser Riesling, Sémillon, Muscat Ottonel, Chenin Blanc and Colombard.

Great attention is paid to detail throughout the whole wine-making process. During harvest time, for example, the grapes are picked and placed in crates of about 500 kilograms each and carefully brought to the cellar. A machine harvester is also used on some of the varieties to ensure that they are harvested both under optimum conditions and at ideal ripeness.

The cellar has also been adapted for the pressing of whole bunches from which the *méthode champenoise* sparkling wine Barouche is made. The range of wines available under the Blaauwklippen label comprises seven white wines, five red wines

Well-preserved wine-making equipment in the Blaauwklippen museum.

(including a Zinfandel which has won numerous awards), a vintage port and a bottle-fermented sparkling wine. Jacques has also made a 1990 Pinotage which he plans to release in 1992. Jacques is a member of the Cape Independent Winemakers' Guild and makes a few wines especially for the guild auction, namely Cabernet Sauvignon Reserve, Cabriolet (a Cabernet/Merlot blend), Chardonnay Reserve and a Reserve sparkling wine.

Besides the 400 000 bottles of wine produced annually, the farm also features an added attraction in the form of a coach museum, and displays of well-preserved wine-making and farming equipment – a private interest the owner shares with his visitors. The collection includes Cape carts, 'plaasbakkies', gigs, a horse-drawn omnibus which last ran between Kuils River and Cape Town in 1905, and two graceful landaus, built in 1833 and 1834, which have given a name to two of the farm's most popular blended wines, the White Landau and the Red Landau. There is also a traditional 'Cape Kitchen', and a Coachman's Lunch is available to visitors in the summer months.

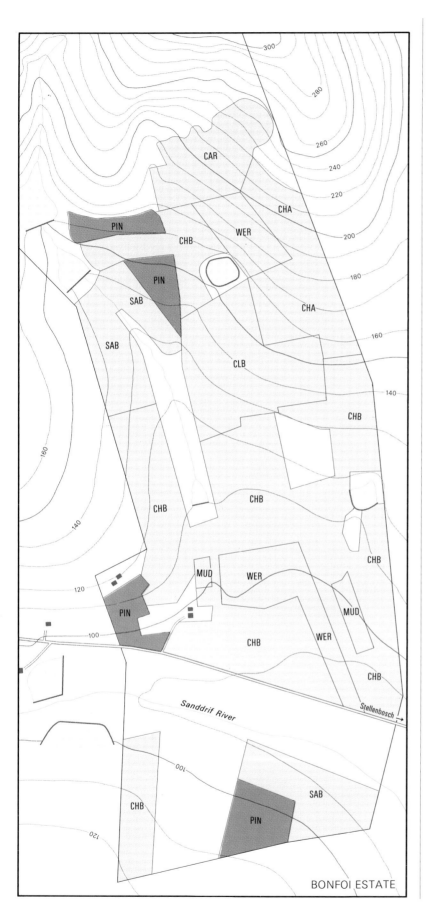

BONFOI ESTATE

—BONFOI—
ESTATE

Bonfoi, on the southern slopes of the Bottelary Hills, is situated in a low-lying part of
the Stellenbosch Kloof. Here the late Christoff van der Westhuizen, who bought Bonfoi
(an old French Huguenot name meaning
'Good faith') in 1958, made both white and
red wines. At present the estate is run by the
Van der Westhuizen family.

The farm has had its share of bad luck: in
1933 and again in 1970 the entire crop of
grapes was destroyed in a violent hailstorm.
The winemakers of Bonfoi continue in their
vocation, however, presently making their
semi-sweet Ouverture wine with a fine balance between sugar and acidity that helps it
to achieve a longer bottle maturation. In
1991 new equipment was installed in the cellar, and the estate looks forward to placing a
dry white wine on the market in the future.

BONFOI ESTATE

Varieties planted (ha)

3-wire trellis
Chenin Blanc 46
Sauvignon Blanc 12,5
Chardonnay 12
Cape Riesling 10
Pinotage 7,5
Cabernet Sauvignon 6
Clairette Blanche 6
Weisser Riesling 3

Total area under vines in 1991/2: 103 ha.
Irrigation: Some 60 ha of vineyards are irrigated.
Average temperatures: Records are not kept.
Average annual rainfall: Records are not kept.
Stock: Rooted vines are bought from a nursery.
Envisaged new variety: Merlot.
First wines bottled under the Bonfoi label:
Clairette Blanche 1974 and Chenin Blanc 1976.
Wine currently bottled under the Bonfoi label:
Ouverture (bottled by The Bergkelder).
Wood ageing: Not practised.
Cellar capacity: 8 500 hl.

Bonfoi Estate is not open to the public.

—BOTTELARY—
CO-OPERATIVE WINERY

In the seventeenth-century heyday of the
Dutch East India Company, the store room
on board its ships, which contained supplies
for men and animals alike, was called the

bottelary. As was its English counterpart *but-
tery,* the word was a corruption of the French
bouteillerie, literally a place for the storage
of bottles. A reference to the origin of the
name survives on the labels of the wines
made by the Bottelary Co-operative Winery,
which feature the innovative design of a
pantry on an old sailing ship.

Now a flourishing and well-equipped,
modern enterprise, the co-operative began
life in the immediate post-World War II
period with limited facilities and support.
Formed in 1946 by eight farmers in the area
under the chairmanship of F.W. Ninow,
the cellar was built on a portion of the farm
Welgelegen, bought from J. Bonthuys. With
all the machinery belt-driven from a single
tractor, and with the building still open to
the sky, the co-operative's first winemaker,
Sakkie Uytenbogaardt, extemporized with
considerable ingenuity whilst attempting to
produce the first wine from the 1947 vintage.
Not surprisingly, however, it ended up as
distilling wine.

Since those early days of hectic improvisa-
tion, the Bottelary Co-operative matured into
a respected winery under winemaker Danie
Zeeman, who came to the cellar in 1972 and
saw it through many developments. These include the replacement of the old concrete
tanks with stainless steel systems, the introduction of cold fermentation for white wines,
the implementation of a Vaslin press, Bucher
separators, Roto tanks for red wines and
whites which benefit from skin contact, and
imported small wood barrels used since the
1988 season.

Ill health forced Danie Zeeman into early
retirement after a 23-year career at the cellar. He has been succeeded by Herman du
Preez, who was previously winemaker at the
Koelenhof Co-operative.

Under the present chairman, George van
der Westhuizen, the 37-member co-operative
draws its annual 11 000 tonnes of grapes
from Devon Valley through to Durbanville
and along the Bottelary Road up to Kuils
River, giving rise to the rather wide range of
variety wines produced. The most important
white varieties are Chenin Blanc, Sauvignon
Blanc, Cape Riesling, Weisser Riesling,
Bukettraube and Gewürztraminer. Bottelary
was the first co-operative to produce a Chardonnay wine in 1989 – the maiden vintage
for the vines of the Carinus family. Red vari-

eties include Cabernet Sauvignon, Pinotage, Shiraz and, more recently, Merlot.

Of the wine made, only 2 per cent is bottled and sold (from the cellar only) under the winery's own label, the balance being sold to local wholesalers, or distilled. Of the good wine produced, 84 per cent is white and 16 per cent red. The Gewürztraminer and Sauvignon Blanc were released on international South African Airways flights in 1985, and the 1988 Gewürztraminer enjoyed the rare honour of being selected for the New World Wine Auction.

— CLOS DU CIEL —

It is not uncommon for talented winemakers to have had another profession. John Platter, the owner of Clos du Ciel, is known to most wine lovers in South Africa through his book *John Platter's South African Wine Guide*. Launched in 1980, this annual publication gives star ratings to all South African wines. Soon after the launch of his book, John started making wine at Delaire, a farm near

John Platter, the author of John Platter's South African Wine Guide *and owner of Clos du Ciel.*

Stellenbosch which he had purchased. The farm was planted to vines but did not produce wine. After a few years, John produced an interesting range of wines from Delaire.

Born in Hungary to an Austrian-Italian father and Scots mother, John spent his earliest years in Italy's South Tyrol, where his relatives still have vineyards. His family moved to Kenya where they farmed cattle. John's father grew a few vines but, as John recalls, made 'terrible' wine. Schooled in Kenya, John became an agricultural correspondent and political columnist for a daily newspaper in Nairobi. He later joined United Press International, covering North Africa, and was subsequently posted to London and finally to southern Africa as bureau chief for United Press.

The desire to farm led John to the Cape in 1979. Cattle would have been his first choice, but for various reasons he and his wife Erica, also a journalist, settled on a fruit and grape farm in Franschhoek, from where he began to write about wine for the *Rand Daily Mail*.

Clos du Ciel is more a hobby than a commercial wine undertaking for John Platter. Approximately 2 hectares are planted exclusively to Chardonnay vines using 10 different clones. The vines are not irrigated. Prior to Platter's first harvest in 1991, Chardonnay grapes were bought in for wine-making. Vinification is almost exclusively in barrel and the 1991 vintage remained on its lees for 10 months without any use of sulphur. John strongly believes in the minimal handling of the grapes and pressing of whole bunches.

Only in special vintages will the wine be bottled under the John Platter label. A second label, the name of which is not yet decided, will be used for the rest of the wine. John intends Clos du Ciel's production to be 1 000 cases and will buy in additional grapes from the nearby slopes of the Helderberg mountains. He also envisages planting Pinot Noir for the production of sparkling wine.

The Clos Malverne Winery, on the slopes of the Devon Valley in Stellenbosch.

— CLOS MALVERNE —

The Clos Malverne winery is situated on the gentle slopes of Devon Valley on a farm previously known as Malvern Heights, so named by its previous owner, Colonel J.W. Billingham, because the surrounding countryside reminded him of the hills around Malvern in his native England. Seymour Pritchard, the present owner, bought the farm in 1970 when the vineyards were still planted with table grapes. In 1976 he decided to plant the Cabernet Sauvignon variety for which the rich Hutton soils are well suited. The situation of the vineyards is further enhanced by the moderate climate of the valley and the sloping terrain which allows good penetration of the cool early-morning sunlight.

The quality yields of the vineyards were sold to one of the major wineries in Stellenbosch until 1986, when Seymour and his friend and winemaker Jeremy Walker de-

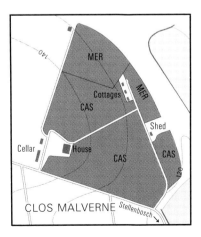

cided to make their own wine for the harvest of that year. They repeated the experiment in 1987 and the results were so encouraging that they decided to make the 25 tonnes of Cabernet Sauvignon pressed from the 1988 vintage commercially available. From this beginning, 7 hectares are now under vines and Merlot and Pinotage grapes are pressed in addition to the Cabernet Sauvignon, albeit in very limited quantities. The present production of Clos Malverne is 3 500 cases.

Large-scale expansion would indeed be anathema to the winery and the beliefs of its management, for it is presently Stellenbosch's smallest wine-producing property – as is proudly stated on their letterhead. The winery has had notable successes at young wine shows in South Africa.

The cellar of Stellenbosch's tiniest winery comprises only two small buildings, namely the 'production' cellar, which is used for the crushing of grapes, fermentation of the must and the pressing of the skins; and the 'maturation' cellar, which is used for barrel and bottle ageing as well as for bottling. All wines under the Clos Malverne label are matured in small 225-litre French oak barrels, new barrels being imported each year to ensure that the ripe fruit aromas and flavours of each vintage are complemented by fine wood characteristics. Elsenburg-qualified Guy Webber took over as winemaker in May 1991.

DE HELDERBERG
CO-OPERATIVE WINERY

Of the nine co-operative wineries originally established with government support in the years immediately after 1905, this is one of the four still in existence. At the turn of the century, with the recovery of the local winelands from the phylloxera epidemic and

Inus Muller, the winemaker at De Helderberg Co-operative Winery.

WINES BOTTLED AND MARKETED

Red: Vin Rouge, Pinotage, Shiraz, Cabernet Sauvignon and De Zoete Roodt.
White: Vin Blanc, Vin Sucre, Chenin Blanc, Cape Riesling, Sauvignon Blanc, Late Vintage and Blanc de Noir.
Sparkling: Brut and Demi-Sec.
Fortified: Port and Jerepigo.

On the Stellenbosch Wine Route, De Helderberg is open on weekdays from 09h00 to 17h30, and on Saturdays from 09h00 to 15h00.

A sweeping view from Delaire Vineyards across the Helshoogte Pass towards Franschhoek.

the improvement of wine-making and viticultural methods, over-production had brought economic crisis to the wine farmers. The law of 'the higher the quantity, the lower the price' drastically reduced the earnings of most of the wine farmers, and drove many of them to bankruptcy.

In this critical situation a proposal to create a co-operative winery system was put forward, and during 1905 a number of farmers in the Helderberg district came together for discussions with a view to rationalizing their activities and making wine co-operatively (the going price then was the equivalent of R3,00 for 577 litres). With little prospect of change in the immediate situation, and with no other available solution to the problem, the decision for co-operation was taken. It was agreed to take up a loan for the erection of a cellar, and a portion of the farm Vredenburg was acquired for this purpose from one of the founder members.

Building commenced towards the end of 1905. Since there were no transport facilities, the 18 founder members turned out in horse-drawn wagons to help convey bricks and sand from Faure, and cement from the Firgrove railway station.

The pressing cellar was completed in time to receive the 1906 crop, with an expected

yield of 3 000 leaguers (17 310 hectolitres). Dawie de Villiers was appointed the first winemaker at the co-operative.

Power to drive the machinery was supplied in the early days by a steam engine of the type used to drive threshing machines. By 1927, however, it was replaced by a diesel machine, which in its turn became obsolete when Eskom made electricity available in 1932. The early years of the co-operative's life were far from easy, and there were a number of defections by members during the difficult time of the Depression years in the early 1930s. Advances in legislation protecting the co-operative movement as a whole, together with the determination of the remaining members, kept it afloat, if somewhat precariously, over the years.

The emergence of this co-operative in recent decades has been largely the work of its former manager and winemaker, J.C. (Christo) Herrer, whose roots lie not far from the Helderberg. He was appointed assistant winemaker under L.T. Sparks in 1952, and when Sparks retired in 1964, he took over as manager and winemaker. On Herrer's retirement in 1983, after 37 years of energetic wine-making, his place was taken by the present manager and winemaker, Inus Muller, previously of Weltevrede Estate just

outside Bonnievale. Under the guidance of Inus, the cellar itself was recently upgraded and modernized. Included in this rejuvenating process was the enlargement of the wine-tasting area which has been equipped with a cosy fireplace and tables where light lunches are served throughout the year. Outside, under the trees, there is a park where children can play to their heart's content.

Most De Helderberg wines are available in 500-millilitre bottles, which have become very popular of late.

DELAIRE
VINEYARDS

Spectacularly situated at the summit of the Helshoogte Pass between Stellenbosch and Franschhoek, the vineyards of Delaire have become known to wine lovers as the 'Vineyards in the Sky'. The tasting room on the farm faces the stately Simonsberg, and from the highest point on the property one can see the Groot Drakenstein Valley to the east, and in the distance to the west Table Mountain and the hazy sweep of False Bay.

Storm and Ruth Quinan of Somerset West bought Delaire from John and Erica Platter in 1987. Chris Keet is in charge of the cellar

Storm Quinan and Chris Keet.

as well as the 18 hectares of vineyards. After graduating from Stellenbosch University in 1987 with a B.Sc. (Agric.) with Oenology and Viticulture, he worked as assistant cellar-master at Delheim, where he gained a great deal of invaluable practical experience. Before joining Delaire, Chris spent about five months in France with the well-known *négociant* Jean-Louis Denois.

Delaire is 38 hectares in extent, of which over 18 hectares are under vines. The 1990 winter saw an extensive replanting programme, with some Cabernet Sauvignon and Weisser Riesling vines making room for

---

DELAIRE VINEYARDS

Varieties planted (ha)

3-wire fence
Pinotage 2,9
4-wire fence
Sauvignon Blanc 3,5
Weisser Riesling 2
3- and 4-wire fence
Merlot 3,9
Cabernet Sauvignon 3,7
Chardonnay 3,3

Total area under vines in 1991/2: 19,3 ha.
Irrigation: None.
Average temperatures:
Maximum 22 °C; minimum 13 °C.
Average annual rainfall: Approximately 850 mm.
Stock: Rooted vines are bought from a nursery.
First wines bottled under the Delaire Vineyards label: Rhine Riesling 1985 and Blanc de Noir 1985.
Wines currently bottled under the Delaire Vineyards label: Joie de l'Air (sparkling wine), Chardonnay, Sauvignon Blanc, Blanc Fumé, Weisser Riesling, Barrique and Cuveé Rouge.
Wood ageing: The wines are aged in wood on the farm.
Cellar capacity: 1 070 hl.

Delaire Vineyards are on the Stellenbosch Wine Route and are open to the public on weekdays from 09h00 to 13h00 and 14h00 to 16h00, and on Saturdays from 09h00 to 13h00, or by appointment.

---

some more Chardonnay. The mainly Hutton soils with their good water-retention abilities, and the cool north- and south-facing slopes, are ideal for the varieties which are currently grown, namely Sauvignon Blanc, Chardonnay, Weisser Riesling, Pinotage, Cabernet Sauvignon and Merlot. Due to the high rainfall (up to 1 000 millimetres per annum), it is unnecessary to irrigate the vineyards. These factors naturally lead to considerably lower yields per hectare which reinforces Delaire's commitment to quality as opposed to quantity.

A number of exciting changes have taken place since the Quinans took over Delaire. The most visible of these is surely the change of logo and label. The new labels were designed by Rose Dendy-Young and have been exceptionally well received by wine lovers. The old 'Volkshuisie' has been turned into a friendly and intimate tasting room. In summer wine lovers can taste the Delaire range outside on the lawns while enjoying the magnificent setting. During the winter months a roaring log fire creates a convivial ambience for tasting the wine.

A new temperature- and humidity-controlled maturation cellar has been built next to the pressing cellar. All barrels, as well as bottled stock awaiting labelling, will be stored here under optimum conditions. The old barrel maturation cellar has been converted into a function room. This venue will be available for intimate functions such as weddings or conferences.

— DELHEIM —

In 1938 a retired master builder, Mr H. Hoheisen, bought the 177-hectare property of De Driesprongh for £5 000 from Charles Nelson (a grand-nephew of Lord Nelson of Trafalgar fame). With no experience in farming, Hoheisen needed someone to help him turn his newly acquired land into a going concern. He finally discovered the ideal partner with the arrival of his wife's nephew, Michael 'Spatz' Sperling.

Neither Hoheisen nor his new assistant knew anything about wine farming, though Sperling's family had farmed in Poland for 150 years and he himself had been trained as a farmer. The only idea they had between them was that of making wines of quality –

Delheim vineyards on the slopes of the Simonsberg in winter.

and this at a time when the general level of local wine-making was far from high.

Enthusiasm and intelligent trial and error soon paid off. Recognition of Sperling's growing skills came in 1957, when he and his uncle came to an arrangement whereby the younger man would run the farm and pay Hoheisen a portion of the profits – if there were any. With an injection of £1 500 from Hoheisen's private capital and the help of his aunt, who grew and sold flowers during the leaner times, Spatz therefore began farming on his own.

The improvement in the quality of Spatz's wines came slowly, but steadily. At this time there were numerous young Ger-

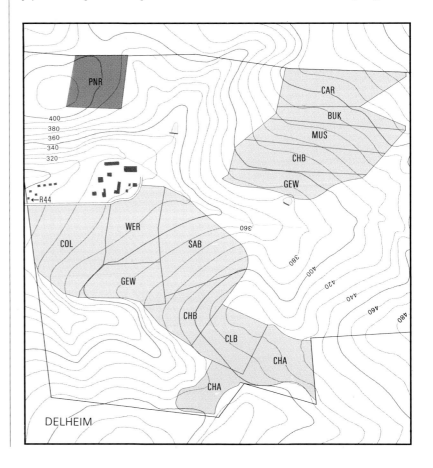

Delheim's owner, Spatz Sperling and winemaker, Philip Costandius.

DELHEIM

Varieties planted (number of vines)

Bush vines
Pinotage 42 000
Bush vines and 5-wire hedge
Chenin Blanc 95 000
Cabernet Sauvignon 94 000
Cape Riesling 29 000
5-wire hedge
Sauvignon Blanc 43 000
White Muscadel 29 000
Pinot Noir 25 000
Gewürztraminer 24 000
Chardonnay 20 000
Colombard 20 000
Weisser Riesling 20 000

Total area under vines in 1991/2:
139 ha (3 ha still to be planted).
Irrigation: Most vineyards can be irrigated
when necessary.
Average temperatures: Records are not kept.
Average annual rainfall: Approximately 920 mm
(Driesprongh); approximately 705 mm (Veracruz).
Stock: Rooted vines are bought from a nursery.
First wines bottled under the Delheim label:
H.O.H. Muscat (dessert), Delheim Cabernet and
Delheim Riesling (all 1949 vintage).
**Wines currently bottled under the Delheim
label:** Heerenwijn, Blanc Fumé, Chardonnay,
Rhine Riesling, Gewürztraminer, Goldspatz Stein,
Spatzendreck Late Harvest, Special Late Harvest,
Edelspatz Noble Late Harvest, Pinotage Rosé,
Dry Red, Pinotage, Shiraz, Cabernet Sauvignon,
Pinot Noir, Merlot, Grand Reserve and
Cuveé Brut Rosé Pinot Noir (sparkling wine).
Wood ageing: Wine is aged in wood at Delheim.
Cellar capacity: 11 821 hl.

Delheim is on the Stellenbosch Wine Route and
is open to the public for tastings and sales on
weekdays between 08h30 and 17h00, and
on Saturdays from 08h30 to 12h00.
Cellar tours are conducted from 1 October to 30 April
on weekdays at 10h00 and 15h00, and
on Saturdays at 10h30.
A Vintner's Platter is offered from 1 October to
30 April from Mondays to Saturdays between
11h00 and 14h00. Soup lunches are served from
1 May to 30 September from Mondays to Fridays
between 11h00 and 14h00.

man winemakers in the Cape, and many of them would visit Driesprongh for the weekend; in return for hospitality they would assist and advise Spatz with his wine-making. It was at this time that one of the estate's most popular wines, the Spatzendreck, originated. When Spatz was struggling with the making of this wine, he gave a sample to a friend who described it bluntly in somewhat agricultural terms. Since Sperling is the German word for a sparrow and Michael's nickname is a more colloquial name for the bird, the wine inevitably became 'Spatzen-dreck'. Spatz vowed he would make his friend eat his words, and with determination went on to develop and refine this fine Late Harvest wine, the label of which shows a cheerful sparrow perched over a barrel, its droppings – the *Dreck* – falling through the bunghole into the wine.

If the high reputation of the Delheim wines is a relatively modern phenomenon, the land from which they come goes back to the time of the earliest grants in this area. De Driesprongh ('where three roads join') was the name of the property originally granted to Lourens Campher by Willem Adriaan van der Stel in February 1600.

Above the homestead and wine cellar, set among magnificent old oaks, are the ruins of the ancient house once inhabited by the Dutch East India Company servant whose job it was to fire the cannon on top of Kanonkop to alert the local farmers to the arrival in Table Bay of a ship bringing provisions. This cannon was the third in a relay, the other two being in Cape Town and on Koeberg. Today this beautiful spot makes a tranquil and serene setting for the cemetery of the farm Driesprongh.

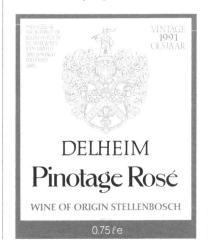

Most of the land which comprised Campher's grant now falls within the boundaries of the farms of Muratie and Nieuwetuin, which lie lower down the valley. The land which today carries the name Driesprongh was first registered when it was transferred to G.A. Berry from William van der Byl in 1903.

Delheim wines are made from grapes grown on two farms: Driesprongh was first planted commercially in the 1940s (the oldest still drinkable wine is the 1949 Muscat-Dessert, of which there are a few bottles remaining); and Veracruz, 3 kilometres away at the foot of Klapmutskop, which was bought in 1975 (the oldest wine from this farm dates from the early 1960s). Apart from the vineyards, Delheim owns 150 hectares of forest on the steep mountain slopes which enclose the valley. The soil on the farms varies slightly, most of the vines being grown on red granite and on a rocky black turf. The enclosed nature of the valley at this point limits the amount of available sunshine. Looking back over several decades of experience, Spatz estimates that his vines receive some 10 to 12 days less sunshine (an advantage in the general South African conditions) at Driesprongh, compared with farms lower down the Simonsberg. The high rainfall here, on the other hand, makes it difficult to produce very full-bodied red wines. Although in most years he can make excellent white wines, Spatz maintains that he can only produce top-quality red wines when there is a drought. Except for one 3-hectare block of Pinot Noir, all red varieties have now been shifted from Driesprongh to Veracruz, the warmer farm, where Delheim's latest red wines such as the Grand Reserve (Bordeaux blend) are produced.

Spatz believes that white wine-making is a specific technical skill which can be acquired by training, whereas the making of red wine is more of an art, and less of a science. This, he feels, is why the technically accurate German winemakers in South Africa make much of the best white wine, and why the locals, who in some cases may not be quite so formally technical, turn out the better reds. Be this as it may, Driesprongh makes very good red wines as well as high-quality whites, especially the sweeter ones.

In view of the farm's inauspicious start, current standards are impressive and competition results equally so. Among the wines

now made under the Delheim label (the name, in memory of Mrs Hoheisen, is coined from her name, Deli, and the German word for 'Home', Heim) are the Delheim Spatzendreck Late Harvest, Gewürztraminer, Goldspatz (featuring another sparrow, this time continent), Riesling Sec, and the 'quaffing wine', Heerenwijn.

Delheim's extensive cellar is modern in all aspects, from grape crushing through to the final bottling and labelling, and can accommodate up to 1 000 tonnes of grapes, of which 400 come from the vineyards of Driesprongh, and the balance from Veracruz.

Since 1973 Spatz has been assisted in his expanded production by a number of young winemakers. The first of these was Otto Helmer, who was succeeded in 1980 by Kevin Arnold, who made wine at Delheim until July 1987. Kevin had as his assistant Jeff Grier, who subsequently acquired his own estate, Villiera. Kevin was thereafter assisted by the present winemaker, Philip Costandius.

— DEVONVALE —
ESTATE

The development of the modern estate of Devonvale began with its purchase in the late 1950s by Simeon Blumberg. Almost concurrently he acquired the firm of Bertrams of Constantia and in 1959 combined his two acquisitions by moving the Bertrams headquarters to the Devon Valley, where he established new and expanded cellars. The enterprise was subsequently taken over by the Gooderson family who severed the connection with Constantia, moving the complete wine-making and merchandising operation to Stellenbosch. In 1972, in their turn, the Goodersons were bought out by Gilbey Distillers and Vintners, for whom the farm is today an impressive showpiece, built up over 16 years by its well-known and highly respected former technical director, Dr Arnold Schickerling, who retired in March 1986.

Brought up on a wine farm in Constantia, Arnold's interest in wine began at an early age. An interest in chemistry intervened, however, leading him to the University of Cape Town and a Masters Degree followed by a Doctorate. During a two-year period of lecturing at Rhodes University, he was invited to join the company then known

DEVONVALE ESTATE

Varieties planted (ha)

5-wire trellis
Cabernet Sauvignon 14
Shiraz 12
Weisser Riesling 5
Chenin Blanc 5 (to be replanted with Cabernet Sauvignon)
Merlot 3
Cabernet Franc 2,5
Chardonnay 1,5

Total area under vines in 1991/2:
Approximately 43 ha.
Irrigation: None.
Average temperatures:
Maximum 25 °C; minimum 8 °C.
Average annual rainfall: 934 mm.
Stock: Heat-treated, virus-free vines are bought from a nursery.
First wines were bottled under the Eikendal Vineyards label in 1902.
Wines currently bottled under the Bertrams label: Robert Fuller Reserve, Cabernet Sauvignon, Shiraz, Pinotage and Zinfandel.
Wood ageing: Wine is aged in wood on the estate.
Cellar capacity: 62 000 hl.

Devonvale Estate may be visited by appointment only.

as South African Distillers and Wines, returning to the Western Cape to take up his new appointment in 1953.

Having thus come full circle back to the world of wine, he set about applying his knowledge of organic chemistry to the problems of wine-making, studying many facets of production both locally and overseas in France, Italy, Germany and California. Then, in 1970, he joined Bertrams Wines to run the Devon Valley Estate for the then owners, the Gooderson family. At present Martin van der Merwe is operations manager and Leo Burger is cellarmaster at Devonvale. He is no newcomer to the estate, having been responsible for making the red wines since 1983. The Devonvale wines are bottled under the Bertrams label.

The Devonvale Estate, its olive-lined vineyards reminiscent of a typical Tuscan scene, is ideally suited to the making of both red and white wines of high quality. Situated on the southern edge of the Bottelary Hills in one of the most beautiful of the wineland valleys, it has good, deep, rich soil in some areas and in others relatively sandy. The approximately 43 hectares of vines are almost without exception laid out on slopes receiv-

ing the benefit of a tamed south-easter. When the wind is howling over the rest of the peninsula, it is rarely more than a stiff breeze in the shelter of the Devon Valley. The vineyards have been replanted with virus-free clonal material of Merlot, Cabernet Sauvignon, Cabernet Franc and Shiraz.

The variety of soils and microclimates here provide a challenge to the winemaker and the inspiration for a broad range of fine wines. Leo Burger leads a small team of dedicated winemakers who place considerable emphasis on the importance of good vineyard practices. Irrigation is not employed, so as to keep the yield low and concentrate the quality of the grapes. Intensive canopy-management that is yield-controlled is of vital importance for the production of top-quality grapes.

The Devonvale winery crushes grapes from its own and lease vineyards. Cellar procedures receive great attention, and in particular much emphasis is given to blending, regarded by Leo as one of the winemaker's most effective tools. The red wines produced at Devonvale are marketed under the Bertrams label, and the white wines mostly under the Alphen label, thus perpetuating two famous old Constantia names, now transplanted to Stellenbosch.

— DISTILLERS' — CORPORATION

This large company is a producing co-subsidiary of Cape Wine and Distillers. Its historical growth begins, however, with the emergence after The Second World War of the Distillers Corporation.

Distillers Corporation (SA) Limited was registered in June, 1945. Early in 1946, the first of its cellars was completed, the first pot still installed, and a modern wine laboratory – the first of its kind in South Africa – established. Combining this modern technology and equipment with traditional processes, the company launched a full range of vine products – the most famous of these being Oude Meester Brandy.

The following years saw an energetic expansion. Marketing relationships were set up with local estates – Alto and Theuniskraal being the first to enter into this now familiar kind of partnership – in 1947.

The early 1960s saw the absorption of the largest privately owned sherry-maturation cellars in the country, those of the Drostdy Co-operative Cellars at Tulbagh. The following year the mother company of Oude Meester Kelders, Distilleerders en Brouerskorporasie, was established.

In 1968, at the instigation of Dr Anton Rupert, chairman of the Oude Meester Group, occurred one of the most important of the company's innovations, with the building of The Bergkelder. These are maturation cellars, tunnelled into the flank of the mountain on the southern slopes of the Papegaaiberg. Here red wines can be matured at ideal temperatures, even in the fierce heat of the Cape summer. Here also are made the well-known Fleur du Cap wines, the Stellenryck 'Collection' and, probably the best known of all the Oude Meester wines, the Grünberger range.

The Oude Meester Group proper was formed in 1970, when the mother company of Distillers Corporation, Oude Meester Kelders, Distilleerders en Brouerskorporasie, merged with another company, South African Distilleries and Wines Limited, the latter consisting of upwards of some 40 wine merchants, including many of nineteenth-century provenance such as Castle Wine and Brandy Company, E.K. Green, Collisons (now revived in London with an injection of capital from the Oude Meester Group to distribute and market the Group's products in the United Kingdom) and the Van Ryn Wine and Spirit Company.

A further ramification of the Group's structure occurred in August, 1974, when it was announced that a number of leading private wine estates had entered into a marketing partnership with The Bergkelder; a fitting tribute to the efforts of Dr Rupert who some two decades earlier had laid the foundation to such partnership with the marketing agreements he had concluded with Alto and Theuniskraal. This meant that independent farmers would continue to make their own individual wines in their own personal style from grapes grown on their estates, but that they would now have the advanced technology of The Bergkelder at their disposal, and that henceforth they would be able to leave the increasingly complicated ageing, bottling and marketing of their wines to the company. Since 1974 the

number of estates in partnership with The Bergkelder has increased from nine to nineteen; in the Stellenbosch district they include Meerlust, Alto, Jacobsdal, Bonfoi, Goede Hoop, Middelvlei, Hazendal, Koopmanskloof, Uitkyk and Le Bonheur; Durbanville is represented by Meerendal; the Swartland by Allesverloren; Tulbagh by Theuniskraal; and the Robertson area by four estates, those of De Wetshof (the first estate to be registered there), Mont Blois, Zandvliet, and Rietvallei; and L'Omarins and La Motte in Franschhoek. Dr Julius Laszlo is responsible for the technical development of Bergkelder wines, and Gerhard Hoffmann is the director in charge of production.

The head office of Distillers Corporation is off Dorp Street in Stellenbosch. The Bergkelder organizes public tours of its underground cellars; these begin at the giant door which opens directly into the side of the hill and continue down dim corridors tunnelled into the earth and lined with thousands of bottles of maturing red wine. To these cellars has now been added a magnificent, air-conditioned wood maturation cellar where the wines are aged in 225-litre oak casks. Further into the hillside are rooms housing hand-carved maturation vats, the tour being completed in the tasting room where visitors may sample a selection of certain of the cellar's wines.

— THE BERGKELDER — VINOTÈQUE

The Bergkelder has also introduced an innovative system which gives the individual wine lover the opportunity of maturing wines in The Bergkelder Vinotèque. This is an underground cellar in which conditions of temperature and humidity are meticulously controlled, providing ideal conditions for the maturation of wine.

The 'Vinotèque Pre-Release Offer' enables the buyer to purchase selected wines while they are still maturing either in the barrel or in the bottle, and therefore not yet available from wine merchants. After purchase, these young wines are left to mature in The Berg-

kelder Vinotèque, but only on the condition that they remain there until the wine is officially released.

The owner of the wine is advised when his wine will be available and he is given the option to leave the wine for further maturation if he wishes. In this way, the wine will improve in character and increase in value.

Bergkelder wines that are currently available may also be ordered through a wine merchant, and further matured in the Vinotèque. The progress of the wine is monitored by the cellarmaster, who sends the owner regular reports on the maturation progress of his wine, advising him when the wine is approaching optimum maturity.

Every year, limited stocks of carefully selected, older vintage wines are offered from the Vinotèque on a 'Special Release Sale'. The quantities are limited, and the wines are sold on a 'first come, first served' basis.

The modern premises of the Eersterivier Valleise Co-operative Winery.

A unique data base, with information on the vintages owned by both wine merchants and private collectors who may wish to sell their wines currently held in the Vinotèque, has been established. Prospective buyers of particular vintages may be put into contact with the owners of those wines, and ownership may be transferred without the wines ever leaving the premises of the Vinotèque. When the owner is ready to receive his wine, delivery anywhere in South Africa or Namibia is free of charge.

The Bergkelder exports its own wines – mainly the Fleur du Cap and Stellenryk ranges and the sparkling wines of the House of J C le Roux. The company also exports the wines of a number of private and individual estates such as Alto, Zandvliet, De Wetshof, Allesverloren, L'Ormarins, Meerendal and Meerlust among various others.

Despite sanctions, The Bergkelder has had successful markets in Europe for many years, and with the current opening up of trade with South Africa, has expanded its agents to include such places as Canada, the United States of America, Scandinavia, Taiwan and Hong Kong. Taking part in international competitions has played an important role in promoting interest in Bergkelder wines. Among other awards, three Chardonnays (all 1989 vintage), from De Wetshof, L'Ormarins and Le Bonheur, were particularly successful at the 1991 Monde Selection International Wine and Spirit Competition in Brussels, and three trophies were awarded to Bergkelder wines at the 1991 International Wine and Spirit Competition in London.

— EERSTERIVIER — VALLEISE
CO-OPERATIVE WINERY

This co-operative, which receives grapes from 17 wine farmers in the vicinity, was built on a subdivision of the Vlottenburg farm, which dates back to 1687 when two French refugees, Pierre Rochefort and Gerard Hanseret (whose name has been given to a number of Eersterivier's products), worked the land and planted the first vines in 1689. The name Vlottenburg is derived from an early owner, Antoine Vlotman, who bought it in 1709, after previously having either rented it or worked on it as a foreman, for it was already known as Vlottenburg at the time he bought it. In the early 1950s Vlottenburg farm was owned by Paul Roux, whose family (still the owners of the farm) have lived here for over 200 years. It was from him that the land for the Eersterivier Valleise Co-operative was originally bought.

Established in August 1953, the co-operative pressed its first vintage in the Deciduous Fruit Board's building in Stellenbosch. At this early stage only distilling wine was made, but building operations were already underway on the selected site, and in 1954 the first vintage was handled in the newly completed cellars by the co-operative's first dedicated winemaker, Malherbe Rossouw, who developed the Eersterivier Valleise Co-operative during the next 15 years into one of the leading local wineries. An innovator and designer, Malherbe Rossouw produced a system of static drainers which in their time were far ahead of anything comparable in the Cape wine industry.

From Rossouw's death in 1970 the co-operative has been run by its present wine-maker and manager, Manie Rossouw. A winemaker of distinction, he combines a hearty and jovial air with an extensive knowledge of his art.

Manie Rossouw started his career as an assistant winemaker with Oom Sarel Ros-souw at the Simonsvlei Co-operative in 1962, and was considerably impressed by both Oom Sarel's hard taskmastership and his at-tention to hygiene. With this invaluable ex-perience behind him, he left in 1966 to become winemaker at the Rooiberg Co-oper-ative in the Robertson district. Here he set about raising the performance of the co-oper-ative from the average level at which he found it to that of one of the top prize win-ners at the Cape Wine Show.

This sure touch in the making of quality wines has been further reflected in Manie's career with the Eersterivier Valleise Co--operative. He receives grapes from the farms of the co-operative's members, all in the Stel-lenbosch district but widely spread across the area, with 13 000 to 14 000 tonnes coming in for processing from the foot of the Helder-berg, and from throughout the Eerste River and Devon valleys, as well as from Stellen-bosch Kloof and Kuils River.

Great changes have been brought about at this winery in recent years, and it is now certainly one of the most modern and techni-cally advanced in the country. With the pro-duction of value-for-money wines as index, the emergence of a Variety Guideline Plan has resulted in members planting Merlot, Chardonnay and Sauvignon Blanc, using quality virus-free clones.

WINES BOTTLED AND MARKETED

Red: Cabernet Sauvignon, Pinotage, Vin Rouge and Grand Reserve.
White: Chardonnay, Sauvignon Blanc, Riesling, Chenin Blanc, Muscat d'Alexandrie, Weisser Riesling, Special Late Harvest and Vin Blanc.
Sparkling: White.

The co-operative is on the Stellenbosch Wine Route and is open to the public on weekdays from 08h30 to 17h00, and on Saturdays from 09h00 to 13h00.

Vineyards on the property of Eikendal, situated on the lower slopes of the Helderberg.

This viticultural innovation is reflected in the recent addition of a red blend – Grand Reserve – to the popular existing red wine range, as well as a Chardonnay and a spar-kling wine to the white wine range. Two new fortified wines, namely a Hanepoot Jerepigo and a port, are also due for release.

These changes, coupled with Manie's skill, have borne fruit. Apart from several awards for wines entered in Cape Wine Shows, Manie Rossouw's Eersterivier Valleise Sauvignon Blanc 1984 won the coveted Diners' Club Award – a noteworthy accom-plishment in that, to date, Eersterivier is only one of two co-operatives to have attained this award for an unfortified table wine.

The Eersterivier Co-operative Winery is one of the most popular stops on the Stellen-bosch Wine Route, welcoming and catering to the diverse needs of its many visitors.

Apart from daily conducted wine tastings, special group visits and tastings in the Vino-tèque, which houses the co-operative's wines dating from 1972, can be made by pre-arrangement with Manie Rossouw. Lunches are offered in season, there is a playground for children and visitors can also spend time in the magnificent rose garden adjoining the large cellar complex.

— EIKENDAL — VINEYARDS

Although the land on which Eikendal stands was first granted in 1793 to Jacobus Carolus van Graan, the first building a visitor to the farm sees today is the cellar which is decided-ly and arrestingly modern.

This large cellar has become something of a landmark on the road between Stellen-bosch and Somerset West. It was designed by an architect who spent some time in Califor-nia. His intention in constructing the cellar at Eikendal was to combine the best ele-ments of traditional Cape and modern Cali-fornian architecture.

Eikendal consists of two old farms on the lower slopes of the Helderberg, namely the famous Longridge and Mietjiesvlei. It is said that the site of what was to become the farm Mietjiesvlei was originally called Moddergat ('mudhole') by Simon van der Stel, whose wagon stuck fast in a mudhole there while he and his entourage were heading for the coast on a fishing expedition.

Extensive plans are afoot to restore the old homestead on the farm as well as the other farm buildings on the Mietjiesvlei part of the property of Eikendal.

A Swiss public company, AG für Plant-agen, owns Eikendal Vineyards. This com-pany had extensive rubber and coffee plantations in Indonesia and Tanzania, but after nationalization of its interests in Tanza-nia in 1976, it was decided to turn to invest-ing in South Africa.

The company bought the two old farms in 1982 and set up Eikendal Vineyards. The managing director of Eikendal Vineyards is Professor R. Saager, who is usually based in Zürich, but visits South Africa regularly.

Jan 'Boland' Coetzee of Vriesenhof is a dir-ector of Eikendal and acts as consultant winemaker. It was with his aid and advice that the winery at Eikendal was set up. The

Eikendal Vineyards' general manager and winemaker, Josef Krammer.

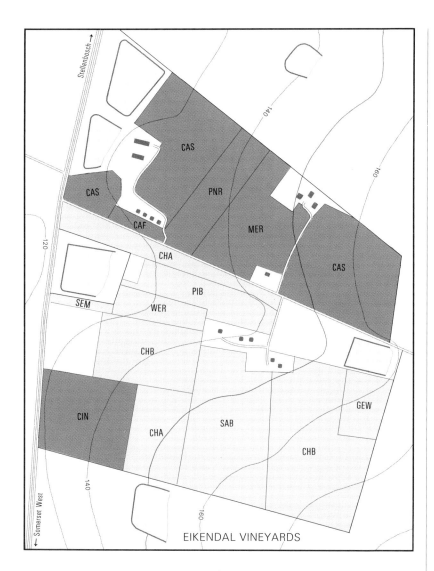

EIKENDAL VINEYARDS

EIKENDAL VINEYARDS

Varieties planted (ha)

2-wire trellis
Chenin Blanc 18
4-wire vertical trellis
Cabernet Sauvignon 13
Sauvignon Blanc 8
Pinot Blanc 7
Chardonnay 7
Merlot 6
Cabernet Franc 2,5
Bush vines
Cinsaut 5,5

Total area under vines in 1991/2: 67 ha.
Irrigation: Overhead irrigation when necessary.
Average temperatures: Records are not kept.
Average annual rainfall: 600 mm.
Stock: Rooted vines are bought from a nursery.
First wines bottled under the Eikendal Vineyards label: Blanc de Blanc 1984, Sauvignon Blanc 1984 and Duc de Berry.
Wines currently bottled under the Eikendal Vineyards label: Eikendal Blanc de Blanc, Chenin Blanc, Sauvignon Blanc, Chardonnay, Special Late Harvest, Cabernet Sauvignon, Pinot Noir, Classique, Merlot, Duc de Berry Stein, Rouge and C'est si Blanc sparkling wine.
Wood ageing: Wines are aged in wood at Eikendal.
Cellar capacity: 6 500 hl.

Eikendal Vineyards are on the Stellenbosch Wine Route and are open to the public for wine tasting and buying on weekdays from 08h30 to 17h00, and on Saturdays from 09h00 to 12h30.

GILBEY DISTILLERS AND VINTNERS

Typical of those early wine firms which have survived in a larger capacity as modern producing wholesalers, is the big Stellenbosch-based company of Gilbey Distillers and Vintners, nowadays commonly referred to simply as 'Gilbeys'.

In 1857, two London wine importers, Walter and Alfred Gilbey, became associated with Cape wines, importing the local port and sherry, Madeira Bucellas and Marsala – an advertisement placed by them in a contemporary London newspaper priced the wines at 20 shillings a dozen, with brandy at 30 shillings per dozen. Within five years the Gilbeys had established a healthy two-way trade between England and the Cape.

It was almost a century later, however, that the company became involved directly in the local production. In July 1950, W. & A. Gilbey, the holding company of Gilbey Distillers and Vintners, was founded in Pietermaritzburg with the opening of a distillery originally designed only to produce gin. Gilbey's gin was the first of the London gins to be made locally.

A decade later the company made a move to include not only spirits but wine in its range of interests. In 1962 Gilbeys acquired R. Santhagens Cape Limited, one of the country's oldest established brandy producers and leading wine merchants. Reiner von Eibergen Santhagens, otherwise known as René, or 'Santy', had imported the refined French methods of brandy-making to the Cape in the 1890s. Among his innovations had been the maturation of brandy in Cognac oak, the introduction of an improved design of brandy-still (which is still the basis for the modern equipment), the production of light Hermitage wine, a form of cold stabilization of the local wine, and the marketing of sparkling grape juice. At Oude Molen they have established a 'working' brandy museum in his memory.

The Santhagens company was based on the old property of De Oude Molen, near the Plankenbrug; and it was here that the new company of Gilbey-Santhagens Limited made its headquarters in the Cape. The amalgamated company began to expand rapidly. It retained the title of Gilbey-Santhagens till 1970, when, to provide a

---

original vineyards were mainly Cinsaut and Chenin Blanc, but on the advice of 'Boland' Coetzee, there have been extensive new plantings of varieties such as Cabernet Sauvignon, Merlot, Pinot Noir, Sauvignon Blanc, Pinot Blanc and Chardonnay. As these vines are still young, some grapes are still bought in to supplement the crop.

The general manager and winemaker of Eikendal is Josef Krammer, who learned his skills in his homeland, Austria. He first came to South Africa in 1971 to gain experience, intending to stay for a year.

Josef stayed for 18 months in South Africa, working at Delheim. At the time he intended to go on to Australia for further experience in the wine industry, but as it happened he hitchhiked across Africa and finally returned to Austria. There he met Helmut Ratz, who wanted to buy a wine farm in South Africa, and as a result Josef found himself back in the Cape winelands in 1975 as winemaker at Villiera, the estate which Helmut Ratz purchased. In 1983 the Grier brothers bought Villiera and Josef stayed on as winemaker for a while before returning to Austria. Finally, he returned in 1986 to take over the general management of Eikendal Vineyards, and the wine-making from Abraham Beukes.

There are six white wines, five red wines and a Duc de Berry sparkling wine available from Eikendal. The label 'Duc de Berry' is used in honour of the third son of King Jean II of France, 'John the Good'. This son, Jean de France (1340-1416), was duke of, among others, the province of Berry, hence the title 'Duc de Berry'. Although his oppressive policies once led to a peasants' revolt, he is also known as a peace negotiator (with, for example, John of Gaunt, Duke of Lancaster) and as a patron of the arts. He spent lavishly on the treasures that remain at his monument, on paintings, tapestries, jewellery and illuminated manuscripts (to such an extent that there was not enough money to pay for his funeral). He commissioned from the Limburg brothers the world-famous *Très riches heures du duc de Berry*, the 'Book of Hours', poetry beautifully illuminated and handwritten in Gothic script. A rare facsimile of this book passed into the hands of the Saagers, and they decided to display it at Eikendal. They also decided to use the name as a wine label. The Duc de Berry label is a print of one of the pictures in the book. In future, it is intended that most of the wines be marketed under the Eikendal label, while the Duc de Berry label will be used mainly for the C'est si Blanc sparkling wine.

A 'Swiss country lunch' (selected cold meats, salad, cheese, etc) is served from November to April. During the winter months Swiss cheese fondues are a speciality of the farm on Friday evenings.

clearer indication of the company's activities, it was changed to the present name of Gilbey Distillers and Vintners.

In 1968 the company bought a wine farm, De Kleine Zalze, which is situated opposite Blaauwklippen on the road between Stellenbosch and Somerset West. The following year their first wine was made there, and incorporated into ranges such as the Alphen Dry Red and Valley. The first Zinfandel to be bottled under its varietal name, made from the 1975 vintage, was marketed by the company under the Kleine Zalze label, and proved an interesting and unusual wine. Alphen wines are produced in the cellar at Kleine Zalze from grapes grown on the farm or from grapes purchased from growers in carefully selected parts of the Stellenbosch district. The Sauvignon Blanc for their Le Fèvre is grown by Ted and Gary Jordan. Other supplies range as far away as the Helderberg and further into the Vergelegen Valley from the Bairnsfather-Cloete farm Morgenster. The winemaker at Kleine Zalze is Marius Lategan. The contemporary homestead of Kleine Zalze was the home of Allan Bell, who was chairman of Gilbeys South Africa from 1963 to 1987, until his retirement. The present chief executive officer of the company is Peter Fleck.

The most important take-over in Gilbey's recent history, the acquisition of Bertrams Wines Limited, occurred in 1972. The Bertrams company had come into being towards the end of the last century, when Robertson Fuller Bertram purchased the Constantia Estate, famous for the quality of its wines for over 200 years. He extended and

modernized the Constantia cellars, and conducted his wine and spirit business from the estate. During the early part of the present century, Bertrams acquired a high reputation for the quality of its wines and other products, including the internationally known Bertrams Van Der Hum, a naartjie (tangerine)-based liqueur.

The Bertram family continued to control the business until 1939, when it was bought by G.N. Maskell who, in 1940, introduced a complete range of wine and spirits to the South African market under the name of 'Bertrams of Constantia'. New cellars were built adjacent to Groot Constantia, and the company extended its operations into the Transvaal and Natal. In 1943 it also acquired control of Groot Constantia vineyards. A few years later Maskell brought together the various companies under his banner under the name of Bertrams Wines Limited.

In the post-Second World War years, the traditional farming structure of Constantia life began to break down under increasing pressures from urban expansion. In 1959, Bertrams Wines passed into the hands of Simeon Blumberg, who had previously purchased a large wine estate in the Devon Valley, outside Stellenbosch. Shortly after taking over his new company, Blumberg moved both its head office and its cellar activities to the Devonvale farm.

The early 1970s saw the brief ownership of the Devon Valley concern by Gooderson Hotels Limited, and a new emphasis on the making of top-quality table wines. After the merger with Gilbeys, further rationalization took place, the Devonvale winery concentrating on the making of the estate's own wines, as well as upon the blending, maturation and bottling of the Gilbey Group's other quality table wines.

The vineyards at Devonvale are now almost totally replanted with varieties of the very best red wines available. Their famous Shiraz has been replanted with material taken from the original ancient vines that produced magnificent fruit but had almost gone out of production with age. In 1991 Gilbeys totally revamped their Bertrams Cellars at Devonvale and also upgraded their production facility at Oude Molen.

Besides the production of its own wines, Gilbeys markets and distributes N.C. Krone's Twee Jongegezellen range of white wines.

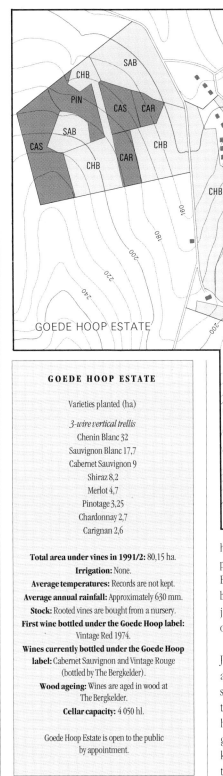

GOEDE HOOP ESTATE

GOEDE HOOP
ESTATE

Once predominantly a white-wine farm growing largely Palomino, Sémillon and Chenin Blanc, the vineyards of Goede Hoop

have been progressively modified by their present owner and winemaker, Johann Bestbier, to enable the making of fine red blended wines. Johann's son, Peter, has now joined his father on the farm and has taken over much of the responsibility of running it.

The estate was bought in 1928 by Johann's father, Petrus Johannes Bestbier, and the qualities of the estate's soil have since been exploited for high-quality production. The steep, gravelly slopes high on the hills of Bottelary are ideally suited to the growing of shy-bearing red varieties of the kind introduced by the elder Bestbier at a time when the demand for such wines still lagged behind the public taste for sweet, white fortified wines.

In recent years, however, this taste has moved towards full red wines. As is normal with most makers of red wines, Johann maintains Chenin Blanc plantings to balance the work programme in his vineyard calendar.

—GRANGEHURST—
WINERY

This property, situated on the slopes of the Helderberg, is owned by Jeremy Walker. The grapes are grown under lease agreements with the local farmers, and the most ideally suited sites were chosen for plantings of the varieties Cabernet Sauvignon, Merlot, Pinotage, Chardonnay and Sauvignon Blanc. The first crush in 1992 will be of small quantities of Merlot, Cabernet Sauvignon and Pinotage. The Chardonnay and Sauvignon Blanc will be made in 1993 and sold in 1994. The red wine will be aged in wood and will be released in about 1995.

Jeremy graduated in 1977 from the University of Stellenbosch with a B.Sc. in Oenology and Viticulture. He then worked for two years with Dr Arnold Schickerling at Bertrams, as well as gaining experience in Rheinhessen in Germany, and Beaujolais and Bordeaux in France. When at Clos Malverne, he produced the 1988 South African Champion Cabernet Sauvignon.
(No statistical information available.)
Grangehurst Winery is not open to the public.

—HARTENBERG—
ESTATE

Known as Montagne for many years, Hartenberg Estate was originally incorporated in Nooitgedacht, which was granted to Christoffel Estreux, or L'Estreux (an ancestor of the South African Esterhuizen family), in 1704. The name Estreux is now used for the estate's Late Harvest wine.

Since those early days the farm has passed through many hands. A famous elephant hunter, Paulus Keyser, owned Hartenberg during the 1720s; subsequently a certain Ari Lekkerwyn was in residence for a while; a freed slave, Aron van Ceylon, also owned it for a few years.

In 1838 the Bosman brothers took over the farm and Johannes Bosman constructed the existing square-gabled house in 1849. There being no Bosman heir to the farm, it was eventually sold to a Swiss immigrant by the name of Doctor Hampf.

The farm's record remained modestly undistinguished until a Cape Town pathologist, Dr Maurice Finlayson, bought it in 1949.

Danie Truter of Hartenberg Estate.

Though wine was being made on the premises, Finlayson and his wife initially concentrated on the development of a chicken hatchery, and later of a dairy herd. No wine of any distinction was made until the Finlaysons' eldest son, Walter, came onto the farm in 1959. At this time dry red wines (including quantities of Cabernet Sauvignon) and sherries were produced for the Castle Wine and Brandy Company, which incorporated the Cabernet and Pontac into their range of Vlottenheimer wines.

Walter Finlayson began his agricultural career by studying to become a dairyman at the West of Scotland Agricultural College. On his return to Hartenberg he was put in charge of the Ayrshire herd, until Dr Finlayson, a veteran lover of good wines, set his son the challenging task of improving the estate's wine production.

Walter took up the challenge with alacrity, and with encouragement from the Castle Wine and Brandy Company and advice from the Wine Institute, quality soon improved. With better techniques went an upgrading of equipment: the original cellar dates back many years, but it was substantially modernized in the early 1960s, when Walter and an agricultural engineer, Johan Murray, collaborated to design a compact crushing and draining plant, which was erected on higher ground alongside the old cellar.

The wines produced were sold under the Montagne label and developed a high reputation, particularly the reds. In 1975 Walter moved off to new pastures, becoming the winemaker at Blaauwklippen, and his younger brother, Peter, took his place.

After Gilbey Distillers and Vintners bought the property a few years later, Peter also moved on, to become winemaker at Hamilton Russell Vineyards. In 1982 he was succeeded at Montagne by Danie Truter, the

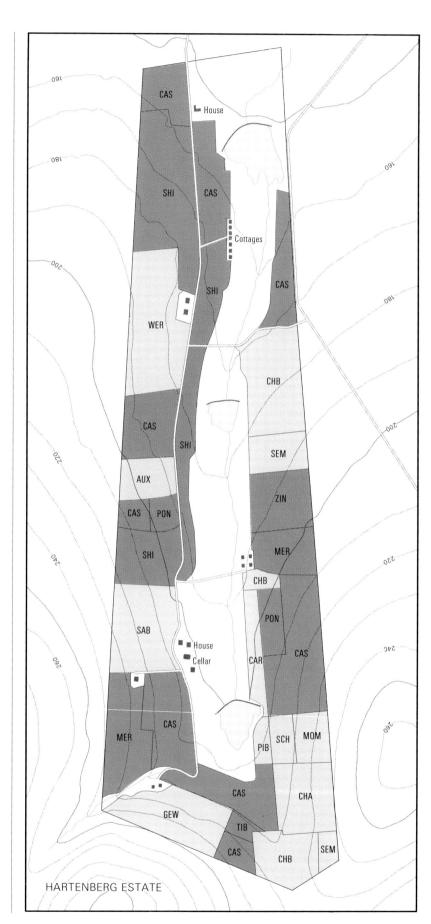

HARTENBERG ESTATE

HARTENBERG ESTATE

Varieties planted (ha)

2-wire vertical trellis
Tinta Barocca 1,75
3-wire vertical trellis
Cabernet Sauvignon 26,83
Shiraz 18,2
Chenin Blanc 12,28
Weisser Riesling 8,64
Merlot 5,68
Gewürztraminer 5,48
Sauvignon Blanc 4,85
Zinfandel 4,03
Chardonnay 3,81
Sémillon 3,5
Auxerrois 3,08
Pontac 2,52
Morio Muscat 1,22
Pinot Blanc 1,22
Schönberger 1,22

Total area under vines in 1991/2: 104,3 ha.
Irrigation: Only young vineyards up to 3 years are irrigated when necessary.
Average temperatures:
Maximum 24 °C; minimum 12 °C.
Average annual rainfall: 750 mm.
Stock: Selected rooted vines are bought from nurseries.
First wine bottled under the Hartenberg label:
Dry Red (vintage approximately 1968).
Wines currently bottled under the Hartenberg label: Chatillon, Weisser Riesling, Sauvignon Blanc, L'Estreux, Bin 3, Bin 6, Cabernet Sauvignon, Shiraz, Zinfandel, Paragon, Bin 9 and Chardonnay.
Wood ageing: A new underground cellar can accommodate up to 1 000 small barrels and six 5 000-*l* vats.
Cellar capacity: 5 514 *hl* in tanks, 62 400 *l* in big wooden vats, 80 000 *l* in small wooden barrels, up to 200 000 bottles.

Hartenberg Estate is on the Stellenbosch Wine Route and is open to the public for wine tastings and sales on weekdays from 08h30 to 17h00, and on Saturdays from 09h00 to 15h00.
Cellar tours are conducted on weekdays at 10h00 and 15h00, and on Saturdays at 10h00.
Vintner's lunches are served all year round Monday to Saturday; in summer vintner's platters are served in the garden and in winter soup lunches are served in the tasting room.

present winemaker. Gilbeys changed the name back from Montagne to Hartenberg. The range of modern Hartenberg wines was launched in 1985 and immediately found favour, especially the red wines. The Cabernet and Shiraz are not released until they have matured for six years after their vintage – one year in 5 000-litre oak barrels and five years in the bottle.

The underground cellar at Hartenberg.

Hartenberg has its own distinctive climate, with early morning mists followed by good sunshine, with the result that the grapes ripen up to two weeks later than the surrounding farms.

Hartenberg Estate is well known for its unique soils, varying from decomposed granite to Malmesbury Shale. This wide range of soils makes the estate ideally suited to many of the world's finest varieties.

Today Hartenberg belongs to businessman Ken Mackenzie, who, together with his two daughters, bought it in 1986. Ken was born in the Cape and educated in South Africa; after serving throughout World War II as a fighter pilot, he started a business which grew into a very successful international enterprise. He is domiciled abroad but has always maintained a keen interest in South Africa and, of course, in particular in Hartenberg Estate. He has, over the past 40 years, put together an enviable private cellar in which are represented some of the top-quality wines from vineyards located all over the world.

The estate is now some 180 hectares in extent, of which 104 are under vines. An extensive replanting programme is being carried out and the estate will eventually produce 70 per cent red wines. These vines will include Cabernet Sauvignon, Shiraz, Merlot, Pontac and Zinfandel. Hartenberg still has 8 000 Auxerrois vines, the produce of which is used in the dry white blend, Chatillon. Chardonnay has been planted and the first barrel-fermented Chardonnay was released in limited quantities in 1990.

—HAZENDAL—
ESTATE

Situated between Stellenbosch and Kuils River on the sandy fringes of the Stellenbosch wine-making region, Hazendal has been the home of the Bosman family for over a hundred and fifty years. The farm itself dates back to a grant of 1704, and features a very fine late eighteenth-century Cape Dutch homestead named after the farm's first owner, Christoffel Hazenwinkel. It was taken over by the Bosmans from the widow Wilhelmina de Waal in 1831. Already well established in the Cape, they were descended from one Hermanus Lambertus Bos-

Michael Bosman, who is the fifth generation of the Bosman family to live on Hazendal Estate.

man, the *sieketrooster*, or sick-comforter, to the Drakenstein congregation in the early eighteenth century. The modern farm Hazendal emerged, however, with Piet Bosman,

HAZENDAL ESTATE

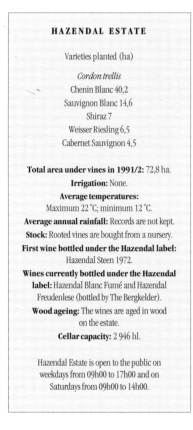

owner and winemaker for the 40 years from
1941 until his death in 1982.

Although Hazendal is particularly well
known for one of its white wines, the prize-
winning Chenin Blanc, the plantings that
Piet established were predominantly of red
varieties. Most of the red varieties were trellised while the whites were left as bush vines,
the exception being in the low-lying alluvial
soils where the white varieties, particularly
the Chenin Blanc, grow vigorously and therefore need the support of trellises to keep
them clear of the ground. Piet never irrigated his vineyards, feeling that the soil retained sufficient moisture for their needs,
leading to a smaller crop of better quality. A
traditionalist, Piet Bosman felt that it was
important that there should be contact between the must of the white grapes and their
skins before fermentation, if only for a few
hours. It was on this basis that the Chenin
Blanc was made. A Special Late Harvest
called Freudenlese is also produced and has
an ageing potential of up to 10 years.

The fifth generation of the Bosmans has
now taken over the running of the farm.
Piet's son Michael is the owner and winemaker while his wife Carita looks after the
tasting and a most attractive country shop.

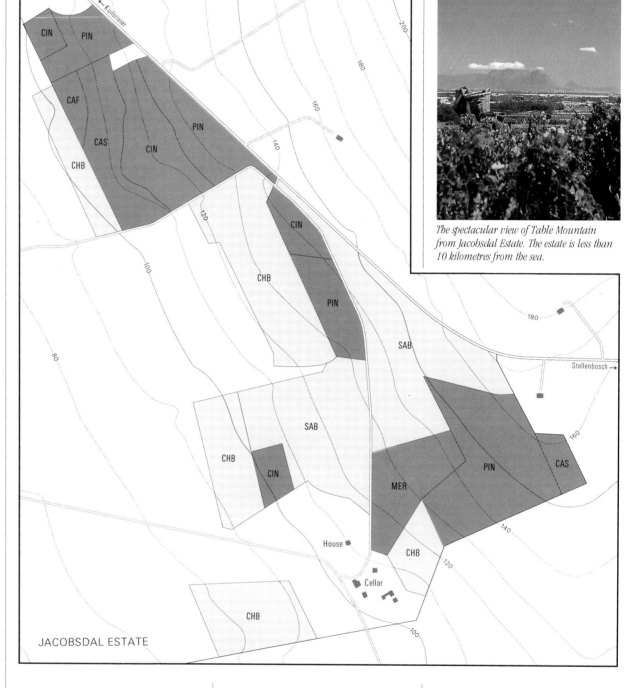

*The spectacular view of Table Mountain
from Jacobsdal Estate. The estate is less than
10 kilometres from the sea.*

JACOBSDAL ESTATE

—JACOBSDAL—
ESTATE

Situated on the extreme southern edge of the
wine-producing area of Stellenbosch and facing the sea less than 10 kilometres distant,
Jacobsdal is a good example of the ingenious
exploitation of limited resources. Combining
deep, predominantly sandy soil with a dearth
of water supply and without the advantages
of a natural reservoir such as that provided
by the water in the Eerste River, Jacobsdal

Estate relies heavily on the 600-millimetre
annual winter rainfall.

Given these unpromising conditions, the
owner and winemaker of Jacobsdal, Cornelis
Dumas, has adapted his vineyard procedures
with the use of extensive pruning. With a
minimum of plant nutrition and moisture
available in the soil, it has been necessary to
concentrate the strength of the growing vines
by cutting back their bearing capacity, and
by growing them as bush vines rather than
training them on trellises.

The result of this approach is that though
the farm features what are generally regarded as prolific varieties, the crop — small
by comparison with those of other local
farms — is of a high quality, the pruning
techniques giving fine, rich colour to such
wines as Jacobsdal's award-winning Pinotage (to date the only one of the estate's products to be bottled under its own label).

Of the total 300 hectares of generally low-
lying land, about 92 are given over to the
vineyards. The bulk of these are shared be-

JACOBSDAL ESTATE

Varieties planted (ha)

Bush vines
Chenin Blanc* 34
Pinotage 18
Sauvignon Blanc 18
Cinsaut 9
Cabernet Sauvignon 6
Cabernet Franc 2
Perold trellis
Merlot 5
* Includes the oldest vine on the estate (65 years)

Total area under vines in 1991/2:
92 ha (15 ha still to be planted).
Irrigation: None.
Average temperatures:
Maximum 30 °C; minimum 5 °C.
Average annual rainfall: 600 mm.
Stock: Rooted vines are bought from a nursery.
First wine bottled under the Jacobsdal label:
Pinotage 1974.
Wine currently bottled under the Jacobsdal label: Pinotage (bottled by The Bergkelder).
Wood ageing: At The Bergkelder.
Cellar capacity: 4 800 hl.

Jacobsdal Estate is not open to the public.

tween Chenin Blanc, Pinotage and Sauvignon Blanc, while smaller blocks are planted to Merlot, Cinsaut, Cabernet Sauvignon and Cabernet Franc. The remaining 200 hectares are mostly used as grazing for Cornelis's large flocks of Dohne Merino sheep.

— JORDAN —
ESTATE

After retiring from 'Jordan Shoes' in 1982, Ted Jordan bought the rather neglected farm called Kanonkop – named after the hill on which it is situated and where the signal cannon still lies. Together, the Jordan family

Ted and Gary Jordan, of Jordan Estate in Stellenbosch.

The Jordan family restored the neglected property of Kanonkop, renamed it Jordan, and today it is a beautiful estate.

turned the dilapidated 74-hectare property into the fine estate it is today. Even Gary, who was completing his B.Sc. degree in geology at the time, was actively involved in the replanting of the vineyards. From 1985 he joined the farm full-time.

Since 1985, the farm has been entirely replanted, mostly with new-clone Cabernet Sauvignon and Chardonnay vines, as well as with smaller amounts of Pinot Noir, Merlot, Sauvignon Blanc, Gewürztraminer, Weisser Riesling and Chenin Blanc. In 1988 a further 10 hectares were bought from a neighbour on the northern farm boundary, increasing the farm size to 85 hectares. The KWV quota was then increased to 710 tonnes. From 1983 to 1990, all the grapes were delivered to the Eersterivier Co-operative where the Chardonnay grapes were used to produce the first Eersterivier Chardonnay. Since 1991 the farm has delivered grapes to the Alphen Winery.

In 1989, Gary and his wife Kathy became the first South African husband and wife team to work in a winery in California. They returned to South Africa with a son, Alexander, who has become affectionately known as 'Alexander the Grape'! His studies at the University of California, Davis, together with his background in geology and viticultural experience, have enabled Gary to select the grape varieties and rootstocks best suited to the particular slopes and soils, and specific clones for individual vineyards.

Gary believes that quality fruit and rigorous grape selection is vital for the production of high-quality wine. He also maintains that hillside vineyards produce the best fruit and that a combination of cool breezes, optimal trellising, leaner soils and lower yields have improved the flavour and quality of the grapes. New-clone, virus-free varieties have been planted, 70 hectares to be under vines once the replanting programme has been completed. Harvesting at the coolest periods of the day and prompt delivery of grapes to the cellar ensure less colour and phenolic extraction at pressing.

Plans are already under way for the building of a winery and the first crush is intended for February 1993. The focus will be to achieve a balance and complexity in the wines, and barrel fermentation of Chardonnay and Sauvignon Blanc will be an important contribution to the Jordan style. A Cabernet blend is also envisaged. The wine will be marketed under the family name of Jordan, as Gary believes: 'a 'New World' name for a new South Africa'.

JORDAN ESTATE

Varieties planted (ha)

Vertical hedge trellis
Chardonnay 16
Cabernet Sauvignon 12,5
Sauvignon Blanc 8
Chenin Blanc 8
Merlot 3,5
Cape Riesling 3
Pinot Noir 2
Weisser Riesling 2
Gewürztraminer 1,5

Total area under vines in 1991/2:
56,5 ha (13,5 ha still to be planted).
Irrigation: 39 ha are under an Israeli-designed, computer-controlled microjet system; the remaining hectares can be irrigated with moveable pipelines if necessary.
Average temperatures:
Maximum 25 °C; minimum 12 °C.
Average annual rainfall: 785mm.
Stock: Rooted vines are bought from a nursery and only certified virus-free clonal material is used.
First wines to be bottled under the Jordan label: Jordan Chardonnay and Jordan Cabernet Sauvignon (maiden vintage 1993).
Wood ageing: Wines to be aged in new small wood on the estate.
Cellar capacity: 4 000 hl plus 180 000-bottle maturation cellar.

Jordan Estate will be open to the public from 1993 by appointment only.

KAAPZICHT
ESTATE

The farm Rozendal was bought by Major D.C. Steytler in 1946 when he and his two sons, David and George, returned from Italy after World War II. George, the younger of the brothers, ran the farm for his father, building up grape production from 250 tonnes in the 1940s to 1 100 tonnes in the 1970s. In 1969 he formed a company called Steytdal Farm (Pty) Ltd, and bought the farm from his father.

George's son, Danie, joined the family company in 1976 as farm manager after finishing his studies in agriculture, and in 1982 Danie tried to register the farm as an estate. He was unable to do so as a company had registered the name 'Rosenthaler', and the well-known farm of Hazendal was already registered as an estate. It was felt that 'Rozendal' was too similar to these names, which meant an alternative name had to be found. As the farm is situated in the Bottelary hills and has a breathtaking view of Cape Town and its mountains, the name 'Kaapzicht' was considered appropriate and the estate was registered in 1984 under this name. In the same year, George Steytler Junior joined the company and with his brother Danie formed a company, Kaapzicht Landgoed (Pty) Ltd, drawing up a lease contract to hire the farm Rozendal from Steytdal Farm (Pty) Ltd for a period of six years starting from February 1985.

As a result of a large vineyard renewal programme, the production of the estate dropped to 750 tonnes in 1986 and in 1991 reached 1 179 tonnes. There is a KWV quota of 1 600 tonnes, which should be reached in time. The wine is bottled by the Stellenbosse Bottleringskoöperasie Beperk, but the family wants to keep its bottling venture small and exclusive, with quality and individuality as its main aims, increasing the range to five wines but not letting it exceed 10 per cent of the total production, so that they can manage their own marketing. At present 99 per cent of the wine produced at Kaapzicht is sold to Stellenbosch Farmers' Winery.

Kaapzicht's first wine, an off-dry Weisser Riesling, was bottled in 1984. The 1985 vintage was better, and a more delicate Weisser Riesling with a lower alcohol level was produced, in the same style. In 1986 the

---

KAAPZICHT ESTATE

Varieties planted (ha)

Bush vines
Chenin Blanc 74,36
Bush vines and 3-wire trellis
Muscat d'Alexandrie 13,2
Cinsaut 3
Colombard 2,5
3-wire trellis
Sauvignon Blanc 11,06
Cabernet Sauvignon 10,38
Merlot 4,5
Shiraz 2,25
Weisser Riesling 1,64
Clairette Blanche 0,89
Pinotage 0,72
Perold trellis
Cape Riesling 2,4

The oldest vineyard comprises 2,4 ha, containing 5 354 Chenin Blanc/Jacquez vines planted in 1929.

Total area under vines in 1991/2: 126,9 ha.
Irrigation: None.
Average temperatures: Records are not kept.
Average annual rainfall: 572 mm.
Stock: Kaapzicht used its own parent stock for grafting until 1977; it now buys from a nursery.
Envisaged new variety: Chardonnay.
First wine bottled under the Kaapzicht label: Weisser Riesling 1984.
Wines currently bottled under the Kaapzicht label: Sauvignon Blanc, Weisser Riesling, Weisser Riesling Special Late Harvest, Cinsaut and Pinotage (all bottled by the Stellenbosse Bottleringskoöperasie Beperk).
Wood ageing: Pinotage is being aged in new Nevers small wood barrels.
Cellar capacity: 5 686 hl.

Wine sales are conducted at Kaapzicht Estate on weekdays from 09h00 to 18h00, and on Saturdays from 08h00 to 12h00. Wine- tastings and cellar tours are by appointment only.

Danie Steytler of Kaapzicht Estate.

Steytlers changed the style of the wine to completely dry, and also introduced night picking, which considerably improved the bouquet of this vintage.

Autumn colours in the vineyards at Kanonkop Estate.

KANONKOP
ESTATE

The land of Kanonkop originally formed part of the farm Uitkyk, the property of the late Senator J.H. Sauer, but in 1930 the larger portion of Uitkyk was sold to Baron Hans von Carlowitz, while the lower section was renamed Kanonkop. (In the days of the Dutch East India Company, sightings of the approach of the Company's fleet were signalled by a cannon on a nearby hill.)

It was on this newly created farm that J.H. Sauer's son, the Honourable P.O. Sauer (Minister of Transport for some time, and respectfully known as 'Oom Paul'), began wine farming, together with Danie Rossouw, in the early 1930s.

Since Oom Paul's death in 1975, the farm has been run by his son-in-law, Jannie Krige, who is today ably assisted by his two sons, Johann and Paul. The making of its high-quality wines, however, was the responsibility of Jan 'Boland' Coetzee, who left in 1980 and was replaced by the innovative winemaker Beyers Truter.

Both Beyers and his forerunner have concentrated on two varieties, namely Cabernet Sauvignon and Pinotage. These two varieties are eminently suited to the soil and climate of Kanonkop, which was one of the first of the local estates to plant Pinotage. Of the three main soil types found on the estate, the most important is the pebbly, granitic soil found on the high sloping western side of the farm. It is in this area that the farm's Pinotage and Cabernet plantings are concen-

trated. Because of the excellent and hotter climatic conditions on the lower and more sandy soils, a five-year programme of soil preparation was started in the early 1980s. New virus-free clones of Merlot, Cabernet Franc, Cabernet Sauvignon and Pinotage were planted and are already in production.

The present winemaker, Beyers Truter, has now put his own individual stamp on the excellent wines produced on Kanonkop.

KANONKOP ESTATE

Varieties planted (ha)

Bush vines
Pinotage 16
5-wire trellis
Cabernet Sauvignon 36
Sauvignon Blanc 10
Weisser Riesling 10
Pinot Noir 8
Cabernet Franc 6
Merlot 6
Chardonnay 3

Total area under vines in 1991/2: 95 ha.
Irrigation: None.
Average temperatures: Records are not kept.
Average annual rainfall: Records are not kept.
Stock: Rooted vines are bought from a nursery.
First wine bottled under the Kanonkop label: Cabernet Sauvignon 1973.
Wines currently bottled under the Kanonkop label: Cabernet Sauvignon, Paul Sauer and Pinotage.
Wood ageing: Wines are aged for 16-18 months in small Nevers French oak barrels.
Cellar capacity: 7 000 hl.

Kanonkop Estate is open to the public during normal office hours.

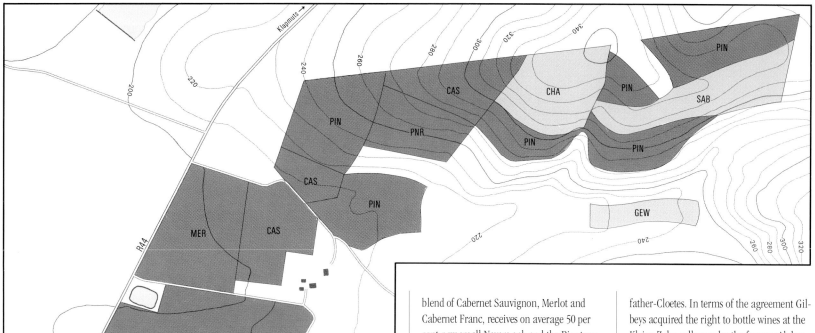

KANONKOP ESTATE

In his first 10 years on the estate he has achieved great success – one of the highlights being the Diners' Club Winemaker of the Year award in 1987 for Kanonkop Pinotage, and another his being chosen as Winemaker of the Year at the 1991 International Wine and Spirit Competition in London.

One of the more important aims on Kanonkop is to restore Pinotage to the posi-

Beyers Truter with the coveted Robert Mondavi Trophy.

tion it deserves in the South African market. To this end Beyers makes sure that the grapes are picked at optimum ripeness – essential for the Pinotage fruit – and that the correct wood contact is given to the wine. After many years of experimentation with Pinotage in new Nevers oak (225-litre barrels), the 1989 vintage was the first to be released with a higher oak level to match the rich fruit of the Kanonkop Pinotages.

Experimentation is done on an ongoing basis on fermentation temperatures, duration of skin contact and optimum ripeness for different seasons and soils. Beyers has also done a lot of experimentation on wood contact to suit the Kanonkop reds – to such an extent that the estate now boasts a small-barrel maturation cellar in excess of 500 barrels from the Seguim Moreau Cooperage in France, besides *barriques* from various other coopers. The Paul Sauer, which is a

blend of Cabernet Sauvignon, Merlot and Cabernet Franc, receives on average 50 per cent new small Nevers oak and the Pinotage 15 per cent (which is now being increased).

The estate has of late cut back on its range of wines and will in future only market the Paul Sauer, Cabernet Sauvignon and Pinotage. All plantings since the last decade were aimed at this mix, yielding gratifying results. In recent years Kanonkop has won an impressive array of awards and medals at wine shows both locally and internationally, strengthening the already sound reputation of this fine estate.

— KLEINE ZALZE —

The original freehold grant of the 57-morgen farm De Groote Zalze by Governor Simon van der Stel dates back to 1695. The land seems to have been granted in two parts, and it is within the boundaries of one of these subdivisions that the present-day farm of Kleine Zalze lies – opposite Blaauwklippen Estate on the road between Stellenbosch and Somerset West.

The original estate had a great many owners, a number of them bearing the names of some of the more famous families of the region, among them Colyn, Krige and Du Toit. In 1968 the portion then known as De Kleine Zalze was bought by Gilbeys, who modernized the name and began developing the farm's wine-making potential. This was done in association with Alphen, the Constantia Estate then owned by the Bairns-

father-Cloetes. In terms of the agreement Gilbeys acquired the right to bottle wines at the Kleine Zalze cellar under the famous Alphen label, and this practice continues today even though direct links with Alphen are no longer in place, following the sale of the Cloete farm to Hans-Joachim Schreiber in 1981. Marius Lategan is the winemaker reporting to Gilbey's production chief, Martin van der Merwe. In addition to the Alphen range, wines were also produced in the early years under the Kleine Zalze label.

Today the Alphen wines, all bottled at the Kleine Zalze winery, are produced from the grapes harvested from a number of individual farms in the Stellenbosch district, where the owners have been commissioned to grow chosen varieties. The association between cellarmaster and grower is very close at Kleine Zalze, starting with the mutual planning of

Wooden barrels in the cellar at Kleine Zalze.

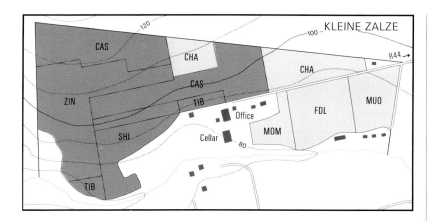

SFW, Distillers and KWV, and a small amount is bottled for sale on the premises. This winery has most modern and technologically advanced wine-making equipment, and was the first to install an automatic pressing cellar, operated by one man

—KOOPMANSKLOOF—
ESTATE

Situated on the northern slopes of the Bottelary hills, this estate is now owned by Stevie Smit, the third generation of his family to own Koopmanskloof. The estate has a long history, having already been part of the Bottelary freeholds in 1701. Izaak Bosman bought a subdivision of the original farm 'Bottelary' from a certain Jan Rotterdam in 1777. According to an inventory of that year, Koopmanskloof had at that time 50 000 vines, 16 leaguers (1 leaguer is equivalent to 127 gallons) of wine and 1,5 leaguers of brandy, making the estate one of the first places in South Africa to have distilled brandy. When Stevie's grandfather, Wynand Stephanus Smit, bought it in 1896, it was run as a mixed farm, with wheat and vines side-by-side. Nowadays the wheat has been replaced by fruit, but the vines are still very much in evidence. The present owner took over the property in 1956, and proceeded to expand its production. Of late Stevie has confined his activities to the vineyards, while his son, Stefan, who returned from four years of wine studies in Weinsberg, Germany, to work in his father's cellar, takes responsibility for making the wine.

In Koopmanskloof's wide range of soils, a representative range of varieties is grown, made possible by the various aspects, slopes and microclimates found on the estate. White wine varieties include Sauvignon Blanc, Chardonnay, Sémillon and Weisser Riesling, while red varieties include Tinta Barocca, Shiraz and Cabernet Sauvignon.

During his studies overseas, Stefan was exposed to the European concern for conservation and ecology. He realized that the emphasis is often placed on productivity at the cost of the environment, and was determined to implement bio-organic farming methods on his return to South Africa. These include higher than normal training methods in order to increase the natural acid of the grapes, and also to allow more air and sunlight to reach the grapes, thereby increasing resistance to disease. With thorough soil analysis, it is possible to plant the ideal varieties in the most suitable soils, therefore soil preparation is carefully planned. A cover crop is sown each winter in order to suppress weed growth and aid humus build-up in the soil, and pest control methods are applied only when absolutely necessary. Only organic fertilizer is used. In the cellar, too, the gentlest and healthiest vinification methods are used to obtain the best possible wines and natural flavours. Fermentation only takes place with genetically stable yeast, and the wines are then fined with natural agents.

At present Koopmanskloof's Marbonne Sauvignon Blanc is marketed by The Bergkelder and from the estate under the estate's label. It is a superb wine and the pride of the estate. First marketed in 1979, it received the Gold Medal at the International Club Oenologique Wine and Spirit Competition in London in its début year. Following the success of the Blanc de Marbonne, the first Koopmanskloof Rhine Riesling, the 1984 vintage, was released to great acclaim.

The neck labels of these wines depict various fynbos species, as proof of the owner's abiding interest in and respect for the wealth of flora in this part of the world – a love for

Stefan Smit of Koopmanskloof Estate.

---

each vineyard and continuing right through the grape-growing and on through the entire wine-making process.

ALPHEN
CHARDONNAY
1990
WINE OF ORIGIN
COASTAL REGION

—KOELENHOF—
CO-OPERATIVE WINE CELLAR

Pieter Carstens, winemaker at Koelenhof Co-operative Wine Cellar.

Established in August 1941, this co-operative began as a family concern involving J.W.S. de Villiers, four of his sons, and Nico de Kock. They had their own winemaker, Hugo de Vries, whose son, Helmie, succeeded him as winemaker and is now manager of the co-operative. The present winemaker is Pieter Carstens.

Today the co-operative has 81 members, mostly in the Stellenbosch district, but some as far away as Constantia, Durbanville and Wellington. The bulk of the wine is sold to

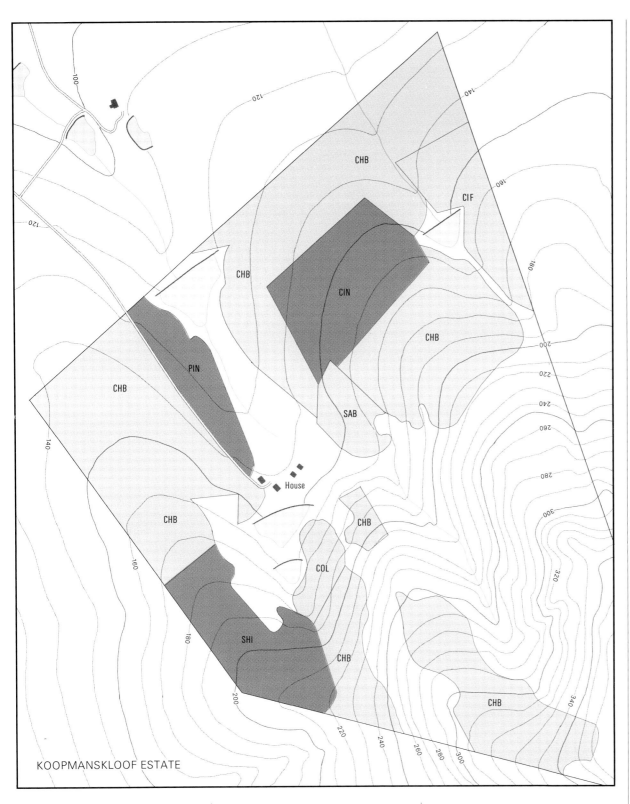

KOOPMANSKLOOF ESTATE

KOOPMANSKLOOF ESTATE

Varieties planted (ha)

Bush vines
Sauvignon Blanc 40
Chardonnay 20
Pinotage 18
Tinta Barocca 12
Sémillon 8
Vertical trellis
Cabernet Sauvignon 36
Weisser Riesling 25
Shiraz 20
Pinot Gris 12
Merlot 4

Total area under vines in 1991/2: Not available.
Irrigation: Some vineyards are irrigated.
Average temperatures:
Maximum 23 °C; minimum 11 °C.
Average annual rainfall: 625 mm.
Stock: Rooted vines are bought from a nursery.
**First wine bottled under the Koopmanskloof
label:** Blanc de Marbonne 1979.
**Wines currently bottled under the
Koopmanskloof label:** Rhine Riesling and
Marbonne Sauvignon Blanc (bottled by
The Bergkelder).
Wood ageing: At present wines are aged in wood
at The Bergkelder but will be aged on the estate
in the future.
Cellar capacity: 25 000 hl.

Koopmanskloof Estate is on the Stellenbosch Wine
Route and is open to the public from 09h00 to 17h00
every day but Sunday and any other time
by appointment.

—LANZERAC—
VINEYARDS

The property of Lanzerac, together with the Lanzerac Hotel buildings, was bought by businessman Christo Wiese in 1991. He is renovating the traditional Cape buildings, and hoping to make the homestead his private residence. The existing rooms and suites of the hotel will continue to be used so that visitors can still relax and enjoy the beautiful rural surroundings. The Lanzerac Coffee Shop Patio, at the entrance to Lanzerac, is already functioning, as is the Malay Kitchen, serving traditional Cape-Eastern dishes.

Jan Boland Coetzee of Vriesenhof is acting as consultant to Lanzerac (as well as to Talana Hill, Eikendal and Madeba Valley, among others). Once the soils and conditions have been carefully analysed, classic varieties such as Chardonnay, Pinot Noir, Cabernet Franc and Merlot will be planted in

nature which has led to the establishment of a 200-hectare fynbos nature reserve on Koopmanskloof. Another feature of the estate is that it is crossed by the Vineyard Trail – a 24-kilometre hiking trail along the crest of the Bottelary hills which Stevie was instrumental

in establishing. At the highest point of this trail – on Koopmanskloof – there is a stone rondavel which is often used as a peaceful retreat from the cares of the world.

Future developments to watch for on the estate include a port made in the traditional

Portuguese style, planned for release in 1993, and an estate brandy made from the best varieties, distilled in copper stills and aged in new barrels for at least five years. The first such brandy made in this way is due for release in 1996.

Established in 1692, Lanzerac houses a well-known restaurant offering traditional Cape dishes and cheese lunches.

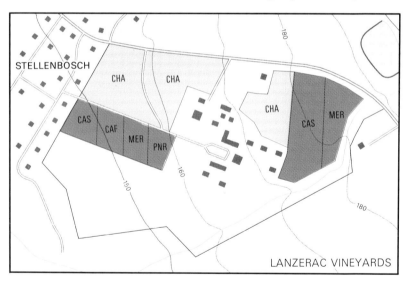

the areas most suited to each variety. Eventually, 24 hectares will be under vine, and about 250 tonnes of grapes should result in some 170 000 bottles of wine.

The development of the property of Lanzerac is a challenging prospect for Christo Wiese. His main intention is to intends to improve the quality of the wines and preserve the historic buildings.

— LE BONHEUR —
ESTATE

Previously known as Oude Weltevreden, this 163-hectare estate with the optimistic name of Le Bonheur ('Happiness') is situated along the slopes of the Klapmuts Hill on the northern point of the Simonsberg. The farm was granted to its first owner, Jacob Isak de

Villiers, by Lord Charles Somerset, and it was De Villiers who built the H-shaped Cape Dutch homestead, the roof of which was destroyed by fire many years ago. When it was rebuilt, the characteristic gables of the period were covered by a corrugated iron roof.

In the early 1970s the farm was bought by Michael Woodhead. Born in Johannesburg, he studied Tropical Agriculture and Soil Science at a university in Holland.

Before becoming a wine farmer, Michael held a variety of positions in agriculture in different parts of the world, working in South America on sugar plantations, raising beef, tobacco and maize in Swaziland, and running a cattle ranch in the Knysna area. He was also once an agricultural adviser to the former president of Tanzania, namely Julius Nyerere.

When Michael acquired Oude Weltevreden, both lands and house were dilapidated, and wine had not been made on the farm for 50 years. He found that the soils were relatively poor: the lower-lying areas were sandy, with a clay subsoil, while those on the higher areas, running from Klapmuts Hill to Klapmuts Nek, though of granitic

origin and deep and well drained, were also poor in quality.

Enrichment of the soil was obviously a priority and large quantities of compost were introduced to improve the organic matter content. Michael has a dairy which produces about half his compost needs; a small stud farm on the property also makes its contribution. Grape husks added to the

The attractive and modern new cellar buildings at Le Bonheur were recently completed.

LE BONHEUR ESTATE

Michael Woodhead, producer of the best Cabernet Sauvignon at the 1991 International Wine and Spirits Competition.

our, took the fancy of the consumers to any extent, and have now been discontinued. The Le Bonheur Blanc Fumé, which followed, has become a bench mark for wines of its type. It is made from Sauvignon Blanc, a selectively cultivated variety which gives a very dry but full wine with a flowery aroma. More recently magnificent Cabernets from the 1982 and 1983 vintages have been released. Made entirely from Cabernet Sauvignon, and well aged in small wood, they show promise of being truly great in the 1990s. The Le Bonheur Chardonnay also promises to be an exceptional wine.

—LIEVLAND—
ESTATE

The tiny eastern European state of Lievland, which since the Second World War has disappeared from the map, gave its name posthumously to this estate. In the early 1930s, the Baron von Stiernhielm of Lievland came to South Africa and bought land at the Cape. The Baron died leaving his widow to bring her four children out alone in 1936.

The farm her husband had purchased, Beyers Kloof, had, until 1820, been part of the property of Natte Vallei. The Dutch-born Baroness promptly renamed it Lievland, in honour of her husband's fatherland. An indomitable woman, she took up the study of viticulture under Dr A.I. Perold, and within four years was making her own wine. At first she was assisted by a winemaker, but soon decided she could do the job herself, and therefore boldly took on the running of the whole operation.

The farm was bought by the Benadé family in 1973. The new owners took Lievland in hand, planting a range of new varieties, including Bukettraube, Kerner, Wiesser Riesling, Sauvignon Blanc and Merlot. A new underground cellar for maturation and storage was completed in 1987, further strengthening the infrastructure of this sound estate. One of the most enterprising newcomers to the winelands, Janey Muller, was approached to become winemaker at Lievland. After two years of hard work, Janey

OVERLEAF: *Rows of vines in Stellenbosch with the Simonsberg in the background.*

soil – a regular practice on most farms – have also helped to improve its quality. Michael has generally tried to restructure his soils along the lines of some of the better vineyard soils that are found in the wine-making areas of France.

Complete replanting of the vineyards was undertaken. Red varieties introduced include Cabernet Sauvignon, Shiraz and Carignan; whites include Chenin Blanc, Sauvignon Blanc and Chardonnay. Michael is one of the few local farmers to grow Carignan, an

important grape in the south of France, but rare here, to use in blending. An ultra-modern and most attractive new cellar was completed, in time for the 1990 vintage.

Some time ago the estate launched a 1981 vintage dry Rosé which was made in the traditional manner for this kind of wine, and exclusively from Cabernet Sauvignon grapes. The 1982 vintage was even better, yet incredibly neither of these excellent wines, which were fresh and fruity with unmistakeable Cabernet character and delightful col-

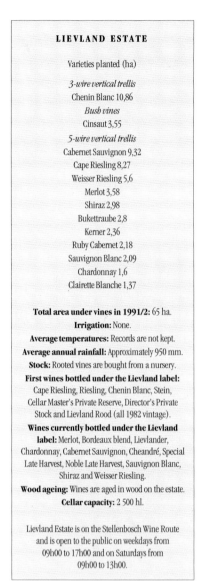

LIEVLAND ESTATE

Varieties planted (ha)

3-wire vertical trellis
Chenin Blanc 10,86
Bush vines
Cinsaut 3,55
5-wire vertical trellis
Cabernet Sauvignon 9,32
Cape Riesling 8,27
Weisser Riesling 5,6
Merlot 3,58
Shiraz 2,98
Bukettraube 2,8
Kerner 2,36
Ruby Cabernet 2,18
Sauvignon Blanc 2,09
Chardonnay 1,6
Clairette Blanche 1,37

Total area under vines in 1991/2: 65 ha.
Irrigation: None.
Average temperatures: Records are not kept.
Average annual rainfall: Approximately 950 mm.
Stock: Rooted vines are bought from a nursery.
First wines bottled under the Lievland label:
Cape Riesling, Riesling, Chenin Blanc, Stein,
Cellar Master's Private Reserve, Director's Private
Stock and Lievland Rood (all 1982 vintage).
**Wines currently bottled under the Lievland
label:** Merlot, Bordeaux blend, Lievlander,
Chardonnay, Cabernet Sauvignon, Cheandré, Special
Late Harvest, Noble Late Harvest, Sauvignon Blanc,
Shiraz and Weisser Riesling.
Wood ageing: Wines are aged in wood on the estate.
Cellar capacity: 2 500 hl.

Lievland Estate is on the Stellenbosch Wine Route
and is open to the public on weekdays from
09h00 to 17h00 and on Saturdays from
09h00 to 13h00.

*Abé Beukes, previously winemaker at
Eikendal and Simonsig.*

left Lievland to concentrate on wine-making
at her own estate, Lemberg.

In 1984 Paul Benadé took over the management of the estate. A B.Com. graduate
from the University of Port Elizabeth, Paul
had previously worked at Stellenbosch

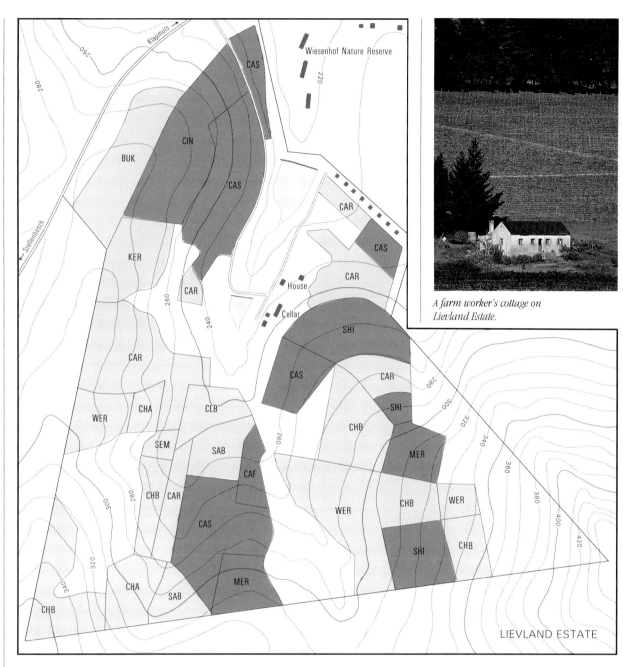

*A farm worker's cottage on
Lievland Estate.*

LIEVLAND ESTATE

Farmers' Winery in the marketing division.
Jako Smit joined the estate as winemaker
that year, and on his departure in 1987 was
succeeded by Abraham Beukes. Abé Beukes
graduated from the University of Stellenbosch with a B.Sc. in agriculture majoring
in viticulture, viniculture and microbiology.
As a student he worked with Jan Coetzee at
Kanonkop, gaining valuable experience. Subsequent to two years of viticultural research
at Nietvoorbij, he worked as winemaker at
Eikendal and Simonsig.

Having bought his father's interest in
Lievland, Paul Benadé is now sole owner of

the estate. Abé and Paul both travel extensively and their shared ambition is that Lievland
should be known both locally and internationally as producing wines of repute. They
have been particularly conscious of creating
an awareness of Shiraz and the Lievland
Shiraz is known to be one of the highest
quality in the Cape. Abé is particularly proud
of the Lievland Noble Late Harvest which
scored higher than any other Noble Late Harvest wine at the 1991 International Wine and
Spirit Competition in London. Paul is an
avid student and successfully graduated as
a Cape Wine Master in 1992.

— LOUISVALE —
FARM

The imposing homestead of this Devon Valley property, built in 1905 and recently renovated, is a classic example of Sir Herbert
Baker's architectural genius. At some stage
the farm probably formed part of a much
larger estate, but in its present form Louisvale is a young farm. The bulk of the bearing vines were planted in the mid-1980s;
prior to this the land had been put to varied
uses, including the cultivation of fruit and
vegetables and cattle-farming. Only when

The homestead and cellar buildings of Louisvale Farm in the beautiful Devon Valley.

Hans Froehling and Leon Stemmet, who acquired Louisvale in 1988.

LOUISVALE FARM

Varieties planted (ha)

Perold trellis
Chardonnay 14

Total area under vines in 1991/2: 14 ha.
Irrigation: Minimal; just after harvesting.
Average temperatures:
Maximum 22,9 °C; minimum 10,7 °C.
Average annual rainfall: Approximately 605 mm.
Stock: Rooted vines are bought from a nursery.
First wine bottled under the Louisvale label:
Chardonnay 1989.
Wine currently bottled under the Louisvale label: Chardonnay.
Wood ageing: The wine is aged in small French oak casks on the farm.
Cellar capacity: 630-730 hl.

Louisvale Farm is open to the public only by prior arrangement.

the present owners, Hans-Dieter Froehling and Leon Stemmet, took over the farm in 1988 did intensive vine cultivation begin.

By their own admission Hans and Leon knew a lot more about the business world and computers than they did about farming, let alone the exacting practice of viticulture and wine-making. However, experts at Niet-voorbij and KWV, as well as farmers in the area, gave freely of their wisdom and experience, and this, coupled with the skill of Neil Ellis, with whom they entered into an agreement whereby Neil makes their wines, is responsible for the success of the two partners.

In 1989 their maiden harvest was pressed. The yield was deliberately kept low in an effort to produce high-quality grapes. The success gave further impetus to the operation and a pressing cellar, cellar and storerooms

were created from a converted shed in time for the 1990 harvest. Additional buildings were constructed to house the French oak maturation barrels.

With characteristic energy and enthusiasm Hans and Leon ensured that their wine-making efforts did not go unnoticed. They set about creating a marketing strategy so successful that the 600 cases comprising their maiden Chardonnay vintage were sold out within three weeks. In 1990 the harvest yield increased to 4,5 tonnes per hectare and 1 000 cases were made, and in 1991 all the vines were harvested, yielding some 80 tonnes of grapes. A further 2,5 hectares were planted in September 1991, bringing the total area of the 17-hectare farm under vines to 14 hectares. For these new plantings Neil Ellis chose a Chardonnay clone which complemented the existing stock.

— MEERLUST —
ESTATE

Situated on the Eerste River near the old Companiesdrift Road to Somerset West, the estate of Meerlust has a long and fascinating history, reaching back to the turn of the eighteenth century. It was then that the first owner of the land, Henning Huysing, built the basic T-shaped house around which the

rest of the complex was subsequently developed. An ambitious and enterprising free burgher, he amassed vast wealth through obtaining the monopoly on the meat trade, supplying the passing ships of the Dutch East India Company's fleet on their way to the Orient. Besides the land at Meerlust, he also secured extensive grazing rights in the Eerste River area on which his enormous herds, reputed to number 20 000 cattle and 60 000 sheep, were fattened.

All this wealth and abundance appears to have aroused the ire of the then Governor of the Colony, Willem Adriaan van der Stel. Among the many enemies made by the younger Van der Stel, Huysing was the most powerful. He became the natural leader for the insurgence of the free burghers against the tyranny of the Company's servants. Arrested and sent with a number of the other rebels to Holland to appear before the Council, he made out a convincing case both for the Governor's guilt and his own innocence: and when Van der Stel went into exile Huysing returned, a free man, to Meerlust. He died in 1713, without leaving an heir. Thereafter, the farm passed through a number of hands until, in 1756, it came into the possession of Johannes Albertus Myburgh.

By this date wine-making was already well established, both in the locality and at Meerlust. Myburgh and his son expanded the farm to its present extent, building the complex of cellars, stables and slave workshops, each with its insignia over the door of the trade carried on within, and the columbarium, or pigeon-house, a rare and beautiful example of its kind. They also made additions to the homestead itself, adding a further T-shape to the front of Huysing's original design to create the local H-shaped Cape Dutch ground plan.

By the time Nicolaas Myburgh, the seventh generation of this family to own the farm, took it over in 1950, the condition of the property had declined sadly from its late eighteenth-century splendour. Its wines, too, were not generally of exceptional quality. Based mainly on two grape varieties, the Chenin Blanc and Green Grape (Sémillon), they were mostly of the sweet fortified type which appealed to the popular taste of the earlier part of the century.

Nicolaas (better known as Nico) set out both to repair and restore the time-worn

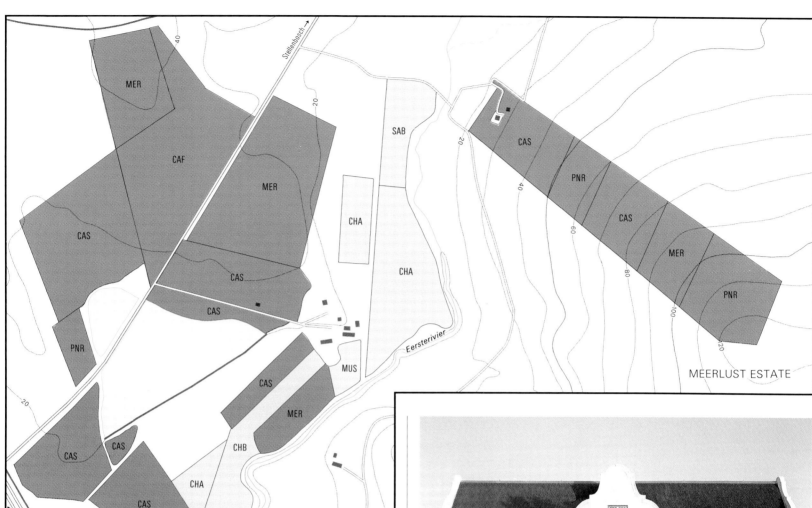

MEERLUST ESTATE

The gracious homestead at Meerlust, in the Myburgh family for eight successive generations.

Hannes Myburgh and Giorgio Dalla Cia.

homestead and to replant the vineyards, introducing new and better vines and developing a range of fine wines, including a number of red wines of exceptional quality. During the last four decades both these acti-

vities have been carried out concurrently, improvements in the wine-making to a large extent financing a superb restoration of the farm complex, one of the largest of its kind.

Crucial to this change to a better quality product was the introduction of adequate water supplies. Nico built a large dam on the estate into which water reserves for the summer season flow. Irrigation is used when inadequate rainfall needs to be supplemented. Further moisture in this area comes from the mists which are known to be a regular feature of the coastal belt.

The area under cultivation has been expanded from its previous 85 hectares to its present 174 hectares. Two main soils are found. The deep-draining alluvial types which flank the river support the farm's white wine varieties. On the higher ground is the pebbly loam soil on which are grown the red varieties of Cabernet Sauvignon, Pinot Noir, Cabernet Franc and Merlot.

In 1975 the first red wine was produced at Meerlust, the 1975 Meerlust Cabernet Sauvignon. In 1980 Nico was able to realize a lifelong ambition; with the help of his

The Meinert Winery, designed by Cape Town architect Michael Dall.

cellarmaster, Giorgio dalla Cia, he produced the Rubicon, a blend of Cabernet Sauvignon, Merlot and Cabernet Franc. That same year saw the birth of the Meerlust Pinot Noir, and in 1984, Nico and Giorgio produced the 1984 Meerlust Merlot.

Since Nico's death in 1988, Meerlust has been in the capable hands of his son, Hannes. He and Giorgio have embarked on an ambitious and extensive renewal programme. Old vineyards are being replanted, Chenin Blanc vines are being replaced with Chardonnay, to be vinified under the Meerlust label, and a new cellar is to be constructed in the foreseeable future.

— MEINERT —
WINERY

In late 1987 Cindy and Martin Meinert bought an 11,5-hectare smallholding with deep Hutton and gravelly Glenrosa soils high up on the slopes of Devon Valley. It faces directly south onto Hangklip and there is a 100-metre height difference from the top to the bottom. They began redeveloping it in 1989, when an extensive replanting programme was instituted, and at present Cabernet Sauvignon, Pinotage and Merlot

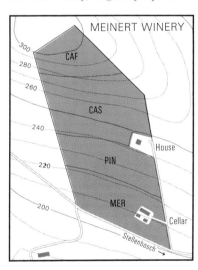

vineyards have been planted. Future plantings will include Petit Verdot and Malbec.

The winery, designed by Cape Town architect Michael Dall – as were all the other buildings on the farm – was completed in 1991. The functional emphasis is on simplicity and gentle handling, which makes the winery decidedly low-tech. The tank room is on three levels, which allows for gravity feed until after pressing. The under-

*Martin and Cindy Meinert, who
intend to specialize in blended
red wines.*

ground barrel and bottle storage cellar is designed for a total of 5 000 cases, 400 225-litre barrels and 150 000 bottles.

The Devon Valley has long been known for its excellent red wines, and the soils and climate on the farm also made it a logical choice to specialize in reds. In 1991 a small quantity of wine was made from Cabernet Sauvignon from the farm, together with Merlot and Cabernet Sauvignon bought from neighbouring farms. The blend was bottled in 1992, and in future strict selection may result in a second blended wine. As soon as the younger vineyards are in full production, only grapes from the farm itself will be used.

The wine-making philosophy at the Meinert Winery is that elegant yet flavourful and complex wines reflecting the slightly cooler mesoclimate should be aimed for. This is done by maximizing aroma, colour and tannin development in the vineyards and by gentle handling and minimal interference in the winery. Grapes are packed into lug boxes and crushed directly into fermentation tanks. The juice is pumped over, and gravity flow and light pressing are employed. The wine is barrelled and blended early and barrel-to-barrel racking is used to eliminate filtration. The emphasis is on the unhurried crafting of individual wines.

— M I D D E L V L E I —
E S T A T E

The neat, carefully tended vineyards of Middelvlei are bounded on one side by houses, gardens and tarred streets. The suburbs of Stellenbosch now extend to the front gate of this lovely estate, where the emphasis has always been on the making of red wines. The winemaker and owner of the farm is 'Stil Jan' Momberg, to be distinguished from his cousin 'Jan Bek' Momberg, formerly of Neethlingshof Estate.

The two Jan Mombergs jointly inherited the farm of Middelvlei (their fathers, who were brothers, had worked the farm together for many years previously). Then in 1963 Jan Bek sold his share of Middelvlei to Stil Jan, and purchased the nearby estate of Neethlingshof, leaving Stil Jan as the sole owner of Middelvlei Estate.

Since those days Jan has done much to develop Middelvlei's potential. In the course of extensive replantings, the ratio of red to white varieties is 56 per cent to 44 per cent. In order to secure registration of Middelvlei as an officially recognized wine estate he rebuilt and re-equipped the farm's antiquated cellar. This involved the installation of cold fermentation equipment for the white wines as well as cooling equipment for the control of the fermentation of the red wines.

The particularly rich granite soil of this area of the Bottelary Hills favours the making of Middelvlei's Pinotage, which has been a consistently fine example of this varietal wine for many years. Jan prunes his Pinotage vines to reduce their otherwise prolific bearing capacity, adding the press-juice to the free-run juice and maturing the wine in wood before bottling.

The success of Jan's Pinotage has led him to expand his plantings of this variety and in addition to plant Cabernet Sauvignon. The first wine was pressed from this in 1981, in almost equal quantities to that of the Pinotage. The Middelvlei Cabernet Sauvignon was released in 1985 and has proved to be an excellent wine.

Nonetheless, despite this success the proportion of wine marketed under the estate's own label remains fairly small, the bulk of the production being supplied to The Bergkelder.

MIDDELVLEI ESTATE

Varieties planted (number of vines)

Bush vines
Pinotage 62 200
2-wire vertical trellis
Cabernet Sauvignon 89 500
Chenin Blanc 79 000
Chardonnay 46 000
Merlot 38 000
4-wire vertical trellis
Sauvignon Blanc 45 000
Shiraz 32 500
Tinta Barocca 14 400
Hárslevelü 4 500

Total area under vines in 1991/2: 126,9 ha.
Irrigation: Only the Tinta Barocca vineyards are irrigated.
Average temperatures: Records are not kept.
Average annual rainfall: 596 mm.
Stock: Rooted vines are bought from a nursery.
First wine bottled under the Middelvlei label: Pinotage 1973.
Wines currently bottled under the Middelvlei label: Pinotage, Cabernet Sauvignon and Shiraz.
Wood ageing: Wines are aged in wood at The Bergkelder.
Cellar capacity: 12 000 hl.

Middelvlei Estate is not open to the public.

— M O R G E N H O F —

The somewhat chequered early history of Morgenhof is reflected not only in the number of times the farm changed hands, but also in its different names. The original farm (granted in 1680) was known as Harmony, but the goodwill inherent in the name seems to have been lost in later years, when it was renamed Onrus.

When 'Stil Jan' Momberg of Middelvlei took over the farm, it was known as Morgenhof. It had been grossly neglected, but the farm thrived on Jan's expertise. Previous owners had taken much from the land without putting anything back, but Jan set about remedying the situation by improving the existing vineyards and developing new ones. He did not concern himself with the restoration of the buildings, however, as his home is at Middelvlei.

In 1982 Morgenhof was bought by Rhine Ruhr Holdings (Pty) Ltd, a Johannesburg-based company. Gert Grobe, the managing director, and his associates have committed themselves not only to improving the vineyards and the farm in general, but also to in-

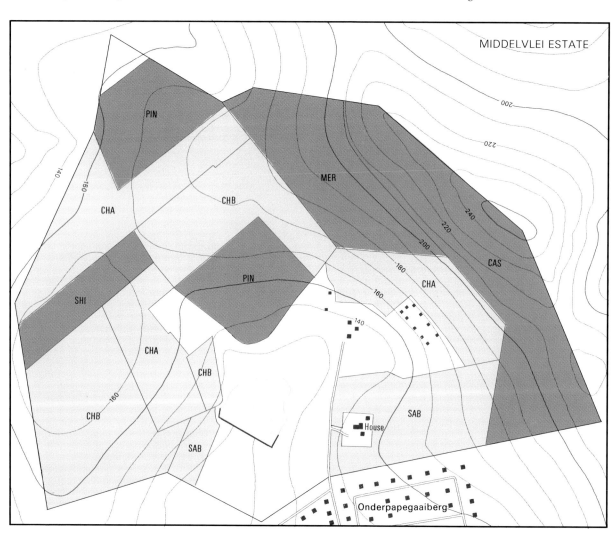

MIDDELVLEI ESTATE

Morgenhof, built in 1820, is situated in the foothills of the Simonsberg.

MORGENHOF

Varieties planted (ha)

Vertical trellis
Sauvignon Blanc 9,22
Weisser Riesling 7,95
Cabernet Sauvignon 6,49
Chenin Blanc 4,95
Chardonnay 4,78
Merlot 2,65
Pinotage 2,43
Tinta Barocca 2,15

Total area under vines in 1991/2:
40,62 ha (12,2 ha still to be planted).
Irrigation: None.
Average temperatures:
Maximum 34 ˚C; minimum 8 ˚C.
Average annual rainfall: 640 mm.
Stock: Rooted vines are bought from a nursery.
First wine bottled under the Morgenhof label:
Cabernet Sauvignon Superior 1984.
**Wines currently bottled under the Morgenhof
label:** Sauvignon Blanc, Cabernet Sauvignon,
Chenin Blanc, Pinotage, Blanc de Noir and
Rhine Riesling (bottled by the Stellenbosse
Botteleringskoöperasie Beperk).
Wood ageing: Wines are aged in wood on the estate.
Cellar capacity: 3 000 hl.

Morgenhof is on the Stellenbosch Wine Route and is
open to the public on weekdays from 08h30 to 17h00,
and on Saturdays from 09h00 to 15h00.

vesting much effort in restoring the dilapidated homestead and outbuildings. The chicken house, built in 1770, has been completely restored and is one of the best examples of a chicken coop of that era. It features a traditional floor, nowadays rare, made of peach pips arranged in a special pattern, with a protective wax covering. A building shown on old drawings of the farm has been completely rebuilt, and a speciality restaurant will open shortly. The final stages of restoration include the renovation of the Morgenhof guest house.

The hilly terrain at Morgenhof provides ideal sites for the various needs of different varieties (the highest ground, at 410 metres, for example, is reserved for Chardonnay). A replanting programme is in progress with new virus-free plant material replacing the old vineyards (to date Cinsaut has been removed in favour of Weisser Riesling). The new production cellar is now complete.

As Gert Grobe is resident in Johannesburg, the farm is in the capable hands of Denzel van Vuuren, who is both the general manager and winemaker.

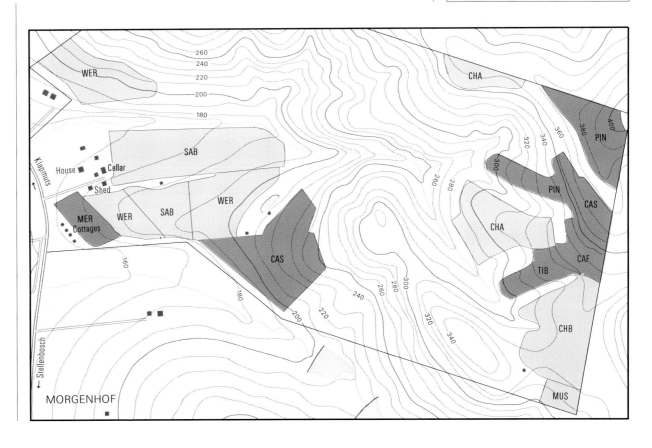

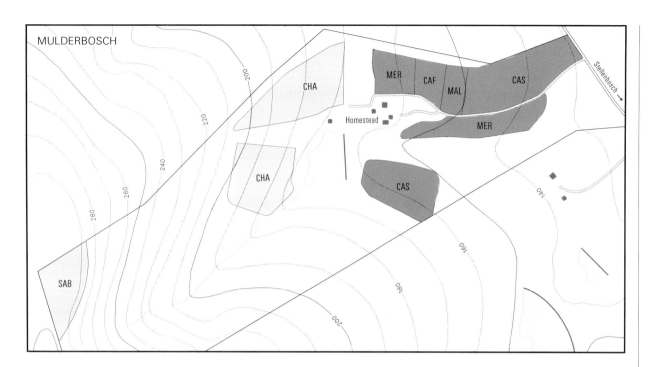

MULDERBOSCH

— MULDERBOSCH —

As with so many of the new vineyards in Stellenbosch and elsewhere, the focus at Mulderbosch is on the present, but human habitation of the land dates to somewhere between 30 000 and 60 000 years ago, as is evidenced by the many well-preserved stone-age tools that were unearthed during the deep soil preparation of the vineyards. These cutting and digging implements will be on permanent display at the Mulderbosch cellar. During the Boer War the property was occupied by a contingent of the British forces and reminders of their presence include an underground water reservoir and the occasional spent cartridge found in the kloof, where the troops had a shooting range.

The renaissance of Mulderbosch began in June 1989 when the farm was bought by Larry Jacobs with the specific purpose of extensively developing it as a wine-producing vineyard of quality.

The challenge was an exciting one, as the land had to be totally replanted and resculpted to realize its high potential. Fortunately the soils are good and the farm has both north-east facing slopes as well as long, cool south-eastern slopes rising from 130 metres above sea level at the Koelenhof Road to 300 metres at the highest point of the farm. Furthermore, in the long hot summer months the vineyards are cooled by the

Mike Dobrovic and Larry Jacobs.

wind-tunnel effect which is unique to the Koelenhof area of Stellenbosch.

Plantings include the Cabernet Sauvignon, Merlot and Malbec varieties required for blended red wines of distinction, and the classic white varieties of Sauvignon Blanc and Chardonnay. No irrigation will be used and yields will be limited to between 6 and 8 tonnes per hectare.

The cellar is designed for underground wood maturation for a minimum of two years and bottle maturation of up to three years, and the equipment has been chosen to ensure that the grapes are pressed without excessive pumping or bruising. Although the quest for quality wines is uncompromising, the development of the farm has not been without attention to the environment. The buildings, though new, are unobtrusive and only 30 hectares of the 48-hectare farm will be used commercially (20 hectares are set aside for vineyards and 10 hectares for other

farming). The balance of 18 hectares is reserved for the existing forest and fynbos flora, home to a family of grysbok (buck) and other small animals including many bird species. Harmony is central to the philosophy of Mulderbosch, where cellarmaster Mike Dobrovic will put his unique stamp upon the quality and character of the wines which are produced.

MULDERBOSCH

Varieties planted (ha)

Extended Perold trellis
Chardonnay 5,7
Cabernet Sauvignon 3
Merlot 3
Sauvignon Blanc 0,7
Cabernet Franc 0,7
Malbec 0,4

Total area under vines in 1991/2: 13,5 ha.
Irrigation: None.
Average temperatures: Records are not kept.
Average annual rainfall: Approximately 600 mm.
Stock: Rooted vines are bought from a nursery.
First wine bottled under the Mulderbosch label: Blanc Fumé 1991 (made from purchased Sauvignon Blanc grapes).
Wine currently bottled under the Mulderbosch label: Blanc Fumé.
Wood ageing: Wines are aged in wood on the farm.
Cellar capacity: 900 hl.

Mulderbosch is not open to the public as yet.

In the early part of this century a German artist named Georg Paul Canitz came to South Africa largely for reasons of health, little suspecting that for many years his family's name would be synonymous with a wine estate named Muratie. Georg's creative imagination was stirred by the wealth of the African landscape, and he stayed on in the country, opening a small art school in Stellenbosch.

In 1925, while riding on horseback with his two daughters to a party in a valley under the Simonsberg, he mistook the way and came upon an old and then almost derelict farm: Muratie, whose name, appropriately enough, comes from an old Dutch word meaning 'ruins'. With this encounter began a lifelong romance between Canitz and the farm, and with the wines he made.

At first little more than an inspired and enthusiastic amateur, he was lucky to include among a wide circle of convivial companions (Canitz's parties were legendary) a key figure in the modern history of South African wine, Professor Abraham Izak Perold of Stellenbosch University. An innovative wine scientist, Perold took the aspiring wine farmer under his wing, advising him to introduce a number of red wine varieties for which he felt the climate and soil of the farm were very suitable. Among these proposed varieties was Pinot Noir, then a hardly known variety in the local vineyards. Within a few years, with Perold's encouragement (the professor spent most of his spare time for two years on the farm) and with the assistance of Wynand Viljoen, Muratie's first wine-maker, Canitz was able to introduce the first of the famous Muratie Pinot Noir wines.

Viljoen was soon to leave the valley to begin farming on his own account in the Karoo, and Georg Canitz continued on his own in his adopted métier, with unabated enthusiasm. But his death in 1959 left his elder daughter, Annemarie, with a decision as to the future course of the farm — female winemakers were then virtually unknown in the winelands. With the determination characteristic of her family, however, Miss Canitz continued to run the estate and to make her father's wines, with the assistance of a new winemaker, Ben Prins. The partnership be-

MURATIE ESTATE

Varieties planted (number of vines)

Perold trellis

Cabernet Sauvignon 21 200

Pinot Noir 17 200

Merlot 15 400

Cinsaut 14 650

Chenin Blanc 10 500

Shiraz 9 750

Clairette Blanche 8 000

Muscat d'Alexandrie 7 100

Cape Riesling 4 250

Port varieties 3 600

Total area under vines in 1991/2:
35 ha (17 ha still to be planted).
Irrigation: None.
Average temperatures: Records are not kept.
Average annual rainfall: Records are not kept.
Stock: Rooted vines are bought from a nursery.
First wines bottled under the Muratie label:
Pinot Noir 1927, Cabernet Sauvignon, Claret,
Amber and Port (vintages not available).
**Wines currently bottled under the Muratie
label:** Pinot Noir, Cabernet Sauvignon, Shiraz,
Dry White, Amber and Port (bottled on the estate or
by the Stellenbosse Bottelerings Koöperasie Beperk).
Wood ageing: Wines are aged in wood on the estate.
Cellar capacity: 3 000 hl.

Muratie Estate is on the Stellenbosch Wine Route
and is open to the public from Monday to Thursday
from 09h30 to 17h00, on Fridays from
09h30 to 16h00 and on Saturdays from
09h00 to 13h00.

George Canitz named Muratie when he came across the near-derelict farm in 1925.

tween Miss Canitz and Ben Prins continued until 1988 when Ronnie Melck bought the farm and Christo Herrer became winemaker.

There is about this charming old tree-enclosed early nineteenth-century farm an air of defiance of time. A rich sense of atmosphere, intensified by the wealth of trees which surround the house and shadow its neo-classical façade and gable, of a refusal to be hurried, lingers about the house and in the wine cellar on the other side of the dusty farm road. Here in the cellar the original concrete fermentation tanks, installed by Canitz more than half a century ago on the advice of Roberto Moni, are still well in use. And other traditions have been retained, in the face of fashion and the developments of scientific viticulture, as Christo Herrer is very much an instinctive winemaker, living with his wine, aiming for quality above quantity.

— NEETHLINGSHOF —
ESTATE

The 300-year-old farm of Neethlingshof was originally granted by Simon van der Stel in 1692 to Willem Barend Lubbe, who named the farm 'De Wolwedans' (The Dance of the Wolves), a name probably referring to the packs of jackals which ranged the area and no doubt harassed the flock of about 100 sheep which Lubbe kept. After experiencing numerous owners, the farm was bought by Johannes Henoch Neethling in 1816 (the Deed of Sale for January 2, 1816, is signed by Lord Charles Somerset). In the same year the farm was extended by a 200-hectare grant. Neethling, after whom the farm came to be named, was a colourful and eccentric character, something of a dandy, whose flamboyant dress and lifestyle earned him the nickname of 'Lord' of Neethlingshof, or simply 'Lord Neethling'. Although Neethling had three sons, he sold Neethlingshof in 1871, the year before his death, to his son-in-law, Jacobus Louw, and the farm stayed in the hands of the Louw family for almost a hundred years. In 1963 Nico Louw sold to Jannie Momberg and his cousin 'Stil Jan'. Jannie Momberg, a public figure (presently an MP) with wide-ranging interests and activities, and popularly known in the winelands as 'Jan Bek', is the son of a wine farmer, born and brought up with the language of wine and its making.

At the time the Mombergs bought Neethlingshof it had the reputation of being one of the best wine farms in the district, but closer

inspection revealed that the cellar facilities were somewhat primitive. In the first few years, until 1970, Jan made no wine, instead selling his grapes to Stellenbosch Farmers' Winery. Soon, however, he set about modernizing the cellar. In due course, he and his cousin came to an arrangement whereby Jan sold his share in Middelvlei to Stil Jan and bought Stil Jan's share in Neethlingshof. After 22 years of successful farming at Neethlingshof, Jan sold the estate to Hans-Joachim Schreiber in March 1985.

Schreiber also owns the farms of Stellenzicht near Stellenbosch and Klein Welmoed (not to be confused with the Welmoed Cooperative, which it adjoins). He is an international financier, a German citizen based in Singapore, and a former managing director of the Dresdner Bank AG of Frankfurt. No sooner was the purchase of the estate finalized than he proceeded to implement a comprehensive and significant development programme comprising not only new farm buildings but also an extended vineyard replanting scheme. Before 1994 all standard varieties will probably have been replaced by noble varieties. Vast and costly renovations and extensions to the office complex and wine cellar provide the latest in wine-making facilities, and a host of features for visitors and tourists. The developments also include the building of an attractive and extensively equipped staff housing complex, housing 26 families, as well as the restoration of the homestead, which is now a large restaurant, 'The Lord Neethling'.

Most important, however, is the comprehensive vineyard programme — now well advanced. Neethlingshof is situated 5,5 kilometres out of Stellenbosch on the Kuils River road, on the eastern slopes of the Bottelary hills and the ridge of the famous Polkadraai basin, enjoying a prime position with opti-

Günter Brözel, vintner for both Neethlingshof and Stellenzicht.

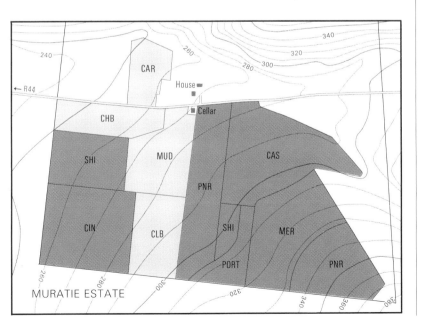

MURATIE ESTATE

NEETHLINGSHOF ESTATE

Varieties planted (ha)

6-wire vertical trellis
Cabernet Sauvignon 30
Chardonnay 19
Sauvignon Blanc 19
Weisser Riesling 15
Cabernet Franc 10
Merlot 10
Gewürztraminer 9
Cape Riesling 8
Shiraz 8
Chenin Blanc 7
Pinotage 4
Tinta Barocca 4
Sémillon 3
Muscadel (white) 3
Gamay 3
Pinot Noir 2
Bukettraube 2

Total area under vines in 1991/2: 156 ha.
Irrigation: Some of the vineyards are
irrigated (about 20 ha).
Average temperatures: Records are not kept.
Average annual rainfall:
About 800 mm per annum.
Stock: Rooted vines are bought from a nursery
after clonal selection.
Envisaged new varieties: Expansion of Pinot Noir
and Pinotage vineyards.
**First wines bottled under the Neethlingshof
label:** Clairette Blanche 1971 and
Chenin Blanc 1971.
**Wines currently bottled under the
Neethlingshof label:** Cape Riesling,
Weisser Riesling, Sauvignon Blanc, Blanc de Noir,
Neethlingshoffer, Gewürztraminer, Bukettraube,
Chardonnay, Rhine Riesling, Noble Late Harvest,
Special Late Harvest, Lord Neethling Blanc, Pinotage,
Lord Neethling Rouge and Cabernet Sauvignon.
Wood ageing: Wines are aged in wood on the estate.
Cellar capacity: 20 000 hl.

Neethlingshof Estate is on the Stellenbosch Wine
Route and is open to the public on weekdays from
09h00 to 17h00, and on Saturdays from
10h00 to 16h00. Cellar tours are conducted on
weekdays at 11h30 and 15h30.

The gracious Neethlingshof manor house is a National Monument and is home to the Lord Neethling Restaurant.

mum growing conditions. Neethlingshof Estate covers 273 hectares which range in altitude from 70 metres to 282 metres above sea level on the northern boundary. Here are found varieties which enjoy cooler temperatures, such as Chardonnay, Pinot Noir and Gewürztraminer.

To make the most of these advantages and establish Neethlingshof as one of the leading Cape wine estates, the vineyard programme has included scientific soil classification, the uprooting of old, redundant

vineyards and the planting of new or additional vines of the noble varieties.

Schalk van der Westhuizen is in charge of the vineyards. He was born on the estate, where his father was estate manager for over 30 years, grew up in the wine industry and has a certificate in viniculture. Günter Brözel is vintner for both Neethlingshof and Stellenzicht. Günter is an almost legendary figure, best known for his long tenure at Nederburg. Heinrich Hesebeck is the winemaker at Neethlingshof. He spent two years at Nederburg and then two years studying at Weinsburg in Germany, returning to Nederburg with a diploma in viticulture and cellar technology. He joined Neethlingshof in 1991. This team has also had the benefit of the assistance of Gyles Webb of Thelema as consultant winemaker.

— NEIL ELLIS —
WINES

As the source of fine wine is top-quality grapes, it follows that the vintner's work begins in the fields. For centuries it has been the practice throughout the world to desig-

nate the very best wines by the individual vineyards from which they originate. Because vines vary greatly in their soil and climatic requirements, however, no single vineyard can satisfy the needs of all the different grape varieties.

Neil Ellis qualified in oenology in 1973 and started his career at KWV under the guidance of Willi Hacker. He was cellarmaster at Groot Constantia until 1982 and at Zevenwacht until 1989. In true *négociant* style, he began searching the winelands to establish where individual varieties excel and to build up associations with grape owners who would cultivate, under his direction, the high-quality grapes he required for his vineyard selection wines. He was given per-

Talented winemaker Neil Ellis.

mission for this venture by Gilbert Colyn, chairman of the publicly owned farm Zevenwacht, where Neil produced a very creditable range of wines. In 1989, when Neil left Zevenwacht, he founded his own cellar in the Devon Valley near Stellenbosch.

Neil Ellis is not the first winemaker to produce, independently, his own range of wines while employed as winemaker by a particular farm. For example, while cellarmaster at Boschendal, Achim von Arnim bought his own estate, Clos Cabrière in Franschhoek, and there produced a sparkling wine by the *méthode champenoise* from the classic varieties of Chardonnay and Pinot Noir.

At present the Neil Ellis range comprises a Sauvignon Blanc, Chardonnay and Cabernet Sauvignon under the Neil Ellis label with Inglewood as an alternative label. Neil's wines are produced in small quantities, because of the limited selection of the crop, as an exercise in quality and nothing else. As a result, the wines have become much sought-after and are regularly supplied to Woolworths. Another of Neil's innovations has been the establishment of Elgin as an area of origin. The Neil Ellis Sauvignon Blanc comes from the Elgin vineyards.

—OUDE NEKTAR—
ESTATE

The history of this farm in the beautiful Jonkershoek Valley, some 5 kilometres from Stellenbosch, can be traced back to 1692, but it was given its evocative name only in 1814 by a certain Gertrude de Villiers. Over the years it changed hands and was subdivided several times.

A variety of wines, including Claret, Cabernet, Riesling, Sauterne and Frontignan, were made and bottled under the Oude Nektar label in the old cellar near the homestead until 1956. Between 1956 and 1983 the grapes grown on Oude Nektar were delivered to The Bergkelder, but in 1983 a new cellar was completed under the management of Gregory Peck, and the first wines from the new cellar were released in November 1983. In 1989 the farm was bought by Hans-Peter Schröder. Hans-Peter grew up in Stellenbosch but made his life in Japan where he had a successful business.

Jonkershoek enjoys a microclimate of its own because of the towering mountains which influence the number of sunlight hours, leading to slower ripening. Thanks to the ample rainfall of the area, the vines do not require additional irrigation. The soils on the farm vary, but the majority are a deep Hutton, which contributes to the making of superior red wines.

At present about 30 hectares of the farm's total 232 hectares are planted with vines. The farm is being totally renovated with one objective in mind, namely to produce, in limited volumes, wines of such quality that they will be able to compete with the best internationally. Thought is also given to the protection of the environment, and the restoration of the natural flora. The feeling is that visitors to the farm must be impressed

Hans-Peter Schröder, who acquired Oude Nektar in 1989.

Oude Nektar is situated in the Jonkershoek Valley, one of the most beautiful valleys in the Cape.

by the natural beauty and harmony of the surrounding environment.

Lacking experience in the wine industry, Hans-Peter has enlisted the help of Dr Eben Archer of the University of Stellenbosch to advise on the viticultural side of the business, and of Neil Ellis on the wine-making side. Pieter Smit is the general manager.

OUDE NEKTAR ESTATE

Varieties planted (ha)

5-wire trellis with movable wires
Cabernet Sauvignon 10
Chardonnay 8
Merlot 4,5
Sauvignon Blanc 3
Cabernet Franc 2
Pinot Noir 1,6

Total area under vines in 1991/2: 29,1 ha.
Irrigation: None.
Average temperatures:
Maximum 24 °C; minimum 16 °C.
Average annual rainfall: 850 mm.
Stock: Rooted vines are bought from nurseries.
First wines bottled under the Oude Nektar label: Chenin Blanc, Nemes Furmint, Olasz Riesling, Cabernet Sauvignon, Shiraz and Pinotage (all 1983 vintage).
Wines currently bottled under the Oude Nektar label: Cabernet Sauvignon, Pinotage, Shiraz, Chardonnay, Sauvignon Blanc and a red wine blend.
Cellar capacity: 1 500 hl.

Oude Nektar Estate is on the Stellenbosch Wine Route and is open to the public on weekdays from 09h30 to 17h00 throughout the year, and from September to April on Saturdays from 11h00 to 16h00. Picnic lunches are offered during the summer months.

—OVERGAAUW—
ESTATE

This estate originally formed part of the historic farm By-den-Weg, granted by Simon van der Stel to Hendrik Elbertz in 1704. In 1784 By-den-Weg was bought by Daniël Joubert, of Huguenot origin, and remained in possession of the Joubert family for five generations.

In 1906 Abraham Julius van Velden bought a portion of By-den-Weg from his maternal grandfather, Willem Joubert, and named it Overgaauw, after the maiden name of the wife of Dirk, the first Van Velden to emigrate to the Cape from Holland. Abraham built a wine cellar on the farm in 1909, and his home the following year.

Abraham's son, David, worked for his father before taking over the farm in 1945. At that stage the area under vines comprised about 40 hectares of the more traditional varieties. David planted better varieties and also introduced Sylvaner, well known in Alsace, Austria and Germany but hardly known in South Africa until it was planted on an experimental plot on a neighbouring farm by the Viticultural Research Station. Using this stock, David planted a vineyard in 1959. Almost unique to Overgaauw, this distinctive dry white wine was first bottled on the estate in 1971, and when it reached the market it brought an immediate response. The range of varieties was further enhanced and expanded by plantings of Pinotage, Merlot, Cabernet Franc, Sauvignon Blanc and Chardonnay, and a selection of five Portuguese varieties for port production, namely Tinta Barocca, Tinta Francisca, Malvasia Rey, Cornifesto and Souzão.

In 1973 David was joined by his son Braam, who had just completed a course in Wine Technology at Geisenheim in Germany. Together the two of them embarked on a programme of systematically replacing mass-produced varieties with shy-bearing noble varieties, and also tackled the costly operation of modernizing and expanding the cellar, while retaining the core of the old cellar with its magnificent old *stukvats*. The new part of the cellar has a double-storeyed air-conditioned store for 1 000 barriques, and the lower floor as well as the bottled wine maturation store are below ground level. For future reference and pleasure of the owner there are two vinotèques in which small quantities of every wine bottled in the past 20 years are stored.

Overgaauw is situated on the south-facing slopes of the Ribbok range of hills,

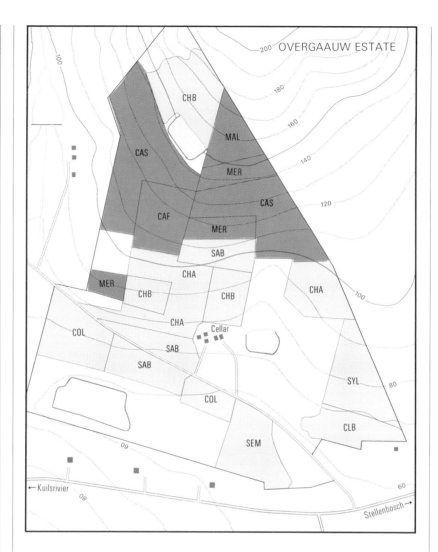

starting next to Stellenbosch with Pape-gaaiberg and ending near Kuils River at Kanonkop. The soil is Hutton, deep and cool with above-average moisture-retaining capacity and moderately fertile, thus discouraging too luxuriant foliage and yield, while encouraging high-quality grapes and consequently high-quality wines.

The first grapes were pressed in Overgaauw's cellar in 1910, and for the past 80 years wine has been made in the same building, now enclosed by a cluster of well-appointed maturation and storage additions. The estate produces excellent wines in the proportion of 55 per cent white to 45 per cent red. The red wine range includes a vintage port, a dry port, a blend of Cabernet Sauvig-

Braam van Velden, the winemaker at Overgaauw Estate.

non, Cabernet Franc and Merlot, known as Tria Corda, as well as wines made entirely from two classic varieties, a Cabernet Sauvignon and a Merlot. All reds are matured in new and old oak for at least two years before being bottled. The whites are the aforementioned Sylvaner, a Sauvignon Blanc and, since 1986, a Chardonnay, which is considered to be one of the quality South African

Chardonnays. A limited quantity of Overgaauw wines are sold in bottle, the balance, including some noble varieties, still being sold in bulk to the wholesale trade.

ROZENDAL
FARM

Kurt Ammann, the owner of Rozendal Farm, trained and worked in restaurants and hotels in Switzerland, France and Germany before coming to South Africa in 1967. In Johannesburg he owned the TV Tower Restaurant and it was here that his keen interest in wine manifested itself.

During 1979 the restaurant was closed for eight months for additions and alterations, and Kurt spent that time visiting and working on wine farms. It was then that he was fired with the desire to one day make his own wine. Among those who inspired him was

the well-known Jan 'Boland' Coetzee of Vriesenhof.

Back in Johannesburg, on completion of the refurbishment of his restaurant, he amassed one of the best wine cellars in the country, but by a cruel turn of fate he was forced to give up the business: just as it was making its mark it was closed by the authorities on the grounds that the television tower was a 'key point', and the restaurant a security risk. Expecting considerable compensation (which he did not receive) for the 13 years his lease still had to run, Kurt looked for a suitable farm in the Cape where he could fulfil his ambition to make his own wine. He found everything he wanted on the 25-hectare farm Rozendal, which he bought in December 1981.

He immediately set about improving the property, which had originally been part of Lanzerac and on which stood a homestead and cellar built in 1864. Wine had been made up until 1955, when Hermitage, Chenin Blanc and a fortified wine were delivered to the well-known and famous old firm of R. Santhagens Limited.

Kurt's first step was to plant 1,5 hectares of Merlot and Cabernet Franc on the farm and to rebuild the wine cellar. He and his family moved onto the property in April 1982 and he set about making his own wine.

Blissfully ignorant of all the ramifications of KWV registration, excise requirements and KWV grape-buying contracts, he bought grapes and made his first wine, breaking a host of regulations in the process. All these problems were eventually solved, however, and the first remarkable Rozendal wine emerged from the 1983 vintage. With the help of his mentor, Billy Hofmeyr of Welgemeend Estate, he produced a blend of Cabernet and Cinsaut which drew harsh criticism when young and yet developed into a fine wine, being sold at the first auction of the Cape Independent Winemakers' Guild held in Johannesburg in 1985. In 1989 it won a silver medal at the International Wine and Spirit Competition in London and the 1986 vintage won a gold medal.

Rozendal is not the only label used. A new label, 'Val de Lyn', was used in 1989 to commemorate Halley's Comet, and 'Doornbosch' is the second label for wines which do not reach the high standards expected of Rozendal. The 'Konstanz' label was used for wines

Kurt Ammann, a chef, is now making his own wine at Rozendal.

from the 1984 and 1986 vintages for export to Switzerland.

Only the best vintages and the best barrels are chosen to be bottled under the Rozendal label. The blend has changed from 75 per cent Cabernet Sauvignon and 25 per cent Cinsaut in 1983 and 1984 to 50 per cent Cabernet Sauvignon and 50 per cent Merlot in 1986 and 80 per cent Merlot, 15 per cent Cabernet Sauvignon and 5 per cent Cabernet Franc in 1987. It will remain in these proportions for the future. Using the traditional methods of Bordeaux, the wines are only fined with egg whites, with no filtration or stabilization. Since the 1989 vintage the wine is matured for two years in small French oak barrels.

Rozendal Farm is situated at the lower end of the beautiful Jonkershoek Valley and is the nearest private cellar to the centre of Stellenbosch. Production varies between 1 500 and 3 000 cases. Since 1990, the farm has been fortunate to have the assistance of

---

ROZENDAL FARM

Varieties planted (number of vines)

Perold trellis
Merlot 20 000
Muscat d'Alexandrie 3 000
Cabernet Franc 3 000
Cabernet Sauvignon 1 000

Total area under vines in 1991/2: 7 ha.
Irrigation: None.
Average temperatures: Records are not kept.
Average annual rainfall: Records are not kept.
Stock: Rooted vines are bought from a nursery.
First wine bottled under the Rozendal label: Rozendal 1983.
Wines currently bottled under the Rozendal label: Konstanz (which is exported to Switzerland), Rozendal, Val de Lyn and Doornbosch.
Wood ageing: Wines are aged in small new wood on the farm for 24 months.
Cellar capacity: 60 tonnes of grapes.

Rozendal Farm is not open to the public.

Schoongezicht, where the wines are made under the Rustenberg label, is located in one of the most picturesque settings in the Cape winelands.

Professor Joël van Wyk, who is the head of the faculty of Oenology and Viticulture at Stellenbosch University.

Kurt has increased his plantings of Merlot, Cabernet Sauvignon and Cabernet Franc to nearly 7 hectares and has improved his wine-making techniques. He is now accepted as one of the new and innovative winemakers. He initially applied for registration of his property as an estate, but later dropped this plan, preferring instead to buy good quality grapes from other farms when necessary, as is common practice in some of the other wine-producing countries.

He operates a small and personal guest house, 'L'Auberge Rozendal', to give wine lovers the opportunity of experiencing the day-to-day routine of a wine farm.

1986
DOORNBOSCH
Wine of Origin Stellenbosch
PRODUCT OF THE CAPE OF GOOD HOPE
750 ml A 244

—RUSTENBERG—
ESTATE

Rustenberg occupies a special place in the regard of the wine lovers of the Cape. Situated on the foothills of the Simonsberg above Ida's Valley, looking away to the south beyond woods of sun-dusted oak trees to False Bay in the distance, and approached by a winding, shaded road intersected by the valley's streams, this is one of the most beautiful of the Cape's traditional wineries. It is in the old cellar at Schoongezicht (part of the original farm) that the estate's fine natural wines are made under the Rustenberg label. Rustenberg has continuously bottled wine since 1892 – as far as is known longer than any other estate. Furthermore the estate has had only three winemakers in the past hundred years, namely Alfred and Reginald Nicholson, and Etienne le Riche.

The property has a long history, dating back to 1682, when Roelof Pasman obtained a grant of land of nearly 93 morgen (80 hectares) from Willem Adriaan van der Stel, certainly a prolific giver of land grants, and named the farm Rustenberg. In 1783 the farm of Rustenberg became the property of Jacob Eksteen, who in 1810 deducted nearly 61 morgen to form the new farm of

Schoongezicht, which he gave to his newly acquired son-in-law, Arend Brink.

Schoongezicht was transferred from Brink to Pieter Lourens Cloete, a scion of the Cloete family of Constantia, in 1813, and it was he who added the present classically Cape Dutch frontage to the existing homestead. In fact the view up the meadows to the high gable of Schoongezicht has become one of the archetypal images of the winelands, and one which has been much reproduced.

Almost 80 years after Cloete's purchase, and in very different economic circumstances from the confident affluence of Cloete's day, the farm was bought by John X. Merriman at a stage when it was under quarantine because of phylloxera. Later to become the last prime minister of the Cape Colony, Merriman was at this time the Minister of Agriculture. Concerned at the poor condition of the local farming, he decided that the most effective way of gaining an insight into the problems concerned would be to become a farmer himself.

Soon after he bought Schoongezicht in 1892, Merriman was joined by a young English immigrant named Alfred Nicholson, whose job it was to oversee the practical aspects of running the almost derelict farm, recovering, as were so many of the local

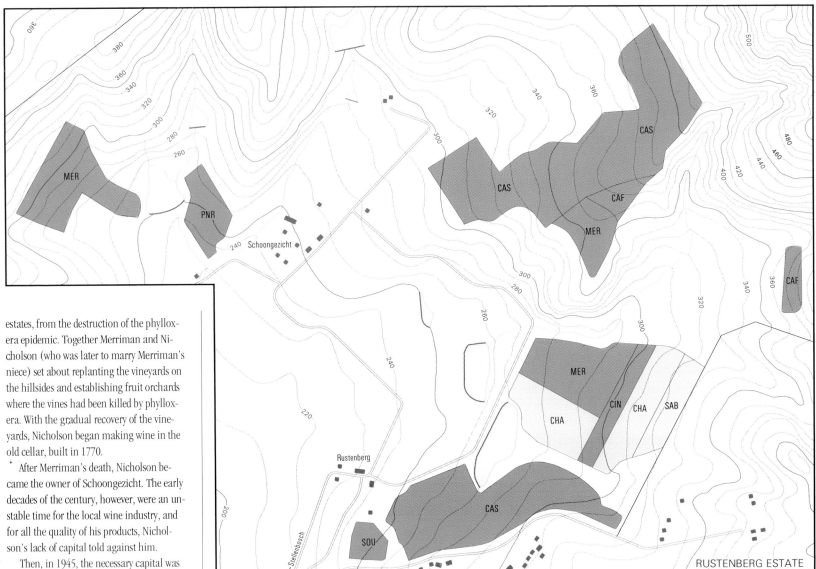

RUSTENBERG ESTATE

estates, from the destruction of the phylloxera epidemic. Together Merriman and Nicholson (who was later to marry Merriman's niece) set about replanting the vineyards on the hillsides and establishing fruit orchards where the vines had been killed by phylloxera. With the gradual recovery of the vineyards, Nicholson began making wine in the old cellar, built in 1770.

After Merriman's death, Nicholson became the owner of Schoongezicht. The early decades of the century, however, were an unstable time for the local wine industry, and for all the quality of his products, Nicholson's lack of capital told against him.

Then, in 1945, the necessary capital was supplied when Peter Barlow bought the farm. This was his second purchase in the valley, for five years earlier he had bought the neighbouring farm of Rustenberg as a family home. Now Peter reunited the two estates after a century of separation, to complete the original but now slightly larger property. He also restored both the homestead and the old cellar. He retained Alfred's son, Reg Nicholson, as winemaker. Later the farm Glenbawn was also added, but it is used for fruit production rather than wine. Since Peter Barlow's death in 1975, the estate has been owned by his widow, Pamela. Peter's son Simon took over the management of the estate in 1987.

Reg Nicholson held to traditional views in his wine-making, and, while he was duly impressed by the changes taking place in wine-making technology in recent years, he

insisted on making his wines by the more traditional methods. The cellar at Schoongezicht still contains few of the new-fangled innovations which would disturb the peace and quiet of its restful atmosphere, though it does now include efficient modern machinery and a handsome new maturation cellar well stocked with Bordeaux barrels.

Etienne le Riche, a graduate in Viticulture, Oenology and Agricultural Economics from Stellenbosch University, joined Nicholson in 1974, taking over on his retirement the following year. He has followed his predecessor in his insistence upon the use of natural yeast but on red wines only. Chardonnay is now produced in what is recognized as the true French manner, aged on the lees in small oak casks.

This individual approach and willingness to experiment with new ideas while respecting old ones, has resulted in a fine range of natural wines. If the wine master's skill is important, however, no less important is the co-operation of climate and setting, and in these respects the estate has been singularly fortunate. In South Africa many wine farmers face a problem not shared by their counterparts in Europe: the excessive heat to which their vineyards are subjected in the late summer. In its high, cool, sheltered valley under the Simonsberg, the estate receives as much as 19 days less sunlight a year than the majority of farms in the Stellenbosch and Paarl areas. The soil here, which is red, granite based and highly fertile, gives the grapes a further natural advantage. The

farm receives an average of 950 millimetres of rain annually.

The vineyards are located at altitudes ranging from 270 to 330 metres. At present 70 hectares are in full bearing. The established vineyards consist of 35 hectares of Cabernet Sauvignon, the next most planted variety being Merlot on 10 hectares.

Rustenberg bottles a 100 per cent Cabernet Sauvignon, as well as the popular 'Dry Red'. This is made up of approximately 66 per cent Cabernet Sauvignon and 34 per cent Cinsaut. There are only 3 hectares of Cinsaut, but since this variety is a prolific bearer compared to Cabernet, the crop is sufficient for the blend, which makes up the major part of the farm's red wine output. Since 1987 10 per cent Merlot and 10 per cent

RUSTENBERG ESTATE

Varieties planted (ha)

3-wire vertical trellis
Cabernet Sauvignon 35
Merlot 10
Pinot Noir 9
Chardonnay 9
Cinsaut 3
Sauvignon Blanc 2
Cabernet Franc 2
Souzão 1

Total area under vines in 1991/2: 71 ha.
Irrigation: None.
Average temperatures:
Maximum 23,6 °C; minimum 9,1 °C.
Average annual rainfall: Approximately 950 mm.
Stock: Rooted vines are bought from a nursery.
**First wines bottled under the
Schoongezicht/Rustenberg labels:**
Schoongezicht Dry Red, Schoongezicht
Hock and Schoongezicht Frontignac
(approximately 1892 vintage).
**Wines currently bottled under the Rustenberg
label:** 'Gold', Cabernet Sauvignon, Dry Red,
Pinot Noir, Chardonnay and Vintage Port.
Exceptional wines are labelled 'Reserve'.
Wood ageing: Wines are aged in small oak casks
and large vats on the estate.
Cellar capacity: 2 300 hl.

Rustenberg Estate is open to the public from
09h00 to 16h30 on weekdays and on
Saturdays during the Christmas season.

Cabernet Franc have been added to the
blend. A handsome Bordeaux-styled blend
called Rustenberg 'Gold' is produced from
the three classic varieties Cabernet Sauvignon, Merlot and Cabernet Franc.

The Rustenberg red wines are matured
for two years in vats and barrels, depending
on the wine. Of the farm's total production,
70 per cent is red wine and 25 per cent white;
the balance includes a vintage port. Exceptional wines are labelled 'Reserve'.

Besides wine, the farm is famous for its
magnificent Schoongezicht Jersey herd, one
of the first to be established in the country.
The flat, low-lying land of the two farms,
where lush kikuyu grass, rye and clover grow
in profusion, is reserved for this herd. As with
most of the older-style farms on the Stellenbosch side of the Simonsberg, the herd's
manure is used on the vineyards and is considered an integral part of the farming cycle.

After the reuniting of the two halves of the
original farm it became a tradition to sell
the red wines under the name of Rustenberg,

and the white wines under that of Schoongezicht. The labels of each feature the respective gables of the contrasting homesteads,
the flowing Cape Dutch of Schoongezicht
and the more restrained neo-classical of
Rustenberg. At present the estate is registered
under the name Rustenberg, and from 1991
all its products have been sold under the
Rustenberg label. A further move has been
greater specialization, and only three main
wines are now produced, namely Cabernet
Sauvignon and blends of this variety, Chardonnay and Pinot Noir.

— RUST-EN-VREDE —
ESTATE

The 50-hectare wine farm of Rust-en-Vrede,
and its homestead, were both in a virtually
derelict condition before being restored by
former rugby Springbok Jannie Engelbrecht.
Born in Namaqualand, he went to high
school and university in Stellenbosch, where
he first came into contact with wine-making
and the lore of wine through contact with
schoolfriends who were the sons of wine
farmers. A developing interest crystallized in
practical form in 1978 when he bought the
old farm of Rust-en-Vrede at the foot of the
Helderberg at Stellenbosch.

Once part of a much larger property
named Bonte Rivier, which was granted by
Simon van der Stel in 1694 to Willem van

The Stellenbosch Mountains provide a spectacular backdrop to the vineyards at Rust-en-Vrede.

der Wêreld, the first vines were planted here
in 1730. By 1790 the existing old wine cellar
was completed, and as the wine-making
flourished, the main house was built and
completed in 1825.

In later years the property of Bonte Rivier
was divided, and in the mid-nineteenth
century one of the subdivisions became the
property of Rust-en-Vrede.

By the 1920s wine-making had died out
on the farm, though grapes continued to be
grown. When Jannie moved onto his newly
acquired farm, he found the old wine cellar
being used as a stable for horses and cows.
Some of the original open cement fermenta-

tion tanks still survived but were of no practical use. In the vineyards there were blocks
of Cabernet Sauvignon, Shiraz, Tinta Barocca, Cinsaut and some Chenin Blanc. Jannie
set about bringing new life to the property of
Rust-en-Vrede. With the help of well-known
architects Gabriel Fagan and his wife Gwen,
well known for many other restorations in
the winelands, he restored the old buildings
to their original glory.

The old vineyards were largely replanted
with new stock, to the extent that of the
30 hectares about half are new plantings.
The emphasis here is strongly upon red varieties, which are particularly suited to the
situation of the farm, with good Hutton and
Clovelly soils on well-drained slopes. Plantings are made up of 47 per cent Cabernet
Sauvignon, 30 per cent Shiraz, 15 per cent
Merlot and 8 per cent Tinta Barocca. Before
making these plantings, Jannie consulted
the viticulturalist Desiderius Pongràcz.

The old cellar was renovated, and Jannie
made his first wine in 1979, working against
time and in response to a sporting challenge
from friends. It wasn't easy; the last equipment for the cellar arrived at the same time
as the first load of grapes. Furthermore an
order for Bordeaux barrels (225 litres) for
this first crop made Jannie one of the first
winemakers in South Africa to mature his entire production of red wine in new Nevers
oak *barriques*.

OVERLEAF: *Vineyards at the foot of the
Simonsberg form a patchwork pattern.*

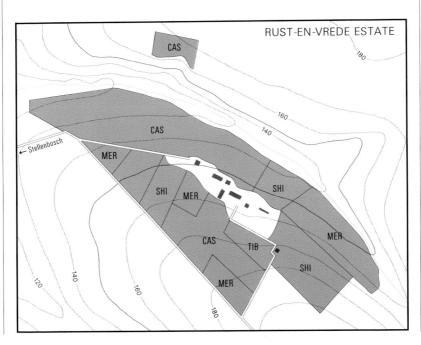

RUST-EN-VREDE ESTATE

Kevin Arnold, who specializes in making red wines and Jannie Engelbrecht, who owns Rust-en-Vrede.

His wines were an immediate success. Jannie himself considers Cabernet Sauvignon to be the 'king of the wines', and an ideal wine for keeping. His ambition to be purely a red wine producer (a matter both of soil and climate and of temperament) was achieved in 1981.

Jannie feels that making red wine is more rewarding, seeing that the time taken from the harvesting of the white grapes to the marketing of that wine can be less than a year, as opposed to the making of red wine, which is a more protracted, lingering and contemplative activity. Outstanding results have been achieved at various wine shows in a relatively short period of time.

Besides the restored original cellar, a new modern cellar – capable of handling

200 tonnes of grapes – has been designed. Its pressing and working cellar is on the ground floor and there are two floors underground. The first of these is for bottle maturation, accommodating 500 000 bottles, and the second for use as a private vinotèque and public wine-tasting area. Now that this building is complete, the old cellar will be used only for ageing the red wines in Nevers oak vats.

During 1987 Jannie handed over his winemaking responsibilities to South Africa's Champion Winemaker in 1986 and red wine specialist Kevin Arnold. Kevin's appointment as cellarmaster of Rust-en-Vrede Estate is seen as a further commitment to specialization and quality.

Kevin obtained a diploma in cellar technology from Elsenburg College in Stellenbosch and then visited France and Germany before taking up a post as winemaker at Delheim. During his nine years at this estate he won both regional and national awards and trophies for his wines. Likewise his first vintages at Rust-en-Vrede had immediate success at the South African Championship Young Wine Show.

Kevin has a simple but wise philosophy, namely that 'Nature is the winemaker's boss' and that 'the winemaker's palate is his encyclopaedia'. He is continuing the tradition of producing wines at Rust-en-Vrede that are characteristic of its terroir.

SAXENBURG
WINE FARM

Saxenburg Wine Farm is situated high on the hills above Kuils River and commands a panoramic view of the Cape Peninsula. In 1693 the land where Saxenburg stands was granted by Governor Simon van der Stel to a free burgher named Joachim Sax (hence the name of the farm). In 1705 the farm was sold to two Swedes, Oloff and Albertus Bergh, and changed hands again a decade later when Oloff sold both Saxenburg and an adjoining farm, De Kuijlen, in order to acquire Groot Constantia. Saxenburg then had a succession of owners, of whom the De Villiers family was probably the best known.

The homestead was built around 1701, the style being the simple farmhouse typical of that era. It was so badly damaged by fire in 1945, however, that it had to be demolished. Fortunately the inner doors, made of stinkwood and yellowwood, and a built-in cupboard – the oldest of its type in South Africa – were saved. In the same year the present manor house was built in almost the same position as the original homestead and in the same style, although with an additional bedroom wing, giving the manor house its present H-shape.

In 1989 Saxenburg became privately owned when it was bought by Adrian and Bir-

Nico Van der Merwe of Saxenburg.

git Buhrer of Switzerland, whose family have been in the wine business for five generations. Together with their young family, the new owners are now resident in the manor house, and apart from overseas visits to maintain his business commitments there, Adrian is very much involved with the management of the farm.

The farm is 200 hectares in extent, with 90 hectares under vines. In the past Saxenburg specialized in white wines, but an extensive planting programme has been completed and the new vintages will include some magnificent red wines.

Work on the administration offices and bottling room has been completed and historic wine cellars have been renovated to house a new restaurant – the Guinea Fowl – as well as a bar and private dining room.

RUST-EN-VREDE ESTATE

Varieties planted (percentage of vineyards)

Vertical trellis
Cabernet Sauvignon 47 per cent
Shiraz 30 per cent
Merlot 15 per cent
Tinta Barocca 8 per cent

Total area under vines in 1991/2: 30 ha.
Irrigation: None.
Average temperatures: Records are not kept.
Average annual rainfall: 650 mm.
Stock: Rooted vines are bought from a nursery.
First wines bottled under the Rust-en-Vrede label: Cabernet Sauvignon, Shiraz, Tinta Barocca (all 1979 vintage).
Wines currently bottled under the Rust-en-Vrede label: Cabernet Sauvignon, Shiraz, Tinta Barocca and Rust-en-Vrede Estate Wine, which is a premium blended wine.
Wood ageing: Wines are aged in wood on the estate.
Cellar capacity: 2 000 hl.

Rust-en-Vrede Estate is on the Stellenbosch Wine Route and is open to the public on weekdays from 09h30 to 16h30, and on Saturdays from 09h00 to 12h00.

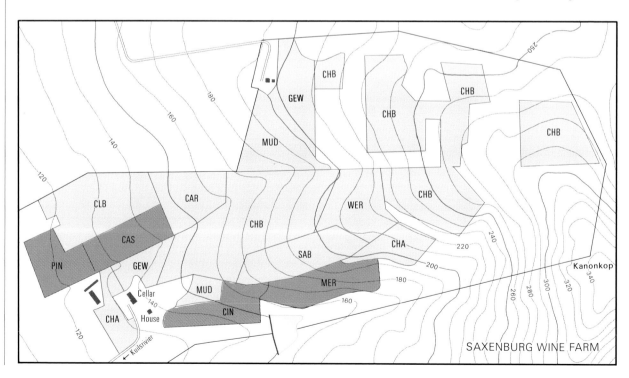

SAXENBURG WINE FARM

There is a new tasting room adjacent to the restaurant. The visitors' car park is being resited and enlarged and extensive landscaped gardens will enhance the manor house and public areas. The entrance to Saxenburg has been re-designed and will complement the Cape Dutch architecture of the manor house.

Saxenburg's winemaker Nico van der Merwe, was Winemaker of the Year for 1991. He is implementing changes at Saxenburg which he believes will make it one of the top wine farms in South Africa. Born on the West Coast, he became interested in wines as a teenager and after completing his Cellar Technology course at Elsenburg, studied for

two years at the Weinsburg Academy in Germany, where his real wine education began and his questions were answered.

Nico feels that in Europe there is real harmony between the grapes and the wine because the winemaker not only makes the wine, but is also responsible for cultivating the grapes on the estate. Such control over the grapes enables the winemaker to produce a quality product, and makes his job in the cellar so much easier.

An organic growing programme has also been recently introduced to Saxenburg's vines, and this is in line with trends in Europe where a more environmentally aware attitude is beginning to be practised in the vineyards. This means that Saxenburg's vineyards will be kept healthy without recourse to excessive spraying, and in so doing nature will be allowed to determine the quality of the produce.

A Saxenburg Connoisseur Wine Club was recently founded and a marketing division established, with the intention that they should help to both strengthen Saxenburg's South African market share, and to help increase the export of its wines to Europe, the United Kingdom and the USA.

Simonsig Estate, which originally formed part of the farm Nooitgedacht, the grant for which dates back to 1682.

SIMONSIG ESTATE

One of the largest of the Cape's private wine estates, Simonsig comprises three original land grants, those of the farms De Hoop, Simonsig and Morgenster, separated by 3 kilometres but unified under the single ownership and organization of the Malan family. One of the originators, in the early 1970s, of the Stellenbosch Wine Route, Frans Malan is a determined and independent man who has concentrated upon establishing a broad foundation of both white and red wines. To this end some 18 varieties are grown on Simonsig, 65 per cent of the total hectares being given to white wine varieties such as chardonnay.

Johan and Frans Malan. Frans was one of the originators of the Stellenbosch Wine Route.

Included in the Simonsig range is the first South African estate sparkling wine produced by the *méthode champenoise*, the Simonsig Kaapse Vonkel, made from Chardonnay and Pinot Noir grapes. In earlier days in the Cape, all sparkling wines were made by this method, but with the perfection of tank fermentation, bottle fermentation all but disappeared, the little that was made being either experimental or purely for own use. Frans has led the re-introduction of *méthode champenoise* sparkling wines with the Simonsig Kaapse Vonkel.

The scale of enterprise at Simonsig is a relatively recent development in the estate's history. Originally, Simonsig formed part of the farm Nooitgedacht, the grant for which dates back to 1682. Its companion farm, De Hoop, is of even earlier origin, being part of the old property of Koelenhof, granted to Simon de Groott in 1682.

The first wine to be made on De Hoop was bottled as recently as 1941, and the farm which Frans Malan took over from his father-in-law in 1953 still largely featured mixed farming. With his M.Sc. in oenology from Stellenbosch University, Frans set about enlarging and streamlining the cellar facilities on De Hoop, planting larger quantities of better vines. Further expansion led Frans in 1964 to purchase the nearby farm of Simonsig. He subsequently made the decision to consolidate the two farms, registering them as a single wine estate – since De Hoop was not available for the estate name, that of Simonsig, named for its sweeping view of the Simonsberg which appears in miniature on many of the estate's labels, was chosen instead. The first wine under a Simonsig label appeared in 1968.

In 1989 Simonsig acquired the grapes from the famous Kriekbult vineyards by means of a long-term lease. These vineyards

---

SIMONSIG ESTATE

Varieties planted (ha)

Perold or extended Perold trellis
Pinotage 36
Chenin Blanc 30,65
Cabernet Sauvignon 30
Weisser Riesling 27,82
Chardonnay 19,67
Clairette Blanche 16,62
Sauvignon Blanc 15,94
Palomino 15,55
Bukettraube 13,3
Gewürztraminer 12,47
Shiraz 11,83
Merlot 7,72
Cape Riesling 7,38
Colombard 5,43
Cinsaut 4,11
Pinot Noir 3,18
Muscat Ottonel 1,82
Morio Muscat 1,80

Total area under vines in 1991/2: 261,29 ha.
Irrigation: 80 per cent of the vineyards can be irrigated if necessary.
Average temperatures: Records are not kept.
Average annual rainfall: Approximately 540 mm.
Stock: Rooted vines are bought from a nursery; clonal material supplied by KWV.
First wines bottled under the Simonsig label: Clairette Blanche, Steen and Riesling (all 1968 vintage).
Wines currently bottled under the Simonsig label: Adelberg, Cabernet Sauvignon, Chardonnay, Chenin Blanc, Franciskaner Special Late Harvest, Gewürztraminer, Kaapse Vonkel, Mustique, Noble Late Harvest, Pinotage, Riesling, Rosé, Sauvignon Blanc, Shiraz, Sonstein, Vin Fumé, Vin Gris and Weisser Riesling.
Wood ageing: Wines are aged in wood on the estate.
Cellar capacity: 230 000 hl.

Simonsig Estate is on the Stellenbosch Wine Route and is open to the public on weekdays from 08h00 to 13h00 and from 14h00 to 17h00, and on Saturdays between 08h30 and 12h30.

---

produce some of the finest Pinotage wines in the country and are suitable for other red varieties such as Cabernet Sauvignon and Merlot. Kriekbult is adjacent to De Hoop.

The soils in the area are predominantly Hutton and Clovelly types. Frans maintains that, although they are relatively poor, the soils encourage the production of quality over quantity. For this reason only light applications of fertilizer are used, though careful analyses of soil and leaves are regularly made so as to diagnose any sudden or unexpected deficiency. This procedure has proved to be most successful.

Though traditional staples such as Chenin Blanc and Cape Riesling are grown on Simonsig and De Hoop (where the cellar is situated), Frans's interest in producing high-quality wines has led to a constant broadening of the range of varieties grown. Eight different clones of Chardonnay are planted in vineyards at Simonsig, as well as Weisser Riesling, Gewürztraminer and Bukettraube, the last two varieties producing particularly notable wines.

Frans's three sons joined him on the farm some time ago and Pieter handles the marketing and administration, while François, a qualified viticulturist, manages the vineyards. Johan, the youngest son, became the winemaker after completing his studies at Stellenbosch University, majoring in oenology and viticulture.

A visit to Simonsig, and in particular to the Kaapse Vonkel cellar, where the inverted bottles undergo *remuage* in wooden racks or *pupitres*, is a fascinating experience. At the 1990 International Wine and Spirit Competition Simonsig's Chardonnay won the Cape Wine Academy Trophy for the best South African dry white wine. Their 1984 Cabernet Sauvignon won the Dave Hughes trophy for the best South African red wine.

— SPIER —
ESTATE

This is an old Cape wine farm run by an old Cape family; the present owner of the Spier complex (which includes some five farms in

all), Niel Joubert, is a descendant of a Huguenot immigrant who first put down tenacious roots in the Cape at the turn of the eighteenth century. Pierre Joubert was a wine farmer from the Loire Valley of France, who joined the 1688 Huguenot emigration to the VOC's colony at the Cape in search of political and religious freedom. Once arrived, he soon settled down to ply his trade, buying a property in the Drakenstein district.

Two centuries later his descendants were established in the Vlaeberg-Polkadraai area. It was here that the father of the present Joubert was born. He was Christian Joubert, and it was he who, in 1908, bought the farm Goedgeloof. His son Niel bought the historic Spier in 1965 and made it the centre of the present flourishing wine-making concern.

One of the oldest wine farms in the Stellenbosch area, Spier was first granted by Governor Simon van der Stel in September 1692 to one Arnout Tamboer Jansz (the original

The old slave quarters, which now house the popular Spier restaurant.

SPIER ESTATE

Varieties planted (number of vines)

Perold trellis

Pinotage 83 530

Chenin Blanc 80 000

Cabernet Sauvignon 66 410

Shiraz 32 170

Clairette Blanche 26 932

Colombard 25 124

Pinot Gris 10 000

Fernão Pires 7 000

Furmint 5 000

Hárslevelü 5 000

Muscat d'Alexandrie 3 700

Pontac 1 875

Fence trellis

Cabernet Sauvignon 63 000

Sauvignon Blanc 56 854

Cape Riesling 34 340

Gewürztraminer 22 500

Chardonnay 20 000

Merlot 20 000

Weisser Riesling 13 450

Bukettraube 8 250

Total area under vines in 1991/2: 203 ha.
Irrigation: All the vineyards are irrigated.
Average temperatures: Records are not kept.
Average annual rainfall: Approximately 600 mm.
Stock: Rooted vines are bought from a nursery.
First wines bottled under the Spier label:
Pinotage 1969 and Colombard 1972.
Wines currently bottled under the Spier label:
Pinotage, Cabernet Sauvignon, Shiraz, Vin Rouge, Chenin Blanc, Sauvignon Blanc, Chardonnay, Riesling, Weisser Riesling, Blanc de Blanc, Fernão Pires, Bukettraube, Special Late Harvest, Noble Late Harvest, Blanc de Noir, Gewürztraminer, Sauvignon Blanc Extra Brut, Vin Doux, Vin Sec, Spumanté, Port and Mistelle.
Wood ageing: Wines are aged in wood on the estate.
Cellar capacity: 21 800 hl.

Spier Estate is on the Stellenbosch Wine Route and is open to the public on weekdays from 08h30 to 13h00 and from 14h00 to 17h00, and on Saturdays from 08h30 to 13h00. Meals are served at both the Jonkershuis wine house and the Spier Restaurant.

title deed, a treasured possession, is preserved by the present owners). In 1712 Jansz disposed of the property to Hans Hendrik Hattingh (who hailed from Speyer in Germany, hence the name Spier), and in the following decades it changed hands a number of times. Cecil John Rhodes farmed here, as did families such as the Cartwrights and the Keppels before its purchase by the present generation of Jouberts. With the assistance of his son Chris, who now manages the estate, Niel Joubert built up a thriving organization

which includes three other vineyards – Olives, Goedgelegen and Goedgevonden – besides Spier and Goedgeloof.

The wide range of Spier wines is made in the extensive cellars at Goedgeloof. Here an annual crop of between 2 000 and 2 500 tonnes of grapes is processed. The estate's red wines are matured in casks in a special maturation cellar which also contains up to 250 000 bottles for ageing.

During its first 10 years of estate bottling, the talented Arthur Boulle was responsible for the wine-making at Spier, with Chris taking an active interest. Since June 1982 Jan Smit has assisted Chris in the cellars of Spier as winemaker.

Earlier in the present century the farm specialized in the production of export fruit, and a certain amount is still grown, but the remaining orchards are being steadily replaced by vines, the emphasis being on the establishment of quality varieties. Considerable care is taken to match the type of variety to the conditions prevailing in the different areas of the estate.

The old Spier homestead has been meticulously restored by the Jouberts; its Jonkershuis has been converted into a charming wine house where meals are also served, while the slave quarters have been developed into the Spier Restaurant. The cellar building is one of the oldest of its kind in the country, dating back to the early eighteenth century. Attractive tasting facilities are also included on the premises.

— STELLENBOSCH — FARMERS' WINERY

Stellenbosch Farmers' Winery makes over half the wine, and a large proportion of the spirits, drunk in South Africa.

The spectacular rise and expansion of Stellenbosch Farmers' Winery is very much a twentieth-century phenomenon. Although this is a winery with a contemporary style, in the forefront of the industry, echoes of the past still linger in the brisk and efficient corridors of the company's headquarters and in its large modern cellars and laboratories; for the land on which Stellenbosch Farmers' Winery stands is that of the historic farm of Oude Libertas, once the property of Adam Tas. It is often forgotten that Tas, besides

Seen from the air Stellenbosch Farmers' Winery is an impressive complex.

being a diarist, agitator and polemicist of some talent, was also a wine farmer.

Legend has it that the farm was named by Tas (Liber + Tas) to commemorate his release from the Castle where he had been held by Willem Adriaan van der Stel on charges of sedition. But Tas was not the first owner of the land. It was first granted by Simon van der Stel in 1689 to Jan Cornelis van Oudenlingenland and, contrary to popular belief, it was he, not Tas, who gave his new property the name of Libertas, meaning 'liberty'. In 1692 Libertas was merged by a subsequent owner with a number of other areas of land, though the original name was retained. This farmer was Hans Jurgen Grimp; after his death Adam Tas married the widow Grimp, and thus gained title to the land – this was a common way in which a presentable but impecunious young man could acquire land of his own in those days.

After Tas' death in 1722, the farm changed hands several times, being eventually divided into two; the properties of Libertas and Oude Libertas. After many vicissitudes, the Oude Libertas portion of the land was bought by the Krige family in 1867. The first of the Kriges on Oude Libertas, Gideon Johannes, was an effective enough wine farmer. The early years of the present century saw the Kriges, father and son, attempting to establish a small private winery and distillery on Oude Libertas. However, they soon ran into difficulties.

It was at this point, in 1924, that William Charles Winshaw made his appearance. Win-

shaw is one of the great characters of modern winelands history.

His career up till this point had been nothing if not chequered. An American immigrant to the Cape, Winshaw had been born in Kentucky, the son of an eccentric doctor. At the age of 12 he ran away from home to begin a wandering life, living by the wits with which he appears to have been well endowed. He tumbled through a series of adventures More dignified ambitions crystallized, and he returned to the life of a gambler to finance medical studies at Tulane. After a visit to Germany to study tropical diseases, he returned to New Mexico, where, in the intervals of treating gunshot wounds, he met a hitherto unencountered species in the person of a British army officer named McGuiness.

McGuiness was buying mules for the army engaged in the Anglo-Boer War, and it was not long before the wanderlusting Winshaw had agreed to organize the transportation of 4 500 mules to Cape Town.

Winshaw and his mules arrived in the Cape in 1899. The mules were taken to Stellenbosch, where they were quartered on the

The Oude Libertas complex, wine and cultural centre of Stellenbosch Farmers' Winery.

— THE CAPE WINE — ACADEMY

The Cape Wine Academy is situated in the Oude Libertas Complex at Stellenbosch Farmers' Winery. It was instigated by Dave Hughes and other senior staff members of SFW at the time. Phyllis Hands has been principal of the academy since its inception in 1979, and today it has over 17 000 registered students.

The courses run by the academy are recognized internationally and cover all aspects of the South African wine industry as well as of the winelands of the world. These courses include a Preliminary course of five lectures, a Certificate course of six lectures, and a two-year Diploma course. The dedicated student may then study for the Cape Wine Master exam, an esteemed and coveted qualification.

In January 1992, KWV's wine courses were merged with those of the Cape Wine Academy and KWV will now be sharing the running costs of the courses.

The Cape Wine Academy is now the only recognized wine and spirit educational body in South Africa.

---

hillside behind Koelenhof and tended by British officers who had been 'Stellenbosched', in other words withdrawn from combat for reasons of incompetence and dumped in camp at Stellenbosch where they could do no further harm. Winshaw himself spent the war as an army doctor, returning to Stellenbosch after the hostilities to the start of a more settled way of life.

He married an English Boer-War nurse named Ada Day and in 1904 he became the tenant of a Cape Town dentist, Dr Lindup, who owned a small farm called Patrys Vlei, some 21 hectares in extent, outside Stellenbosch. Here Winshaw began to experiment with the making of wine, mostly from the varieties Hermitage and Pontac.

Unfortunately Winshaw's first attempts at wine-making were not a great success. However, he very quickly discovered new ways of improving his humble product. In a short while he began selling his 'raisin wine', or 'processed Hermitage', to Fred Green of the wine merchants E.K. Green and Company. Greatly encouraged by a current shortage of wine owing to a bad

harvest, his products soon gained in quality, and thus in popularity.

Then, in February, 1909, Winshaw went into business on a serious scale. With a capital of £1 000 he opened his Stellenbosch Grape Juice Works, from which he sold both wine and unfermented grape juice. This was complemented in 1913 by a part-ownership in the Stellenbosch Distillery.

William Charles Winshaw was finding his feet. He was also beginning to make his personality felt in a more general way in the local wine-making milieu. In the years before the First World War, he began shrewdly buying up good unsold wine from the local growers, at double its normal price of £2 a leaguer, thus outbidding the other merchants who were manipulating a depressed post-war market to their advantage and at the expense of the growers.

In this tactic Winshaw found support from Charles Kohler, the most active proponent of the budding co-operative movement. In return Winshaw gave Kohler much support (particularly against the wine merchants) in the formation of KWV in 1918.

Winshaw's first adventure in the wine trade lasted little more than a decade. With 'too many irons in the fire', his company ran into financial trouble, followed by insolvency, a process hastened by KWV which (momentarily forgetting previous loyalties and any principle of co-operation) advised the growers who were supplying Winshaw to insist on their payments in advance. The *coup de grâce*, however, was delivered by the

merchants who raised their prices to the farmers (as Winshaw himself had once done to them), forcing him to bid beyond his financial strength. On the twelfth of January, 1921, he was declared insolvent, KWV moving in quickly to buy up his company, its stocks and its fustage, its extensive cellar and wine-making equipment.

Now over 50 years of age, Winshaw returned to the United States of America for a brief spell as a doctor. But within a few years, ever dogged, he was back in the Cape, and on the third of March, 1924, at the age of 53, he was formally rehabilitated from his state of insolvency, the court pointedly noting, 'in a measure the applicant has been misled by the farmers themselves'.

Winshaw's *wandeljahre* were now finally over. Looking for a new point of entry into the local wine market, he soon discovered Gideon Johannes Krige Junior and his faltering distillery on the northern banks of the Eerste River. With an entrepeneurial instinct for a 'good thing', Winshaw first entered into partnership with the Kriges of Oude Libertas, then later bought them out for the modest sum of £5 500.

Back in business with a vengeance, Winshaw brought his two sons, Bill, who was at university, and later Jack, into his new concern. Soon they were making and selling their own wine on a rapidly expanding scale. They were also making changes in the type and style of this wine, making radical departures from the prevailing norm.

During this period very little natural wine was drunk in South Africa; almost all was sweet fortified wine, such as Muscadel, sweet ports, brown sherries, and jerepigos with col-

Francis (Duimpie) Bayly, group operations director of SFW.

ourful names such as Worcester Hock, Polly Hock and Paarl Rock. Not only were these wines strengthened with the addition of wine spirit or brandy, but the addition of cane sugar, in the event of a poor summer, was common practice.

Either sensing an impending change of taste or feeling that he might be able to help make it himself, Winshaw had long argued against this practice, finally bringing the Prime Minister, General Smuts (whose wife was related to the Kriges of Oude Libertas), around to his viewpoint. One result of this lobbying was Act 15 of 1924, which forbade the use of cane sugar in the flavouring and fermenting of wine.

A further element in Winshaw's reasoning was medical. As a doctor, he felt that a natural wine, with its relatively low sugar and alcohol content, would be better for the public health than the rich and powerful concoctions of old. From the beginning, therefore, the Winshaws concentrated upon making natural wines. Among the most famous of these were the Chateau Libertas and La Gratitude wines – the latter named after the beautiful old house in the now historic Dorp

Street in Stellenbosch, now a National Monument, which was (and still is) the Winshaw family home. In other wine ranges the name of Adam Tas is remembered, in Tasheimer, Oom Tas, Taskelder and Tassenberg, to the extent that 'Tassies' has gone into the vernacular. Winshaw attached great importance to names and labels, defending them ardently against plagiarism by other winemakers. He also continued to make it a fixed policy to buy only good wines from the growers, and only at good prices.

In these years the younger William Winshaw (universally known as 'Bill') began to take a larger share in the emerging character of the firm, following study of modern wine-making methods in Europe; in 1930 he introduced Grand Mousseux, still one of the most famous and best-selling of the Cape's sparkling wines.

The business operation at Oude Libertas remained a private concern until 1935 when

---

WINES MARKETED AND DISTRIBUTED BY STELLENBOSCH FARMERS' WINERY GROUP

Autumn Harvest range
Crackling, Late Vintage, Ausberger, Country Claret, Grand Crû, Stein and Rosé.

Kellerprinz range
Stein, Grand Crû, Rosanne and Late Harvest.

Nederburg range
(see Nederburg, page 201)

Taskelder range
Claret, Premier Grand Crû, Late Vintage and Blanc de Noir.

Zonnebloem range
Cabernet Sauvignon, Special Late Harvest, Noble Late Harvest, Grand Crû, Pinotage, Shiraz, Rhine Riesling, Premier Grand Crû, Chardonnay, Gewürztraminer, Cabernet Blanc de Noir, Blanc de Blanc and Sauvignon Blanc.

Overmeer range
Grand Crû, Late Harvest, Stein and Red.

Individual labels
Tasheimer Goldtröpfchen, La Gratitude, Lieberstein, Roodendal Cabernet Sauvignon, Casa de Ouro Graça, Roma White, Virginia, Zonnheimer, Chateau Libertas, Tassenberg, Capenheimer, Oom Tas, Lanzerac Rosé and Lanzerac Chardonnay.

Sparkling wines
Grand Mousseux: Grand Cuvée, Grand Rouge, Vin Doux, Vin Sec, Spumanté and 5th Avenue Cold Duck.
Nederburg: Cuvée Brut and Kap Sekt.

Fortified wines
Monis: Full Cream, Medium Cream and Dry Sherries, Moscato, Very Old Port and Special Reserve.
Sedgwick: Old Brown Sherry, Government House Port, Libertas White Muscadel and Ship Sherry.

---

it was converted into a public company. With this move, the basic structure of the present-day Stellenbosch Farmers' Winery was laid down. With further expansion came mergers with other companies, one of the more important of these being the amalgamation in November 1950 with the firm V.H. Matterson, first established in Pietermaritzburg in 1851; this merger led to the establishment of a group under a holding company, Stellenbosch Farmers' Wine Trust Limited. Further large mergers took place in 1966 and 1970. In the first of these Stellenbosch Farmers' Wine Trust Limited merged with Monis Wineries Limited of Paarl (which also owned the famous Nederburg farm) and the new holding company of the resulting group was named Stellenbosch Wine Trust Limited. With the creation of this large new group the paths of two other pioneers of the local wine industry, Roberto Moni and Johan Georg Graue, were linked with Stellenbosch Farmers' Winery. Large sums were then allocated for the further development of Nederburg. With a heavy investment in the natural wine industry, the group achieved a bigger share of the spirits and fortified wine market with their 1970 takeover of Sedgwick Tayler Holdings Limited.

Together with these expansions into new areas went major developments both in marketing – the winery allocated R2 million in 1962 for advertising their products – and in production and research facilities, reflected in the 1964 purchase of two farms for viticultural research.

The most spectacular expression of this new thrust was in the meteoric career of a Stellenbosch Farmers' Winery product which first appeared in 1959. In that year a semi-sweet table wine, largely made from Chenin Blanc, was launched with the name of Lieberstein. Three decades later, the following table still brings a misty look to the eyes of Stellenbosch Farmers' Winery executives:

AMOUNT OF LIEBERSTEIN SOLD

Year	(litres)
1959	30 000
1960	700 000
1961	4 500 000
1962	12 700 000
1963	22 300 000
1964	31 200 000

The peak achieved in 1964 made this the largest selling bottled wine in the world at the time, and though public taste has moved on, Lieberstein retains a devoted, if somewhat diminished, following.

During all these developments, William Charles Winshaw remained at the head of his company. Seemingly immortal, it was only at the indomitable old age of 92 that the founder retired from his creation, handing over the running of the company to his son, Bill Winshaw. The elder Winshaw died in 1968 at the age of 96.

His memorial on the northern banks of the Eerste River is an impressive one. The extensive cellars and winery produce a quantity of wine which gives the company turnover in excess of R600 million a year. Public tours of the premises are laid on; these include not only a view of the winery itself, from the enormous steel tanks of the cold fermentation process to the teams of skilled coopers assembling the red wine maturation vats from staves of imported Limousin oak, but also films on wine and a tasting of the company's products in the elegant tasting-rooms. Sophisticated educational courses are also housed in the complex.

One further attraction of Oude Libertas needs mention. This is the Oude Libertas complex, comprising a private underground cellar-restaurant and the Oude Libertas Amphitheatre, built in 1977 on the slopes of the Papegaaiberg, and opened with a performance by Vladimir Ashkenazy. Based on the design of the ancient Greek theatres of Athens and Epidauros, it seats some 430 theatre-goers.

Bill Winshaw retired as chairman of the holding company in 1980, but remains on the board of directors. His son John is general manager of the Stellenbosch operation. Lothar Barth, who had been managing director since 1970, succeeded Bill Winshaw as chairman. He retired in 1986, but remained on the board until 1989. Lothar's son, John, is cellarmaster. Ronnie Melck joined the company in 1956, became managing director in 1981, and retired in 1990. Frans Davin is the present chairman and Frans Stroebel the managing director. The director in charge of operations is Francis (Duimpie) Bayly, a graduate of Stellenbosch University, and the University of California, Davis in the USA.

—STELLENZICHT—
VINEYARDS

The 228-hectare farm of Stellenzicht (then known as Alphen) was bought in 1981 from the Bairnsfather-Cloete family of Constantia by Hans-Joachim Schreiber, a German financier. Subsequently, in 1985, Schreiber also bought Neethlingshof, also in Stellenbosch, from the Momberg family.

As at Neethlingshof, an extensive and ongoing replanting programme is well under way under the direction of winemaker Marinus Bredell, and Jan Bester, who, with his assistant Willem Burger, manages the vineyards. Marinus, a winemaker of more than 20 years' experience, studied at the

---

STELLENZICHT VINEYARDS

Varieties planted (ha)

6-wire vertical trellis

Cabernet Sauvignon	25
Chardonnay	15
Merlot	12,5
Sauvignon Blanc	8,5
Zinfandel	7
Shiraz	7
Sémillon	6,4
Cabernet Franc	5,8
Gewürztraminer	5,1
Muscadel (white)	4,6
Pinot Gris	4
Erlihane	3,9
Auxerrois	3,4
Weisser Riesling	2,6
Pinot Noir	2,5
Malbec	2,5
Chenin Blanc	1,7
Morio Muscat	1,5
Cape Riesling	1,3

Total area under vines in 1991/2: 120,3 ha.
Irrigation: The vineyards are irrigated.
Average temperatures: Records are not kept.
Average annual rainfall: 800 mm.
Stock: Rooted vines are bought from a nursery.
First wines bottled under the Stellenzicht Vineyards label: Heerenblanc, Grand Vin Blanc, Rhine Riesling and Rhine Riesling Noble Late Harvest.
Wines currently bottled under the Stellenzicht Vineyards and Bergendal labels: Heerenblanc, Grand Vin Blanc, Rhine Riesling, Rhine Riesling Noble Late Harvest, Fragrance, Bergenblanc, Bergendal Late Harvest and Bergenrood.
Wood ageing: Wines are aged in wood on the estate.
Cellar capacity: 12 000 hl.

Stellenzicht Vineyards are on the Stellenbosch Wine Route and visits can be arranged by appointment.

Elsenburg College and in 1968 joined Gilbeys as an assistant at the Kleine Zalze estate (previously Alphen), where he rose to become winemaker and manager. In 1983 he won the General Smuts trophy as Winemaker of the Year at the South African Champion Wine Show. Marinus was no stranger to the Stellenzicht Vineyards when he joined the newly renamed farm, as he had been involved in the replanting programme from the start.

The vineyards are situated between 150 and 380 metres above sea level on predominantly western-facing slopes. The high potential of the area is evidenced by the high quality of the wines made on the neighbouring estates of Alto, and Rust-en-Vrede, and Hans-Joachim and his management team, which includes the renowned Günter Brözel, believe that Stellenzicht is now poised to take its place amongst the most celebrated producers of fine Cape wines.

Only the best in wine-making equipment and technology has been used in the construction of the new cellar, which has the capacity to handle some 1 200 tonnes of grapes. The stainless steel fermentation tanks have capacities ranging from 410 litres to 20 000 litres, while the maturation cellar can hold 800 000 litres in 2 500- to 5 000-litre vats and 420 225-litre barrels of French oak from Allier, Nevers and Vosges. Following the practice at Neethlingshof, the Stellenzicht red wines are matured in wood for up to three years before being matured for a further two years in bottles before release. In ad-

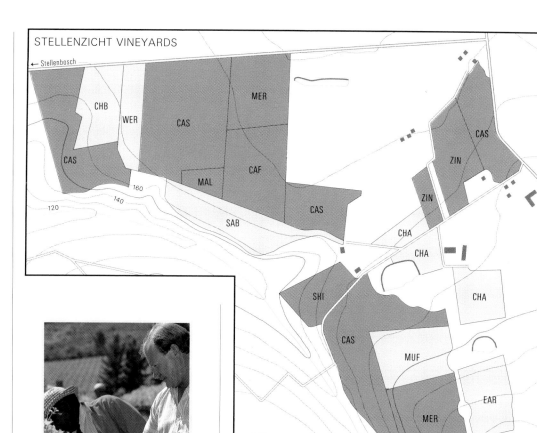

STELLENZICHT VINEYARDS

← Stellenbosch

—TALANA HILL—
WINERY

Marinus Bredell of Stellenzicht.

dition to the range of Stellenzicht wines (which include Grand Vin Blanc and Rhine Riesling), it is also the intention to market blends made from Neethlingshof and Stellenzicht wines under the Bergendal label. To cope with this extra volume a blending cellar has been added to the winery.

—TALANA HILL— WINERY

Like so many of the new wine-making ventures which have revitalized the Cape wine industry, Talana Hill is the result of a collaboration of investment capital, professional expertise and great enthusiasm. This tiny 7,2-hectare property lies in the Paradyskloof valley bounded by the Stellenbosch Mountain looming high over the area, and the Helderberg range with its attendant foothills.

The maturation cellar at Stellenzicht, where the wines are matured in wood for up to three years

Talana Hill Winery's underground cellar.

The views from the sloping vineyards are spectacular, facing south-west and overlooking the Stellenbosch winelands with Table Mountain and False Bay in the distance.

The farm has Jan 'Boland' Coetzee's winery, Vriesenhof, as its neighbour and the association is a very close one indeed. The land belonged to Jan until 1987 when he sold it to his old rugby friend, Doug Smollan, and Doug co-investors Carlos dos Santos, Alan Silverman, Les Weil and Jonny Frankel, all of whom share Doug and Jan's commitment to making great wines. Jan had

---

TALANA HILL WINERY

Varieties planted (ha)

(Trellising system being changed)
Chardonnay 3
Merlot 2
Cabernet Franc 1
(Cabernet Sauvignon grapes are selected from neighbouring farms under long-term contracts)

Total area under vines in 1991/2: 6,5 ha.
Irrigation: None
Average temperatures: Records are not kept.
Average annual rainfall: Records are not kept.
Stock: Rooted vines are bought from a nursery.
First wine bottled under the Talana Hill Winery label: Chardonnay 1987.
Wines currently bottled under the Talana Hill Winery label: Royale and Chardonnay.
Wood ageing: Wines are aged in wood on the estate.
Cellar capacity: The cellar is to be expanded to handle 80 tonnes of grapes.

Talana Hill Winery is not open to the public.

---

already planted the vineyards, so the winery was ready for immediate production from the Chardonnay, Merlot and Cabernet Franc varieties, and by agreement he undertook to continue managing the vineyards and to lend his consummate skill to making wine under the Talana Hill label.

Between 1987 and 1990 the wine was made in Jan's cellar, but in 1990 a partially underground cellar was built at Talana Hill and it was in this brand new facility that the 1991 harvest was pressed. Only French oak is used for maturation, the 225-litre *barriques* coming from Tronçais, Nevers and Allier. Only two wines are made: a Chardonnay and a Bordeaux-style blend. The Chardonnay made its debut at the first New World Wine Auction and was well received. This was then released locally and soon sold out. For the 1990 vintage the wine was racked and then allowed to mature in oak for a further seven months before final blending and bottling. The first vintage of the Bordeaux-style blend, named Royale, was launched in limited quantities in 1991.

—THELEMA—
MOUNTAIN VINEYARDS

In July 1983 the McLean Family Trust bought the old fruit farm Thelema, situated at the top of the Helshoogte Pass about 6 kilometres outside Stellenbosch. It was the culmination of a long search by Gyles and Barbara Webb for that rare location where exceptional wines could be made.

The 157-hectare farm lies on the slopes of the Simonsberg at an elevation that ranges from 370 to 640 metres above sea level. Aspects are mainly south-facing, and there are spectacular views of the Simonsberg, Drakenstein and Jonkershoek mountains. Thelema is, therefore, one of the highest and probably coolest wine farms in the Stellenbosch area. Although wine had been made on the farm in the early part of the century and table grapes were produced until the late 1960s, there were no vines on the farm at the time of purchase, only neglected orchards. The run-down state of the farm was part of its charm, augmented by the views, huge 150 year-old oak trees surrounding the dilapidated house and the quiet disturbed only occasionally by raucous peacock shrieks.

Gyles Webb of Thelema, who believes in keeping wines 'as natural as possible'.

It has, however, involved an enormous effort to convert Thelema into a wine farm. The labourers' housing has been renovated and new cottages built, and the old Cape Victorian homestead restored. The orchards have gradually made way for vineyards, and virgin mountainside has been cleared and prepared to increase the arable land to about 45 hectares. Exhaustive tests of the soil revealed it to be high-potential, deep, red, decomposed granite with excellent water-retention capacity.

These qualities of climate and soil have prompted the planting of the classical varieties only. To date 31 hectares have been planted and a further 10 hectares will be planted in the next few years. Of the total, 70 per cent will be white varieties (mainly Chardonnay) and the remainder red (mainly Cabernet Sauvignon).

In October 1987 building started on the winery, designed to handle the expected annual crop of 400 tonnes, and in February 1988 the first load of Chardonnay was received and processed. This harvest yielded 55 tonnes of grapes, which have produced the first range of Thelema wines: Sauvignon Blanc, Rhine Riesling, Chardonnay and Blanc Fumé. The 1988 Cabernet Sauvignon was bottled in 1991. The policy is to use farm grapes only and to bottle on the premises in order to maintain complete control.

Thelema's winemaker, Gyles Webb, had an unusual beginning in the industry, having qualified as an accountant after attending school in Natal. Although an enthusiastic wine consumer, it was a chance encounter with Puligny-Montrachet in Kimberley in the mid-1970s that persuaded him to pack away his green pen and bring his wife and infant son to Stellenbosch, where he completed a B.Sc. (Agric.) degree in 1979, majoring in Viticulture and Oenology.

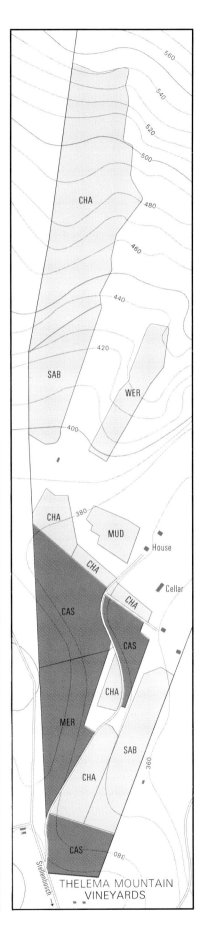

THELEMA MOUNTAIN VINEYARDS

THELEMA MOUNTAIN VINEYARDS

Varieties planted (ha)

Vertical hedge
Chardonnay 13
Cabernet Sauvignon 8
Sauvignon Blanc 7
Weisser Riesling 2,5
Muscat de Frontignan 1

Total area under vines in 1991/2: 31,5 ha.
Irrigation: None.
Average temperatures: Records are not kept.
Average annual rainfall: 1 000 mm.
Stock: Rooted vines are bought from a nursery.
First wines bottled under the Thelema Mountain Vineyards label: Thelema Sauvignon Blanc, Riesling, Blanc Fumé and Chardonnay (all 1988 vintage).
Wines currently bottled under the Thelema Mountain Vineyards label: Sauvignon Blanc, Cabernet, Chardonnay, Riesling and Muscat de Frontignan.
Wood ageing: Wines are aged in wood on the estate.
Cellar capacity: 2 800 hl.

Thelema Mountain Vineyards are open to the public for sales and tastings from 09h00 to 12h30 and from 13h00 to 17h00 on weekdays and from 09h00 to 12h30 on Saturdays.

Gyles then worked as experimental wine-maker in the Small-Scale Cellar at the Stellenbosch Farmers' Winery, gaining useful experience in many aspects of wine-making, including *méthode champenoise* procedures, making special and noble late harvests and nouveaus, wood experiments, yeast trials and also making basic red and white wines. In 1982 he left for California where for four months he lived with and worked for Joseph Heitz in his Napa Valley winery. From this colourful Californian wine pioneer he gained invaluable practical experience in aspects of fine wine-making, with special emphasis on the handling of wines in wood. He also experienced and endorsed Joe's 'keep it simple' approach of minimal finings, filtrations and manipulation of the wine to ensure as natural a product as possible. Above all he confirmed the importance of regularly tasting and appreciating wines from other parts of the world.

On his return to South Africa in 1983 he worked as assistant winemaker at Neethlingshof. Two wines for which he was responsible – the Weisser Riesling Special Late Harvest 1983 and the Cabernet Sauvignon 1983 –

were later sold on the Nederburg Auction. He continued at Neethlingshof as wine-making consultant until the end of 1985 when he left to concentrate full-time on the development and running of Thelema which, during the intervening years, had been bought by his wife's family.

Gyles's aim as a winemaker is to produce flavourful, long-lasting, dry white and red wines with distinctive character. He is convinced that good fruit is the single most important quality determinant in wine-making, so great emphasis is placed on vineyard management. The role of wood is also regarded as crucial, so his Chardonnay and all his red wines are aged in classic 225-litre French oak barrels. Although this is the most expensive form of wood maturation, it is considered sufficiently important to warrant the additional cost. He believes in keeping wine as natural as possible, with low sulphur dioxide levels and minimal handling – his policy is one of benign neglect.

— UITERWYK —
ESTATE

One of the oldest estates in the Stellenbosch area, Uiterwyk was once situated on the main road from Cape Town to Stellenbosch which wound through this panoramic valley. Named after an area in Holland, the land was first settled in 1682 by Dirk Coetzee, and formally granted to him by Willem Adriaan van der Stel in 1699.

It began to make its mark as a wine farm in the late eighteenth century, with the advent of the Krige family. It was they who built the present homestead – a beautiful example of the Cape Dutch type – in 1791. An adjacent cellar was added in 1798, and the stables in 1812. A further smaller house was added at the back to complete the complex in 1822.

In the present century Uiterwyk came into the ownership of another old South African family, the De Waals. The first De Waal to be born in the country farmed vines in what is now Wale (or Waal) Street in Cape Town. His son, Pieter, moved away to farm at Alphen, and subsequent generations crossed the Cape Flats to the Stellenbosch area. After various further moves the family finally settled at Uiterwyk when it was bought by Jan Christoffel de Waal in 1912. When he retired in 1946 his son, Danie, the present owner, took over. Danie's eldest son, Chris, studied winemaking at the Elsenburg Agricultural College. He gained practical experience in wine-making in West Germany and now makes the white wines on Uiterwyk. Pieter, the second son, studied Economics at the University of Stellenbosch and worked in the Napa Valley, California, to gain experience in the marketing of wine. He is responsible for the marketing and sales of Uiterwyk wines. The youngest son, Daniël, studied for a B.Sc. in viticulture and oenology at the University of Stellenbosch and gained experience in red wine-making at Château l'Angelus in

France. He is now responsible for making the red wines at Uiterwyk.

The estate's impressive cellar was opened in 1979. Danie designed it so that it can be enlarged and it incorporates a reception, tasting and selling area, an office, laboratory and a cellar for ageing bottled wines. For visitors to Uiterwyk the old wine cellar remains rich in atmosphere; with many of its massive oak casks still intact (they were erected with the building), it has seen continuous yearly production of wine since it was built in 1798.

The estate covers 150 hectares, of which about 112 are presently under vines. Here Danie de Waal concentrates about two thirds of his production on Chenin Blanc and Clairette Blanche, followed by Pinotage, Colombard and Cabernet Sauvignon. The balance is made up of relatively small quantities of Cape Riesling, Müller-Thurgau, Bukettraube, Sauvignon Blanc, Weisser Riesling, Merlot and Cabernet Franc. From these varieties, eight wines are bottled and sold under the estate's own label.

UITERWYK ESTATE

Varieties planted (ha)

1-wire trellis
Chenin Blanc 38,69
Clairette Blanche 28,32
Pinotage 9,05
Cabernet Sauvignon 7,93
Colombard 7,2
Merlot 3,7
Sauvignon Blanc 3,03
Cape Riesling 2,9
Müller-Thurgau 2,72
Cabernet Franc 2,66
Chardonnay 2,14
Weisser Riesling 2,05
Bukettraube 1,63

Total area under vines in 1991/2: 112,02 ha.
Irrigation: All vineyards are irrigated.
Average temperatures: Records are not kept.
Average annual rainfall: Approximately 900 mm.
Stock: Parent stock is used for grafting; rooted vines are also bought from a nursery.
First wines bottled under the Uiterwyk label: Colombard 1972 and Cabernet Sauvignon 1973.
Wines currently bottled under the Uiterwyk label: Cabernet Sauvignon, Pinotage, Merlot, Kromhout, Sauvignon Blanc, Müller-Thurgau, Rhine Riesling and Riesling.
Wood ageing: Wines are aged in wood on the estate.
Cellar capacity: 10 000 hl.
Uiterwyk Estate is on the Stellenbosch Wine Route and is open to the public from 09h00 to 16h30 every day except Sundays.

The Uiterwyk manor house, built in 1791 is now a National Monument.

—UITKYK—
ESTATE

Once the domain of aristocratic Hans von Carlowitz, this wine farm went through lean times in the period following World War II before a change of ownership in the early 1960s brought with it a rebuilding and expansion of the vineyards and the restoration of the striking and beautiful homestead. A neo-classical masterpiece and one of the rare architect-designed homesteads in the winelands, its designer was almost certainly the French immigrant Louis Michel Thibault, who abandoned a career as a designer of military fortifications to devote himself to the graceful embellishment of the local burgher architecture.

Thibault often collaborated with the German sculptor and designer Anton Anreith, who was responsible for the carving of Uitkyk Estate's monumental front door.

First granted to Jan Oberholzer in 1712 and largely used for grazing in the early years, by the late eighteenth century the farm had become the property of one of the most successful self-made immigrants of his day, the formidable Martin Melck. By hard work and shrewd investment he had accumulated a large number of farms, including the area of the present estates of Uitkyk, Kanonkop and Elsenburg. Then, in 1776, Melck ceded the land of Uitkyk to his son-in-law, Johan David Beyers, as a wedding gift. It was Beyers who built the present splendid townhouse-style mansion for himself and his large family. During the following century the farm continued to be used mainly for grazing or as a country seat for various wealthy families. In 1929, however, it was purchased by an immigrant Prussian nobleman, Hans von Carlowitz. It was Von Carlowitz who recognized the wine-making possibilities inherent in the high slopes of the farm, with their good soil and drainage. With his two sons, Hans and Georg, he divided his land between vines, timber on the steeper slopes, and wheat on the lower-lying areas. Responsibility for the different kinds of farming was shared by Von Carlowitz between his sons, with Hans attending to the wheat and timber and Georg being in sole charge of the vineyards.

In 1939 the elder son returned to Germany, leaving Georg in full control of the es-

The neo-classical Uitkyk homestead which was designed by the French immigrant Louis Michel Thibault.

tate's operations. In the following years Georg developed the vineyards, planting predominantly Chenin Blanc, Cape Riesling, Cinsaut and Cabernet; it was a blend made from the last-mentioned two varieties for which the family is still remembered. This was the famous Carlonet (the few remaining bottles of this blend are prized collector's items), which was complemented by a fine white blend of Chenin Blanc and Cape Riesling, the sweet and fruity Carlsheim.

In the post-World War II period these outstanding wines gained for Georg von Carlo-

witz a secure reputation among Cape Town's discerning wine lovers. Unfortunately, this reputation was not accompanied by financial security. The area of the vineyards was small; its 35 hectares provided quality, but not the quantity to ensure a working profit, or the capital needed for expensive developments such as the cooling equipment introduced to the country in the 1950s, or the planting of new vines to replace Uitkyk's ageing vineyards.

In 1963, in the face of these pressures, Von Carlowitz was forced to sell. The man who bought the farm at this juncture in its fortunes, Gerry Bouwer, was at least as interested in the old homestead as in the farm which went with it. At the same time Bouwer's dentist son-in-law, Dr Harvey Illing, switched careers and became the well-known and successful winemaker of Uitkyk — a position he held until his retirement.

An aesthetically appropriate new cellar was built during this period and the vineyards were extensively expanded. The next stage in Uitkyk's history was the building of an architecturally and technically modern

cellar and the arrival of Jan du Preez as winemaker. Jan joined Uitkyk in 1989 after having trained as a winemaker in Stellenbosch. He then made wine for several private estates at the Cape and in Germany and had five years of marketing experience in Europe before settling at Uitkyk.

Jan is challenged by the complexity of conditions at Uitkyk. The estate has some 600 hectares with a great variety of terroirs — different combinations of many different soils, slopes, heights, rainfall, etc. He feels he has the perfect infrastructure to expand the vineyards with classic grape varieties. Jan is also determined that Uitkyk will not be dictated to by constantly fluctuating wine fashions but only by the best quality and the suitability of varieties to the different terroirs. He is planning new vineyards of the Cape Riesling variety, which he considers the best 'drinking' wine of the Cape, and plans to increase plantings of varieties such as Sauvignon Blanc, Chardonnay, Pinot Gris, Cabernet Sauvignon, Pinot Noir, Merlot and Shiraz plantings with a possibility of adding

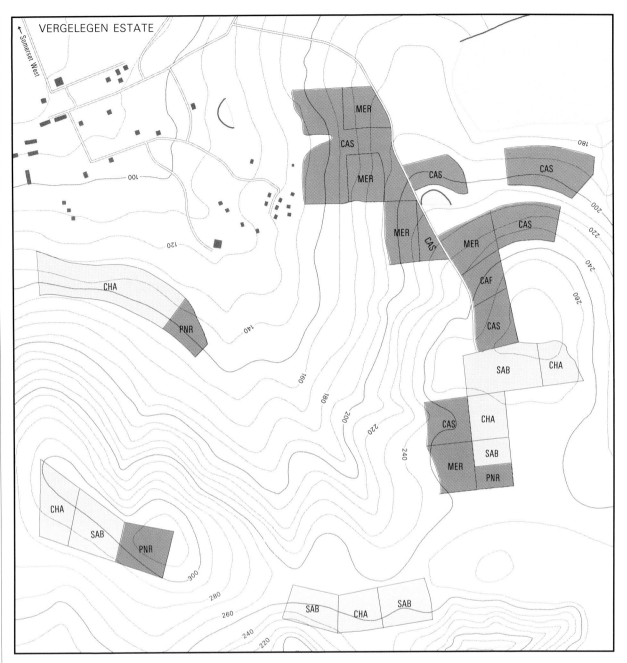

Gewürztraminer, Cabernet Franc, Sémillon and Pinot Blanc.

Uitkyk is establishing an initial 30 hectares of narrow planting (80 by 150 centimetres). Whereas 3 300 vines per hectare is the norm, this system allows for 8 300. vines.The greater density will not increase the crop drastically, however; the normal planting density results in a Cabernet Sauvignon vine producing 1,8 to 2 kilograms of grapes per vine, but under the new system – with proper soil preparation, trellising and canopy management – a vine will produce only 1 kilogram per vine. The advantage is that these grapes will be much more concentrated. The new system will yield about 8 tonnes per hectare as against 6,5 tonnes under the old system. Narrow planting has necessitated the importation of a specially adapted tractor from the wine-producing Champagne region of France – assembled in the Cape by a French technician.

— VERGELEGEN —
ESTATE

The story of Vergelegen is almost as old as the story of the Cape itself, for this was the estate of Willem Adriaan (more accurately Wilhem Adriaen), eldest son of Simon van der Stel and his successor in the post of governor of the Colony. Overwhelmingly arrogant and an administrative martinet, his rise and fall at the turn of the seventeenth century adds a nice note of villainy to the historical record at the tip of Africa. For all his faults Willem Adriaan was the owner of a curious and intelligent mind, more at home with the theory of agriculture than the practice of rule. On his 400-morgen estate of Vergelegen near what is now Somerset West, he established a vast experimental farm where he tested a wide range of stock and crops, both European and Oriental. Vvines were planted in 1700, the same year the estate was granted, and within six years some 500 000 vines were yielding 55 leaguers of wine. The treatment of the vine under local conditions is recorded with precision in Simon van der Stel's *Gardener's Almanack*, intended as a guide for farmers of the Cape.

Martin Meinert, who is winemaker at Vergelegen, as well as at his own winery

Some of his own practices, however, brought his ambitions up short. Conflict with the emerging society of the free burghers, now acting with increasing independence from the Dutch East India Company, came to a head in open rebellion against the governor's tyranny. A brief game of bluff and counterbluff ended in the governor's defeat, humiliation and exile. He returned to live out the rest of his life in Holland, his researches into the farming potential of the Cape abandoned.

Following Van der Stel's demise, the estate passed through a succession of owners and though it retained evidence of its former glory it became progressively more rundown. In 1798 the Theunissen family acquired the property and it was to remain in their family for a full century. Under the Theunissens the vineyards flourished and a new cellar was built. In the early years of the present century, however, the estate again fell into disrepair and when it was bought by Sir Lionel and Lady Florence Phillips in 1917, Lady Phillips immediately set to work, with her architect, to restore the homestead, in the process adding two new wings and replacing the plain gable at the back with a copy of the Old Paarl Pastorie gable. During restoration, traces of the original octagonal wall mentioned by François Valentijn were discovered, and the wall rebuilt on the old foundations. The Theunissen's wine cellar was modified to house Sir Lionel's magnificent collection of books.

Florence Phillips not only restored the old homestead, library and gardens, but also spent vast sums of money on the estate itself. An old footbridge was replaced by a structure wide enough to accommodate motor traffic, roads were constructed and dams built. Lady Phillips decided to remove all the vineyards, which she replaced with mixed agriculture. After the deaths of Sir Lionel and Lady Florence Phillips, her heirs in England decided to exercise their option to sell Vergelegen, which was then bought by Charles 'Punch' Barlow and his wife Cynthia in June 1941. The Barlows resumed farming operations on Vergelegen and began planting vines on a small scale. In 1987 the estate was acquired by Anglo American Farms Limited and one of the many projects undertaken was to begin replanting the vineyards, following intensive climatic and soil tests.

Of the 100 hectares presently being planted, 60 per cent will be red varieties and

In 1917, Vergelegen underwent extensive restoration.

VERGELEGEN ESTATE

Varieties planted (ha)

Perold trellis
Cabernet Sauvignon 24
Chardonnay 17
Sauvignon Blanc 15
Merlot 13
Pinot Noir 5
Cabernet Franc 2

Total area under vines in 1991/2:
76 ha (24 ha still to be planted).
Irrigation: All but 19 ha of the vineyards can be irrigated if necessary.
Average temperatures: Records are not kept.
Average annual rainfall: 850 mm.
Stock: Rooted vines are bought from a nursery.
First wines to be bottled under the Vergelegen label from 1992.
Wood ageing: Wines are aged in wood on the estate.
Cellar capacity: 6 750 hl.

Vergelegen Estate is not open to the public as yet.

the balance white. The reds are Cabernet Sauvignon, Merlot, Cabernet Franc, Petit Verdot and Pinot Noir, while the whites are Chardonnay, Sémillon and Sauvignon Blanc. The plantings are on Clovelly, Glenrosa and Pinedene soil types, and varieties and rootstock have been selected to match the soils as well as the aspect. The climate at Vergelegen is mild, but there are two distinctly different areas. The north- to north-west-facing slopes vary in altitude from 140 to 260 metres and, being the warmer part of the farm, are where the red varieties have been planted. The south-facing slopes overlooking False Bay (which is only 5 kilometres away) rise to 305 metres and experience tempera-

tures which are on average 2 °C lower, being constantly fanned by the sea breezes, and are the site of the white variety plantings. The moisture-holding soils and mild climate have resulted in minimal irrigation being required – 19 per cent of the vines are not irrigated at all.

Every effort is being made towards the rehabilitation of Vergelegen as a major wine producer, and as much attention has been paid to the construction of the winery as to vineyard practices. The cellar complex is the result of expert input from various authorities around the world and has been built to be as productive as possible while being economical and practical.

The hilltop site of the winery commands sweeping views of the estate beneath the crags and kloofs of the Helderberg, and care has been taken with the new buildings to ensure that they complement the surroundings and the elegance of the traditional Cape Dutch architecture of the homestead and old outbuildings. Functionally the winery is designed to allow gravity flow, and reveals the influence of a return to simplicity and craftsmanship in the wine-making industry around the world. The complex is on four levels, comprising a harvest plaza and visitors' platform, a red wine fermentation platform, the main tank floor and the barrel cellar. For functional and aesthetic reasons the excavations needed to house the winery are 10 metres deep.

1992 was an auspicious year for Martin Meinert, Vergelegen's winemaker, as it was the year of the maiden vintage of the reconstituted estate. The range of wines be limited to Sauvignon Blanc, Chardonnay, Pinor Noir and red blends. The quality is uncompromisingly aimed at establishing a worldwide reputation. In terms of international markets Vergelegen has already shown the way by hosting, in 1990, the first New World Wine Auction, an event conceived to provide a showcase for the best wines of the Cape, California, Oregon, Australia, New Zealand, Argentina, Chile and Mexico.

VERGENOEGD ESTATE

Jac and John Faure of Vergenoegd, one of the oldest estates in the Cape.

VERGENOEGD ESTATE

Varieties planted (ha)

Bush vines and vertical trellis
Chenin Blanc 28
Vertical trellis
Merlot 13
Cabernet Sauvignon 12
Shiraz 9
Sauvignon Blanc 5
Cape Riesling 2
Cabernet Franc 2
Perold trellis
Cabernet Sauvignon 23
Shiraz 13
Bush vines
Tinta Barocca 9
Cinsaut 9

Total area under vines in 1991/2: 125 ha.
Irrigation: All the vineyards can be irrigated if necessary.
Average temperatures: Records are not kept.
Average annual rainfall: 400-450 mm.
Stock: Rooted vines are bought from a nursery.
First wines bottled under the Vergenoegd label: Cabernet Sauvignon and Shiraz 1969 (bottled by KWV); Cabernet Sauvignon 1972 (bottled on the estate).
Wines currently bottled under the Vergenoegd label: Reserve, Cabernet Sauvignon, Shiraz, Tinta Barocca, Sauvignon Blanc, Cinsaut and Port.
Wood ageing: Wines are aged in wood on the estate. (Some Vergenoegd wines are also aged in wood and bottled at KWV, but this is a completely separate venture.)
Cellar capacity: 5 000 hl.

Vergenoegd Estate is open to the public every Wednesday from 14h00 to 17h00 and by appointment on other days

— V E R G E N O E G D —
E S T A T E

Situated on the lower reaches of the Eerste River, the estate of Vergenoegd, like Groot Constantia, enjoys the cooling winds of False Bay even if it does not have the 1 000 metre-high Constantiaberg to lend it shade in the late afternoon. This well-chosen site has had an influence on the growing of the vines and the making of the extremely good wines of Vergenoegd, produced by the brothers Jac and Brand Faure, now assisted by their respective sons John and Alex, the fifth and sixth generations of the family to live there.

The red wines of the estate have certainly come into their own, featuring prominently in the local wine shows.

One of the oldest farms in the Eerste River area, the land of Vergenoegd was originally

granted to Pieter de Vos in 1696. After a series of changes it became, in 1772, the property of Johannes Nicolaas Colijn, the son of the Colijn who had acquired Groot Constantia in 1720. It was he who built the present gable, dated 1773, onto the already existing homestead (it is believed that one of Johannes Colijn's slaves was responsible for the curious spelling of the name Vergenoegd on this gable).

In 1820 the farm was sold to the first of the Faure family, Johannes Gysbertus Faure. (The local proliferation of the Faures gave their name to the area at large.) Johannes Faure continued the making of wine which had begun here in the eighteenth century, but the course of the nineteenth century saw a diversification of the farm's activities, particularly in the breeding of race-horses, for which numerous stables were added. During

the Boer War a thriving horse-dealing business was run from here, to the extent that horses were exported to India and a groom had to be sent out to look after the horses on the boat during their voyage from the Cape.

But it was during the present century that Vergenoegd began to establish its own marked identity as a wine farm, under the guidance of John Faure, the father of the present owners. A committed wine farmer, he set about building up the vineyards, and in doing so concentrated, at the suggestion of Dr Charles Niehaus, upon two specific areas of development.

Niehaus is an important figure in modern South African wine history. He 'fathered' the sherry industry in the 1920s and 1930s,

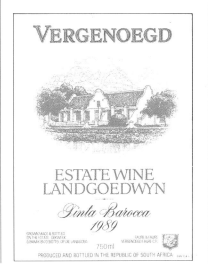

making a study of the distribution in the local vineyards of the naturally occurring 'flor' yeasts of the kind traditionally associated with the making of the fine, dry Spanish *fino* sherries. Vergenoegd was among the first of the 18 local farms where he discovered this yeast. His advice to plant varieties for sherry production was adopted by John Faure, whose sons have continued the cultivation of these varieties.

The second piece of advice given by Niehaus was to plant Cabernet Sauvignon. Though it was not taken up immediately, on Niehaus' further insistence vineyards of Cabernet were laid out, replacing many of the old Shiraz vines. The foundation for the excellent Vergenoegd Cabernet of today, one of the most respected wines of its kind in the country, was thus laid.

The soil on the estate varies considerably, from deep alluvial alongside the Eerste River, through all types of sandy soil to deep, yellow pot-clay types. It is on this latter, water-retaining type that the Cabernet vines are grown, and most of the other noble red varieties are also planted in soil with a high clay content.

The summers are hot but tempered by the south-easter, which appears to live up to its title of the 'Cape Doctor', for the vineyards suffer little from disease, and only light dusting is needed to counteract oïdium and downy mildew. The rainfall here is lower than in most of the other areas which fall under the Stellenbosch Wine of Origin district, particularly those which are close to the mountains, but most of the grapes are given only one irrigation.

Vergenoegd is situated on the irrigation canal which emerges from the Eerste River in Stellenbosch and runs down the length of the valley. During winter heavy rainfall in Jonkershoek causes the Eerste River to run very full, and with its shallow fall from Faure to the sea — Vergenoegd itself is only 10 to 13 metres above sea-level — this last meandering stretch of the river tended in the past to silt up, causing it to burst its banks and flood the adjacent vineyards. Today a good deal of the silt has been removed, and flooding reduced with the construction of artificial banks, or levées, along the river. With heavy winter rains, however, the possibility of flooding still causes the Faure brothers some anxiety — in some parts of the farm it is not unusual to find the odd patch of poor growth among the vines owing to lack of drainage.

Originally the property covered an extent of about 736 hectares, but it was reduced by 51 hectares to allow for the main Cape Town to Strand highway and the road to Stellenbosch which leads from it. Of the remaining 685 hectares some 125 are currently under wine grapes, though the planted area is being extended yearly. The main white varieties are Chenin Blanc, Sauvignon Blanc and Cape Riesling, which make up roughly a third of the area under vines, with the remainder being red varieties. Besides the Cabernet Sauvignon, these include plantings of Shiraz, Cinsaut, Tinta Barocca, Merlot and Cabernet Franc. In the old days Vergenoegd also produced a quality Chenin Blanc

wine which was supplied to KWV, but with the development of KWV's extensive modern white-wine cellars the organization has handled the farm's output of Chenin Blanc, leaving the Faures to concentrate on the production of their red wines. Some white wine is made from the free-run juice which is taken off the Cinsaut before the skins are allowed to ferment in the smaller quantity of juice needed for a darker and fuller red wine.

Since the death of John Faure in 1969 the activities of Vergenoegd have been divided between his two sons. The younger, Brand Faure, is responsible for the vineyards, while the elder brother, Jac Faure, concentrates upon the making of the wine. Jac's son, John, joined them in 1983, after graduating in Cellar Technology from Elsenburg Agricultural College, and Brand's son Alex, joined the vineyard section in 1990. In recent years the fine old buildings of Vergenoegd have been renovated and restored (including the charmingly florid gateway, bearing the same date as the main homestead, which leads to the courtyard at the rear of the house).

The outbuildings, too, have been restored, refurbished, and converted to offices, wine sales rooms, and maturation stores for Vergenoegd Estate's wine — the Cabernet Sauvignon receives a minimum of three years in wood and a further six months in bottle before being sold to the public. The old homestead itself is occupied by Jac Faure and his family. Filled with paintings of and trophies won by magnificent horses, its atmosphere is a legacy from the late nineteenth-century days of horse-breeding and racing. But it is the making of Vergenoegd's red wines which remains the consuming interest of the twentieth-century Faures.

— VLOTTENBURG —
CO-OPERATIVE WINERY

The establishment of the Vlottenburg Co-operative Winery in the mid-1940s can be traced to the inordinate congestion of grape deliveries to KWV's Stellenbosch depot, which was regularly besieged at harvest time by farmers who had gathered their grapes at dawn, only to find themselves waiting through the following night to deliver loads of already fermenting grapes.

WINES BOTTLED AND MARKETED

Red: Cabernet Sauvignon, Pinotage, Gamay and Merlot.
White: Riesling, Chenin Blanc, Premier Grand Crû, Gewürztraminer, Chenin Blanc, Sauvignon Blanc, Weisser Riesling, Chardonnay, Special Late Harvest and Muscat de Hambourg.
Fortified: Hanepoot.

The co-operative is on the Stellenbosch Wine Route and is open to the public on weekdays from 08h30 to 17h00, and on Saturdays from 08h30 to 12h30.

To relieve the pressure on these inadequate facilities the Vlottenburg Co-operative was built, after being launched at a meeting in September 1945. The cellar, completed in time for the 1947 harvest, was built on part of the farm Vlottenburg (on which the Eersterivier Winery also stands). Its first few seasons' activities were supervised by Charlie Sparks of the Castle Wine and Brandy Company, before the appointment of a full-time winemaker and manager. The present incumbent is Kowie du Toit, who took over the winery in 1973, after the death of the then winemaker, Nico Mostert.

Today the co-operative has an up-to-date cellar and 30 members distributed around the Lynedoch, Stellenbosch Kloof and Kuils

River areas. Of the 12 000 tonnes of grapes received annually, 50 per cent is Chenin Blanc and 10 per cent Clairette Blanche. The remaining 40 per cent is mainly made up of Cape Riesling, Chardonnay, Weisser Riesling, Sauvignon Blanc, Cabernet Sauvignon, Pinotage, Cinsaut, Colombard and Muscat d'Alexandrie. The first Cabernet Sauvignon was added in 1977, when plantings in the Stellenbosch Kloof area by the Co-operative's chairman, Mr E.P. Andrag, began to yield. All the good wine made here is sold to Stellenbosch Farmers' Winery, while the distilling wine goes to Oude Meester.

— VREDENHEIM —
ESTATE

Boasting a history that goes back more than 300 years, this estate counts among the oldest in the Boland. The Eerste River that flows through the property, the manor house with its handsome baroque gables, the lovely gardens and the spectacular backdrop of the impressive Stellenbosch mountains all make for a beautiful setting.

Vredenheim boasts a dynamic young woman winemaker, Elzabé Bezuidenhout, whose parents acquired the farm in 1986. She originally trained as an industrial psy-

The homestead at Vredenheim, one of the oldest estates in the Boland.

Elzabé Bezuidenhout, winemaker at her parents' farm since 1987.

chologist but found her vocation in wine-making, making her début in the wine industry in 1987. Most of the wine made on the estate is supplied to Stellenbosch Farmers' Winery, and only a small percentage is bottled under the estate's own label. Currently these wines are only available from the estate itself. Vredenheim is also one of the few estates making a red and a white sparkling grapejuice.

VREDENHEIM ESTATE

Varieties planted (ha)

3-wire vertical trellis
Chenin Blanc 24
Cabernet Sauvignon 13,8
Sauvignon Blanc 9,5
Colombard 9,4
Merlot 5,3
Pinotage 4,8
Weisser Riesling 4,4
Cape Riesling 3,7
Tinta Barocca 0,43
Shiraz 0,28
Carignan 0,12

Total area under vines in 1991/2: 75,73 ha.
Irrigation: Micro-irrigation and overhead irrigation are used when necessary.
Average temperatures: Records are not kept.
Average annual rainfall: 700 mm.
Stock: Rooted vines are bought from a nursery.
First wines bottled under the Vredenheim label: Blanc de Noir, Chenin Blanc, Colombard, Debuut and Cabernet Sauvignon (all 1987 vintage).
Wines currently bottled under the Vredenheim label: Blanc de Noir, Chenin Blanc, Colombard, Debuut, Cabernet Sauvignon, Sauvignon Blanc, Pinotage, Weisser Riesling and Special Late Harvest.
Wood ageing: Wines are aged in wood on the estate.
Cellar capacity: 800 tonnes of grapes.

Vredenheim Estate is on the Stellenbosch Wine Route and is open to the public on weekdays from 09h00 to 16h00, and during December and January on Saturdays as well from 09h00 to 12h00.

—VRIESENHOF—

Towards the end of the Paradyskloof Road almost on the outskirts of Stellenbosch lie the 25 hectares of Vriesenhof. Little is known of its earlier wine-making history, though previous owners, Mr and Mrs G. Gerryts, found a good Chenin Blanc made on the farm when they bought it in 1946. In subsequent years grapes were delivered at harvest time to a local winery.

Then, in 1980, the farm was bought by Jan 'Boland' Coetzee, the famous Western Province and Springbok rugby player, who during his rugby-playing career also made a name for himself as a winemaker. He began the active practice of his craft at Kanonkop, where he spent 10 years, quickly making his presence felt, particularly with fine red wines.

For Jan the purchase of Vriesenhof represented a strong desire to strike out on his own. Within a few months of his settling at the farm he had made a first 26 000 litres of Cabernet Sauvignon wine, which after being aged in wood was further aged in the bottle and released in 1984. His first priority on arrival was to get his cellar in order; in due course he intends to renovate and refurbish the old homestead, built at the beginning of the nineteenth century.

At present the bulk of the vineyards are planted with Cabernet Sauvignon, but he has introduced other noble varieties such as Merlot, Pinot Noir, Pinot Blanc, Cabernet Franc, Sauvignon Blanc and Chardonnay. All the vines are trellised and no irrigation is used.

Jan feels very strongly about the importance of the use of wood in the production of the best red wines, in combination with the factors of varieties, soil and the local climate. A major expense in the setting up of the Vriesenhof cellar was the purchase of

Winemaker Jan Coetzee, who also acts as consultant to several other estates and farms.

wooden vats made to his specifications by the well-known French cooper Jean Demptos; other, smaller casks (*barriques*) of varying sizes were also acquired. Jan feels that casks should be renewed reasonably often and not, as is sometimes the case in the Cape, used for decades on end. The *barriques* are used for the first period of maturation and then the wine is put into big wood for further maturation. To date 1981, 1982, 1983 and 1984 vintages of Vriesenhof Cabernet Sauvignon have been released. The 1984 and 1985 vintages are blends of Cabernet Sauvignon and Merlot. Only the pick of Jan's wine is used in these blends and the rest is bottled under the Paradyskloof label.

Jan's reputation at Kanonkop was for wines of robust quality; this has changed, as the microclimate at Vriesenhof is considerably cooler than that at Kanonkop. With the relief of cooling breezes off the Indian Ocean as well as the beneficial effect of the relatively fewer sunshine-hours at the foot of the Stellenbosch Mountains, Vriesenhof wines are lighter and both elegant and complex in character as a result.

At Kanonkop and at Vriesenhof Jan never submitted his wines for the now discontinued Superior rating as he has never believed in the system. His wines sell well because of their quality. As he puts it, 'The wines must fight their own battle in the market place and not with the Wine and Spirit Board!'. He has also chosen not to register Vriesenhof as an estate. He is a member of the Cape Independent Winemakers' Guild, which holds an annual auction on the first Saturday in September each year. The first auction was held in 1985. For these auctions Jan and the other members of the Guild choose some specially selected barrels of wine which differ completely from the usual wines offered for sale. The wines are tasted blind by all the members of the Guild and a wine that is not approved as being of a particularly high standard will be withdrawn and not considered for the auction. A number of Vriesenhof wines have been auctioned and are available for collectors only in very small quantities at specialized liquor outlets. To avoid confusion all the wines sold at the auction have an additional special seal. Jan also acts as a consultant for numerous wineries and farms and gives invaluable assistance to those concerned, such as Buiten-

---

VRIESENHOF

Varieties planted (ha)

Perold trellis
Cabernet Sauvignon 4
Chardonnay 3
Merlot 3

Total area under vines in 1991/2: 10 ha.
Irrigation: None.
Average temperatures: Records are not kept.
Average annual rainfall: Records are not kept.
Stock: Rooted vines are bought from a nursery.
First wines bottled under the Vriesenhof label: Cabernet Sauvignon 1981 and Chardonnay 1986.
Wines currently bottled under the Vriesenhof label: Chardonnay, Cabernet Sauvignon and Kallista (a blend of Cabernet Sauvignon, Cabernet Franc and Merlot). Wines not qualifying for the Vriesenhof label are marketed under the Paradyskloof label (Red, White and Pinotage).
Wood ageing: Wines are aged in wood on the farm.
Cellar capacity: A new cellar has been completed and will be used for the first time for the 1991 vintage.

Vriesenhof is open to the public by appointment only.

---

verwachting, Madeba, Talana Hill, Lanzerac and Eikendal Vineyards.

During the European 1981 vintage Jan, his wife Annette, two small daughters and baby son went to France where Jan spent time in the famous cellars of Joseph Drouhin in Beaune, adding to the spectrum of his knowledge and experience. One of France's most respected négociants, Drouhin owns numerous vineyards in Burgundy, and also buys wines from selected vineyards in the region and blends them. Inspired by the wines of Burgundy, Jan hopes to produce his own definitive Cape Style. Many knowledgeable wine drinkers feel that he is already fulfilling this ambition.

—WARWICK—
ESTATE

In the valley enclosed by the Simonsberg, Kanonkop and Klapmutskop lies Warwick Estate, originally part of Good Success, a vast eighteenth-century farm that extended over most of the catchment area. The founder of Warwick farm was one Colonel Alexander Gordon, who renamed his portion of Good Success in honour of the Warwickshire Regiment, which he commanded during the Boer War. Like so many of his compatriots, Gordon decided to stay in South Africa after hostilities ended. He subsequently decided to settle on Warwick farm, raising livestock and growing fruit trees.

Stan Ratcliffe bought Warwick in 1964 without a vine on the farm, but had the foresight to begin planting noble Cabernet Sauvignon vines, which are still used in the production of Warwick wines. The Cabernet Sauvignon vines produced high-quality grapes and were soon sought after by wholesalers and other wineries.

The serious business of wine-making, however, lies mostly in the hands of one of the two 'Ladies of Warwick', namely Norma Ratcliffe. It was with Norma's arrival in 1971 that the Ratcliffes made a few experimental wines from Cabernet Sauvignon, with extremely encouraging results.

After many trips to Bordeaux, and an investigation of all possibilities, Stan and

Norma decided to build their own cellar and to make wines in the Bordeaux style. Norma began to study wine-making in earnest; Merlot and Cabernet Franc were planted in 1980; one of the historical buildings, which had very likely been a winery, was restored; and Stan, a genius with his hands, transformed second-hand equipment into working items. By 1984, Stan and Norma Ratcliffe launched their initial pilot project and by 1985 they were in full production.

In 1991 the first of the Ratcliffe's new virus-free clones came into bearing. These comprise only 5 per cent of the total and will be used for blending so as to add more complexity to the blend. Many of the older vines will be replaced with the original clone which is now virus free. By retaining this old classic clone, the Ratcliffes feel that they will retain the original character and unique style of their wine.

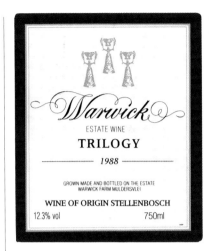

Norma Ratcliffe, the highly successful winemaker at Warwick Estate.

A member of the Cape Independent Winemakers' Guild, Norma produces several very special casks of wine for the Cape Independent Winemakers' Guild auction, which takes place in the first week of September every year. Chosen in a blind tasting by the members, these are of a particularly high standard and are rated very highly by collectors both here and abroad. The Guild holds frequent tastings and members exchange technical knowledge on a regular basis.

The original label for the Cabernet Sauvignon, with its striking blue border, sets off the second 'Warwick Lady'. She is the gold image of the original quaint drinking vessel that has pride of place on the Ratcliffes' dining table. Called a marriage or wager cup, it was used originally for toasting a marriage or waging a bet. The 'Warwick Lady' is in Elizabethan costume, and holds a small swivel cup in her outstretched arms. The skirt of her dress forms a second cup, which, like the smaller one she holds, is made of silver on copper and is gilt-lined. When the figure is inverted, both cups can be filled with wine, but the utmost care must be taken when drinking from the larger vessel not to spill the contents of the smaller one, and not to put the cup down until all the wine is finished. The same emblem and style is used for all the Warwick labels; the blue being replaced by deep pink for their Trilogy label; a deep purple for their Merlot label and an emerald green for the Cabernet Franc.

At the end of 1989, the existing cellar was enlarged, to accommodate two new rotor tanks. Warwick more than doubled their production capacity and this also meant an increase in their wood maturation cellar.

In 1991 the Ratcliffes installed innovative new tanks which are copies of smaller ones that they had seen in restaurants in Burgundy in France. They are extremely useful for bottling, fermenting or storage.

However, the philosophy with which the Ratcliffes started making wine still prevails. Norma prefers the traditional methods of red wine-making.

In keeping with tradition, Norma gives the fermenting grapes maximum skin contact to extract the flavours and tannins. The grapes are left on the skins until they are dry and, time permitting, are subsequently left macerating on the skins for up to three weeks in order to soften these tannins, increase fruit character and reduce herbaceousness. Without artificial fining agents or filtration and through careful racking, the wine gradually settles and clarifies itself. Several egg white finings (approximately three egg whites to every hectolitre of wine according to the tannins and also to the vintage of the wine) are used to assist the settling without stripping any of the colour, flavour or tannin. The individual components are vinified separately and racked separately into 225-litre Bordeaux *barriques*. Only when the wine has begun to develop (this can take from nine months to a year), is the blend entirely assembled. It is kept in wood, in a temperature-controlled maturation cellar, and time completes the maturation of the red wine. Two hundred and fifty 225-litre Bordeaux *barriques* are packed into the maturation cellar to give the wine the unique 'new wood' character that Norma loves.

The Ratcliffes have achieved their ultimate goal – to specialize in superb red wines. They started small, with their first vintage (1985) being 100 per cent Cabernet Sauvignon (only 1 500 cases). In 1986 they produced their first Bordeaux blend, in a

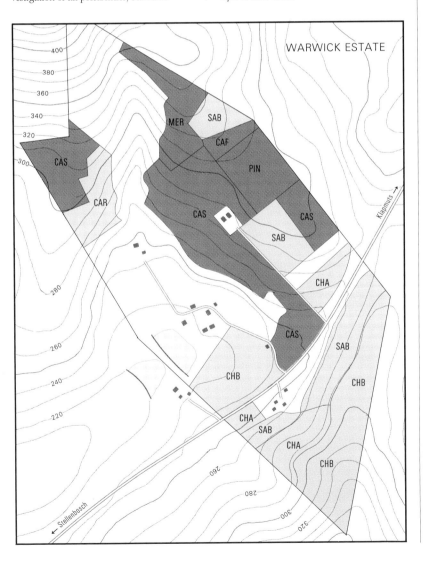

Table Mountain, a well-known feature of Cape Town, can be seen from Warwick.

Medoc style, with a Muldersvlei bias, when their Cabernet Franc and Merlot came into production. This is called the 'Warwick

WARWICK ESTATE

Varieties planted (ha)

4-wire trellis
Cabernet Sauvignon 16.5 ha
Merlot 5.34 ha
Cabernet Franc 1 ha

Total area under vines in 1991/2: 56 ha.
Irrigation: None.
Average temperatures:
Maximum 22.9 °C; minimum 10.7 °C.
Average annual rainfall: 605.8 mm.
Stock: Rooted vines are bought from a nursery.
First wines bottled under the Warwick label:
Cabernet Sauvignon 1985 and Trilogy 1986.
Wines currently bottled under the Warwick label: Cabernet Sauvignon, Merlot, Cabernet Franc and Trilogy (blend of the three).
Wood ageing: Wines are wood aged on the estate.
Cellar capacity: 450 hl.

Warwick Estate is not open to the public.

Trilogy', and emphasizes the importance of each variety in the classic blend. Each vintage reflects its own character, as Norma feels that they must be kept separate and not blended to produce a uniform neutral wine. New plantings of Cabernet Sauvignon, Merlot and Cabernet Franc are in the pipeline.

In 1990 Stan and Norma expanded their cellar to accommodate the optimum number of cases. From the 20 tonnes they started with, they are now up to 75 tonnes, but having reached their goal, they plan to keep it at this. 'We have only four people to run the entire operation, other than the vineyard staff,' says Norma. Stan, running the financial side; Norma as winemaker and marketer; the very able Lola Hunting as cellar manager; and Marcus Milner as assistant.

The Merlot and Cabernet Franc have found such a happy home at Warwick that Norma has started to bottle small quantities of these varieties as varietal wines. She is delighted with the results and will continue with these wines.

— WELMOED —
CO-OPERATIVE WINE CELLARS

This is the first co-operative on the road from Cape Town to Stellenbosch through Faure, and is built on a site between the road and the Eerste River. As with the estates in the vicinity, the wines of Welmoed reflect the felicity of the local climate and the moderating influence in the summer months of the wind from False Bay.

The farm of Welmoed was granted to Henning Huysing by Simon van der Stel in 1690, though Huysing had already occupied the land for a decade. Three years later, in 1693, Van der Stel also granted Meerlust, adjoining Welmoed, to Huysing. In 1696 Huysing sold Welmoed to his friend Jacobus van der Heyden who put up the buildings and the bell-tower which are now part of the nursery of Rosarium, adjacent to the winery which retains the right to use the image of the bell-tower on its labels. Van der Heyden was one of those who, with Huysing and his nephew, Adam Tas, were responsible for the unseat-

ing of Willem Adriaan van der Stel. During the course of events leading up to this Van der Heyden was arrested by Van der Stel and sentenced to death. Van der Stel was relieved of his post before the sentence could be carried out, but not before the unfortunate Van der Heyden had spent 27 miserable days in the Donker Gat ('Black Hole') at the Castle.

Pieter Gerhard van der Bijl acquired Welmoed in 1797 and on his death in 1831 it was divided between his two sons, Philipus Johannes calling his portion Klein Welmoed and Pieter Voltelen retaining the original name, Welmoed, for his larger portion.

Many years later the Castle Wine and Brandy Company built a winery at Welmoed, where farmers from the surrounding areas delivered their grapes, but in 1940 the company decided to close down the operation. Eight of the farmers who had delivered grapes there then bought the property and founded Welmoed Koöperatiewe Wynkelders Beperk on 15 October 1941. The following season 500 tonnes of grapes were pressed. Today there are 45 members with 55 different farms and 10 500 tonnes of grapes are pressed and made into wine annually. The co-operative had a somewhat lacklustre period in the early 1960s but its organization and wine-making were much improved and overhauled with the advent of Jassie Coetzee in 1966. Previously at the Stellenbosch Farmers' Winery, when he arrived at Welmoed he found himself in charge of a run-down wine cellar and a set of books in decidedly precarious condition.

Jassie Coetzee was succeeded in 1980 by Kobus Rossouw, who achieved great success for Welmoed, with many awards being won at wine shows. Kobus took over as wine-

WINES BOTTLED AND MARKETED

Red: Cabernet Sauvignon, Pinotage, Shiraz, Rouge Sec and Zinfandel.
White: Weisser Riesling, Sauvignon Blanc, Cape Riesling, Chenin Blanc, Dry Steen, Chardonnay, Grand Crû, Late Vintage, Special Late Harvest and Blanc de Noir.
Sparkling: Sec and Cuveé Brut.
Fortified: Sweet Hanepoot, Red Jerepiko and Port.

The co-operative is on the Stellenbosch Wine Route and is open to the public on Mondays to Saturdays from 08h30 to 17h00. Traditional Cape lunches are served.

Welmoed Co-operative Wine Cellars, founded on the fifteenth of October 1941.

maker at Simonsvlei from his father, Oom Sarel Rossouw, in December 1985, and when Oom Sarel retired at the end of April 1986, Kobus became manager of Simonsvlei as well. Nicky Versveld, an Elsenburg graduate, succeeded him as winemaker at Welmoed. Co-incidentally, after leaving Elsenburg, Nicky received further training at Simonsvlei, under the experientcued tutelage of Oom Sarel and Johan Rossouw.

Nicky Versveld and his board of directors have moved Welmoed into the modern era with much improved overall quality and with a bold approach to marketing. 1991 saw the co-operative celebrating its fiftieth anniversary and the introduction of an exciting set of labels. They have built substantial storage for bottled products, the tasting facilities have been considerably improved, and a full restaurant is now in operation.

— ZEVENWACHT —

In 1974 a Cape Town architect, Gilbert Colyn, bought a small 39-hectare farm named Avonduur in the Banghoek Valley, with the intention of using it both as a private retreat and for farming on a modest scale. This farm later became Delaire , and his involvement sparked an ambition to start an estate wine farm. To this end Colyn acquired a further two farms, buying Zevenfontein in 1979 and increasing its size by the addition of the adjacent property of Langverwacht. Together they cover some 353 hec-

tares between Kuils River and Stellenbosch, spread over the Bottelary Hills.

At the time of purchase, Zevenfontein Farm was in a neglected condition. The existing vineyards were replaced and extended with plantings of a range of varieties, including Cabernet Sauvignon, Merlot, Shiraz, Chenin Blanc, Weisser Riesling, Cape Riesling, Gewürztraminer, Pinot Gris, Pinot

Noir, Sauvignon Blanc and Chardonnay. Gilbert's first wines, including a Rhine Riesling, were released at the end of 1983.

The soils on the two farms - registered as a limited company and known collectively as Zevenwacht - are varied and of good quality, with a mix of Clovelly and Glenrosa forms, well suited to the growing of quality grapes. Most of the vineyards are located on south- or southwest-facing slopes, towards the prevailing wind from the sea.

Gilbert (who is descended from the Colijn family with long-standing connections with the Constantia Valley and, for a period, with Groot Constantia itself) has built compact modern housing for his farm workers and manager, and has restored the fine old late eighteenth-century homestead on Zevenfontein. As an architect he was responsible for the design of the new Groot Constantia cellar, and has built a new cellar not far away from the Zevenwacht homestead. In establishing his cellar he worked closely with his winemaker at the time - Neil Ellis, who came to the farm having proved his talents at Groot Constantia. Eric Saayman, who has been with Zevenwacht for many years, is now the cellarmaster.

The future of Zevenwacht is uncertain as, in March 1992, an application was brought in the Supreme Court for the provisional liquidation of the estate.

Zevenwacht will however continue making wine and selling it under the same management.

ZEVENWACHT

Varieties planted (number of vines)

Extended Perold trellis
Chenin Blanc 74 000
Chardonnay 48 000
Weisser Riesling 39 000
Cabernet Sauvignon 30 000
Sauvignon Blanc 30 000
Cape Riesling 26 000
Merlot 20 000
Shiraz 20 000
Gewürztraminer 15 000
Pinotage 15 000
Pinot Noir 12 000
Cabernet Franc 10 000
Pinot Gris 8 000

Total area under vines in 1991/2: 160 ha (40 ha more to be planted by 1997).

Irrigation: The vineyards can be irrigated if necessary.

Average temperatures:
Maximum 24 ℃; minimum 16 ℃.

Average annual rainfall: 700-750 mm.

Stock: Rooted vines are bought from a nursery.

First wines bottled under the Zevenwacht label: Rhine Riesling, Cabernet Sauvignon, Chenin Blanc, Blanc de Blanc and Bouquet Blanc (all 1983 vintage).

Wines currently bottled under the Zevenwacht label: Blanc de Blanc, Sauvignon Blanc, Rhine Riesling, Gewürztraminer, Bouquet Blanc, Chardonnay, Zevenwacht (blended red), Cabernet Sauvignon, Shiraz, Pinotage, Pinot Noir and red and white house wines.

Wood ageing: Wines are aged in wood on the farm.

Cellar capacity: 1 000 tonnes of grapes are being processed at present, but the cellar is being enlarged to accommodate up to 1 400 tonnes.

Zevenwacht is not open to the public, but its shareholders and their friends enjoy a private wine farm and its facilities. Wine is sold to the public, however, from the old wine cellar on the lower farm, Langverwacht.

The elegant late-eighteenth century manor house at Zevenwacht.

PAARL

On a clear, windless morning in February 1658, a party of 15 explorers authorized by Commander Jan van Riebeeck set out from the Dutch East India Company's fort at the Cape. They were led by Sergeant Jan van Herwaarden, and included a surveyor named Pieter Potter whose job it was to record and map the journey. Accompanied by several Khoikhoin as well as oxen burdened with their equipment, food and weapons, they followed the route taken six months earlier by Abraham Gabbema, travelling north and east towards a large hill which Gabbema had named Klapmuts – a landmark still known by this name. Van Herwaarden's expedition passed the hill on the third day (the pace of an ox being about 5 kilometres an hour on easy terrain, with time taken off for rest and grazing during the heat of noon). The following day at the foot of a chain of seemingly impassable mountains they came to a stream running north, which they named the Berg River. It seemed an ideal place to pass the night and they were able to enjoy a welcome change of diet by catching fish in the river pools.

On the fifth day the party continued its journey along the river, passing on the left a low mountain whose crest was domed with bare granite rocks, previously christened Paarl and Diamant for the way they glistened in the morning light after a night of rain. The only sign of life on this still, brilliant morning as they walked along, were the herds of sleek zebra which warily studied these intruders in their ancestral domain.

At a certain point of the visitors' approach, as if at a silent signal, the herd would break and canter away snorting, only settling down to graze again at a safe distance. Later that day they saw many rhinoceros, which took off at a lumbering trot, shy unless provoked. There were also many hippopotami, which never strayed far from the large pools in the river, shaded by the magnificent trees which filled the valley. The sergeant and his party had wandered into a natural paradise. But within the next few decades this valley beneath the shining rocks was to become a settled farming community: the first 23 farms, each of 52 hectares, were marked out along the Berg River in October 1687, and within a century it became a wine-making centre second only to Stellenbosch in importance.

The soil, climate and setting are ideally suited to the making of wine. Rising in the south, the Berg River flows through the length of the valley, supplying a ready source of irrigation.

To the south, south-east and east, the area is bordered by the ranges of the Groot Drakenstein, Franschhoek and Klein Drakenstein mountains. In the west the valley broadens into a plain which allows cool breezes from the Atlantic some 60 kilometres distant to penetrate and influence the Paarl climate which, typically Mediterranean in character, features good winter rainfall and comparatively long, hot summers. The average rainfall here is some 650 millimetres, compared with the generous 1 000 millimetres of Constantia, the low 357 millimetres of Durbanville, and the similar 600 to 800 millimetres of the Stellenbosch area. The average temperature is between 19 and 21 °C compared with a maximum of 19 °C in Constantia in the growing season alone, to an average of 19 °C in Durbanville and between 18 and 19 °C in Stellenbosch.

The vineyards of Paarl are distributed across three main types of soil. In the area along the Berg River they are grown on the sandy soils of Table Mountain Sandstone origin; in the town of Paarl and its immediate vicinity they are located on granitic soils; and along the slopes of the mountains to the south-east they are also found on this type of granite-based soil; while to the north-east they are mainly located on soils of Malmesbury Shale origin.

The lower-lying lands in the valley often require mechanical drainage by means of underground pipes, as well as supplementary irrigation during December and January. Deep ploughing and the application of agricultural lime is generally needed during soil preparation (the soils of both Paarl and Stellenbosch lack naturally occurring lime). The cooler soils against the eastern slopes normally require higher lime applications during preparation but, because of their greater water-holding capacity, are not usually irrigated.

The wine-making life of the Paarl district has been dominated by two major organizations, the first being KWV, whose headquarters are at Suider-Paarl, and the second being Nederburg, under the aegis of Stellenbosch Farmers' Winery. In terms of the legislation governing the proclamation of South African wine-making districts, the fertile Franschhoek valley forms part of the Paarl district. However, due to the very distinctive character of the Franschhoek valley and its estates and wineries, it was decided that, in this book, the area would be accorded its own chapter (see pages 208 to 221).

LEFT: *The slopes of Paarl Mountain, on which the Afrikaans Language Monument stands, overlooking the Groot Drakenstein Valley.*

An aerial view of Backsberg Estate, purchased in 1916 by Charles Back.

— BACKSBERG —
ESTATE

The history of the Backsberg Estate is a three-generation success story. In a few decades the Back family have put this estate and its wines firmly on the map of the winelands. The achievement is all the more remarkable in that the estate had virtually no historical or viticultural tradition when it was bought in 1916 by Charles Back, an immigrant from Lithuania. In those days the farm was called 'Klein Babylonstoren' and its first wines, made and sold under this name, were supplied either in barrels to KWV, or exported to the United Kingdom

In 1938 the elder Back was joined by his son, Sydney, who now owns the farm. In the post-war years the two men worked hard to expand and improve the vineyards, and at the same time to adapt to coming trends in wine-making technology. By 1973, when the farm was registered as the Backsberg Estate Winery, the emphasis in its production was firmly on the making of quality red wines. Sydney Back was also the pioneer of Char-

Michael and Sydney Back with Backsberg Estate winemaker Hardy Laubser.

donnay in South Africa, having been the first to plant this variety.

The reward for this industry and expertise has been an impressive range of wine awards. The climax of Sydney Back's wine-making career came in 1978, when he was voted Champion Winemaker of the Year at the Cape Championship Wine Show; this outstanding achievement was repeated in 1982. In 1989 Backsberg Estate received the trophy for the best South African white wine at the International Wine and Spirit Competition in London for their 1986 Chardonnay.

The Backsberg vineyards now cover 160 hectares and consist predominantly of Cabernet Sauvignon, Shiraz, Merlot, Chardonnay, Sauvignon Blanc and Weisser Riesling. They are grown on the slopes of the Simonsberg in soils which are largely of decomposed granite. The cellars on the estate are a model of their kind, and include a beautifully designed cave cellar where much of the wine is stored for bottle maturation before sale.

In 1971 Sydney Back's son, Michael, returned to the farm after studying viticulture and oenology at the University of Stellenbosch. Together with a team of young managers, Michael has taken over much of the running of the estate. The wine-making is now in the capable hands of Hardy Laubser, a graduate of Elsenburg College.

The 'Backsberg John Martin', a wood-fermented and further wood-aged wine is named after the late John Martin, who handled the administration of the farm.

A new venture is the distillation of brandy. In 1991 Backsberg imported from

---

BACKSBERG ESTATE

Varieties planted (ha)

Vertical 5-wire trellis
Cabernet Sauvignon 40
Chardonnay 25
Chenin Blanc 18
Pinotage 15
Sauvignon Blanc 15
Weisser Riesling 12
Merlot 8
Pinot Noir 8
Shiraz 8
Bukettraube 4
Gewürztraminer 4
Muscat d'Alexandrie 3

Total area under vines in 1991/2: 160 ha.
Irrigation: Only when necessary.
Average temperatures: Records are not kept.
Average annual rainfall: 800 mm.
Stock: Only virus-free material is used.
First wines bottled under the Backsberg label: Late Harvest, Steen, Clairette Blanche, Rosé, Perlé, Pinotage and Hanepoot (all 1970 vintage).
Wines currently bottled under the Backsberg label: Bouquet Blanc, Rhine Riesling, Bukettraube, Kerner, Special Late Harvest, Chenin Blanc, Sauvignon Blanc, Sauvignon Blanc John Martin, Chardonnay, Rosé, Cabernet Sauvignon, Shiraz, Pinotage, Merlot, Klein Babylonstoren, Dry Red, Pink Sparkling, White Sparkling and Hanepoot.
Wood ageing: Wines are aged in small French oak casks of 225 litres each.
Cellar capacity: 10 000 hl.

Backsberg Estate is on the Paarl Wine Route and is open to the public on weekdays from 08h30 to 17h00, and on Saturdays and public holidays from 08h30 to 13h00 (closed on religious holidays). There is a small wine museum on the premises and an added attraction is the self-guided tour aided by closed-circuit television, demonstrating vineyard practices and wine-making practices not generally seen by visitors.

Cognac the first automated pot still for the production of Backsberg Estate Brandy which will be matured for three years in Limosin oak barrels before the first release at the end of 1994. At this stage results of the first samples, sent to France for analysis, indicate an excellent quality. This new development is directly under Hardy's control.

— BELCHER —
WINE FARM

When Ronnie Belcher, the Afrikaans poet and academic, bought this wine farm in January 1990, he immediately set about

---

BELCHER WINE FARM

Varieties planted (number of vines)

Perold trellis
Sémillon 10 028
Palomino 900
5-wire cordon trellis
Chenin Blanc 38 935
Cape Riesling 25 840
Colombard 7 400
Muscat d'Alexandrie 1 000
Bush vines
Pedro Luis 9 900

Total area under vines in 1991/2:
30 ha (10 ha still to be planted).
Irrigation: The vineyards are irrigated using microjet and overhead irrigation.
Average temperatures: Records are not kept.
Average annual rainfall: Records are not kept.
Stock: Rooted vines are bought from a nursery.
First wines bottled under the Belcher Wine Farm label: Riesling Special Reserve, Blanc de Blanc and Stein (all 1991 vintage).
Wines currently bottled under the Belcher Wine Farm label: Riesling Special Reserve, Sémillon, Bouquet Blanc, Late Harvest, and Vin Sec Sparkling.
Wood ageing: Wines are aged in wood on the farm.
Cellar capacity: 2 530 hl.

Belcher Wine Farm is on the Paarl Wine Route and is open to the public on weekdays from 08h30 to 17h00 and on Saturdays and public holidays from 08h00 to 13h00.

---

building and equipping a stone wine cellar. This was designed to fit in with the other attractive buildings constructed from stone by Italian prisoners of war during the Second World War. The cellar became operational the following year, featuring controlled cold fermentation inside the barrel by means of chilling plates which fit through the bung-hole, and a reversion to spun concrete fermentation tanks with chilling plates from top to bottom. The tasting room and sales area is built in the form of a bell-towered chapel, and will be used as a venue for various musical and other cultural events, a small outdoor amphitheatre serving the same purpose during the summer months.

The 45-hectare farm is planted to some 35 hectares of vines including the traditional Cape varieties such as Cape Riesling, Chenin Blanc, Sémillon, Colombard and Palomino on the sandy loam and decomposed granite soils. The vineyards are irrigated from three large dams and two rivers. To ensure quality

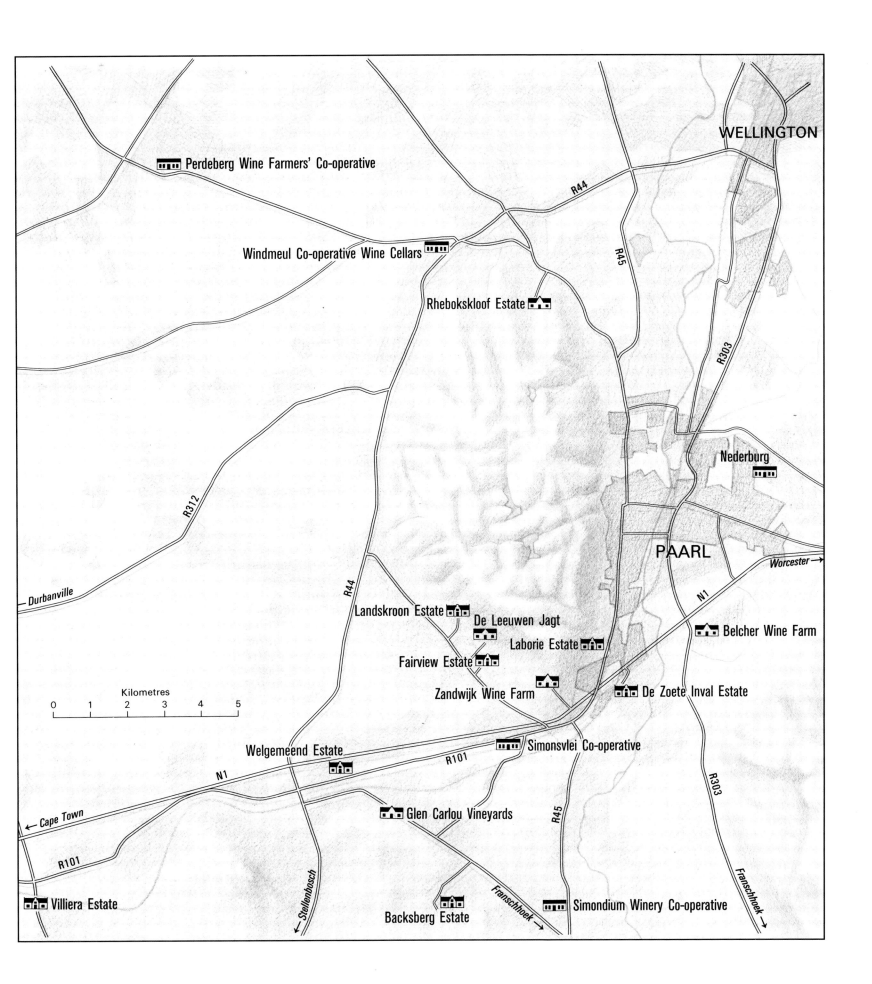

WELLINGTON

Perdeberg Wine Farmers' Co-operative

Windmeul Co-operative Wine Cellars

R44

R45

Rhebokskloof Estate

R303

Nederburg

R312

PAARL

Worcester →

Durbanville —

R44

Landskroon Estate

De Leeuwen Jagt

Laborie Estate

N1

Belcher Wine Farm

Fairview Estate

Zandwijk Wine Farm

De Zoete Inval Estate

Kilometres

0   1   2   3   4   5

Welgemeend Estate

Simonsvlei Co-operative

N1

R101

R303

R45

Cape Town ←

Glen Carlou Vineyards

R101

Stellenbosch

Villiera Estate

Backsberg Estate

Franschhoek ↓

Franschhoek

Simondium Winery Co-operative

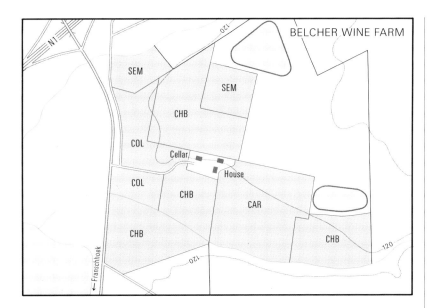

BELCHER WINE FARM

Ronnie Belcher in front of his cellar built by Italian prisoners during World War II.

grapes from the vines, the crop is limited by not fertilizing the vineyards, pruning severely, and removing as much as 50 per cent of the bunches. For the most part, this ensures an average yield of 15 tonnes per hectare. While some of the vineyards are still being replanted, other varieties of grapes will be brought in. The grapes that are not wanted in the Belcher cellar are delivered to the Boland Co-operative.

In 1992, Ronnie was joined by winemaker Ernst Gouws, formerly of Saxenburg and, more recently, Rhebokskloof. Ernst began his career as a wine controller in the certified wine section of KWV. He then

studied at the Weinsburg Wine School in Germany, returning to South Africa to become manager and winemaker at the Du Toitskloof Co-operative. He subsequently worked for a year in France to gain experience in the *méthode champenoise* and spent the harvesting season in Bordeaux making Cabernet Sauvignon and Merlot wines. The intention is to produce a Cabernet, a Chardonnay, and a Sémillon along the lines of a dry Graves. Ronnie, as former publicity officer, journalist, and editor, and Ernst, as a talented winemaker, should prove to be a formidable team in the competitive world of wine.

— BODEGA —

The ebullient South African cricketing legend Eddie Barlow has now swopped bat and ball for grape and glass. In 1988, he bought the 60-hectare property of Bodega on the Joostenberg Vlakte. On New Year's Eve, he was picnicking with friends on the property when a wild fire swept across the flats, con-

---

BODEGA
(no other information available)

Varieties planted (ha)

Cabernet Sauvignon (traditional) 8
Cabernet Sauvignon (new-clone) 4
Merlot 2
Pinotage 1
Total area under vines in 1991/2: 15 ha.
Bodega is not open to the public.

---

tinuing up towards the West Coast for another three days before being extinguished. The farm was right in its path, and Eddie battled with a handful of friends and other landowners to save the buildings but all else was destroyed, except for the vines — only three vines had been burned.

Eddie, his wife Julienne, and the then farm manager set to work with the typical Barlow verve and converted the tractor shed into a small winery into which three 6-tonne open concrete fermenters were built and two 6 200-litre holding tanks installed. An area to house wooden barrels under refrigerated conditions was also prepared. An Italian filter used in the winery was found on a farm in Sussex, England.

The varieties grown are Cabernet Sauvignon, Merlot and Pinotage. The first 'commercial' quantities were crushed in 1990 from Cabernet Sauvignon grapes. The light-styled, distinctive Cabernet aged in French oak was bottled in February 1992, and will be released in late 1992. The first 30 barrels were sold to the public, and these 30 people have become founder members of the 'Bodega Barrel Club'.

Julienne and Eddie enjoy Bordeaux reds, with Eddie having a particular preference for Pinotage, and so these are the two types of wines in which they intend to specialize. They are also going to plant Shiraz for a more traditional Cape blend. Julienne's first love is her thoroughbred horse stud but she has also become a dab hand in the cellar.

— BOLANDSE —
CO-OPERATIVE WINE CELLAR

This is one of the biggest and best known of the coastal co-operatives and was enlarged some years ago when it incorporated the Paarl Vallei Wine Co-operative, which itself had been formed in 1976 by the merger of the Pêrelse Wine Cellars and Bergrivier Co-operative. Situated on the slopes of the Paarl Mountain, this concern now has over 149 members who supply some 24 000 tonnes of grapes from an area, reaching as far afield as Durbanville, Klipheuwel and Malmesbury.

The Bolandse Co-operative winery pressed its first grapes, some 3 000 tonnes, in 1948. Built on a section of the farm Nieuwedrift on the outskirts of Noorder-Paarl, the co--

Jacques du Toit, co-winemaker at the Bolandse Co-operative Wine Cellar.

operative served an initial 18 members under its first chairman, Willie de Waal. Altus le Roux joined the co-operative in 1984 as winemaker with a diploma from Elsenburg in cellar technology. In 1991 he became the manager with Anthony de Jager and Jacques du Toit as winemakers and Charl du Plessis as assistant winemaker.

The co-operative has an excellent reputation, particularly for red wines, and especially for its Cabernet Sauvignon. The co-operative's prestige is reflected in its splendid collection of awards over the years . The Bolandse Co-operative Wine Cellar makes a wide range of wines, of which only a proportion is bottled under its own label, other labels being personalized.

WINES BOTTLED AND MARKETED

Red: Grand Rouge, Pinotage, Cabernet Sauvignon and Shiraz.
White: Stein, Bukettraube, Special Late Harvest, Gewürztraminer, Natural Sweet, Grand Crû, Sauvignon Blanc, Chardonnay, Riesling and Weisser Riesling.
Sparkling: Semi-Sweet and Dry.
Fortified: White and Red Hanepoot and Port.

The co-operative is on the Wellington Wine Route and is open to the public on weekdays from 08h30 to 12h30 and from 13h30 to 17h30, and on Saturdays from 08h30 to 12h30.

—BOVLEI—
CO-OPERATIVE WINERY

Founded in 1907 with government support, and therefore one of the earliest of the co-operatives, Bovlei (known in the early years as the Boven Vallei Co-operative Winery) was also one of the few to survive the rigorous early years before the advent of KWV and the ensuing legislation which stabilized the struggling co-operative movement.

Today, under its manager and wine-maker, Tinus Broodryk, the Bovlei Winery handles 11 500 tonnes of grapes a year, produced by 72 members

Although wine has been made at Bovlei Co-operative since 1908, it was only with the 1982 vintage that its range of wines was made available to the public, including its particularly good Cabernet and Pinotage. The bulk of its production is sold to the major merchants.

WINES BOTTLED AND MARKETED

Red: Cabernet Sauvignon, Bon Vino Dry Red and Pinotage.
White: Bukettraube, Chenin Blanc, Riesling, Stein, Late Vintage, Bon Vino Dry and Semi-Sweet, Chardonnay and Sauvignon Blanc.
Sparkling: Demi-Sec.
Fortified: Muscadel, Port and Hanepoot Jerepigo.

The co-operative is on the Paarl Wine Route and is open for wine sales during the week from 08h30 to 13h00 and 13h30 to 17h00, and on Saturdays from 09h00 to 12h00.

—DE LEEUWEN JAGT—

On the fifteenth of January 1992, this 360-hectare property was purchased by a Swiss gentleman, who prefers to remain unnamed. Gideon Theron, formerly of Bergsig Estate, has continued as the cellarmaster and manager of the farm, with Mr L. Meintjies acting as Managing Director. Old buildings on the

Winemaker Gideon Theron.

DE LEEUWEN JAGT

Varieties planted (number of vines)

Perold trellis
Cabernet Sauvignon 39 260
Chenin Blanc 32 482
Chardonnay 26 314
Cape Riesling 16 700
Weisser Riesling 6 804
Merlot 5 300
Cabernet Franc 5 000
Sauvignon Blanc 4 400
Muscadel 3 150
Cinsaut 1 400

Total area under vines in 1991/2:
47 ha (4,5 ha still to be planted).
Irrigation: The vineyards are irrigated.
Average temperatures: Records are not kept.
Average annual rainfall: 680 mm.
Stock: Rooted vines are bought from a nursery.
First wines bottled under the De Leeuwen Jagt label: Leeuwen Blanc and Paarl Riesling (both 1989 vintage).
Wines currently bottled under the De Leeuwen Jagt label: Leeuwen Blanc, Riesling, Chardonnay, Late Harvest, Cabernet Sauvignon, Merlot and Muscadel.
Wood ageing: The wines are aged in wood on the estate.
Cellar capacity: 1 600 hl.

De Leeuwen Jagt is open to the public on Mondays to Fridays from 08h30 to 12h30 and from 13h30 to 17h00 and on Saturdays from 08h30 to 13h00.

---

farm, in particular the main house, have been beautifully restored. The tasting area in the underground cellar has an atmosphere reminiscent of a European cellar. Above this new cellar, is the traditional old cellar, where the wines are made. All the red wines are matured in wood for one year and then for two to three years in the bottle before release. The Chardonnay is fermented in French oak barrels.

—DE ZOETE INVAL—
ESTATE

Den Zoeten Inval, the old Dutch name for this farm, can be roughly translated as 'Happy event', or 'Welcome arrival'. The land was first granted by Simon van der Stel in 1688 to Hercule des Prés (or du Preez) — literally 'Hercules of the Meadows', a felicitous name for a farmer. The lower portion of the farm adjacent to the Berg River changed hands regularly in the early years because of

---

the almost annual flooding of the river. Its modern history, however, began with its purchase in 1878 by the first member of the Frater family in South Africa.

Robert Frater was one of three brothers born in the lowlands of Scotland who grew up to make their living from sheep and wool. About 1870 they emigrated to North America, but Robert did not settle and instead came to South Africa, hoping to make his fortune in diamonds at Kimberley. He soon decided to return to the business he knew best, however, and moving to Cape Town, entered into partnership with Thomas Mossop, founder of the former Rondebosch tannery, with the intention of starting a woolwashery.

He chose Paarl as the most suitable site, since it was within easy reach of the wool-producing areas and yet close enough to Cape Town to make export relatively easy. The decisive factor, however, was the good supply of soft water from the Berg River. To obtain the necessary water rights, the farm De Zoete Inval was bought from the then owner, Jac de Villiers, together with two neighbouring farms which were then added to the main property. This not only gave a large frontage along the Berg River itself but incorporated the supply from Van Wyk's River which joined the main river within the new farm's boundaries.

A fine supply of water was thus secured and the washery was soon built and in operation. But the farm was not neglected, for while the acquisition of the land had been almost incidental to the main business of wool-washing, the farm itself had been productive and had included a modest amount of wine-making. The new owners therefore decided to keep it as a sideline.

The sideline turned out to be a success. Soon Mossop and Frater extended the wine cellar to cope with increased production, and when Mossop died in 1918 and the partnership was dissolved, Frater found himself in possession of both wool and wine.

In the following years wine gradually prevailed, the Scottish wool-farming family becoming South African wine farmers. Adrian Robert Frater, the current owner of De Zoete Inval, is the fourth generation to farm the land and is the winemaker. A science graduate from the University of Cape Town, he has further developed the farm, building wine grapes into its most important crop.

DE ZOETE INVAL ESTATE

Varieties planted (ha)

1-wire vertical trellis
Cabernet Sauvignon 31,5
Chenin Blanc 6,5
Cinsaut 5,75
Port varieties 4
Pinot Noir 1
Factory system
Sauvignon Blanc 7
Chardonnay 5,5

Total area under vines in 1991/2: 66 ha.
Irrigation: The vineyards are irrigated using sprinklers and drippers.
Average temperatures: Records are not kept.
Average annual rainfall: Records are not kept.
Stock: Parent stock is used for grafting.
First wine bottled under the De Zoete Inval label: Cabernet Sauvignon 1976.
Wines currently bottled under the De Zoete Inval label: Blanc de Blanc, Capri, Blanc de Noir, Rosé Sec, Grand Rouge, Cabernet Sauvignon and Extra.
Wood ageing: None.
Cellar capacity: 6 000 hl.

De Zoete Inval Estate is open to the public on Mondays to Saturdays from 09h00 to 17h00. Wine can be bought on the farm and a wine tasting centre has been opened.

Recently he was joined by his eldest son Gerard and his daughter Elizabeth, the latter running the newly opened tasting room in the old wine cellar.

Today De Zoete Inval has some 66 hectares under vines. At one stage over 15 hectares supported table grape varieties, but these are gradually being replaced by white-wine varieties — Sauvignon Blanc has already replaced all the Waltham Cross and Chardonnay has replaced most of the Alphonse Lavalle and New Cross. Cabernet Sauvignon is the major wine variety grown, but a moderate quantity of good quality Cinsaut and some Chenin Blanc are also grown. The ground not used for vines is used for fruit.

Some 3 500 hectolitres of dry red wine are made annually in De Zoete Inval's cellar. Prior to concentrating on dry wines, the estate produced excellent port which was sold to KWV (in 1955 a port from the farm was judged 'Grand Champion' of the Cape Wine Show). However, the decline in the English port market in the post-war years forced the Fraters to cut back on this branch of their production.

—DOUGLAS GREEN— OF PAARL

Shortly after the turn of the century, a wine farmer named Piet le Roux sold wine to customers who brought their own containers – bottles, cans, or even buckets – to his address at 360 Main Street, Paarl (now long associated with the headquarters of KWV).

Evidently his wine was palatable, for his business prospered, being expanded in 1930 after its acquisition by the Forrer brothers of Paarl. The new owners started a bottling line and opened a retail outlet which still survives as a local landmark today, the Stukvat Bottle Store.

WINES MARKETED AND DISTRIBUTED BY DGB

Douglas Green range
Premier Grand Crû, Blanc de Blanc,
St Vincent of Saragossa, Chenin Blanc,
Rhine Riesling, Paarl Riesling, Sauvignon Blanc,
St Morand, Stein, St Anna Schloss,
St Clare Blanc de Noir, St Raphael, St Augustine,
Shiraz, Pinotage and Cabernet Sauvignon.
Sparkling: Blanc de Noir, Cuvée Brut and Demi-Sec.
Fortified: Rubi and Bianco Port and
Flor Extra Dry, Flor Medium Cream and
Flor Full Cream Sherry.

Culemborg range
Diamanté Blanc de Noir, Blanc de Noir,
Crystal Blanc, Bijou Blanc, Late Harvest, Stein, Grand
Crû, Blanc de Blanc, Light, Claret Light, Pinotage
and Dry Red.

Bellingham range
(see Bellingham, page 210)

Heerenhof range
Late Harvest, Stein, Grand Crû, Dry Red and
Paarl Perlé.

Durhams fortified wines
Dry Sherry, Medium Sherry, Durham's Port
and Marsala.

Villa Rossini range
Bianco, Rosso and Oudo Rosso.

Oude Heerengracht fortified wines
Marsala, Sultana, Hanepoot, 7-year Port,
Pale Dry Sherry and Medium Cream Sherry.

Fortified wines
Purple Domino, Royal Amber, Prize Cup,
Old Brown Sherry, Invalid Port, Cape Port,
Cape Jerepigo, Boland Soet Hanepoot, White and
Red Muscadel, White and Red Malmsey, White Port,
Worcester Hock, Sacramento and Club Sherry.

Then in 1942 the Forrer brothers sold their company to a young man named Douglas Green. The son of a well-known local wine merchant, he had been brought up in close contact with the liquor trade, and had spent some time in France studying wine-farming and -making. On his return to South Africa, and with the help of a loan from his mother, he bought up the Forrer's concern, changing its name to Douglas Green of Paarl. With his new company well situated near the centre of town, he soon began to expand the operation, extending the office block and building new premises for Stukvat. Soon the company's reputation was expanding too, owing to its good and moderately priced wines, matured brandies, ports and high-quality sherries.

In the post-war years Douglas Green of Paarl changed hands, being bought by 'Cappy' Sinclair in 1973, though it retained both its name and the style of its wines. Then, in March 1976, a new chapter in its fortunes began, when it was bought by Rennies to form a new merchant and national liquor distributor, also under the name of Douglas Green of Paarl. Rennies, the then

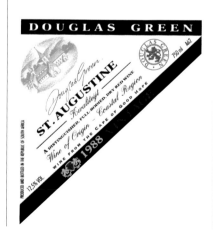

Johannesburg-based subsidiary of the Jardine Matheson Group of Hong Kong, took over two further wine companies, those of J.D. Bosman & Company of Johannesburg and Avrons Limited of Cape Town.

The three companies then amalgamated into a single large operation, but within a few years increased demand for Douglas Green wines and subsequent growth in its market shares over-taxed the capacity of the original Paarl bottling and warehousing organization; and in July 1980, the company transferred its headquarters to a new large-scale depot at Montagu Gardens, on a 3-acre site near Milnerton Racecourse. The head office and marketing is now centralized under the new DGB set-up in Johannesburg. The company also distributes the full ranges of Delheim and Blaauwklippen wines and is the largest importer of liquor, except for whisky, into South Africa.

The Jardine Matheson Group sold Rennies, the then holding company of Douglas Green, to Old Mutual. In December 1984 Rennies merged with Safmarine to form a new company, Safren, which then became the holding company of Douglas Green of Paarl. In April 1985 Douglas Green was sold to Kersaf Liquor Holdings, part of Kersaf, the giant group formerly controlled by Sol Kerzner which also includes the Sun International Group.

Douglas Green did not actually make any of their own wines (relying largely on KWV as a source of their regular ranges and their special releases), but blended, bottled and marketed them. Every season they selected quality wines, skilfully blending them to their vintners' requirements and according to continuous research undertaken to test consumer's tastes. This practice will continue under the new Douglas Green Bellingham set-up but will be modified as time progresses as the Union Wine set-up did not use KWV as a major supplier.

—DOUGLAS GREEN— BELLINGHAM

Graham Beck of Kangra Holdings purchased Union Wine from Jan Pickard. Knowing that Douglas Green had previously began negotiations with Pickard, he initiated further discussions on the possibility of a joint venture.

Considering the excellent portfolio of imported products and the distribution network of Douglas Green, a merger could only be beneficial to both companies. A combination of the extensive range of imported products of Douglas Green and the superior cellar facilities of Union Wine promised a partnership of great potential. Beck therefore sold Picardi Holdings' 50 per cent stake in Picardi Liquors to Liquor retailer Jacques Kempen. He then sold 50 per cent of the Union Wine production, marketing and distribution to Kersaf who already owned Douglas Green of Paarl to form the new DGB company which is managed by Kersaf, creating a wine and spirit company second only (in South Africa) to the Rupert controlled Distillers Corporation and Stellenbosch Farmers' Winery. Douglas Green Bellingham was therefore established on the first of July 1991. DGB's managing director is Tim Hutchinson who has a sound record of hotel management and is ably supported by experienced liquor marketer Henry Kempen.

The DGB portfolio is split into three ranges represented by three sales teams; Douglas Green, Bellingham and the import division Pagan International. Pagan International specializes in Portuguese wines and will now include the prestigious range of products available from Remy Martin. The Liquor Inn retail group operates independently of the wholesale section and comprises some 15 stores. The wines of Blaauwklippen, Delheim, Weltevrede, Groot Constantia and Rhebokskloof are also sold and distributed by DGB. Beck kept the Franschhoek properties of Bellingham and La Garonne out of the deal and will run these along with the Madeba operation at Robertson. Quite how the major brand of Bellingham will be organized with the limited production of the Bellingham farm is not yet decided. Obviously the big Bellingham brand is too valuable to be tampered with but Beck has made moves to improve the quality of the production at Bellingham and La Garonne and will surely want to differentiate this production from the giant brand.

—FAIRVIEW—
ESTATE

At the turn of the century a large area of the Paarl mountain belonged to a certain Mr Hugo, owner of the farm Bloemkoolfontein. Short on water and with soil which was largely sand, it made an unprepossessing property, but it supplied enough nutrition to support a limited quantity of Cinsaut from which Hugo made dry red wine which he purveyed to the public and the wine merchants in small wooden barrels.

When he died in 1937 his farm was bought by an immigrant from Lithuania named Charles Back, who had bought the Drakenstein farm now known as Backsberg in 1916. Reduced in extent (Hugo had sold off the highest part of the farm in 1917), his new acquisition nevertheless had a working cellar and, Back realized, considerable potential for the production of shy-bearing, high-quality wines for which the poor nature of the soil and the limited water supply would be relatively less of a disadvantage.

He set about rooting out the old Cinsaut vineyards and replanting them with quality varieties. After his death in 1954, his son Cyril continued this process of replacement with noble vines such as Cabernet Sauvignon, Pinotage, Shiraz, Pinot Noir and Chenin Blanc. More recently all Cabernet Sauvignon vines were replaced with an earlier-ripening clone, and some Chenin Blanc vines have made way for Chardonnay. Cyril Back consolidated his father's efforts, winning numerous awards for his red wines at the Boberg Show where in 1974, 1976 and 1978 he won the KWV trophy for the Champion Red Wine. For Woolworths Fairview produces white and red wines with no sulphur added; as far as can be established, the red is the first of this kind in the world.

The Backs have always worked as a team. From the early years Cyril's wife, Beryl, has been involved in everything to do with Fair-

---

---

view. Cyril's eldest son, Charles, has been cellarmaster since 1978 although Cyril still helps in the winery during the vintage. Charles was trained at Elsenburg, where he also did an extra cellarmaster's course. He is not only an extremely talented winemaker but also has a natural flair for marketing. In 1986 Charles was the first to make a Gamay Nouveau by the traditional method of carbonic maceration. In 1987 he produced a similar wine but used mostly Pinotage, as the Gamay crop had suffered severe hail damage. A fortified sweet Shiraz is also one of Charles's innovations.

Cyril and Charles Back.

White varieties are well represented at Fairview, but there are more red wine varieties than white. Situated on the southern slopes of the Paarlberg, Fairview's soils range from the decomposed granite of the upper slopes – derived from the mountain itself – through the middle section of the farm made up mostly of sandy loam, down to the lower reaches which are too poor to support vines. Further still to the south the land rises again to present a very good, clay-based soil, well suited to shy-bearing varieties.

None of these soils is fertile enough to give high production. Of the 200 hectares of Fairview, 125 are currently devoted to vineyards. The remainder of the land, mostly comprising the areas of poorer soil, is occupied by 12 000 laying hens and 8 000 pigs and goats. In 1981 Fairview imported Swiss Saanen goats and became the only commercial goat's milk cheese producing unit in South Africa. The herd has now increased to 600 and Fairview produces a range of excellent cheeses which include pecorino, rabiola, chevin, formagini, and feta. The Backs also have a flock of special milk-yielding sheep from Germany and make a popular Portuguese cheese called 'Cesa de Serra', or Cheese of the Mountains. The poultry and animals produce enough organic fertilizer to enrich the vineyards – an impressive 4 000 tonnes a year. Virtually no inorganic fertilizer is used at Fairview, other than the lime needed to supply a common deficiency in the districts of Paarl and Stellenbosch.

In 1974 the estate scored a notable 'first' in the industry with the highly successful private auction of its wines. This was first of its kind for the general public of South Africa. One and a half thousand cases of wine were successfully auctioned.

Fairview offers a comprehensive range of wines, which includes a Sweet Red, made entirely from Shiraz. A *méthode champenoise* sparkling wine made from the traditional Pinot Noir grape was released in 1990. Although Fairview has, of late, been better

---

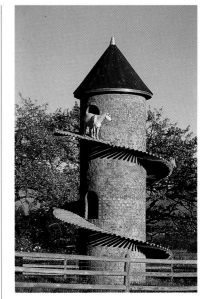

The famous goat tower at Fairview.

known for its red wines, Charles denies any preference for either white or red wines. Like most other estates, Fairview has made a considerable investment in new Bordeaux *barriques*, and Charles is ageing some red wines to be released when ready.

—GLEN CARLOU—
VINEYARDS

Glen Carlou Vineyards, situated in the foothills of the Simonsberg, was established in 1985 by winemaker Walter Finlayson, formerly of Hartenberg and Blaauwklippen. The 108-hectare farm once formed part of the original Simonsvlei land grant 'Skilpadjie', named after the now endangered geometric tortoise. It was given the name Glen Carlou by a previous owner, in honour of his three daughters Lena, Carol and Louise. Today the farm is owned by Walter Finlayson and Sarah and Dan Clarke-Krige.

Walter Finlayson outside his new cellar at Glen Carlou Vineyards.

Following extensive preparation of the soil, the first vineyards were planted in 1985 with varieties best suited to the climate and soil type, such as Cabernet Sauvignon and Chardonnay.

Walter Finlayson, known for his unorthodox and innovative ideas, has produced many fine wines. In recognition of his suc-

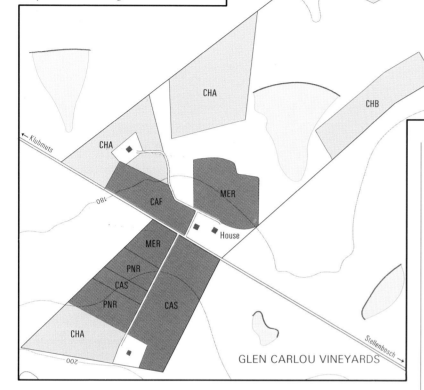

Rows of oak barrels in the new cellar at Glen Carlou Vineyards.

cess, he has twice received the coveted Diners' Club Winemaker of the Year Award, and over the past 20 years his wines have been awarded numerous medals and trophies. The quality of his first few vintages at Glen Carlou have surpassed even his expectations — he did not anticipate such early results — and at the 1990 Cape Independent Winemakers' Guild Auction the Glen Carlou 1989 Chardonnay fetched the highest bid for a white wine.

GLEN CARLOU VINEYARDS

Varieties planted (number of vines)

Perold trellis
Chardonnay 36 000
Cabernet Sauvignon 12 500
Merlot 12 000
Pinot Noir 10 000
Cabernet Franc 3 700
Petit Verdot 1 700

Total area under vines in 1991/2: 38 ha.
Irrigation: None.
Average temperatures: Records are not kept.
Average annual rainfall: 660 mm.
Stock: Rooted vines are bought from a nursery.
First wines bottled under the Glen Carlou Vineyards label: Merlot 1988 and Glen Carlou Chardonnay 1989.
Wines currently bottled under the Glen Carlou Vineyards label: Chardonnay, Reserve Chardonnay, Les Trois (Bordeaux blend), Grande Classique (Bordeaux blend), Merlot, Cabernet Sauvignon and Pinot Noir (Pinot Noir and Reserve Chardonnay only on C.I.W.G. Auction).
Wood ageing: Wine is aged in wood on the estate.
Cellar capacity: 900 hl.

Glen Carlou Vineyards are open to the public by appointment only.

— KWV —

The dominant organization of the winelands, KWV is very much a twentieth-century phenomenon. Market problems attendant upon over-production and a lack of organizational unity resulted in an acute depression in prices, and by the early years of the present century, the winelands of the Cape were in an advanced state of crisis.

To be effective in controlling prices and stabilizing the market, the farmers had to present a united front; they needed a body to represent them and to bargain on their behalf, and at the same time to handle the increasing bulk of excess wine. It was from these two requirements that the basic idea for the structure of KWV was developed.

To a great extent the inspiration for this new system was that of one man, Dr Charles William Henry Kohler. A dentist by training, he was born in 1862 at Calvinia in the northern Cape, and after qualifying in Cape Town settled in Paarl for a while before moving to the Transvaal to become involved in mining investments. But in 1909 he returned to the Cape, and bought the farm Riverside in the Paarl district. He then decided to settle down to become a wine farmer.

As a farmer he shared in the problems and concerns of his time; and he soon became aware that only a centralized body would be able to deal with them. At a meeting of the Paarl Wine Farmers' Association on the thirteenth of December 1916, convened by Kohler himself, it was decided to form a Co-operative Viticultural Union of South Africa. Financed by voluntary contributions from the farmers, the Union held its first meeting in Paarl in December 1917, and on the eighth of January 1918 it was converted into a co-operative and registered under the Companies Act of 1892 as Ko-operatieve Wijnbouwers Vereniging van Zuid-Afrika Beperkt (it still retains this Dutch form of the title).

The two-fold aims of the new organization were set out in its constitution. With regard to the market, KWV was 'So to direct, control and regulate the sale and disposal by its members of their produce, being that of the grape, as shall secure or tend to secure for them a continuously adequate return for such produce'. At the same time, the organization undertook to dispose of its members'

WINES DISTRIBUTED BY KWV

Cathedral Cellar range
Cabernet Sauvignon and Sauvignon Blanc and Chardonnay.

Cape Country range
Cabernet Sauvignon and Pinotage, Steen, Sauvignon Blanc, Colombard, Chardonnay and Chenin Blanc.

OTHER WINES DISTRIBUTED BY KWV

Red: Roodeberg, Cabernet, Pinotage, Cinsaut, Shiraz, Bonne Esperance and Laborie Red.
White: Riesling, Steen, Chenin Blanc, Sauvignon Blanc, Bonne Esperance Dry White and Stein, Weisser Riesling, Kerner, Late Vintage, Noble Late Harvest Superior, Cape Forêt, Cape Bouquet, Cape Nouveau Blanc and Laborie White.
Sparkling: Petillant Blanc and Rosé, Mousseux Blanc Brut, Blanc Demi-Sec, Musanté and Laborie Blanc de Noir.
Rosé: Bonne Esperance, Cape Blush and Cabernet Sauvignon Blanc de Noir.
Fortified: VO Sherry, Light Tawny Port, Tawny, Muscadel Jerepigo and Hanepoot Jerepigo.

surplus produce – at this stage powers vested in the company by law were limited to wine for distilling purposes only.

For KWV to be fully effective both in terms of dealing with over-production and in controlling prices, it had to ensure that all the wine farmers joined its ranks. Given the straitened economic circumstances and Kohler's energy, determination and persuasiveness, it was not long before the great majority – up to 95 per cent – had joined.

The result of this unity of purpose was that, at least as far as distilling wine was concerned, minimum prices could be fixed, though there was some initial confusion about the rights of the remaining growers who were not members of KWV to sell directly to the merchants. Since they did not have to deduct any surplus, they received better prices than if they had sold their wine to KWV, while at the same time the merchants could buy more cheaply from these growers than from the co-operative. Notwithstanding this manipulation, however, the effect of the new organization's presence was a sharp rise in prices, reaching £10 a leaguer in 1919.

In these early years, short of staff and funds, KWV converted all its surplus into distilled ethyl alcohol. In the same period considerable quantities of this alcohol were

being distilled from unsaleable molasses by the sugar farmers of Natal. Collaboration between the two industries led to the development of a petrol substitute named 'Natalite', KWV's first product. Unfortunately, it was more expensive than petrol, the return of which to the market after the blockade of the war years caused Natalite to fade away. Further problems came in the early 1920s with particularly heavy crops in the years 1921 and 1923; and a recurrence of the earlier pattern took place, with a price drop to £3 a leaguer and the destroying of over 50 million litres of unsaleable wine.

But 1924 saw an important turning-point in KWV's fortunes: the Government ratified its powers with Act 5 of 1924, the Wine and Spirit Control Act, which empowered KWV to fix on a yearly basis the minimum price to be paid to farmers for their distilling wine. That same year, too, saw the organization begin its second major project for the disposal of excess wine by making mature brandy; and round this main product the co-operative's range was gradually expanded to include dry table wines, fortified wines and liqueurs. This was well-timed, for the following year saw the introduction by Britain of a preferential tariff in respect of high-strength wines imported from Commonwealth countries; which had a marked effect in reviving the local industry by providing a protected outlet for KWV's growing export produce (by its constitution, the co-operative had agreed to share its markets abroad with the producing wholesalers, selling its wares in Africa only in countries north of the Equator).

With increased quantity came improved quality. In these years KWV began a concerted programme of technical improvement aimed at every level of the wine-making process. In 1927 one of the most important of South Africa's viticultural pioneers, Dr. Izak Abraham Perold, became the organization's principal research scientist. A decade later he was joined by another wine scientist, Dr. Charles Niehaus, who as his assistant, investigated local sherry production, before turning to the improvement of table wines.

Subsequent decades have seen a progressive enlargement of the KWV's scope and power. By Act 23 of 1940, the organization's control was extended to cover not only distilling wine but also good wine (it had originally been assumed, erroneously, that the

The central window at La Concorde, the headquarters of KWV in Paarl.

stabilization of distilling-wine prices would lead to a similar stability in good wine prices as well). Control was extended to include the whole wine industry. All transactions between merchants and producers had to be approved by KWV, and all payments made through the organization. The Act further stipulated that no person might produce wine except under a permit issued by KWV, such permits only being granted if the co-operative was satisfied that the producer was in possession of the necessary cellar facilities and fustage. The legislation concerning the annual surplus to be delivered to KWV was further expanded and refined.

The post-war years saw an accelerating pace in the local wine industry. Stimulated by new methods and despite the controls introduced in 1940, the old problem of over-production now returned, as fresh as ever. In response, new legislation was devised. In 1957, after over half a century, controls were put on production at source. A detailed scheme, known as the Quota System, was introduced for the limitation of production; the first of these quotas was fixed in terms of the vines growing on the farmer's property on the twenty first of June 1957 .

A major change took place on the first of April 1992 when KWV announced the lifting of the 35-year-old quota system, in a move to help create a free-market system.

The present structure and policy of KWV continues to reflect its legal and administrative evolution. The co-operative principle

with which it began remains firmly at its centre. Membership is not compulsory, although minimum prices and production quotas are applicable to all members, currently amounting to 5 000 wine farmers, 79 estates, 71 private wineries and 70 co-operative cellars. Members are represented by a Board of Directors elected by the farmers themselves – in theory at least, the farmers have the power to dissolve the organization at any time they may wish. For the purposes of election the winelands are divided into eight geographic regions without any specific 'Wine of Origin' connotation. The 12 directors who represent these districts, generally known as 'KWV districts', are headed by the present chairman of KWV (the fourth to hold office in the organization's history), Mr P.B.B. Hugo.

KWV products are not generally available on the local market since, by agreement, the organization sells only to members, personnel, merchants and distillers for domestic consumption. The major emphasis remains upon production for export. KWV handles 70 per cent of the country's wine and spirit exports – the remainder being divided largely between the Stellenbosch Farmers' Winery and Distillers Corporation, with important contributions also from Gilbeys, Douglas Green Bellingham and some leading estates.

Considerable research is undertaken by KWV, and liaison takes place with other research centres such as the Viticultural and Oenological Research Institute at Stellenbosch. In the late 1980s it instituted a levy on wine production quotas to raise funds for research. It also raised funds to facilitate for an extension of services to farmers.

A further important responsibility of KWV is that of publicity and image-building for the industry in general, in particular with the creation of overseas markets. On home ground, the headquarters of KWV at Paarl – the target of over 20 000 visitors every year – is the scene of popular conducted tours, film shows and wine-tastings.

Visibly or invisibly, KWV is everywhere in the modern Cape winelands. Born of a series of defensive gestures, this vast organization provides both a controlling and a mediatory role between producers, co-operatives, wholesalers and retailers: indeed, on a larger scale, through its export function, this role extends beyond the Cape to the wine world in general.

The Laborie restaurant has become a popular venue for residents of, and visitors to, Paarl.

Paul de Villiers the fifth, who has been in charge of wine-making at Landskroon since 1980.

LABORIE ESTATE

Varieties planted (ha)

Extended Perold trellis
Cabernet Sauvignon 8,42
Weisser Riesling 3,68
Pinotage 3,24
Merlot 3
Sauvignon Blanc 2,43
Gewürztraminer 1,97
Chardonnay 1,72
Pinot Noir 1,47
Pinot Gris 1,43
Gable trellis
Shiraz 2,25

Varieties to be planted by 1997 (ha)

Extended Perold trellis
Cabernet Sauvignon 9,99
Chardonnay 9,29
Merlot 4,72
Pinot Noir 3,08
Pinotage 2,95
Pinot Gris 1,39
Sauvignon Blanc 0,96

Total area under vines in 1991/2:
29,61 ha; by 1997: 32,38 ha.
Irrigation: Only supplementary irrigation is used,
depending on the rainfall during the growing season.
Average temperatures:
Maximum 23,8 °C; minimum 11,7 °C.
Average annual rainfall: Approximately 1040 mm.
Stock: All planting material used originates from the
KWV Plant Improvement Scheme.
First wine bottled under the Laborie label:
Laborie Red 1979.
**Wines currently bottled under the Laborie
label:** Laborie Red, Laborie White,
Laborie Blanc de Noir, Laborie Taillefert Red
and Laborie Taillefert White.
Wood ageing: None.
Cellar capacity: 4 250 hl.

While the Laborie cellar is not open to the public,
Laborie wines and other wines from the region
may be purchased from the Wine House at Laborie on
weekdays from 09h00 to 17h00 and
on Saturdays from 09h00 to 14h00.
Laborie Estate is on the Paarl Wine Route.

— LABORIE —
ESTATE

In 1972 KWV bought Laborie, the old French Huguenot wine farm in Paarl, and since then has restored the nineteenth-century Cape Dutch style Manor House, as well as developing it into a flourishing wine estate where the cellarmaster, Kobus Jordaan, makes the Laborie and Laborie Taillefert range of wines. Today the wine farm is a bustling KWV complex and showpiece, of which the 'Historical Cellar' is used as a wine training centre, and the Manor House is used to host KWV's guests. On 15 July 1977 the Manor House, with its spectacular view of the Drakenstein Mountains, was proclaimed a National Monument.

Soon after the 1972 purchase, an extensive vineyard renewal programme was introduced during which the existing fruit trees and vineyards (mainly table grapes) were uprooted. The soil – derived from the granite boulders of Paarl mountain – is ideally suited to wine grapes and underwent careful preparation before the first new vineyards were planted. This comprised deep ploughing on the level surfaces, while a trencher was used on the terraces; lime was added to the soil in order to regulate the pH balance of the subsoil. Irrigation is only used on a supplementary basis, and a minimum of fertilization is needed.

Today about 31 hectares of the total area of 45 hectares are under vines; when they are all fully productive, the farm will yield about 450 tonnes of grapes, of which 60 per cent will be red and 40 per cent white. A replacement programme is in progress which should be completed in 1997.

The Laborie Taillefert range is named in honour of Jean Taillefert, who was the original French Huguenot owner of Laborie. It

---

was introduced during the French Huguenot festival in 1988 to commerate the tercentenary of their arrival at the Cape in 1688. The estate boasts a modern wine cellar with the latest wine-making equipment and stainless steel tanks.

— LANDSKROON —
ESTATE

Located on the southern slopes of the Paarlberg, this farm was given its name in 1692 by its first owner, a Swede named Jan Holsmit. It remained in the hands of a number of free burgher farmers throughout the eighteenth century, but in 1872 a subdivision of the property, under the name of Weltevreden, was bought by a member of the De Villiers family which still owns the farm.

They were of Huguenot descent from one Jacques de Villiers who, early in the eighteenth century, had established himself at the Groot Drakenstein farm of Boschendal. When Jacques and his two brothers first arrived at the Cape in 1689 on the packetboat *Zion*, they carried a letter from the Here XVII to Governor Simon van der Stel recommending their skill in the art of wine-making. The family continued to farm at Boschendal until 1874, when they sold their two-century-old property, leaving Paul de Villiers, newly established on the slopes of the Paarl mountain, to continue the dynasty.

He soon set about enlarging and consolidating the family's new base, within years acquiring the rest of Landskroon Farm and further adding to it the neighbouring property of Schoongezicht (not to be confused with the farm of the same name in the Stellenbosch district).

Settled on their substantial piece of land, the new branch of the De Villiers family steadily developed the wine-making side of the farm. These developments can be traced through a series of De Villiers owners – all of them, with a fine sense of dynastic continuity, named Paul. The present owner is the fourth Landskroon patriarch of this name, and the fifth Paul de Villiers has been in charge of wine-making since 1980.

The first Paul de Villiers, of the 1874 vintage, found an area of the farm planted with vines, though there is no record of their type. In the next few years he planted Chenin

---

Blanc, Cinsaut and Muscadel vines and built a cellar where he made sweet fortified wines of the type popular at that time. Borne by ox-wagon to Cape Town and sold in small wooden casks, these luscious wines fetched

---

LANDSKROON ESTATE

Varieties planted (number of vines)

Bush vines
Cinsaut 238 000
Chenin Blanc 107 000
Cabernet Sauvignon 99 000
Pinotage 62 000
Pinot Noir 35 000
Sauvignon Blanc 33 000
Souzão 29 000
Cabernet Franc 28 000
Tinta Barocca 28 000
Shiraz 27 000
Tinta Roriz 21 000
Merlot 20 000
Alicante Bouschet 18 000
Gamay 12 000
Morio Muscat 10 000
Pinot Gris 9 000
Pinot Blanc 8 800

Total area under vines in 1991/2: 265 ha.
Irrigation: The vineyards are irrigated.
Average temperatures:
Maximum 37 °C; minimum 6 °C.
Average annual rainfall: 660 mm.
Stock: Rooted vines are bought from a nursery.
First wine bottled under the Landskroon label:
Cinsaut 1974.
**Wines currently bottled under the Landskroon
label:** Cinsaut, Chenin Blanc Dry, Bouquet Blanc,
Cabernet Sauvignon, Blanc de Noir,
Chenin Blanc (semi-sweet), Pinotage,
Sauvignon Blanc, Pinot Noir, Shiraz,
Cabernet Franc, Pinot Gris, Pinot Blanc and Port.
Wood ageing: Wine is aged in wood on the estate.
Cellar capacity: 10 500 hl.

Landskroon Estate is on the Paarl Wine Route
and is open to the public on weekdays from
08h30 to 17h30, and on Saturdays from
08h30 to 12h30. Cheese lunches are served from
November to April between 11h30 and 14h30.

good prices both for local consumption and for export.

The second Paul de Villiers brought the farm into the twentieth century and to the period of the inception of KWV in 1918. From then until 1973 almost all Landskroon wine was sold to KWV.

The third Paul de Villiers developed the variety side of the farm and, in a period when the bulk of the local wine produced was white, began producing dry red table wine. He also planted an assortment of port

LANDSKROON ESTATE

Hugo runs this dairy farm, while Paul concentrates on the vineyards and cellars.

In the past two decades the vineyards of Landskroon have seen radical change. The port-type varieties have been retained, but extensive new plantings of high-quality red varieties, such as Cabernet Sauvignon, Pinotage, Pinot Noir and Shiraz, have been made. Since 1973 the wines made from these quality varieties have been bottled under the estate's own label. Since 1918 KWV has used Landskroon port in the blending of its own ports, but a limited quantity bottled under the Landskroon label is now sold at two years old for further laying down. This vintage port is made from Tinta Barocca, Tinta Roriz and Souzão.

The majority of Landskroon's vineyards are found on the lower slopes of Paarl mountain. The sun rises behind the granite domes, with the result that the farm receives little early morning warmth, which permits the high-quality grapes to mature slowly.

Out of a total of 265 hectares of vines, about 75 per cent of them are high-quality varieties. The new departures of recent years have paid off and the estate has been a consistent prize winner at the various annual wine shows.

wine varieties, including a number such as Tinta Barocca, Souzão and Tinta Roriz still grown on Landskroon. In this enterprise he was encouraged by KWV and by Dr. Charles Niehaus (often described as the 'father of the South African sherry industry'), who was at this time investigating the occurrence in the local vineyards of *flor* type yeasts, of the kind found in the vineyards of Spain and associated with the making of the traditional *fino*

styles of sherry. Landskroon was among the 18 or so farms in the Cape where this naturally occurring yeast was found.

Paul de Villiers senior, together with his brother Hugo, inherited the farm in 1963. Since then they have divided the running of the estate between them. Part of the property has been developed as a Jersey stud and dairy farm (as at nearby Fairview, the animals provide the organic fertilizer for the vineyards).

— MONIS OF PAARL —

Now part of the Stellenbosch Farmers' Winery Group, Monis of Paarl was founded in the early years of the century by Roberto Moni, one of three immigrant sons of a prominent Tuscan wine-making and merchandising family.

Applying their inherited skills in the local context, the brothers began making wine, concentrating in the early years on fortified dessert wines. With experience came innovation. The hot South African summers complicated the making of the delicate noble wines; to overcome this problem Roberto Moni imported large-scale refrigeration equipment from Europe – the first of its kind on the local scene and an important development in the improvement of the Cape wines.

With post-war expansion, Monis took over the Nederburg farm in 1956, with a subsequent shift of emphasis towards the making of the kind of natural wines for which Nederburg was already well known. A new market was opened in 1962 when the company became the first in South Africa to successfully market a *perlé* wine, Capenheimer. This is now marketed by Stellenbosch Farmers' Winery.

Roberto Moni was quick to appreciate the excellence of fortified wines made at Montagu and he brought them to his own cellar where they were matured and blended. In so doing he established a tremendously popular and high-quality range of sweet fortified wines of which Marsala and Moscato were perhaps the best known.

Moni also began producing *flor* sherry by the traditional Spanish method and today the winery boasts one of the finest private *soleras* in the country.

In recent years Monis have released a series of 'Collectors' Ports' with interesting labels. Some have depicted rare South African stamps, and for the Johannesburg Centenary the labels were sketches of the 'Randlords'. The latest 'Collectors' Port', to commemorate the three hundredth anniversary of the arrival of the Huguenots and the founding of Paarl, is contained in most attractive replicas of a ship's decanter, which cannot tip over.

Monis have always been producers of high-quality grape juice and following the modern trend have entered the growing market for health-giving, natural fruit juices, producing juices such as citrus, apricot, peach and litchi. A full list of Monis products appears together with others of the Stellenbosch Farmers' Winery Group.

—NEDERBURG—

Situated in the Klein Drakenstein area of the district of Paarl, the land of Nederburg was first granted, relatively late for this area, in 1792. In that year the Dutch East India Company sent out one of its officials, Commissioner-General Sebastiaan Cornelis Nederburgh, to perform one of its periodic checks on the behaviour and probity of its servants at the Cape – though by now the Colony's days as a Dutch possession were numbered. In the course of his stay, he granted a piece of land to a German immigrant named Philip Wolvaart, who gratefully remembered his debt to the Commissioner in the name of his new property.

It was he who in 1800 built the fine Cape Dutch homestead, based on the classic 'inland' ground plan of an H-shape. Thereafter the farm continued in the nineteenth century in the hands of a succession of owners, few of whom showed more than a minimal interest in wine farming: indeed, Nederburg remained generally undistinguished until 1937 when, with the advent of a new owner, Johann Richard Georg Graue, the real life of the estate began.

A German immigrant, Graue had begun his working life in a prominent German brewery, and by the early 1930s had achieved a secure position as managing director of the firm. Although his personal security seemed assured, the shadow of uncertainty loomed in the days after the collapse of the Weimar Republic, and the coming to power of Adolf Hitler precipitated a choice for Graue and his family. In particular, he wished to find a secure future for his only son, Arnold.

There were shadows over Europe, and South Africa, a young country, appeared to offer a refuge from the mounting tensions at home. From the point of view of the Graue family it offered something more, for despite the elder Graue's many years in the brewery, both father and son were possessed by the wine-making spirit. For Johann, South Af-

The Cape Flemish Nederburg homestead, built in 1800 by Philip Wolvaart.

rica appeared the ideal creative opportunity for an ambitious winemaker searching for something new. With its dependable soil and climate, its steady sunshine and mild winters, it offered conditions of stability rarely to be found in the erratic climate of northern Europe.

So for the Graues the acquisition of Nederburg was the start of a great wine-making adventure. Not that the immediate prospects were prepossessing; the farm taken over by the newly arrived immigrants in 1937, though enchanting in aspect with its beautiful old homestead and its stately setting of mountains, was undeveloped and limited in extent with 93 hectares of ill-tended vines. Fired with a sense of new opportunities, Graue remained undaunted, and immediately plunged into his first task – planting new vineyards.

To this task he brought a degree of knowledge and thoroughness not always found locally. His motto was simple and direct. 'Good wine,' he maintained, 'starts in the vineyards.' He kept the fullest possible records of all plantings made, and of the lineage and performance of every vine on the farm. Setting the highest standards for his vines, he ruthlessly culled those which fell short. At the same time he made a close study of the varieties themselves, making a number of important discoveries about them. At the time of his purchase of the farm, the vineyards contained limited amounts of Chenin Blanc, Cape Riesling, Clairette Blanche, Cinsaut and Cabernet Sauvignon; he found, though, that the Chenin

Blanc was a superior variety and set about selecting and developing it as the basis for a high-quality white wine.

So the foundation of Nederburg's future vineyards was laid during these early years, but little large-scale technical progress was possible during World War II. It was only with the end of the war that the Graues began to emerge, not only as vine growers, but as winemakers, and in little short of a spectacular manner.

It was based on an innovation of Johann's which turned out to be a stroke of genius – the perfecting of the process now known as 'cold fermentation', a method which was to revolutionize the whole structure of the South African wine industry.

If there is a major fault in the local climate, it lies in the high summer temperatures, reaching a peak at harvest time, which, particularly in the case of white wines, can have an adverse effect. The natural reaction of fermentation is speeded up to an alarming degree, to the extent that the high temperature can stop the process altogether. With the knowledge of German white wine-making behind him, Graue's instinct told him that only cool conditions, even if artificially created, would give the precision of control in the wine-making which he had already successfully obtained in the Nederburg vineyards.

In the exciting years of expansion after the war, Graue and his son developed the technique of cooling the tanks in which the white wine fermentation took place with refrigerated water. The equipment required

was installed, and the farm's facilities enlarged and modernized. While the elder Graue concentrated upon these innovations, the son returned to Europe for periods of study at the famous Geisenheim Wine Institute in the Rhineland, at Wadenswiel in Switzerland, and in the château wineries of Bordeaux, for the Graues had realized that if cold fermentation could help them perfect their white wines, the optimum use of the soils and climate of the Cape could do the same for their reds.

With well-rationalized vineyard procedures and controlled and technically sophisticated methods for the production of both white and red wines, the ground plan for the future success of Nederburg was laid. In 1951 Arnold returned to South Africa, to be put in charge of the technical control of the winery. A year later, at the 1952 annual Cape Wine Show, the first wines made by the younger Graue achieved recognition with a spectacular array of prizes.

It was a success which appeared to mark the beginning of a fine career, and the consummation of the father's work. The dream, however, was brutally ended, almost at the moment when it had begun: in September 1953, Arnold was killed when his private aeroplane was involved in a collision with a military training aircraft at Youngsfield in Cape Town.

For Johann it was both a personal tragedy and the end of his life's adventure. Though he took control of the winery again for a while, the burden of its rapid expansion soon proved too heavy. Within a few years of his son's death he had merged his company with that of Monis of Paarl. Johann Graue died in April 1959, a broken man, having withdrawn increasingly from taking an active part in the wine-making.

Although his personal life ended in tragedy, his creation and his wine-making ideas survived him, largely in the person of the man who took over the role of wine master at Nederburg after the death of Arnold Graue – Günter Brözel. Since he had arrived at Nederburg from Germany in 1956, Günter had exploited and developed all the elements inherited from the Graues, building up a broad and varied spectrum of wines, made at a remarkably high level of quality and consistency. The meticulous control of vineyard standards is a part of this quality, as is the ex-

Cellarmaster Newald Marais.

tensive and streamlined modern technology of the large Nederburg cellars, including the massive cold fermentation complex for the white wines. Together with these goes a further aspect, based upon a practice originated by the elder Graue, that of blending and using grapes grown in different areas but well suited to his particular needs.

As the demand for Nederburg wines increased rapidly in the early 1950s, Johann Graue had begun supplying vines for farmers in many different parts of the Western Cape to grow grapes in optimum conditions for use in making Nederburg wines. In doing so he maintained the strictest control over quality, taking advantage of the range of different soils and mesoclimates available to select the best possible quality of grapes of each specific variety. Many of the vines grown by these other farmers came from the Nederburg nurseries. By this method the problems attendant upon making wine from grapes grown on a limited area of land were greatly reduced.

A good deal of Nederburg's wines are still made on this basis, with grape deliveries at harvest time being made from across a wide area from specially selected farms.

Then in 1966, together with Monis of Paarl, Nederburg was merged with Stellenbosch Farmers' Winery and thereupon entered a new era. Around this time, too, the Nederburg land became the subject of complex law-making. In 1972 the Wine of Origin legislation was introduced, in terms of which individual farms were invited to apply for registration as officially designated estates. Hitherto, the wines made from the vineyards around the Nederburg winery were incorporated as an integral part of the winery's production. In terms of the new law, however, the conflation of a local with a more widespread operation debarred Nederburg from

claiming the status of an estate – notwithstanding the fact that its cellars were among the most advanced in the country and its wines demonstrably of a superior quality.

The estate portion of the project was therefore renamed Johann Graue, while the bulk of the wines continued to be made under the Nederburg label. To expedite this scheme a number of practical obstacles had to be overcome, chief among them being the problem of keeping the two wine-making operations

separate while still under the same roof. Assurances that this could be done secured the go-ahead for the company, which duly produced the first of what was intended to be an extensive range of Johann Graue Estate wines. In the event, however, only six of these superb wines (now collector's items) in fact appeared before a combination of political problems brought their production to a standstill three years later.

The question of the status of the Johann Graue Estate wines abides. In the meantime, the wine-loving public is more than content with a spectrum of wines from Nederburg which includes many of the country's classics, among them the famous Edelkeur, made with the help of *Botrytis cinerea*, otherwise known as 'noble rot'. In this instance Nederburg winemaker, Günter Brözel, was granted an indulgence by the Department of Agriculture. Commonly used in the making of natural dessert wines such as Trockenbeerenauslesen in Germany when it occurs on the grapes at harvest time, the mould attacks the fruit, reducing its moisture and greatly increasing the concentration of natural sugar. Thus it enabled a wine with a sugar content of as much as 200 grams a litre to be made – far above the legal limit which was applied at that time. Eventually, having been granted special dispensation, Brözel added this magnificent sweet wine to his considerable range of Auction wines.

Günter Brözel left Nederburg in 1989, marking the start of yet another new era at Nederburg. The outstanding genius of Günter Brözel was recognised in 1985 when he won the coveted Robert Mondavi Trophy for the International Wine Maker of the Year at the Club Oenologique Internationale Wine and Spirit Competition held in London. He has won the Diners' Club Award on two occasions and was further honoured in 1986 for his outstanding contribution to the advancement and international recognition of the South African wine industry.

Under the diligent guidance of managing director Ernst le Roux, cellarmaster Newald Marais and group farm manager Hannes van Rensburg, the Nederburg tradition of ensuring outstanding quality of wine-making through up-to-date vineyard practices and state-of-the-art wine-making techniques continues.

—ONVERWACHT—
ESTATE

Although Onverwacht can trace its origins to grants of land to the French Huguenots along the Krom River in 1699, the estate is a newcomer to the competitive environment of the wine industry. To compensate for its 'youth', however, Onverwacht Estate is being innovative and original in its methods and outlook.

Acquired by Trevor Harris in 1986, the farm is now almost fully planted at 51 hectares, with those varieties best suited to the Wellington region, which is well known for its more robust wines. These include new plantings of Sémillon, Muscadel and Sauvignon Blanc.

The winemaker, Mark Ravenscroft, previously a water analyst, travelled for two years after graduating from Elsenburg Col-

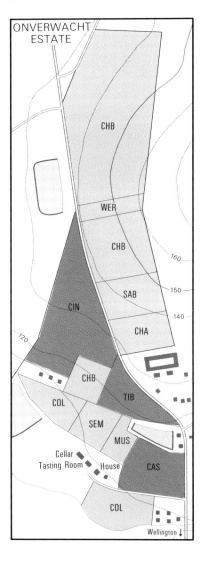

lege, and maintains contact with producers in Australia where he worked. He will no doubt benefit from the exchange of technology and wine-making concepts from that continent. In line with international trends, the estate has already experimented with different barrel sizes and wood types.

A further innovation is the packaging and marketing concept of 'blending art and wine'. The label of the first *méthode champenoise* wine (made by Laurent Berger) features a reproduction of a painting that was commissioned from artist André Naude. A numbered and signed poster of the painting is sold together with the wine, limited to the first 500 bottles only.

Inventiveness, skill, enthusiasm and hard work have been combined to put Onverwacht on the map. Hopefully these same qualities will prepare the estate to meet the challenges of the future.

— PERDEBERG —
WINE FARMERS'
CO-OPERATIVE

On 22 August 1941 a meeting was held in the vicinity of the Perdeberg (the *perde*, or horses, were the zebra which once roamed the area) on Jan Rossouw's farm Vryguns, and as a result the Perdeberg Wine Farmers' Co-operative was formed under the chairmanship of S.F. Dreyer. Jan Rossouw sold 2 hectares of Vryguns at a nominal price to provide the land on which to build a cellar, and in 1942 it was ready to receive its first intake of 1 322 tonnes of grapes.

Pieter Dreyer, the chairman's brother, became the winemaker, while Jan Rossouw's brother, D.J. Rossouw, was manager, but the functions of manager and winemaker were combined by the time Joseph Huskisson joined the co-operative in 1956.

Joseph had had the privilege of working with experienced and respected winemakers, for example at Nederburg, where he trained under Arnold Graue for five years. Early in 1956 he moved to the Bolandse Co-operative, where he gained invaluable experience in handling large volumes of grapes.

Joseph Huskisson's dedication to quality has made Perdeberg a regular trophy and prizewinner at the Cape Young Wine Show. The co-operative receives grapes from 47 member farmers, processing 18 000 tonnes annually. Only a small amount of its wine is bottled for the public, as most of the production is sold to merchants.f

— RHEBOKSKLOOF —
ESTATE

Rhebokskloof dates back to 1692 when Simon van der Stel granted the land to free burgher Dirk van Schalkwyk. The present owners, Mervyn Key and his wife Michelle,

No expense is being spared in the restoration of the beautiful Rhebokskloof Estate.

have enthusiastically set about restoring the estate, and today it is one of the most beautiful properties in the area, with views of Table Mountain, horse paddocks, Île de France sheep stud, and historic Cape Dutch buildings. A pair of rare Black Eagles are often seen circling over the estate, and the rhebok that gave the estate its name roam freely in the kloofs. The estate also runs three different styles of restaurant; visitors may choose to dine in the traditional Cape Dutch homestead, the elegant Victorian dining-room, or, during the summer months, outside on a terrace overlooking the vineyards and mountains, from where one can see beautiful black swans on a dam below the buildings.

The 450-hectare farm has a comparatively warm mesoclimate and therefore needs careful viticultural practice to extract the best from the vines. At present vines cover 80 hectares of the farm and grow on the west- and east-facing slopes of the mountain in soil that is granitic throughout (Glen Rosa and Clovelly types). Wine is made solely from grapes grown on the estate. Rhebokskloof's philosophy is that a lower yield per hectare produces flavourful, characterful grapes and therefore more complex and noble wines. Table grapes are also grown for export and now form a large part of the farm's activities.

The winemaker at Rhebokskloof is Californian-born John Reagh, who graduated from Fresno University in California in 1979 with a B.Sc. in Agricultural Science, majoring in Oenology and Viticulture. John has worked at various wineries in California as vineyard manager, planting and maintaining vineyards; as assistant winemaker responsible for the cellar operations at a 15 000-case winery; and as maker of *méthode champenoise* sparkling wine.

To gain overseas experience, John then went to Germany where he worked on Pinot Noir and barrel-fermented Chardonnay programmes. Rhebokskloof is very fortunate that he subsequently chose to settle in the Cape, believing that the Cape winelands have the potential to be the wine area of the future.

RUSTENBURG
FARM

Claridge Fine Wines are made at Rustenburg Farm on the slopes of the Groenberg, near Wellington, by Roger and Maria Jorgensen. Having farmed in Kent, the Jorgensens decided to find a property for the purpose of producing wine.

After much deliberation, the Jorgensens settled on South Africa, buying this 33-hectare farm in 1987. Since then, Roger has replanted 8 hectares, planting only the best slopes with varieties such as Chardonnay, Merlot, Cabernet Sauvignon and Cabernet Franc. 'Red Wellington' is a classic blend of the three noble reds, and the Chardonnay is made as naturally as possible to reflect the

---

terroir more than the winemaker's influence. Both wines will be bottled by June 1992 in 500-millilitre returnable bottles, which are handmade in Italy.

The deep soils of the mountain vineyards are composed of rotted granite with a 26 per cent clay content. Only the minimum of water is applied to avoid overly stressing the vines. Pruning is always severe, often savage, limiting yields to 5 tonnes per hectare. The Jorgensens like to keep the farm and cellar as uncommercial as possible, 'a family affair of modest, homespun proportions', preferring to rely more on traditional techniques than on technology.

SIMONDIUM
WINERY CO-OPERATIVE

The Simondium Winery Co-operative was formerly known as the Drakenstein Co-operative, which was founded by a group of eight local farmers in October 1906.

In the first decades, between 1909 and 1948, brandy was distilled at the co-operative, and its first Hanepoot Jerepigo was made in 1909 and long remained one of its best-known products. In the early days, too, fine Cabernet, Pontac and Cinsaut wines were made.

The first official winemaker at the Co-operative was a Mr Boettgen, succeeded in 1921 by Wolfram Wagener, whose son, Willie, took over from him in 1950. After a break of a few years Willie Wagener has now returned to the co-operative as the manager and winemaker.

Visitors to the winery are greeted by the many-gabled façade of the building which houses the co-operative, as well as the two well-preserved brandy stills from which the early brandy was made. There are also a number of the first cork-sealed bottles of brandy produced.

With the giant wine bottle that stands in front of the winery's cellar, Simonsvlei Co-operative is difficult to miss.

SIMONSVLEI
CO-OPERATIVE

Established in 1945 and situated in the shadow of the Afrikaanse Taalmonument in Suider-Paarl some 50 kilometres from Cape Town, Simonsvlei produces a wide range of wines, including delicate dry and semi-sweet whites, sparkling wines, matured reds and full-bodied sweet dessert wines.

The cellar gathers about 18 000 tonnes of grapes per year, grown in a wide area stretching from the cool Wemmershoek and Klein Drakenstein areas, along Paarlberg and the Simonsberg to the gravelly soil of Muldersvlei. As a result, Simonsvlei is able to produce quality wines of a wide variety year after year.

Sarel Rossouw was Simonsvlei's first cellarmaster. During his 34-year tenure he received many awards for his wines, culminating in 1981 when he was named South African Champion Winemaker. He was also the inspiration for a range of distinguished wines, including the Simonsvlei Cabernet Sauvignon of 1973, the first wine made by a co-operative to receive a Superior certification (now defunct). Simonsvlei was also the first co-operative to participate at the Nederburg Auction.

Johan Rossouw followed in his father's footsteps, becoming Simonsvlei's cellarmaster in 1982. He was succeeded in 1985 by

---

his brother, Kobus, formerly South African Champion Co-operative Winemaker.

Having won many awards at young wine shows over the years, Simonsvlei still produces champion wines under the supervision of Kobus Rossouw, and, since 1991, that of newly appointed production manager Philip Louw.

In 1989 Simonsvlei completed a modern new tourist centre where wines can be tasted and cellar tours are offered. Simonsvlei wines are available at various bottle stores throughout South Africa or can be ordered directly from the winery.

RUSTENBURG FARM

Varieties planted (number of vines)

Perold trellis
Cabernet Sauvignon 17 000
Chardonnay 7 500
Merlot 2 500
Cabernet Franc 600

Total area under vines in 1991/2: 8 ha.
Irrigation: None.
Average temperatures:
Maximum 35 °C; minimum 8 °C.
Average annual rainfall: 670 mm.
Stock: Confidential source.
First wines to be bottled under the Claridge Fine Wines label: Red Wellington and Chardonnay.
Wood ageing: Wines are aged in wood on the farm.
Cellar capacity: 500 hl.

Rustenburg Farm is open to the public for sales and tasting by appointment only.

WINES BOTTLED AND MARKETED

Red: Claret.
White: Grand Crû and Vin Blanc

The co-operative is on the Paarl Wine Route and is open to the public on weekdays from 08h30 to 17h30, and on Saturdays from 08h30 to 13h00.

WINES BOTTLED AND MARKETED

Red: Cabernet Sauvignon, Shiraz, Pinotage, Simonsrood and Pinot Noir.
White: Chardonnay, Blanc Fumé, Sauvignon Blanc, Cape Riesling, Blanc de Blanc, Premier Grand Crû, Rhine Riesling, Chenin Blanc, Blanc de Noir, Special Late Harvest, Late Vintage, Stein and Bukettraube.
Sparkling: Vin Sec and Vin Doux.
Fortified: Port, Humbro, Hanepoot, Red and White Muscadel.
A rosé is also made.

The co-operative is on the Paarl Wine Route and is open to the public on weekdays from 08h00 to 17h00, and on Saturdays from 08h30 to 17h00. Light meals are served in the cellar's wine garden on weekdays during the December school holidays.

— UNION WINE —
LIMITED

The Wellington-based firm of Union Wine Limited was established on the tenth of April 1946 in Graaff-Reinet by a group of farmers and businessmen headed by Mr J.C. van Rensburg. The first company on the platteland to be granted a listing on the Johannesburg Stock Exchange, it operated numerous outlets, both hotels and bottle stores. It soon developed into a flourishing concern and in 1956 the head office was moved from Graaff-Reinet to Oudtshoorn, its headquarters for the next 15 years.

In 1966 Robertson Distillers used their considerable shareholding in Oude Meester Cellars to take over control of Union Wine. Jan Pickard was made chairman. In 1967 the Germiston depot opened to serve the Witwatersrand and with the acquisition of Stag Breweries in mid-1968, a strong distribution network in the Transvaal was established.

A further acquisition was that of Culemborg Wineries (Pty) Limited of Wellington, which already marketed the well-known Bellingham range of wines, and on the first of January 1972 the head office of the greatly enlarged company was moved from Oudtshoorn to Wellington, to establish close ties and communication with the wine industry and the primary producers. In 1973 another company, Picardi Hotels Limited, was formed, to administer the retail operations. Union Wine purchased a further 75 retail licences during 1979, thereby increasing the total to 97.

Union Wine Limited became one of the bigger liquor-producing companies, with bottling plants and branches throughout the country, marketing products such as the Bellingham range of wines, Culemborg wines, Private Stock Brandy and Long John Whisky. The company was one of the few independents left in the industry.

In 1991, Union Wine was bought out by Graham Beck. He sold the retail interests of Picardi and then sold the half share of Union Wine production and distribution to Douglas Green, keeping the focus of Bellingham and La Garonne out of the deal. These properties will be developed separately and their products will be promoted with those of Madeba and distributed by Douglas Green Bellingham.

VILLIERA ESTATE

Simon Grier, the estate manager.

— VILLIERA —
ESTATE

Villiera's vineyards form the north-western extremity of the Koelenhof-Stellenbosch vine-growing area, though the estate is technically in the Paarl Wine of Origin area. The farm is 170 hectares in extent and has widely varying soil conditions, ranging from near dune consistency to chalky, pebbly loams. These soils form a layer one to three metres deep over a relatively impervious clay base. The mature vineyards have no difficulty in finding moisture at root level above this clay barrier, even during the most extreme drought. Careful study of these conditions

has permitted the planting of a wide range of varieties. The estate has now become very successful in the production of grapes from Cabernet Sauvignon, Merlot, Sauvignon Blanc, Rhine Riesling, Pinot Noir and Chardonnay.

The original cellar was built by the De Villiers family, from whom the estate took its name. At that time, the estate had not featured as a wine farm and at the time of purchase, there were no vineyards on the land. However, Josef Krammer (who had purchased the farm with Helmut Ratz) embarked on a vineyard planting programme which was later to be continued by the Grier family.

The Villiera wine-making project really started in 1983 when the Grier family purchased the estate. They chose the farm for its moderate fertility and exposed position, which makes it ideally suited, in vineyard terms, to producing small quantities of intensely flavoured grapes. The Griers had been introduced to the Denois family of the Champagne region in France, and were inspired to enter into an agreement with them for the production of sparkling wine made by the *méthode champenoise* process. For the Griers the meeting realized a long-nurtured dream to become owners of an estate winery and to specialize in the *méthode champenoise* process, culminating in the creation and subsequent success of the 'Tradition de Charles de Fère'. Their philosophy was that management and hands-on involvement were as important as *terroir*.

This French influence has also led to a better understanding of other wine-making techniques. It is not uncommon on Villiera for healthy vineyards to produce as little as 5 tonnes per hectare, or even less, even though most of the new vineyards are planted with a high density of vines. These influences work together to provide grapes with a high density of flavour at comparatively low sugar content.

Five family members are involved in the estate with Jeffrey as cellarmaster and Simon estate manager.

Vineyards in Wellington, an area also famous for its fruit.

—WAMAKERSVALLEI—
CO-OPERATIVE WINERY

Wamakersvallei was originally known as Limietvallei, at one time an outpost of the Cape settlement. With the arrival of the French in the area in 1688 the name changed to 'Val du Charron', later translated by the Dutch to 'Wamakersvallei', meaning 'wagon maker's valley'. Whether wagons were ever made here is uncertain, but there is no doubt that one of the first farms in the area belonged to a blacksmith, and it is not unlikely that he repaired wagons.

The Wamakersvallei Co-operative was formed by a number of discontented farmers, whose grape production was limited, as their main production was other types of fruit. They were not members of the long-established Bovlei or Wellington Co-operative and so delivered their grapes to the Sedgwick Wellington Distillery. Their discontent arose from the distillery's delayed handling of their produce – a delivery could take up an entire day.

In 1941 two farmers, by the names of Peterson and Jordaan, rallied together 45 others to form a co-operative winery and elected its first board of directors. A semi-constructed cellar was purchased and, once complete, it was ready to receive its first crop of approximately 2 000 tonnes in 1942.

Nowadays more than 11 000 tonnes of grapes, from 70 members, are pressed annually under the capable supervision of Chris Roux, who has been winemaker since 1975. The pressing cellar was totally rebuilt in 1991 to celebrate the co-operative's fiftieth anniversary. The bulk of wine is sold to the trade, only a small amount being retained for the members of the co-operative.

—WELLINGTON—
WYNBOERE CO-OPERATIVE

This is one of the original co-operatives, founded as it was in 1906, when the government of the time made available a considerable amount of money for the building of the winelands' first co-operative. Wellington Wynboere faced a number of problems in its early years, to the extent that it had to be re-established in 1934 by 12 local farmers. In more recent years its membership has increased from 37 to 52 growers.

The average tonnage crushed annually has increased from 10 000 to 11 500 tonnes. The varieties planted have also changed, with Chenin Blanc and Cinsaut having proved to be the growers' main choice. Pinotage has also been planted and the first crush of Cabernet Sauvignon was in 1987. More recently Merlot, Sauvignon Blanc and Chardonnay vineyards have been established. In the earlier years, the co-operative's entire production was sold to wholesale merchants, but a certain percentage is now available for sale to the public.

A blockhouse in Paarl dating back to the Anglo-Boer War.

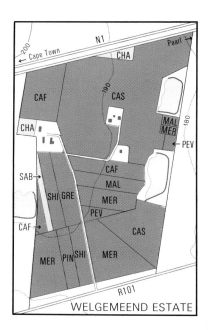

— WELGEMEEND —
ESTATE

On the site where the Jan van Riebeeck High School in Cape Town now stands was once situated the last working vineyard within the city's boundaries; its name was Welgemeend and it belonged to the Hofmeyr family. When the well-known wine connoisseur and writer W.A. (Billy) Hofmeyr finally realized a life-long ambition of buying a wine farm of his own – in the Paarl district – this was the name he gave it. Billy's daughter Louise, who has worked closely with him for four years, is now taking over the wine-making on the estate.

The farm at Klapmuts which he chose in 1974, then named Monte Video, soon showed the imprint of his personal taste. A passion-ate aficionado of the noble wines of Bor-deaux, he and his wife Ursula, who is both farm and cellar manager, set about reorgan-

izing the estate's vineyards according to the traditional plantings in certain wine-producing regions of France, the first of the South African estates to do so. To this end he replaced the straggly and neglected Mus-cat d'Alexandrie, Chenin Blanc and Cinsaut vines with Cabernet Sauvignon, Cabernet Franc, Merlot, Petit Verdot and Malbec, the varieties that more often than not are those blended to make the elegant clarets of Bordeaux. Pinotage began to be planted in 1971, with Shiraz and Grenache in 1976. Most of the Pinotage was replaced with Merlot in 1984, leaving only 800 vines.

Some of the vines on Welgemeend are not trellised and this, combined with soil type and no irrigation, produces a low yield by South African standards. But this is by de-sign, for Billy wants quality rather than quantity, and intends to limit his production to a very low six tonnes per hectare, as is the

---

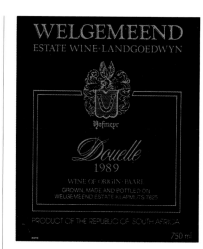

practice in Bordeaux. The present produc-tion of the estate is 5,5 tonnes per hectare, as some 15 per cent of the vines are not fully mature.

During the replanting of his vineyards Billy also devoted considerable energy and ingenuity to the task of putting together a wine-making cellar for his modest 16-hec-tare property. Equipment for the cellar came from a variety of sources, including a dump from which one item was rescued.

Some of his equipment may have been second-hand, but his enthusiasm was in mint condition. In 1979 it bore fruit in the first two wines produced on the estate, the one being the appropriately named 'Welge-meend' and the other Amadé. Welgemeend is a classic Bordeaux blend of Cabernet Sauvig-non, Merlot and Cabernet Franc. Amadé, akin to the Rhône wines, is a blend of Gre-nache, Shiraz and Pinotage, in the ratio of 5:4:1. Douelle, a blend of equal proportions of Malbec and Cabernet Sauvignon, first ap-peared in 1985, when the Malbec was removed from the Welgemeend Bordeaux blend. Cabernet Sauvignon has been pro-duced in the past and will be re-introduced in the future.

— WINDMEUL —
CO-OPERATIVE WINE CELLARS

During the 1880s there were some 27 mills in the Paarl area, but only one of them was a windmill, and it was situated at Agter-Paarl.

In 1927 the mill was demolished to a height of 3 metres, a roof was constructed over the circular base and the building was used as a farm store room. It still stands

---

Hein Koegelenberg & Bernard Luttich

today, and some of the old millstones can be found at the local primary school.

In 1944 a group of export table-grape farmers wanted to form a co-operative winery, in order to make use of those grapes not suitable for table use. They were unable to provide the minimum requirement of 1 500 tonnes needed to form a co-operative, and so several wine-grape growers were in-vited to join in their venture. On the fourth of September 1944 the Windmeul Co--operative was registered and its 23 members undertook to deliver 1 700 tonnes of grapes. In 1946 the first crop was pressed in the newly completed cellar.

In 1963 the composition of the board changed to predominantly wine farmers and the production was sold to wholesalers. The present winemaker, German-born Bernhard Lüttich, was appointed. Among the innova-tions he introduced were an automatic off-loading system, a modern crusher, and juice separators. A novel cooling system for the fer-mentation and settling tanks was also intro-duced, the only one of its kind in South Africa, designed jointly by Lüttich, the late Dieter Thielhelm of SFW and Günter Brözel, a director of Windmeul.

In 1988 the co-operative appointed Hein Koegelenberg as co-winemaker. In 1990 he was sent for further study at the Winzergenos-senschaft Breisach in Germany. In 1991 the co-operative installed two skin coolers to cool the skins and juice during the juice separation.

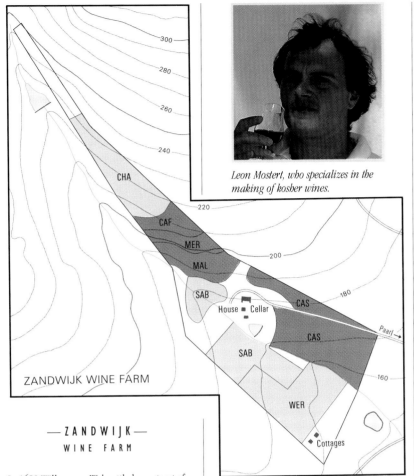

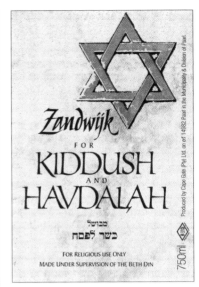

Leon Mostert, who specializes in the making of kosher wines.

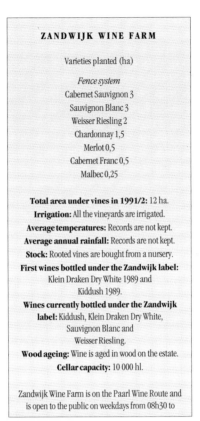

Zandwijk

FOR

KIDDUSH
AND
HAVDALAH

מבושל

כשר לפסח

FOR RELIGIOUS USE ONLY
MADE UNDER SUPERVISION OF THE BETH DIN

750ml

ZANDWIJK WINE FARM

Varieties planted (ha)

Fence system
Cabernet Sauvignon 3
Sauvignon Blanc 3
Weisser Riesling 2
Chardonnay 1,5
Merlot 0,5
Cabernet Franc 0,5
Malbec 0,25

Total area under vines in 1991/2: 12 ha.
Irrigation: All the vineyards are irrigated.
Average temperatures: Records are not kept.
Average annual rainfall: Records are not kept.
Stock: Rooted vines are bought from a nursery.
First wines bottled under the Zandwijk label:
Klein Draken Dry White 1989 and
Kiddush 1989.
**Wines currently bottled under the Zandwijk
label:** Kiddush, Klein Draken Dry White,
Sauvignon Blanc and
Weisser Riesling.
Wood ageing: Wine is aged in wood on the estate.
Cellar capacity: 10 000 hl.

Zandwijk Wine Farm is on the Paarl Wine Route and
is open to the public on weekdays from 08h30 to

— ZANDWIJK —
WINE FARM

In 1689 Willem van Wyk settled on a tract of land on the slopes of Paarl Mountain. As a farmer, Van Wyk was a dismal failure and it was only in 1742, when the farm was sold to Jacobus Bosman, that Zandwijk was to come into its own. Bosman died in 1782, leaving his wife and five daughters a well-developed wine farm.

By the time a group of Johannesburg businessmen, collectively known as Cape Gate, acquired Zandwijk in 1983 it had changed hands 22 times and was once again in disrepair, producing only table grapes and plums. What was needed was a reputable winemaker to re-establish the vineyards and the wine cellar. Nathan Friedman of Cape Gate approached Leon Mostert, at the time an assistant winemaker, and, impressed by his forthrightness and determination, offered him the position at Zandwijk. They set about restoring the mid-eighteenth century homestead, and today the visitor will find the Zandwijk farmhouse not dissimilar to the original residence as it was in 1785.

Having cleared the grounds, planted the vineyards, and built a new wine cellar incor-

porating the most recent technology, Leon Mostert made a trip to Israel for an intensive course on the making of kosher wines. Creating a distinctive wine within the restrictive kosher laws is a challenge: all operations must be supervised by the Beth Din, in some cases the winemaker may not deal with the wine on a 'hands on' basis and it is essential that only additives from kosher origins are used. The cellar is closed on the Sabbath and tours are conducted by appointment. Although these constraints are daunting,

Leon has done a remarkable job of integrating his expertise in the creation of non-kosher wines with his newly gained knowledge of those that are kosher.

The mid-eighteenth century homestead at Zandwijk.

FRANSCHHOEK

The Franschhoek ward is a relatively small area, but one with a marked character and tradition of its own. In the two-year period between 1688 and 1690, some 200 Protestant Huguenot immigrants fleeing from Catholic persecution in France arrived at the Cape. They were mainly settled by the governor of the time, Simon van der Stel, at the upper end of the Drakenstein valley, an enclave to which they first gave the name *Le Quartier Français* (the French Quarter), subsequently known as *Franschhoek* (French Corner). Here they introduced their skills of wine-growing to the local free burgher population. Becoming socially and culturally integrated within a few generations, they established farms, many of which are still worked by their descendants. The legacy of their names survives – Fouché, De Villiers, Du Plessis, Joubert, Rousseau, Nortier, Malherbe, Fourie, Vivier, Roux and Du Toit (literally 'of the roof': the thatcher) to name only a few – even if with altered pronunciation. The names of their farms – L'Ormarins, La Provence, La Bourgogne and many others – are a nostalgic memory of the distant French countryside. To commemorate the first Huguenot settlement at the Cape, a monument symbolizing the freedom of religious belief was inaugurated in 1948. Situated at the top of Huguenot Road, it has since become a landmark of the region.

The general topography of the Franschhoek Valley resembles that of Paarl, though the average rainfall here is higher, at an annual 900 millimetres. The climatic and soil conditions vary considerably from one farm to another, and this, together with the differing geographical location of the vineyards (some riverside and some hillside), results in an unusually wide range of wines. Nevertheless, viticulture in Franschhoek has not been without its hardships; in 1885, the vineyards were devastated by an outbreak of phylloxera. Accustomed to adversity, the farmers merely replaced some of the vines with fruit trees, and Franschhoek thereafter became renowned for its fruit.

Today, Franschhoek is once again a wine-growing area of note, principally due to an enthusiastic group of winemakers who initiated the *Vignerons de Franschhoek* in 1984. The primary objectives established by their honorary president, Dr Anton Rupert, were: to promote the growing and enjoyment of quality wine, to uphold as high a standard as possible, and to follow the French wine-growing tradition of helping the needy of the valley. These admirable goals have been attained, and wines from Franschhoek are respected and enjoyed both locally and internationally.

LEFT: *Seen from the air, the Huguenot Memorial is a landmark of the Franschhoek region.*

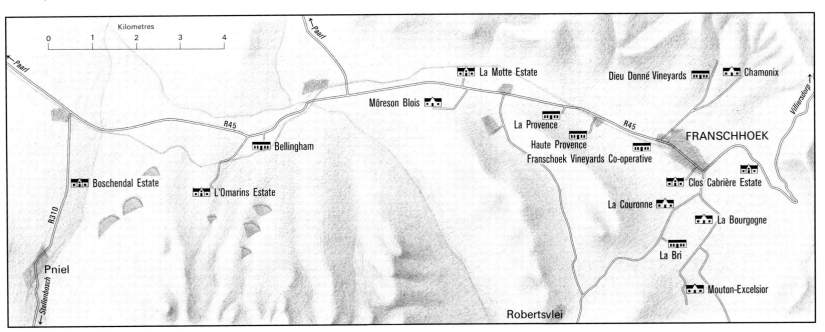

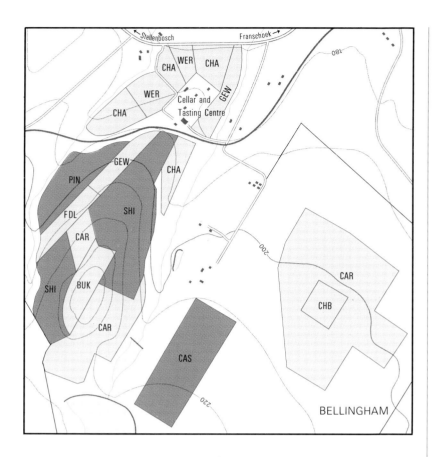

The entrance to Bellingham at the foot of the Groot Drakenstein Mountains.

─ BELLINGHAM ─

The original grant for this 37-hectare farm in the Groot Drakenstein district was made to Gerritt Jansz van Vuuren in October 1693. During the late nineteenth century the estate was expanded, but by the Depression years of the 1930s it had declined into a near derelict condition. It was in this state that it was purchased by Bernard and Fredagh Podlashuk in 1943. Invalided out of the South African Air Force, Bernard had come to the Cape with a vague but powerful desire to become a farmer.

The raw material of Bellingham – the name is surmised to be a corruption of the French *Bellinchamp*, or 'beautiful fields' – was unpromising in the extreme, nor did Podlashuk have any professional training for his chosen occupation, but he was a man of determination and ingenuity. He was supported, too, by a wife who fully shared his aspirations. In the post-war years they began an extensive overhaul and re-creation of the Bellingham farm and its beautiful though somewhat Victorianized homestead. He replanted the farm's decayed vineyards with new, high-quality varieties, cheerfully mort-

gaging himself to the hilt in the process. To provide himself with the necessary technical and theoretical background to his work he made extensive visits to the French winelands, penetrating with his enthusiasm and charisma their winemakers' reserve to gather advice and insights for the kind of wines he planned to make, especially the fine dry white wines which appealed to his taste but which at that time had little influence on the local South African palate.

Within a few years, in their characteristically designed Bellingham flask, the first of Podlashuk's wines, his Johannisberger, Shiraz and Premier Grand Crû, began to appear. This last in particular was to make the Bellingham name, opening

The winemaker, Charles Hopkins.

up a new wine category in the local market. Although the number of cellars making this type of wine has increased rapidly in recent years, the Bellingham Premier Grand Crû remained alone in its field for two decades. Bellingham wines were exported and served on the great liners sailing between Cape Town and Southampton.

Bellingham draws grapes for the making of its blends from a number of sources in the Groot Drakenstein and Franschhoek areas, and for this reason is not classified as an estate. During 1970 Union Wine Limited bought the farm. A new cellar was built and in 1985 Jan Pickard opened the new tasting centre, where visitors to Bellingham can be received and entertained. The Bellingham railway siding has become a feature on the farm, with groups of visitors to the winery arriving by steam train from Cape Town. Bellingham was one of the founder members of the *Vignerons de Franschhoek* wine route, established as a tribute to the French Huguenots who settled in the valley of Franschhoek more than three centuries ago.

Painstaking attention to detail and quality provides Bellingham wines with constant high standards . While perpetuating the traditional Bellingham wines the new winemaker, Charles Hopkins, has also initiated Bellingham's first Chardonnay, a Sauvignon Blanc, and a new sparkling wine. Bellingham has also expanded its frontiers and currently exports wines to Europe, the Far East, and elsewhere in Africa.

Since July 1990 Bellingham has been the property of Graham Beck of Kangra Holdings, who merged his wine and spirit inter-

ests with that of Sol Kerzner's Kersaf in 1991 to form Douglas Green Bellingham.

BELLINGHAM

Varieties planted (ha)

4-wire vertical trellis
Cape Riesling 45
Shiraz 20
Cabernet Sauvignon 11
Chardonnay 9
Weisser Riesling 7
Pinotage 7
Bukettraube 6
Gewürztraminer 5
Ferdinand de Lesseps 3,5
Chenin Blanc 3,5

Total area under vines in 1991/2: 117 ha.
Irrigation: The vineyards are irrigated.
Average temperatures:
Maximum 23 °C; minimum 11 °C.
Average annual rainfall: Approximately 1 300 mm.
Stock: Rooted vines are bought from a nursery.
First wines bottled under the Bellingham label:
Riesling 1950, Premier Grand Crû 1951, Rosé 1951, Johannisberger 1957 and Shiraz 1957.
Wines currently bottled under the Bellingham label: Almeida Rosé, Paarl Riesling, Noble Late Harvest, Chardonnay, Cabernet Sauvignon, Classic Thirteen, Blanc Fumé, Johannisberger, Pinotage, Premier Grand Crû, Rosé Sec, Shiraz, Special Late Harvest, Blancenberger, and Brut, Vintage Rosé Brut and Gold sparkling wines (all Bellingham wines are bottled by DGB Wellington).
Wood ageing: Wines are aged in wood.
Cellar capacity: 21 000 hl.

Bellingham is on the Franschhoek Wine Route and is open to the public from the beginning of December to the end of April on weekdays for conducted wine-tastings at 09h30, 10h30, 14h30 and 15h30. There is a wine-tasting on Saturdays at 10h30 by appointment only.

─ BOSCHENDAL ─
ESTATE

Granted in 1685 and originally named 'Bossendaal' by its first owner, a Huguenot immigrant named Jean le Long, this farm was sold in 1715 to another Huguenot, Abraham de Villiers, in whose family it was to remain for the next 160 years. He was one of three brothers who had arrived in 1689 bearing a letter from the Lords XVII, the board of directors of the Dutch East India Company in Amsterdam, to the governor of the Cape, Simon van der Stel, recommending the brothers for their knowledge of viticulture.

It was a knowledge which was to find full expression in the coming decades in the beautiful valley of Groot Drakenstein, with its wide flow of land and soaring mountains. Through the eighteenth century the generations of the De Villiers family built up one of the finest farm complexes of its kind in the area, completed in 1812 with the Cape Flemish-style manor house built for Anna Susanna Louw, the wife of the then owner, Paul de Villiers.

The sumptuous style of those early days of affluence crumbled during the nineteenth century before the increasing economic difficulties which affected the wine-farming world of the Cape, and in 1879 the last of the De Villiers family was forced to sell his home. (A scion of the family, Paul de Villiers, bought the Paarlberg farm of Landskroon in the same period, however, thus keeping alive the De Villiers' wine-making tradition to the present.)

Like Groot Constantia, Boschendal passed out of family ownership, and within a few years of the sale the farm was acquired as one of the Rhodes Fruit Farms, the 30-odd farms in the district which were brought together in a project by Cecil John Rhodes. His intention was to provide the farmers of

Hilko Hegewisch in the cellar.

The beautifully restored Boschendal Manor House in the Groot Drakenstein valley.

the region with alternative crops to the devastated vines which they were forced to destroy by the million in the wake of the phylloxera epidemic. An export fruit trade to Britain, Rhodes argued, would provide a more secure market than that of the vulnerable grapes. Moreover, the recent introduction of refrigeration on cargo ships made the move practically feasible. An alternative view, suggested by Harry Pickstone, Rhodes's fruit-growing expert, was that the scheme might have been motivated by Rhodes's need to re-establish himself in the eyes of the farmers after the *débâcle* of the Jameson Raid, but whatever the motive, altruistic or otherwise — and Rhodes was an inherently secretive per-

sonality — he invested large amounts of his fortune in the purchase of these farms.

Rhodes died in 1902, and in the coming decades his dreams of extended Empire were to fade. His modest fruit farm scheme, however, has survived, given a new lease of life in recent years by its take-over in 1969 by the Anglo American Corporation, which has assumed management of the Rhodes Fruit Farms, and restored both the farms and their old homesteads. The restoration of the buildings at Boschendal was undertaken by the architect Gabriel Fagan. The complex as it stands today consists of the Manor House itself, the *Waenhuis* (now a gift shop), the - *Taphuis*, one of the oldest buildings on the

estate, and the modern winery. The Manor House, meticulously restored to reflect the transitional period in local taste from Dutch to English influence at the turn of the nineteenth century, has among its treasures a fine collection of Ming porcelain – dubbed *Kraakporselein* by the Dutch since they first encountered it in the hold of a captured Portuguese carrack, or *kraak*.

The present winery was originally the cellar for the Rhône Manor House which dates back to 1795, and has been declared a national monument. In 1977 the cellar was modernized and has since kept abreast of technological advancements. The pressing capacity of the winery is now sufficient to cope with the estate's full grape quota, taking in an average of 120 tonnes per day during the harvest season. A mash cooler has been installed which reduces the temperature of the grapes to 5 °C within minutes.

The vineyards comprise 425 hectares and geographically extend for 14 kilometres from the banks of the Berg River in the Franschhoek Valley to the lower slopes of the Simonsberg. The soils comprise loamy-stone Clovelly types near the river, a variety of Shortland, loam, and clay. The highest parts of the estate have red loam-clay Hutton soil types. The geographical range of the vineyards results in grapes that ripen in the valley at 19 or 20 °Balling, while those higher up are ideally ripe at 22 or 23 °Balling.

Developments in the wine-making side of the estate have been successful; the structure of the vineyards was extensively revised, with new varieties carefully matched to soil and conditions on the farm. The vineyards were established by and are now managed by Herman Hanekom, while the wines were the province of Achim von Arnim until November 1988, when he was appointed director of the Boschendal and Vergelegen Estate wines and his assistant, Hilko Hegewisch, became cellarmaster. A graduate of Elsenburg, Hilko has travelled extensively in Europe, studying at the Weinsberg College in Germany and also gaining experience in France and Italy.

In 1980 Boschendal was the first winery to produce Blanc de Noir, a white wine made from red grapes. In 1985 a Grand Vin Blanc was produced to celebrate a 300-year-old tradition of fine wine-growing — an early example of small wood being used for both fermentation and maturation.

BOSCHENDAL ESTATE

Varieties planted (ha)

Extended Perold trellis
Chardonnay 75
Cape Riesling 65
Cabernet Sauvignon 45
Sauvignon Blanc 45
Merlot 34
Weisser Riesling 34
Chenin Blanc 29
Pinot Noir 25
Pinotage 16
Mixed Muscats 14
Gewürztraminer 13
Shiraz 12
Sémillon 8
Pinot Gris 6
Tinta Barocca 4

Total area under vines in 1991/2: 425 ha.
Irrigation: Only if necessary.
Average temperatures:
Maximum 21,8 °C; minimum 12,6 °C.
Average annual rainfall: 1 500 mm.
Stock: Parent stock is used for grafting; rooted vines are bought from a nursery.
First wines bottled under the Boschendal label: Chenin Blanc 1976, Steen 1976, Blanc de Blanc 1978, Riesling 1978, Vintage Steen 1978, Bouquet des Fleurs 1978, Le Mirador 1979, Le Pavillon 1979 and Vin d'Or 1979.
Wines currently bottled under the Boschendal label: Blanc de Blanc, Blanc de Noir, Brut, Cabernet Sauvignon, Chenin Blanc, Grand Vin Blanc, Lanoy, Le Bouquet, Riesling, Gewürztraminer, Rhine Riesling, Chardonnay, Sauvignon Blanc, Pavilion Blanc, Vin d'Or, Blanc de Blanc Méthode Champenoise and Grand Vin.
Wood ageing: Wines are aged in wood on the estate.
Cellar capacity: 2 000-3 000 tonnes of grapes.

Boschendal Estate is on the Franschhoek Wine Route and is open to the public on weekdays from 08h30 to 17h00, and on Saturdays from 08h30 to 12h30. There is an audio-visual presentation on weekdays at 11h00 and 15h00, or upon request.

Boschendal's limited but distinctively styled red wines are set to assume a higher profile in about 1996 when the 40 hectares of newly planted Cabernet Sauvignon, Merlot, Cabernet Franc and Pinot Noir vines will come into mature bearing to hopefully produce some fine varietal and Bordeaux-style additions to its range.

Among the many other innovations introduced by the Anglo American Group, both at Boschendal and at other farms belonging to Rhodes Fruit Farms, have been improved conditions of employment, amenities and health services for their staff. The housing

scheme for workers on the estate is a model of its kind. Attractions for the visitor include the restored Boschendal Manor House, the restaurant housed in the original farm cellar, the Waenhuiswinkel and 'Le Pique-Nique', a lunch hamper available in Boschendal's spacious gardens between November and April.

— CHAMONIX —

The farm Waterval, now called Chamonix, was originally part of La Cotte, one of the first farms granted to the French Huguenots in 1688. One of the largest farms in the Franschhoek Valley, it was fairly undeveloped for many years. This is probably due to the hilly topography, as Chamonix, which covers 270 hectares, has some of the highest vineyards in the Cape. In 1947 Judge Malan bought the farm, built the main homestead and began developing the land. After his death, the farm was bought by the Pickering family in 1965, and they continued to develop it on the excellent infrastructure created by its former owner.

Although Chamonix is planted mainly to fruit and timber, the cool south-eastern slopes are ideal for the growing of grapes. The vineyards comprise some 33 per cent of the cultivated area, and the varieties planted are Clairette Blanche, Chenin Blanc, Cabernet Sauvignon, Weisser Riesling, Pinotage and Chardonnay. Pinot Noir is planned for the future. The deep, cool Hutton soil, the wide range of mesoclimates and the prevailing south-easterly breezes allow for a lengthy ripening period, and the grapes of Chamonix are the last to be harvested in the area.

In 1983 the Franschhoek Vineyards Cooperative agreed to keep the grapes of Chamonix and of Michael Trull's farm, La Bri, separate from those of all the other members of the co-operative, thereby ensuring that Wines of Origin would be made from them. In this way the grape farmer can avoid the

expense of providing his own cellar, and have his wine made by an expert winemaker at the co-operative. Several different Wines of Origin are now made under one roof at the Franschhoek Vineyards Co-operative and then sent back to their farms of origin, from where they are sold.

Towards the end of 1983 Chamonix marketed its first wines, a Vin Blanc and a Blanc de Rouge. In 1985 a Rhine Riesling was added to the range, and the name Blanc de Rouge was changed to Blanc de Noir due to an objection by the Wine and Spirit Board. The first two Chamonix wines submitted to the *Vignerons de Franschhoek* received the *Vignerons Controlée* seal.

In 1986 Robbie de Villiers of Janice Ashby Design Partnership designed a new range of labels, to reflect the contemporary orientation of Chamonix wines. These labels won a Loerie Award and were nominated for the International Cleo award in New York. The entire range is bottled in claret bottles to increase recognition among consumers.

CHAMONIX

Varieties planted (ha)

Perold trellis
Clairette Blanche 5,4
Chardonnay 5,2
Vertical trellis
Cabernet Sauvignon 4,2
Weisser Riesling 3,8
Pinotage 1,6
Perold and vertical trellis
Chenin Blanc 9,0

Total area under vines in 1991/2:
30 ha (14 ha still to be planted).
Irrigation: None.
Average temperatures: Records are not kept.
Average annual rainfall: Approximately 900 mm.
Stock: Rooted vines are bought from a nursery.
First wines bottled under the Chamonix label: Vin Blanc and Blanc de Rouge (both 1983).
Wines currently bottled under the Chamonix label: Bouquet Blanc, Rhine Riesling, Blanc de Noir, Cabernet Sauvignon, Courchevel Cuvée Brut and Courchevel Demi-Sec (bottled by the Stellenbosse Botteleringskoöperasie Beperk).
Wood ageing: Wines are aged in wood at the Franschhoek Vineyards Co-operative.
Cellar capacity: The wines are made at the Franschhoek Vineyards Co-operative.

Chamonix is on the Franschhoek Wine Route and is open to the public by appointment only. Wine tasting and sales are at the Franschhoek Wine Centre.

— CLOS CABRIÈRE —
ESTATE

The first estate in South Africa to specialize solely in *méthode champenoise* wines, Clos Cabrière is now owned by the well-known director of Boschendal and Vergelegen, Achim von Arnim. In 1694 the farm at Olifantshoek, so called because elephants had been encountered there, was granted to Pierre Jourdan, a Huguenot settler. He named his farm Cabrière, after the French village of his birth, Cabrière-d'Aigues.

The initial 17 hectares of the farm (known as Cabrière) have been expanded by the purchase of a further 20 hectares on the western slopes of the valley in 1989, the site now known as Haute Cabrière. The vines on both Cabrière and Haute Cabrière — together being the estate of Clos Cabrière — are under the care and management (Achim likes to think guardianship) of Deon Carstens. On Haute Cabrière, Achim and Deon are determined to challenge Burgundy with its most demanding variety, Pinot Noir. For this purpose they have chosen the best site, soil and clones, and intend using each part of the vineyard for what it is best suited — the Burgundian notion of expressing the *terroir*, allowing the vine to interpret fully the nuances of soil and climate.

This fundamental wine-growing philosophy of Achim's is embodied in a pillar in the vineyards with a weather-beaten sundial depicting on its four sides the Sun, Soil, Vine and Man. As integral as each element is to the creation of a good wine, no single aspect is solely responsible. 'A wine is born', says Achim, 'and not made', and this can only ensue from a perfect harmony and balance between the four factors, each relinquishing their autonomy to become an intrinsic part of the eventual wine.

Subsequent to this philosophy, Achim decided to specialize in the style of wine best suited to the situation and soils on the estate. This is sparkling wine produced in the true *méthode champenoise*, 'a civilized drink designed from the soil upwards'.

Achim uses only the classic champagne varieties to create his wine, namely Chardonnay and Pinot Noir. Chardonnay has been planted in the alluvial river soils, and more Chardonnay and Pinot Noir in the gravelly and clayey soils on the slope on the side of

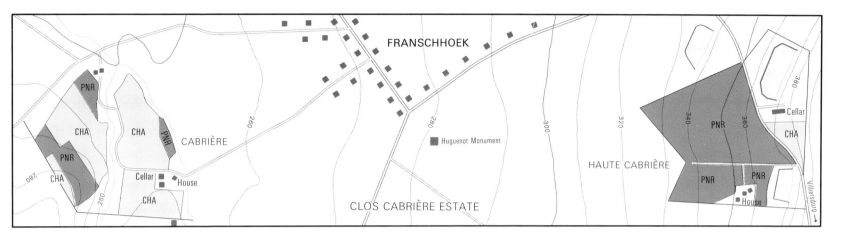

the Franschhoek River opposite to the farm buildings.

In addition, on the advice of viticulturist Dr. Eben Archer, Achim and Deon are challenging traditional viticultural practices with a very high vine population of 10 000 vines per hectare, compared with the norm of about 5 000 vines per hectare. This venture is especially exciting for Dr Archer as he can watch the theory of his doctoral thesis in plant population growing into a reality.

CLOS CABRIÈRE ESTATE

Varieties planted (ha)

Cabrière Cordon trellis
Chardonnay 8 ha
Pinot Noir 3,6 ha
Haute Cabrière Cordon Trellis
Pinot Noir 10,2 ha
Chardonnay 1 ha

Total area under vines in 1991/2: 22,8 ha (3 ha still to be planted).
Irrigation: Supplementary irrigation only.
Average temperatures: (A weather station has been installed with a data chip for accurate reading of weather conditions.)
Average annual rainfall: 1 561 mm.
Stock: Clonal material grafted by nursery and KWV motherblock system of Burgundian clones.
First wine bottled by the Clos Cabrière Estate: Pierre Jourdan 1984.
Wines currently bottled by the Clos Cabrière Estate: Pierre Jourdan Cuvée Brut, Cuvée Brut Sauvage, Cuvée Reserve, Blanc de Blanc, Cuvée Belle Rose.
Wood ageing: The Blanc de Blanc is fermented and matured in *pièces champenoises*.
Cellar capacity: 1 200 hl.

Clos Cabrière Estate is on the Franschhoek Wine Route and is open to the public by appointment only.

A modern cellar has been installed in the picturesque old outbuildings without spoiling their outward appearance. The first release from the cellar came from the 1984 vintage. Although this was not the first sparkling wine made in South Africa by the *méthode champenoise*, it was the first made in this traditional manner to contain the classic Champagne varieties. Subsequent releases have been internationally acclaimed. Clos Cabrière is also the first estate to produce its own estate brandy. In 1990 for the first time the *deuxième taille* or second pressing was distilled in a traditional pot still into a *fine*, as is the cultural practice in Champagne. This distillate, to be called Fine de Jourdan, will be matured in Limosin oak for three years before release is considered.

Achim von Arnim of Clos Cabrière.

Intrinsic to Clos Cabrière is the sense of affinity, not only between Sun, Soil, Vine, and Man, but also between the past, present, and future. The name Pierre Jourdan has been perpetuated along with the name of his home village so many miles away. The names of other Huguenots who settled in the Franschhoek valley will also not be forgotten, their signatures now in evidence on the wine labels. Even the memory of the Olifantshoek elephants has been maintained, having become somewhat of a motif on the estate in the form of a myriad collection of carvings and pictures. The sense that progression and constancy coexist is ultimately embodied in a recent replacement of much of the exotic vegetation on the banks of the Franschhoek River with indigenous yellowwood and white stinkwood. These new trees will grow up together with the seasoned oaks which have become so much a part of the Cape, thereby conserving the old while at the same time encouraging the new.

— DIEU DONNÉ — VINEYARDS

The two farms Dieu Donné and De Lucque lie within the municipal area of Franschhoek, and are owned and run as one venture by Robert Maingard. Unlike so many of the other wine farms in the Franschhoek valley, this winery does not have its wines made at the local co-operative, but produces them on its own property. The winery consists of four buildings against the north-eastern slopes of the Franschhoek mountains, where the winemaker François Malherbe makes wine with a slight French manner and style. The four

DIEU DONNÉ VINEYARDS

Varieties planted (ha)

Vertical trellis
Cabernet Sauvignon 7
Chardonnay 4,3
Chenin Blanc 1,2
Merlot 1,2
Sauvignon Blanc 1,2
Weisser Riesling 1,2

Total area under vines in 1991/2: 16,1 ha.
Irrigation: Only young vines are under irrigation.
Average temperatures: Records are not kept.
Average annual rainfall: 1 280 mm.
First wines bottled by the Dieu Donné and De Lucque Vineyards: Chiara de Lucque and Fait de Foi (both 1986 vintage).
Wines currently bottled by the Dieu Donné and De Lucque Vineyards: Cabernet Sauvignon, Sauvignon Blanc, Grand Cuvée, 60/40, St Dominique and Rhine Riesling.
Wood ageing: Wine is aged in wood on the farms.
Cellar capacity: 1 900 hl.

Dieu Donné Vineyards are on the Franschhoek Wine Route and are open to the public for wine sales and tastings during normal hours. Cellar tours are by appointment only.

Winemaker François Malherbe, of Dieu Donné Vineyards.

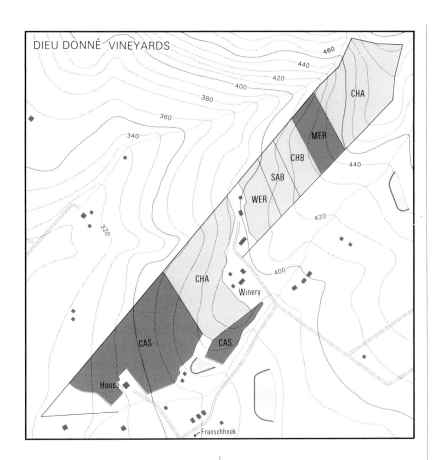

DIEU DONNÉ VINEYARDS

winery buildings have been carefully designed to blend in with the atmosphere of
the Franschhoek valley, and were modelled
on some 200-year-old buildings in the Cape
Flemish style. The five-gabled Cape Dutch
homestead has also been restored.

Six varieties are grown on the farms and
from these the wines are made. Only small
quantities of these wines are produced.

In 1988 the farm was replanted in some
areas to rationalize production. Mark Tanner, the wine manager, visited France in
1991 to establish contact with the proprietors
of Château de Montmirail, and this has
brought Dieu Donné in direct contact with
the ideas, technology and wine-making philosophy of the southern Rhône Valley.

FRANSCHHOEK
VINEYARDS CO-OPERATIVE

The Franschhoek Vineyards Co-operative was
founded in 1945, and its winery was built in
a commanding position at the head of the
beautiful and historic Franschhoek valley on
La Cotte, one of the original Huguenot
farms. Its first winemaster was an immigrant from Italy, Alberto Agostini, who developed the winery, which receives its grapes
from most of the farmers in the valley, and
experimented with new cellar methods. In
particular, he worked on the problems of
controlling fermentation in the heat of summer (this, of course, was before the advent of
cold fermentation). One method he devised
involved adding sulphur to the must to halt
the fermentation during the summer, and
then desulphuring it again in winter when
the cool temperatures would permit a slower
fermentation rate.

On his death in 1969, Agostini's place was
taken by Johan Theron. Son of a Tulbagh
wine farmer and a graduate in viticulture
and oenology from the University of Stellenbosch, he guided the fortunes of the co--
operative for 18 years. On his departure in

1984 his assistant, Deon Truter, who has a
diploma in cellar technology from Elsenburg
Agricultural College, took over as winemaker. Deon, too, has wine-making in his
blood, as his father, Bennie Truter, was also
a winemaker. He has been assisted by Driaan
van der Merwe since 1984 and between them
they have further developed and refined the
wines characteristic of this area with its high
winter rainfall and relatively mild summers,
which favour the making of light, dry and
semi-sweet wines such as Sémillon and
Chenin Blanc.

Deon has been fundamental in the successful development of the scheme – unique,
so far, to Franschhoek – whereby certain
members of the co-operative request that
their grapes be kept distinct from the bulk of
the members' contributions. Wine is then
made from these batches of grapes and bottled separately as well, so that the individual
members of the scheme can market their
own wines from their premises. In this way
relatively small farmers, and in some cases
relatively inexperienced ones, enjoy the benefits of a well-equipped cellar and the invaluable expertise of Deon and Driaan, and still
have the satisfaction and pride of marketing
their own wines.

The Franschhoek Vineyards Co-operative
annually receives approximately 8 000
tonnes of grapes from its 123 members.
About 2 per cent of the total is selected to be
bottled under the La Cotte label, a further
small percentage goes back to the six mem-

bers who have their wines made separately in
terms of the scheme previously mentioned,
and the rest is made into wines which are
sold to the large wholesalers.

HAUTE PROVENCE

Haute Provence is a portion of the original
farm La Provence, granted to the Huguenot
Pierre Joubert in 1694 by Governor Simon
van der Stel. The farm, once owned by well-
known wine writer John Platter, is now
owned by another journalist, Peter Younghusband, who is leaving behind his career as
an award-winning foreign correspondent to
become a full-time wine farmer.

Peter has replaced all remaining orchards
on the farm with vineyards, and Haute

WINES MADE AND BOTTLED

Red: Franschhoek Claret and La Cotte Cabernet.
White: La Cotte Sauvignon Blanc, Franschhoek Cape
Riesling, Franschhoek Premier Grand Crû,
La Cotte Sémillon, La Cotte Pinotage Blanc de Noir,
La Cotte Chenin Blanc and Franschhoek Sémillon.
Sparkling: Medium Sweet and
Sauvignon Blanc Brut.
Fortified: Port and Sweet Hanepoot.

The co-operative is on the Franschhoek Wine
Route and is open to the public on weekdays from
08h30 to 13h00 and from 14h00 to 17h30
(from May to September to 17h00), and on
Saturdays from 09h00 to 13h00. Cellar tours are
conducted by prior arrangement only.

The entrance to the Franschhoek Vineyards Co-operative, founded in 1945.

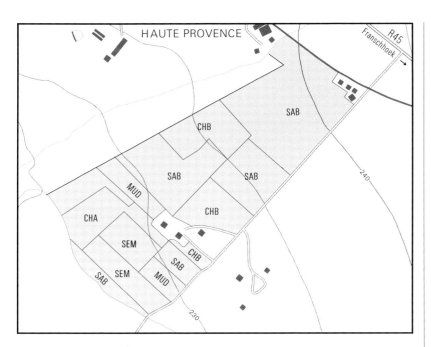

HAUTE PROVENCE

Provence is now devoted entirely to wine production, mainly dry whites. Five varieties are grown, namely Sauvignon Blanc, Chenin Blanc, Chardonnay, Sémillon and Muscat d'Alexandrie.

HAUTE PROVENCE

Varieties planted (number of vines)

Perold trellis
Sauvignon Blanc 33 000
Chenin Blanc 7 500
Chardonnay 6 500
Muscat d'Alexandrie 2 500
Bush vines
Sémillon 19 000

Total area under vines in 1991/2: 13 ha.
Irrigation: The vineyards are irrigated.
Average temperatures: Records are not kept.
Average annual rainfall: Approximately 1 080 mm.
Stock: Rooted vines are bought from a nursery.
First wines bottled under the Haute Provence label: Grand Vin H4 Series, Grand Vin H5 Series and Grand Vin Doux.
Wines currently bottled under the Haute Provence label: Grand Vin, Larmes des Anges, Blanc Fumé, Chardonnay, Blanc Royale and Brut.
Wood ageing: Wines are aged in wood at the Franschhoek Vineyards Co-operative.
Cellar capacity: The wines are made at the Franschhoek Vineyards Co-operative.

Haute Provence is on the Franschhoek Wine Route and is open to the public from 10h00 to 12h00 and 14h00 to 16h00 on weekdays and on Saturdays from 09h30 to 12h00.

Haute Provence's two best-selling wines are its Grand Vin – a blend of Sauvignon Blanc and Sémillon, – and its Blanc Fumé, a wooded Sauvignon Blanc aged in small French oak casks. There is also a Larmes des Anges (Angel's Tears), a semi-sweet wine (a blend of Chenin Blanc and Muscat d'Alexandrie) with a back label which carries a charming tribute to the origin of the name.

Peter Younghusband.

Younghusband, the first owner to introduce wooded wines to Haute Provence's range, went on to produce another dry table wine, Blanc Royale, a wooded blend of Sémillon and Sauvignon Blanc. A dry sparkling wine is also produced. At present all Haute Provence's wines are made at the Franschhoek Vineyards Co-operative, but Younghusband has begun designs for his own cellar for vinification on the farm.

— LA BOURGOGNE —

La Bourgogne is situated on land first cultivated by the Huguenots when they came to Franschhoek in 1688. Located at the southeastern end of the valley, the 13,3-hectare farm is protected by hills on three sides. The climate and soil conditions are ideal for the production of the fine Sémillon and Muscat d'Alexandrie for which the district of Franschhoek is renowned.

Grapes have been grown on La Bourgogne for many years but it was only when Sonny and Michael Gillis bought the farm in 1990 that it was decided to produce wine. Their wine is called Joie de Vivre, meaning the Joy of Life. The name epitomises the pleasure they experience from their participation in the wine-making process, spanning the cultivation of the grapes to the production of the wine.

The first Joie de Vivre, produced in 1991, was a dry, single-variety Sémillon with a distinctive bouquet and a good sugar/acid balance. The limited production of 750 cases

LA BOURGOGNE

Varieties planted (number of vines)

Perold trellis
Sémillon 5 328
Muscat d'Alexandrie 1 090
Chardonnay 461
Untrellised
Sémillon 4 998

Total area under vines in 1991/2: 2,7 ha.
Irrigation: The young vines are irrigated by moveable metal pipes.
Average temperatures: Maximum 23 °C; minimum 16 °C.
Average annual rainfall: 1 000 mm.
Stock: Rooted vines are bought from a nursery.
First wine bottled under the Joie de Vivre label: Joie de Vivre Sémillon 1991.
Wood ageing: Information not available.
Cellar capacity: The wines are made at the Franschhoek Vineyards Co-operative.

La Bourgogne is on the Franschhoek Wine Route and is open to the public by appointment only.

proved so popular, both in the South African and overseas markets, that demand exceeded supply. Future plans include a wooded Sémillon and a blend of Muscat and Sémillon for which vines have already been planted.

— LA BRI —
VINEYARDS

La Bri Vineyards, owned by Michael and Cheryl Trull, date from 1694 when Huguenot Jacques de Villiers was granted the farm by Governor Simon van der Stel. La Bri is situated at the eastern end of the beautiful Franschhoek valley and has an historic H-shaped homestead and a centuries-old sales and tasting cellar in a setting of unparalleled beauty.

La Bri's unique combination of altitude (more than 300 metres above sea level) together with a rainfall that exceeds the Cape average, and its central position in the valley with the best soils, results in wines which tend to be more complex, fruitier and European in style than is the norm. The vineyards' top-selling wine is the Sauvignon Blanc – Sauvage de La Bri – which has a grassy style reminiscent of Sancerre and New Zealand Sauvignon Blancs. This wine won a commendation in the *Wine Magazine* International Challenge for two years running.

Rows of vineyards at La Bri at the upper end of the Franschhoek valley.

LA BRI VINEYARDS

Varieties planted (ha)

Extended Perold trellis
Sauvignon Blanc 13
Cabernet Sauvignon 3,5
Weisser Riesling 3,5
Chardonnay 1,5
Merlot 1
Bush vines
Sémillon 1,5

Total area under vines in 1991/2: 24 ha.
Irrigation: None.
Average temperatures: Records are not kept, but temperatures are lower than in most of the Cape.
Average annual rainfall: 1 300 mm.
Stock: Parent stock is used for grafting; rooted vines are bought from a nursery.
First wine bottled under the La Bri label: Blanc de La Bri 1983.
Wines currently bottled under the La Bri label: Sauvage de La Bri, Blanc de La Bri, La Briette and Weisser La Bri.
Wood ageing: Wines are aged in wood at the Franschhoek Vineyards Co-operative.
Cellar capacity: The wines are made at the Franschhoek Vineyards Co-operative.

La Bri Vineyards are on the Franschhoek Wine Route and are open to the public on Monday to Saturday from 10h00 to 17h00.

In addition to their vineyards in the Cape, Michael and Cheryl are partners in the Denbies Wine Estate in Surrey, England, where they are developing the largest vineyard (100 hectares) in Britain.

— LA COURONNE —

Businessman Mike Stander and former doctor Glennie van Hoogstraten purchased this property in 1987 with the purpose of turning it into a model wine farm. After careful evaluation of the soil, the vineyards were extensively replanted with the varieties that were most suited to each location. Most recently, Chardonnay, Cabernet Sauvignon and Merlot vines have been planted. Land is also given over to plums and pears, which are exported. Sakkie Daniels acts as farm manager. The remaining land has been made into pastures for the Beauvoir stud horses, and in 1990, the adjoining property of Goede Hoop was acquired for the same purpose. A wine-tasting complex, and a restaurant which also arranges picnic lunches, looks out onto these graceful paddocks. A winery is being built adjacent to these

LA COURONNE

Varieties planted (ha)

High trellising system
Cabernet Sauvignon 6
Chardonnay 6
Sauvignon Blanc 4
Merlot 2
Pinot Noir is being planted

Total area under vines in 1991/2: 18 ha.
Irrigation: The fruit orchards are irrigated.
Average temperatures: Records are not kept.
Average annual rainfall: 650 mm.
Stock: Rooted vines are bought from a nursery.
First wines bottled under the La Couronne label: Richesse and Sauvignon Blanc (both 1989 vintage).
Wines currently bottled under the La Couronne label: Chardonnay, Blanc Fumé, Sauvignon Blanc Reserve and Richesse.
Wood ageing: The Blanc Fumé and Chardonnay are barrel fermented on the farm.
Cellar capacity: 10 000 cases a year.

La Couronne is on the Franschhoek Wine Route and is open to the public on Monday to Sunday from 10h00 to 17h00.

facilities. The wines are also available from the Franschhoek Vineyards Co-operative.

— LA MOTTE —
ESTATE

The Huguenot Pierre Joubert, progenitor of the family of that name, owned a number of farms in the Franschhoek valley, one of which he named La Motte for a part of France which had once been his home. He bought the land in 1709 from a German named Hans Heinrich Hattingh to whom it had been granted in 1695, but who used it merely for grazing his cattle. Joubert's widow sold the farm to Jan Hendrik Hop, and he in turn was succeeded by Gabriel du Toit who erected the original house which is incorporated in the present beautiful homestead. Du Toit was a wealthy man and planted about 20 000 vines on La Motte. Ownership of the property reverted to the Jouberts when Gideon Joubert, great-grandson of Pierre, bought it in 1815, enlarging the homestead and improving the farm during the 43 years he lived there.

In 1897 Cecil Rhodes bought La Motte from his friend Lewis Lloyd Michell, then chairman of De Beers, and it later became part of Rhodes Fruit Farms. Thereafter he exchanged La Motte for the farm Excelsior. Some thirty years later it once more passed into private ownership. The Rupert family bought the farm in 1970 and extensively restored the outbuildings and the old homestead, which has been altered from a T-shape to a more spacious H-plan. Noble varieties were planted on more than half of the extensive property, one of the largest in the Franschhoek area. A modern pressing cellar was built in 1985 while the old cellar, suitably converted, continues to be used for maturation purposes.

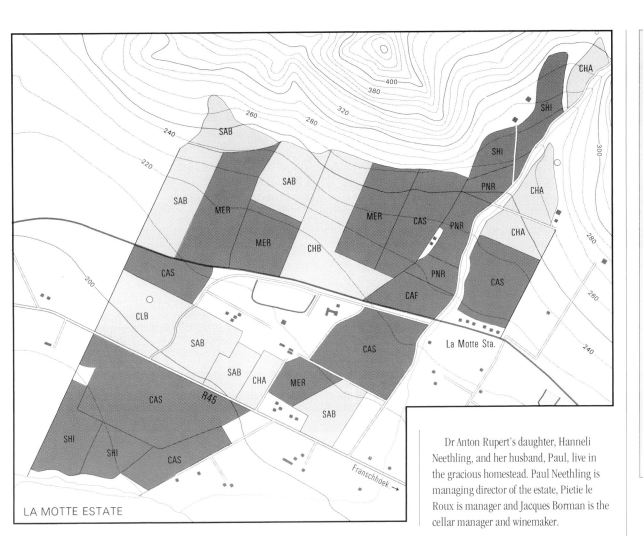

LA MOTTE ESTATE

LA MOTTE ESTATE

Varieties planted (ha)

Extended Perold trellis
Cabernet Sauvignon 38
Sauvignon Blanc 19
Merlot 15,5
Shiraz 11
Chenin Blanc 8,5
Chardonnay 7,5
Pinot Noir 5,5
Cabernet Franc 2

Total area under vines in 1991/2: 107 ha.
Irrigation: The vineyards are irrigated.
Average temperatures:
Maximum 23 ℃; minimum 11,9 ℃.
Average annual rainfall: 810 mm.
First wine bottled under the La Motte label:
Château La Motte Cabernet Sauvignon
(vintage uncertain – approximately 1969).
**Wines currently bottled under the La Motte
label:** Cabernet Sauvignon, Millennium, Shiraz,
Sauvignon Blanc and Blanc Fumé.
Wood ageing: Wines are aged in wood on the estate,
in 225-litre Nevers oak barrels.
Cellar capacity: 6 000 hl.

La Motte Estate is on the Franschhoek Wine Route
and is open to the public from 09h00 to 16h30 on
weekdays and from 09h00 to 12h00 on Saturdays. It
is closed on Sundays and public holidays.

Dr Anton Rupert's daughter, Hanneli Neethling, and her husband, Paul, live in the gracious homestead. Paul Neethling is managing director of the estate, Pietie le Roux is manager and Jacques Borman is the cellar manager and winemaker.

A quaint old watermill at La Motte is evocative of the estate's Huguenot past.

Jacques Borman, the winemaker.

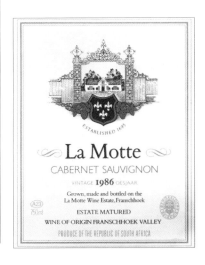

The homestead at La Provence, which was damaged by an earthquake in 1969, and subsequently restored by the well-known architect, Gabriel Fagan.

LA PROVENCE

Varieties planted (number of vines)

4-wire vertical trellis
Sauvignon Blanc 25 954
Weisser Riesling 13 876
Chenin Blanc 9 040
Chardonnay 5 666
Sémillon 3 000
Cabernet Sauvignon 1 750
Cape Riesling 461

Total area under vines in 1991/2: 18,5 ha.
Irrigation: The vineyards are irrigated.
Average temperatures:
Maximum 22,7 °C; minimum 10,4 °C.
Average annual rainfall: 830 mm.
Stock: Some parent stock is used for grafting;
rooted vines are bought from a nursery.
First wine bottled under the La Provence label:
Cuvée Blanche 1985.
**Wines currently bottled under the La Provence
label:** Cuvée Blanche, Sauvignon Blanc
and Rougeance.
Wood ageing: Wine is aged in wood on the farm.
Cellar capacity: The wines are made at the
Franschhoek Vineyards Co-operative.

La Provence is on the Franschhoek Wine Route and
is open to the public for tastings every day from
09h30 to 16h00 or by special appointment.

—LA PROVENCE—

The original owner of the La Provence wine farm was Pierre Joubert from the Provençal village of La Motte d'Aigues, where he was born in 1664. A French Huguenot, he was granted the land in 1694, and in 1712 was awarded the title of La Provence, then measuring 60 morgen.

Extremely hard-working, Pierre Joubert was a considerably wealthy man when he died in 1732, having become owner of half a dozen other farms, among them Bellingham, L'Ormarins and La Motte. His widow and ten children were left thousands of hectares of land, 30 000 vines and hundreds of farm animals.

John Rudd, the owner of La Provence.

The original dwellings of the French Huguenots and other settlers at the Cape were quite humble until the second half of the eighteenth century.

Building operations on the La Provence homestead as we know it today were started by Pieter de Villiers in about 1756 and completed by his widow. Severely damaged by the earthquake of September 1969, La Provence was meticulously restored by one of South Africa's most talented and well-known architects, Gabriel Fagan.

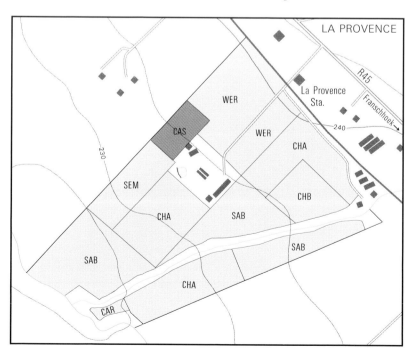

John Rudd's company, Trelew Investments Ltd, acquired the farm in 1981. Besides an extensive replanting programme, Trelew also engaged Jan Roux, the well-known Franschhoek-based builder, to reconstruct the old wine cellar, which was reopened in 1986 to coincide with the release of Cuvée Blanche, La Provence's first wine this century.

Trelew acquired the neighbouring property Trouvé in 1988 and added a small dairy farm to the La Provence wine-farming and olive-plantation activities. The cottage or Jonkershuis, where the founder Pierre Joubert first established his abode, has been most attractively redecorated in the same style (part Cape, part Oriental) that characterizes the main homestead. In fact much care has been lavished on the entire property, making it one of the gems of this beautiful and famed Huguenot valley, and a magnet for a great number of local and international visitors.

After a three-year agreement with nearby Bien Donné vineyards, which undertook the vinification of La Provence's grapes (nearly 200 tonnes were harvested in 1990), the La Provence Sauvignon Blanc is now vinified at the Franschhoek Vineyards Co-operative, while its Cabernet Sauvignon is made in the restored cellar.

A dynamic international businessman, John sets high standards for anything he does, and his exceptional marketing expertise has a great deal to do with the success of his wines, and exports make up about 20 per cent of La Provence's production.

— L'ORMARINS —
ESTATE

Mountains tower behind the particularly beautiful homestead of L'Ormarins, and its perfect proportions and dignified neo-classical gable, dated 1811, are reflected in a willow-fringed ornamental lake in front of it. This lovely old Huguenot farm was acquired in 1969 by Dr. Anton Rupert and is now owned by his younger son, Anthonij. The farm has been modified for the production of good red wines such as Cabernet Sauvignon, Merlot, Pinot Noir and Shiraz, together with white-wine varieties such as Sauvignon Blanc, Weisser Riesling, Chenin

L'ORMARINS ESTATE

Varieties planted (ha)

Perold trellis
Sauvignon Blanc 40
Chardonnay 40
Cabernet Sauvignon 25
Cape Riesling 20
Chenin Blanc 20
Weisser Riesling 15
Pinot Gris 12
Pinot Noir 10
Merlot 10
Gewürztraminer 6
Shiraz 5
Cabernet Franc 4
Souzão 3
Bukettraube 2
Port varieties 1

Total area under vines in 1991/2: 213 ha.
Irrigation: All the vines can be irrigated.
Average temperatures: Records are not kept.
Average annual rainfall:
Approximately 1 200–1 500 mm.
First wines bottled under the L'Ormarins label:
SA Riesling, Rhine Riesling and Sauvignon Blanc
(all 1982 vintage).
Wines currently bottled under the L'Ormarins label: Sauvignon Blanc, Franschhoek Riesling, Rhine Riesling, Blanc Fumé, Pinot Gris, Noble Late Harvest, Guldenpfennig, Cabernet Sauvignon, Shiraz and Optima.
Wood ageing: Wines are aged in wood on the estate.
Cellar capacity: 20 000 hl.

L'Ormarins Estate is on the Franschhoek Wine Route and is open to the public on weekdays from 09h00 to 13h00 and from 14h00 to 17h00, and on Saturdays from 09h00 to 13h00 by appointment. Wine is sold on the farm.

Anthonij Rupert and Nico Vermeulen.

Blanc, Chardonnay and Cape Riesling. The wines are made by Anthonij Rupert and Nico Vermeulen in their very modern cellar which has been built in a position where it will not detract from the splendid beauty of the original farm buildings. The bottling and marketing of the wine is done by The Bergkelder from their well-equipped cellar.

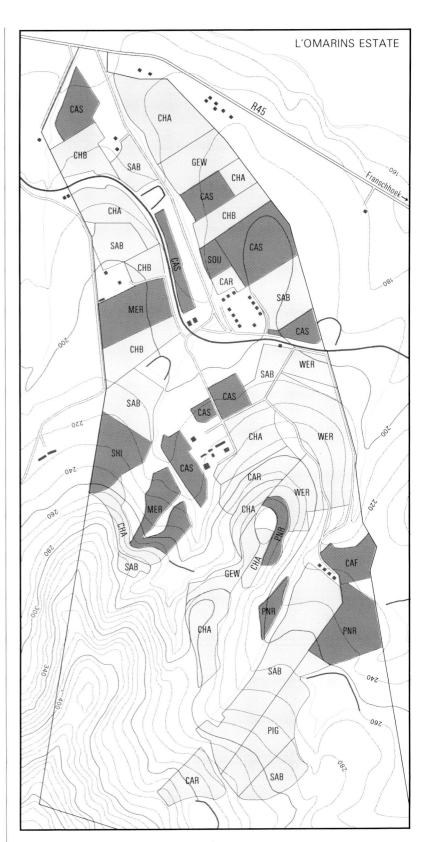

L'OMARINS ESTATE

Now some 213 hectares of vineyards in extent, L'Ormarins was initially granted in 1694 to a Huguenot refugee, Jean Roi. It later passed into the ownership of the De Villiers family, one of whom built the oldest surviving structure on the property, a T-shaped dwelling now occupied by a farm manager. The farm's cellar, now used only for storage,

The gracious L'Ormarins homestead, completed in 1811.

dates from 1799 and contains a number of casks, each of which is beautifully carved with the coat of arms of one of the original French Huguenot settlers.

In the early years of the nineteenth century L'Ormarins appears to have thrived: by 1825 its then owner, Izaak Jacob Marais, could number an impressive 114 000 vines on his land, and an equally impressive array of prizes won at contemporary wine shows. After the Cape of Good Hope Agricultural Society's show of 1833, for example, he rode home with a prize of 100 rixdollars (for his Cape Madeira) and a silver trophy.

Fanatically interested and very well travelled, Anthonij Rupert has an astute talent for marketing and is determined to produce only the best. He and Nico Vermeulen have certainly proved their talents beyond any doubt. They are able to release their Chardonnay and red wines after a longer bottle-maturation period than most, so the whites are quite accessible when they are released on the market.

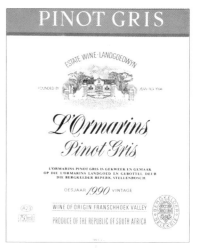

A hoek (corner) in the Drakenstein Mountains forms the beautiful Franschhoek valley.

The Mouton Excelsior sign, indicating that the farm is on the Franschhoek Wine Route, developed in 1984 to promote the wines of the region.

Chardonnay and Sauvignon Blanc have been planted over the years; the first harvest of 1990 Merlot and 1991 Chardonnay was bottled in 1991 and released in December of that year. The Le Moutonné labels won a Clio award in 1986.

—MÔRESON BLOIS—

Môreson and its adjoining farm, Blois, originally formed part of La Motte, which was granted to the Huguenot Hans Heinrich Hattingh in 1695. Over the centuries the lands were divided and the farms changed hands many times. Now a member of the *Vignerons de Franschhoek*, Môreson was bought by Pauline and Charles Friedman in 1986 and is managed by Neil le Roux, assisted by Kobus Mostert.

After assessing the different soil conditions on the farm, the Friedmans set about planting the best available varieties suited to

Matin Soleil

VIN BOUQUET

LIMITED 1991 RELEASE

CHENIN BLANC

WINE OF ORIGIN FRANSCHHOEK

750ml PRODUCED AND BOTTLED IN THE REPUBLIC OF SOUTH AFRICA A175

MÔRESON BLOIS

Varieties planted (ha)

Perold trellis
Sauvignon Blanc 7
Chardonnay 5
Chenin Blanc 4,6
Weisser Riesling 3,8
Sémillon 2,5

Total area under vines in 1991/2: 22,9 ha.
Irrigation: Micro-irrigation is practised.
Average temperatures:
Maximum 22,7 °C; minimum 10 °C.
Average annual rainfall: 1 115 mm.
Stock: Rooted vines are bought from a nursery.
First wine bottled under the Matin Soleil label:
Chenin Blanc 1989.
Wines currently bottled under the Matin Soleil label: Chenin Blanc and Sauvignon Blanc.
Wood ageing: Wood ageing is not practised.
Cellar capacity: The wines are made at the Franschhoek Vineyards Co-operative.

Môreson Blois is on the Franschhoek Wine Route and may be visited by appointment only.

---

the soil. They retained the excellent mature Chenin Blanc vineyard, but gradually pruned these vines for low-quantity and therefore high-quality grapes. The 1989 harvest from this vineyard was used to make the crisp and fruity Chenin Blanc which was the first wine to appear under the simple and elegant label, Matin Soleil. The Matin Soleil wines are made by Deon Truter at the Franschhoek Vineyards Co-operative.

—MOUTON-EXCELSIOR—

Ben Mouton, a descendant of the Huguenot Jacques Mouton, who settled in the Franschhoek valley in 1699, bought the well-known hotel Swiss Farm Excelsior in 1984. The hotel is situated on a farm where Ben has replanted the vineyards with a number of noble varieties.

His first wines were a Cabernet Sauvignon, and a Sémillon. Noble varieties of Merlot, Cabernet Franc, Cabernet Sauvignon,

---

MOUTON-EXCELSIOR

Varieties planted (number of vines)

5-wire Perold trellis
Cabernet Sauvignon 26 000
Chardonnay 18 000
Merlot 17 000
Sauvignon Blanc 6 000
Sémillon 6 000
Cabernet Franc 6 000

Total area under vines in 1991/2: 25 ha.
Irrigation: The vineyards are dryland and irrigated.
Average temperature: 17 °C.
Average annual rainfall: 800 mm.
Stock: Rooted vines are bought from a nursery.
First wines bottled under the Mouton-Excelsior label: Le Moutonné Sémillon and Cabernet Sauvignon (both 1985 vintage).
Wines currently bottled under the Mouton-Excelsior label: Le Moutonné Merlot, Le Moutonné Sémillon, Le Moutonné Chardonnay and Le Moutonné Cabernet Sauvignon.
Wood ageing: Wines are wood-aged in Alliers oak.
Cellar capacity: 820 hl.

Mouton-Excelsior is on the Franschhoek Wine Route and is open for wine-tastings and light lunches from Monday to Friday from 09h00 to 17h00, on Saturdays from 10h00 to 14h00, and on Sundays from 12h00 to 13h00.

SWARTLAND

The first mention of *'Het Zwarte Land'* occurs in a report made in Willem Adriaan van der Stel's journal on the twenty sixth of August 1701, which described a skirmish that had taken place four days earlier between a party of soldiers led by Corporal Daniel Taus of the Riebeek Kasteel outpost and a group of San hunters. It is a moot point why the land is thus named, for the soil in the area is not black; an explanation may be that the name is derived from the colour of the indigenous vegetation, which appears almost black ('swart') at certain times of the year.

Whatever the source of the name, the land itself, open and undulating, proved fertile. For most of its recorded history the district has been used for large-scale wheat farming, and this continues to be its main crop. As a wine-producing area the region is comparatively new, the biggest expansion having taken place in the last three decades, concentrated mainly in the southern areas of Malmesbury, Darling and Riebeek West.

The Swartland district is bounded on the south by the Durbanville and Paarl regions, on the east by the Berg River, and on the west by the Atlantic Ocean, whose cool breezes modify many of the microclimates in the area. The generally low-lying landscape is interrupted by mountains at Perdeberg, Riebeek West and Riebeek Kasteel, and between Darling and Mamre.

The predominant soil type is Malmesbury Shale. Isolated granitic patches occur, while the soils in the south originate from Table Mountain Sandstone. Vineyards are cultivated on all three soil types, on deep Hutton and Clovelly as well as sandy Fernwood and Kroonstad forms. The low-pH soils are deep ploughed, with lime and phosphate added to the subsoil.

Apart from the cool Saldanha area near the sea, this is a hot region and the rainfall is marginal, the average annual supply varying between approximately 450 and 600 millimetres, but with a low annual average of 242 millimetres in the vicinity of Malmesbury. The average summer temperatures range from 19,5 °C to 21 °C, depending on the location.

LEFT: *Swartland vineyards near Riebeek Kasteel, named after Jan van Riebeeck.*

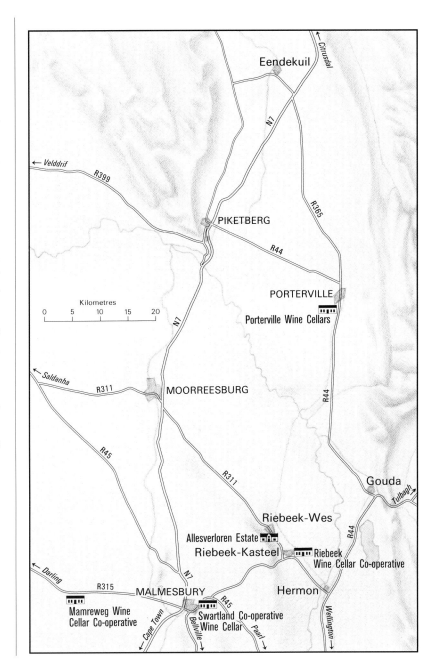

—ALLESVERLOREN—
ESTATE

Situated at the foot of the Kasteelberg between Riebeek Kasteel and Riebeek West, this estate is now the property and the wine-making domain of Fanie Malan, a specialist in red table wine-making.

This estate was originally granted in 1704 by Willem Adriaan van der Stel to a widow named Cloete. The farm acquired its unusual name during the eighteenth century, when one of its owners returned from a church visit to Stellenbosch to find that his property had been wiped out in a raid by San hunters, his cattle stolen and his buildings

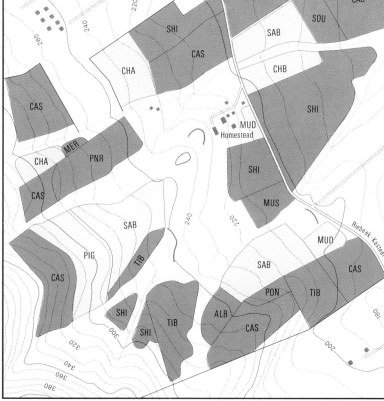

ALLESVERLOREN ESTATE

The homestead at Allesverloren Estate, situated at the foot of the Kasteel Mountains.

razed. The event received its bleak commemoration in the new name for the farm: 'Allesverloren' (All is lost).

Daniel François Malan, the first of his family to farm at Allesverloren, arrived from the Wellington district in 1870. He found a farm where all was far from lost: 700 fertile hectares of wheatland rolled down from the Kasteelberg, whose summit gathered wel-

come rainclouds when the lower land lay dry. By this time there were already a few vineyards established on the farm, and he made wine from these vines for local consumption. His principal claim to fame, however, was posthumous and lay outside the realm of the wine farmer: His elder son, also Daniel François Malan, took the long road from the farm to become a minister of the

Dutch Reformed Church, a Member of Parliament and the first nationalist Prime Minister in 1948.

It was left to Malan's younger son, Stephanus, to take over Allesverloren in 1904. He introduced a few new vines, but did little to develop the land beyond its traditional role as a wheat farm. In 1945 it was inherited by his two sons, who divided it between them,

the elder, Daniel François, receiving the half on which the old homestead stood.

It was he who made Allesverloren into a wine farm. On his 500 hectares of land he set out to develop a red port and, assisted by advice and encouragement from Professor Theron and the Department of Viticulture at Stellenbosch University, he introduced a range of suitable varieties. Over a decade he

ALLESVERLOREN ESTATE

Varieties planted (number of vines)

4-wire vertical trellis
Cabernet Sauvignon 80 000
Shiraz 76 000
Sauvignon Blanc 57 248
Tinta Barocca 30 000
Pinot Gris 21 350
Chardonnay 18 000
Merlot 11 760
Alicante Bouschet 6 000
Tinta Roriz 6 000
Pontac 4 000
Cabernet Franc 3 800

Total area under vines in 1991/2: 180 ha.
Irrigation: None.
Average temperatures:
Maximum 25 °C; minimum 12 °C.
Average annual rainfall: 550 mm.
Stock: About 50 per cent of the parent stock is used for grafting and rooted vines are bought from a nursery.
First wines bottled under the Allesverloren label: Tinta Barocca 1972 and Cabernet Sauvignon 1974.
Wines currently bottled under the Allesverloren label: Cabernet Sauvignon, Port, Tinta Barocca and Shiraz (bottled by The Bergkelder).
Wood ageing: Wines are aged in wood at The Bergkelder.
Cellar capacity: 12 000 hl.

Visits to Allesverloren Estate can be made only by appointment through The Bergkelder or directly with the estate. The estate is on the Swartland Wine Route.

Fanie Malan and his son Danie, from the estate of Allesverloren.

established varieties which included Tinta Barocca, Malvasia Rey, Muscadel, Shiraz, Pontac and Tinta Roriz.

A clear identity for the farm had been created, and recognition of Daniel Malan's achievement came with prizes for his port

wines in the mid-1950s – the Cape Wine Show trophy for the best port wine went to Allesverloren in both 1956 and 1957.

In 1961 family history was repeated when Daniel sold the farm to his two sons who divided it between them. The elder, who is the present winemaker of Allesverloren, Fanie Malan, chose the area with the homestead, while the younger, Gerard, took the larger but less promising sector.

The post-war years had seen changes in the market and in the demand for port wines. In the early 1960s port simply fell out of fashion. On his 200 hectares Fanie then concentrated on red wine production and extensive new plantings, mostly of red wine varieties, took place. Some port varieties, though, particularly Tinta Barocca, were retained. These port varieties impart a unique character to the Allesverloren red wines in which they are used. Fanie's famous Swartland Rood, for example, is a blend of Shiraz, Cabernet Sauvignon and the port variety, Souzão. Three separate wines are made from each variety, matured separately and only then blended to make Swartland Rood. Since 1988 Fanie Malan's son Danie has been taking increasing responsibility for the making of the wines in the same tradition of full-bodied reds.

In general the Swartland is hot and dry. Stretching down the slopes of the Kasteelberg, and with an altitude differential of more than 170 metres (from 130 to 300 metres above sea level), however, Allesverloren has to cope with varying soils and microclimates. Soils range from sandy alluvial loam to clay, and to other mixtures of clay and sand, with a pebbly, gravelly structure throughout. There is also a considerable variation in rainfall, with a difference of 200 millimetres a year between the upper and lower reaches of the mountain.

This double set of variables of soil and climate necessitates great care when planting vineyards and when choosing varieties. At a distance of 50 kilometres from the coast and therefore with minimum benefit from a cooling sea breeze, with fertile soil and a mountain rainfall, the grapes here are capable of attaining a high sugar content of 30 °Balling at harvest time.

Besides developing the vineyards and experimenting with new varieties, Fanie Malan has made innovations in the cellar tech-

nology of Allesverloren. The high quality of Allesverloren's red wines has won them many awards over the years. At the 1985 South African Wine Show, Allesverloren Port was judged the champion fortified wine, and in the same year Fanie won the trophy as the Champion Estate Winemaker at the Stellenbosch Wine Show. At present all four of Allesverloren's wines, three natural wines and a port, are marketed under the estate's label by The Bergkelder.

— MAMREWEG —
WINE CELLAR CO-OPERATIVE

The Mamreweg Wine Cellar Co-operative is situated between Malmesbury and Darling on the rolling slopes of the Dassenberg mountain range. The co-operative was founded in 1949 and today has 29 members, who produce about 12 000 tonnes of grapes per year.

The principal reason for the founding of the co-operative was to produce better quality wines under the supervision of a winemaker, because the farmers were making wine of an inferior quality in their individual farm cellars.

Most of the vineyards of the co-operative's members are planted on the slopes of the Dassenberg. The area is included in the Swartland district, but in actual fact fits more easily into the Cape Coastal Region because of the nature of the deep red soil and the cool climate. The area therefore has the potential to produce top-quality wines, given that the correct varieties are

planted and that the correct viticultural practices are administered.

Most of the vines are pruned to a bush vine shape, although some of the farmers have already begun trellising some of the new stronger-growing clones. This will definitely increase the quality of the grapes, but one must bear in mind that only the best soils can be used for trellising.

At the moment the variety spectrum is limited, but the farmers have already started planting quality white and red varieties, including Cape Riesling, Bukettraube, Weisser Riesling, Gewürztraminer and Cabernet Sauvignon. The quality of the grapes is further improved by the proximity of the cold Atlantic Ocean, which has a cooling effect in the heat of the afternoons.

Groenkloof Drankhandelaars is the sole bottler and distributor of Mamreweg wines. The company was founded in 1949 to promote and sell the co-operative's products. It is also one of the few wholesale licences with the privilege of selling directly to the public on the premises.

Vines grow alongside wheat in this dry area, where irrigation is extensively used to compensate for the low rainfall.

— PORTERVILLE —
WINE CELLARS

As the only co-operative winery in the Piketberg district, the Porterville Cellars receive virtually the entire annual grape crop of the district. With a current membership of 131 farmers it processes an impressive 14 500 tonnes a year, under the direction of its manager and winemaker, Klaas de Jongh, who is assisted by Bunny Rossouw.

WINES BOTTLED AND MARKETED

Red: Pinotage and Dry Red.
White: Grand Crû, Blanc de Blanc, Sauvignon Blanc, Late Vintage, Emerald Riesling and Hárslevelü.
Fortified: Golden Hanepoot Jerepigo and Red Jerepigo.

The co-operative is on the Swartland Wine Route and is open to the public on weekdays from 08h30 to 13h00 and from 14h00 to 17h00, and on Saturdays from 08h30 to 11h00.

Established in 1941, the Porterville Wine Cellars now concentrates mainly on Chenin Blanc, Colombard and Sauvignon Blanc; improvements in quality in recent years have been reflected in a number of awards, including three gold medals at the South African Championship Wine Show. Only a fraction of the co-operative's produce is bottled for sale to the public.

— RIEBEEK —
WINE CELLAR CO-OPERATIVE

Most of the grapes pressed by the Riebeek Wine Cellar Co-operative are grown on the cooler eastern slopes of Kasteelberg (Riebeekberg) in low-yield, dryland vineyards — factors which concentrate flavours and aromas and contribute to the winemaker's consistent success at wine shows. New plantings of Pinot Gris, Merlot and Chardonnay indicate a belief that the area has been underrated in the past, and has a high potential.

On 4 February 1661 Pieter Cruythoff became the first European to reach Riebeek Kasteel, and for many years he featured on the wine labels of the co-operative, which was founded in 1941. New limited releases in 1991 under new Pieter Cruythoff labels include a 1991 Sauvignon Blanc and a 1988 Cabernet Sauvignon.

The co-operative is one of the main attractions of the Swartland Wine Route and

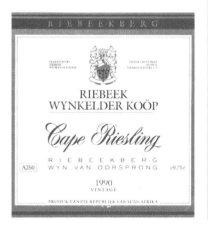

prides itself in offering warm hospitality. The Riebeek area itself is one of the most beautiful valleys on the Swartland Wine Route.

Various other new releases include two sparkling wines, namely a brut made from Sauvignon Blanc, and a demi-sec made from Weisser Riesling.

WINES BOTTLED AND MARKETED

Red: Pinotage, Shiraz, Nouveau (Merlot), Tinta Barocca, and Pieter Cruythoff Cabernet Sauvignon.
White: Special Late Harvest, Late Harvest, Nouveau (Chenin Blanc), Blanc de Noir, Chenin Blanc, Weisser Riesling, Colombard, Cape Riesling, Grand Crû and Pieter Cruythoff Sauvignon Blanc.
Sparkling: Brut and Demi-Sec.
Fortified: Port, Hanepoot Jerepigo and Red Jerepigo.

The co-operative is on the Swartland Wine Route and is open to the public on weekdays from 07h30 to 12h30 and from 13h30 to 17h30, and on Saturdays from 08h30 to 12h00.

Swartland is an area with a low annual rainfall, and grapes are grown under dryland conditions.

—SWARTLAND—
CO-OPERATIVE WINE CELLAR

The award of a second prize at the 1972 International Wine Show in Budapest for a 1969 vintage Pinotage made by the Swartland Co-operative Winery first brought this cellar to the attention of the public. However, it had already been established for some 24 years. In April 1948 a group of 15 farmers in the Malmesbury area assembled at the old Malmesbury 'bioscope' to

Johan de Villiers, Albie van Vuuren, and Christo Koch of Swartland Co-operative.

vote for the formation of the new winery. A month later a Board of Directors was elected, and the co-operative was registered in due course.

Four hectares of land were donated by the Chairman, Mr P.L. Loubser, taken from his farm, Doornkuil, 3 kilometres outside the town of Malmesbury. By 1950, when the winery's cellars were completed, the membership had grown to 48 farmers, who supplied 2 500 tonnes of grapes in the first year alone. The bulk of the wine made was white, with an emphasis on Palomino, but including substantial quantities of Chenin Blanc, Sémillon and False Pedro. The red wine contribution in those early days was restricted to the production of Cinsaut.

Since then Swartland Co-operative has grown to almost double its original membership. At present 90 growers deliver some 22 000 tonnes of grapes at vintage time to the modern and streamlined wine-making plant which includes heat fermentation, or thermo-vinification, equipment and rotating tanks to aid colour extraction in the making of increasing amounts of red wine.

This fairly hot, dry region with a low annual average rainfall of 500 millimetres falling mainly in the winter produces grapes high in sugar content. The Swartland Co-operative's range includes a variety of sweet and semi-sweet, rich and full-bodied wines, both white and red. The first manager and winemaker was Nico Botha who held the post for over 30 years. He was subsequently assisted as winemaker by Albie van Vuuren, who has now succeeded him as production and marketing manager. Johan de Villiers is now responsible for the white wines, while Christo Koch makes the red and sweet wines.

As the Swartland is included under Stellenbosch for the Young Wine Shows, the co-operatives of the area compete with a great number of wineries at these shows and competition is stiff. It is no mean feat, therefore, to be the champion cellar. Swartland achieved that accolade four times, in 1980,

1981, 1985 and 1986. The co-operative sells a large range of 'good-value-for-money' wines and bottles considerable quantities for various retailers as 'own labels' and 'no-name' brands.

Swartland Co-operative wines are also exported to the United Kingdom and Europe as well as to Central Africa.

TULBAGH

On a hot afternoon in February 1658, a group of men reached the top of a mountain pass and looked down into the valley below. Of the 15 under Sergeant Jan van Herwaarden who had left the fort at the Cape days earlier, the majority had turned back, discouraged by dysentery (of which two of the party were to die before the end of the journey), the intense heat and an absence of cattle for which to barter. But Pieter Potter, the surveyor commissioned by Van Riebeeck to map and record the journey, had struggled to the top of the steep pass with five others, including two Khoikhoin, and there a magnificent view met their eyes.

It was an enormous rocky basin, completely enclosed by great mountains. In the distance a river threaded through the floor of the valley. Potter was not impressed, however: he had expected to find verdant pastures like those of the Table Mountain area, but here in the shimmering midday heat the valley looked dry and infertile, in spite of the many trees along the river and in the kloofs of the mountains. Moreover, it appeared to be completely uninhabited. Seeing no sign of the Khoikhoin from whom they had hoped to barter cattle, the party turned back and started on their homeward journey.

Potter and his companions were the first whites to look down into what was later to be named the Tulbagh basin, a vast mountain cul-de-sac enclosed on the north by the Winterhoek range, on the east by that of the Witzenberg, and on the west by the Oukloof and Elandskloof mountains, divided by the Roodezandt Pass up which Potter had climbed. The river he had glimpsed flows out of the valley to meet the Berg River and was appropriately if unimaginatively named the Klein Berg River, the major source of water for the farms that lie in the valley today.

If Potter came, saw, and retreated, the next important visitor to the valley some 40 years later showed a more constructive interest in its possibilities. In November 1699 Willem Adriaan van der Stel, the new governor of the Colony, eager to make his mark on the rapidly expanding community, set out on a tour of inspection of the Stellenbosch and Drakenstein areas. By this time scattered farms had been established as far as what is now the Wellington area. Having inspected the already settled farming areas and searching for more land to allocate to ever more colonists, Van der Stel moved on to explore further and on a summer's day he and his party broke through the narrow defile where the Klein Berg River leaves the valley of Tulbagh.

Impressed with his discovery, he celebrated it in gubernatorial fashion by giving names to several of its outstanding landmarks. The great range of mountains to the east was to be called the Witzenberg, in honour of Nicolaas Witzen, burgomaster of Amsterdam. In contrast, the range to the west over which he had just climbed became the Obiqua mountains, for they were the haunt of San hunters, and *obiqua*, meaning 'robbers', was what the Khoikhoin commonly called them. The valley itself he called the 'Land of Waveren', in honour of a well-known family of that name in Amsterdam, to whom he was related.

Within a year or so the first pioneers had settled in the valley, but at this stage, and for many years to come, the land was used mainly for grazing sheep and cattle. The first farms were on loan from the Dutch East India Company, but by 1720 eight had been granted freehold – four to Dutch settlers and four to French Huguenots.

In 1743 a small church, described as 'a very humble and simple edifice', was built. Between it and its *pastorie* a row of about a dozen small houses was strung out. These humble dwellings were occupied mainly by traders and handicraft workers who appeared to earn a solidly comfortable living from the 40 families who had chosen to make their home there by the end of the eighteenth century.

It is uncertain when wine-making was first introduced to the valley. Given the climate and soil, the vines must have made a natural complement to the wheat crop, particularly in stony areas where the wheat was hard to establish. No doubt the quantities made were small because of the difficulties of transportation to markets outside the valley, and most of it must have been consumed locally. Primitive stills made their appearance at this time, too, their rough brandy not only providing consolation at the end of a hard day in the sun, but being used for medicinal purposes as well.

By the turn of the nineteenth century the 'Land of Waveren' had become a stable if not affluent community. It had also gained a measure of administrative independence, given official form in 1804 when the commissioner-general issued a proclamation formally cutting the valley off from the Stellenbosch district and establishing it with a name and an identity of its own. The name he chose was that of an earlier and much-respected governor, Ryk Tulbagh. From now on the valley would have complete charge of its own affairs, obviating the necessity for the long journey to Stellenbosch for such legal matters as powers of attorney, contracts and wills. In particular, it meant that the perpetual arguments over land, boundaries and water-rights which were apt to preoccupy farming communities could now take place on home ground.

The seat of the law in Tulbagh was the drostdy, or local magistrate's court. In a piece of benign eccentricity the newly established ward contrived to erect its new drostdy a full

LEFT: *Vineyards in the Tulbagh basin, initially thought to be a dry and infertile area.*

half-hour's walk from the village – perhaps in the hope that the walk would cool off the citizens' ardour for litigation.

Self-sufficient and largely self-supporting, the valley passed quietly and unobtrusively into the twentieth century, with only an occasional tremor in the smooth passage of its years. But on the twenty ninth of September 1969, in a matter of a few minutes, the most severe earthquake in South Africa's recorded history split the sun-baked village asunder. Hardly a house in the area was unaffected, while many, particularly in the oldest area of the main thoroughfare of Church Street, tumbled to the ground.

The story of the rebuilding and restoration of Tulbagh is well known. Supervised by the architect Gabriel Fagan, the reconstruction included the incorporation of reinforcements as a safeguard against further tremors. With many of its houses now National Monuments, Tulbagh has been preserved as one of the most enchanting of the surviving early Cape villages and one which has remained almost entirely free of the encroachments of industrial civilization.

Much of the wheat-growing land of the early farmers has been taken over for fruit farming, but the most profitable form of agriculture is now wine-farming, with an emphasis upon white wines. Compared with other wine-making districts, Tulbagh is small, with only five producing estates and one co-operative at present. Included with Paarl in the Boberg region, it is also the first of the true 'inland' areas, that is, those generally mountainous areas at a remove from the cooling influence of the winds from the sea.

The soils of the Tulbagh valley vary considerably. Along the river banks, deep sand and loose stone cover clay subsoils; an unpromising-sounding combination but one which has in fact proved generally fertile. The soils most represented are the low-pH Hutton forms against the lower slopes, which require large-scale additions of lime during soil preparation. The soils of the higher slopes also vary considerably, with mountain clay from a depth of 1 to as much as 2,5 metres providing a seepage which acts as a natural, laid-on form of irrigation. The drawback of these mountain soils, and one which applies to much of the valley, is that the slopes carry more stone than soil, and making a vineyard requires the preliminary removal of tonnes of stone – on one site vines were planted in earth which was still intractable after 30 000 tonnes of stone had been removed from 10 hectares of land.

Within the district there are numerous microclimates, represented by the different altitudes of the farming land. Temperatures vary greatly between winter and summer: those of summer range from an average of 19 °C in the Winterhoek area to 21 °C in the Wolseley area, while the winters are cold, with recurrent frost and snow on the higher mountains for up to two months of the year. Rainfall also varies from 750 millimetres in the Winterhoek to 450 millimetres in the Wolseley area, necessitating supplementary irrigation – mainly from the Klein Berg River in most vineyards during the dry summers.

— KLOOFZICHT —

Kloofzicht's owner, Swiss-born Roger Fehlmann, studied political science in Geneva and comparative religion in India, and worked as a translator in Tokyo, all of which is a far cry from the farming lifestyle he sought when he came to South Africa in 1982. Once here, Roger enjoyed three years of training in agriculture, and became interested in the concept of wine-making. Inspired by winemakers such as Kurt Ammann

and Billy Hofmeyr, he set about making Kloofzicht's first wine by foot-crushing and hand-pressing Chenin Blanc grapes, using his baby son's paddling pool as a substitute for the cold fermentation process. Nicky Krone, from Twee Jongegezellen, was persuaded to taste this first attempt, and pronounced it 'Not South African – foreign in approach – cheesy overtones – Swiss!'.

Kloofzicht has, however, come a long way since this inauspicious beginning. In January 1989 the first fruit was picked from

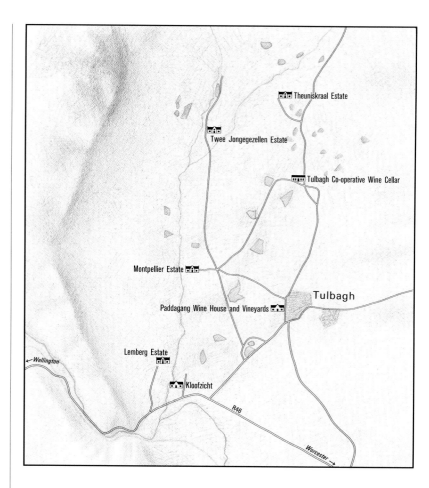

newly planted, three-year-old vines. The planting pattern used is tramlines, accommodating 5 555 vines per hectare, a relatively high density population which ensures that the roots compete for water and consequently limits the output per vine. Fortunately the alluvial clay soils are capable of high water retention and allow dryland cultivation. Although in Tulbagh trade winds replace the sea breezes of the coastal regions, the grapes ripen early and need to be harvested before the stifling heat of summer.

The first wine from Kloofzicht was named Alter Ego and is the first Bordeaux-styled wine to carry the appellation 'Wine of Origin Tulbagh'. The red wine produced is of a depth and quality previously unknown in this 'white' wine area. Maturation and pressing was initially carried out in an old stable, but in 1990 an underground cellar was built with a storage capacity of 100 000 bottles and 150 *barriques*. Above the cellar is an art studio where Roger's wife Sharon draws, paints and sculpts, and on a landing above is a cosy wine-tasting lounge. For those who wish to spend a night or two on the farm to

enjoy fishing, hiking or merely relaxing in the picturesque surroundings, there is even a

---

KLOOFZICHT

Varieties planted (ha)

2-wire vertical trellis
Merlot 3,5
Cabernet Sauvignon 1
Chardonnay 0,5

Total area under vines in 1991/2:
5 ha (4 ha still to be planted).
Irrigation: None.
Average temperatures: Records are not kept.
Average annual rainfall: 550 mm.
Stock: Rooted vines are bought from a nursery.
First wine bottled under the Kloofzicht label:
Alter Ego 1989.
**Wine currently bottled under the
Kloofzicht label:** Alter Ego.
Wood ageing: The wine is aged for a period of
12 months in new and second-fill French and
American *barriques*.
Cellar capacity: 120 hl.

Kloofzicht is on the Tulbagh Wine Route and is
open to the public on weekdays from 10h00 to 16h00
and on weekends by appointment.

fully equipped quaint three-bedroomed cottage near the homestead which has become most popular among tranquillity-seeking visitors to the valley.

— LEMBERG — ESTATE

In the Klein Berg River valley, at the foot of the Witzenberg, Winterhoek and Obiqua mountains, lies one of the Cape's smallest estates: Lemberg, the property of Jan and Janey Muller. Its vineyards and cellar are the culmination of the life's ambition of Janey Muller, a rare case in South Africa of a woman winemaker responsible for the creation of her own style of wine.

Born and brought up in Cape Town, Janey Provan accompanied her father on wine-hunting tours of the Stellenbosch area after the opening of the first Wine Route there in the early 1970s. A passion for wine was kindled, together with a determination to become personally involved in its making. To this end, while still in Standard Seven, she sat down and fired off letters to all the farmers on the Wine Route, asking to be allowed to work on a farm during her school holidays, to learn wine-farming and to improve her Afrikaans. She received a single encouraging answer, from Koelenhof farm's Attie Joubert, who visited Janey's parents and arranged for her to work on his farm during the holidays until she matriculated.

During the next few years she worked at Koelenhof at every opportunity, gaining invaluable early experience 'from soil to glass'. At the same time it became clear that without a farming background formal academic weapons would be needed to fight her way into the winelands. She therefore decided to

Janey Muller, who honed her wine-making skills at Lievland Estate and at Lemberg.

Lemberg, a 'miniature winery' which is nevertheless fully equiped with stainless steel tanks and oak barriques.

enroll for a four-year course under the well-known Professor Joël van Wyk at the University of Stellenbosch, eventually obtaining her B.Sc. (Agric), majoring in viticulture, oenology and microbiology.

Developments in this period were not all academic: while working as a tour guide with a local firm of bus-tour operators during her first university vacation she met a young law student named Jan Muller, a fellow Capetonian who was doing the same job. They were married in 1977 after Jan's graduation, by which time he had caught the infection of Janey's enthusiasm for her calling. Soon they began to look around for a small and inexpensive property which would be ideal to start a wine farm.

In late 1978 the Mullers bought a modest 13-hectare farm in the Tulbagh valley. Then called Vergelegen, the Mullers changed the name to Lemberg, the German name for the Ukrainian town from which Jan's maternal family had emigrated to South Africa.

To gather extra experience and capital the couple worked in a variety of other places while taking their new farm in hand, in particular at Le Bonheur, where Jan learned much of the practice of viticulture from the owner, Michael Woodhead. It was at Le Bonheur, too, that Janey met Gert van der Merwe of Lievland. Gert was in search of a winemaker to be employed on an ad hoc basis, and soon Janey found herself commuting between her own estate and Lievland. At the same time, with increasing knowledge and confidence, Jan took on the running of the viticultural side of the Lemberg enterprise.

The Mullers, aware of the limitation in size of their land, have concentrated their efforts on the planting of high-quality varieties. Old blocks of Palomino, Cinsaut and Kanaan were cleared away, the soil was enriched with lime, and the land planted with Sauvignon Blanc and Hárslevelü, the latter being a Hungarian variety little known in South Africa but a vigorous grower and well suited to the low-lying terrain of Lemberg. Jan and Janey have been inspired by the traditional wine-making philosophy of the Old World, modelling Lemberg on the small château vineyards of Bordeaux and the 'boutique' vineyards of California. They feel that small ventures are at a distinct advantage, as the vintner can become more personally involved in the vineyard and its wines.

Traditional methods are employed in the care of the vineyards. Only natural fertilizers are used and the vineyards are never irrigated. By means of careful training and pruning, the crop yield is restricted to less than 40 hectolitres per hectare, allowing the grapes to ripen without stress in order to reach optimum quality.

By South African standards the cellar at Lemberg is very small. It is fully equipped, however, with new stainless steel wine tanks and additional oak *barriques*, and a watchful eye has been cast upon it by Professor Chris Theron, now retired to his ancestral Tulbagh valley, but still much involved in wine and its ways.

With the help and encouragement of many people, coupled with a tenacity of purpose, the Mullers have found a small but se-

cure place for themselves in the future of the winelands, and their wines have already acquired a loyal following.

— MONTPELLIER — ESTATE

The white wines in which this estate specializes are now made in collaboration by two brothers, Jan and Hendrik Theron, with Hendrik in charge of the vineyards and Jan responsible for the cellar operation. The modern history and development of Montpellier were largely the creation of the late De Wet Theron, father of the present generation.

The origins of Montpellier reach back from the thriving present of the Theron family to the early years of Tulbagh's history, and to the grant of a modest 50 morgen of fertile alluvial soil on the banks of the Klein Berg River. It was the first deed issued by the landdrost of Drakenstein in 1714, signed by the then governor of the Cape, Maurits Pasques de Chavonnes, and made to a Huguenot immigrant named Jean Joubert. A refugee from the Languedoc town of Montpellier, his birthplace, he named his new farm after it, and there built the first simple homestead, a three-room mud-brick dwelling with a main room, a kitchen and a bedroom.

During the early years the farm was used exclusively for grazing cattle. Joubert himself appears to have died without issue, for it passed into the hands of a widow, Suzanna

LEMBERG ESTATE

Varieties planted (ha)

4-wire vertical trellis
Sauvignon Blanc 2
Hárslevelü 2

Total area under vines in 1991/2: 4 ha.
Irrigation: None.
Average temperatures: Records are not kept.
Average annual rainfall: 525 mm.
Stock: Vines are propagated from parent stock.
First wine bottled under the Lemberg label:
Sauvignon Blanc 1983.
Wines currently bottled under the Lemberg label: Lemberg Aimée and Lemberg.
Wood ageing: Wines are aged in wood on the estate.
Cellar capacity: 300 hl.

Lemberg Estate is on the Tulbagh Wine Route and is open to the public by appointment only.

The Montpellier homestead today, very different from the mud-brick dwelling of 1714.

Gardé, who ran it until her death in 1771. In 1778 it was acquired by the first of the Theron family, Jan Theron, who enlarged and modified the house and added the fine *bolbol* gable dated 1714.

During the nineteenth century Montpellier saw a succession of different owners, who did not change its basic stock-farming character but expanded its grazing land to cover a substantial proportion of the valley – the extent of the present 600 hectares. In the early 1880s Montpellier became the property of the Theron family once again, and this time finally. Three brothers – Hendrik, Jan and Gawie – bought it jointly but in 1884 De Wet Theron's grandfather, Hendrik, bought out his brothers to become sole owner.

The original vineyards at Montpellier were laid out during the last years of the nineteenth century, and from these, modest leaguers of wine were made in 1926. Although a certain amount of wine, mostly from Sémillon, Cape Riesling and Cinsaut grapes, was made prior to World War II, both the farm and its produce lacked distinction.

When De Wet Theron inherited Montpellier in 1945, he sought to achieve the quality the farm had hitherto lacked. He made radical changes in the structure of the farm, the most important being its conversion to the exclusive making of white wine. The old Cinsaut vines were uprooted and replaced with good white varieties, and realizing that the commitment to white wine-making would require a concomitant technology, he also set about improving his cellar conditions and methods.

The crucial problem in this period before the introduction of cold fermentation was that of controlling the rate of white-wine fermentation during the hot summers.

Under the direction of the then cellarmaster Karl Werner, a system of cold fermentation was introduced and later modified to allow for pressing in the absence of oxygen. Accent was also placed upon the careful choice of the right yeast cultures for specific types of wines.

The result of these innovations was a spectacular improvement in the quality of Montpellier wines, and in December 1967 the first Montpellier white wine, a Cape Riesling, was made. Bottled and labelled by hand, this initial 1 000 bottles of Riesling was kept as an experimental product – as were the wines made in the following three vintages.

In 1968 Werner, having launched the new style of cellar technology on the estate, went back to Geisenheim, and in the years since his departure the Therons have steadily confirmed the reputation of their fine white wines. In 1973 two Montpellier wines, the Montpellier Riesling and the Montpellier Gewürztraminer, were the first of their kinds to receive Superior classification (now defunct) from the Wine and Spirit Board.

The development of the cellar had been accompanied by attention to detail in many other areas. The Theron family has continued to improve the vineyards, introducing new clones to enhance quality, among them clones of the varieties Chenin Blanc and Weisser Riesling, which De Wet christened Tuinwingerd Riesling.

MONTPELLIER ESTATE

Varieties planted (ha)

3-wire vertical trellis
Chenin Blanc 23,26
Weisser Riesling 20,05
Colombard 14,61
Sauvignon Blanc 8,71
Clairette Blanche 8,66
Hárslevelü 6,92
Roter Traminer 5,82
Bukettraube 5,15
Cape Riesling 5,10
Pinot Noir 4,04
Pinot Gris 3,34
Pinot Blanc 1,00

Total area under vines in 1991/2: 110,46 ha.
Irrigation: All the vineyards are irrigated.
Average temperatures: Records are not kept.
Average annual rainfall: 545 mm.
Stock: Parent stock is used for grafting.
First wines bottled under the Montpellier label: Riesling 1967 and Traminer 1971.
Wines currently bottled under the Montpellier label: Suzanna Gardé, Huiswyn, Blanc de Blanc, Tuinwingerd and Special Late Harvest, and Gleno Rhine Riesling, Blanc Fumé and Pinot Noir.
Wood ageing: The Blanc Fumé is aged in wood on the estate.
Cellar capacity: 7 000 hl.

Montpellier Estate is on the Tulbagh Wine Route and is open to the public on Mondays to Fridays from 09h00 to 12h00 and from 13h30 to 17h00, and on Saturdays from 09h00 to 12h00.

With the purchase of 17 adjoining properties over the years, Montpellier has grown to almost 600 hectares, of which 110 are devoted to vineyards. Harvested in 20-kilogram plastic lug-boxes to prevent undue

crushing, the grapes are made into specific varietal wines and rarely blended – a central tenet of De Wet's code as a winemaker for he felt that blending leads to standardization of wines.

In the smooth process of improving the Montpellier wines only the year of the earthquake marked a hiatus. The September night which shook the valley brought down in ruins the beautiful old Cape Dutch homestead, built of friable local mud-brick. Given the choice of rebuilding the homestead or erecting a new building, De Wet Theron elected to restore the first Jan Theron's ancestral home. The result is witness to the passion for good workmanship and fine finish which are themselves the hallmark of the Montpellier white wines.

Since 1989 wines such as Suzanna Gardé, Huiswyn, Blanc de Blanc, Tuinwingerd and Special Late Harvest have been certified under the Montpellier label (Suzanna Gardé owned the farm in the late 1700s). The 'Gleno' selection, consisting of a Rhine Riesling, Blanc Fumé and Pinot Noir (Montpellier's first red wine), was released late in 1990. This is a prestige range and will be released only if the quality warrants it.

— PADDAGANG —
WINE HOUSE AND VINEYARDS

Many towns in South Africa have a Church Street, but Church Street, Tulbagh, is unique in that every building along it has been meticulously restored. They form the largest

Paddagang ('frog alley') restaurant, which specializes in traditional Cape cuisine.

concentration of National Monuments in the country, one of them being Paddagang, a restaurant and winehouse run by the Paddagang Vignerons.

The building dates back to 1809, when it was constructed as a private residence, but subsequently, in 1821, it became established as one of the first Tap Houses in the country. In 1974 Paddagang was opened as a KWV Wine House, but was sold to the Tulbagh Wine Association in 1986.

The origin of the name is not certain, but a popular theory is that the area was a thoroughfare for frogs (paddas) during the mating season. Frogs have become the emblem of Paddagang – the range of boutique wines features quaint frogs on the labels and carries equally quaint names such as Paddasang (song), Paddajolais (merriment), Paddamanêl (tailcoat), Paddapoot (foot), and Brulpadda (bullfrog). The wines are chosen by 'ten friends', including Nicky Krone from Twee Jongegezellen.

Paddagang intends becoming the focal point for the wine industry in Tulbagh. Other local wines besides the 'Padda' range, such as Montpellier and Lemberg, may be sampled at the new wine-tasting centre and tours of the Tulbagh estates and wineries are also organized from the Wine House.

WINES CURRENTLY BOTTLED UNDER THE 'PADDA' LABEL: Paddarotti, Paddamanêl, Paddajolais, Paddadundee, Paddasang, Platanna, Paddapoot and Brulpadda.

—THEUNISKRAAL—
ESTATE

Kobus and Rennie Jordaan make the wine on this estate at the northern end of the Tulbagh valley between the twin shadows of the Obiqua and Witzenberg mountains. Since 1964, when they took over the running of the farm, these two brothers have introduced varieties such as Sémillon, Chenin Blanc and Gewürztraminer. The one for which the estate is famous, however, remains the Cape Riesling introduced by their father, Andries Jordaan, in the late 1940s. It was with this Theuniskraal Riesling that the elder Jordaan achieved one of the great moments of local wine-making with the award of a gold medal at the Commonwealth Wine Show in 1950. This achievement was all the more striking in that Jordaan was a first-generation winemaker, with little or no knowledge of the craft before his mother bought the farm in 1927. Up till then, Theuniskraal's winemaking record had been generally undistinguished. First granted in 1714 to a Huguenot named Theunis Bevernage, grapes were grown during the nineteenth century, but it was only in 1905 that a winery was built on the property.

The Jordaan family came from the Hex River valley, where they had grown table grapes. Mrs Jordaan's intention in buying Theuniskraal was to launch her son on a

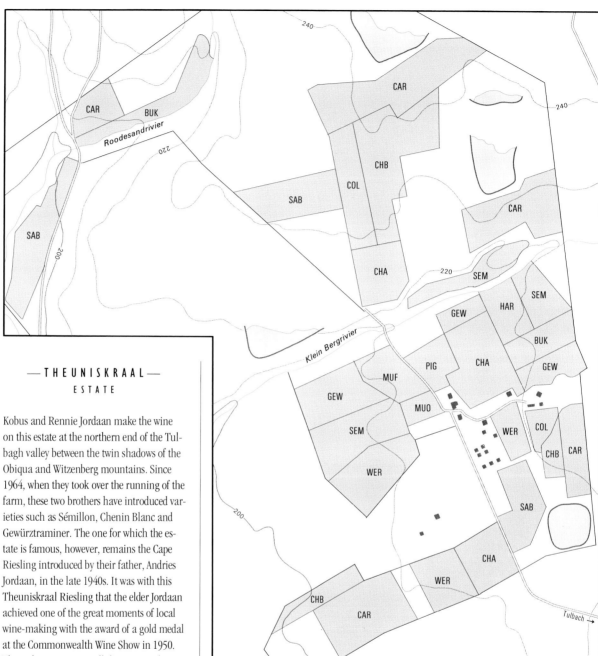

THEUNISKRAAL ESTATE

wine-making career, for the Tulbagh valley was already well known for its good white wines. When they moved onto their new farm the Jordaans found it planted with White French (Palomino), Green Grape – now identified as Sémillon – and Cape Riesling. The young Jordaan's efforts to make wine from these crops were not at first a success. These were the years before the advent of cold fermentation, and although the problems of uncontrolled fermentation in white

wines were recognized, as yet no viable solution had been found. It was at this point that the struggling winemaker received much assistance from Frank Myburgh of the Drostdy Co-operative, under whose expert guidance he made the farm's first blended wine. Named simply 'Theuniskraal', it was a sweet and delicate blend of Palomino, Sémillon and Cape Riesling. It was an immediate success. But the wine which was to put the seal on this success was the Theuniskraal Ries-

Kobus Jordaan, the winemaker at Theuniskraal Estate.

ling, a wine which, since its introduction in 1948, has remained the centrepiece of the farm's production.

The land at Theuniskraal is generally extremely stony but much of the soil is alluvial, fertile and well drained. The present generation of Jordaans, Kobus and Rennie, use irrigation to balance the effects of the drainage and to boost production of their range of new white varieties. These include Colombard, Pinot Gris, Hárslevelü and Bukettraube, as well as the spicy Gewürztraminer, with its elusive fragrance.

THEUNISKRAAL ESTATE

Varieties planted (ha)

4-wire vertical trellis
Cape Riesling 28,5
Sauvignon Blanc 16,5
Chenin Blanc 16
Chardonnay 14
Sémillon 10,5
Bukettraube 9
Colombard 8
Gewürztraminer 8
Weisser Riesling 6
Muscat Ottonel 5,5
Pinot Gris 4
Hárslevelü 2

Total area under vines in 1991/2: 128 ha.
Irrigation: The vineyards are all irrigated.
Average temperatures: Records are not kept.
Average annual rainfall: 700 mm.
Stock: Rooted vines are bought from a nursery.
First wine bottled under the Theuniskraal label: Theuniskraal 1948 (Riesling).
Wines currently bottled under the Theuniskraal label: Riesling and Gewürztraminer (bottled by The Bergkelder).
Wood ageing: Not practised.
Cellar capacity: 17 000 hl.

Theuniskraal Estate is on the Tulbagh Wine Route and is open to the public by appointment only.

—TULBAGH—
CO-OPERATIVE WINE CELLAR

On April 30, 1906, a meeting took place at the old drostdy outside the village of Tulbagh. A small gathering of six worried local farmers was convened under the leadership of Sir Meiring Beck, the resident at the drostdy. The subjects under discussion were the problems caused by over-production, the lack of marketing opportunities, and the generally chaotic state of the Cape wine industry as a whole.

At the conclusion of the meeting it was proposed that a co-operative wine cellar be built in the valley – Beck had been much impressed by the success of the co-operative system in Europe. The proposal was further approved in principle on May 14, when it was decided to erect a cellar which could handle an initial 500 to 1 000 tonnes of grapes a year. The basic function of the cellar was to receive grapes, process them, and sell the resultant natural wine to wholesalers. On the seventeenth of July the first board of directors was chosen, with Mr G. Euvrard, who had donated the property on which the co-operative's cellar was about to be built, as chairman.

The building was completed, and the first crop of grapes taken in. The first wine to be sold was the 1907 vintage, for which E.K. Green & Company's offer of £5 5s a leaguer was accepted by the directors. By 1908 the grape crop delivered to the cellar had increased to 650 tonnes. In the same year a three-year contract with the merchants was signed and the company appointed Frank Myburgh, at a salary of £200 a year, as the co-operative's winemaker. Within a few years his Witzenberg range of wines had become a feature of the cellar's produce.

In spite of the improved quality of the wine, the times were difficult. In 1909 the co-operative's members received no more than £1 10s for a tonne of grapes. By 1921 the situation had deteriorated to the extent that members were obliged to pay in their harvest. And in 1923, with no ready market for their produce, it was decided to let all the wine of the 1922 harvest drain away.

Against all odds, the Drostdy Co-operative (as it was then known) survived. In 1924 the directors decided to market the Witzenberg wines themselves; the shareholders signed a bank security, and Mr P.F. Theron offered all his assets as security for the co-operative's debts. At the same time a considerable sum was spent on advertising.

By 1928 a slow recovery had begun. The Drostdy cellars were by then supplying exports to England which later were extended to Sweden. In 1933 KWV asked the Drostdy to produce Witzenberg wines for them for export to the USA, having secured permission to trade under the name.

The co-operative's first sparkling wine, known as Winterhoek, was being marketed by 1937. The outbreak of World War II, however, brought new problems for the exporters, with a lack of shipping space and a premium on bottles – indeed, while the bottle shortage lasted, permission was granted to sell Witzenberg wines in tomato sauce bottles! In the 1940s, the co-operative's range was enlarged to include sherry, liqueurs and brandy, and in 1979 the directors decided to bottle small amounts of wine for sale to members; demand grew to such an extent, however, that it was later decided to make the wine available to the general public as well. The present winemakers at the co-operative are Mr S. Smit and Mr L. Knoetze.

In 1964 the Distillers Corporation took over the marketing of the co-operative's Wit-

---

WINES BOTTLED AND MARKETED
Red: Claret.
White: Grand Crû, Late Harvest, Chenin Blanc, Sauvignon Blanc, Riesling and Blanc de Noir.
Fortified: Port, Jerepigo and Hanepoot.

The co-operative is on the Tulbagh Wine Route and is open to the public on weekdays from 08h30 to 12h30 and from 13h30 to 17h00, and on Saturdays from 08h30 to 12h00.

zenberg range and their Drostdy sherry range. Confusion arose, however, with Distillers' Drostdy-Hof range of wines, and this prompted the co-operative to change its name to Tulbagh Co-operative Wine Cellar in August 1989.

—TWEE JONGEGEZELLEN—
ESTATE

Generally acknowledged as one of the country's great estates, Twee Jongegezellen is also the oldest family farm in the Tulbagh district, and one with a tradition of growing grapes that goes back some 275 years. The image most commonly associated with the estate and its wines – two cheerful young men in period garb and feathered hats – reflects a colourful period of its long history.

The initial grant of the land which includes the present estate was made in 1710. In the early part of the eighteenth century the farm became the property of two Dutchmen who had been friends in Holland. They joined forces and named their farm 'Twee Jongegezellen', or 'Two Young Bachelors'. Since 1745, the family line has continued unbroken to the present, inheritance passing impartially, and most unusually, through both sons and daughters.

The present owners of the farm, the Krone family, owe much to this enlightened tradition of inheritance. In 1916 the first Krone of Twee Jongegezellen – christened N.C., as have all Krone first-born sons down to the present day – married the daughter of the then owner, Christiaan Jacobus Theron, who had failed to produce a male heir. Krone, who bought the farm from his father-in-law, was the son of a Dutch immigrant who had spent 14 years in the wine and brandy trade in Holland before making his way to the Cape in 1869. The first N.C. Krone did much to consolidate wine-making at the estate of Twee Jongegezellen, but it was his son and

*Nicky Krone and André Rousseau of
Twee Jongegezellen Estate.*

namesake, father of the present Nicky
Krone, who was to establish the farm firmly
on the winemaker's map.

N.C. Krone's career covered the major developments in modern South African wine-
making. He took over the running of the
farm in 1939 after graduating from the
University of Stellenbosch in viticulture and
oenology, having already done practical
work on the farm in 1936 during his university course. He was therefore well aware of
the farm's strengths and limitations, and
during the course of shaping it, became well
known as the maker *par excellence* of white
wines. Every aspect of the wine-making process at Twee Jongegezellen Estate bore the
imprint of his personality and of the stringent standards he set both for himself and
for those who worked for him.

When N.C. Krone took over the farm, the
bulk of the vineyards was concentrated on
the alluvial soil close to the river, but he
soon developed new vineyards on the mountain slopes. There is an old winemaker's
adage which holds that 'the poorer the land,
the better the grapes'. N.C.'s studies of his
land had proved that vines grown closer to
the mountain produced a higher quality
wine and in the following years he steadily,
and successfully extended his vineyards to
encroach on these slopes.

With abundant irrigation and sunshine,
the new noble white varieties which N.C. introduced, the Cape Riesling, Sauvignon
Blanc, Chenin Blanc and Sémillon,
flourished. And on the lower slopes of the
original farm he replaced the old heavy-
bearing Palomino and Sémillon stock with
these new varieties. At the same time he set
about modifying and improving the estate's
cellar facilities, adapting them to the making of high-quality white wine. He began experimenting with methods of controlled

fermentation of white wines, based on the
concept of keeping the whole cellar at a uni-
formly cool temperature. The first of the
Cape wine farmers to use the cold fermentation process in the mid-1950s, his enterprise
paid off impressively in 1959, when his new
wines made by this process won a decisive 13
first prizes at the Cape Wine Show – a success which persuaded many of the more sceptical makers of white wine to invest in steel
and cold water.

N.C.'s son Nicky, a graduate of Elsenburg
Agricultural College and of the famous
Geisenheim Institute in Germany, now runs
the farm and has explored new avenues in
wine-making technology, for example experimenting with the use of a wide range of
imported yeasts. He was awarded the trophy
for the Champion Estate Winemaker in 1979
and 1981 at the South African Championship Wine Show.

Twee Jongegezellen's 296 hectares of vineyards (out of a total of 600 hectares) are situated on the western edge of the Tulbagh
basin. The farm starts along the alluvial
soils of the northern bank of the Klein Berg
River and extends up the slopes of the mountain range to the northwest. Most of the estate's best vineyards lie on the recently
developed slopes at the foot of the Obiqua
Mountain. The slopes are in the rain shadow
of the mountain and receive more rain than
other parts of the Tulbagh area. The soils are
thoroughly mixed with small and large
stones and are much more difficult to cultivate than the alluvial soils in the valley
below. In order to plant vineyards on these
slopes, it is necessary for the ground to be
terraced. Adding to the difficulty is a layer of
ferrocrete conglomerate stone approximately
a metre under the terraces, which has to
be deep-ripped to allow the roots of the vines
to penetrate.

The sloping ground faces east and com-
pensates the vineyards for the relatively high
temperatures recorded in the Tulbagh valley.
Vines on the slopes receive the early-
morning sun while the dew is still on the
leaves, and when the sun sets in the evening
behind the Ou Kloof Mountain, these vineyards fall into shadow before the vineyards
on level ground.

Tulbagh is one of the most northerly of
the recognized quality wine areas in South
Africa, and summer temperatures are normally high. To minimize the extreme effects
of the summer sun, Nicky has positioned all
his recently planted vineyards east to west.
Furthermore the vines' summer canes are
trained to keep the bunches out of direct sunlight until they are harvested; sunburned
grapes have always presented problems in
Cape cellars, due to the fact that a certain
amount of oxidation is inevitable once the
berries are damaged.

Although Twee Jongegezellen is in the
coolest part of the valley, Nicky believes that
the quality of the wines improves when the
grapes are picked at the lowest temperatures.
He experimented with night picking small
batches of grapes between 1977 and 1981
and compared the analyses of juice obtained
from night-picked grapes with that of juice
from comparable grapes picked by day. Working with cool, night-harvested grapes helps
to improve both the flavour and longevity of
the wine. The cooler grapes allow better skin
contact at temperatures below 12 °C whereby
more flavour is extracted and there is less
chance of the negative release of the polyphenols or tannic substances.

The night-picking teams are equipped
with waterproof jackets and trousers to combat the dew, and wear lightweight battery
packs to power the miners' lamps on their
helmets. They work at a faster rate than their
counterparts during the day, as the temperatures are lower and the lights clearly illumi-
nate the bunches.

Although there are so many different varieties on the farm, Nicky has come to the
conclusion that there only five classic white
varieties, namely Chardonnay, Sauvignon
Blanc, Gewürztraminer, Weisser Riesling
and Sémillon, and he intends concentrating
on these in the future. He feels that the introduction of the cold fermentation process has
caused winemakers to lose their way, as it

made them forget that great wines are not
made in the cellar, but in the vineyards.

In recent years Nicky has often been successful with young wines in competitions.
One of Twee Jongegezellen's major successes
has been the introduction of Schanderl
(named after Nicky's esteemed teacher at
Geisenheim), a blend based on Weisser Riesling and Muscat de Frontignan, and TJ 39, a
blend of 17 varieties which has become the
estate's most successful seller.

A new cellar at Twee Jongegezellen has
been custom-built for the production of
'Krone Borealis', a *méthode champenoise*
made from a blend of Chardonnay, Pinot
Blanc and Pinot Noir. The making of this
champagne is supervised by André Rousseau.

The fanciful name of this wine is an
adaptation of 'Corona Borealis', the con-
stellation of stars which, according to Greek
mythology, was created when Bacchus, god
of wine, threw his crown into the heavens
to prove his love for Ariadne, daughter of
the King of Crete.

TWEE JONGEGEZELLEN ESTATE

Varieties planted (ha)

Perold trellis
Weisser Riesling 79
Chenin Blanc 60
Frontignan 40
Sauvignon Blanc 30
Chardonnay 26
Gewürztraminer 21
Sémillon 12
Pinot Blanc 8
Pinot Noir 7
Sylvaner 7
Furmint Nemes 6

Total area under vines in 1991/2: 296 ha.
Irrigation: The vineyards can be irrigated
if necessary.
Average temperatures: Night average 15 °C.
Average annual rainfall: 1 700 mm.
Stock: Parent stock is used for grafting.
**First wine bottled under the Twee
Jongegezellen label:** TJ 39 (about 1955 vintage).
**Wines currently bottled under the Twee
Jongegezellen label:** TJ 39, TJ Light, Schanderl,
Night Harvest, Engeltjiepipi Special Late Harvest
and Krone Borealis.
Wood ageing: Wines are aged in wood on the estate.
Cellar capacity: 23 000 hl.

Twee Jongegezellen Estate is on the Tulbagh Wine
Route and is open to the public on Mondays to
Fridays from 09h00 to 12h30 and from 13h00 to
17h00, and on Saturdays from 09h00 to 12h00.

OLIFANTSRIVIER

By the middle of the nineteenth century vineyards were planted along the banks of the southern reaches of the Olifants River. The wine produced was mainly for local consumption, and included a percentage of dessert wine, as the creative enthusiasm of the wine farmers was reserved for the making of brandy. These were balmy days for the brandy industry in the mountains, for permits for distilling wine were issued with cheerful abandon (the owner of the Matjiesrivier farm in the Cederberg received a permit to distil the produce of a single vine!). Given such official encouragement, brandy-making flourished through to the 1920s, when the issue of distilling permits became the responsibility of the Department of Customs and Excise and KWV. The resultant stringency cast a shadow over the distillers of the high valleys, and within a few years the healthy flow of brandy had dwindled to a trickle. But while brandy is no longer so important along the Olifants River, a substantial amount of grapes is still grown here and processed in the seven local co-operatives.

The district reaches from Citrusdal in the south to Lutzville in the north, and includes the areas of Clanwilliam, Klawer, Vredendal and Koekenaap. It is a hot, dry part with the lowest rainfall near the sea. At Citrusdal and Clanwilliam the farming of citrus and rooibos tea predominates, and the vineyards are largely concentrated to the north, along the Olifants River and between Trawal and Koekenaap, where they receive intensive irrigation from the Clanwilliam and Bulhoek dams.

Three soil types are mainly used for viticulture – the fertile soils near the rivers, medium-potential red sandy soils, and high-potential Karoo soils. On the mountain range between Clanwilliam and Graafwater the vineyards have an average rainfall of approximately 400 millimetres, and a summer temperature of 21 °C. In the Trawal and Koekenaap areas the annual rainfall at about 300 millimetres is appreciably lower and the winters are very mild. The vineyards here are planted on terraces to provide flood irrigation, and are intensively trellised to give active leaf surface so that heavy crops can ripen under cool microclimate conditions in the shade of the leaves.

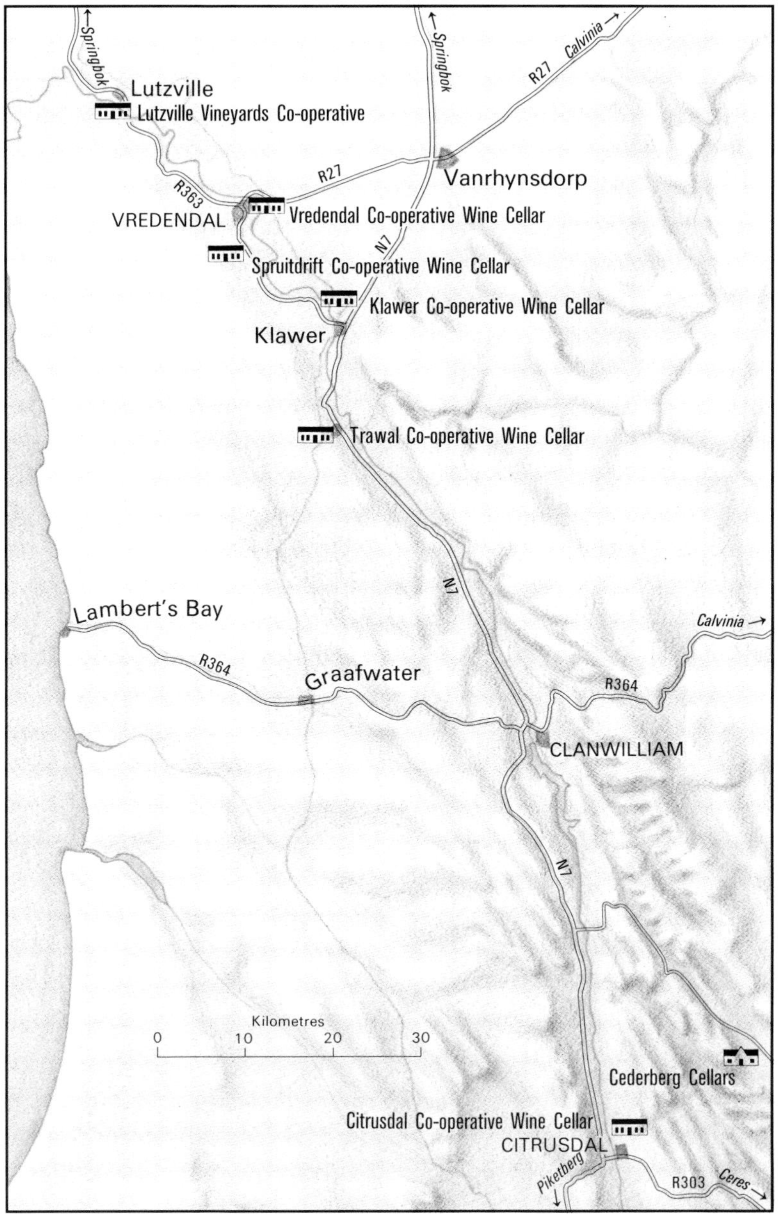

LEFT: *Vineyards have been planted along the banks of the Olifants River since the middle of the nineteenth century.*

—CEDERBERG—
CELLARS

Overlooked by the Sneeuberg, the Tafelberg and the Wolfberg Cracks in the Cederberg mountains, this family-run winery is part of Dwarsrivier, the farm owned by David Josephus Nieuwoudt, universally known as 'Oom Pollie'. The running of the cellars, as well as the 18-hectare vineyard, is the responsibility of Pollie's son, Frikkie, while the remainder of the farm, comprising fruit orchards, livestock and tobacco, is in the charge of his elder brother, Ernst.

At a lofty 1 200 metres above sea level, Dwarsrivier has a cool, mild climate for most of the year, with an annual rainfall of 450 to 500 millimetres. Much of the higher ground is stony, but the lower reaches have good, fertile red soils on which is grown a mix of Cabernet, Pinotage, Barlinka (a table grape), Riesling and Bukettraube.

Until 1964 there were no vines on Dwarsrivier. Then, following a suggestion by Attie Rabie of the Deciduous Fruit Board, Oom Pollie introduced a small block of Barlinka table grapes. With his modest vineyard doing well, he and Frikkie then built a small wine cellar, later enlarged at Frikkie's insistence. Registered in 1973 as the Cederberg Cellars Company, they at first made only a small amount of *boerewyn* ('farmers' wine') from the Barlinka grapes.

Within a few years, however, they had increased their plantings with blocks of Cabernet and Pinotage, causing much local comment with their investment in these high-quality red varieties in an area largely given to white-wine production. It was a bold move, but it paid off, and with startling speed: the 1978 Cabernet made local history as, with its first entry in 1979 in the Olifants

---

WINES BOTTLED AND MARKETED

Red: Pinotage, Merlot, Cabernet Sauvignon and Ceder Rouge.
White: Bukettraube, Riesling, Sauvignon Blanc, Pinot Gris, Dwarsrivier Weissberger, Dwarsrivier Cederberger, Blanc de Noir and Chenin Blanc.

The Cederberg Cellars are on the Olifantsrivier Wine Route and are open to the public on weekdays from 08h00 to 17h00, and on Saturdays from 08h00 to 13h00.

River Wine Show, it won the Distillers Corporation Trophy. In the same year this Cabernet also won the Gold Medal at the Cape Championship Wine Show.

Now firmly on the map of the Olifantsrivier district, Cederberg Cellars currently bottles Pinotage and Cabernet Sauvignon under its own label. One of the more recent labels is most attractive, featuring the 'Maltese Cross Rock' in the Cederberg mountains. The wines can be bought on the farm, by postal order, or at retail outlets.

—CITRUSDAL—
CO-OPERATIVE WINE CELLAR

Situated at the foot of the Sneeuberg in the heart of Citrusdal, Citrusdal Co-operative Wine Cellar, which markets its wines under the Goue Vallei label, boasts extensive modern technology which enables the winery to produce a wide range of quality wines. The grapes for the production of these wines are harvested, inter alia, from vineyards nearest to the snow-line in South Africa. Grapes are harvested from farms situated along the Oli-

---

WINES BOTTLED AND MARKETED

Red: Pinotage, Tinta Barocca, Cabernet Sauvignon and Chianti.
White: Bukettraube, Blanc de Blanc, Premier Grand Crû, Late Vintage, Special Late Harvest, Sauvignon Blanc, Riesling and Weisser Riesling.
Sparkling: Rosé and Vin Doux.
Fortified: Red and White Jerepigo, Hanepoot Jerepigo and White Muscadel.

The co-operative is on the Olifantsrivier Wine Route and is open to the public on weekdays from 08h00 to 12h30 and from 14h00 to 17h00, and on Saturdays from 09h00 to 12h30.

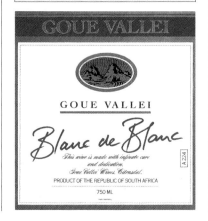

---

fants River and in the Cederberg mountains. The cellar has been awarded several trophies for excellent products, as well as recognition and laurels from many of South Africa's foremost tasting clubs.

The cellar furthermore produces a number of original series of collector's wines, of which the Blou Bulle (in honour of the Northern Transvaal rugby team) and the Flower series are particularly popular. The cellar's regular wine list includes Jerepigo, Pinotage, Tinta Barocca, Bukettraube, Riesling, Cabernet Sauvignon and Sauvignon Blanc as well as two sparkling wines.

—KLAWER—
CO-OPERATIVE WINE CELLAR

One of the larger co-operatives, the Klawer Wine Cellar receives some 25 000 tonnes of grapes annually from 82 members in the Vredendal and Klawer districts. The co-operative is run by manager-winemaker Manfred van Heerden, the other winemaker being Wynand Hamman, formerly of Backsberg. There is now an impressive new tasting centre and sales complex next to the cellar where visitors may sample and buy the wines. A dining room seating 80 people is also available for lunches by appointment.

WINES BOTTLED AND MARKETED

Red: Pinotage, Vin Rouge and Shiraz.
White: Late Vintage, Special Late Vintage, Premier Grand Crû, Colombard, Nouveau, Blanc de Noir and Blanc de Blanc.
Sparkling: Vonkelwyn Sec, Vonkelwyn Demi-Sec and Michelle Vin Doux.
Fortified: Soet Hanepoot, Red Muskadel and Wit Muskadel.

The co-operative is on the Olifantsrivier Wine Route and is open to the public on weekdays from 08h00 to 17h00 and on Saturdays from 09h00 to 12h00.

—LUTZVILLE—
VINEYARDS CO-OPERATIVE

Established in 1962, this co-operative receives 30 000 tonnes of grapes annually from 109 members . Most of the grapes are processed into rebate wine for brandy production and only the best grapes are reserved for the making of wine. Before it became Lutz-

---

---

ville, the town was called Vlèrmuisklip after a rock where early explorers sheltered and were evidently pestered by bats and now the most notable wines in the range are sold under the Fleermuisklip label. Lutzville Co-operative is under the management of Johan Theron and the winemaker is Gerhard van Deventer.

WINES BOTTLED AND MARKETED

Red: Robyn.
White: Fleermuisklip Sauvignon Blanc, Grand Crû, Chardonnay, Chenin Blanc, Bukettraube, Blanc de Noir, Late Harvest and Special Late Harvest.
Fortified: Sweet Hanepoot.

The co-operative is on the Olifantsrivier Wine Route and is open to the public on weekdays from 08h00 to 12h30 and from 14h00 to 17h00, and on Saturdays from 08h30 to 12h00.

—SPRUITDRIFT—
CO-OPERATIVE WINE CELLAR

One of the younger co-operatives in the Vredendal area, the Spruitdrift Co-operative, which is quite spectacular in size, has the benefit of advanced cellar technology and equipment in handling its annual intake of 25 000 tonnes of grapes from 118 members.

The winemaker is Johan Rossouw, formerly winemaker at the Simonsvlei Co-operative. Under his guidance a number of new varieties have been planted, including Gewürztraminer, Weisser Riesling, Sauvignon Blanc, Morio Muscat and Merlot. Several awards at wine shows have popularized the name among wine lovers far and wide of the Spruitdrift Co-operative.

Wine tastings and lectures are regularly conducted in the attractive vinotèque, and snoek braais can be organized for large groups if bookings are made in advance.

WINES BOTTLED AND MARKETED

Red: Pinotage and Cabernet Sauvignon.
White: Premier Grand Crû, Riesling, Sauvignon Blanc, Special Late Harvest, Late Harvest, Chenin Blanc, Colombard, Gewürztraminer, Weisser Riesling, Morio Muscat and Blanc de Noir.
Sparkling: Demi-Sec.
Fortified: Red and White Muscadel and White Hanepoot.

The co-operative is on the Olifantsrivier Wine Route and is open to the public on weekdays from 08h30 to 17h30, and on Saturdays from 08h30 to 12h00.

Modern stainless steel equipment at the Vredendal Co-operative Wine Cellar, formerly known as the Olifantsrivier Co-operative.

—TRAWAL—
CO-OPERATIVE WINE CELLAR

Situated near Klawer, this co-operative was started in 1969, and is currently run by J.P. (Kobus) Basson. All wine made here is supplied in bulk to the trade. The co-operative is on the Olifantsrivier Wine Route.

—VREDENDAL—
CO-OPERATIVE WINE CELLAR

Formerly known as the Olifantsrivier Co-operative, this is the largest co-operative winery under one roof in the country, and up to 55 000 tonnes of grapes, supplied by 175 members, have been delivered to the co-operative annually, with a maximum of 1 700 tonnes per day. Situated in Vredendal, it was established in 1948, and is run by Gielie Swiegers, who took over from Corrie de Kock when the latter retired in 1986. Gielie spent four years at the Spruitdrift Co-operative. and before then had made a name for himself at the McGregor Co-operative.

Mostly white wine varieties are grown in the ward of Vredendal, among them Fernão Pires, Hárslevelü, Bukettraube, Sauvignon Blanc and Weisser Riesling. Some reds, such as Pinotage and Tinta Barocca, are also grown, and of late these varieties have been augmented with Chardonnay, Merlot, Cabernet Franc and Ruby Cabernet. Although much of the crop is turned into distilling wine, the cellar is designed to give equal attention to a range of light table wines and good-quality single-variety wines. Small French oak barrels are now used for ageing some of the wines. Vredendal's Nouveau has the unusual name Gôiya Kgeisje, which is the San for 'first wine'. The 1989 Koekenaap Chardonnay was awarded a silver medal at the 1990 International Wine and Spirit Competition in London.

The co-operative's attractive emblem is the Namaqua dove, which symbolizes the peace (*vrede'*) of Vredendal. The wine labels depict the area covered in spring blossoms, and incorporate the coat of arms of the Vredendal Municipality, which also features the same bird in the design.

WINES BOTTLED AND MARKETED

Red: Dry Red.
White: Classic Dry White, Chardonnay, Sauvignon Blanc, Meisje (low-alcohol), Gôiya Kgeisje, Chenin Blanc, Fernão Pires, Bukettraube, Late Harvest and Noble Late Harvest.
Fortified: Red Muscadel and Hanepoot Jerepigo.

The co-operative is on the Olifantsrivier Wine Route and is open to the public on weekdays from 08h30 to 12h20 and from 14h00 to 17h30, and on Saturdays from 08h00 to 12h00.

WORCESTER

In the early days the main route through the great mountain barrier which stretches northwards from the Hottentots-Holland, Wemmershoek and Slanghoek mountains to the Groot Winterhoek mountains, lay through the Roodezand pass into the valley of Tulbagh. From here the road gave access in the south-east to the wide valley of the Breede River.

In the course of the eighteenth century scattered farms and settlements grew up in this valley. Much of the land was used for grazing and remained otherwise undeveloped until the early nineteenth century when Governor Lord Charles Somerset shifted the seat of the magistracy from Tulbagh to Worcester, near the banks of the Breede River. Tulbagh was granted its own administrative independence in 1804.

The fortunes of the Breede River community improved, but difficulties of access still limited development and it was only with the building of the Bain's Kloof road, completed in 1853, that a viable commercial route was established between Cape Town and Worcester. By this time flourishing vineyards were settled in the area, and by the 1860s production compared favourably with that of the Stellenbosch and Paarl valleys. Much of the crop was dried for raisins, and this continued to be an important aspect of the local industry into the present century. But a decline in the demand for raisins after World War II persuaded most of the farmers to convert to growing wine grapes, and in response to this change an extensive network of co-operative wineries sprang up – a total of some 32 across the whole Breede River region.

The results of these developments have been spectacular. Approximately 25 per cent of the total national crop is processed in the Worcester district, making it – in terms of volume – the most important of South Africa's wine-making districts.

Geographically the district is delimited mainly by mountain ranges, while the border to the eastern side is formed by a natural watershed with the Robertson area. There are a number of wards within the official Worcester district, reflecting a marked internal variation in soil types and microclimates. Worcester and its surroundings form part of the Breede River catchment area, which is fed by a number of smaller rivers supplemented by the run-off from the winter snows in the mountains.

In the Breede River, Botha, Slanghoek and Goudini areas the soils are sandy loams with a varying loose stone content and fairly high free-water table. As a result they often require artificial drainage during soil preparation. Other types include deep fertile alluvial soils along the river banks, and calcareous clayish soils which require intensive ripping during prepara-

LEFT: *Rawsonville vineyards in the spring.*

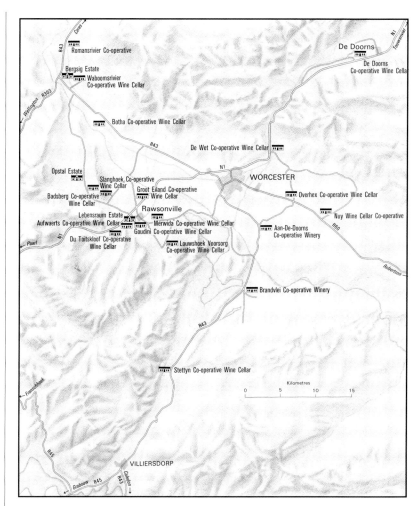

tion. Average summer temperatures range between 19 and 22 °C. Rainfall varies considerably, the annual average in the Slanghoek area to the west being approximately 1 500 millimetres, in contrast with a low 300 millimetres in the Nuy and Scherpenheuvel areas to the east.

Vineyards in the Worcester district are mostly found along river banks. Many of the farmers depend on the Brandvlei Dam for irrigation, especially in the lower rainfall regions where all the vineyards must be intensively irrigated. Where the rainfall is higher some vineyards are grown without, or with only supplementary, irrigation.

—AAN-DE-DOORNS—
CO-OPERATIVE WINERY

Situated in the Aan-de-Doorns ward of the Worcester district, this winery came into production in 1955. Some 43 member farmers in the district supply 15 000 tonnes of grapes at harvest time to Alwyn Mostert, the cellar's winemaker and manager.

Alwyn produces a range of approximately 18 wines, of which the Cabernet Sauvignon and the Chenin Blanc show consistently good quality. The co-operative's sweet dessert wine, Muscat d'Alexandrie, is particularly popular. The latest addition to the cellar's range of red wines, a Ruby Cabernet, is a particularly good example of this variety. The co-operative produced its first Chardonnay – which was also the first to be bottled in the area – from the 1991 vintage.

WINES BOTTLED AND MARKETED

Red: Vin Rouge, Dry Red, Pinotage, Cabernet Sauvignon and Ruby Cabernet.
White: Chenin Blanc, Premier Grand Crû, Sauvignon Blanc, Clairette Blanche, Riesling, Sparkling Wine, Muscat d'Alexandrie, Chardonnay, Colombard, Late Harvest, Special Late Harvest and Blanc de Noir.
Fortified: Port and Muscadel.

The co-operative is on the Worcester Wine Route and is open to the public on weekdays from 08h00 to 12h00 and from 13h00 to 17h30 and on Saturdays from 09h00 to 12h00.

—AUFWAERTS—
CO-OPERATIVE WINE CELLAR

Situated near Rawsonville in the Worcester district, the Aufwaerts winery was started as a family concern in 1974 and serves only three farms. The chief executive is W.T. Hanekom and the winemaker H.L.D. de Villiers. The bulk of the co-operative's production is table and dessert wines, which are sold to wholesale merchants.

WINES BOTTLED AND MARKETED

White: Weisser Trocken and Leicht Trocken.
Fortified: Hanepoot Jerepigo and White Jerepigo.
The co-operative is on the Worcester Wine Route and is open to the public by appointment only.

—BADSBERG—
CO-OPERATIVE WINE CELLAR

Badsberg was inaugurated in 1951 and wine-making began the following year. Since then its winemaker, Lourens de Jongh, has achieved remarkable success with his Hanepoot. A consistently excellent dessert wine, it has been a prolific award winner at both Worcester and National Championship shows. The co-operative also produces a number of natural wines.

Lourens de Jongh retired at the end of 1988 after 31 years at the cellar. Gerrit van Zyl, a B.Sc. graduate from the University of Stellenbosch, is the new winemaker. New wine labels and plantings of Chardonnay, Merlot and Ruby Cabernet in 1991 indicate the possibility of very different wines in the future from this cellar. A new addition to the range is a carbonated sparkling wine.

WINES BOTTLED AND MARKETED

White: Riesling, Sauvignon Blanc, Chenin Blanc, Tafelwyn, Badslese, Hanepoot (dessert), Laat Oes and Sparkling Wine.

The co-operative is on the Worcester Wine Route and is open to the public on weekdays from 08h00 to 12h00 and from 13h00 to 17h00 and on Saturdays from 09h00 to 12h00.

—BERGSIG—
ESTATE

Bergsig Estate – situated in the fertile Breede River Valley, where Willem Hendrik Lategan settled in 1843 and planted the first vines – became established as a wine-producing farm in the 1930s, but only in 1978 was the property of the present owner consolidated and Bergsig Estate formally established.

One of the largest wine estates in the country, Bergsig in recent years has been developed by the Lategan family. It is now run by 'Prop' Lategan, his three sons, and his winemaker, Kas Huisamen. An impressive range of varieties is grown on 370 hectares of irrigated vineyards, including Chenin Blanc, Colombard, Cape Riesling, Cinsaut and Cabernet Sauvignon, as well as more unusual varieties such as Fernão Pires and Furmint. Approximately 2 per cent of the total

The cellar at Bergsig Estate, at the foot of Bain's Kloof.

BERGSIG ESTATE

Varieties planted (ha)

Various trellising systems are used
Chenin Blanc 150
Muscat d'Alexandrie 60
Colombard 40
Cape Riesling 30
Sauvignon Blanc 20
Tinta Barocca 12
Cabernet Sauvignon 10
Cinsaut 10
Weisser Riesling 10
Chardonnay 8
Pinotage 7
Gewürztraminer 5
Furmint 4
Fernão Pires 2
Merlot 2

Total area under vines in 1991/2: 370 ha.
Irrigation: The vineyards are irrigated.
Average temperatures:
Maximum 23,8 °C; minimum 11,2 °C.
Average annual rainfall: 900 mm.
Stock: Rooted vines are bought from a nursery.
First wines bottled under the Bergsig label:
Cabernet Sauvignon, Colombard, Sweet Hanepoot and Chenin Blanc (all 1978).
Wines currently bottled under the Bergsig label: Sauvignon Blanc, Riesling, Weisser Riesling, Fernão Pires, Furmint, Gewürztraminer, Bouquet Light, Weisser Riesling Special Late Harvest Superior, Gewürztraminer Special Late Harvest, Noble Late Harvest Superior, Pinotage Blanc de Noir, Painted Lady sparkling wine, Pinotage, Cabernet Sauvignon, Sweet Hanepoot and Port (bottled by the Breërivier Bottling Co-operative).
Wood ageing: Wines are aged in wood on the estate.
Cellar capacity: 3 500 tonnes of grapes.

Bergsig Estate is on the Worcester Wine Route and is open to the public on weekdays from 08h45 to 16h45, and on Saturdays from 09h00 to 12h00.

---

crop is bottled, while the remainder is sold to wholesalers. Over the years Bergsig Estate has won a considerable number of awards for its wines.

—BOTHA—
CO-OPERATIVE WINE CELLAR

The prolific Botha family in this area of the Breede River Valley have given their name both to the locality and to the small railway station on the line between Worcester and Wolseley, as well as to the co-operative which was established here in July 1949. Originally named the Botha's Halt Co-operative Wine

---

WINES BOTTLED AND MARKETED

Red: Cabernet Sauvignon and Pinotage.
White: Weisser Riesling, Sauvignon Blanc, Vin Blanc, Chenin Blanc, Chenin Blanc Late Harvest, Riesling and Blanc de Noir.
Fortified: Port and Sweet Hanepoot.

The co-operative is on the Worcester Wine Route and is open to the public on weekdays from 08h30 to 12h30 and from 13h30 to 17h30, and on Saturdays from 10h00 to 12h00.

The Botha Co-operative Wine Cellar.

Cellar, the cellar is now run by winemaker André Stofberg, his assistant Johan Morkel, and the winery's secretary, Fourie de Kock.

Improvements in quality control in recent years have been matched by increases in production: the annual crop taken in is now 18 400 tonnes. Recent awards for this co-operative's wines include those won at the Cape Championship Wine Show.

—BRANDVLEI—
CO-OPERATIVE WINERY

The co-operative was built in 1955 on 5 hectares of land donated by Danie de Wet from his farm Brandvlei. Extensions to the Brandvlei Dam forced the winery to move to a new site in 1974. Here a new and improved modern cellar was constructed, much of its operation now being automated, which allows the winemaker to produce good quality-wines. The co-operative has 40 members and crushes 12 500 tonnes of grapes annually. Winemaker Theuns le Roux took over from Booysen Maree as general manager and winemaker at the end of 1989. He is assisted by Willie Burger.

The Brandvlei Co-operative's main claim to fame is its Chenel wine. In 1965 Danie van Tubbergh obtained a few cuttings from Professor Chris Orffer, who developed this Chenin Blanc-Trebbiano crossing. Danie planted them on his father's farm, Riverside,

---

WINES BOTTLED AND MARKETED

Red: Ruby Cabernet and Cabernet Sauvignon to be available by 1993.
White: Grand Crû, Late Vintage and Colombard.
Fortified: Soet Hanepoot Jerepiko and Port.

The co-operative is on the Worcester Wine Route and is open to the public on weekdays from 07h30 to 12h30 and from 13h30 to 17h30.

The Brandvlei Co-operative Winery, which channels one third of its crop into brandy.

along the banks of the Breede River. Further plant material was propagated from these vines, and wine from the new variety was made commercially for the first time in 1978 at the Brandvlei Winery.

Brandvlei's bottled wine, however, accounts for only a small portion of production, the bulk being sold to the trade. Thirty per cent of the grapes that are crushed go to brandy production.

—DE DOORNS—
CO-OPERATIVE WINE CELLAR

Pieter Hamman is the winemaker and manager of this winery, which is situated just outside De Doorns in the Hex River Valley. Besides wines, the cellar also handles large quantities of export table grapes grown by member farmers, who now number 210. The first bottled wine under the De Doorns label came on to the market in 1977; nowadays about a dozen different wines, including a sparkling wine, are bottled annually.

WINES BOTTLED AND MARKETED

White: Sauvignon Blanc, Grand Crû, Chenin Blanc, Stein, Perlé Blanc, Laatoes, Late Vintage and Colombard.
Rosé: Perlé Rosé.
Sparkling: From Sauvignon Blanc.
Fortified: Hanepoot.

The co-operative is on the Worcester Wine Route and is open to the public on weekdays from 08h00 to 12h30, and from 13h30 to 17h00 and on Saturdays from 08h30 to 12h00.

—DE WET—
CO-OPERATIVE WINE CELLAR

The De Wet Co-operative Wine Cellar at the base of the pass leading through the mountains into the Hex River Valley is situated directly on the N1 national road. Wine-making began in 1946 and today approximately 16 000 tonnes of grapes are pressed annually, with two wines now sold in the United Kingdom. The responsibility for the wine-making rests on the shoulders of Zakkie Bester, who is the winemaker and manager, and joint winemaker Kobus de Wet, who has been with the cellar since 1966.

Vines at De Wet Co-operative growing alongside the railway line.

WINES BOTTLED AND MARKETED

Red: Dry Red.
White: Sauvignon Blanc, Cape Riesling, Clairette Blanche, Fernão Pires, Blanc de Noir, Special Late Harvest, Pétillant Fronté and Noble Late Harvest.
Sparkling: Cuvée Brut and Vin Doux.
Fortified: Red Muscadel, White Muscadel and Hanepoot.

The co-operative is on the Worcester Wine Route and is open to the public on weekdays from 08h00 to 17h00, and on Saturdays from 09h00 to 12h00.

At the end of 1989, the co-operative split into two independent co-operatives, the one handling export table grapes and the other exclusively devoted to wine-making. This arrangement has enabled the co-operative to concentrate on the quality of its wines. The co-operative is also engaged in a variety renewal programme and premium varieties such as Chardonnay, Merlot and Cabernet Sauvignon have been planted. Production of these wines will mark the start of a new era for the De Wet Co-operative.

—DU TOITSKLOOF—
CO-OPERATIVE WINE CELLAR

Du Toitskloof Co-operative Wine Cellar is situated in a valley at the entrance to the Du Toitskloof Pass about 100 kilometres from Cape Town. The winery began production in 1962 and serves 12 farmers who harvest on average 10 000 tonnes of grapes per season. Philip Jordaan, present winemaker and manager, joined the cellar in 1984. The small number of members enables Philip to choose grapes from selected vineyards for pressing separately in order to make specific wines. A batch of reds (maiden vintages of Merlot, Cabernet Franc, Ruby Cabernet and Shiraz are due in 1992) and Chardonnay will in future allow him to extend his skills.

WINES BOTTLED AND MARKETED

Red: Cinsaut, Pinotage, Cabernet Sauvignon and Vino Uno dry red.
White: Sauvignon Blanc, Riesling, Blanc de Blanc, Weisser Riesling, Colombard, Chenin Blanc, Bukettraube, Muscat d'Alexandrie, Special Late Harvest, Noble Late Harvest Superior, wood-matured Chardonnay, Blanc de Noir, Vino Uno Dry White and Vino Uno Semi-Sweet white.
Sparkling: Sparkle.
Fortified: Port and Hanepoot Jerepigo.

The co-operative is on the Worcester Wine Route and is open to the public on weekdays from 08h30 to 12h30 and from 13h30 to 17h30 (17h00 on Fridays), and on Saturdays from 08h30 to 12h00.

Philip Jordaan, of the Du Toitskloof Co-operative Wine Cellar.

Philip's 1985 Hanepoot Jerepigo was the first ever Nederburg Auction wine from this cellar. New World-influenced labels designed by local artist Cecily Rocher are a striking match for the wines Philip Jordaan makes for his cellar.

— GOUDINI —
CO-OPERATIVE WINE CELLAR

This co-operative – situated on the Smalblaar River near Rawsonville – was established in June 1948 with a membership of 25, and is the second-oldest co-operative in the Worcester district. In 1949 the first harvest of 6 000 tonnes of grapes was received by Chris van Reenen, who later became a lecturer at the Elsenburg College.

Goudini means bitter honey (it is believed that honey made from the flowers of the smalblaar trees is bitter), and the co-operative's label depicts a honeycomb surrounded by leaves of the smalblaar tree and the well-known Sneeukop in the background.

The Goudini Co-operative Wine Cellar, from where some of the country's champion muscat wines have been produced.

> ### WINES BOTTLED AND MARKETED
>
> **Red:** Pinotage.
> **White:** Chenin Blanc, Chenin Blanc Late Harvest, Special Late Harvest, Gouvino, K'Gou Dani, Clairette Blanche, Riesling and Blanc de Noir.
> **Fortified:** Sweet Hanepoot.
>
> The co-operative is on the Worcester Wine Route and is open to the public on weekdays from 08h30 to 12h00 and from 13h00 to 17h00.

In 1971 Mr C.P. le Roux succeeded Chris Van Reenen as manager and winemaker, and in 1985 he in turn was succeeded by Hennie Hugo. Hennie has produced wines of good quality since his arrival.

At present 16 000 tonnes of grapes are handled annually by Hennie Hugo, Sakkie Bosman and Faan Langenhoven.

— GROOT EILAND —
CO-OPERATIVE WINE CELLAR

This cellar was established near Rawsonville in December 1961 with an initial 13 members. The first crop of 5 295 tonnes of grapes was delivered in 1962 and the pressing was supervised by the newly appointed winemaker and manager, Cecil Bredell, formerly of Santhagens in Stellenbosch.

The present winemaker and manager is Willem Loots, who receives 8 000 tonnes of grapes annually from 15 members. Only white-wine varieties are used for the production of wine from this co-operative.

> ### WINES BOTTLED AND MARKETED
>
> **White:** Nouveau, Riesling, Pinot Gris, Perlé Dali, Hönigtraube and Chenin Blanc Late Harvest.
> **Fortified:** Sweet Hanepoot.
>
> The co-operative is on the Worcester Wine Route and is open to the public on weekdays from 08h30 to 12h30 and 13h30 to 17h30, and on Saturdays from 09h00 to 12h00.

— LEBENSRAUM —
ESTATE

Originally a part of the farm 'Het Groote Eiland', this estate was given independent life in 1943. The fifth generation of the family to farm in this area was Philip Deetlefs who was succeeded by his son after Kobus had graduated from Stellenbosch University. In 1989 and 1990 Kobus won three gold medals at the South African Wine Show but has not bottled his 1990 and 1991 harvests, the wines having been taken up by wholesalers.

> ### LEBENSRAUM ESTATE
>
> (No other information available)
> **First wines bottled under the Lebensraum label:** Stein, Clairette Blanche and Soet Hanepoot Superior (all 1978 vintage).
> **Wines currently available under the Lebensraum label:** Cape Riesling and Weisser Riesling.
>
> Lebensraum Estate is on the Worcester Wine Route and is open to the public on weekdays from 14h00 to 18h00.

— LOUWSHOEK VOORSORG —
CO-OPERATIVE WINE CELLAR

Grapes grown only in the Louwshoek and Voorsorg regions are used at this winery which has been in production since 1957. The co-operative's wines are made under the supervision of winemaker and manager, Jacob Potgieter. It has 32 members and crushes 13 000 tonnes of grapes annually.

> ### WINES BOTTLED AND MARKETED
>
> **Red:** Dry Red.
> **White:** Chenin Blanc, Colombard, Riesling, Premier Grand Crû, Noble Late Harvest, Late Harvest and Muscat d'Alexandrie (dessert).
> **Fortified:** Nectar de Provision.
>
> The co-operative is on the Worcester Wine Route and is open to the public on weekdays from 08h00 to 12h30 and from 13h30 to 17h00 and on Saturdays by appointment.

— MERWIDA —
CO-OPERATIVE WINE CELLAR

One of the dense concentration of co-operatives in the Rawsonville district (whose 10 co-operatives make it the highest-producing area in the winelands), the Merwida Co-operative is also one of the few family concerns. After its formation in November 1962 it was bought out by the Van der Merwe family, already majority shareholders in the company and owners of much of the land in the vicinity. Now under the chairmanship of Schalk van der Merwe, the co-operative draws a wide range of grape varieties from some 700 hectares in the vicinity. Of the wines made by winemaker Jacobus 'Wollie' Wolhuter and his assistant, Sarel van Staden, seven are currently bottled under the Merwida label.

> ### WINES BOTTLED AND MARKETED
>
> **White:** Riesling, Sauvignon Blanc, Colombard and Chenin Blanc.
> **Sparkling:** Cuvée Brut.
> **Fortified:** Port and Sweet Hanepoot.
>
> The co-operative is on the Worcester Wine Route and is open to the public on weekdays from 07h30 to 12h00 and from 13h30 to 17h30.

Merwida, a family-owned co-operative in the Rawsonville district.

— NUY —
WINE CELLAR CO-OPERATIVE

With just 20 members, Nuy is one of the smallest co-operative wine cellars in the country. Despite its size, however, it has earned an enviable reputation for superior wines. To ensure this quality, only the top 3 per cent of production is bottled under the Nuy label, the rest being sold to wholesalers for blending into their own products. Situated at the foot of the Langeberg some 14 kilometres from Worcester, Nuy serves 13 farms and presses some 8 000 tonnes of grapes annually. It produces primarily dry and semi-sweet white wines as well as sweet dessert wines.

Although Nuy was established only in 1963, most of its members come from

Wilhelm Linde, winemaker at the Nuy Wine Cellar Co-operative.

families who have been growing or making wines for generations. The first winemaker, C.P. le Roux, was succeeded in 1971 by Wilhelm Linde, who is still at the helm. Linde believes in making classically styled wines,

The gateway to Nuy Co-operative, one of the smallest co-operative wine cellars in South Africa.

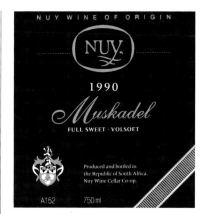

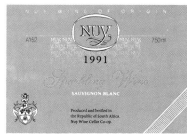

where the nature of the varieties and the vineyards are allowed to speak for themselves. His wines have won numerous prestigious awards, twice winning the Diners' Club Award, in 1988 for the 1985 White Muscadel and in 1991 for the Riesling. In 1987 he won the General Smuts Trophy for that year's Red Muscadel, which was named South African Championship Wine. Since 1983 Nuy wines have also featured at the Nederburg Auction, where the muscadels in particular have fetched excellent prices.

WINES BOTTLED AND MARKETED

Red: Rouge de Nuy.
White: Riesling, Sauvignon Blanc, Colombard Dry, Chant de Nuit, Fernão Pires, Bukettraube, Colombard Semi-Sweet and Steen Late Harvest.
Sparkling: From Sauvignon Blanc.
Fortified: Red and White Muscadel.

The co-operative is on the Worcester Wine Route and is open to the public on weekdays from 08h30 to 16h30 and on Saturdays from 08h30 to 12h30.

— OPSTAL —
ESTATE

Situated near Rawsonville in the Slanghoek Valley, this estate, in its early years a large cattle farm, was first settled in the middle of the nineteenth century by 'Lang Jan' Ros-

---

OPSTAL ESTATE

Varieties planted (ha)

1- and 3-wire vertical trellis
Chenin Blanc 36
Muscat d'Alexandrie 16
Colombard 14
Clairette Blanche 10
Sauvignon Blanc 5
Cinsaut 3
Cabernet Sauvignon 2
Ferdinand de Lesseps 1
Weisser Riesling 1

Total area under vines in 1991/2: 88 ha.
Irrigation: Computerized drip and micro-irrigation.
Average temperatures: Records are not kept.
Average annual rainfall: Approximately 1 100 mm.
Stock: Rooted vines are bought from a nursery.
First wines bottled under the Opstal label:
Chenin Blanc and Volsoet Hanepoot
(both 1978 vintage).
Wines currently bottled under the Opstal label:
Dry Steen, Chenin Blanc, Colombard, Weisser Riesling, Blanc de Noir, Cabernet Sauvignon, Sweet Hanepoot (bottled by the Breërivier Bottling Co-operative).
Wood ageing: Not practised.
Cellar capacity: 10 000 hl.

Opstal Estate is on the Worcester Wine Route and is open to the public for wine sales on weekdays from 09h00 to 11h00 and from 15h00 to 17h00.
Cellar tours can be arranged by appointment.

---

souw. The name of its homestead, *'De opstal bij de fonteinen'* (the homestead by the spring), in due course became attached to the farm itself.

The former owner and winemaker, the late Attie Louw, planted a number of white varieties such as Clairette Blanche, Chenin Blanc and Colombard, as well as the red variety Cabernet Sauvignon, on the upper slopes of the farm. The first wines bottled under Attie's guidance and the estate's own label were a Chenin Blanc and a Sweet Hanepoot in 1978.

Opstal is now run by Stanley Louw, the sixth generation of the Louw family. In 1987 he won the Vineyard Competition run by Stellenbosch Farmers' Winery for the best vineyard block of Chenin Blanc. The overseas trip which was the prize for the Vineyard Competition enabled Stanley to visit the wine-growing countries of Europe and the Californian vineyards.

Each year, a harvest day is held, at which the public can pick grapes themselves, which are then taken to the cellar for processing.

Vineyards in the region flourished after the completion of the Bain's Kloof road in 1853, which created a link between Cape Town and Worcester.

—OVERHEX—
CO-OPERATIVE WINE CELLAR

The Overhex Co-operative was started in 1963 with Doug Lawrie, an M.Sc. graduate from the University of Cape Town, in charge of its design, construction and eventual wine-making, which included the installation of the first Bucher separator to be used in a local winery. Hennie Verster, a student in cel-

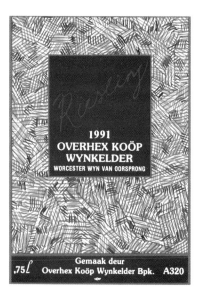

WINES BOTTLED AND MARKETED

White: Sauvignon Blanc, Cape Riesling, Clairette Blanche, Colombard, Late Harvest and Chenin Blanc Special Late Harvest.
Fortified: White Muscadel.

The co-operative is on the Worcester Wine Route and is open to the public on weekdays from 08h00 to 13h00 and from 14h00 to 17h00, and on Saturdays from 09h00 to 12h00.

---

lar technology at the Elsenburg College, took over as manager and winemaker in December 1990, with Alkie van der Merwe being appointed joint winemaker in the same month.

—ROMANSRIVIER—
CO-OPERATIVE

In the immediate post-Second World War years the rapid expansion of the wine industry in the Breede River area led to a heavy congestion at harvest time at the KWV depot in Worcester – farmers were allowed only two days in 14 on which to deliver their grapes. The founding of the Romansrivier

Co-operative grew out of a response to this crisis, and was initiated by two local farmers, H.F. Conradie and D.J. Viljoen. The winery was built in 1949 and the first crop, some 4 000 tonnes, delivered by the 18 founder members, was pressed in 1950. The co-operative now has 65 members and crushes 10 000 tonnes of grapes annually.

Romansrivier Co-operative was, under the guidance of Monis of Paarl, one of the early users of cold fermentation and its wines were

---

WINES BOTTLED AND MARKETED

Red: Cabernet Sauvignon, Pinotage, Vino Rood and Rovino dry red (500ml).
White: Riesling, Dry Colombard, Off-Dry Colombard Semi-Sweet, Vin Blanc Special Reserve, Grand Crû, Chenin Blanc, Late Harvest,
Special Late Harvest, Rovino Dry White, Rovino Semi-Sweet, Blanc de Blanc, Chardonnay, Noble Late Harvest, Sauvignon Blanc Sec and Vin Doux.
Fortified: Port and Hanepoot.

The co-operative is on the Worcester Wine Route and is open to the public on weekdays from 08h30 to 12h00 and from 13h30 to 17h00, and on Saturdays from 08h30 to 10h00.

---

much sought after by wine merchants. The present winemakers are Olla Olivier and Bartho Eksteen who joined the co-operative in 1974 and 1990 respectively. Most of the wine produced at Romansrivier is sold in bulk to merchants. Although only part of the crop is bottled, the co-operative provides an extensive range of products: some 22 different wines are bottled annually.

The Romansrivier Co-operative's wines are of a very good quality. Olla's success can be attributed partly to his excellent rapport with the farmers, as well as to his knowledge of their vineyards, enabling him to advise the farmers to harvest the grapes in exactly the condition he requires, providing the raw material he needs.

—SLANGHOEK—
CO-OPERATIVE WINE CELLAR

Tucked away in a valley of the Slanghoek Mountains about 2 kilometres from Goudini Spa, this winery was formed in 1951, taking in its first crop of 3 000 tonnes of grapes in the following harvest. Izak (Bill) Pretorius was the winemaker at that first vintage, and he still occupies the post, though he has been assisted by Carel van Breda since 1964.

Since the early days both the membership and the crop received have increased dramatically: 36 farmers now supply the winery with nearly 19 000 tonnes of grapes annually. In spite of this bulk, however, the emphasis at Slanghoek has always been on the making of quality wines, and it has performed consistently well at regional wine shows. The 1979 Colombard was sold at the Nederburg Auction.

Technical innovations have in part been responsible for this high quality. One

---

WINES BOTTLED AND MARKETED

Red: Pinotage.
White: Chenin Blanc, Colombard, Riesling, Premier Grand Crû and Late Harvest.
Fortified: Sweet Hanepoot.

The co-operative is on the Worcester Wine Route and is open to the public on weekdays from 07h00 to 08h30, from 09h00 to 12h00 and from 13h30 to 17h30 (16h30 on Fridays). On Saturdays, it is open from 10h00 to 12h00.

Slanghoek Co-operative, tucked away in the Slanghoek Mountains near the Goudini Spa.

The buildings of the Waboomsrivier Co-operative Wine Cellar.

example is the centrifugal pump developed by the Slanghoek winemakers in collaboration with Professor Joël van Wyk of Stellenbosch University; this gives a cleaner must than the pumps previously used. During 1989 a new insulated storage cellar was completed; the new Cape Georgian-styled front of the cellar housing the 26 stainless-steel tanks looks quite impressive against the background of the majestic mountains. The first harvest of Chardonnay took place in 1992 and new plantings of Cabernet Sauvignon are in the pipeline.

—STETTYN—
CO-OPERATIVE WINE CELLAR

Situated on the road between Worcester and Villiersdorp, the Stettyn Co-operative was started in 1964, the first wine being made

the following year. The co-operative has nine members operating from six farms, who deliver an annual 4 000 tonnes of grapes. The cellar is supervised by winemaker and manager Tienie Crous.

—WABOOMSRIVIER—
CO-OPERATIVE WINE CELLAR

The design of the wine labels of the Waboomsrivier Co-operative features the flower of *Protea arborea,* the 'waboom' from whose sturdy wood the local wagon wheels were made. Established in 1949, this co-operative wine cellar concentrated from the outset on the making of quality wines. An area of the farm Kleinberg was bought as the site of the winery, which pressed its first crop of 4 148 tonnes in 1950.

In the post-war years capital was limited, and the initial 22 members of the co-operative loaned their farm tractors to the winery to power the cellar machinery until finance for electricity was available. While electricity powered the machinery, much of the co-operative's human energy and resources were supplied by its winemaker and manager, Mynhardus Cloete. His career was distinguished by fine wine-making and a commitment to the founders' ingenuity and inventiveness. In 1956, for example, he designed a drainer made of wood which improved the yield of free-run juice in white wine-making. Twelve such drainers, soon known as the Cloete drainer or separator, were installed, and by 1958 virtually the en-

tire crop at the co-operative was processed by means of these. Other inventions which were developed by him included a special tank for the fermenting of quality red wines, and a quick-fermenter for the fermentation of husks for distilling. Some of these aids have been superseded, but in their time they helped to improve both quality and efficiency of production.

In 1987 Cloete went on pension and was succeeded by Chris van der Merwe – only the second winemaker at the co-operative. Chris has had previous experience as winemaker at the Porterville and Villiersdorp co-operatives. Currently the co-operative comprises 44 members who provide 22 different grape varieties.

The labels have been changed, and among Chris's innovations is a pink demi-

sec sparkling wine made from Pinotage and Chenin Blanc varieties. The resultant wine is called Rubellite. New plantings of Merlot and Shiraz varieties are planned, and the use of wood maturation is to be implemented in the future.

View over the Stettyn area, near Lake Marais, better known as the Brandvlei Dam.

O V E R B E R G

The Overberg district is on the coastal belt in the south-western part of the Cape Province east of the Hottentots Holland Mountains. Previously known as the Caledon district, it includes Villiersdorp, Caledon, Riviersonderend, Bredasdorp, Hermanus and Bot River. A mountainous region, it is mainly given over to wheat and fruit production – the most important being apples, pears and peaches.

One of the principal towns of the district, Caledon grew up around the famous hot springs. Ferdinand Appel, the first white settler in the area, obtained 44 acres of land from the Dutch East India Company in 1709. In 1810, the farm was purchased and a village called Zwartberg founded. Three years later it was renamed after the Earl of Caledon, the first civilian governor of the Cape Colony.

Villiersdorp, around which most of the vines in the district are grown, was established in 1844 on the farm Radyn, on which one of the five old water-mills erected by the Dutch East India Company still stands. The Villierdorp Moskonfyt and Fruit Co-operative receives and markets most of the grapes, onions, peaches, apricots and apples grown in the area. The *moskonfyt* ('grape-syrup') factory in the town is the only one of its kind in the world.

One of the most well-known fishing towns in the area, Hermanus was founded in the 1830s by Hermanus Pieters, a fisherman. The small natural harbour provided safe anchorage for fishing boats, and has now been converted into an open-air museum. The village has become a popular tourist resort.

The soil in the Overberg district is mainly sandy, which facilitates straightforward preparation and cultivation. The climate is cool, and the vines do not receive as many hours of sun as in other districts because of the proximity of mountains. The cool climate causes the grapes to ripen late in the season. The mean annual rainfall is high, at some 700 millimetres.

Although there are only two vineyards in the ward of Elgin producing commercial quantities of grapes (fruit is still much more profitable), the area, being one of the coolest in the country, has great potential for producing wines with very distinctive characteristics.

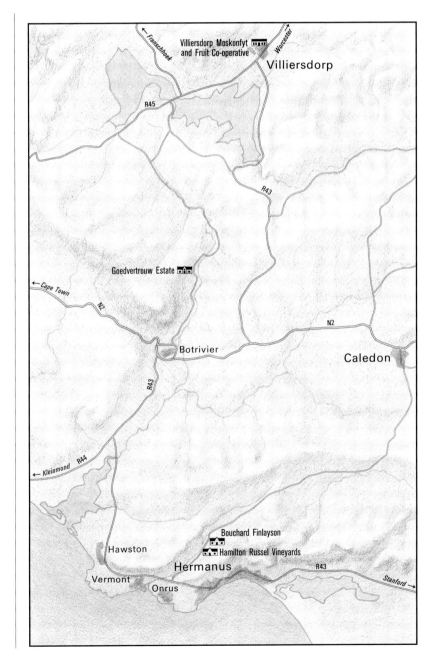

LEFT: *Fynbos and vineyards in the Hemel-en-Aarde Valley in the Overberg district.*

The Bouchard Finlayson cellar, with the sea in the distance.

—BOUCHARD FINLAYSON—

The Bouchard Finlayson farm was part of a Moravian Mission Station from 1818 to 1845. In 1847 it was granted to J.F. Joubert and J.D.K. Reitz by the governor of the Cape, Sir Henry Pottinger. Since then it changed hands several times before being acquired by the present owners, Peter Finlayson and Paul Bouchard, in January 1990.

It is intended to plant 15 hectares of vineyard, to be known as Klein Hemel-en-Aarde. This vineyard is set on the slopes of the Glen Vauloch mountains 9 kilometres from Hermanus in the Hemel-en-Aarde Valley. Nearly 70 per cent of the land is not suitable for vineyard, but is rich in fynbos and will be maintained as a wilderness area and water catchment source. The vineyard development programme will not be completed before 1996. The first 7 hectares are being established on the gentle west-facing slopes below the winery and comprise mainly Pinot Noir, with Chardonnay, Pinot Blanc and Sauvignon Blanc on the deeper soils. The arable land is described as a duplex structure having a heavy consistency with a clay underlayer and soils are prepared with generous

Michael Clark, with owners Peter Finlayson and Paul Bouchard.

additions of lime. Planting and trellising have been based on the Burgundian method of narrow rows, high vine density and low yields from the individual vines.

The attractive new winery is designed with practicality in mind – the wide veranda assists in keeping the interior cool, and the thatch roof provides its own natural insulation. The 16-metre long maturation cellar will house 150 *barriques*. Wine-making follows the traditional crushing and destalking methods, much of the operation done by hand to ensure that no bitter character enters the wine through pumping the mash. The red wine fermentation takes place in traditional open fermenters and all wines undergo malolactic fermentation.

Winemaker Peter Finlayson is a graduate oenologist from Stellenbosch University. He furthered his studies at the wine school of Geisenheim in the Rhinegau in 1975 and he has since travelled abroad regularly, returning to Burgundy five times in the last 10 years. Peter spent valuable years at the fledgling Boschendal winery between 1976 and 1979 before taking on the daunting challenge of building the winery at Hamilton Russell Vineyards. He was particularly successful at the now neighbouring cellar with the Pinot Noir grape, winning the coveted Diners' Club Winemaker of the Year award in 1989 for a 1986 Pinot Noir. His prize included staying four days in Beaune, France, as the guest of Paul Bouchard. Paul now assists in the styling of wines and advises on international markets and developments with Michael Clark acting as administrator and financial director.

The first wine was made in 1991 from grapes purchased from a carefully selected nucleus of grape-growers whose grapes will form the basis of the wines for some years to come. Two labels will distinguish between the two styles of wine made – one for varietal wines and one for a blended white wine.

The first wines, a blended white and a Sauvignon Blanc, were released towards the end of 1991. Early in 1992 a limited quantity of Chardonnay was released, and by 1993 the first Pinot Noir and Merlot will be available to the public.

BOUCHARD FINLAYSON

Varieties planted (number of vines)

Burgundian system
Pinot Noir 20 000
Sauvignon Blanc 6 000

Hedge system
Chardonnay 3 000
Pinot Blanc 3 000

Total area under vines in 1991/2:
7 ha (9 ha still to be planted).
Irrigation: The vineyards are only irrigated in times of drought.
Average temperatures: 1 620 degree-days.
Average annual rainfall: Approximately 750 mm.
Stock: Parent stock is used for grafting.
First wines bottled under the Bouchard Finlayson label: Sauvignon Blanc 1991 and Blanc de Mer 1991.
Wines currently bottled under the Bouchard Finlayson label: Sauvignon Blanc, Blanc de Mer, Chardonnay and Pinot Noir.
Wood ageing: Wines are aged in wood on the estate.
Cellar capacity: 700 hl.

Bouchard Finlayson is open to the public by appointment only.

—GOEDVERTROUW—
ESTATE

A retired engineer, Arthur Pillmann came to know and love the French Burgundy and German Moselle wines on his frequent trips to Europe. He dreamed of making his own wines and, in 1984, he and his wife Elreda left city life in Johannesburg behind them and retired to this 240-hectare farm near Bot River. They began planting in 1985, only to have the farm ravaged by drought three years later. However, they installed irrigation and by 1991 had 10 hectares under vines and 24 hectares given over to apricots

Arthur Pillmann of Goedvertrouw Estate in his cellar.

(which are exported) and pastures. The remaining 200 hectares is fynbos in which some extremely rare proteas exist.

The vineyards face either east or south and are planted with four different varieties, including Pinot Noir – Arthur's favourite wine. They will produce only 3 to 4 tonnes per hectare, the cellar handling only about 1,5 tonnes per day. Arthur is now building a smoking room in which he will smoke pork to serve in his wine-tasting room.

GOEDVERTROUW ESTATE

(No information on plantings available)
Total area under vines in 1991/2: 10 ha.
Irrigation: All the vineyards are irrigated.
Average temperatures: No records are kept.
Average annual rainfall: 300 mm.
Stock: Rooted vines are bought from a nursery.
First wine bottled by Goedvertrouw Estate: Chardonnay 1990.
Wines currently bottled by Goedvertrouw Estate: Chardonnay, Cabernet Sauvignon, Sauvignon Blanc and Pinot Noir.
Wood ageing: The wines are aged in wood on the estate.
Cellar capacity: 100 hl.

Goedvertrouw Estate is open for sales on Saturdays from 09h00 to 13h00, and otherwise by appointment.

—HAMILTON RUSSELL—
VINEYARDS

Hamilton Russell Vineyards are situated in the Hemel-en-Aarde Valley, behind the Raed-na-Gael mountains which form the backdrop to Hermanus. These steep mountains protect the vineyards from the harmful effects of the strong salt-laden south-east

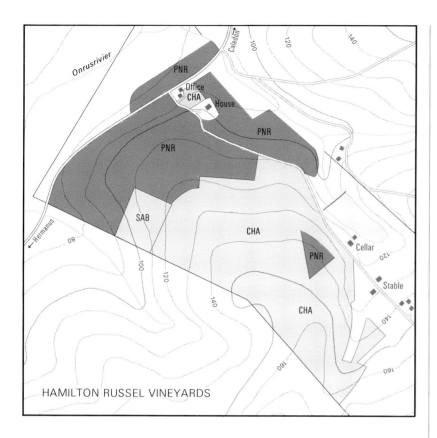

HAMILTON RUSSEL VINEYARDS

The Hamilton Russell vineyards in the Hemel-en-Aarde Valley.

winds that blow off the sea only 2 kilometres away. Approximately 8 kilometres from the town, the vineyards fall under the Walker Bay ward of the Overberg district. The concern is owned by a business executive, Timothy Hamilton-Russell, and the winemaker is Storm Kreusch-Dau.

Much of Hamilton-Russell's youth was spent in Constantia and it was there in the early 1950s that his interest in wine was nurtured. Later, while taking a degree at Oxford, he came into contact with French wines, particularly the red and white wines of Burgundy. He became convinced that excellent red and white wines could be produced from noble varieties such as Pinot Noir and Chardonnay in carefully selected cool areas of South Africa (although his only regret is that the country does not extend a further

Anthony Hamilton-Russell, Storm Kreusch-Dau and Tim Hamilton-Russell.

200 kilometres to the south which would temper its climate to that of central France).

During a career in the firm of J. Walter Thompson in Johannesburg, Timothy nursed this ambition. Then, in 1975, it found practical form with the purchase of land in the Hemel-en-Aarde Valley. The choice of land was carefully made, bearing in mind the kinds of wine he wanted to produce. He undertook a thorough study of a broad spectrum of different areas and microclimates, before finally settling in the Hermanus area.

The great advantage of this area is the cool climate during the growing months. At latitude 34 35' south, as compared for instance to Constantia, at a latitude of 34 02' south, it has fewer than 3 000 degree-days of heat a year. During the summer months it is cooled by breezes off the sea, only 2 kilometres distant. The rainfall in the area is about 750 millimetres a year. The soil is primarily an arenaceous shale, part of the Bokkeveld Series and varies in depth, but on average is about 600 millimetres deep.

In the year after purchase the first serious planting of vines began. In the following years approximately 20 000 vines have been planted annually, with an emphasis upon

two high-quality varieties, Pinot Noir and Chardonnay. Small numbers of Sauvignon Blanc vines have also been established.

While the vineyards were being planted, a cellar was built in 1980, specifically designed to deal only with wines of high quality; its capacity, therefore, is limited. Producing its first wine from the 1981 vintage, it now produces about 16 000 cases a year and is one of the smaller premium wine cellars in the

---

HAMILTON RUSSELL VINEYARDS

Varieties planted (ha)

3-wire vertical trellis
Chardonnay 30
Pinot Noir 20
Sauvignon Blanc 2

Total area under vines in 1991/2: 52 ha.
Irrigation: The vineyards are irrigated only in times of drought, never to increase yield.
Average temperatures: 1 620 degree-days.
Average annual rainfall: Approximately 750 mm.
Stock: Parent stock is used for grafting.
First wines bottled by the Hamilton Russell Vineyards: Hemel-en-Aarde Blanc de Blanc and Grand Crû, Hamilton Russell Grand Vin Blanc and Grand Vin Noir (all 1981 vintage).
Wines currently bottled by the Hamilton Russell Vineyards: Chardonnay, Pinot Noir, Sauvignon Blanc, Premier Reserve and Grand Vin Blanc, and Hemel-en-Aarde Vin Blanc and Vin Rouge.
Wood ageing: Wines are aged in wood on the estate.
Cellar capacity: 1 852 hl.

Hamilton Russell Vineyards are not open to the public, but the wines may be tasted and are for sale at the Hamilton Russell Vineyards Tasting Room in the marketplace behind the Burgundy Restaurant in Hermanus.

---

country. Peter Finlayson, the original winemaker, was fundamental in establishing the cellar's good reputation.

In 1991, Timothy Hamilton-Russell was joined by his son Anthony who is managing director of the enterprise. Anthony spent seven years overseas completing a degree at the university of Oxford and an M.B.A. from the Wharton Business School.

With his two top wines, the Pinot Noir and Chardonnay, Timothy strives for the Burgundy style. All Hamilton Russell wines are wooded in French oak, mainly from Nevers, for periods ranging from 18 months in the case of the Pinot Noir and up to nine months for the Chardonnay. The yields at Hamilton Russell Vineyards are deliberately low, the wines are among the Cape's very best, and their prices, not surprisingly, among the highest in the country.

— VILLIERSDORP —
MOSKONFYT AND FRUIT CO-OPERATIVE

This co-operative is situated in the town of Villiersdorp. It was started in 1922 with the intention of concentrating on moskonfyt and processing fruit, but was expanded to include wine production in 1976. The first bottling took place in 1978.

Classic quality varieties such as Chardonnay, Sauvignon Blanc, Cape Riesling, Sémillon and Cabernet Sauvignon have been planted. In 1991 the first Chardonnay was harvested and released at the end of that year, an exciting occasion for winemaker J.P. Steenekamp. Most of the wine produced at the co-operative is sold to merchants, but a small quantity is retained for sale at the co-operative.

WINES BOTTLED AND MARKETED

Red: Overberg Pinotage and Pinot Noir.
White: Overberg Sauvignon Blanc, Chardonnay, Chenin Blanc, Colombard and Blanc de Noir, and Villiersdorp Grand Crû and Late Vintage.
Fortified: Overberg Port and Villiersdorp Hanepoot Jerepigo.

The co-operative is on the Worcester Wine Route and is open to the public on weekdays from 08h00 to 17h00 and on Saturdays from 08h00 to 11h00.

ROBERTSON

The first farmers in what is now the Robertson district arrived at the beginning of the nineteenth century, thereby extending the settlement of the Breede River Valley into its lower reaches. Here, on the wide expanses of wild grass, the pioneers herded sheep and cattle, but later in the century crops of lucerne were planted in the lime-rich soils as feed for the racehorses that farmers started to breed.

In this period little wine farming was seen in the area. As is so much of the Cape hinterland, it is a hot, dry region, and without irrigation the chances of survival for the vineyards were slender. Two factors changed this bleak prognosis. The first was the building of the Brandvlei Dam at the turn of the century, providing a supplement to the Breede River, which regularly runs dry in the heat of summer. The second was the advent of the cold fermentation process.

LEFT: *Vineyards near the town of Bonnievale, between Swellendam and Robertson.*

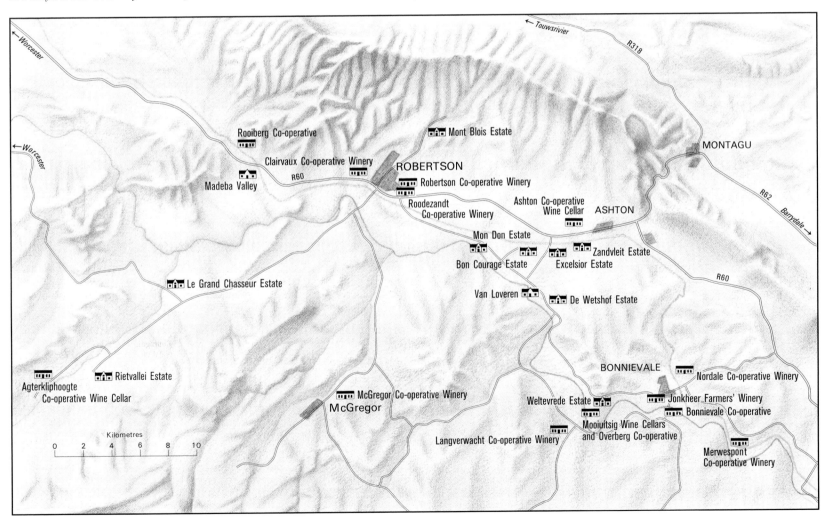

—AGTERKLIPHOOGTE—
CO-OPERATIVE WINE CELLAR

Situated in a dry and inhospitable area 28 kilometres from Robertson is the Agter-kliphoogte Co-operative Wine Cellar. It was started in 1965 and by 1982 some 4 500 tonnes of grapes were being pressed here, of which 2 000 tonnes were Chenin Blanc and the balance was made up of Muscadel, Pinot-age, Cabernet Sauvignon, Colombard and Raisin Blanc.

The present winemaker and manager is Helmard Hanekom. Of the 24 members, four draw water from the *Le Chasseur* Canals which run from Brandvlei Dam; the other 20 members rely on their own dams to collect the natural winter run-off from the mountains and thus supplement the insufficient and unpredictable rainfall. Most of the wine made here is delivered in bulk to merchants, but some is bottled under the Agterklip-hoogte Co-operative Wine Cellar label.

WINES BOTTLED AND MARKETED

White: Chenin Blanc, Colombard and Sauvignon Blanc.
Fortified: Muskadel.

The co-operative is on the Robertson Wine Route and is open to the public on weekdays between 08h00 and 12h30 and between 13h30 and 17h30. Cellar tours are conducted by appointment.

—ASHTON—
CO-OPERATIVE WINE CELLAR

This large co-operative winery is situated on the Robertson side of Ashton, at the foot of the Langeberg. Inaugurated in 1962, the first wine-making season was in 1963, when the first 6 000 tonnes of grapes were crushed. Because many of the grapes delivered to the cellar were too low in sugar to allow good quality wine-making, a grape juice concentrating plant was successfully installed and its product exported to the extent of 50 000 hectolitres annually.

The present winemaker is Tertius Siebrits and the co-operative's current membership stands at 84, with an annual delivery of 21 180 tonnes of grapes of 29 varieties. A consistent prizewinner at young wine shows, the co-operative bottles a substantial range of

wines. All the wines, except the Cabernet Sauvignon, Blanc Fumé and Chardonnay, are marketed in screw-top bottles in an endeavour to keep costs as low as possible.

WINES BOTTLED AND MARKETED

Red: Cabernet Sauvignon and Dry Red.
White: Colombard, Riesling, Blanc Fumé, Chardonnay, Weisser Riesling, Pétillant Blanc, Bukettraube, Late Harvest and Gewürztraminer.
Fortified: Sweet Hanepoot and Red and White Muscadel.

The co-operative is on the Robertson Wine Route and is open to the public on weekdays from 08h00 to 13h30 and from 14h30 to 17h30. It is closed on Saturdays, except during the summer school holidays when it is open from 08h00 to 12h00.

—BON COURAGE—
ESTATE

Bon Courage has been owned since the 1920s by the Bruwer family. The name 'Bon Courage' is a French translation of Goede-moed, the farm of which it was once a part. André Bruwer, the present owner and wine-maker, took over the farm in 1965 and registered it as an estate some 12 years later.

With the installation of cold fermentation equipment on his property in 1966, André began making dry white table wines, then a new development in this generally hot and dry region. Plantings of the traditional Chenin Blanc and Muscadel were extended with a range of varieties suited to dry wine-making, including, Kerner, Riesling, Chardonnay and Gewürztraminer.

The original cellar was redesigned by André in 1974 to allow for more modern methods of wine production. The many awards won since 1983 testify to the quality of the estate's wines. These achievements include trophies, double gold and gold medals and class winners at the South African Championship Wine Show. André Bruwer has been South African Estate Winemaker of the Year in 1984, 1985 and 1986, and in 1990 he received the Diners' Club Wine-maker of the Year award. In 1986 André started night harvesting, accepting the fact that the quality of the grape, especially the subtle flavouring of the skin, is better if the grape is cool. In 1989 André also imported a mechanical harvester from France.

The cellar at Bon Courage Estate, situated about 9 kilometres outside Robertson.

Bon Courage has an interesting range of certified dry, off-dry, semi-sweet and dessert wines as well as a Chardonnay Vin Sec sparkling wine, all of which are on sale from the beautifully thatched and well-preserved Goedemoed homestead, built in 1818.

André Bruwer, Diners' Club Winemaker of the Year for 1990.

OESJAAR 1991 — VINTAGE 1991

Bon Courage

WINE OF ORIGIN ROBERTSON

LE BOUQUET

Estate Wine

GROWN AND MADE BY ANDRÉ BRUWER ON THE BON COURAGE ESTATE AND BOTTLED BY BREERIVIERVALLEI BOTTELERINGSKOÖPERASIE BPK. HIGH STREET, WORCESTER
750ml PRODUCE OF THE REPUBLIC OF SOUTH AFRICA

BON COURAGE ESTATE

Varieties planted (ha)

Perold trellis
Colombard 30
Chenin Blanc 30
Muscadel 27
Clairette Blanche 10
Chardonnay 10
Weisser Riesling 6
Sauvignon Blanc 6
Cape Riesling 5
Gewürztraminer 4
Kerner 3
Merlot 3
Pinot Noir 2
Shiraz 2
Cabernet Sauvignon 2

Total area under vines in 1991/2: 140 ha.
Irrigation: All the vineyards are irrigated.
Average temperatures:
Maximum 25 °C; minimum 16 °C.
Average annual rainfall: Approximately 300 mm.
Stock: Rooted vines are bought from a nursery.
First wines bottled under the Bon Courage label: Colombard, Blanc de Noir and Kerner Late Harvest (all 1983 vintage).
Wines currently bottled under the Bon Courage label: Riesling, Sauvignon Blanc, Chardonnay, Rhine Riesling, Bouquet Blanc, Blanc de Noir, Le Bouquet, Kerner Late Harvest, Gewürztraminer Special Late Harvest, Noble Late Harvest, Red Muscadel, Chardonnay Vin Sec sparkling wine and Shiraz.
Wood ageing: Wines are aged in wood on the estate.
Cellar capacity: 20 000 hl.

Bon Courage Estate is on the Robertson Wine Route and is open to the public on weekdays from 09h00 to 17h00 and on Saturdays from 09h00 to 12h30.

The Bonnievale Co-operative, where Piet Linde has been winemaker since the co-operative was established in 1964.

—BONNIEVALE—
CO-OPERATIVE

Established in 1964, this cellar now has 60 members and presses a substantial 13 000 tonnes of grapes a year, of which approximately 2 300 tonnes are Chenin Blanc and 1 000 tonnes Colombard.

Depending upon the vintage, 30 to 40 per cent of good wine is made by winemaker, Piet 'Kelder' Linde.

WINES BOTTLED AND MARKETED

Red: Pinotage.
White: Blanc de Blanc, Colombard Semi-Sweet, Colombard and Late Vintage.
Fortified: Hanepoot Jerepigo.

The co-operative is on the Robertson Wine Route and is open to the public on weekdays from 08h30 to 12h30 and 13h30 to 17h00.

—CLAIRVAUX—
CO-OPERATIVE WINERY

This co-operative, situated on the outskirts of Robertson, was developed from a private cellar owned by Rial Kloppers in the 1920s and was established as a co-operative in 1963. The winemaker and manager, Kobus van der Merwe, makes a range of wines under the Clairvaux label from grapes received from the winery's 15 member farmers.

WINES BOTTLED AND MARKETED

Red: Pinotage and Cabernet Sauvignon.
White: Rhine Riesling, Special Late Harvest and Blanc de Noir.
Fortified: Port, Red Muscadel Jerepigo and Golden Jerepigo.

The co-operative is on the Robertson Wine Route and is open to the public on weekdays from 08h30 to 17h30, and on Saturdays from 08h30 to 12h30.

—DE WETSHOF—
ESTATE

In 1968, Johann de Wet, the owner of De Wetshof since 1952, sent his son, Danie, to the viticultural institute at Geisenheim in Germany, to acquire an up-to-date education in the ways of modern wine-making. Two years later the younger De Wet arrived back at the family farm in the Robertson area to begin putting his new discoveries into action.

Other advantages included a father with many years of experience in his craft, and fertile land of good extent – recent expansion has brought it up to a present 165 hectares. De Wetshof boasts the country's highest lime content in its soils, giving a high fixed acid content to the wines made here. Besides a supply of irrigation water from the Breede River, special climatic conditions help in the growing of high-quality grapes: at night the cool sea air from the Agulhas coast mingles with the warmer air from the hinterland and causes a thick mist which blankets the land well into the following morning. Together with a heavy dew, this mist helps to protect the farm and its vineyards from the full ferocity of the sun.

On his return from Geisenheim, one of Danie's first moves was the installation of cold fermentation equipment, enabling him to begin making light, fragrant, white table wines. Thereafter, he began systematically to experiment with new varieties and new clones of familiar varieties, while retaining old and trusted favourites such as the traditional Chenin Blanc. New introductions by the mid-1970s included Weisser Riesling and Pinot Gris, as well as Sauvignon Blanc and Chardonnay – two clones of the latter were tried. Danie observed that the Chardonnay from the Champagne region gave a bigger crop under his particular conditions, but that its Burgundy counterpart gave better acids and sugar. Of these, the Weisser Riesling, Sauvignon Blanc and Chardonnay have proved the most successful. Other experiments include investigations into different kinds of oak for wood maturation, though the traditional Limosin oak still came out ahead with a higher tannin content than Nevers or Balkan oaks.

All this energy and innovation soon paid visible dividends. The first farm in the

Danie de Wet, whose innovative approach to wine-making has ensured the success of De Wetshof.

Robertson district to be granted estate status, De Wetshof carried off the champion wine prize at the Robertson Wine Show in 1973 for the De Wetshof Riesling, contrary to all expectations. It was followed by a Sauvignon Blanc, the first to be designated 'Superior' and the South African Champion White Wine in 1984, and the Edeloes, a 'Superior' botrytis or noble rot wine. Released for the first time in 1980 (it is made only in years when there is a heavy dew), the latter is made from Riesling and Chenin Blanc grapes; the must for this wine is kept at a

DE WETSHOF ESTATE

Varieties planted (ha)

Fence system
Chardonnay 76
Chenin Blanc 20
Sauvignon Blanc 17
Weisser Riesling 12
Colombard 10
Cape Riesling 6
Other varieties 3
Gewürztraminer 2
White Muscadel 2
Pinot Gris 2

Total area under vines in 1991/2: 150 ha.
Irrigation: All the vineyards of De Wetshof are irrigated.
Average temperatures:
Maximum 36 °C; minimum -6 °C.
Average annual rainfall: Approximately 375 mm.
Stock: Parent stock is used for grafting.
First wines bottled under the De Wetshof label: Steen Dry 1973, Steen 1974 and Riesling Dry 1974.
Wines currently bottled under the De Wetshof label: Blanc Fumé, Rhine Riesling, Finesse, Chardonnay Reserve and Edeloes.
Wood ageing: Chardonnay and Sauvignon Blanc are aged in wood on the estate.
Cellar capacity: 18 000 hl.

De Wetshof Estate is on the Robertson Wine Route and is open to the public on weekdays from 08h30 to 17h00 and on Saturdays from 09h00 to 13h00.

constant low temperature and is allowed to ferment for two to three months. The estate also makes a wood-matured Chardonnay, the first of its kind in the country to achieve a 'Superior' classification. In 1987 this Chardonnay (from the 1985 vintage), containing 20 per cent Auxerrois, was judged the best wine at the world's most extensive wine and wine machinery exhibition in Bordeaux. Known as 'Vinexpo', this show coincides with a judging of wine held by the Oenological Department of the University of Bordeaux, and it was here that Danie de Wet's wine claimed highest honours.

— EXCELSIOR —
ESTATE

This estate on the Cogmanskloof River is run as a partnership by the brothers Stephen and Freddie de Wet. As do many of the farmers in this lime-rich district, they devote their energies both to growing and making wine and to breeding aristocratic racehorses. In the case of Excelsior, the horse stud, vineyards and cellars are divided between the brothers: Stephen takes charge of the horses and the cellar, Freddie is responsible for the vineyards with their complex irrigation systems – so necessary in this hot, dry region which is,

---

EXCELSIOR ESTATE

Varieties planted (ha)

Extended Perold, factory and vertical trellis
Sauvignon Blanc 46
Colombard 37
Red Muscadel 36
Muscat d'Alexandrie 11
Cabernet Sauvignon 10
Chenin Blanc 9
Chardonnay 5
St Emilion 4
White Muscadel 4
Raisin Blanc 2

Total area under vines in 1991/2: 164 ha.
Irrigation: All the vineyards are irrigated.
Average temperatures: Records are not kept.
Average annual rainfall: 250 mm.
Stock: Rooted vines are bought from a nursery.
First wines bottled under the Excelsior label:
Red and white Muscadel (both 1977 vintage).
Current wines are still to be bottled.
Cellar capacity: 16 000 hl.

Excelsior Estate is not open to the public.

---

however, partly cooled by the mists which occur on summer mornings and the prevailing winds which generally blow off the cold Benguela Current approximately 120 kilometres to the west.

Traditionally, Muscadel varieties were grown here, and still are, but, to cater for the changes in public taste towards dry white wines, other varieties have been planted during the last decade. These include Chenin Blanc, Sauvignon Blanc, Colombard and Trebbiano. Wines for export will soon be bottled on the estate, while the rest is sold in bulk to merchants.

— JONKHEER —
FARMERS' WINERY

This winery was originally established in the early 1900s as an ostrich farm by the grandfather of the current chairman, Nicolaas Jonker. When the ostrich boom collapsed, the Jonkers changed to wine, planted their own vineyards and sold their products direct to the public.

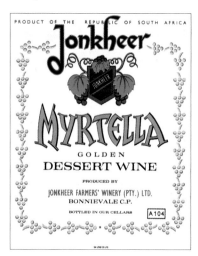

WINES BOTTLED AND MARKETED

White: Bakenskop Riesling, Colombard, Grand Crû, Late Harvest, Edelweiss Stein and Edelstein.
Fortified: Jonkheer Old, White, Cape and Invalid Port. Matador Medium Cream, Medium Dry and Pale Dry Sherry. Jonkheer Old Brown, Golden, Milk, Club and Full Cream Sherry. Red and White Muscadel, Red and White Myrtella, Melita, Marsala, Red and White Muscadel Liqueur Wine, Red and White Malmsey and Medium Sweet Hanepoot.

Jonkheer products are available to retailers only.

Business developed in the 1950s and in 1964 a bottling and distribution plant was established in De Aar. Various retail outlets were bought in an arc from Mossel Bay, across the Klein Karoo and into the Great Karoo, as well as in Worcester and Bonnievale, from which to sell Jonkheer's wide range of wines.

Existing farms were replanted, then two more north of the Breede River were added to put some 260 hectares under irrigation. These supply less than 20 per cent of Jonkheer's needs, with the remainder coming from co-operatives ranging from the area around Bonnievale to Du Toitskloof.

— LANGVERWACHT —
CO-OPERATIVE WINERY

The Langverwacht Co-operative Winery, about 10 kilometres from Bonnievale on the road between Robertson and Stormsvlei, was established in 1954. Originally called the Boesmansrivier Co-operative, this winery was given its present name after objections by the Boesmansrivier Co-operative Cheese Factory. The cellar was designed by Pon van Zyl, formerly of the Robertson Co-operative, and was completed in time to receive the 1956 crop. At present an annual crop of approximately 9 000 tonnes is supplied by 25 members to the co-operative.

Johan Gerber was appointed winemaker and manager in 1986. The co-operative's range of wines is certified as Bonnievale Wine of Origin, and only natural white wines and fortified wines are produced. Modern wine-making techniques and outstanding grapes ensure that white wines of high quality are produced, with the Colombard at the top of the list. New plantings include the varieties Chardonnay, Sauvignon Blanc and Cape Riesling.

WINES BOTTLED AND MARKETED

White: Colombard, Blanc de Blanc and Late Harvest.
Fortified: White Hanepoot Jerepigo and White Muscadel Jerepigo.

The co-operative is on the Robertson Wine Route and is open to the public on weekdays from 08h00 to 12h30 and 13h30 to 17h00.

— LE GRAND CHASSEUR —
ESTATE

Until the early 1950s this farm on the Breede River near Robertson was mainly limited to the production of raisins and sultanas, with a moderate amount of Muscat d'Alexandrie being supplied to KWV for export.

Then, in 1950, Wouter de Vos de Wet inherited the family farm, and soon set about enlarging the existing vineyards. In the course of planning these new blocks in 1956, he ordered a supply of St Emilion vines.

In good faith he planted the vines he received only to discover when they came to bearing that he had been given the then little-known variety of Colombard by mistake. With little idea of the potential of these new arrivals in his vineyard, Wouter approached KWV for advice.

Told to experiment with the making of sweet and semi-sweet wines of the kind long made in this region, he continued to cultivate his Colombard, and was soon followed by many of the local farmers. Against all expectations, the resultant wine has since gained in popularity.

LE GRAND CHASSEUR ESTATE

Varieties planted (ha)

Modified Perold trellis
Chenin Blanc 47,8
Colombard 33,1
Muscat de Frontignan 19,9
Clairette Blanche 7,7
Sauvignon Blanc 7
Cape Riesling 4,6
St Emilion 1,5
Weisser Riesling 1
Morio Muscat 0,9

Total area under vines in 1991/2: 123,5 ha.
Irrigation: All the vineyards are irrigated.
Average temperatures:
Average maximum 30 °C; average minimum 6 °C.
Average annual rainfall: Records are not kept.
Stock: Rooted vines are purchased from a nursery.
First wines bottled under the Le Grand Chasseur label: Chenin Blanc, Colombard, Late Harvest and Cape Riesling (all 1984 vintage).
Wines currently bottled under the Le Grand Chasseur label: Sauvignon Blanc, Cape Riesling, Colombard and Late Harvest.
Wood ageing: Not practised.
Cellar capacity: 16 000 hl.

Le Grand Chasseur Estate may be visited by appointment only.

In 1968 the discovery of the good wine capabilities of Colombard by Pon van Zyl of the local Robertson Co-operative resulted in further extensive plantings of the variety in this area. Since those days Wouter, assisted since 1979 by his son, Albertus, has added further varieties to his almost exclusively white grape vineyards. These include Chenin Blanc, Cape Riesling, Sauvignon Blanc and St Emilion, which go to the production of dry table wines. In 1986 a harvester was bought and today about 60 per cent of the estate's grapes are harvested mechanically.

Limited quantities of Le Grand Chasseur wines are bottled. Wines are mainly sold in bulk to leading wholesalers.

—MADEBA VALLEY—

Travelling from Worcester towards Robertson, you can see one of the Cape's newest and boldest winery ventures set up against the hillside. In architectural style it could not be further from the traditional Cape Dutch whitewash and gables with its orange walls and long curved green roof. The property has been replanted by vineyard manager Alex le Roux since its purchase in 1983 by Graham Beck, and the vines are now in full production. Prior to the first crush in 1991, the grapes were delivered to Rooiberg.

There are two cellars, Madeba I having been purpose built for sparkling wine production by the *méthode champenoise*. In this cellar, the bottle line is centrally situated, surrounded by the stabilization tanks, bottle maturation area, and the bottle fermentation area with *remuage* and *dégorgement* facilities. The temperature is kept at a constant 14 °C. Modern 'gyro-pallates' will be mainly used although some traditional *pupitres* will also be available for special productions. In charge is winemaker Pieter Ferreira, who served his apprenticeship at Clos Cabrière, also having worked in Champagne

Pieter Ferreira, in the méthode champenoise *cellar at Madeba Valley.*

and California. He aims to produce the first *méthode champenoise* wine from Madeba by Christmas 1992. The first fermentation will be in wood, and the second, of course, in bottle. The base wines are of a high quality and early tastings have proved promising. Initially, two wines will be produced from this cellar, with others being added at a later stage. The first available will be a classic Brut under the Graham Beck label, to be released at two years of age, and a Blanc de Blanc from 100 per cent Chardonnay will be

MADEBA VALLEY

Varieties planted (ha)

Extended Perold trellis
Chardonnay 39,2
Weisser Riesling 29,3
Colombard 13,5
Gewürztraminer 11,4
Cape Riesling 11,4
Sauvignon Blanc 10,6
Cabernet Sauvignon 9,6
Shiraz 7,4
Pinot Noir 6,5
Chenin Blanc 5,7
Cabernet Franc 3,9
Merlot 3,7
Muscat d'Alexandrie 3,7
White Muscadel 1,5

Total area under vines in 1991/2: 157,4 ha.
Irrigation: All the vineyards are irrigated.
Average temperatures: Records are not kept.
Average annual rainfall: Records are not kept.
Stock: Rooted vines are bought from a nursery.
First wine bottled under the Madeba Valley label: Chardonnay 1991.
Wines to be bottled under the Madeba Valley label: Sparkling wines: Blanc de Blanc, Brut and Rosé.
Wood ageing: Wines are aged in wood in the cellar.
Cellar capacity: 2 100 hl.

Madeba Valley is open to the public every day from 10h00 to 20h00.

MADEBA VALLEY

available after five years, three of which will have been spent on the lees in the bottle. A portion of the base wines will be barrel fermented and wines from four different woods will be cross blended to give complexity and uniformity of style. The Brut will be 30 per cent wood fermented and the Blanc de Blanc 70 per cent wood fermented.

Manie Arendse has been appointed assistant winemaker for Madeba II. This cellar has been built to handle some 2 400 tonnes of grapes destined for the production of still wine. This cellar is also well equipped, and most of the wine produced here will be sold in bulk to other merchants.

— MERWESPONT —
CO-OPERATIVE WINERY

Situated on the road between Bonnievale and Swellendam, the Merwespont Winery was formed in 1955, the building being completed in 1957. The main thrust of production in the past has been on rebate wine for brandy distillation, but good wine now makes up about 25 per cent of the winery's output, supervised by the winemaker, Dirk Cornelissen. This percentage should increase as other varieties are planted by the co-operative's members, now numbering 50 and growing a combined annual crop of approximately 9 000 tonnes. At present a limited range of wines is available under the Merwespont label.

WINES BOTTLED AND MARKETED

White: Riesling, Late Vintage and Morlé.
Rosé: Vin Rosé.

The co-operative is on the Worcester Wine Route and is open to the public on weekdays from 08h00 to 12h30 and from 13h30 to 17h00.

— McGREGOR —
CO-OPERATIVE WINERY

The McGregor winery is situated 18 kilometres from Robertson on the road to the beautiful historic town of McGregor – possibly the best-preserved and most complete example of a mid nineteenth-century townscape in the Cape.

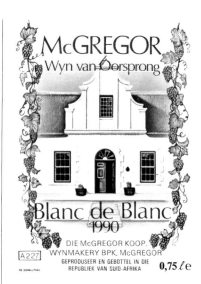

WINES BOTTLED AND MARKETED

Red: Cabernet Sauvignon and Ruby Cabernet.
White: Blanc de Blanc, Colombard, Rhine Riesling and Late Harvest Steen.
Sparkling: Demi-Sec.
Fortified: Port and Red and White Muscadel.

The co-operative is on the Robertson Wine Route and is open to the public on weekdays from 08h00 to 12h00 and from 13h00 to 17h00.

The winery was started in 1948 and made its first wine in 1950. Today the membership of the McGregor Winery is 47, producing a total of 8 500 tonnes of grapes a year, which is made into wine by the winemaker at the co-operative Carel van der Merwe.

The winery specializes in white wines, though a little Red Muscadel and Cabernet Sauvignon form part of the grape crop. Chenin Blanc and Colombard (which does exceptionally well in this area) make up the bulk of the grape varieties produced, but in the past few years there has been an increase in the amount of Sauvignon Blanc, Weisser Riesling and Cape Riesling. The first Chardonnay vines were planted in 1991. Most of the wine is sold in bulk to wholesalers, but a range is bottled under the cellar's label.

— MON DON —
ESTATE

The name of this estate – it means 'My gift' – commemorates the transfer for a nominal sum of the property from Hannetjie Marais

---

MON DON ESTATE

Varieties planted (ha)

Extended trellis
Colombard 31,1
Chenin Blanc 20,2
Clairette Blanche 7,2
Sauvignon Blanc 3,5
Trebbiano 3,5
Weisser Riesling 1,5

Total area under vines in 1991/2: 67 ha.
Irrigation: All the vineyards are irrigated.
Average temperatures:
Maximum 25-28 °C; minimum 12 °C.
Average annual rainfall: 330 mm.
Stock: Rooted vines are bought from a nursery.
First wine bottled under the Mon Don label:
Colombard 1983.
Wines currently bottled under the Mon Don label: Blanc de Blanc and Late Harvest, Chenin Blanc, Mystère, Sauvignon Blanc, Weisser Riesling and Colombard.
Wood ageing: Wood ageing is not practised.
Cellar capacity: 10 420 hl.

Mon Don Estate is on the Robertson Wine Route and is open to the public on weekdays between 08h00 and 17h00, and on Saturdays by appointment.

---

to her son, Pierre, the owner and winemaker since 1962. Since then Pierre has refurbished the near-derelict vineyards, making first sweet wines and sherry and then extending the range to include dry wines which he supplies to merchants. He has bottled small quantities of white wine, which he has released to the public under the Mon Don label. The Sauvignon Blanc is particularly good. Varieties grown here now include Chenin Blanc, Weisser Riesling, Colombard, Clairette Blanche and Trebbiano.

— MONT BLOIS —
ESTATE

Situated in the De Hoop Valley near Robertson, this farm was described in its original title deed as '*De Hoop in het Land van Waveren aan de Witter water*'. By the 1880s it had been acquired by the Bruwer family, descendants of a Huguenot named Estienne Bruère who had come to the Cape from the French town of Blois in 1688. The name of De Hoop was retained by the Bruwer family until 1920, when it was changed to the present name in honour of their ancestor and his distant origins on the River Loire.

MONT BLOIS ESTATE

Varieties planted (ha)

Extended Perold trellis
Chenin Blanc 22,96
Colombard 17,37
Sauvignon Blanc 15,25
Chardonnay 14,26
Weisser Riesling 9,4
Cape Riesling 4,38
Gewürztraminer 4,25
Pinot Noir 1,02
2-wire vertical trellis
Muscadel 40,93
Muscat d'Alexandrie 5,53
St Emilion 5,53
Raisin Blanc 3,74
Palomino 3,68

Total area under vines in 1991/2: 148,3 ha.
Irrigation: All the vineyards are irrigated on the drip system.
Average temperatures:
Maximum 27 °C; minimum 12 °C.
Average annual rainfall: Approximately 500 mm.
Stock: Rooted vines are bought from a nursery.
First wine bottled under the Mont Blois label:
White Muscadel 1974.
Wines currently bottled under the Mont Blois label: White Muscadel, Sauvignon Blanc and Chardonnay. Mont Blois wines are bottled by The Bergkelder.
Wood ageing: The Chardonnay is aged in wood at The Bergkelder.
Cellar capacity: 16 000 hl.

Mont Blois Estate is not open to the public.

Mont Blois is now owned by Ernst Bruwer, who has added two further farms, La Fontaine and Sunshine, to create a substantial spread of some 3 500 hectares. Of these, about 148 hectares are under vines, including Chenin Blanc, Colombard and Muscat d'Alexandrie. The range also includes Red and White Muscadel, and it is the wines from these which are the pride of the estate and the main source of its renown.

The gravelly soil in this high, narrow valley – it is less than 2 kilometres across – is particularly suited to Muscadel grapes, which have been grown here by the Bruwers since the turn of the century. Fortified with pure spirit, these rich, luscious wines are made from late harvested grapes supported on the drip-irrigation system which is carefully controlled. The Mont Blois White Muscadel has consistently received a formidable array of prizes; these include awards over many years at both the Robertson and

Breede River Young Wine Shows, numerous trophies and gold medals at the South African Young Wine Championships, and has won gold medals every year since 1977 in the Club Oenologique International Wine and Spirit Competition.

— MOOIUITSIG —
WINE CELLARS AND
— OVERBERG —
CO-OPERATIVE

Mooiuitsig is a producing wholesale liquor concern owned by the Jonker and Claassen families. Situated in the Breede River Valley in the Bonnievale ward, it markets a range of wines, many of which are made from grapes supplied to the Overberg Co-operative, This co-operative, under the guidance of Boet

---

WINES BOTTLED AND MARKETED

Red: Oude Rust Cabernet Sauvignon and Rusthof Red Table Wine.
White: Oude Rust Range: Riesling, Colombard, Late Vintage and Gewürztraminer Special Late Vintage. Rusthof Range: Premier Grand Crû, Stein and Late Harvest. Bonselect Semi-Sweet, Bonistein, Hanepoot Semi-Sweet, Bonperlé and Mooiuitsig Dry White.
Sparkling: Clairvaux Mousseux.
Fortified: Oude Rust Red and White Muscadel, Medium Sweet Red and White Muscadel, Oude Rust Hanepoot, Bonvin Ruby Liqueur Wine and Golden Liqueur Wine, Overberg Hanepoot, Mooiuitsig Muscana, Mooiuitsig Red and White Jerepigo, Red and White Malmsey, Marsala, Nagmaalwyn, Sweet Hanepoot, Monte Vista, Mooiuitsig Old Brown and Milk Sherry and Mooiuitsig Ports.

The co-operative is open to the public on weekdays from 08h00 to 12h30 and from 13h30 to 17h30 (17h00 on Wednesdays and Fridays).

Jonker, the chairman of the co-operative and managing director of Mooiuitsig Wine Cellars, receives and processes the grapes from the family farms including Mooiuitsig, De Rust, Aan-die-Drift, Ardein and Rheenen. The original winery, dating from the early 1930s, was modernized and converted into the Overberg Co-operative Winery in 1979. François Claassen with fellow winemakers Chris Versfeld and Wrensch Roux produce a range of some 50 wines with the emphasis on sweeter wines, under a variety of labels including Mooiuitsig, Oude Rust, Monte Vista, Overberg, Rusthof and Bonwin.

— NORDALE —
CO-OPERATIVE WINERY

When it was first established in the early 1950s, this co-operative's entire production was sold to the Castle Wine and Brandy Company for distillation. Rebate wine still accounts for 60 per cent of the winery's output, but since the introduction of cold fermentation in 1965, good wine production has been increased to its present 20 per cent of the total. Winemaker Emile Schoch currently bottles five of his quality wines under the Nordale Co-operative Winery label.

WINES BOTTLED AND MARKETED

Red: Dry Red.
White: Sauvignon Blanc, Colombard and Late Harvest.
Fortified: Red Muscadel.

The co-operative is on the Robertson Wine Route and is open to the public on weekdays from 08h00 to 12h30 and from 13h30 to 17h00.

— RIETVALLEI —
ESTATE

The present owner of this estate at Klaasvoogds is Johnny Burger, the fifth generation of his family to own Rietvallei, which the family bought in 1864. On leaving school in 1968 Johnny served an apprenticeship under the elderly foreman of the farm, Jan Vytjie, and was well rewarded when his first wine was judged the South African Champion Muscadel. Although the cellar has been thoroughly modernized, the formula, or recipe,

---

RIETVALLEI ESTATE

Varieties planted (ha)

3-wire vertical trellis
Chenin Blanc 35
St Emilion 30
Clairette Blanche 15
Colombard 15
Weisser Riesling 15
Chardonnay 12
Cinsaut 10
Raisin Blanc 10
Sauvignon Blanc 8
Shiraz 5
Tinta Barocca 5
3-wire vertical trellis and bush vines
Red Muscadel 15

Total area under vines in 1991/2:
175 ha (50 ha still to be planted).
Irrigation: All the vineyards are irrigated.
Average temperatures:
Maximum 22-32 °C; minimum 5 °C.
Average annual rainfall: Approximately 300 mm.
Stock: Parent stock is used for grafting; rooted vines are bought from a nursery.
First wine bottled under the Rietvallei label:
Red Muscadel 1975.
Wines currently bottled under the Rietvallei label: Chardonnay, Rhine Riesling, Red Muscadel (bottled by The Bergkelder).
Wood ageing: Wines are aged in wood on the estate.
Cellar capacity: 22 000 hl.

Rietvallei Estate is not open to the public.

---

of Rietvallei's Muscadel, which was tacked on to the cellar door for many decades, has hardly changed. Johnny believes that part of the success of his excellent Muscadel is due to the use of some grapes from vines which are over 70 years old.

— ROBERTSON —
CO-OPERATIVE WINERY

Founded in 1941, this co-operative has since become renowned for its Colombard wines. The introduction of this variety to the gamut of natural wines is intimately bound up with the career of the Robertson winery's former winemaker and manager, the late Pon van Zyl, who turned a happy accident into a major development.

In 1954 a local farmer, Wouter de Wet, of the farm Le Grand Chasseur near Robertson, ordered a supply of St Emilion vines from a nursery run by Wynand Viljoen at Ladismith in the Little Karoo. De Wet duly planted the vines with which he was supplied, but discovered when they came to bear that he had been given Colombard by mistake. Since, however, both vines were equally adapted to the making of rebate wine, he proceeded to press his vintage as usual. In the following years other farmers in the vicinity began to plant cuttings of Colombard, but it was left to Pon van Zyl to recognize the real potential of this variety. Walking through the Robertson Co-operative Winery's cellars in 1968, he was assailed by a heady perfume which he later compared to the scent of the koekmakranka flower (*Gethyllis* spp.) and at that moment he decided to make the Colombard into a good wine rather than a rebate wine for brandy.

It was an inspired move, and one which was to earn him a modest but secure place in the local winemaker's pantheon. The Robertson Co-operative's Colombard has become one of the area's finest wines, and a consist-

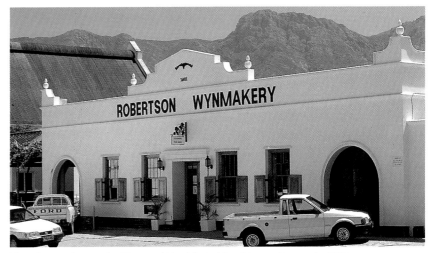

The Robertson Co-operative Winery, which celebrated its golden anniversary in 1991.

ent prize-winner at wine shows. Its success has encouraged others to follow suit to the extent that plantings of Colombard in the Cape vineyards now exceed 14 million vines.

Apart from the Colombard, a further 10 wines are now bottled under the guidance of the present winemaker, Mr Bowen Botha, who joined the winery in 1986. These include the first commercial wine made from a new variety, Therona Riesling, recently developed at the University of Stellenbosch and named after Professor C.J. Theron.

— ROODEZANDT —
CO-OPERATIVE WINERY

W.F. (Robbie) Roberts is the cellarmaster at this winery situated on Voortrekker Street in Robertson. The Robertson wards of Hooprivier and Le Chasseur are represented by the wine cellar's current 52 members, who deliver more than 19 000 tonnes of grapes a

ROODEZANDT
KOÖP WYNMAKERY

1990
TINTA BAROCCA

ROBERTSON
WYN VAN OORSPRONG

750ml A136

year. Assisted by winemaker Christie Steytler, Robbie supervises the production of a range of wines under the Roodezandt label, many of which have won prizes at both local and national shows.

One of these, the White Muscadel, is his particular pride and joy, and each vintage of this wine is very personal to him.

The wine is produced from a single block of 5 000 vines planted in 1960. Over the years the wine has only been bottled in the even years under the Roodezandt label, but the 1991 vintage was an exception because it is the last vintage of this wine from this particular block of vines, as they are being removed due to old age.

Robbie is going to great lengths to promote Muscadel to the wine-drinking public both locally and abroad as he feels the excellent Muscadels produced in the Robertson area go largely unnoticed by the public. He was delighted that 50 cases of his 1986 Superior, sold at the 1991 Nederburg Auction, went to Taiwan. He is always willing to show visitors to the winery the different ways to serve Muscadel.

— ROOIBERG —
CO-OPERATIVE

Rooiberg Co-operative was established in 1964 by 11 farmers near Vinkrivier in the Robertson district, and now has 36 members contributing from individual farms under the guidance of the winemakers Dassie Smith and Tommy Loftus. A graduate of Stellenbosch University where he studied under

Dassie Smith, who is responsible for over 30 wines under the cellar label and 300 under personalized labels.

Professor Chris Orffer, Dassie has placed Rooiberg firmly on the co-operative map since he took over as winemaker in 1970. He has won an impressive array of wine awards within a few years, including the champion Cabernet Sauvignon at the Cape Wine Show in 1979; at the 1982 show Dassie was awarded, jointly with Sydney Back of Backsberg, the General Smuts Trophy for the best winemaker, and was champion winemaker in 1984. Rooiberg was champion co-operative for the first time in 1978 and thereafter for three successive years in 1982, 1983 and 1984 and in 1986.

Drawing grapes from the wards of Vinkrivier and Eilandia, the modern and streamlined Rooiberg winery bottles a comprehensive selection of some 33 different, 'good-value-for-money' wines. Dassie was responsible for the introduction of wood ageing of white wines to the Robertson area and now bottles a selection of oak-matured red and white wines.

— VAN LOVEREN —

A tract of land on the banks of the Breede River, between Robertson and Bonnievale, was once a large farm called Goudmyn. This farm thrived during the ostrich boom, but eventually had to be divided amongst the nine offspring of the Potgieter family. In 1937 Nicholaas Retief bought one of these 28-hectare sections of land for his son Hennie, and the farm at that time was known simply as 'Goudmyn F'.

Hennie's wife Jean felt strongly about the lack of originality in the name, and, having been born a Van Zyl, a descendant of Guillaume van Zyl who had arrived at the Cape in 1692 with his wife Christina van Loveren,

The cellar at Van Loveren, situated at the confluence of the Breede and the Cogmanskloof rivers.

persuaded her husband to name their new farm 'Van Loveren'. The new bride had brought her trousseau to the Cape in a beautiful Philippine mahogany kist, and as a reminder of the past this cherished piece of furniture today continues to have pride of place in the Retief home.

The Van Loveren cellar was one of the first to produce sweet wines, particularly Red Muscadel, for delivery to the Stellenbosch Farmers' Winery. This was the main activity at Van Loveren until 1972 when cold fermentation facilities were installed. This led to the

planting of natural white wine varieties, including Colombard and Chenin Blanc. Since the 1980s the Retiefs have planted all the noble white varieties including Chardonnay, Weisser Riesling, Gewürztraminer, Pinot Gris and Pinot Blanc. In 1992 they started planting reds such as Cabernet Sauvignon, Merlot and Shiraz.

At present Van Loveren consists of five farms which are run by the brothers Nico and Wynand Retief. The farm Schoemanskloof was bought for Nico when he married in 1964. Prior to that Nico had studied at the

Elsenburg Agricultural College, where he was awarded a gold medal for his achievements. Wynand, after completing a B.Com. degree at the University of Stellenbosch, had planned to enter the business world. He changed his mind, however, and bought the farm Jacobsdal when he married in 1968. In 1980 a portion of the farm Goedemoed, with its rich lime soils, was bought, and a fifth farm, Spes Bona, was bought in 1988. In 1980 the Van Loveren cellar was extensively modernized to include only cement and fibreglass tanks, and in 1989 it was further

Wynand and Nico Retief, innovative producers of characterful wines.

enlarged and modernized. It now includes space for the storage of bottled wines and barrels for wood ageing. The total capacity of the cellar is 2 000 tonnes, although a storage wing has been added in the hope of reaching a total pressing quota of 2 700 tonnes.

The brothers have been farming in partnership since the death of their father in 1982. Nico's son Hennie joined the partnership in 1991 after finishing an agricultural degree at Stellenbosch University. Nico is the viticulturist and also manages the fruit and

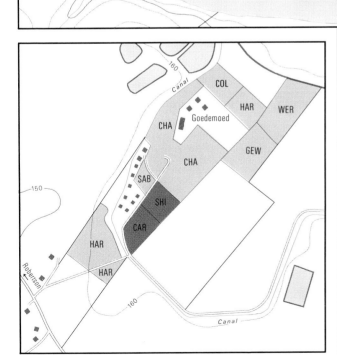

VAN LOVEREN

Weltevrede Estate vineyards, well watered by the Breede River.

— WELTEVREDE —
ESTATE

The name Weltevrede can be translated as 'well-satisfied' and suggests the pleasure that three generations of the Jonker family have derived from farming alongside the Breede River. Situated just outside Bonnievale, Weltevrede provides a picturesque scene of green vineyards and lucerne fields, the wine cellars along the highway and the homestead with its fine garden, the whole set against the backdrop of the Langeberg.

On 30 August 1912, Klaas Jonker, grandfather of the present owner, Lourens Jonker, acquired 280 hectares of shrub veld and named it Weltevrede. The land was divided into four parts, to be farmed by his four sons. The youngest son, Japie, commenced farming in 1933 on the part closest to Bonnievale and retained the name of the original farm, after his three brothers had decided to rename their farms.

Lourens Jonker, Elsabé Ferreira and Pon van Zyl, respectively chairman, P.R. and judge at the National Wine Show, 1991.

Vines were planted on a small scale, and wine production commenced during the Depression, when, on occasion, taps had to be opened and the wine allowed to run out in order to dispose of a product for which no market existed. Japie persevered, however, and as more vines were planted, the cellars were extended. The wines, mainly sweet wine and sherries at that stage, were initially marketed by the barrel but eventually bottled and sold to the public until 1948, when Japie and his brother, Herman, started a wholesale liquor business. This partnership was terminated four years later, when Japie decided to concentrate mainly on farming and wine was sold in bulk to various wholesalers.

After qualifying as a pilot in the South African Air Force, Japie's only son, Lourens, decided to follow in his father's footsteps. He studied viniculture at the University of Stellenbosch and, after graduating in 1961,

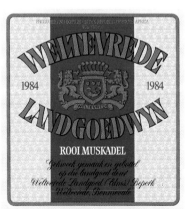

vegetable enterprises and Wynand, in spite of having no formal wine-making training, took on the role of Van Loveren's winemaker.

Although Van Loveren is known for its innovative Hárslevelü and Fernão Pires wines, its Blanc de Noirs have also gained recognition. The Blanc de Noir Muscat has been a class winner at local wine shows. In recent years they have been doing exceptionally well with barrel-fermented Chardonnays. New plantings of Cabernet, Merlot, and Shiraz, will be coming into the cellar in 1995.

visited the wine-growing areas of California and Western Europe. In late 1962 he started farming with his father, devoting himself to wine-making. He was soon rewarded by winning various prizes at a number of wine shows. With Lourens in full control of the farm, Japie was able to devote more time to public service and, among other things, became a director of KWV, a prestigious

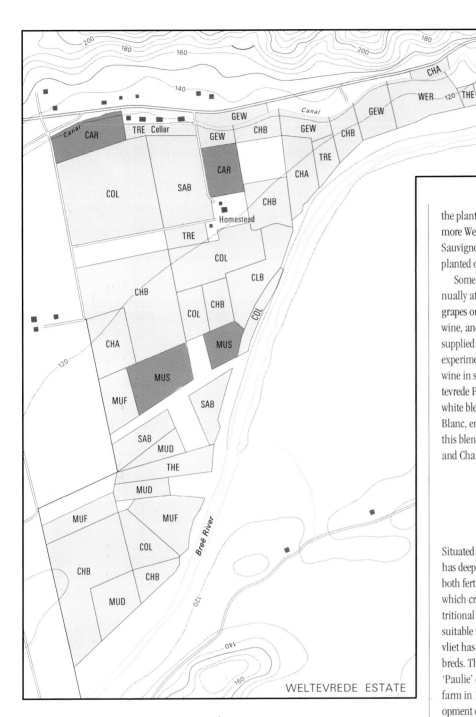

WELTEVREDE ESTATE

ZANDVLIET ESTATE

Varieties planted

3- and 4-wire vertical trellises
(size of vineyards not available)
Chardonnay
Chenin Blanc
Colombard
Pinot Noir
Sauvignon Blanc
Shiraz
Cabernet Sauvignon

Total area under vines in 1991/2: 125 ha.
Irrigation: All the vineyards of Zandvliet are
irrigated.
Temperatures: Maximum 30 °C; minimum 20 °C.
Average annual rainfall: 200 mm.
Stock: Parent stock is used for grafting;
rooted vines are purchased from a nursery.
First wine bottled under the Zandvliet label:
Shiraz 1976.
**Wines currently bottled under the Zandvliet
label:** Shiraz and Cabernet Sauvignon. Zandvliet
wines are bottled by The Bergkelder.
Wood ageing: Wine will be aged in wood on
the estate.
Cellar capacity: 12 000 hl.

Zandvliet Estate is on the Robertson Wine Route and
will be open to the public before the end of 1993.

the planting of classic varieties. Each year more Weisser Riesling, Gewürztraminer, Sauvignon Blanc and Chardonnay vines are planted on Weltevrede.

Some 16 different wines are bottled annually at Weltevrede. Wine from selected grapes only is bottled and marketed as estate wine, and most of the good quality wine is supplied to wholesalers in bulk. Since 1979 experiments have been conducted with white wine in small French oak casks and the Weltevrede Privé du Bois, a wood-matured dry white blend of Colombard and Chenin Blanc, enjoyed wide recognition. In 1991, this blend was changed to Sauvignon Blanc and Chardonnay.

— ZANDVLIET —
ESTATE

Situated on the Cogmans River, the estate has deep alluvial soil and red Karoo soil – both fertile and rich in lime, with a high pH which creates good acidity in grapes. The nutritional value of the soil makes it eminently suitable for the breeding of horses, and Zandvliet has long been famous for its thoroughbreds. The horse stud flourished under 'Paulie' de Wet, but since he took over the farm in 1947 there has been a parallel development of wine farming. His sons, Dan and Paul, now manage the stud farm and the vineyards respectively.

The Robertson district has long been renowned for its brandies, Muscadels and white wines. However, employing certain vineyard practices, Zandvliet has proved that this area can also produce noteworthy red wines from its vineyards. Stable and winecellar wastes are turned into a compost used on the vines up to the age of four years to ensure good root development. All plant rests are put back every winter. Pruning is severe,

and tillage is kept at an absolute minimum to limit the yield.

Firmly believing in the suitability of the estate for Shiraz, the De Wets planted extensive vineyards of this variety and, in 1975, the first Shiraz was yielded. The Shiraz is left in small wood for as long as Paul sees fit and then it is transferred to large oak vats for a year before bottling, after which it matures for a year before being released. In 1984, the first Cabernet Sauvignon was produced.

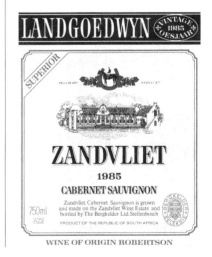

appointment to which Lourens was to take up nearly twenty years later.

After the death of his father in 1969, Lourens acquired the neighbouring farm, Muscadel, from his uncle. Being an ardent supporter of the law for Wines of Origin, he consolidated the two farms and registered Weltevrede as an estate with the Wine and Spirit Board in 1974.

With the marketing of its first bottled estate wine in 1976 – the 1975 Colombard – Weltevrede became the first estate in the

Breede River Valley to bottle and supply wine direct to the public. In 1977 the estate marketed the first Red Muscadel sweet wine in the country, and it was the champion muscat fortified wine at the South African Wine Show in 1986. Gerhard van Deventer assists Lourens as winemaker.

In May 1981, Lourens bought another neighbouring farm, Riversedge, and consolidated the entire 150 hectares as one estate. This farm, with its south-facing slope and gravelly soil, is extremely suitable for

KLEIN KAROO

The Klein Karoo district is narrow from north to south, but stretches a considerable distance from west to east, running north of the Langeberg range from Montagu and eastwards through Barrydale, Ladismith and Calitzdorp to Oudtshoorn and De Hoop. The name 'Karoo' derives from a Hottentot word meaning arid, hard and sparsely covered; a fair description of the region. It is a harsh area, with intense sunshine, low rainfall and extremes of hot and cold. The aridity is the dominant feature of the climate, and has resulted in a unique vegetation. Characteristic of the Klein Karoo are succulents such as aloes, crassulas, euphorbias and stapelias.

Some producers consider this inclement climate to be conducive to the growth of vines since it is tempered by the presence of the mountain ranges, namely the Swartberg to the north and the continuous range of the Langeberg and Outeniqua Mountains to the south. Because of inadequate supplies of irrigation water, vineyards are restricted to deep alluvial soils along the river banks, as well as to deep, red clayish soils of a shale origin with a tendency to salinity and compaction. All must be extensively irrigated, for the climate here is dry to arid, with an average rainfall of less than 300 millimetres a year. The average summer temperatures vary between 20 and 22 °C, though in this inland region late frosts often occur during the winter. The area was originally known only for its brandy and fortified wines, but many producers are planting classic varieties and making new styles of wine.

In the town of Oudtshoorn, the main centre of the Klein Karoo, a few examples still survive of the 'ostrich palaces', those ornately splendid Edwardian houses which sprang up at the height of the ostrich-feather boom in the late 1800s. At this time, there were over 700 000 domesticated ostriches in the Klein Karoo, and more than 400 000 kilograms of feathers were being exported each year to the fashion centres of the world, including London, Paris and New York. The magnificent black and white feathers from the cocks were most lucrative, fetching up to R420 a kilogram. With the advent of World War I, the market collapsed. The threat of bankruptcy forced many of the farmers to turn to alternative farming possibilities, ultimately resulting in the production of wine.

Near to Oudtshoorn are the Cango Caves. The entrance was occupied by San, who painted the walls. But it was only in 1780 that an expedition was led deeper into the caves. Further exploration has revealed the system to have one of the most superb and extensive collections of drip formations in the world.

Prominent co-operatives here include the Rietrivier Wine Cellar Co-operative, the Barrydale Co-operative Winery and Distillery (the only co-operative brandy distillery in the country), and the Kango Co-operative Tobacco and Wine Company – a rare case of two kinds of production under one roof.

LEFT: *The town of Barrydale, renowned for its apples, peaches, apricots and brandy.*

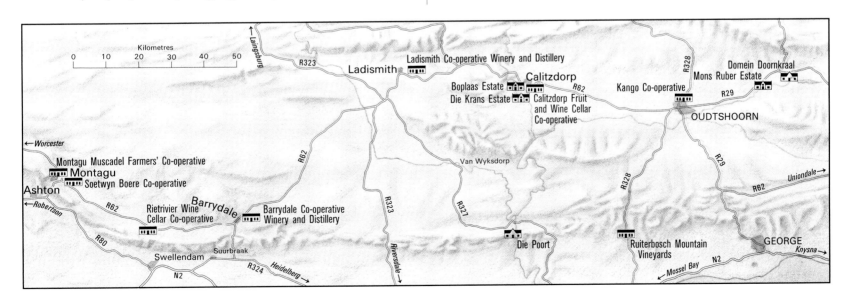

—BARRYDALE—
CO-OPERATIVE WINERY AND DISTILLERY

The Barrydale Co-operative is situated in the Tradouw Valley and began life as a distillery in the early 1940s; it remains the only co-operative to distil brandy, delivering its product to Distillers Corporation. It was soon found, however, that the wine made by individual members was not of sufficient quality for distilling into fine brandy, and wine-making facilities were therefore provided at the distillery.

In 1980 wine was made in its own right on an experimental basis, and this activity has gone from strength to strength. Since 1991 all noble varietal wines have been marketed under the Tradouw label. In 1991, winemaker Bob de Villiers was responsible for the co-operative becoming the first in the country to produce a *méthode champenoise* sparkling wine.

Winemaker Bob de Villiers.

WINES BOTTLED AND MARKETED

White: Late Harvest, Special Late Harvest, Colombard, Sauvignon Blanc, Blanc de Noir, Blanc Fumé and Chardonnay.
Sparkling: Demi-Sec.
Fortified: White Muscadel and Hanepoot Jerepigo.

The co-operative is on the Klein Karoo Wine Route and is open to the public on weekdays from 08h30 to 12h30 and from 13h30 to 17h00.

—BOPLAAS—
ESTATE

Boplaas Estate is situated on the outskirts of Calitzdorp at the foot of the Swartberg mountain range. The estate is about 80 kilometres from the sea and lies directly in line with the two gaps in the Gamka mountains through which flow the Gamka and Gouritz rivers. Although the summers in this area are warm, these gaps channel the cool southerly sea breezes which blow in the afternoons and create the cooler ripening conditions which are perfect for the cultivation of quality grape varieties.

Grapes have been grown on Boplaas for the making of wine and brandy for more than 150 years, and in 1860 Danie Nel, the grandfather of the Danie who currently owns the farm with his son Carel, exported brandy to London. Boplaas is a family enterprise with Danie Nel taking care of the vineyards with Carel, who is also a Cape Wine Master, looks after the general management and wine-making. Their wives, Roline and Jeanne, are responsible for sales, distribution and administration of the estate.

BOPLAAS ESTATE

Varieties planted (ha)

Vertical hedge system
Chenin Blanc 6
Colombard 4
Tinta Barocca 4
White Muscadel 4
Cabernet Sauvignon 2,5
Chardonnay 2
Merlot 2
Pinotage 2
Cabernet Franc 1,5
Pinot Noir 1,5
Other varieties 31,5

Total area under vines in 1991/2: 61 ha.
Irrigation: Flood irrigation.
Average temperatures:
Maximum 38 °C; minimum 12 °C.
Average annual rainfall: 175 mm.
Stock: 20 000 cases sold a year.
First wines bottled under the Boplaas label:
Tinta Barocca and Sauvignon Blanc (both 1982 vintage).
Wines currently bottled under the Boplaas label: Sauvignon Blanc, Blanc Fumé, Vin Blanc, Late Harvest, Special Late Harvest, Sparkling Wine (*doux*), Sparkling Wine (*méthode champenoise*), Pinot Noir, Cabernet Sauvignon, Merlot, Grand Vin Rouge, Blanc de Noir, White Port, Ruby Port, Vintage Port, Vintage Reserve Port, White Muscadel and Sweet Hanepoot.
Wood ageing: Wines are aged in wood on the estate.
Cellar capacity: 5 000 hl.

Boplaas Estate is on the Klein Karoo Wine Route and is open to the public for wine sales and tastings on weekdays from 08h00 to 17h00, and on Saturdays from 09h00 to 12h00.
During the December and April school holidays a light lunch is served on the estate.

Carel Nel, the recipient of five double gold medals at the 1991 Southern Cape Bottled Wine Show.

Ports are the flagship wines of Boplaas. In 1986 and 1987 Boplaas ports were crowned as South African champions, and since 1982 the estate has won more than 30 gold medals for its ports. It is also the only estate which offers port options and futures. Boplaas port originates from poor but well-drained soils; only Tinta Barocca grapes from ungrafted vines are used (4 hectares are planted), as this variety is regarded in Portugal as one of the finest port grapes.

Great effort is made to limit the harvest and to assure quality wines with flavour and deep colour extraction. Carel has an excellent relationship with Peter Symington, winemaker and director of the family company in Portugal which makes Graham and Dow's port. Mutual visits to each other's cellars ensure that Carel is right at the forefront of the latest developments and technology. At present Boplaas markets a White, Ruby, Vintage and Vintage Reserve Port. Other quality wines which are marketed include a sparkling wine, white and red wines and dessert wines. Boplaas was also the first estate to distil an estate brandy, which is still maturing in barrels and will be ready for release in 1994. Boplaas wines are exported to several countries in Europe.

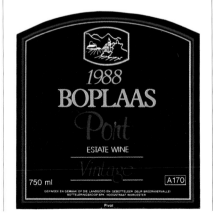

—CALITZDORP—
FRUIT AND WINE CELLAR CO-OPERATIVE

The Calitzdorp Fruit Exporters Co-operative was founded in 1928 by 15 farmers to export Muscat d'Alexandrie grapes. Ironically not a single bunch was dispatched abroad and in spite of its present name, fresh fruit plays no part in its activities. Wine production began during World War II and after somewhat shaky fortunes in their first decades, the cellar was considerably modernized in the mid-1970s. At present 106 member farmers supply over 3 000 tonnes of grapes annually. The main emphasis is on Muscat d'Alexandrie, though Palomino, Chenin Blanc, Colombard and Pinotage are also important, with Pinotage doing exceptionally well. The winemaker is James O'Kennedy.

The bulk of the wine goes to wholesale merchants, while the distilling wine is delivered to KWV; a range of wines, mostly dessert wines, is bottled under the co-operative's Buffelskroon label.

WINES BOTTLED AND MARKETED

Red: Pinotage and Cabernet Sauvignon.
White: Blanc de Noir, Colombard, White Table Wine and Chenin Blanc.
Fortified: White and Golden Jerepigo, White and Red Muscadel, Sweet Hanepoot and Port.

The co-operative is on the Klein Karoo Wine Route and is open to the public on weekdays from 08h00 to 17h30, and on Saturdays from 08h00 to 12h00.

—DIE KRANS—
ESTATE

Situated in the picturesque valley of the Gamka River, on the edge of the town of Calitzdorp, the estate of Die Krans was formerly part of a larger property owned and farmed by brothers Chris and Danie Nel, whose grandfather bought the farm in 1890. Brandy and sweet fortified wines were produced, some of which were exported to Britain. Ninety years later, when the land was divided, Chris and his son, 'Boets', retained the 53,5 hectares of Die Krans, while Danie and his son, Carel, settled on the subdivision which was registered as the new estate of Bo-

DIE KRANS ESTATE

Varieties planted (ha)

2-wire vertical trellis

Muscat d'Alexandrie 17
Chenin Blanc 5
White Muscadel 5
Tinta Barocca 5
Pinotage 3
Cabernet Sauvignon 2
Chardonnay 2
Colombard 2
Fernão Pires 2
Gewürztraminer 1
Hárslevelü 1
Sauvignon Blanc 1
Shiraz 1

Total area under vines in 1991/2:
53 ha (6 ha are planted to table grapes).
Irrigation: All the vineyards are irrigated.
Average temperatures:
Maximum 25 °C; minimum 10 °C.
Average annual rainfall: 240 mm.
Stock: Rooted vines are bought from a nursery.
First wines bottled under Die Krans label:
Wit Muscadel, Pinotage, Tinta Barocca and Port
(all 1979 vintage).
Wines currently bottled under Die Krans label:
Sauvignon Blanc, Grand Vin Blanc, Gewürztraminer,
Bouquet Blanc, Fernão Pires, Muscat d'Alexandrie,
Late Harvest, Special Late Harvest, Blanc de Noir,
L'Enchanté (Blanc de Noir sparkling wine),
Shiraz, Tinta Barocca, Pinotage, Port,
White Muscadel Jerepigo, and Heritage Collection.
Wood ageing: Wines are aged in wood on the estate.
Cellar capacity: 9 000 hl.

Die Krans Estate is on the Klein Karoo Wine Route
and is open to the public on weekdays from
08h00 to 13h00 and from 14h00 to 17h00,
and on Saturdays from 09h00 to 12h00.
Cellar tours, wine tastings and cheese lunches
can be arranged throughout the year;
during December cheese lunches are available
every day from 12h00 to 14h00.

Boets Nel, who has succeeded in making quality wine in an inhospitable area.

plaas. In 1964 the present cellar was built and in 1979 Die Krans was registered as an estate, the first in the Klein Karoo district.

On Chris Nel's death in 1981, Boets took over the running of Die Krans, and its wine-making. The elder generation of the Nels had established a comprehensive range of varieties, including Chenin Blanc, Muscat d'Alexandrie and White Muscadel among the white varieties, and Pinotage, Tinta Barocca and Red Muscadel among the reds.

In 1985 the first Hárslevelü in the region was bottled under the estate's label and in 1986 the first Fernão Pires was bottled in the Klein Karoo, also from Die Krans. A dry red blend and a Tinta Barocca are wood-matured in new small French oak for at least six months, and the estate's port for a year or more.

— DIE POORT —

Nelis Jonker farmed with his father near Bonnievale for 15 years until, in 1957, he bought the undeveloped farm, Die Poort, on the banks of the Gouritz River. The farm is situated on the coastal side of the Langeberg at the spot where the river penetrates the mountain range, hence the name Die Poort. It was originally 120 hectares in extent but in 1960 Nelis purchased two adjoining farms across the river, Waterval and Die Hoek, thereby adding 82 hectares to the property. Nelis had found his father's Bonnievale farm too cramped, with almost every available square metre planted to vines. He revelled in the space at Die Poort and planned to introduce livestock as well as vines. He planted Hanepoot originally, as he had no KWV quota at the time and Hanepoot could be marketed as table grapes, and later, once the quota was obtained, would be acceptable for wine-making. A quota (the system is now defunct) was obtained in 1963, a cellar erected and the first grapes were crushed. Meanwhile, Nelis had established a Jersey herd and built a dairy on the farm. Nowadays, however, the vineyards are the main source of income with Jannie Jonker as the winemaker.

Prior to the flood of 1981, there were deep alluvial soils along the river, with rich, red soil away from the river up the slopes of the foothills of the Langeberg range, but with the flood most of the riverside vineyards were washed away. Those that were not were covered with new deposits of silt, up to 10 metres deep in places. New vineyards have

DIE POORT

(No other information available)
First wine bottled under Die Poort label:
Sweet Hanepoot (1971 vintage).

Wines currently bottled under Die Poort label:
Sweet, Raisin, White, and Golden Jerepigo,
White and Red Port and Fröhlich Stein.

Die Poort is open to the public on weekdays
from 08h00 to 18h00 and on Saturdays from
08h00 to 13h00.

since been planted in these deposits on top of the old.

Most of the wine made is fortified although small amounts of natural wine and distilling wine are made. Some of the natural wine finds its way to the Reef and Cape Town markets but most of the production is sold through three 'farm depots'. The farm does not produce enough grapes for the winery's needs and so grapes are bought in from the surrounding area. In total some 2 500 tonnes are pressed annually. Many visitors to Mossel Bay and the Garden Route call at the winery, which is equipped with an attractive tasting room.

— DOMEIN DOORNKRAAL —

The Le Roux family has been making wine on this farm for three generations. In 1987 Gerrit le Roux, the owner and winemaker, broadened the range of wines after having planted Muscat Ottonel, Sauvignon Blanc and Merlot in addition to his established varieties (Muscadel, Colombard, Chenin Blanc, Pinotage and Tinta Barocca). Also in 1987 the first port was made and in 1990 it was the only port to receive a double gold at the

DOMEIN DOORNKRAAL

Varieties planted (ha)

Extended Perold trellis

Red Muscadel 8
Pinotage 4
Tinta Barocca 3
White Muscadel 2
Sauvignon Blanc 1
Merlot 0,5
Y-trellis
Chenin Blanc 8
Colombard 6
Muscat d'Alexandrie 4
Sémillon 0,7

Total area under vines in 1991/2:
41 ha (3 ha still to be planted).
Irrigation: All the vineyards are irrigated.
Average temperatures:
Maximum 25,3 °C; minimum 9,4 °C.
Average annual rainfall: 160 mm.
Stock: Parent stock is used for grafting; rooted vines
are bought from a nursery.
**First wines bottled under the Doornkraal
label:** Muscadel, Pinta, Hanepoot, Serenade, Port,
Kuierwyn and Tinta Bianca (all 1987 vintage).
**Wines currently bottled under the Doornkraal
label:** Pinta, Hanepoot, Muskadel, Majoor, Kaptein,
Luitenant, Serenade, Tinta Bianca, Kuierwyn, Merlot,
Kannaland and Port (bottled by the Breërivier
Bottling Co-operative, Worcester).
Wood ageing: Wines are aged in wood on the farm.
Cellar capacity: 7 100 hl.

Domein Doornkraal is on the Klein Karoo Wine
Route and is open to the public for tastings on
weekdays from 09h00 to 17h00 and on
Saturdays from 08h00 to 13h00 and in season on
weekdays from 08h00 to 18h00 and on
Saturdays from 08h00 to 13h00.

Southern Cape Bottled Wine Show. Although the production is relatively small, the quality of the wine is exceptional.

In the past the entire production went to wholesalers, but as a result of an effort to promote the Klein Karoo and because of a wider variety of wines now possible, he opened a wine house on the main road between De Rust and Oudtshoorn. This venture is very much a family affair, from the typical Karoo style and décor of the house to the interesting and innovative names and labels of the wines, which all came into being around the dinner table at Doornkraal.

Swepie le Roux believes that a Klein Karoo white wine should have a touch of muscat, whether d'Alexandrie, Frontignan or Ottonel, to distinguish it from those in the Boland. He also believes that blended wines give more scope to the winemaker, and more interesting titillation to the imbiber.

There are also varietal wines: the Muscadels and Hanepoots are indispensable and very much part of the country living. Merlot has proved very successful in the region.

—KANGO—
CO-OPERATIVE

This company began life as a tobacco cooperative in 1926. It was expanded in 1974, however, to take in the making of wine as well — many of the grape farmers in this area of the Klein Karoo had traditionally delivered their grapes to the Union Wine Cellar at Oudtshoorn, an arrangement which ended in that year, leaving the farmers in urgent need of alternative facilities.

The winery section of the Kango Cooperative began production the following year, with 70 members, with both sections of the enterprise under the former general manager, Mr P.K. Steyn. Since then the former winemaker, Pieter Conradie, has taken over as manager and the membership has increased to 86, supplying an annual 5 000 tonnes of grapes, the main varieties being Palomino, Chenin Blanc, Muscat d'Alexandrie, Muscadel and Colombard, together with some Pinotage and Tinta Barocca. The winemaker is Pieter Conradie. Some 11 wines now comprise the winery's marketed range — the 'Rijckshof' label depicts a now-demolished 'ostrich palace', Oliver Towers.

In this arid area small yields from suppliers are not uncommon. In 1991 their maiden vintage for Chardonnay, Weisser Riesling and Gewürztraminer together totalled 800 kilograms.

WINES BOTTLED AND MARKETED

Red: Claret.
White: Sauvignon Blanc, Colombard, Bouquet Petite, Xandré, Premier Blanc, Herfsgoud and Blanc de Noir.
Fortified: Red Muscadel, White Muscadel, Red Jerepigo, Golden Jerepigo, Hanepoot and Port.

The co-operative is on the Klein Karoo Wine Route and is open to the public on weekdays from 08h30 to 13h00 and from 14h00 to 16h30 (the cellar closes at 16h00 on Fridays).

—LADISMITH—
CO-OPERATIVE WINERY AND DISTILLERY

This company began as a distillery in 1939, but in the early 1970s its production was expanded to include wine, and modern equipment for cold fermentation was installed. In 1975 Alex Rossouw was appointed manager and winemaker, assisted from 1991 by André Simonis. The Ladismith wines (the present range is five) are sold under the name Towerkop ('Bewitched Mountain') after the highest peak of the Klein Swartberg which rises behind the town and which legend claims was split asunder by a witch.

WINES BOTTLED AND MARKETED

Red: Towerkop Dry Red.
White: Towerkop Chenin Blanc, Riesling and Stein, and Swartberg Aristaat.
Fortified: Hanepoot Jerepigo.

The co-operative is on the Klein Karoo Wine Route and is open to the public on weekdays from 08h00 to 13h00 and from 14h00 to 17h00.

—MONS RUBER—
ESTATE

Situated 27 kilometres from Oudtshoorn, Mons Ruber constitutes the central portion of the original farm 'Rietvallei' which was granted to Carolus Minnie in 1764. The farm changed hands a number of times until 1929 when the Meyer family, ravaged by the effects of the 1913 crash in the ostrich feather trade, took it over. The farm was badly neglected and reconstruction began, even though times were difficult: those were the days of the Depression, the great drought and the Second World War.

Mixed farming was practised, as it still is. Wine was also made, but with the emphasis on 'witblits' production. This was a crude local brandy which was made by distilling the pulp of skins and pips left at the bottom of the tank when the fermented must had been run off at the end of the wine-making process. Once prohibited, it is now making a tentative official comeback.

In 1936 Basie Meyer replaced the eight distilling kettles on the farm with a single large one. From then onwards, lees and must

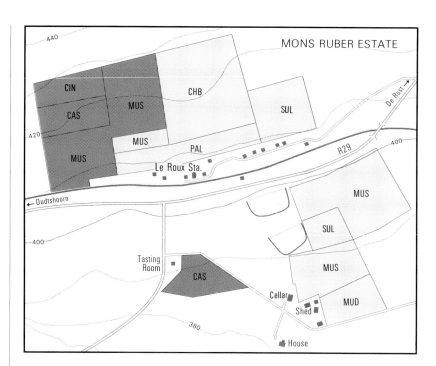

MONS RUBER ESTATE

were separated and wine production in addition to witblits production commenced. The original 1936 kettle is still in use at Mons Ruber today — by distilling the wine at the farm before it is delivered to KWV, the bulk is reduced substantially, with a resultant economy in transport costs.

In 1946 Basie's son Raadus joined him on the farm after obtaining a B.Sc. degree in Chemistry and Zoology. At this time ostriches were a viable farming enterprise once more, but as it had become a firm policy of the farm never again to rely solely on ostrich farming, viticulture gained in importance.

Muscadel was found to be well suited to the soil and climate and was consequently the main variety planted with excellent re-

sults. In 1972 some Cabernet Sauvignon vines were planted — a move which was con-

---

MONS RUBER ESTATE

Varieties planted (ha)

Perold trellis
Red Muscadel 6
Chenin Blanc 5,3
Palomino 5,1
Muscat d'Alexandrie 1,7
Cinsaut 0,84
V-trellis
Cabernet Sauvignon 2,8
V- and Perold trellis
White Muscadel 6,7
Factory trellis
Sultana 4,2

Total area under vines in 1991/2: 35 ha.
Irrigation: The vineyards are irrigated.
Average temperatures: Records are not kept.
Average annual rainfall: 300 mm.
Stock: Rooted vines are bought from a nursery.
First wines bottled under the Mons Ruber label: Cabernet Sauvignon, Hanepoot Jerepigo and Muscadel Jerepigo (all 1986 vintage).
Wines currently bottled under the Mons Ruber label: Cabernet Sauvignon, Conari, Elegantia, Regalis, Bonitas, Muscadel Jerepigo, Red Jerepigo, Cabernet Sauvignon Port, Port and Sherry.
Wood ageing: Not practised.
Cellar capacity: 4 400 hl.

Mons Ruber Estate is on the Klein Karoo Wine Route and is open to the public on weekdays from 08h30 to 17h00, and on Saturdays from 08h30 to 13h00.

natural wines, and in 1970 the winery began making concentrated grape juice for export to West Germany. A further diversification is to take place with the cellar's first crop of Chardonnay appearing in 1992. Membership is now about 75, and each year these farmers deliver some 11 000 tonnes of grapes, made into wine under the supervision of Mr S.B. (Sonnie) Malan. The co-operative's Volsoet Rooi Muskadel has an excellent show record; in 1980 it was the South African Champion Muscat fortified wine and has been a regular trophy winner ever since. The cellar also produces good natural dry white wines.

— RIETRIVIER —
WINE CELLAR CO-OPERATIVE

Situated 20 kilometres east of Montagu on the road to Barrydale, the Rietrivier Wine Cellar was completed in 1967 under the aegis of Piet Frick, the winemaker and manager. The winery, which is one of the few co-operatives to sell directly to the retail market, specializes in making quality wines under several labels. It also produces top-quality rebate wine for brandy production, for which it has won numerous prizes and trophies over the years. The 45 member farmers deliver an annual 5 000 tonnes of grapes.

WINES BOTTLED AND MARKETED

White: Chenin Blanc, Blanc de Blanc, Colombard and Late Harvest.
Sparkling: Vin Doux.
Fortified: Red Muscadel.
White and red semi-sweet wines sold to the retail market in plastic containers ranging from 500 ml to 25 l include Honeybird, Special Stein, Rietrivier and Monselect.

The co-operative is on the Klein Karoo Wine Route and is open to the public on weekdays from 08h00 to 13h00 and from 14h00 to 17h00.

— RUITERBOSCH —
MOUNTAIN VINEYARDS

In 1985 Danie and Carel Nel of Boplaas Estate bought a vineyard at Ruiterbosch in the Outeniqua mountains near Mossel Bay — the only vineyard in the country overlooking the Indian Ocean. Experiencing nearly the coolest average temperatures in the Cape, a

---

RUITERBOSCH MOUNTAIN VINEYARDS

Varieties planted (ha)

Vertical hedge system

Chardonnay 10
Pinot Noir 5
Sauvignon Blanc 3
Weisser Riesling 3
Merlot 2

Total area under vines in 1991/2: 23 ha.
Irrigation: None.
Average temperatures:
Maximum 28 °C; minimum 15 °C.
Average annual rainfall: 625 mm.
Stock: Rooted vines are purchased from a nursery.
First wine bottled under the Ruiterbosch Mountain Cuvée label: Sauvignon Blanc 1989.
Wines currently bottled under the Ruiterbosch Mountain Cuvée label: Sauvignon Blanc, Weisser Riesling, Chardonnay, Pinot Noir and Ruiterbosch Sparkling Wine (*méthode champenoise*).
Wood ageing: Wines are aged in wood on the farm.
Cellar capacity: 5 000 hl.

Ruiterbosch Mountain Vineyards are on the Klein Karoo Wine Route and are not open to the public, but wines are available on the Boplaas Estate and at selected bottle stores.

---

lengthy, even ripening period is experienced which ensures well-structured and flavourful wines from noble varieties.

The Ruiterbosch plantings are in poor, hard, gravelly soils. Dense plantings (7 000 vines per hectare), no irrigation and ripening under optimum conditions produce quality grapes for excellent white wines. Only 23 hectares have been planted at Ruiterbosch and the wines will therefore always be available in limited quantities only. The grapes from these vineyards are transported the short distance across the Outeniqua mountains to be vinified in the Boplaas cellars near Calitzdorp.

The maiden vintage for Sauvignon Blanc was 1989, and it established an immediate reputation for excellence. Chardonnay was first harvested in 1990 and was fermented in small French oak barrels and matured for a further four months on the lees before bottling. In 1990 a small quantity of Pinot Noir was made with some success.

The white wines are available in limited quantities from the Boplaas Estate and certain selected bottle stores, and are also exported to several countries in Europe.

Montagu, named after John Montagu, the colonial secretary, was founded in 1851.

sidered bold by some and foolhardy by others — yet these vines have come to exert a major influence on the development of the estate. Although the major part of its harvest was absorbed by the wholesale trade, Mons Ruber's Cabernet Sauvignon was not of a sufficient quantity to merit transportation over long distances, and furthermore the local public had a definite bias towards white wine. In desperation, a jerepigo was made from the Cabernet Sauvignon grapes and it was such a success that this wine is currently considered to be one of the best wines of the estate. In 1988 Cabernet Sauvignon grapes were used sucessfully in the base wine of a port.

The farm was declared an estate in October 1986 and it was decided to concentrate on the making of dessert wines and dry red wines. In 1990 Raadus passed away and the estate is now jointly owned and managed by the two Meyer brothers, Erhard and Radie.

— MONTAGU —
MUSCADEL FARMERS' CO-OPERATIVE

This co-operative was established in 1941 and was 50 years old in 1991. The original intention of this co-operative was to concentrate upon fortified Muscadel wines, other grapes not suitable for this purpose being sent to KWV for distillation. In 1968, however, the cellar was modified to produce dry

---

WINES BOTTLED AND MARKETED

White: Chenin Blanc, Colombard, Sparkling, Late Vintage and Monte Bouquet.
Sparkling: Demi-Sec.
Fortified: Volsoet Rooi Muskadel.

The co-operative is on the Klein Karoo Wine Route and is open to the public on weekdays from 08h30 to 12h30 and from 13h30 to 17h00.

Soetwyn Boere Co-operative, situated in the centre of Montagu, is renowned for its dessert wines.

The general produce of the scheme is handled by the Vaalharts Agricultural Co-operative. The growing of grapes has steadily increased, and with it the making of wine, to the extent that the area previously known as the ward of Vaalharts was declared a district in its own right and renamed Andalusia. It has since reverted to the status of a ward, but it does not fall under any region or district.

—JACOBSDAL—
WINE CELLAR CO-OPERATIVE

The Orange Free State's sole co-operative winery, the Jacobsdal Cellar (part of the South-Western Transvaal Agricultural Co-operative) was started in 1974. Much of the setting up of the vineyards was overseen by the Viticultural and Oenological Research Institute, mostly from its Jan Kempdorp station, which advised on the most appropriate varieties for this arid climate. The first wine was made from the 1977 vintage under the supervision of the former winemaker,

—SOETWYN—
BOERE CO-OPERATIVE

Founded in 1941, the Soetwyn Boere Co-operative was built under conditions of war-time shortage, and the original cellar had to be thatched. In 1951 Kenneth Knipe was appointed winery manager and winemaker, retiring in 1990 due to ill-health. He was succeeded by Jako Smit. Despite its name, the cellar also makes dry natural wines and an excellentr ebate wine for the production of brandy. The 54 members supply between 5 000 and 6 000 tonnes of grapes per year.

WINES BOTTLED AND MARKETED

Red: Claret.
White: Colombard, Chenin Blanc, Late Harvest, Grand Crû and Muscat d'Alexandrie.
Sparkling: Vin Doux and Vin Sec.
Fortified: Red and White Muscadel and Hanepoot.

The co-operative is on the Klein Karoo Wine Route and is open to the public on weekdays from 08h30 to 12h30 and from 13h30 to 17h00, and on Saturdays from 09h00 to 12h00.

DOUGLAS

Originally part of the Orange River wine area, and sharing its generally hot, dry climate, the Douglas district was given separate Wine of Origin status in 1981.

The town of Douglas was settled at a fording place on the Orange River. In 1775, it was the scene of one of the last battles between the Korana and the San, but is now the peaceful centre of the Douglas district.

—DOUGLAS—
CO-OPERATIVE WINERY

Established in 1968, and this winery now receives grapes from the Douglas, Prieska and Hopetown areas. The intake comprises about 25 per cent Sultana grapes and 10 per cent each of Muscat d'Alexandrie and Palomino, with the balance being shared between Fernão Pires, Chenin Blanc and Colombard. 'Pou' le Roux makes a range of wines bearing the Douglas label from a small percentage of the winery's output, the bulk of the wine being sold to merchants.

WINES BOTTLED AND MARKETED

Red: Pinotage.
White: Colombard, Fernão Pires, Gewürztraminer, Late Vintage, Stein and Blanc de Noir.
Fortified: Rooi Muscadel, Soet Sultana and Muscat d'Alexandrie.
A Rosé is also made.

The co-operative is open to the public on weekdays from 08h00 to 17h00. Cellar tours are by appointment only.

ANDALUSIA

In 1933 the then Minister of Lands, Colonel Deneys Reitz, announced the establishment of the Vaalharts Irrigation Scheme. Based on ideas put forward by Cecil Rhodes (for his own profit) as far back as 1881, the Minister hoped instead to settle farmers who were enduring hardship as a result of drought and economic depression.

Developed at the confluence of the Vaal and Harts rivers some 80 kilometres north of Kimberley, it has become one of the world's largest irrigation schemes.

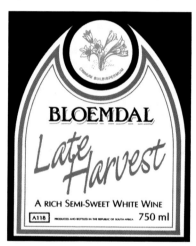

'Bertie' Bruyns. The winery's produce is marketed under the Bloemdal label and the present winemaker is Ian Sieg.

The Sarel Hayward canal, which brings water from the Orange River, was completed in 1987. With this development and sufficient water, new varieties such as Colombard, Chenin Blanc, Chardonnay, Pinotage, Cabernet and Red Muscadel are being planted. About 80 per cent of the crop of approximately 3 000 tonnes is bottled.

— VAALHARTS —
FARMERS' CO-OPERATIVE

This modern, well-equipped cellar is the only co-operative north of the Vaal River, and was started in 1977 under the aegis of the Vaalharts Agricultural Co-operative. The Vaalharts irrigation area is about 100 kilometres north of Kimberley in a shallow, wide valley between the Vaal and Harts rivers. It is the largest irrigation area in the southern hemisphere, drawing water via a complicated canal system from the Vaal River near Warrenton, and was started in 1933 during the Depression, when the State made irrigated farmland available to ex-soldiers. Today the area supports huge crops of wheat, maize, groundnuts, table grapes and wine grapes. The co-operative is situated near Hartswater, one of the two towns in the area, the other being Jan Kempdorp.

Roelof Maree is the manager of the cellar and also the winemaker, having previously been a wine blender with Distillers' Corporation, and assistant at the Franschhoek Co-operative and cellar manager at Frans Malan's Simonsig Estate. His assistant is Joshua du Toit. Johan Cronje acts as viticulture adviser for the members.

A number of varieties such as Colombard, Chenel, Fernão Pires, Emerald Riesling, Ruby Cabernet, Chardonnay and Erlihane have been planted on about 450 hectares of vineyards. The certified wines are marketed as Andalusia Wines of Origin while the uncertified range is marketed under the Overvaal label.

BENEDE ORANJE

Centred around the town of Upington on the Lower Orange River, this very hot area is the most northerly of the country's wine-making regions. As with the ward of Andalusia, it is based on a large-scale irrigation scheme along the banks of the river, and, like Andalusia, this ward does not fall under any region or district. The Benede Oranje vineyards extend between the Boegoeberg Dam and the Augrabies Falls, and yield heavy crops on deep, fertile soils.

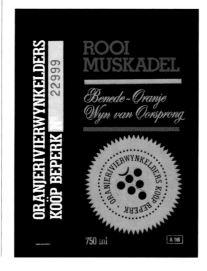

— ORANJERIVIER —
CO-OPERATIVE WINE CELLARS

Established in 1965 with its headquarters at Upington, this co-operative has branches along the Orange River at Groblershoop, Grootdrink, Kakamas and Keimoes. Under the general managership of Noel Mouton, the combine handles a massive 98 000 tonnes of grapes a year of which a fair amount goes to make the co-operative's range of wines.

BRONKHORSTSPRUIT

This is the magisterial (not wine) district in which the most northerly estate in South Africa is situated. The name derives from the water-cress (*bronkers*) found on the river (*spruit*) by early settlers. The town of Bronkhorstspruit was the scene of the opening battle of the First Anglo-Boer War. Mixed farming is now practised in the area.

— LOOPSPRUIT —
ESTATE

The only registered estate north of the Orange River, Loopspruit was established by retired policeman Eric Olivier who concentrated on producing fortified wines and a limited quantity of sparkling wine.

The estate was taken over by the Kwa Ndebele Agricultural Company (KAC) in 1983, and since then the range has been extended. At present, Loopspruit has 20,5 hectares of vines. From these it used to produce its KWV quota of 240 tonnes per annum. The varieties planted on the estate consist of

Colombard, Chenin Blanc, Cabernet Sauvignon, Raisin Blanc, Muscat d'Alexandrie and Chardonnay.

Cellarmaster B.W. Myburgh is confident that the combination of fertile soil and mild temperatures that the area experiences, will contribute towards quality vines. Kwa Ndebele's limited summer rainfall makes irrigation of the vineyards necessary.

G L O S S A R Y

Acetaldehyde The principal aldehyde of wine, occurring in amounts of up to about 100 parts per million. It is generated during the yeast fermentation of a must and contributes much to the bouquet and characteristic flavour of the wine and the other alcoholic drinks distilled from it.

Acetic A vinegary smell, caused by the action of acetobacteria which spoil the wine if it is left in contact with air for extended periods of time. The taste of the wine is also affected by these bacteria.

Acetic acid A volatile acid present in virtually all table wines in small quantities. The legal limit varies from country to country but is usually less than 1,5 grams per litre; the flavour threshold is around 0,5 to 0,6 grams per litre. A wine described as volatile suffers from an excess of acetic acid.

Acidic The sharp taste from an excess of various acids which cause an imbalance in the wine.

Acids There are two kinds of organic acid which occur in wine. The first of these are the fruit acids or fixed acids. These are present both in the grape and in the wine and are indispensable to high quality wines. The principal acids of this type are tartaric acid and malic acid. Their ratio varies, depending upon the grape variety, the soil type, and the weather during growth and ripening and when the grapes are harvested. These acids play an essential role in the maturation of wine; better wines tend to be higher in acid content, and take longer to mature. If the wine contains too little acid it will taste insipid; too much and the result will taste sharp. The correct balance of organic acids lends freshness and individuality to the wine.

The second type of acid is volatile acid. This is the acid of vinegar, acetic acid. It is not found in the grape but develops after alcoholic fermentation. In minute quantities it can be attractive, especially in red wines, but larger amounts represent substantial bacterial spoilage and an eventual deterioration towards vinegar.

Aftertaste Appreciation of the aftertaste is the final stage of the ritual of tasting a wine and is important for its complete assessment. When a wine is swallowed new sensations are experienced by the taste buds on the part of the tongue beneath the uvula and in the throat itself. These taste buds are highly sensitive, and a wine which may have appeared sound through the colour, bouquet and tasting stages may carry a fault which is only revealed in the aftertaste.

Ageing The ageing or maturation of most wines is a continuous process from the time of fermentation, whether in vat, tank, cask or bottle. The rate of ageing varies; in general, white wines usually mature more quickly than red, but there are notable exceptions among whites, for example, special late harvests and particularly noble late harvests such as Nederburg Edelkeur.

Alcohol The alcohol present in wine and spirits is ethyl alcohol. This primary alcohol, or pure spirit, is a colourless liquid with a faint but pleasant smell; it is derived from the fermentation of sugar and has the formula CH_3CH_2OH. Ethyl alcohol is the only pure spirit which is safe to drink.

Alcoholic strength The strength of a wine depends upon the proportion of alcohol present which can be expressed in percentage by volume or as degrees Proof Spirit. In wine the range is usually from 8 to 14% by volume. Fortified wines are between 17 and 22% alcohol, and spirits are from 30 to 40% alcohol in general (in South Africa 43%) though some spirits can be purchased with a content of up to 80% volume.

Absolute alcohol is denoted as being 100% by volume, which on the Sykes scale is 175,35 degrees Proof Spirit (PS). Similarly 100° PS is 57,1% by volume, while a wine of 21° PS has 12% alcohol by volume.

— COMPARATIVE ALCOHOLIC STRENGTHS—

By Volume	Proof Spirit Degrees
Pure alcohol -	175,35° PS
100%	(75,35° over proof)
Gin, brandy -	75,25° PS
if 43%	(25° under proof)
Liqueur -	63° PS
if 36%	37° under proof)
Sherry -	35° PS
if 20%	(65° under proof)
Natural white wine -	21° PS
if 12%	(79° under proof)

Aldehydes A group of chemical compounds derived from dehydrogenated alcohols. There are many forms, such as acetaldehyde, which is produced from ethyl alcohol. *See separate entry on* acetaldehyde.

Alluvial soils These are soils which have been laid down by the action of rivers through the ages. Specific kinds of alluvial soils, known as Dundee soils, show alternating layers of different textures, commonly of silt and sand.

Ampelography The scientific study of the description and classification of the vine and the grape.

Anthocyanin A colouring pigment found in grape skins and playing an important part in both the colour and keeping qualities of a red wine.

Anthracnose (*Gloeosporium ampelophagum*) A vine disease. It appears on the leaves as small circular, greyish-black spots which are sometimes bordered by a yellow discoloration. The spots gradually enlarge, the middle portion often falling out. Sunken cankers form on the shoots till the bark is destroyed, the shoot becoming hard and black. Modern organic fungicides are used to control the disease.

Appearance The first step in wine appreciation which is the assessment of colour and clarity.

Appellation Contrôlée A system of laws which guarantees the authenticity of a wine with a given label, extending both to region, grape variety, methods of viticulture and (occasionally) methods of vinification. In South Africa this is known as the Wine of Origin.

Aroma To be distinguished from the bouquet. The aroma is the smell of the fresh ingredients of the grape, largely contained in its skin, which are carried through into the wine. A young wine will tend to have an aroma, but relatively little bouquet. As the wine ages and matures the aroma slowly diminishes while the bouquet increases. In a good wine there should be a nice balance of aroma and bouquet, and in judging a wine both qualities should be assessed.

Astringency Not to be confused with dryness, acidity or sourness. Some red wines make the mouth pucker – this depends on the amount of tannin absorbed by the wine from the skins, seeds and stalks of the grapes, as well as from the casks. A moderate astringency is desirable in some wine.

Baked A 'hot' earthy smell caused by burned and shrivelled grapes due to excessive sunshine and little rainfall.

Balance A well-balanced wine is one which is completely harmonious and balanced in its make-up, with no quality overpronounced and with no striking deficiency in bouquet, flavour or aftertaste. If light it will be delicate, if full-bodied it will have a corresponding amount of flavour and character. Although the term praises the wine, it need not be a great wine but merely what it should be in type and class.

Balling *See also* Hydrometer. A measure of the concentration of sugar in grape juice or wine, named after the inventor of the saccharometer, the instrument with which this measurement is taken and which is calibrated in degrees Balling. The reading gives the grams of sugar in 100 grams of juice. As a rough rule-of-thumb, the Balling reading multiplied by 0,55 will give the wine's future alcoholic content; juice of 22° Balling, for example, should give a 12% alcohol content.

Bead The bubbles in sparkling wine. The smaller the beads the longer they continue to rise in the glass, the better the quality of the wine. Bottle fermentation produces the smallest beads and the longest-lasting; carbonation produces the largest, which are also the quickest to disperse.

Bentonite This is a type of clay used as a clarifying or fining agent for the protein stabilization of wine. It is mined mainly in Wyoming in the USA, and when properly used has no effect on the bouquet and flavour of the wine.

Big A big wine is one which has more than the average amount of flavour and body, and is high in alcohol, tannin acidity and grape extract. It is not necessarily a term of distinction, since this wine could be coarse and heavy.

Bin A repository for wines where they can be suitably stored, lying horizontally.

Bitter Usually an unpleasant taste detected on the palate, on the back of the tongue and in the aftertaste; however, it may be desirable in certain wines and vermouths.

Black-mould rot (*Aspergillus rot*) A vine disease; it is usually a secondary infection, following on botrytis rot.

Blanc The French word for 'white'.

Blanc de blanc A French term used traditionally for champagne when it has been made only from white grapes, but now widely used for other wines as well.

Blanc de noir This term, literally 'white from black', refers to wine made from red grapes. The skins, however, are removed at the time of pressing and thus they impart only the slightest blush to the wine. Blanc de noir wine is lighter in colour than a rosé. There are some excellent Cabernet Sauvignon blanc de noirs available, but a blend of varieties may also be used. Pinotage is probably the most commonly used grape at the moment. These wines should be drunk young and always served chilled.

Blending The art of mixing together wines or spirits to obtain a better product, or uniformity from year to year, to create a specific style of wine, or to enhance the final product by bringing together each element with its own outstanding feature, thus creating a masterpiece.

Bloom The waxy, water-resistant layer which forms on the outside of ripe grapes and in which yeast cells are found.

Body Used for a 'mouth-filling' wine of good substance which contains a high quantity of 'solid' matter or extract in solution. A wine lacking in body tends to be thin.

Botrytis cinerea (Noble rot) This is a fungus disease which attacks ripe grapes under certain conditions of temperature and humidity. During the growth of the fungi, the mycelia penetrate the skin and in feeding to develop the botrytis growth extract moisture from the grapes, causing them to shrivel and to increase in relative sugar content. This phenomenon has been turned to good account by winemakers, who use 'noble rot' to make rich, sweet wines. The classic Sauternes, Trockenbeerenauslese and Tokay wines of Europe as well as the local Nederburg Edelkeur and various other noble late harvest wines are made from grapes affected by this co-operative fungus. If the fungus does not have optimum weather conditions it can rapidly turn to vulgar rot and absolutely ruin the harvest.

Bottle age Mellow development observed in the bouquet of a wine and in its smoothness across the palate.

Bottle sickness A temporary loss of flavour and bouquet usually found straight after bottling – it is caused by too much contact between air and wine at the bottling stage.

Bouquet The fragrance of the wine as it arises when first poured into t he glass. Unlike the aroma, which is the wine's memory of the natural ingredients of the grape, the bouquet is specifically a product of the fermentation process and of the complex reactions of ageing and mellowing, both in the cask and in the bottle.

Brandy A spirit distilled from wine and usually made anywhere that wine is made. The world's most celebrated brandy comes from Cognac in France where it is distilled in pot stills; in South Africa the law requires that a minimum 30% of a brandy blend be distilled in pot stills. Elsewhere the word is also used to refer to distillates from other fruits besides grapes.

Breathing *See also* Decanting. A wine is allowed to 'breathe' after it has been opened as contact with the air animates the bouquet and enhances its effect.

Brut The French word for 'dry' as applied to wines, in particular to sparkling wines and dry champagnes with a sugar content of 1,5% or less.

Bung The 'cork' for a wine cask, usually made of wood, but can also be of earthenware, glass or other patent material.

Bush vine A term used in South Africa to describe an untrellised vine. *See* Goblet.

Butt From the old French *bot*, this is a barrel or cask for holding approximately 400 litres of wine.

Butyric The smell of rancid butter or spoiled cheese.

Callus The woody outgrowth which develops and joins scion and rootstock in the formation of a graft.

Cane The mature shoot of the vine.

Cap During the fermentation of red grapes the carbon dioxide gas which is released during the reaction forms as bubbles around the solid matter of skins and pips in the must, lifting it to the surface. There it forms a floating layer known as a 'cap'. This has to be frequently roused so that contact between the skins and the liquid can be re-established.

Capsule The plastic or lead cap which protects the cork of bottled wines.

Caramel burned sugar added to spirits as colouring matter; it is tasteless and virtually odourless.

Carbonated wines These are sparkling wines in which the bubbles have been introduced under pressure.

Carbonic maceration Vinification without crushing grapes. Whole bunches are placed into pressure tanks and intercellular fermentation under oxygen-free conditions occurs. This process is used for Beaujolais Nouveau production.

Cask A wooden wine barrel, varying in capacity; it is usually made of oak and bound with steel hoops.

Cellar A suitable place (cool, quiet and away from direct sunlight) for the storage of wine.

Chambre To bring a wine to the temperature of the room in which it is to be drunk by letting it stand there.

Champagne The classic sparkling wine from the Pinot Noir and Chardonnay grapes, made by the *methodé champenoise* to specific atmospheric pressures and sugar content. The 'singing wine' has its own separate mythology. Champagne is a specific region of France and the term 'champagne' should only be used for the wines of this area. However, it is often used to describe any sparkling wine.

Chaptalization *See* Sugaring.

Character As with many wine-tasting terms, this one is generated by human analogy. A wine of character is like a person of character: unique, individual, distinctive.

Clean A wine smell without any foreign or off colours.

Clone This is a vegetatively reproduced plant from one superior parent plant.

Cloying Excessively sweet taste, usually that of a wine of low acidity.

Coarse A generally dismissive word for a badly made, low quality wine of rough texture.

Cold fermentation This is the general name for a number of related technical processes all having the same basic principle, that of cooling and so controlling, often with the use of refrigerated water, the fermenting must of white wine. Its use counteracts the effects of the high temperatures generated by fermentation when weather temperatures are such that they cannot cool the reaction.

Common A flat and dull taste – although a drinkable wine.

Cooked or burned Wines which have been subjected to a heating process to extract colour or to pasteurization.

Co-operative Any one of about 70 organizations in the local winelands, now producing about 85% of the South African good wine crop. The member-farmers deliver their grapes at harvest time to the co-operative's winery, where they are made into wine. Some of this wine may be bottled under the co-operative's own label, but in general the bulk is supplied to KWV or to one of the large producing wholesalers.

Corked wine, corky wine, corkiness All meaning the same thing: microbial infection in the cork introduces a disagreeable smell and taste into the wine. This is fortunately a rare occurence.

Crisp Good acid; a clean and refreshing wine.

Crushing The first stage of wine-making, when the skins of the grapes are mechanically split to release the juice.

Crust Sediment precipitated on the inside of a bottle of wine, especially port, after long bottle maturation.

Cultivar *See* variety.

Cuvée Literally, the contents of a cask, generally applied to a specially prepared blend of wine.

Dead arm (*Phomopsis viticola*) This is a vine disease which is indicated by the formation of small cankers on the basal parts of the shoots and small black spots bordered with yellow on the leaves.

Decanting Slowly pouring a wine into a decanter sometimes enhances and releases the aroma and bouquet of a wine (see Breathing). The main reason for decanting is to separate a wine from its sediment and therefore care must be taken that any sediment in the wine is not disturbed during the operation (a light, traditionally a candle, under the neck of the bottle enables one to see if the sediment is moving).

Delicate Balance and charm in quality light wine.

Demijohn A wicker-covered wine container with a large body and small neck.

Deposit A sediment that is commonly precipitated from red wines during their normal development in the bottle and is completely harmless; it comprises pigment and tannin complexes. Some rich white wines might also form slight sediments which are usually made up of tartrate deposits.

Depth Richness with many flavour nuances.

Dessert wine Wine to which a small amount of spirit has been added to arrest fermentation and to preserve the unfermented grape sugar which lends the wine its sweetness.

Dionysus The ancient Greek god of wine, vegetation and fertility, the son of Zeus and Semele. He was later adopted by the Romans as Bacchus.

Distillation When wine is heated to a certain temperature the alcohol vaporizes with little or no vaporization of the water. In the process of distillation, the vapour is collected and cooled, condensing to form a colourless and, with high refining, almost odourless spirit.

Downy mildew (*Plasmopara viticola*) A vine disease which appears as a white downy mass of spores on the underside of the vine leaf. On the upper surface of the leaf an oily-looking spot appears. A white powdery covering may also appear on young bunches of grapes, causing them to shrivel and drop. The disease is treated with copper oxychloride and a variety of fungicides.

Dry wine A natural wine in which the grape sugar has been converted into alcohol during fermentation, leaving few fermentable sugars.

Dull Uninteresting and insipid, although drinkable.

Dundee soils *See* Alluvial soils

Duplex soils These soils exhibit a marked contrast of texture between topsoil and subsoil. A large proportion of the soils in the western Cape coastal region are made up of three local types of Duplex soils, the Kroonstad, Sterkspruit and Estcourt forms, which feature a relatively sandy topsoil over an underlying clay pan. In the Kroonstad form these two layers are separated by a further layer of *ouklip*, which is rough, iron-bearing pan.

Earthy An earth-like taste not necessarily derived from soil.

Egrappoir A machine for removing stalks and crushing grapes at the start of the wine-making process.

Elegant A description of a graceful and finely made wine which is well-balanced and shows finesse.

Estate In terms of the Wine of Origin legislation, this is a wine farm which both grows its own grapes and makes wine from them in its own cellar. The wines are generally bottled on the estate, although some estate wines are bottled and matured by wholesalers.

Estcourt soils *See* Duplex soils

Esterification This is the production of esters in a wine. One of the reasons for the softening of a wine with age is the reduction of acidity by the process of esterification.

Esters Responsible for the aroma and bouquet of a wine, these are sweet-smelling compounds which derive from the fruit and from reactions between acids and ethyl alcohol during maturation.

Extract Soluble solids that are non-volatile and non-sugars.

Farewell A term used to describe the flavour as well as the length of time that the flavour remains in the mouth after swallowing the wine.

Fat A 'fat' wine is one showing considerable 'body' or substance when held in the mouth; it is usually high in glycerol and grape extract.

Feel The term used to describe the sensation that the wine gives in the mouth before swallowing.

Fermentation The chemical and biochemical reaction upon which all wine-making is based. Derived from the Latin *fervere*, to boil, the word describes the process whereby sugar in the grape is transformed through the action of yeast into alcohol and gaseous carbon dioxide. Although fermentation has been observed since the dawn of history, it was thought to be a wholly spontaneous phenomenon until Pasteur showed in 1864 that it was the work of living organisms – more specifically of zymase, the enzyme of the naturally occurring yeasts found in the waxy 'bloom' on the surface of the grape. In most cellars and wineries today the reaction is carefully and scientifically controlled. A further kind of fermentation can occur in respect of wines. This is secondary, or malolactic fermentation. Malic acid is a natural acid present in most fruit and vegetables. By the action of bacteria the malic acid which is contained in wine is converted into the milder lactic acid with the release of carbon dioxide gas. This happens without adverse effects provided it takes place before the wine is bottled; after bottling gasiness and off-odours may be formed in the bottle.

Fernwood soils *See* Structureless soils

Filtering In the wine-making process the wine is clarified prior to bottling by passing it through any one of many different types of filter.

Finesse The breed, class or natural distinction which separates a wine from its more ordinary fellows. A wine lacking in finesse will be heavy and dull. A great wine is often one which is full-bodied, yet possesses an innate finesse.

Fining This is the traditional method of clarifying wine (called *collage* by French winemakers) known since Roman times, whereby certain substances are added to the wine after fermentation to precipitate insoluble suspended particles such as dead yeast cells. These gradually settle in the form of a sediment, or lees, on the bottom of the tank, leaving the wine clear and bright. Examples of fining agents used in the modern winery are bentonite, gelatine and, more traditionally, egg albumen. *See also* Isinglass.

Finish The term is sometimes used to describe how a wine 'finishes' in the mouth; in other words, the aftertaste. Finish can also refer to the final preparation of the wine before bottling, for example, polish filtration, sweetening with grape juice or sweet reserve, or final sulphur dioxide adjustment.

Fino The palest, lightest, most delicate, and generally the driest of sherries.

Firm A term usually applied to the finish of a wine, and denoting the impact of tannin and possibly acid.

Fixed acids *See* Acids

Flat Dull, insipid, often lacking acidity.

Flor This word, derived from the Spanish for 'flower', refers to a particular kind of yeast, *Saccharomyces beticus*, used especially in the making of sherry. Soon after fermentation it forms a white film or 'flower' on the surface of the must, covering a large surface area as the casks are only three-quarters full. The yeast multiplies rapidly under these conditions, covering the surface and separating the wine from the air as it gradually forms a layer which is up to 15 millimetres deep and resembles chunky cottage cheese. It has an important effect on the final bouquet and flavour of the sherry.

Flowery A term of praise when applied to the bouquet of certain varieties, particularly used for white wines.

Fortification The addition of alcohol to wine to raise its strength. Port and sherry are examples of fortified wines.

Fruit(y) Descriptive of a wine with an aroma reminiscent of other fruits; either of a single fruit such as guava, apple or pineapple, or a combination. If the wine has the aroma of grapes then it is described as having a 'varietal' nose.

Fruity can also indicate acidity and as such show a freshness of taste in young wines. This attribute is lost with age.

Free-run juice As opposed to the press-juice, this is the juice which is released at the start of the cellar process when the grapes are mechanically ruptured but not pressed.

Fresh Having natural vitality and youthful character.

Fruit acid *See* Acids.

Full Refers to a wine of good body, possessing a heavy degree of substance.

Gewürz Spicy flavour or bouquet.

Glycerine A byproduct of fermentation which adds to the texture of a white wine.

Goblet A term describing the shape of an untrellised vine.

Good wine This phase is used in South Africa not only to describe the wine, but to distinguish it from rebate wine, which is distilled for brandy. Because 'good wine' is good does not necessarily indicate that rebate wine is of poor quality; on the contrary, it must reach exacting standards before being accepted for brandy production.

Grafting Developed in answer to the phylloxera aphid, this is a technique in which a scion of the desired variety is allowed to form an organic union with phylloxera-resistant rootstock. Various kinds of cuts – long-whip, short-whip, Jupiter and Omega are examples commonly used – have been evolved to ensure the best join at the interface of the two parts. Most modern vineyards contain only grafted vines.

Grapey The grapes of certain vines – the Muscat and Concord grapes are examples – tend to transmit their special flavour to the wine; in general, though, a wine should taste like wine, not like fresh grapes.

Great An accolade: as a taster's term it should not be used lightly, but reserved for the most outstanding of the best wines, those without flaw, perfect in balance and possessing real character and distinction of their own.

Green Acid-type smell of the unripe, raw or young wine.

Hard Refers to an austere wine, lacking in suppleness. This is not necessarily a fault, since many excellent wines are hard in their youth.

Harsh A harsh wine is one in which 'hardness' is carried to an extreme and is usually accompanied by astringency. In red wines, it can be an indication of youth and the harshness will disappear with time.

Hazy Often the first symptom of a 'sick' wine. A good wine should be clear and brilliant; a hazy wine may be reasonably clear initially but will soon develop the cloudiness of a poorly made product.

Heady High in alcohol – intoxicating.

Heavy A full bodied wine without delicacy or distinction; it is an unfavourable word in general but is used as a less severe term than 'coarse'.

Hectare Metric measure of area of 10 000 square metres or 2,471 acres.

Hectolitre A metric measure of volume equal to 100 litres and the equivalent of 22,3 British Imperial Gallons or of 26,42 US Gallons.

Hock A general term used in nineteenth-century England for wines produced along the banks of the River Rhine – it is an abbreviation of the name of the town of Hochheim.

Honest No great attribute, but a good well-made wine.

Hot Not to be confused with 'hot' as in 'peppery'; this term is descriptive of some wines, usually dry wine of high alcohol content, made from grapes grown in very warm regions. It is often considered a negative quality and is sometimes associated with wines coloured with caramel.

Hot bottling Bottling wine immediately after pasteurization, while it is still hot; used for inexpensive wines.

Husk The skin of the grape.

Hutton and Clovelly soils *See* Structureless soils

Hybrid A cross between an American and a European vine achieved by cross-pollination as opposed to grafting.

Hydrogen sulphide The smell of rotten eggs found in red wines resulting from the reduction of sulphur dioxide or elemental sulphur. Detectable in tiny quantities (one part per million); when bound into the wine it becomes mercaptan.

Hydrometer An instrument for measuring the specific gravity of a liquid, that is, its density relative to that of water. In wine-making a hydrometer is used for measuring the sugar content of a must and the sugar and alcohol content of a wine.

– HYDROMETER GRADUATIONS –

Specific Gravity	Degrees Baume	Degrees Twadell	Degrees Brix/Balling
1,005	0,7	1,0	1,3
1,010	1,4	2,0	2,5
1,015	2,1	3,0	3,8
1,075	10,0	15,0	18,5
1,080	10,7	16,0	19,8
1,085	11,3	17,0	20,8
1,090	11,9	18,0	22,0
1,095	12,5	19,0	23,0
1,100	13,1	20,0	24,2
1,105	13,7	21,0	25,3
1,110	14,3	22,0	25,4

Implicity sweet Apparent sweet taste from elements other than sugar, e.g. glycerol.

Inky or metallic A tinny or metallic taste derived from the presence of tannate of iron.

Isinglass Sometimes used by the winemaker as a fining agent to clear a hazy white wine. It is made from the swim bladder of fresh water fish, and is a form of gelatine.

Kroonstad soils *See* Duplex soils

Lactic acid *See also* Fermentation. A byproduct of fermentation and therefore present in wine in small quantities, lactic acid can also form as a result of malolactic fermentation.

Late harvest, special late harvest, noble late harvest The term 'late harvest' is a specifically South African usage and refers to a sweetish, medium- to full-bodied white wine with sugar levels of more than 20 but less than 30 grams per litre. Special late harvest wines, for example, require a residual sugar content of between 20 and 50 grams a litre, obtained without the addition of any sweetening. *See also* sugar level laws.

Lathuis A 'shade-house', it houses the young vine at an interim stage in its progress from nursery to vineyard. The lathuis, made of vertical wooden slats set at intervals, allows the young rooted vines to receive sun and air but protects them from the force of the wind.

Leaguer One leaguer equalled slightly more than 577 litres, or 127 gallons. However, the traditional measure of Cape wine is now superseded by metrication.

Lees During fermentation and maturation wines deposit a heavy, coarse sediment of insoluble matter at the bottom of the tank; this residue or 'lees' is left behind when the wine is 'racked', an operation which is performed several times before the wine is bottled.

Legs Wine vernacular for the drops which appear on the side of the glass after the wine has been swirled.

Light The opposite of full-bodied or heavy. Light wines are usually slightly lower in alcohol than full rich wines, and though they often possess grace and charm, rarely have the complexity of a great wine.

Lime The calcium oxide content of the soil is important to the growth of the vine in that it balances the acidity of the soil. It can occur naturally or can be artificially introduced to the vineyard where it is lacking.

Liqueur A strongly alcoholic liquor, sweetened and flavoured with aromatic extracts of fruit and plants, intended to be drunk after a meal.

Little or poor Hardly any bouquet or aroma in a wine lacking character or quality.

Lively When a wine stimulates the palate with a pleasant but not dominant acidity; a wine lacking in this quality tends to be flat or dead.

Long Denotes the capacity of flavours of the wine to linger in the mouth and palate after the wine has been swallowed.

Luscious Soft, sweet, fruity, ripe and fat – all in balance with each other.

Maderization A condition of oxidation which afflicts white wine which has been kept for too long or held at too high a temperature. The wine turns a gold-brown colour, and acquires a characteristic 'baked' taste. It is a requirement of Madeira style wines, hence the name.

Malic acids *See* Acids

Malolactic fermentation *See* Fermentation

Maturation The process of ageing wine and spirits until they reach peak condition and are ready for drinking.

Measures (see Table)

Meaty rich, almost chewable

Mealy bugs These are lice which form a sticky, shiny deposit on the bunches of grapes, making them unfit for normal wine-making purposes. The deposit attracts ants which protect the mealy bug from its natural enemy, the ladybird. Spraying the ants leaves a clear field for the ladybirds, providing a natural control on the mealy bugs.

Medium dry Containing traces of sugar but tasting predominantly dry.

Medium sweet Tasting quite sweet but not a dessert wine.

Mellow A rounded and well-matured wine.

Mercaptan Produced by ethyl mercaptan and ethyl sulphides in wine deriving from hydrogen sulphide and produced during the fermentation process. It manifests itself in a range of unpleasant odours ranging from burned rubber to garlic, onion, gamy meat, stale cabbage and asparagus. While hydrogen sulphide can easily be removed, once mercaptan is formed it is much more difficult to eliminate.

Méthode champenoise The method of making sparkling wine employed in Champagne in which the all-important second fermentation takes place in the bottle in which the wine is ultimately sold. The method is being used more and more in the Cape.

Mildew *See* Downy mildew *and* Powdery mildew

Millerandage The occurrence of small and immature grapes among the normally developing grapes in the bunch.

Mispah *See* Shallow soils

Mouldy An unmistakable smell or taste caused by rotten grapes or unclean casks.

Mousse The froth or foam produced when perlé or sparkling wines are poured.

Mousy The smell of mouse droppings – a sign of bacteriological disease affecting only wine in a cask.

Must Fermenting grape juice.

Musty A musty odour and flavour, often the result of poor cellar techniques related to uncleanliness.

Natural wine As distinguished from fortified wine, this is wine to which no alcohol is added.

Nematodes Otherwise known as eelworms, these are microscopic worm-shaped pests which attack the roots of the vine, causing damage similar to that of phylloxera; unlike phylloxera, they prefer moist and sandy soils. Fumigation of the vineyard soil before new plantings and the use of resistant rootstock effectively control nematodes.

Neutral Having no marked physical characteristics.

Noble Can be used when referring to wine or to certain grape varieties. A noble variety of grape is one capable of giving outstanding wine under optimum conditions and, within reason, good wine almost wherever it is planted. A noble wine is one that will be recognized as exceptional quality even by a novice wine drinker.

Noble rot *See* Botrytis cinerea

Nose Wine jargon for the aroma or bouquet of a wine. It can be average, good, excellent, disappointing or bad.

Nutty An aroma and flavour reminiscent of hazels and other nuts. The term is usually used in describing sherries.

Oak This is the preferred wood used for the casks and barrels in which wine is matured. All the finest red wines, most of the fortified wines and some white wines owe part of their quality to the flavour imparted by the oak.

Oaky An odour of oak apparent in wines aged too long in casks. It is desirable in fine red table wines but is unpleasant when excessive and especially so in white table wines.

Oenology The science of wine-making – that is, the science of the cellar as opposed to that of the vineyard, which is the province of viticulture.

Off The broadest and least specific term of disapproval which can be levelled at a wine; it is a permanent fault.

Off-taste An unclean foreign or tainted flavour.

Oïdium *See* Powdery mildew

Olfactory Pertaining to the sense of smell.

Oloroso One of the two basic types of Spanish sherry – Fino being the other. It has a recognizable and typical bouquet and is darker in colour than the Fino and fuller-bodied. Oloroso sherries are developed in 'soleras', but without the use of the particular flor yeasts which are responsible for giving the Finos their special character.

Organoleptic This term is gaining currency among wine tasters and refers to the ability to perceive a sensory stimulus, for example taste, touch and smell.

Overripe A raisin-like odour and taste.

Oxidized The smell is generally found in white table wines which have been in bottle for many years. This odour is usually accompanied by a darkening in colour.

Oxidation Various oxidative reactions occur at every stage in the life of wine. Excessive oxidation, usually from prolonged contact with the air, causes browning of the wine and a marked and unpleasant flavour.

Ouklip *See* Duplex soils

Palate Technically, the roof of the mouth, though it can be used as a compliment to a wine taster who is said to have a 'good palate'.

Pasteurization This is a process of sterilizing wine (it is used for other commodities such as milk as well) by heating it to a temperature of about 80° C(185° F) for one minute; this destroys micro-organisms in the wine, making it microbiologically stable. The treatment is not usually given to high quality wines, but to those destined for early consumption. A method known as 'flash' pasteurization is more commonly used in 'hot' bottling where the wine is raised to the required temperature only momentarily.

Penetrating A powerful content smell on the nostrils – indicating high alcohol and volatile esters formed from malic, acetic and tartaric acids.

Peppery A raw harshness – due to immature or unsettled compounds which have not yet intermingled.

Perlé, Perlant Somewhere between a still wine and a sparkling wine, this is one to which some bubbles of carbon dioxide have been introduced, giving it a slight effervescence.

Perfumed An aroma usually derived from the grape, e.g. Muscadel, Traminer.

Pétillant Originally used only by the French, this word is now used to describe wines which, like perlé wines, contain a little gas, causing a prickle in the mouth and giving them a slight lift. These wines may not have a pressure in excess of two atmospheres, while most have far less – in contrast to sparkling wines, including champagne, which contain a minimum of four atmospheres pressure.

pH This is a measure of the hydrogen-ion concentration of a liquid and records its relative degree (not the amount) of acidity or alkalinity. The neutral point is a pH of 7 (that of water); the higher the reading above 7 the greater the alkalinity, the lower the reading below 7 the greater the acidity. The optimum pH range for musts and wine is from 3,1 to 3,4

Measures	Metric	USA	Imperial
Half pint	284 ml	8 fl.oz	10 fl.oz
Pint	568 ml	16 fl.oz	20 fl.oz
Quart	1,136 litres	32 fl.oz	40 fl.oz (2 pints)
Gallon	4,546 litres	128 fl.oz	160 fl.oz (8 pints)
Half bottle wine	(37 cl)		13,33 fl.oz
Bottle wine	(75 cl)		26,66 fl.oz
One litre wine	(100 cl)		35,50 fl.oz
Magnum	(1,5 litres)		2 bottles
Jeroboam	(3 litres)		4 bottles
Rehoboam (1 gallon)	(4,5 litres)		6 bottles
Methuselah	(6 litres)		8 bottles
Imperiale (as above)			
Salmanazar (2 gallons)	(9 litres)		12 bottles
Balthazar	(12 litres)		16 bottles
Nebuchadnezzar	(15 litres)		20 bottles
Hogshead varies from			
46 gallons to 65			
gallons	(210 to 300 litres)		
Butt (Sherry)	(491 litres)		108 gallons
Pipe (Port)	(523 litres)		115 gallons
Pipe (Madeira)	(418 litres)		92 gallons
Pipe (Marsala)	(423 litres)		93 gallons
Tun	(955 litres)		210 gallons
(All cask sizes vary slightly as they are handmade)			

but some wines show an acid reading as 'high' as 2,7 and others as 'low' as 3,9.

Phylloxera (*Phylloxera vastatrix* now sometimes classified as *Dactylasphaera vitifoliae*) An aphid or plant louse which attacks, at different stages of its life cycle, both the roots and branches of the vine which, unable to heal the lesions, succumbs to secondary infection. It originated in the eastern part of the United States where it lived on the local wild vines which were resistant to its predations. Released accidentally in Europe, it caused widespread destruction of the vineyards; this was followed by the devastation of the vineyards of the Cape. Most modern vines are grown on phylloxera-resistant rootstocks derived originally from the American indigenous vines; no permanent chemical control of phylloxera has yet been found.

Pipe A cask made of oak and tapered sharply towards the ends, it is used to mature port. It comes in varying sizes, the most common holding 522 litres; the standard Madeira pipe is considerably smaller. Those used in South Africa are imported from Europe.

Piquant Fresh, mouth-watering bouquet – a result of balanced acidity.

Plastering In sherry production this is the addition of calcium sulphate, or gypsum, to grapes before fermentation, increasing the total acidity and improving the colour and clarity of the resulting wine; it is a normal procedure in the making of sherry and certain other wines.

Polishing The final filtration of a wine before bottling.

Port A sweet, heavily fortified dessert wine. It originated in the region of Oporto, Portugal – hence the name – and some of the best port still comes from a delimited district in the upper Douro Valley in Northern Portugal.

Positive A marked or noticeable fragrance, as opposed to 'little' or 'dumb'.

Powdery mildew (Oïdium) This vine ailment first made its appearance in the Cape vineyards in the 1850s. It is a form of fungus which appears on the lower surface of the leaf of the vine as small spots and on the upper surface as a white powdery, cobweb-like growth. The grapes are its normal target, though the shoots may be affected as well. It causes mature berries to crack and dry up, opening the way to further micro-organism infections, such as *Botrytis cinerea*. It is controlled with sulphur and other modern compounds.

Premier Grand Crû A term used in South Africa as a name for a class of blended dry wines. This wine should be as dry as vinification techniques allow.

Pungent This term refers to a very aromatic wine with a high level of volatiles.

Punt Indentation at the base of a bottle originally introduced to strengthen the bottle.

Racking Drawing off or decanting clear must or wine after allowing the lees to settle.

Red wine Made by fermenting red grapes in the presence of their skins so that the pigments in the skin can colour the wine. Red wines usually contain more tannin than whites

and are often aged for a year or two in wooden barrels before being bottled.

Residual sugar All grapes contain sugar and it is the conversion of this sugar by yeast into alcohol and carbon dioxide that gives wine. The portion that is not converted and remains behind in the wine, is termed residual sugar.

Remuage An essential operation in the making of champagne, this is the slight shaking and turning of the bottles in their racks, or *pupitres*, so that the sediment is brought down against the cork. After this the neck of the bottle is frozen and the temporary stopper removed, bringing with it the sediment locked in ice, before the wine is made ready for sale.

Rhoicissus capensis An indigenous vine of the Cape, encountered by the early Dutch pioneers.

Rich A wine which has an abundance of bouquet and flavour. A symphony of fruitiness, flavour, alcohol and grape extract well blended together.

Ripe A mature wine ready for drinking.

Robust A tough wine – although it can also be full-bodied and well-rounded.

Rootstock One of a wide range of especially developed phylloxera-resistant vine-stocks onto which the scion of the fruiting variety is grafted.

Rosé A 'pink' wine. It is normally made on the same basis as a red wine, that is, by leaving the heavily pigmented skins of the red grapes in the fermenting must till sufficient colour is extracted. In a rosé wine the period of contact is much shorter than for a red wine, just enough to give the wine its characteristic tinge.

Rouge The French word for 'red'; used in most countries for red wine.

Rough Lacking in finesse. A coarse, rough-edged wine, resulting from high tannin content, which is harsh and not particularly pleasant to drink.

Rounded Without a major defect, the wine is well-balanced and complete – never used to describe a poor wine. When described thus, a wine is not necessarily a wine of great quality.

Rubbery The most common manifestation of hydrogen sulphide in the form of mercaptan.

Saccharometer An instrument for measuring the sugar content of the grape juice or must; it is often calibrated in degrees Balling.

Saccharomyces A generic name for the various yeasts used for wine fermentation.

Sack Sir John Falstaff's favourite beverage was sack, the name by which sherry was known in Elizabethan England.

Scion A cutting of a vine cane bearing fertile buds, which is grafted onto the rootstock variety to become the fruiting part of the vine.

Sediment The deposit or precipitate of crystals and other solids which most red wines tend to throw as they are aged; it has no effect on the wine.

Severe Hard and probably immature.

Shallow soils These are soils which feature a layer of topsoil directly over rock. Otherwise known as 'Mispah', they are

not normally suitable for grape-growing unless the underlying rock can be broken or ripped.

Sharp An unpleasant prickly acidic taste.

Sherry A fortified wine, originally from a specific delimited district in southern Spain round the town of Jerez de la Frontera, between Seville and Cadiz.

Short Lacking in finish. The aftertaste is with you very briefly, whereas in a really good wine it lingers.

Shy bearer A variety which produces a small crop of high-quality grapes.

Semi-sweet A term used in South Africa to describe wines that have an excess of four grams per litre of residual sugar but not more than 30 grams. In practice wines so described normally have about 20 grams per litre and are usually white.

Sick Usually cloudy, with an unpleasant bouquet.

Silky Particularly smooth and fine-textured.

Skin The peel of a grape, often called the 'husk'.

Smooth A soft texture without rough edges.

Snout beetle These are insects which eat young shoots, leaf petioles and young flower clusters, and, given the chance, can devour all the green parts of the plant. They spend the daylight hours in the soil or under the bark of the vines, coming out at night to eat. They are controlled with pesticides from October onwards.

Soft Not harsh, the acidity and tannin being well-balanced; however, this wine could still be flat and dull.

Soil series The classification of soil types based on texture and chemical composition.

Solera A system by which all quality sherries are matured and progressively blended in tiers of casks; the object is to produce wines of consistent quality from year to year.

Sound Without abnormal qualities or defects, in other words a well-made wine. After this general comment a taster would go into more detail of bouquet and other qualities, defining the wine in greater depth and precision.

Sour Not to be confused with dry, tart or astringent, this term is used to describe a wine that has been spoiled by acetic acid and is practically vinegar.

Sour rot (*Rhizopus* rot) It is usually a secondary infection following an attack of botrytis rot. It is controlled with the use of rot-resistant varieties and with fungicides.

Sour-sweet Disagreeable taste associated with lactic bacteria development in fortified sweet wines.

Sparkling Carbon dioxide gas effervescence in wine.

Spicy Often used to describe a wine with an especially pronounced aroma or taste; Gewürztraminer is perhaps the best-known example with its herb-like smell.

Stabilization The chilling of a white wine to near-freezing point to precipitate tartaric crystals.

Stalky The smell of damp twigs – resulting from too long contact of the must with grape stalks during wine-making.

Steely Extremely 'hard'.

Stein Should not be confused with the variety Steen and its wine, though Steen, otherwise known as Chenin Blanc, is normally the basis of the local Stein wines. The name applies specifically to the style in which the wine is made, being semi-sweet with over four grams of sugar per litre and usually between 12 and 20 grams, and with a fruity flavour.

Sterkspruit soils *See* Duplex soils

Stretch A wine is said to stretch when, after the bottle has been opened, it takes up oxygen and develops its bouquet.

Structureless soils These are well-drained soils without restrictive layers in the subsoil which would impede growth. They are therefore generally suitable for grape-growing. Two important forms of structureless soils are found in the Cape, the Hutton and Clovelly and the Fernwood forms. Hutton and Clovelly are well-drained red and yellow soils, while Fernwood soils are deep, dry and sandy.

Sturdy Lacking the finesse of a robust wine.

Sugaring Called *Chaptalization* by the French, this is the adding of sugar to must to bring the final alcohol content obtained by fermentation up to a determined level. It is forbidden in South Africa, California and Italy (where weather conditions normally give good sugar content to the grapes), but authorized in France and Germany. An exception is usually made for champagne and sparkling wines where the secondary fermentation is usually effected by the addition of refined sugar.

Sugar level laws
These are the regulations that strictly define any claims that may be made on a label to the wine's degree of dryness or sweetness:

Extra Dry Wine
Residual sugar not more than 2,5 grams per litre.

Dry Wine
Residual sugar not more than 4,0 grams per litre.

Semi-Dry Wine
Residual sugar more than four but not more than 12 grams per litre (if more than nine the total acid content shall not be more than two grams per litre lower than the sugar content).

Semi-Sweet Wine
Residual sugar more than four but not more than 30 grams per litre (if sugar less than 12 grams per litre then the total acid content must be lower than for semi-dry wine).

Late Harvest Wine
Residual sugar more than 20 but less than 30 grams per litre.

Special Late Harvest Wine
Residual sugar more than 50 grams per litre.

Further requirements for late harvest wine are stated in the Government Gazette of December 19, 1980.

Late Harvest Wine
a.Shall be obtained by the complete or partial fermentation of must;
b.Shall not be fortified;

c.Shall have an alcoholic strength of at least 10 per cent alcohol by volume;
d.Shall have a residual sugar content, expressed as invert sugar of more than 20 grams per litre but less than 30 grams per litre, irrespective whether such residual sugar content has been obtained through the addition of sweet must or concentrated must to the wine concerned.

Special Late Harvest Wine
a.Shall be produced from must of which the sugar content prior to fermentation is at least 22° Balling: provided that:
 1.grapes of a sugar content of less than 21° Balling may not be pressed to obtain such must;
 2.such must may not be concentrated (dehydrated);
 3.no sweetening agent of any kind whatsoever may be added to such must;
b.Shall be obtained from partial alcoholic fermentation of such must;
c.Shall not be fortified;
d.Shall have an alcoholic strength of at least 10 per cent alcohol by volume;
e.Shall have a residual sugar content of more than 20 grams per litre but not more than 50 grams per litre: provided that such residual sugar content will be derived solely from the grapes from which such wine has been produced, and that no sweetening agent of any kind whatsoever may be added to such wine;
f.Shall have a sugar free extract of not less than 19 grams per litre;
g.Shall possess the character which is distinctive of wine which was produced from grapes which were harvested at a full-ripe stage.

Noble Late Harvest Wine
a.Shall be produced from grapes of which the sugar content at the time of pressing thereof is at least 28° Balling.
b.Shall be obtained from the partial alcoholic fermentation of the must of such grapes; provided that:
 1.such must may not be concentrated (dehydrated);
 2.no sweetening agent of any kind whatsoever may be added to such must;
c.Shall not be fortified.
d.Shall have a residual sugar content, expressed as invert sugar, provided that such residual sugar content shall be derived solely from the grapes from which such wine has been produced and that no sweetening agent of any kind whatsoever may be added to such wine;
e.Shall have a sugar free extract of not less than 30 grams per litre;
f.Shall have the character which is distinctive of wine which was produced from grapes that were harvested late.

Sulphur dioxide (SO$_2$) The use of sulphur to sterilize wine is almost as old as wine itself – in the *Iliad* Achilles fumi-

gated his cup with sulphur before pouring libation to Zeus. In the modern wine cellar small but effective amounts of sulphur dioxide are used as the standard sterilizing agent for casks and barrels. It is also extensively used in the vineyards to control vine disease. Compared to some European countries the sulphur level in South African wines is very low. For natural table wines the permitted maximum is 200 parts per million. This can be exceeded only in noble late harvests.

Supple Easy to taste yet hard to define; a combination of juiciness; liveliness and good texture.

Sweet Honeyed or grapey sweet smell which is often affirmed in tasting.

Sweetish Unpleasant sweet taste due to low fruit acid.

Syrupy Very sweet taste – usually low in ethanol.

Table wine A term usually applied to unfortified wine which is drunk with meals. It is normally between 10 and 12% alcohol by volume with a legal maximum in South Africa of 16% alcohol.

Tank carbonation A method of making sparkling wines. Syrup is added to the wine (to obtain the degree of sweetness required), which is then refrigerated. Carbon dioxide is passed through a porous 'candle' and dissolved in the wine as it circulates through the candle. It is then stored in pressurized tanks till the carbon dioxide is fully absorbed, before being filtered and bottled under pressure.

Tannin A group of organic compounds occurring in the bark, wood, roots and stems of many plants and fruits, including the grape.

Tart Sharp and tongue-curling from too much acidity and/or too much tannin.

Tastevin A flat, shallow, silver wine taster's cup that reflects light very effectively. It is widely used in Burgundy for sampling wines, especially young wines from the vat.

Tawny Applied to wines which have turned from red to a brownish colour with maturation, or a type of port.

Temperature Wine is sensitive to the temperatures at which it is stored and served. A white wine served too warm is dull and unresponsive, while a red wine which is served too cold seems numbed, almost entirely lacking in bouquet.

Terpene An odourous component found in certain varieties including ageing Rhine Riesling and some Muscats.

Thin Describes a wine deficient in alcohol and body; it therefore tastes watery and is generally poor.

Tinge Refers to a wine slightly tinted by another colour, seen at the edge of the wine where wine and glass meet.

Tint A grade of colour: for example, a red wine may have a purple tint when young and a mahogany tint when aged.

Tired A wine which has been aged for too long in the bottle, but is not yet completely oxidized.

Topping
 1. The refilling of casks or barrels of young wine to prevent ullage, or air space, between the wine and the bung.
 2. The removal of the first 15 to 20 centimetres of young growing vine shoots, usually by hitting them off with a strong switch or thin stick.

Total Acidity (TA) This is the collective amount or volume of fruit and volatile acids in a wine and is usually expressed in this country as grams per litre.

Tough A term used to describe a wine that is full-bodied but immature, with an excess of tannin.

Training Encouraging a vine plant to grow in the direction most convenient for the farmer, for yield of grapes, for accessibility to the sun and the cooling wind and for convenience of harvesting; most vines are trained onto a trellis.

Trellising A wire-and-wood structure to support the vine through its productive life. A deciduous creeper, the vine takes well to trellising which both provides it with support, keeping it clear of the ground with its moisture and insects, and providing it with access to sun and air and ease of harvesting. The type of trellis used depends on many factors, including the type of soil.

Ullage The empty space above the liquid in an incompletely filled wine container, be it tank, cask or bottle.

Unctuous Cloying and overly sweet.

Unfortified wine A table wine produced naturally, without the addition of spirit.

Vaaljapie Traditionally the wine produced in the Cape for the vineyard labourers. It was usually of indefinite colour (vaal) and a mixture of all varieties. Often turbid.

Variety One of the many different cultivated vine-types, each of which yields its own characteristic wine.

Velkuipe A primitive container used for fermentation in the very early days of wine-making in the Cape winelands, it consisted of an ox-hide suspended on four poles and filled with fermenting must.

Velvety Smooth on the tongue owing to lower acidity and high glycerol content.

Vermouth A fortified herbal wine, dry or sweet, flavoured with aromatic herbs. Most wine-producing countries produce vermouth-type wines.

Vigneron The winemaker or grower of vines.

Vin gris A pale pink wine made, as with blanc de noir wines, from red grapes. Not to be confused with the wine-grape variety of Pinot Gris.

Viniculture 'From soil to glass'; a general term covering the whole science of the growing of wine grapes, the making of wine and the wine's preparation for marketing.

Vin ordinaire An inexpensive wine often sold by the glass or carafe. Taken to mean everyday wine, or house wine.

Vinosity This refers to the depth or the degree to which a wine shows vinous qualities.

Vintage The word 'vintage' originally meant the gathering of the grapes, the gatherer being called the vintager. This meaning is retained but has a further connotation with reference to a vintage wine, which is one of a specific year or a specific gathering.

Vintner Strictly, a wine merchant; but the word is often and incorrectly applied to a winemaker as well.

Viscosity This term refers to the resistance of wine to flow. For example, light dry wines flow freely (low viscosity) while heavy, thick, sweet wines such as ports flow more deliberately and slowly (high viscosity).

Vitaceae The family to which all the genera, species and varieties of the grapevine belong.

Viticulture 'From soil to grape', in other words, the science of grape-growing.

Vitis One of the 10 genera of the family Vitaceae.

Vitis vinifera The most important of the species of the *Vitis* genus, *Vitis vinifera* comprises several thousand varieties throughout the world.

Volatile acidity *See* Acids.

Weeper This is one of a number of terms which is used to describe the effect of wine seeping between the neck of the bottle and the cork. If the bottle has been 'weeping' unnoticed for some time and the level of the wine has dropped considerably as a result, it should be checked for quality and, if acceptable, consumed forthwith; otherwise it should simply be recorked. If this is impossible remove the top of the capsule covering the cork and wipe the cork with a cloth that has been dipped in warm water. Allow it to dry and seal generously with melted candle wax.

Weight A term applied to the feel of the wine in the mouth.

Wine of Origin South African legislation controlling the division of the winelands area into official wine-making districts, the granting of estate status to certain farms, and the affixing of an official Wine of Origin seal to about 10% of wines marketed. It is for the producer to apply for the seal if he so wishes.

If a variety claim is made for a wine in terms of the Wine of Origin legislation it must comply with the provisions laid down by the Wine and Spirit Board. These have changed over the years and are summarized in the table below.

Witblits Otherwise known as Dop, White Lightning, Boerblits, Cape Smoke, or Kaapse Smaak. With a potent tradition of its own, Witblits was a rough local brandy which was made by distilling the wet mash of skins and pips left at the bottom of the tank when the fermented must had been run off at the end of the traditional wine-making process. Long outlawed (though the subject of defiant moonshining for many years), it is now beginning to make a tentative official come-back. It is the equivalent of the French 'Marc' and the Italian 'Grappa'.

Woody A table wine which has acquired a specific aroma and flavour from the cask; usually more noticeable in a young wine, it is a criticism if the woody character is the predominant quality.

Yeast Unicellular micro-organisms, some of which (*Saccharomyces cerevisiae*) bring about the fermentation of grape juice into the wine.

Yeasty Smelling of yeasts from fermentation.

Yield In viticultural terms, this is the production of a given area of vines, expressed in tonnes of grapes per hectare.

Young Recently bottled, and in the case of some white wine and more red wines, it has not yet reached its peak, but is still improving.

— B I B L I O G R A P H Y —

Burger, J. and Deist, J. (ed.), *Windgerdbou in Suid-Afrika*, Maskew Miller Limited, Cape Town, 1981.

Burman, Jose, *Wines of Constantia*, Human and Rousseau, Cape Town, 1979.

De Bosdari, C., *Wines of the Cape*, Balkema, 1966.

De Jongh, S.J., *Encyclopedia of South African Wine*, Butterworths, Durban, 1981.

Hughes, Dave, *South African Wine Buyers' Guide*, Struik Publishers, Cape Town, 1992.

Johnson, H., *The World Atlas of Wine*, Mitchell Beazley Publishers, London, 1977.

Knox, G., *Estate Wines of South Africa*, David Philip, Cape Town, 1982.

KWV., *Wine: A Guide for Young People*, KWV, Paarl, 1975.

Leipoldt, C. Louis, *Three Hundred Years of Cape Wines*, Tafelberg, Cape Town, 1952.

Opperman, DJ (ed.), *Spirit of the Vine*, Human and Rousseau, Cape Town, 1968.

Orffer, C.J. (ed.), *Wine Grape Cultivars in South Africa*, Human and Rousseau, Cape Town, 1979.

Perold, I.A., *Handboek oor Wynbou*, Pro Ecclesia, Stellenbosch, 1926.

Platter, J., *John Platter's South African Wine Guide*, John and Erica Platter, Stellenbosch, 1992.

Pongrácz, Desiderius, P., *Practical Viticulture*, David Philip, Cape Town, 1978.

Rappoport, Simon, Contributions to *Wynboer*, April 1978 to May 1983.

Scholtz, Merwe (ed.), *Wines of the World*, McGraw-Hill, New York, 1973.

Ribéreau-Gayon, Pascal (ed.), *The Wines and Vineyards of France*, Viking Penguin, London, 1990.

Robinson, Jancis, *Vines, Grapes and Wines*, Mitchell Beazley Publishers, London, 1987.

Simpson, Sally, *Wine of Good Hope*, Saayman and Weber, Cape Town, undated.

Van Zyl, D.J., *Kaapse Wyn en Brandewyn 1795 – 1860*, H A U M, Cape Town, 1975.

Wynboer. Official journal of KWV, published monthly, KWV, Paarl.

INDEX

— A —

Aan-de-Doorns Co-operative Winery 242
Aden (*farm*) 54
Agostini, Alberto 214
Agricultural Research Council (ARC) 48,
    53-4
Agterkliphoogte Co-operative Wine Cellar 254
Alfa Laval Trophy 122
Alicante Bouschet 85
Allesverloren Estate 137, 138, 224-5
Allied-Hiram Walker 33
Alphen (*farm*) (Stellenbosch) 175-6
Alphen Estate (Constantia) 25, 147, 178
    wines 33, 137, 141, 147
Alphen Winery 145
Alto Estate 127-8, 137, 138, 176
Altydgedacht Estate 100, 120-1
Ammann, Kurt 35, 164-5, 230
Andalusia 270-1
Andrag, E.P. 183
Anglo-American Group 181, 211, 212
Anreith, Anton 99, 113, 179
anthracnose (*Gloeosporium ampelopha-
    gum*) 51-2, 56, 57, 77, 272
Antinori, *Marchese* Piero 32
ants 51, 55
appreciation of wine 89-92, 272
Archer, *Prof* Eben 48, 163, 213
Arendse, Manie 258
Arnold, Kevin 35, 136, 170
aroma of wine 91, 272
Aron van Ceylon 142
Ashton Co-operative Wine Cellar 254
Aspergillus rot (black-mould rot) 273
auctions 32-3
    Cape Independent Winemakers' Guild 33,
        35, 131, 164, 184, 185, 196
    Fairview 195
    Nederburg *see under* Nederburg Auction

New World Wine 133, 177, 181
Aufwaerts Co-operative Wine Cellar 242
Austin, Diana *and* Ian 25
Auxerrois 85, 143
Avonduur (*farm*) 187
Avontuur Winery 128-9
Avrons Ltd 33, 194

— B —

Back, Charles 190, 195
Back, Charles jnr 195
Back, Cyril 195
Back, Michael 190
Back, Sydney 79, 190, 260
Backsberg Estate 65, 70, 79, 101, 190, 195
Badsberg Co-operative Wine Cellar 242
Bairnsfather-Cloete family 25, 141, 147, 175
Baker, Sir Herbert 154
Balthazar bottle 71
Barbera 121
Barlow, Charles 'Punch' 181
Barlow, Cynthia 181
Barlow, Eddie 192
Barlow, Pamela 166
Barlow, Peter 166
Barlow, Simon 166
Barnard, *Lady* Anne 19
barrels 66-7, 70-1
Barrydale Co-operative Winery and Distillery
    105, 266
Barth, John 175
Barth, Lothar 175
Basson, J.P. (Kobus) 239
Bayly, Francis (Duimpie) 174, 175
Beck, Graham 32, 33, 194-5, 204, 210, 257
Beck, *Sir* Meiring 234
beer 27, 97
Belcher, Ronnie 190, 192

Belcher Wine Farm 102, 190, 192
Bell, Alan 141
Bellevue (*farm*) 54, 129
Bellingham 32, 33, 103, 194-5, 204, 210
Benadé, Paul 154
Benadé family 151
Benede Oranje 271
Berger, Laurent 202
Bergh, Albertus 170
Bergh, Oloff 170
The Bergkelder 29-32, 65
    estates linked with
        Durbanville 100, 123
        Franschhoek 219
        Stellenbosch 127, 137, 148, 158, 163
        Swartland 225
Bergkelder Vinotèque 30-1, 137-8
Bergrivier Co-operative 192
Bergsig Estate 193, 242
Bergvliet 25, 111-12
Berry, G.A. 136
Bertram, Robertson Fuller 141
Bertrams Wines Ltd 32-3, 136-7, 141
Bestbier, Johann 141
Bestbier, Peter 141
Bestbier, Petrus Johannes 141
Bester, Jan 175
Bester, Zakkie 243
Beukes, Abraham (Abé) 35, 140, 154
Beyers, Jan Marthinus 129
Beyers, Johan David 179
Beyers family 129
Beyers Kloof (*farm) see* Lievland Estate
Beyerskloof (Stellenbosch) 129
Bezuidenhout, Elzabé 183-4
Bien Donné 219
Billingham, *Col* J.W. 133
Blaauwklippen 35, 130-1, 141, 142, 194, 195
black-mould rot (*Aspergillus rot*) 273
Blanc de noir 64, 90, 211, 262, 273

blending 61, 273
    varieties used in 82, 84, 87
Bloemaris, Johan 47
Bloemendal Estate 100, 121
Bloemkoolfontein (*farm*) 195
Blumberg, Simeon 136, 141
Blush wine 64
Boberg region 69, 107
Boberg Show 195
Bodega 192
Boesmansrivier Co-operative 256
Boettgen, Mr 203
Bolandse Co-operative Wine Cellar 192, 202
Bon Courage Estate 254
Bonfoi Estate 132, 137
Bonnievale Co-operative 255
Bonte River (*farm*) 167
Bonthuys, J. 132
Boom, Hendrik 12-13
Boonzaier, Graham 130
Booysen, Eugene 54
Boplaas Estate 35, 105, 266, 269
Borman, Jacques 217
Boschendal Estate 32, 35, 103, 198, 211-12,
    250
    wines 64, 65
Bosheuvel (*farm*) 14
Bosman, Hermanus Lambertus 143
Bosman, Izaak 148
Bosman, J.D. & Co. *see* J.D.Bosman & Co.
Bosman, Jacobus 207
Bosman, Johannes 142
Bosman, Michael 143-4
Bosman, Piet 143
Bosman, Sakkie 244
Bosman brothers 142
Botha, Bowen 260
Botha, Nico 227
Botha Co-operative Wine Cellar 242-3
Botha family 242-3

Botrytis (grey mould) 52, 57, 76
Botrytis cinerea (noble rot) 51-2, 74, 201, 273
Bottelary Co-operative Winery 100, 132-3
Bottelary (*farm*) 148
bottles 71
   opening of 95-6, 97
   pouring from 97
Bouchard, Paul 250
Bouchard Finlayson (*farm*) 250
Bouchet *see* Cabernet Franc
Boulle, Arthur 173
bouquet 90-1, 273
Bouwer, Gerry 179
Bovlei Co-operative Winery 23, 102, 193, 205
boxed wine 68
Brading, William 25
Brandvlei Co-operative Winery 243
brandy 30, 69-70, 121, 137, 148, 197, 237, 273
   museums 101, 140
   production 101-2
      on estates 103, 149, 190, 213, 266
      in wine co-operatives 105, 203, 243, 258, 266, 269, 270
   varieties used in distilling of 73, 77, 82, 88
Bredell, Cecil 244
Bredell, Marinus 175-6
Breede River Valley 77, 88, 103, 107; *see also* Robertson, Worcester
Breede River Young Wine Show 259
Brink, Arend 25, 165
Brink, Cornelis 25, 112
Bronkhorstspruit 271
Broodryk, Tinus 193
Brözel, Günter 161-2, 176, 206
   at Nederburg 66, 85, 117, 200-1
Brunt, Jacob Willem 25
Bruwer, André 254
Bruwer, Ernst 258
Bruwer, P. 54
Bruwer family 254, 258
Bruyns, 'Bertie' 271
Buchinsky, Julius 32
Buhrer, Adrian *and* Birgit 170
Buitenverwachting 25, 35, 99, 112-13, 184
Bukettraube 37, 57, 78, 172
Burchell, John 25
Burger, Dr Johan 47
Burger, Johnny 259
Burger, Leo 137
Burger, Willem 175
Burgundy bottles 71
By-den-Weg (*farm*) 163

— C —

Cabernet Franc 57, 80, 81, 164-5, 185-6
Cabernet Sauvignon 52, 73, 74, 79, 80, 81, 82, 94, 115
   accompanying food 97
   award winners 181-2, 203, 238
   maturation & ripening 49, 57, 95
   used in blending 84, 127-8, 166-7, 184
   used in cross 86
Cabrière *see* Clos Cabrière
Caldwell, W. 21
Calitzdorp Fruit and Wine Cellar Co-operative 105, 266
Calitzdorp wine route 105
Campher, Lourens 136
Canitz, Annemarie 160-1
Canitz, Georg Paul 81, 160
cans 68
Cape Championship Young Wine Show 77
Cape Championship Wine Show 122, 190, 238, 243
Cape Gate 207
Cape Independent Winemakers' Guild 33, 35, 131
   auctions 33, 35, 131, 164, 184, 185, 196
Cape Riesling 38, 57, 76, 94, 97, 233-4
'Cape Smoke' 70, 279-80
Cape Wine Academy 20, 93, 174
Cape Wine and Distillers (CWD) 20, 27-9, 137
Cape Wine Farmers' & Wine Merchants' Association 23
Cape Wine Show 129, 139, 225, 260
Cape Wine Tasters Guild 92
Cape Young Wine Show 202
Carignan 57, 85, 86, 151
Carlowitz, *Baron* Hans von 146, 179
Carlowitz, Hans jun. von 179
Carlowitz, Georg von 179
Carstens, Pieter 148
Carstens, Deon 212-13
Cartwright family 172
Castle Wine and Brandy Co. 137, 142, 183, 186, 259
Cedarberg Cellars 104, 238
cellars
   home 94
   underground 116, 137-8, 151, 157, 160
Chamonix 212
champagne 64, 65, 81, 273; *see also méthode champenoise*
Chardonnay 57, 79, 85, 86, 92, 94, 115, 132
   award winners 138, 190, 196, 255-6, 262
   champagne production 64, 171-2
Chenel 38, 52, 57, 73, 79-80, 243

Chenin Blanc 13, 38, 52, 74, 97, 114, 221
   award winners 144, 200, 245
   development of Chenel 79
   used in brandy 70, 73
   used in fortified wines 69
Cia, Giorgio dalla *see* dalla Cia, Giorgio
Cinsaut 57, 69, 70, 73, 81-2, 85
   development of Pinotage 24, 38, 48
   used in blending 80, 83, 127, 166
Citrusdal Co-operative Wine Cellar 238
Claassen, François 259
Clairette Blanche 37, 57, 75, 178, 183
Clairvaux Co-operative Winery 255
Claret bottles 71, 212
Claridge Fine Wines 102, 203
Clark, Michael 250
Clarke-Krige, Sarah *and* Dan 195
climate 46-7, 51; *see also under* regions
Cloete, Dirk Gysbert 25
Cloete, Hendrik 19, 25, 99, 111-14
Cloete, Hendrik jun. 25, 111
Cloete, Johan Gerhard 25
Cloete, Mynhardus 247
Cloete, Peter Bairnsfather *see* Bairnsfather-Cloete
Cloete, Pieter Lourens 25, 165
Cloete, Ryk Arnoldus 25, 112
Cloete family 19, 20, 22, 83
Clos Cabrière Estate 35, 65, 70, 103, 162, 212-13
Clos du Ciel 133
Clos Malverne 133-4, 142
co-operative movement 11, 23-4, 27-9, 42, 196-7, 274
coach museum 131
Coastal region 107
Coetzee, Dirk 178
Coetzee, Jackie 121-2
Coetzee, Jan 'Boland' 35, 146, 154, 164, 177, 184
   as consultant 139-40, 149
Coetzee, Jassie 186
Coetzee, Koos 121
cold fermentation
   development of 20, 24, 60, 175, 232, 253
   results of 75, 259, 261
      Paarl 190, 200-1
      Robertson 255, 259, 261
      Tulbagh 103, 232, 235
      Worcester 246
Colijn, Johannes 19
Colijn, Johannes Nicolaas 182
Colijn family 187
Collison, Henry C. & Sons 128, 137
Colombard 52, 57, 70, 77, 94, 246, 256-60

colour 90-1
Colyn, Gilbert 162, 187
Colyn family 147
Conradie, H.F. 246
Conradie, Pieter 268
Constantia 13, 23, 99-100
   climate 46, 111, 117
   district 111-17
   estate 16-17, 111-12, 141
   wines 19, 25, 32, 54, 83, 111-14
Constantia Uitsig (*farm*) 25
coopering 70-1
corks 67-8, 95-6
corkscrews 95-6
Cornelissen, Dirk 258
Cornifesto 123, 163
Costandius, Philip 35, 136
Cronje, Johan 271
Crous, Tienie 247
Cruchen Blanc 38
Cruythoff, Pieter 226
Culemborg Wineries (Pty) Ltd 204

— D —

Dactylosphaera vitifoliae see phylloxera
Dall, Michael 157
dalla Cia, Giorgio 156-7
Daneel, Jean 35, 112
Daniels, Sakkie 216
Dave Hughes Trophy 172
Davin, Frans 175
De Doorns Co-operative Wine Cellar 243
de Groott, Simon 172
De Helderberg Co-operative Winery 23, 134
De Hoop (*farm*) 171-2
de Jager, Anthony 192
de Jongh, Klaas 226
de Jongh, Lourens 242
de Kock, Corrie 239
de Kock, Fourie 243
de Kock, Nico 148
De Kuilen 170
De Leeuwen Jagt 193
De Lucque (*farm*) 213
de Man, Andries 120
de Pass, Alfred Aaron 25
de Smidt, Abraham 25
de Villiers, Abraham 17, 211
de Villiers, Abraham Lochner 25, 115
de Villiers, Bob 266
de Villiers, Dawie 134
de Villiers, Gertrude 163
de Villiers, H.I.D. 242

de Villiers, Hugo 198
de Villiers, J.W.S. 148
de Villiers, Jac 193
de Villiers, Jacob 17
de Villiers, Jacob Isak 150
de Villiers, Jacques 198, 215
de Villiers, Johan 227
de Villiers, Paul 198, 211
de Villiers, Pierre 17
de Villiers, Pieter 218
de Villiers, Robbie 212
de Villiers family 170, 204, 211, 219
de Vos, Pieter 182
de Vries, Helmie 148
de Vries, Hugo 148
de Waal, Chris 178
de Waal, Danie 178
de Waal, Daniël 178
de Waal, Jan Christoffel 178
de Waal, Pieter 178
de Waal, Pieter jun. 178
de Waal, widow Wilhelmina 143
de Waal, Willie 192
de Wet, Albertus 257
de Wet, Dan 263
de Wet, Danie 243, 255-6
de Wet, Freddie 256
de Wet, Johann 255
de Wet, Kobus 243
de Wet, Paul 263
de Wet, Paulie 263
de Wet, Stephen 256
de Wet, Wouter de Vos 77, 256-7, 259
De Wet Co-operative Wine Cellar 243
De Wetshof Estate 137, 138, 255-6
De Zoete Inval Estate 193
dead arm (*Phomopsis viticola*) 51-2, 56,
    274
decanting 96, 274
Deetlefs, Kobus 244
Deetlefs, Philip 244
Deist, Dr Jacob 54
Delaire 133, 134-5, 187
Delheim 35, 99, 135-6, 140, 170, 194
Dendy-Young, Rose 135
Devereux, Peter 93
Devonvale Estate 136-7, 141
Die Krans Estate 105, 266-7
Die Poort 267
Diemer, Christina 117
Diemersdal Estate 54, 100, 122
Dieu Donne Vineyards 103, 213-14
Diners' Club SA 129
    awards 139, 201, 245
    Winemaker of the Year 147, 196, 250, 254

diseases and pests 15, 21-3, 27, 39, 51-2; *see
    also* Phylloxera epidemic and specific
    names of diseases
Distillers Corporation 20, 27-30, 32, 71, **137,
    194, 197, 234, 266**
distilling wine varieties 87-8
Dobrovic, Mike 160
Dog Ridge rootstock 51
Domein Doornkraal 105, 267-8
Doornboom 54
Doornkuil (*farm*) 227
Doringboom (*farm*) 54
dos Santos *see* Santos, Carlos dos
Douglas district 270
Douglas Co-operative Winery 270
Douglas Green Bellingham 20, 103, 105,
    194-5, 197, 204, 210
Douglas Green of Paarl 32, 33, 194
downy mildew (*Plasmopara viticola*) 51-2,
    56-7, 274
Drakenstein Co-operative 203
Drakenstein Draai 102
Dreyer, Cas 93
Dreyer, Pieter 202
Dreyer, S.F. 202
Dreyer, W. 54
Driesprongh 135-6
Drostdy Co-operative *see* Tulbagh Co-opera-
    tive Wine Cellar
Drouhin, Joseph 184
Drouhin, Robert 32
D'Urban, *Sir* Benjamin 119
du Plessis, Charl 192
du Plessis, Fred 27
du Preez, Hercule 193
du Preez, Herman 132
du Preez, Jan 179
du Toit, François 17
du Toit, Gabriel 216
du Toit, Guillaume 17
du Toit, Hempies 127-8
du Toit, J. 54
du Toit, Jacques 192
du Toit, Joshua 271
du Toit, Kowie 183
du Toit, Piet 128
du Toit, Pieter 35
du Toit, Pieter Daniël 114
du Toit, R. 54
du Toit, S. 54
du Toit family 147
du Toitskloof Co-operative Wine Cellar 192,
    243-4
Dumas, Cornelis 144
Durban Wine Society 93

Durbanville 85, 100, 119-23
Durbanville Food and Wine Feast 100
Durbanville Wine Trust 100, 120
Dutch East India Company 11-20, 25, 120,
    122, 146, 155, 181
Dwarsrivier (*farm*) 238
dying arm disease 79

— E —

E.K.Green & Co. 137, 174, 234
eelworms *see* nematodes
Eersterivier Valleise Co-operative Winery 138-
    9, 145, 183
Eikendal Vineyards 139-40, 149, 154, 184
Eksteen, Bartho 246
Eksteen, Jacob 165
Elbertz, Hendrik 163
Elgin 162
Ellis, Neil 35, 155, 162, 163, 187
Elsenberg Agricultural College 47-8, 54, 125,
    179
    research and development 79, 87, 129
    see also University of Stellenbosch. Depts
        of Viticulture & Oenology
Emerald Riesling 85
Engelbrecht, Jannie 35, 167, 170
Erasmus, D. 54
Erasmus, L.S. 47
erinose 56, 57
Ernita Nursery 47, 116
estate status 108
estates 274 *see under* specific names
Estreux, Christoffel 142
eutypa disease 79
Euvrard, G. 234
Excelsior (*farm*) 216
Excelsior Estate (Robertson) 256
export of wine 21, 22, 23, 25, 27, 127, 138
    Constantia wines 19, 20, 25

— F —

Fagan, Gabriel (Gawie) 116, 167, 211, 218,
    230
Fagan, Gwen 167
Fairview Estate 102, 195
False Pedro 121
Faure, Alex 182-3
Faure, Brand 182-3
Faure, Jac 182-3
Faure, Johannes Gysbertus 182
Faure, John 182-3

Faure family 123
Fehlmann, Roger 230
Ferreira, Pieter 257
fermentation 59-61, 64-6, 274
    red wine 65-6
    white wine 60-1, 64; *see also* cold fermen-
        tation
Fernão Pires 57, 85, 262
fining 16, 61, 274-5
Finlayson, Dr Maurice 142
Finlayson, Peter 142, 250, 251
Finlayson, Walter 35, 130-1, 142, 195-6
Fleck, Peter 141
food and wine 97
Forrer brothers 194
fortified wines 68-9, 174, 189, 267, 275; *see
    also* port; sherry
Fouche, S. 54
Frankel, Jonny 177
Franschhoek 17, 103, 209-21
Franschhoek Vineyards Co-operative 103,
    214, 216
    wines made at 212, 215, 219, 221
Frater, Adrian Robert, 193
Frater, Elizabeth 193
Frater, Gerard 193
Frater, Robert 193
Frick, Piet 269
Friedman, Nathan 207
Friedman, Pauline *and* Charles 221
Froehling, Hans-Dieter 155
Furmint 57, 85

— G —

Gabbema, Abraham 189
Gamay Noir 57, 84-5, 113
Gardé, Suzanna 231-2
Gerber, Johan 256
Gerryts, G. 184
Gewürztraminer 57, 77-8, 94, 97, 132-3,
    172
Gilbey, Alfred 140
Gilbey, Walter 140
Gilbey Distillers and Vintners 27, 32-3,
    140-1
    estates owned by 136, 142, 147
Gilbey-Santhagens Ltd 140-1
Gilbeys South Africa 20, 141, 197
Gillis, Sonny *and* Michael 215
gin 140
glasses 89-90, 96-7
Glen Carlou 35, 131, 195-6
Glenbawn (*farm*) 166

Gloeosporium ampelophagum see anthracnose
goats' milk cheese 102, 195
Goede Hoop Estate (Stellenbosch) 137, 141
Goede Hoop (Franschhoek) 216
Goedemoed (*farm*) 254, 261
Goedertrou 54
Goederust 102
Goedgelegen (*farm*) 173
Goedgeloof (*farm*) 172-3
Goedgevonden 173
Goedvertrouw Estate 250
Goldberg, Bennie 32
Good Success (*farm*) 184
Gooderson family 136-7
Gooderson Hotels Ltd 141
Gordon, *Col.* Alexander 184-5
Goudini Co-operative Wine Cellar 244
Goussard, *Prof* Pieter 48
Gouws, Ernst 192
Gower, Ross 115, 116-17
Graaff-Reinet vine 49
Grachen 85
grafting 23, 38-40, 275
Grangehurst Winery 142
grape juice 140, 184, 199, 254, 269
Graue, Arnold 200, 202
Graue, Johan Georg 175
Graue, Johann Richard Georg 200-1
Graue family 24
Green, E.K. *see* E.K. Green & Co.
Green, Fred 174
Green, Douglas 194
Green Grape *see* Sémillon
green manure crop 55-6, 57
Grenache 57, 69, 86
grey mould (*botrytis*) 52, 57, 76
Grier, Jeff 35, 136, 205
Grier, Simon 205
Grier family 140, 204-5
Grimp, Hans Jurgen 173
Grobe, Gert 158-9
Groenkloof Drankhandelaars 225
Groenrivier (*farm*) 127
Groot Constantia 22, 35, 99, 113-14, 130, 187, 194
Groot Drakenstein Co-operative 23
Groot Eiland Co-operative Wine Cellar 244
Groote Zalze 147
Grubb, Patrick 32

— H —

Hacker, Willi 162
Hamilton Russell Vineyards 142, 250-1
Hamilton-Russell, Anthony 251
Hamilton-Russell, Timothy 251
Hamman, Pieter 243
Hamman, Wynand 238
Hampf, Dr 142
Hands, Phyllis 174
Hanekom, Helmard 254
Hanekom, Herman 211
Hanekom, W.T. 242
Hanepoot *see* Muscat d'Alexandrie
Hanseret, Gerard 138
Harmony *see* Morgenhof
Harris, Trevor 201
Hárslevelü 57, 85, 231, 262
Hartenberg Estate 35, 130, 142-3, 195
harvesting 15, 16, 57, 59; *see also* night harvesting
Hattingh, Hans Heinrich 173, 216, 221
Haute Provence 214-15
Hazendal Estate 137, 143-4
Hazenwinkel, Christoffel 143
Hegewisch, Hilko 35, 211
Heitz, Joseph 178
Helderfontein Co-operative 23
Helmer, Otto 136
Hengl grafting machine 39
Hermitage *see* Cinsaut
Heroldrebe 85
Herrer, J.C. (Christo) 134, 161
Hesebeck, Heinrich 162
Het Groote Eiland (*farm*) 244
Het Sluis 54
Heydenrych, Hennie 120
Hexvallei (*farm*) 54
Hock 275
  bottles 71
Hoffmann, Gerhard 137
Hofmeyr, Louise 206
Hofmeyr, W.A. (Billy) 35, 164, 206, 230
Hoheisen, H. 135
Holsmit, Jan 198
Hooggenoeg 54
Hoop op Constantia 25
Hop, Jan Hendrik 216
Hopkins, Charles 210
Hopkins, Henry 93
'Houd de Mond' *see* Bellevue
Hughes, Dave 172, 174
Hugo, Mr 195
Hugo, Hennie 244
Hugo, P. 54

Hugo, P.B.B. 197
Hugoskraal 54
Huguenots 16-17, 20, 83, 209
Huisamen, Kas 242
Huskisson, Joseph 202
Hussey, Clara 25, 115
Hutchinson, Tim 194
Huysing, Henning 17, 122, 155, 186

— I —

Illing, Dr Harvey 128, 179
Intercontinental Breweries 27-8
International Club Oenologique Wine & Spirit Competition 148, 259
International Distillers and Vintners 32
International Wine and Food Society 93
International Wine & Spirit Competition (I.W.S.C.) 66
  (1989) 164, 190
  (1990) 172, 239
  (1991) 129, 138, 147, 151, 154
International Winemaker of the Year
  (1985) 201
  (1991) 129,147

— J —

J.D.Bosman & Co 33, 194
Jacobs, Larry 160
Jacobsdal (*farm*) (Robertson) 261
Jacobsdal Estate 137, 144-5
Jacobsdal Wine Cellar Co-operative 270-1
Jacquez rootstock 39
Janssen, Christiaan 15
Jansz, Arnout Tamboer 172-3
Jardine Matheson Group 194
jar 71
Jereboam 71
jerepigo 69, 94, 269
Johann Graue Memorial Trophy 117
Johannesburg Consolidated Investments (JCI) 117
Johannesburg Stock Exchange 28, 29
Johnston, Mrs Arlene 32
Jonker, Boet 259
Jonker, H. 54
Jonker, Herman 262
Jonker, Jannie 267
Jonker, Japie 262-3
Jonker, Klaas 262
Jonker, Lourens 66, 262-3
Jonker, Nelis 267

Jonker, Nicolaas 256
Jonkheer Farmers' Winery 256
Jooste, Duggie 25, 54, 100, 115, 117
Jooste, Lowell 117
Jordaan, Andries 233
Jordaan, Kobus (Klein Constantia) 117
Jordaan, Kobus (Laborie) 198, 233-4
Jordaan, Philip 243-4
Jordaan, Rennie 233-4
Jordan, Alexander 145
Jordan, Gary 141, 145
Jordan, Ted 141, 145
Jordan Estate 145
Jorgensen, Roger *and* Maria 203
Joubert, Attie 231
Joubert, Chris 173
Joubert, Christian 172
Joubert, Daniël 163
Joubert, Gideon 216
Joubert, H. 54
Joubert, J.F. 250
Joubert, Jean 231
Joubert, Niel 99, 172-3
Joubert, Pierre 172, 216, 218-19
Joubert, Willem 163
Jourdan, Pierre 212-13, 214
jug 71

— K —

Kaapzicht Estate 146
Kaapzicht Landgoed (Pty) Ltd 146
Kanaan 88
Kango Co-operative 105, 268
Kangra Holdings 33, 194, 210
Kanonkop 35, 129, 145, 146-7, 154, 179, 184
Keet, Chris 134-5
Kempen, Jacques 194
Kempen, Henry 194
Keppel family 172
Kerner 57, 80, 122, 151
Kersaf Liquor Holdings 33, 194, 210
Kerzner, Sol 194, 210
Key, Mervyn *and* Michelle 202
Keyser, Paulus 142
Klawer Co-operative Wine Cellar 54, 238
Klein Constantia 25, 54, 100, 111, 115-17
Klein Karoo 66, 69, 105, 107, 265-70
Klein Welmoed (*farm*) 161, 186
Kleinberg 247
Kleine Zalze 141, 147-8, 176
Kleinplasie Farm Museum 103
Kloofzicht 230-1

Kloppers, Chris 85
Kloppers, Manie 128
Kloppers, Rial 255
Knipe, Kenneth 270
Ko-operatiewe Wijnbouwers Vereniging van
    Zuid-Afrika Beperkt (KWV) *see* KWV
Koch, Christo 227
Koegelenberg, Hein 206
Koelenhof 129
Koelenhof (*farm*) 172, 231
Koelenhof Co-operative Wine Cellar 100,
    132, 148
Kohler, Dr Charles William Henry 20, 23,
    174, 196-7
Kok, Christo 'Kokkie' 54
Koopmanskloof Estate 137, 148-9
kosher wine 101, 207
Kotze, J. 54
Krammer, Josef 140, 204
Kreusch-Dau, Storm 251
Kriekbult Vineyards 172
Krige, Gabriel jnr 24
Krige, Gideon Johannes 173
Krige, Gideon jnr 174
Krige, Jannie 146
Krige, Johann 146
Krige, Paul 146
Krige family 147, 173, 178
Kromme Rhee Agricultural College 48
Krone, N.C. 24, 141, 234-5
Krone, Nicky 230, 233, 235
Krone family 32, 103, 234-5
Kruger, Jacques 35, 131
Kwa Ndebele Agricultural Company (KAC)
    271
KWV 31, 33, 101, 164, 194, 196-8
    advice supplied by 54, 93, 155, 174
    bulk wine purchases 122, 123, 129, 148,
        183
    formation of 20, 23-4, 27-9, 174
    price setting 20, 24, 28, 59, 197
    quota system 24, 28, 145, 146
    research & development 47, 66, 87
    wine houses 233

— L —

La Bourgogne 215
La Bri 212, 215-16
La Cotte 212, 214
La Couronne 216
La Fontaine 258
La Garonne 194-5, 204
La Motte Estate 103, 137, 216-17, 221

La Provence 17, 214, 218-19
Laborie Estate 32, 102, 198
Ladismith Co-operative Winery & Distillery
    268
Landskroon Estate 198-9, 211
Langenhoven, Faan 244
Langverwacht (*farm*) 187
Langverwacht Co-operative Winery 256
Lanzerac Hotel 149
Lanzerac Vineyards 149-50, 164, 184
Laslo, Dr Julius 137
Late Harvest 94, 275, 278
Lategan, Daniel 25
Lategan, Marius 141, 147
Lategan, 'Prop' 242
Lategan, Stephanus Petrus 25
Lategan, Stephen 25
Lategan, Willem 25
Lategan, Willem Hendrik 242
Lategan family 25, 112
Laubser, Hardy 190
Laubser, N. 54
Lawrie, Doug 246
Le Bonheur Estate 137, 138, 150-1, 231
Le Grand Chasseur Estate 256-7, 259
Le Long, Jean 211
Le Riche, Etienne 35, 165-6
Le Roux, Alex 257
Le Roux, Altus 192
Le Roux, C.P. 244, 245
Le Roux, Ernst 47, 115-16, 201
Le Roux, Gerrit (Swepie) 267-8
Le Roux, Neil 221
Le Roux, Piet 194
Le Roux, Pietie 217
Le Roux, 'Pou' 270
Le Roux, Theuns 243
Le Vaillant, François 25
Lebensraum Estate 244
Leef-op-Hoop 54
Lekkerwyn, Ari 142
Lemberg Estate 35, 154, 231
Lever, Abraham 25
Libertas (*farm*) 24, 173
Lievland Estate 35, 151, 154, 231
Linde, Piet 'Kelder' 255
Linde, Wilhelm 245
Lindup, Dr 174
Little Karoo *see* Klein Karoo
L'Ormarins Estate 17, 57, 103, 137, 138, 219-
    20
Loerie Award 129, 212
Loftus, Tommy 260
Longridge (*farm*) 139
Loopspruit Estate 271

Loots, Willem 244
Loubser, P.L. 227
Louisvale Farm 154-5
Louw, Anna Susanna 211
Louw, Attie 245
Louw, Beyers 122
Louw, George *and* Olivia (Lategan) 25
Louw, Jacobus 161
Louw, Johannes Wynand 25
Louw, Nico 93, 161
Louw, Philip 203
Louw, Stanley 54, 245
Louw, Tienie *and* Joanita 54, 122
Louw, Tossie 47
Louw family 112, 161
Louwshoek Voorsorg Co-operative Wine
    Cellar 244
Lower Orange River Irrigation Scheme 54
Lubbe, Willem Barend 161
Lüttich, Bernhard 206
Lutzville Proefplaas 54
Lutzville Vineyards Co-operative 238

— M —

Maastricht (*farm*) 122
Mackenzie, Ken 143
Madeba Valley 149, 184, 194, 204, 257-8
Magnum 71
Maingard, Robert 213
Malan, *Judge* 212
Malan, Danie 225
Malan, Daniel François 224-5
Malan, Fanie 224-5
Malan, François 172
Malan, Frans 99, 171-2, 271
Malan, Gerard 225
Malan, Hennie 127
Malan, Johan 35, 172
Malan, Manie 127-8
Malan, Pieter 172
Malan, S.B.(Sonnie) 269
Malan, Stephanus 224
Malbec 57, 84, 157, 160
Malherbe, François 213
Malmesbury 86, 87, 223, 225, 227
Malvasia Rey 163
Mamreweg Wine Cellar Co-operative 225
Marais, Hannetjie 258
Marais, Izaak Jacob 220
Marais, J. 54
Marais, Newald 201
Marais, Pierre 258
Maree, Booysen 243

Maree, Roelof 271
Martin, John 190
Maskell, G.N. 141
Mataro 69
maturation 94, 137-8, 272, 276
McGregor Co-operative Winery 239, 258
McLean Family Trust 177
mealy bugs 51, 55, 57, 276
Meerendal Estate 100, 121, 122-3, 137, 138
Meerland, Jan 122
Meerlust Estate 122, 137, 138, 155-7, 186
Meinert, Cindy & Martin 157, 181
Meinert Winery 157-8
Meintjies, L. 193
Melck, Martin 47, 125, 179
Melck, Ronnie 161, 175
Merlot Blanc 84
Merlot Noir (Merlot) 57, 84, 94, 97
Merriman, John X. 165-6
Merwespont Co-operative Winery 258
Merwida Co-operative Wine Cellar 244
Messina 54
méthode champenoise 192, 266, 276
    Franschhoek 162, 212-13
    Paarl 195, 202, 203, 204-5
    Robertson 257
    Stellenbosch 65, 131, 172, 178
    Tulbagh 103, 235
Methuselah 71
Meyer, Basie 268
Meyer, Erhard 269
Meyer, Raadus 268-9
Meyer, Radie 269
Mgt 101-14 rootstock 39
Michell, Lewis Lloyd 216
Middelvlei Estate 137, 158
Mietjiesvlei (*farm*) 139
mildew *see* downy mildew, powdery mildew
Minnie, Carolus 268
Mondavi, Robert 32
    trophy 66, 129, 201
Momberg, 'Jan Bek' (Jannie) 158, 161
Momberg, 'Stil Jan' 158, 161
Momberg family 175
Mon Don Estate 258
Moni, Roberto 161, 175, 199
Monis Wineries Ltd of Paarl 20, 31, 120, 175,
    199-201, 246
Mons Ruber Estate 268-9
Mont Blois Estate 137, 258-9
Montagne *see* Hartenberg
Montagu Muscadel Farmers' Co-operative
    23, 269
Montpellier Estate 231-2
Mooiuitsig Wine Cellars 259

Môreson Blois 221
Morgenhof 131, 158-9
Morgenster (*farm*) 141, 171
Morio Muscat 57, 87
Morkel, Dirk Cloete 129
Morkel, Johan 243
Morkel, Pieter Krige 129
Mossop, Thomas 193
Mostert, Alwyn 242
Mostert, Kobus 221
Mostert, Leon 207
Mostert, Nico 183
Mouton, Ben 221
Mouton, Jacques 221
Mouton, Noel 271
Mouton-Excelsior 221
Mulderbosch 160
Muller, Inus 134
Muller, Jan 231
Muller, Janey 35, 151, 154, 231
Müller, Richard *and* Christine 99, 112
Müller-Thurgau 76, 178
Munkerus, Henricus 120
Muratie Estate 136, 160-1
Murray, Johan 142
Muscadel 94, 256, 259, 268, 269; *see also*
       Red & White Muscadel
Muscat group 87
Muscat d'Alexandrie 13, 38, 56, 57, 75-6, 87
    Constantia 113, 114
    Klein Karoo 266
    Worcester 242
Muscat de Frontignan 16
Muscat Ottonel 57, 87, 131
museums
    brandy 101, 140
    coach 131
    cultural history 99
    farm 103
    wine 101, 114
Myburgh, B.W. 271
Myburgh, Frank 233-4
Myburgh, Hannes 156-7
Myburgh, Johannes Albertus 155
Myburgh, Nicolaas (Nico) 155-7

— N —

Natte Vallei 151
National Bottled Wine Show 66
National Oenothèque 54
National Vinotèque 54
National Young Wine Show 66
Naudé, L. 54

Nebuchadnezzar 71
Nederburg 24, 100, 120, 162, 200-1, 202
    Auction 20, 31-2, 35, 85, 102
       wine sold at 178, 203, 244, 245, 246, 260
Nederburgh, Sebastiaan Cornelis 200
Neethling, Johannes Henoch 161
Neethling, Paul & Hanneli 217
Neethlingshof Estate 101, 158, 161-2, 175,
       176, 178
Neil Ellis Wines 35, 162
Nel, 'Boets' 266-7
Nel, Carel 35, 266, 269
Nel, Chris 266-7
Nel, Danie 266, 269
Nelson, Charles 135
nematodes 39, 46, 51, 276
Nemes Furmint 85
New World Wine Auction 133, 177, 181
Nicholson, Alfred 165-6
Nicholson, Reginald 165-6
Niehaus, Dr Charles 123, 182, 197, 198
Niehaus, Dr J.G. 21
Nietvoorbij Institute for Viticulture & Oeno-
       logy 20, 48, 52-4, 78, 101, 125, 154,
       155
Nieuwetuin 136
Nieuwedrift (*farm*) 192
Nieuwoudt, David Josephus 'Oom Pollie' 238
Nieuwoudt, Ernst 238
Nieuwoudt, Frikkie 238
night harvesting 57, 59, 103, 146, 235, 254
Ninow, F.W. 132
Noble Late Harvest 94, 154, 275, 278-9
noble rot *see Botrytis cinerea*
Non Pareil (*farm*) 102
Nooitgedacht 129, 142, 172
Nordale Co-operative Winery 259
nose 90-1, 276
Northumberland, Duke of 114
Nuy Wine Cellar Co-operative 244

— O —

O'Kennedy, James 266
Oberholzer, Jan 179
oenology 54, 101, 276
    study of 47-8; *see also* Nietvoorbij
oïdium *see* powdery mildew
Olasz Riesling 85
Olifantshoek (*farm*) 212
Olifantsrivier
    region 42, 54, 86, 107, 237-9
    wine route 104-5
    wine show 66

Olifantsrivier Co-operative *see* Vredendal Co-
       operative Wine Cellar
Olives (*farm*) 173
Olivier, Eric 271
Olivier, Olla 246
Omega grafting machine 39-40
Onderplaas 54
Onrus *see* Morgenhof
Onverwacht Estate 102, 201-2
Opstal Estate 54, 245
Oranjerivier Co-operative Wine Cellars 271
Orffer, Prof Christiaan 38, 40, 48, 84, 85,
       115, 125
    development of Chenel 73, 79, 243
organic farming methods 113, 148, 171, 231
Ou Muratie 81
Oude Drostdy 103
Oude Libertas (*farm*) 24, 173, 175
Oude Meester Brandy Museum 101
Oude Meester Group 27, 29, 137, 183
Oude Meester Kelders, Distilleerdes en
       Brouerskorporasie 137, 204
Oude Molen 140, 141
Oude Nektar Estate 163
Oude Weltevreden 150
Overberg 79, 249-51
Overberg Co-operative Winery 259
Overgaauw Estate 35, 54, 100, 163-4
Overhex Co-operative Wine Cellar 23, 246

— P , Q —

Paarl Co-operative 23
Paarl Nouveau Festival 102
Paarl Riesling *see* Cape Riesling
Paarl Rock Brandy Cellar 101-2
Paarl Vallei Wine Co-operative 192
Paarl Valley 15, 189-207
    wine route 101-2
    wine show 66
    wines, red 84-7
    wines, white 74, 76, 79
Paarl Wine Farmers' Association 196
Paddagang Vignerons 103, 233
Paddagang Wine House and Vineyards 232-3
Pagan International 33, 194
Palomino 38, 57, 69, 70, 74-5, 141, 227
Pampoenkraal 119
Parker, Daisy 120
Parker, Dennis 120
Parker, Jean 120-1
Parker, John 120-1
Parker, Oliver, 120-1
Pasman, Roelof 165

Pasteur, Louis 20, 21-2, 24, 64
Patrys Vlei 174
Peatling, Hugh 129
Peck, Gregory 163
Pedro 69
Perdeberg Wine Farmers' Co-operative 202
Pêrelse Wine Cellars 192
Perold, Prof Abraham Izak 21, 125, 160, 197
    merlot 84
    pinotage 20, 24, 48, 82, 129
    port 87, 123
    research 24, 38, 74, 75, 83, 86
pests *see* diseases and pests
Petit Verdot 37, 157, 181
Phillips, *Sir* Lionel *and Lady* Florence 181
Phomopsis viticola see dead arm disease
phylloxera (*Dactylosphaera vitifoliae*) 11,
       22-3, 25, 27, 51, 277
Phylloxera Commission 23
Phylloxera Epidemic 11, 20, 25, 39, 74, 134,
       165-6, 209, 211
Phylloxera vastatrix see phylloxera
Picardi Hotels Ltd 204
Picardi Liquors 194
Pickard, Jan 194, 204, 210
Pickard family 33
Pickering family 212
Pickstone, Harry 211
Piketberg 15
Pillmann, Arthur 250
Pinot Blanc 57, 86, 140, 180
Pinot Gris 57, 85, 86, 94, 122, 179
Pinot Noir 47, 57, 64, 81, 82, 94, 97
    awards 113, 122, 160, 250
    champagne produced from 172
    development of Pinotage 24, 48
Pinotage 82, 86, 97, 123, 146-7, 158, 172
    awards 144
    development of 24, 38, 48, 129
    maturation and ripening 49, 57, 94
Plasmopara viticola see downy mildew
Platter, John *and* Erica 133, 134, 214
Podlashuk, Bernard *and* Fredagh 210
Pongràcz, Desiderius 167
Pontac 16, 37, 57, 60, 69, 83-4
Pontallier, Paul 66
port 24, 67, 69, 71, 94, 277
    awards 193, 199, 225, 266, 267
    varieties 37, 82, 83, 86, 87
Porterville Wine Cellars 226
Potgieter, Jacob 244
Potgieter family 260
Potter, Pieter 15, 189, 229
powdery mildew (oïdium) 21, 22, 51, 56, 57,
       277

Pretorius, Izak (Bill) 246
Prins, Ben 160-1
Pritchard, Seymour 133
Provan, Janey *see* Muller, Janey
pruning 49-51, 55-6, 57
Puligny-Montrachet 177
Quinan, Storm *and* Ruth 134-5
quota system 20, 24, 27-8, 197, 267

— R —

R. Santhagens Cape Ltd 140, 164, 244; *see
        also* Santhagens, Reiner
racking 61, 65, 66, 69, 277
Radoux family 71
rainfall ; for rainfall of specific regions *see
        under* name of region
Raisin Blanc 37, 57, 88
raisins 42, 75-6, 241, 256
Ramsey rootstock 39, 51
Ras, Catharina 117
Ratcliffe, Norma 35, 185-6
Ratcliffe, Stan 185-6
Ratz, Helmut 140, 204
Ravenscroft, Mark 201-2
Reagh, John 202-3
red wine 31, 90, 96, 277
        varieties 37, 57, 80-6
Red Muscadel 87, 258, 261, 263
regions 107 *see also* under specific names
Reitz, J.D.K. 250
Rembrandt Group 27-9, 31-2, 33
remuage 65, 277
Remy Cointreau 33
Remy Martin 194
Rennies Group 33, 194
Research Institute for Plant Protection 54
restaurants 105
Retief, Dan 102
Retief, Hennie & Jean 260-1
Retief, Nico 261-2
Retief, Nicolaas 260-1
Retief, Piet 102
Retief, Wynand 261-2
Rheboam 71
Rhebokskloof Estate 102, 192, 194, 202-3
Rhine Ruhr Holdings (Pty) Ltd 158
Rhine Riesling *see* Weisser Riesling
Rhizopus see sour rot
Rhodes, Cecil John 22, 23, 130, 173, 270
Rhodes Fruit Farms 211-12, 216
Rhoicissus capensis 12, 37, 277
Richter 99 rootstock 39, 51

Riebeek Wine Cellar Co-operative 226
Rietrivier Wine Cellar Co-operative 269
Rietvallei (*farm*) 268
Rietvallei Estate 137, 259
Riverhouse 54
Riversedge (*farm*) 263
Riverside (*farm*) 196, 243
Robert Mondavi trophy 66, 129, 201
Roberts, W.F.(Robbie) 260
Robertson 42, 54, 86, 253-63
        wine route 104
        wine show 66, 255, 259
Robertson Co-operative Winery 77, 114,
        256-7, 259-60
Robertson Distillers 204
Robertson Wine Trust 104
Rochefort, Pierre 138
Rocher, Cecily 244
Roi, Jean 219
Romansrivier Co-operative 246
Roobernet 85
Roodeplaat 54
Roodezandt Co-operative Winery 260
Rooiberg Co-operative 139, 257, 260
rosé wine 64, 67, 82, 90, 277
Rossouw, Alex 268
Rossouw, Bunny 226
Rossouw, D.J. 202
Rossouw, Danie 146
Rossouw, Jan 202
Rossouw, Johan 187, 203, 239
Rossouw, Kobus 186-7, 203
Rossouw, 'Lang Jan' 245
Rossouw, Malherbe 138-9
Rossouw, Manie 139
Rossouw, Sarel 139, 187, 203
rot 51 *see also Botrytis cinerea*, sour rot,
Rosarium Nursery 186
Rotterdam, Jan 148
Roussouw, Frederik 117
Roux, Chris 205
Roux, Jan 219
Roux, Paul 138
Roux, Wrensch 259
Rozendal Farm 35, 146, 164-5
Ruby Cabernet 86
Rudd, John 218-19
Ruiterbosch Mountain Vineyards 269
Rupert, Dr Anton 30, 137, 194, 209, 219
Rupert, Anthonij 219-20
Rupert family 29, 32, 33, 216-17
Rust-en-Vrede Estate 35, 167, 170,
        176
Rustenberg Estate 35, 80, 165-7
Rustenburg Farm 54, 102, 203

— S —

Saager, *Prof* R. 139-40
Saayman, Eric 35, 187
Salmanazar 71
Sanlam Group 27
Santhagens, Reiner von Eibergen (René) 70,
        140 *see also* R.Santhagens Cape Ltd
Santos, Carlos dos 177
Sauer, *Senator* J.H. 146
Sauer, *Hon.* Paul O. 129, 146
Sauvignon Blanc 57, 78-9, 94, 97, 117, 269
Sax, Joachim 170
Saxenburg Wine Farm 170-1, 192
Schickerling, Dr Arnold 136-7, 142
Schoch, Emile 259
Schoemanskloof (*farm*) 261
Schoongezicht (Paarl) 198
Schoongezicht (Stellenbosch) 35, 165-7
Schreiber, Hans-Joachim 147, 161, 175-6
Schröder, Hans-Peter 163
screw tops 67-8
scurvy 13
Sedgwick Tayler Ltd 25, 31, 175
Sedgwick Wellington Distillery 205
Sémillon 38, 57, 69, 70, 77
Serrurier, Jan 25
sherry 37, 67, 69, 71, 94, 97, 277, 278
        establishment of industry 21, 24, 182, 197,
            199
        Paarl 199
        Stellenbosch 142
        Tulbagh 103, 137
Shiraz 37, 49, 57, 69, 83, 97, 123, 263
        used in blending 82, 94, 127
shows 66
        Boberg 195
        Breede River Young Wine 259
        Cape Championship Wine 122, 190, 238,
            243
        Cape Championship Young Wine 77
        Cape Wine 129, 139, 225, 260
        Cape Young Wine 202
        Klein-Karoo 66
        Olifantsrivier 66, 238
        Paarl 66
        Robertson 66, 258
        South African Championship Wine 226
        Stellenbosch 66, 113, 225
        Worcester 66, 103, 242
        see also International Wine & Spirit
            Competition
Siebrits, Tertius 254
Sieg, Ian 271
Signal Hill (*farm*) 54

Silverman, Alan 177
Simon, André 93
Simondium Winery Co-operative 203
Simonis, André 268
Simonsig Estate 35, 65, 68, 154, 171-2, 271
Simonsvlei Co-operative 139, 187, 203
Sinclair, 'Cappy' 194
Sinclair, Roger 92
Slanghoek Co-operative Wine Cellar 246-7
slavery 14, 20, 21
Smit, Jako 154, 270
Smit, Jan 173
Smit, Pieter 163
Smit, S. 234
Smit, Stefan 148
Smit, Stevie 148
Smit, Wynand Stephanus 148
Smith, Dassie 260
Smollan, Doug 177
Smuts, Gen. Jan Christiaan 104, 174
        Trophy 176, 245, 260
snails 51
Sneewind, Hendrik 122
snout beetles 51, 56-7, 278
societies, wine 92-3
Soetwyn Boere Co-operative 270
soil 42-6; for soil in particular areas *see
            under* names of districts or estates
Somerset, *Lord* Charles 103, 150, 161, 241
Sotheby Park Bernet 32, 33, 35
sour rot (*Rhizopus*) 52, 76, 278
South African Breweries (SAB) 27-8, 31
South African Champion Co-operative Wine-
            maker 203
South African Champion Estate Winemaker
            235, 254
South African Champion Winemaker 176,
            203
South African Champion wines
        Cabernet Sauvignon 142
        Dry white wine 117
        fortified wine 225
        Muscadel 259
        Red Muscadel 245, 263, 269
South African Championship Wine Show 66
        awards 121-2, 176, 226, 235, 244, 254
South African Championship Young Wine
        Show 170, 259
South African Distillers and Wines Ltd 137
South African Riesling *see* Cape Riesling
South African Society of Wine Tasters 92-3
South African Vintage Wine Auctions 32
Souzão 57, 73, 87, 123
        used in port 37, 69, 163
Sowter, Norman 71

sparkling wine 64-5, 67, 71, 75, 94, 96-7
    see also méthode champenoise
Sparks, Charlie 183
Sparks, L.T. 134
Special Late Harvest 94, 144, 275, 278
Sperling, Michael 'Spatz' 99, 100, 135-6
Spes Bona (*farm*) 261
Spier Estate 99, 100-1, 172-3
Spruitdrift Co-operative Wine Cellar 239
St Emilion *see* Trebbiano
Stander, Mike 216
Starke, Kosie 122-3
Starke, William 122-3
Starke, 'Oom Willie' 121, 123
Stassen, D. 54
Steen *see* Chenin Blanc
Steenberg 93, 117
Stellenbosch 16, 66, 125-87, 225
    wine route 20, 99, 100-1, 171
Stellenbosch Distillery 174
Stellenbosch Farmers' Wine Trust Ltd 175
Stellenbosch Farmers' Winery (SFW) 27-32,
    47, 65, **173-5**, **197**
    formation of 20, 24
    grapes delivered to 100, 161
    mergers 25, 71, 194, 199, 201
    public relations 54, 93, 245
    wine sold to 129, 146, 148, 183, 184
Stellenbosch Food and Wine Festival 101
Stellenbosch Grape Juice Works 174
Stellenbosch University *see* University of
    Stellenbosch
Stellenbosch Wine Trust Ltd 175
Stellenbosch Young Wine Show 113
Stellenbosse Botteleringskooperasie Beperk
    146
Stellenryk Wine Museum 101
Stellenzicht (*farm*) 161-2; *see also* Alphen
Stellenzicht Vineyards 175
Stemmet, Leon 155
Stephen Welz and Co. 32, 33
Stettyn Co-operative Wine Cellar 247
Steyn, P.K. 268
Steytdal Farm (Pty) Ltd 146
Steytler, Christie 260
Steytler, *Maj* D.C. 146
Steytler, Danie 146
Steytler, David 146
Steytler, George 146
Steytler, George jun. 146
Steytler, W. and son 54
Stiernhielm, *Baron* von 151
Stofberg, A. 54
Stofberg, André 243
storage 94; *see also* cellars, underground

Stroebel, Frans 175
Stukvat Bottle Store 194
Sultana (Thompson's Seedless) 88
sultanas 256
Sunshine (*farm*) 258
Superior Imports Ltd 33
Swaansweide *see* Steenberg
Swartland Co-operative Wine Cellar 227
Swartland district 74, 104, 223-7
Swartvalle 54
Sweerts, Jean-Luc 128
Swiegers, Gielie 239
Swiss Farm Excelsior 221
Sylvaner 57, 76, 163
Symington, Peter 266

— T —

Taillefert, Jean 198
Talana Hill Winery 149, 176-7, 184
Tanner, Mark 214
Tas, Adam 17, 24, 173, 175, 186
Les Tastevins du Cap 92
tasting 89-92, 272
Thelema Mountain Vineyards 35, 54, 162,
    177-8
Theron, *Prof* Christiaan Jacobus 20, 38, 83,
    87, 125, 224, 231, 260
    development of Pinotage 24, 48, 129
Theron, Christiaan Jacobus 234
Theron, De Wet 231-2
Theron, Gawie 232
Theron Gideon 193
Theron, Hendrik 231-2
Theron, Jan 231-2
Theron, Johan 214, 238
Theron, P.F. 234
Therona Riesling 85, 260
Theuniskraal Estate 137, 233-4
Theunissen family 181
Thibault, Louis Michel 19, 99, 103, 113, 179
Thielhelm, Dieter 206
Thompson's Seedless (Sultana) 88
Tinta Barocca 37, 49, 57, 73, 87, 97
    production of port 69, 163, 225, 266
Tinta Francisca 37, 87, 163
Tinta Roriz 37, 87
tipping 56
Tonnellerie Radoux 71
topping 56-7, 279
Torres, Miramar 32
Trawal Co-operative Wine Cellar 239
Trebbiano 57, 70, 73, 79, 88
Trelew Investments Ltd 219

trellises and trellising 49, 55, 279
Trollinger 80
Trouvé (*farm*) 219
Trull, Michael *and* Cheryl 212, 215-16
Truter, Bennie 214
Truter, Beyers 35, 66, 129, 146-7
Truter, Danie 35, 142-3
Truter, Deon 214, 221
Tulbagh, Ryk 229
Tulbagh 42, 79, 103, 229-35
Tulbagh Co-operative Wine Cellar 20, 23,
    103, 137, 234
Tulbagh Wine Association 233
Twee Jongegezellen Estate 32, 65, 103, 141,
    234-5
    night harvesting 59, 103, 235

— U —

Ugni Blanc *see* Trebbiano
Uiterwyk Estate 178
Uitgezocht 54
Uitkyk (Klein Karoo) 54
Uitkyk Estate (Stellenbosch) 137, 146,
    179-80
Uitsig (Paarl) 54
Uitsig (Worcester) 54
Union Wine Ltd 33, 194, 204, 210
United Distillers Group 30
University of Stellenbosch. Depts of Oenology
    & Viticulture 20, 24, 48, 125; *see also*
    Elsenberg Agricultural College
Uys, D.C.H. 53
Uytenbogaardt, Sakkie 132

— V —

V.H.Matterson 175
Vaalharts Agricultural Co-operative 270-1
Vaalharts Farmers' Co-operative 271
Vaalharts Irrigation Scheme 270
Valentijn, François 181
van Breda, Carel 246
van der Bijl, Pieter Gerhard 186
van der Bijl, Pieter Voltelen 186
van der Bijl, Philipus Johannes 186
van der Byl family 25
van der Byl, William 136
van der Heyden, Jacobus 186
van der Merwe, Alkie 246
van der Merwe, Carel 258
van der Merwe, Chris 247
van der Merwe, Driaan 214

van der Merwe, Gert 231
van der Merwe, Kobus 255
van der Merwe, Martin 137, 147
van der Merwe, Nico 170-1
van der Merwe, Schalk 244
van der Merwe, W. 54
van der Stael, Pieter 14
van der Stel, Simon 16-20
    and Constantia 25, 99-100, 111-13
    and the Huguenots 209, 211, 214, 215
    Gardener's Almanack 17, 111, 180
    grants farms 117, 120, 125, 130, 139, 147,
        161, 163, 167, 170, 172, 173, 186, 193,
        202
van der Stel, Willem Adriaan 16, 17-18, 20,
    155
    and Adam Tas 155, 173, 186
    and Vergelegen 16, 17-18, 180-1
    grants farms 122, 136, 165, 178, 223-4,
        229
van der Wêreld, Willem 167
van der Westhuizen, Christoff 132
van der Westhuizen, George 132
van der Westhuizen, Schalk 162
van Deventer, Gerhard 238, 263
van Graan, Jacobus Carolus 139
van Heerden, Manfred 238
van Herwaarden, Jan 189, 229
van Hoogstraten, Glennie 216
van Kempen, Jacob Cloete 13, 25, 111
van Lill, J. 54
van Loveren, Christina 260-1
Van Loveren 104, 260-2
van Oudenhove de St Géry, Dr I.C. 92
van Oudenlingenland, Jan Cornelis 173
van Reenen, Chris 244
van Rensburg, Hannes 201
van Rensburg, J.C. 204
van Rensburg, Johannes 47
van Riebeeck, Jan 11-15, 20, 21, 27, 37, 75,
    83, 189
Van Ryn Brandy Distillery 71
Van Ryn Wine & Spirit Co. 137
van Schalkwyk, Dirk 202
van Schalkwyk, Theunis Dirkz 25
van Staden, Sarel 244
van Suurwaarde, Elsje 120
van Tubbergh, Danie 243
van Velden, Abraham Julius 163
van Velden, Braam 35, 54, 163-4
van Velden, David 163
van Velden, Dirk 163
van Vuuren, Albie 227
van Vuuren, Denzel 159
van Vuuren, Gerritt Jansz 210

van Wyk, Joël 48, 125, 165, 231, 247
van Wyk, Willem 207
van Zyl, Gerrit 242
van Zyl, Guillaume 260
van Zyl, J. 54
van Zyl, Pon 77, 256-7, 259
Venter, Dr Piet 129
Veracruz (*farm*) 136
Vergelegen Estate 17, 180-1, 211
Vergenoegd Estate 122, 123, 182-3
Vermeulen, Nico 219-20
Verster, Hennie 246
Versveld, Chris 259
Versveld, Nicky 187
Vignerons de Franschhoek 103, 209, 210, 221
Viljoen, D.J. 246
Viljoen, Wynand 160
Villeria Estate 35, 65, 140, 204-5
Villiersdorp Moskonfyt and Fruit Co-operative 251
vinegar fly 83
Vinexpo 66, 113, 256
vineyard calendar 54-7
vineyard competition 54
Vineyard Trail 149
Vineyards Protection Act 23
vintage guide 94-5, 138, 279
virus detection 47
Visser, Gerrit 130
viticulture 37-57
   study of 47-8
Vitis aestivalis 39

Vitis berlandieri 39
Vitis cinerea 39
Vitis riparia 39
Vitis rupestris 39
Vitis vinifera 23, 37, 38, 39, 51, 76, 279
Vlotman, Antoine 138
Vlottenburg (*farm*) 138
Vlottenburg Co-operative Winery 183
Vlottenheimer wines 142
von Arnim, Achim 35,162, 211, 212-13
von Babo, *Baron* Carl 22-3
von Carlowitz family *see* Carlowitz, von
Vredenburg (*farm*) 134
Vredendal Co-operative Wine Cellar 104, 239
Vredendal Irrigation area 74
Vredenheim Estate 183-4
Vriesenhof 35,177, 184
Vryguns (*farm*) 202
Vytjie, Jan 259

— W —

W. & A. Gilbey 140
Waboomsrivier Co-operative Wine Cellar 247
Wagenaar, Zacharias 16
Wagener, Willie 203
Wagener, Wolfram 203
Walker, Jeremy 133, 142
Walters, Mike 47
Wamakersvallei Co-operative Winery 205
Wansbek (*farm*) 54
Wardrup, Sue 32

Warwick Estate 184-6
Warwick Farm 35
Waterval (*farm*) 212
Webb, Gyles *and* Barbara 35, 54, 162, 177-8
Webber, Guy 134
Wedgewood, Jeff 32
Weil, Les 177
Weisser Reisling 38, 57, 76, 78, 80, 97, 114, 178
Weldra 52, 57, 85
Welgelegen 132
Welgemeend Estate 35, 164, 206
Welgemoed 100
Welgevallen (*farm*) 24, 48
Wellington Co-operative Winery 23, 102, 205
Wellington wine route 102-3
Welmoed Co-operative Wine Cellars 161, 186-7
Weltevrede Estate 134, 194, 262-3
Weltevreden (*farm*) 198
Welvanpas Cellars 102
Werner, Karl 232
whisky 30, 31
White French *see* Palomino
white grape varieties 74-80, 86
White Muscadel 87, 258, 260
white spirits 31, 32
white wine 42, 60-1, 64, 90
   varieties 37, 57, 74-80, 86
Wiese, Christo 149-50
'Wijnbergen' 14
Windmeul Co-operative Wine Cellars 206
Wine and Spirit Board 64, 108, 121, 129

Wine and Spirit Control Act 24, 27, 70, 197
Wine and Spirit Education Trust 48
Wine Grape Improvement Board 47
Wine of Origin legislation 20, 82, 107-9, 201, 263, 279
Wine of Origin Superior 108
Wine Tasters' Guild of South Africa 93
Winemaker of the Year Award *see* Diners' Club of SA
Winshaw, Bill 174-5
Winshaw, Jack 174
Winshaw, John 175
Winshaw, William Charles 20, 24, 31, 173-5
Witblits 70, 103, 268, 279-80
Wolhuter, Jacobus 'Wollie' 244
Wolvaart, Philip 200
De Wolwedans *see* Neethlingshof
Woodhead, Michael 150-1, 231
Woolworths wines 162, 195
Worcester 42, 66, 79, 86, 103-4, 241-7
'Die Wynboer' 93

— Y , Z —

Younghusband, Peter 214-15
Zandvliet Estate 137, 138, 263
Zandwijk Wine Farm 101, 207
Zeeman, Danie 132
Zevenfontein (*farm*) 187
Zevenwacht 35, 162, 187
Zinfandel 57, 85, 86, 97, 141